# The Abandoned Empress

1

INA

Original Story by
Yuna

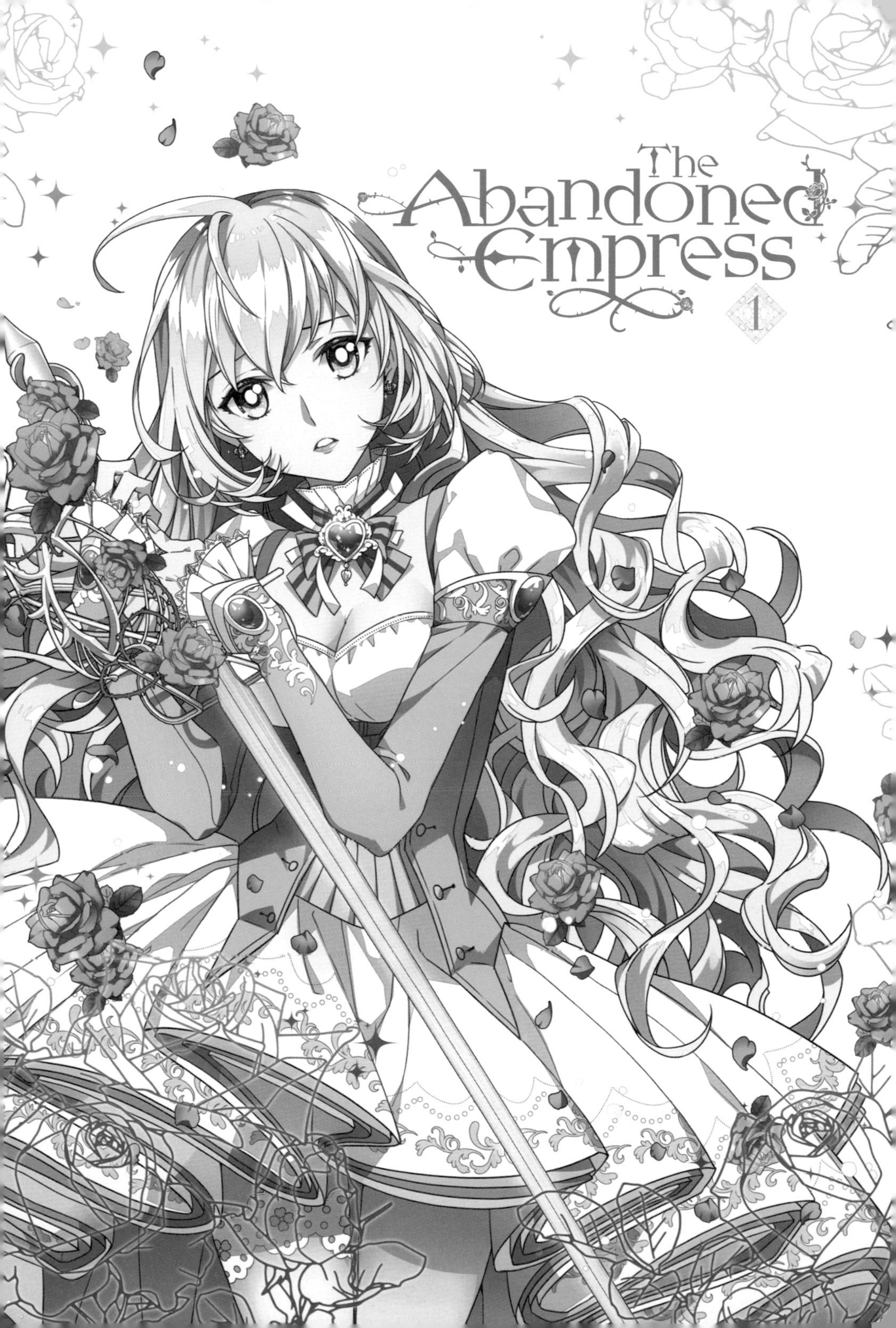
The Abandoned Empress
1

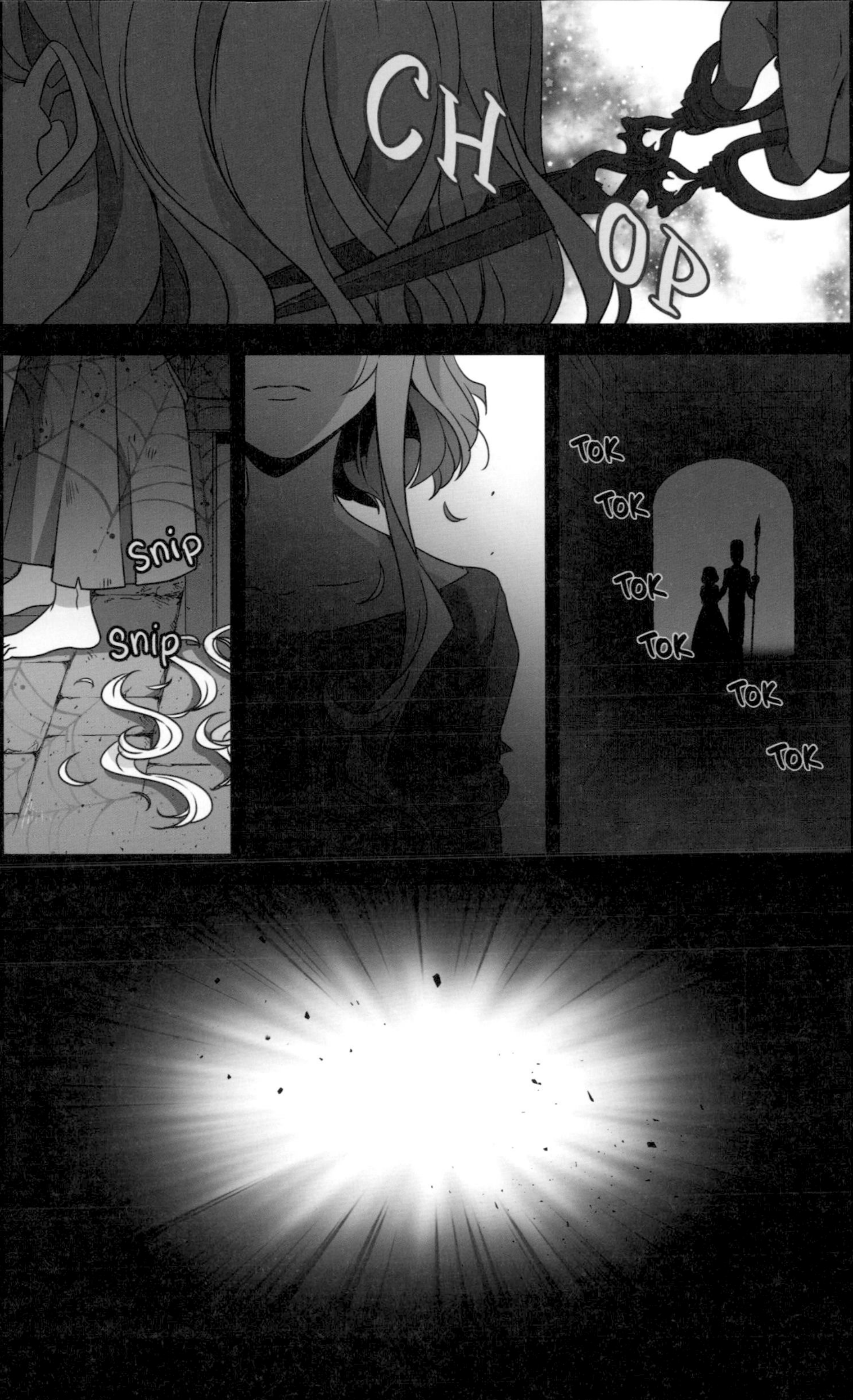

CHOP
snip
snip
TOK
TOK
TOK
TOK
TOK
TOK

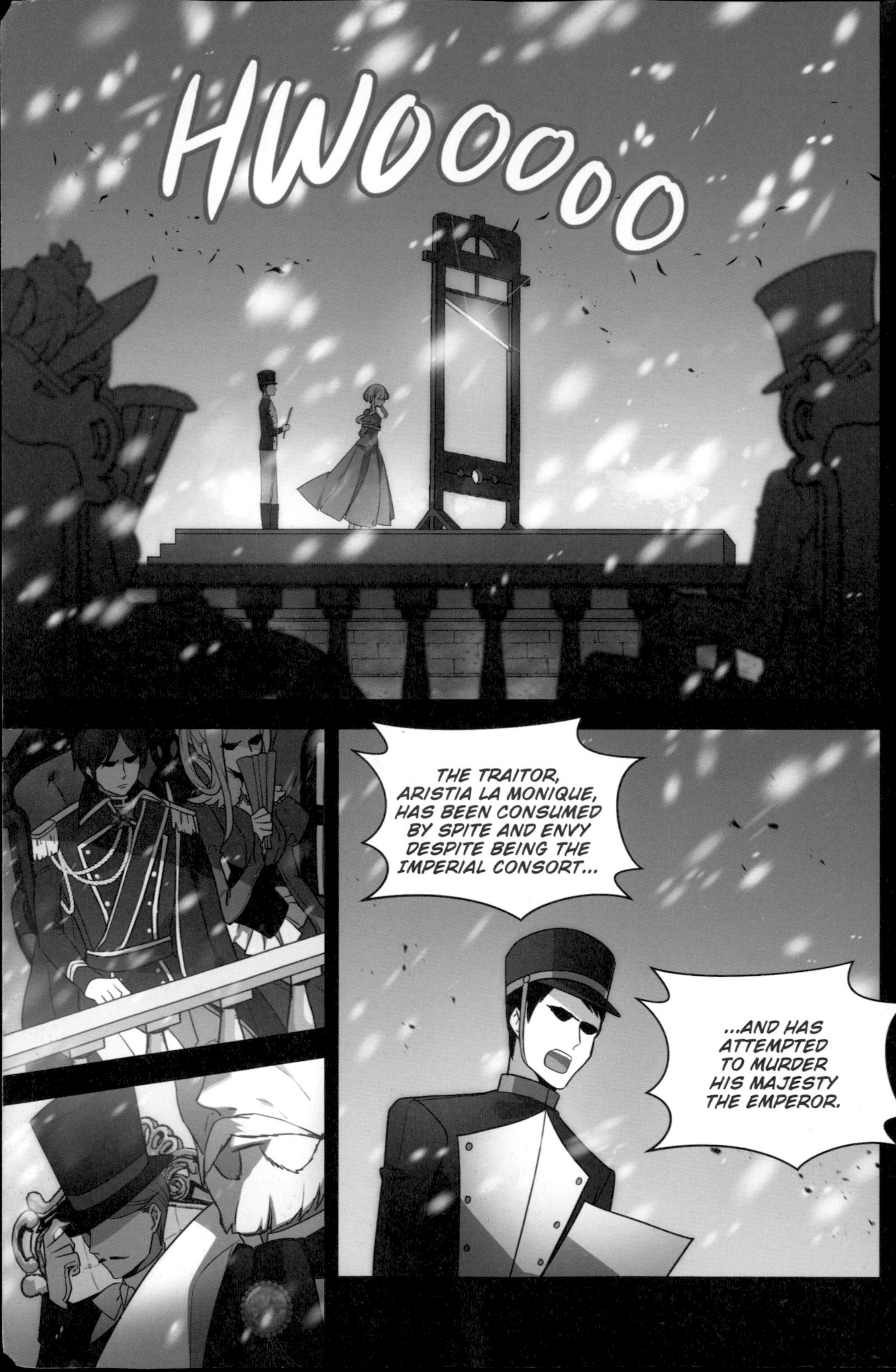
HWOOOOO
THE TRAITOR, ARISTIA LA MONIQUE, HAS BEEN CONSUMED BY SPITE AND ENVY DESPITE BEING THE IMPERIAL CONSORT...
...AND HAS ATTEMPTED TO MURDER HIS MAJESTY THE EMPEROR.

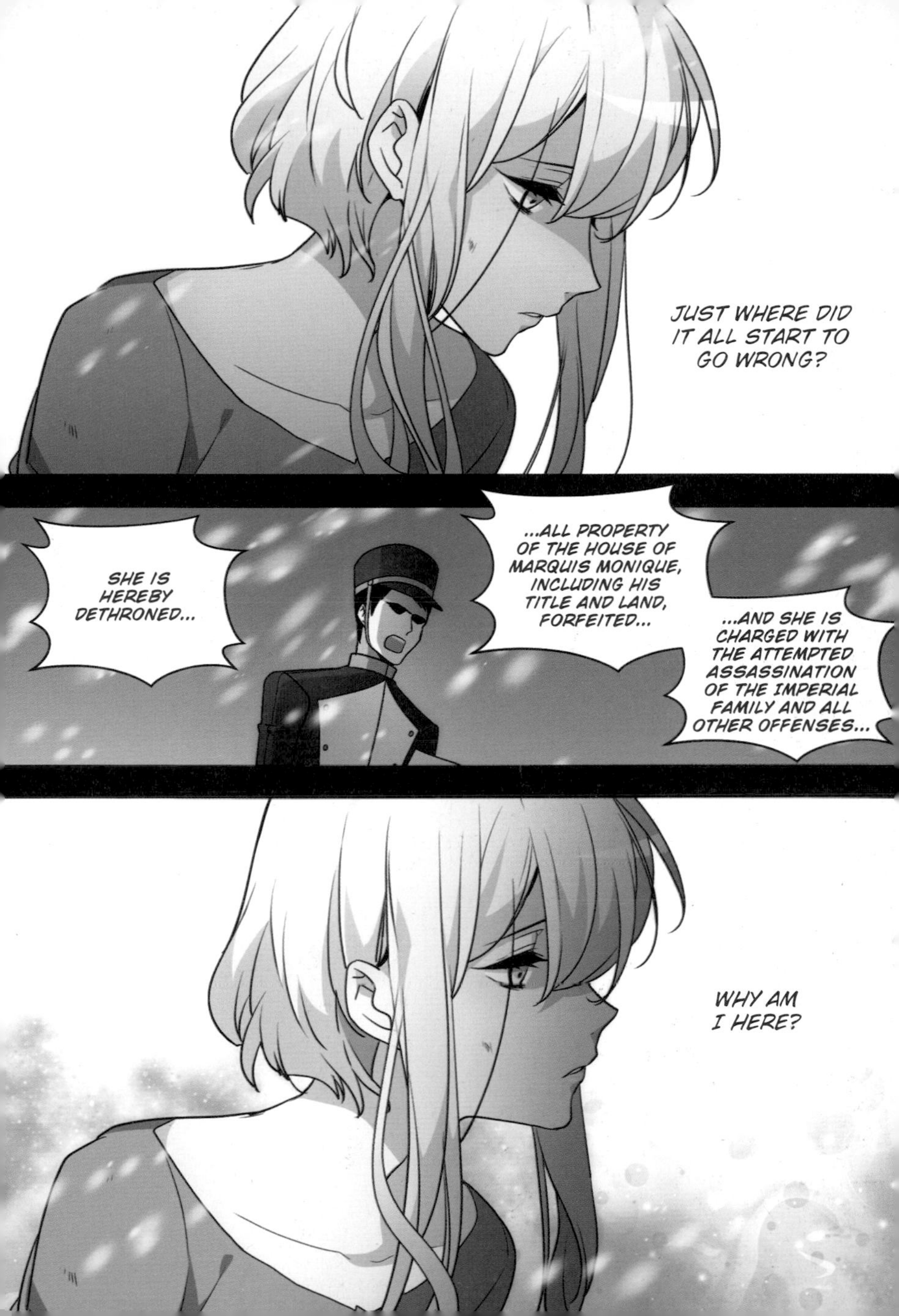
JUST WHERE DID IT ALL START TO GO WRONG?
SHE IS HEREBY DETHRONED...
...ALL PROPERTY OF THE HOUSE OF MARQUIS MONIQUE, INCLUDING HIS TITLE AND LAND, FORFEITED...
...AND SHE IS CHARGED WITH THE ATTEMPTED ASSASSINATION OF THE IMPERIAL FAMILY AND ALL OTHER OFFENSES...
WHY AM I HERE?

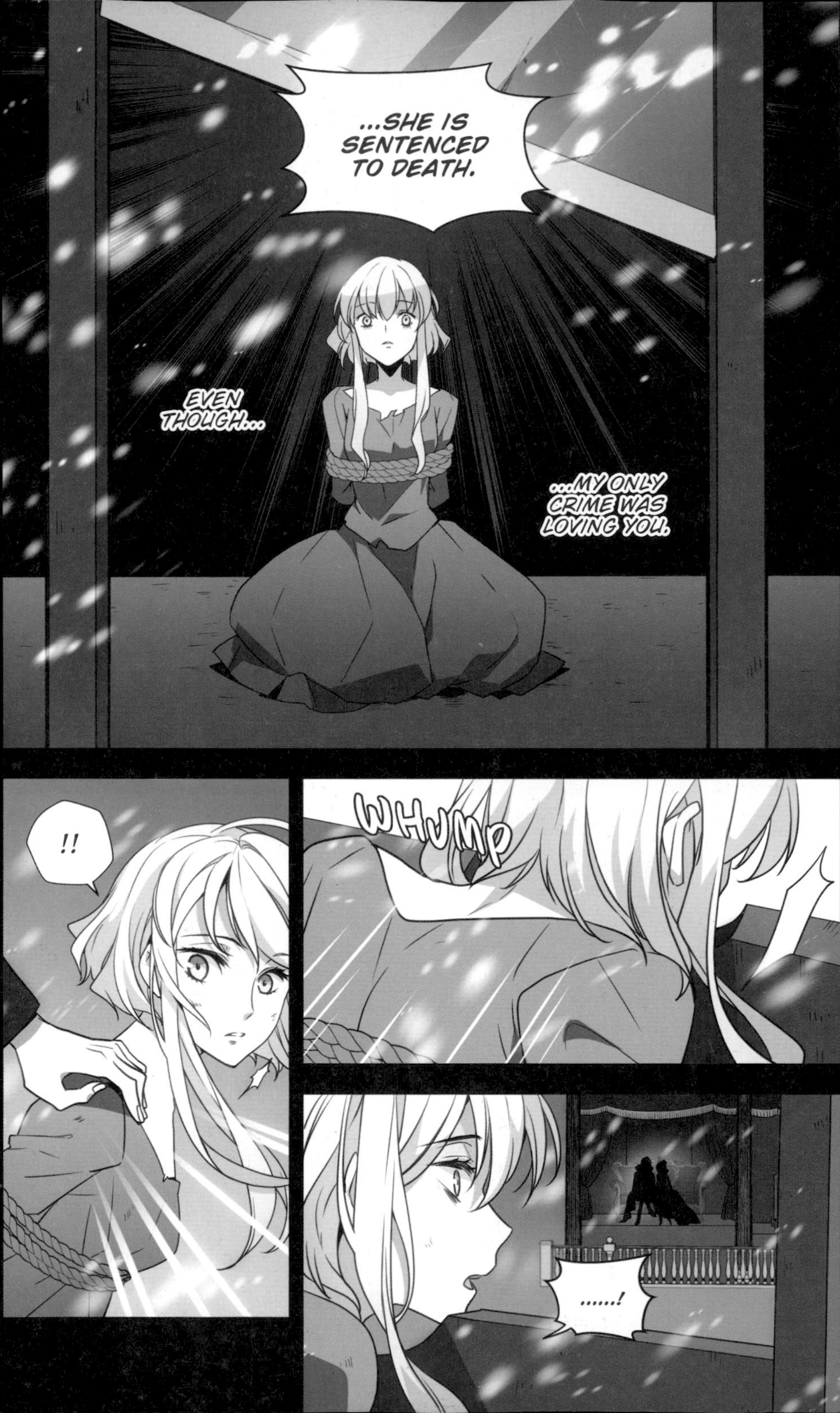
...SHE IS SENTENCED TO DEATH.
EVEN THOUGH...
...MY ONLY CRIME WAS LOVING YOU.
!!
WHUMP
......!

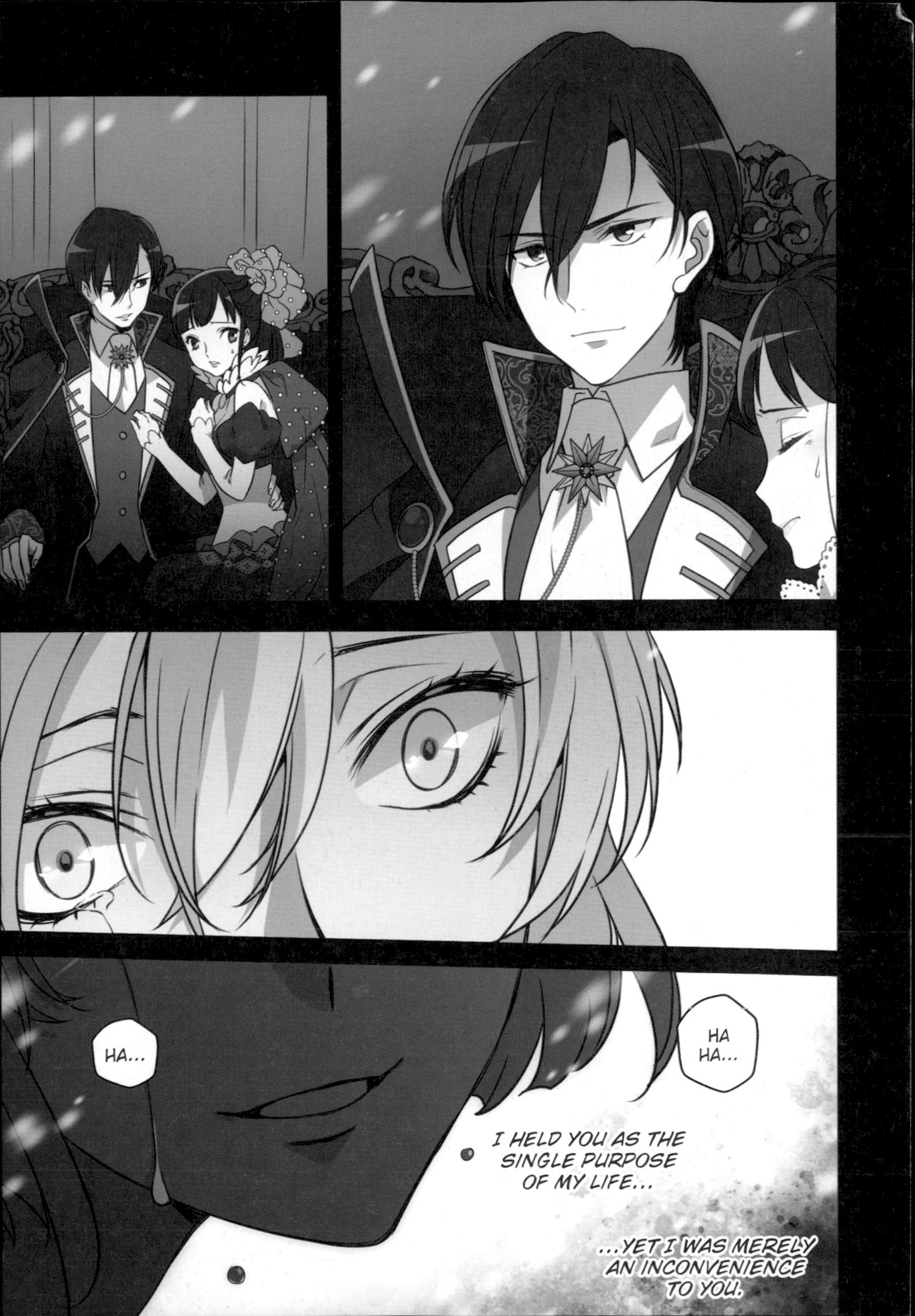
HA HA...
HA...
I HELD YOU AS THE SINGLE PURPOSE OF MY LIFE...
...YET I WAS MERELY AN INCONVENIENCE TO YOU.

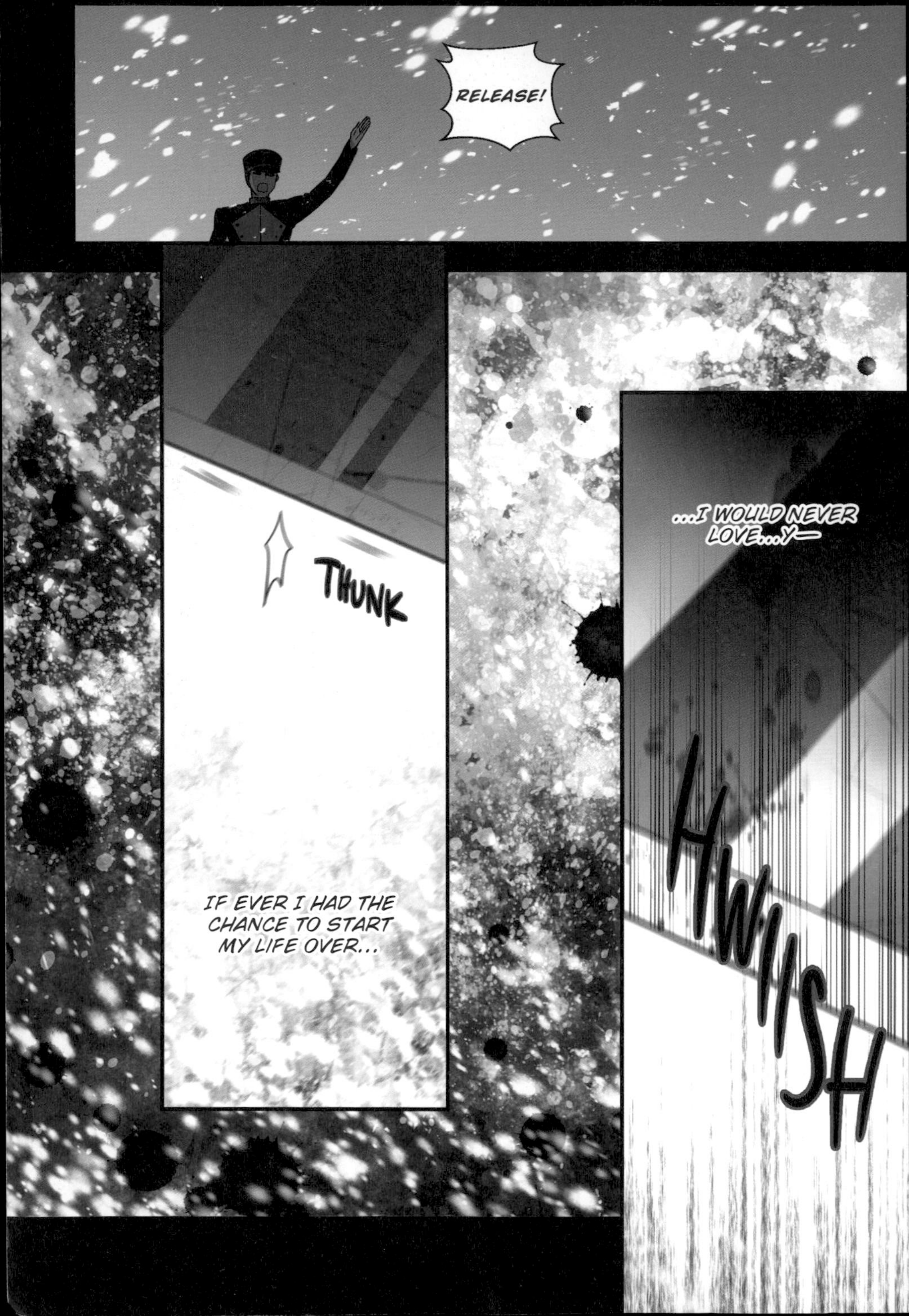
RELEASE!
THUNK
IF EVER I HAD THE CHANCE TO START MY LIFE OVER...
...I WOULD NEVER LOVE...Y—
HWIISH

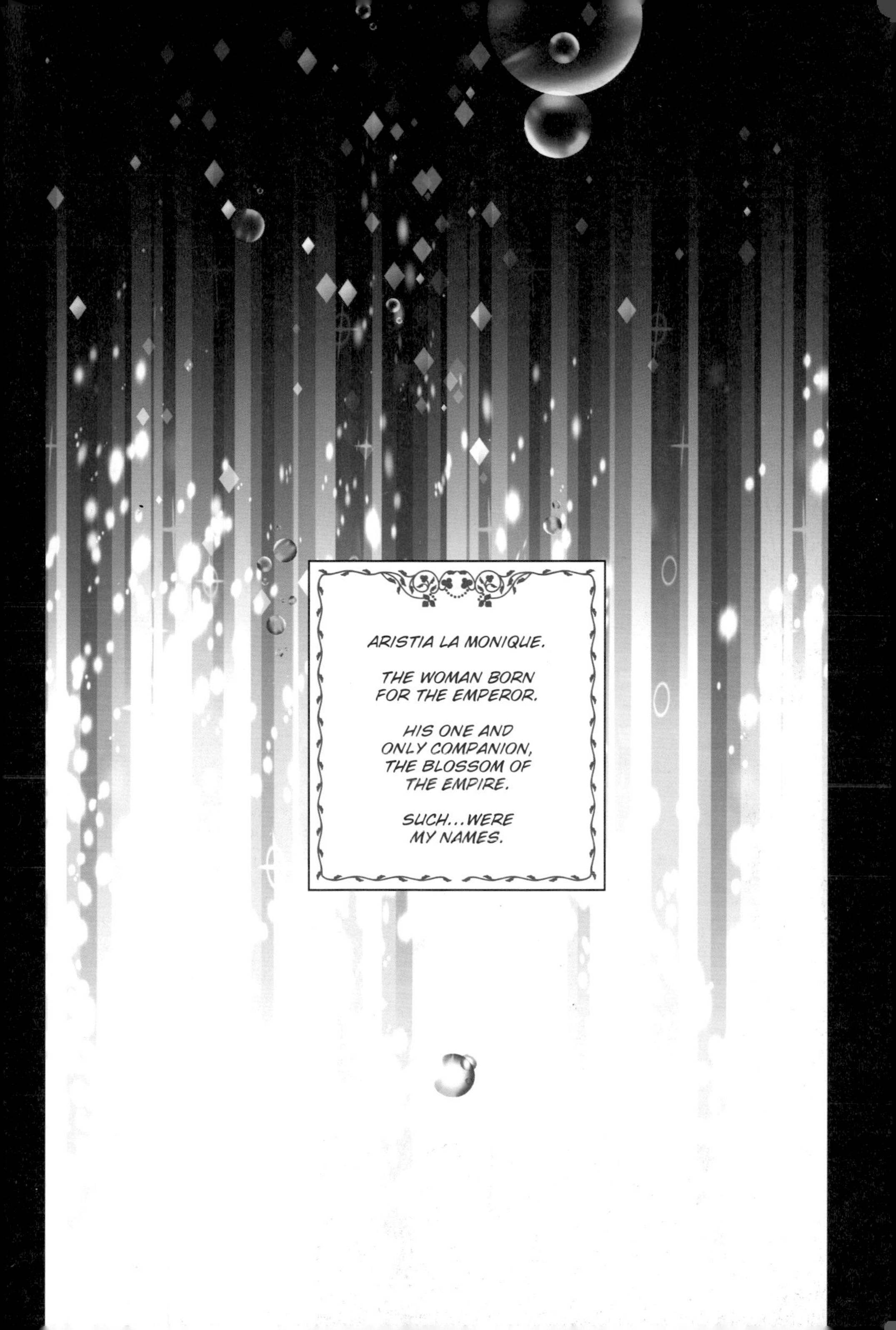
ARISTIA LA MONIQUE.
THE WOMAN BORN FOR THE EMPEROR.
HIS ONE AND ONLY COMPANION, THE BLOSSOM OF THE EMPIRE.
SUCH...WERE MY NAMES.

# The Abandoned Empress

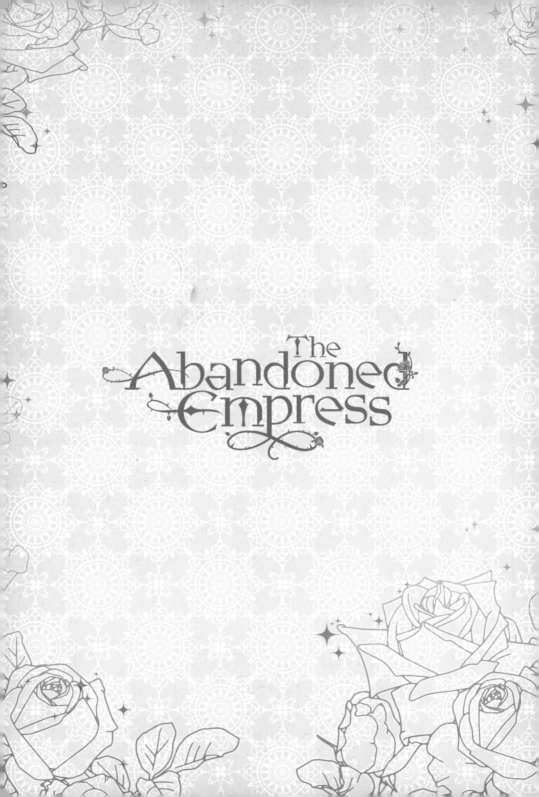

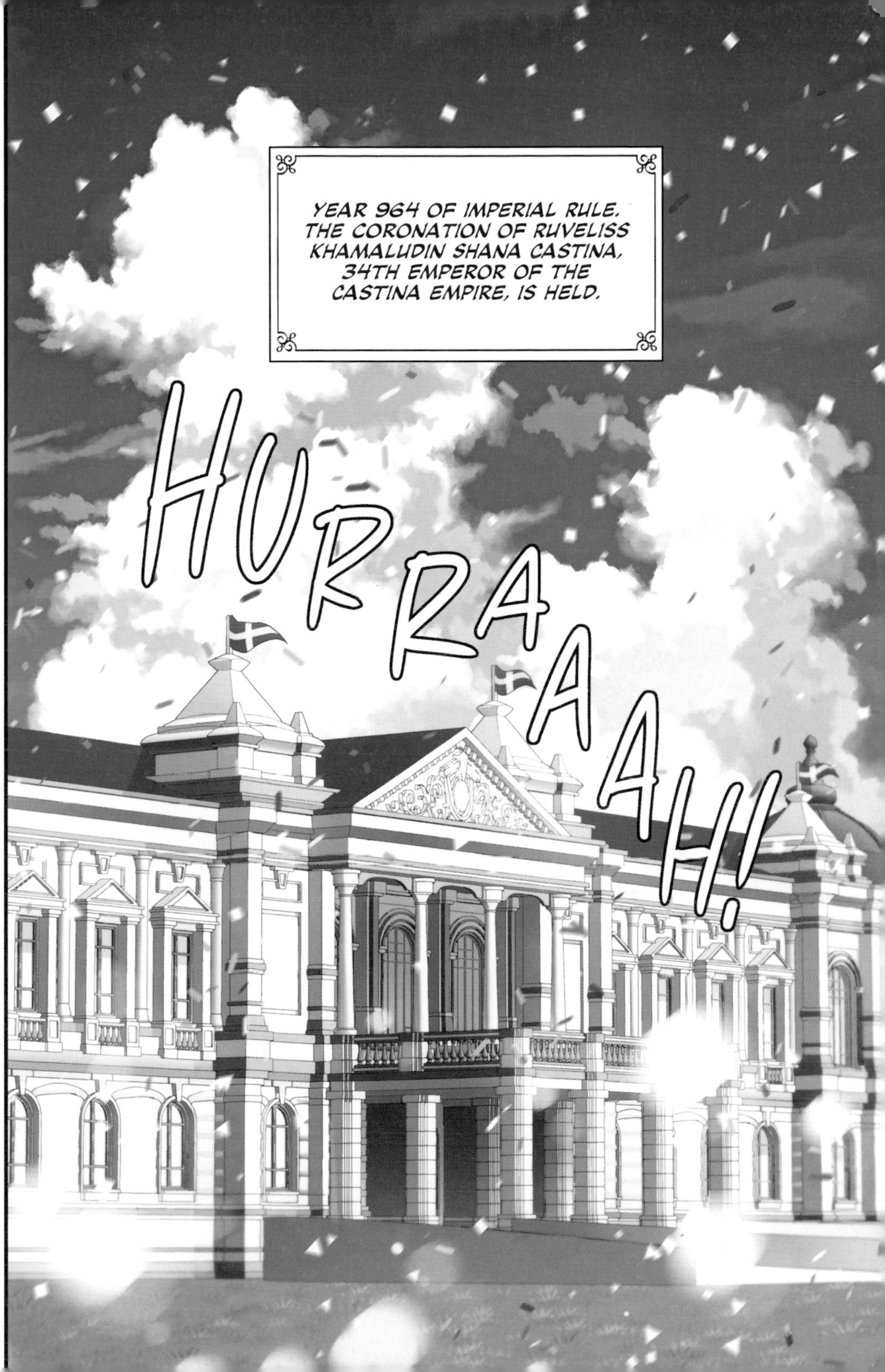
YEAR 964 OF IMPERIAL RULE. THE CORONATION OF RUVELISS KHAMALUDIN SHANA CASTINA, 34TH EMPEROR OF THE CASTINA EMPIRE, IS HELD.
HURRAAAH!!

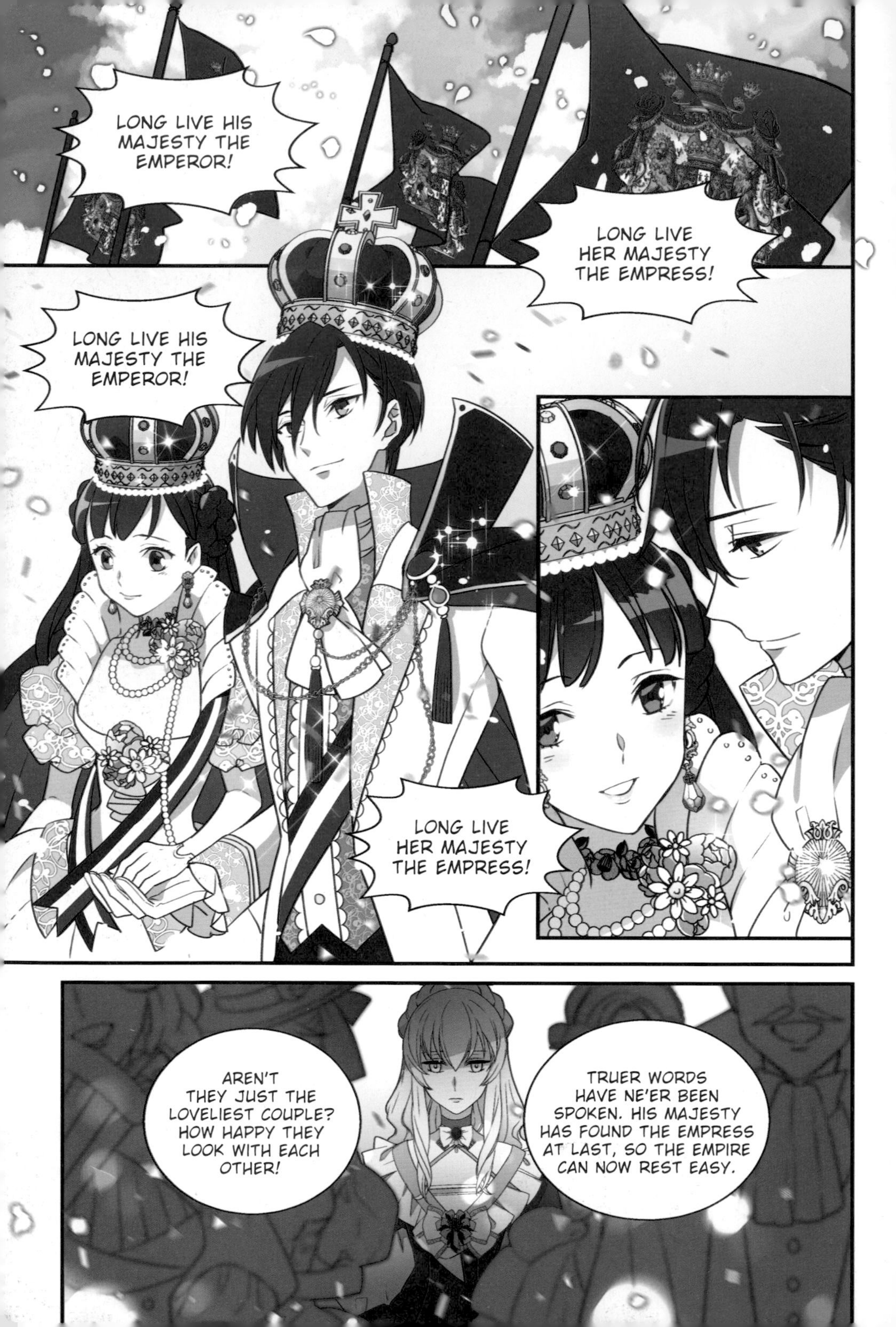
LONG LIVE HIS MAJESTY THE EMPEROR!
LONG LIVE HER MAJESTY THE EMPRESS!
LONG LIVE HIS MAJESTY THE EMPEROR!
LONG LIVE HER MAJESTY THE EMPRESS!
AREN'T THEY JUST THE LOVELIEST COUPLE? HOW HAPPY THEY LOOK WITH EACH OTHER!
TRUER WORDS HAVE NE'ER BEEN SPOKEN. HIS MAJESTY HAS FOUND THE EMPRESS AT LAST, SO THE EMPIRE CAN NOW REST EASY.

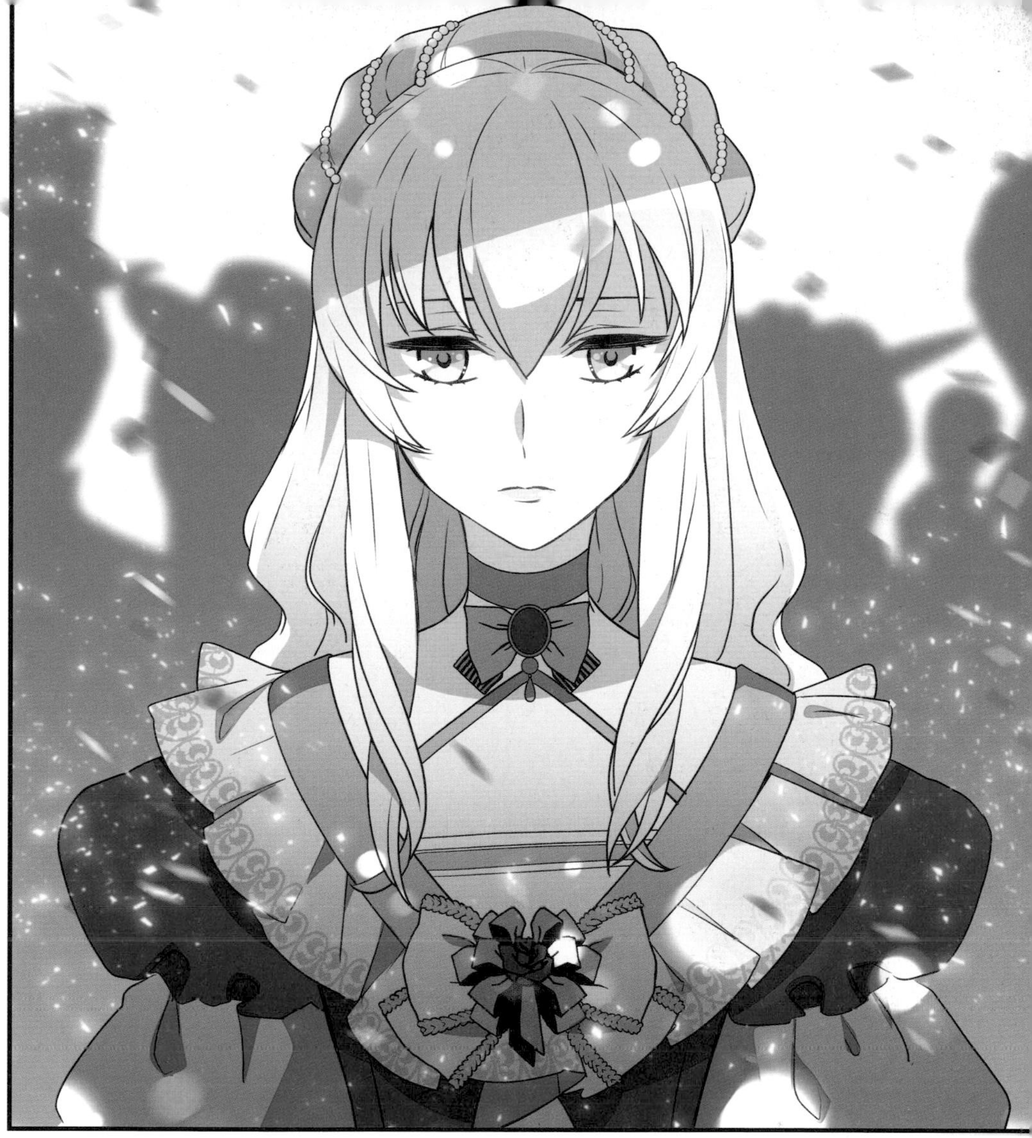

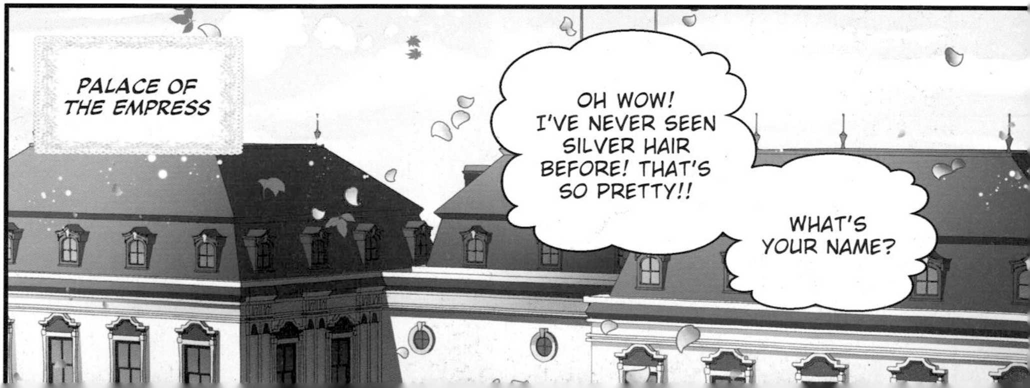
PALACE OF THE EMPRESS
OH WOW! I'VE NEVER SEEN SILVER HAIR BEFORE! THAT'S SO PRETTY!!
WHAT'S YOUR NAME?

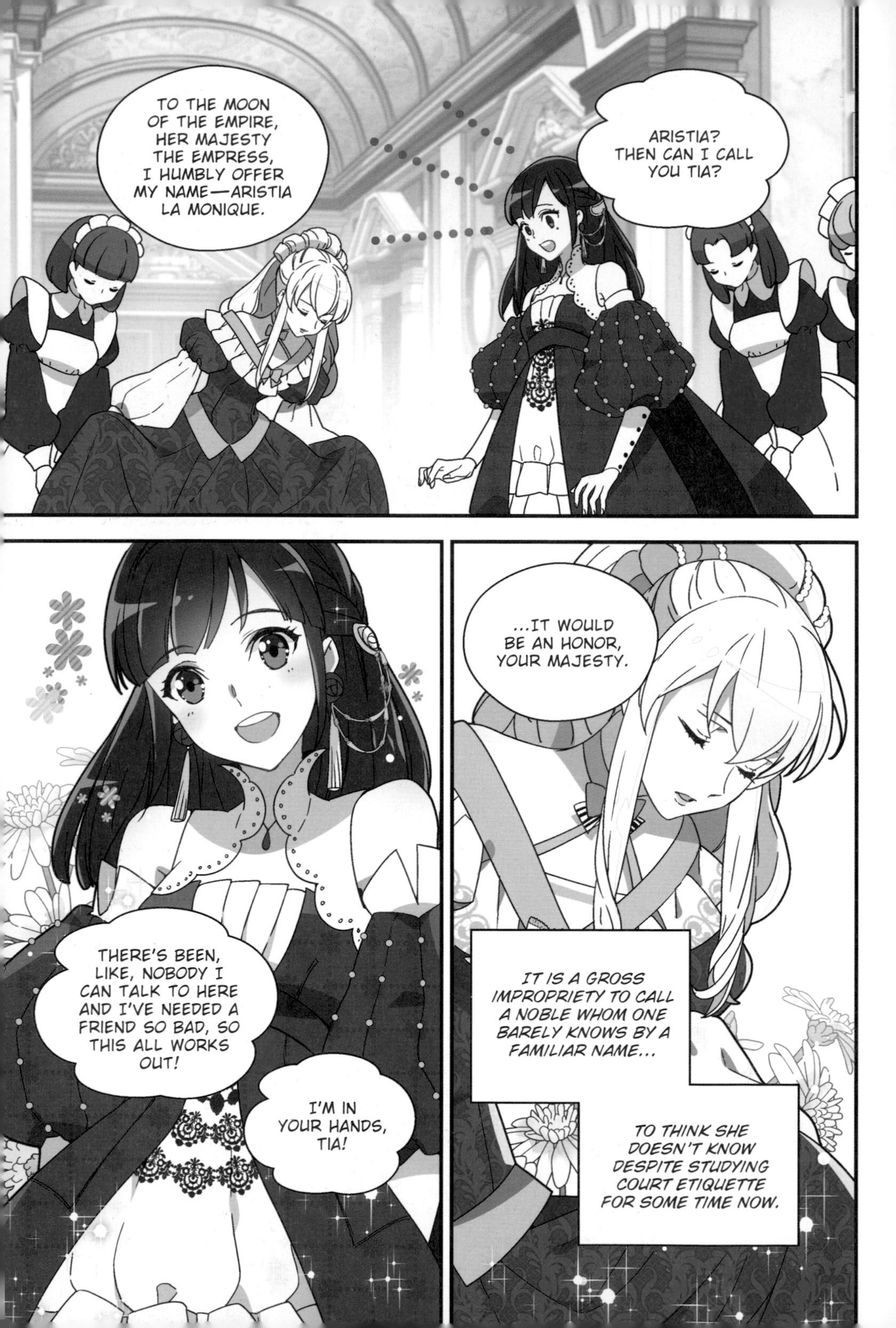
TO THE MOON OF THE EMPIRE, HER MAJESTY THE EMPRESS, I HUMBLY OFFER MY NAME—ARISTIA LA MONIQUE.
ARISTIA? THEN CAN I CALL YOU TIA?
THERE'S BEEN, LIKE, NOBODY I CAN TALK TO HERE AND I'VE NEEDED A FRIEND SO BAD, SO THIS ALL WORKS OUT!
I'M IN YOUR HANDS, TIA!
...IT WOULD BE AN HONOR, YOUR MAJESTY.
IT IS A GROSS IMPROPRIETY TO CALL A NOBLE WHOM ONE BARELY KNOWS BY A FAMILIAR NAME...
TO THINK SHE DOESN'T KNOW DESPITE STUDYING COURT ETIQUETTE FOR SOME TIME NOW.

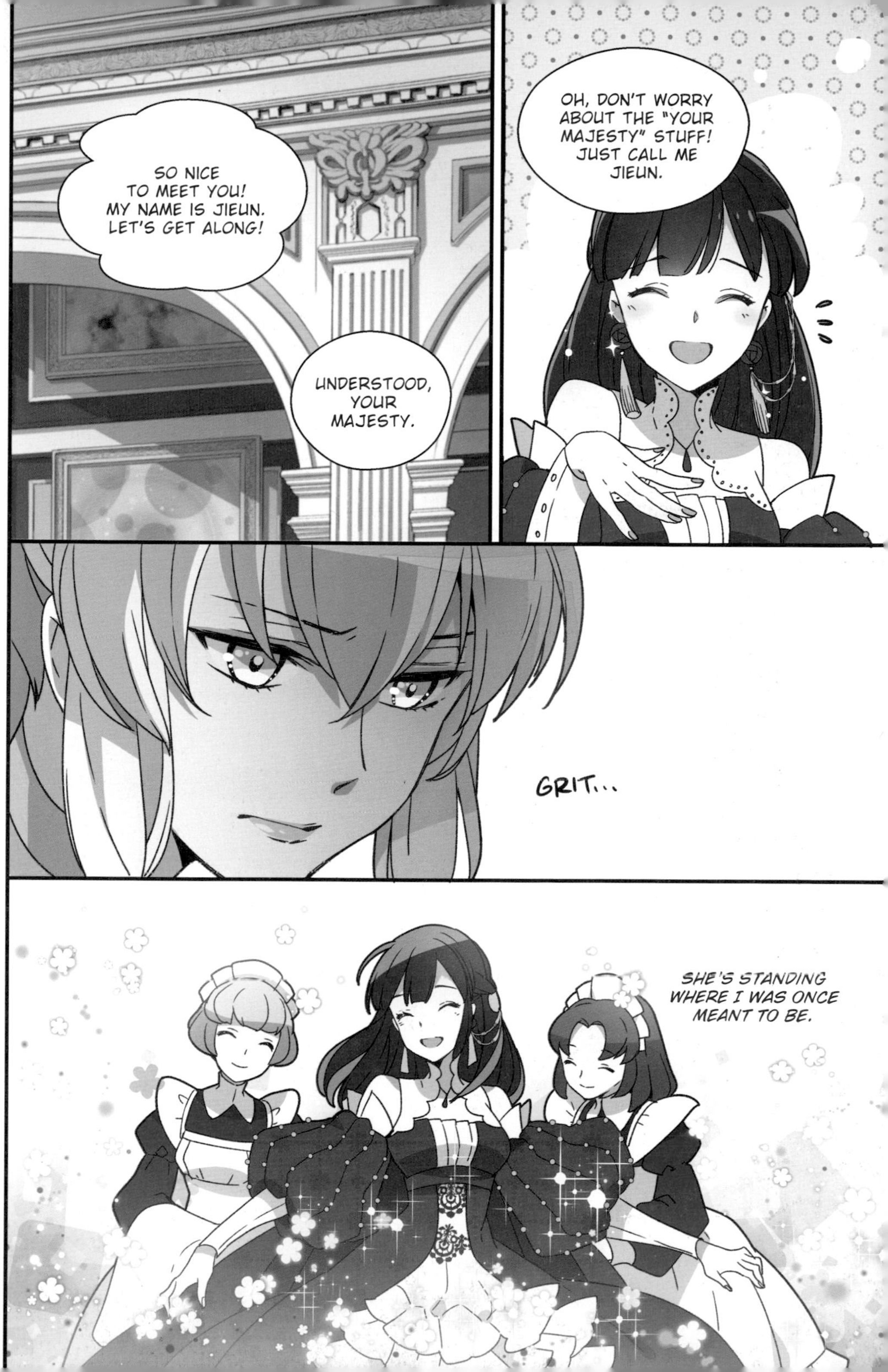
SO NICE TO MEET YOU! MY NAME IS JIEUN. LET'S GET ALONG!
UNDERSTOOD, YOUR MAJESTY.
OH, DON'T WORRY ABOUT THE "YOUR MAJESTY" STUFF! JUST CALL ME JIEUN.
GRIT...
SHE'S STANDING WHERE I WAS ONCE MEANT TO BE.

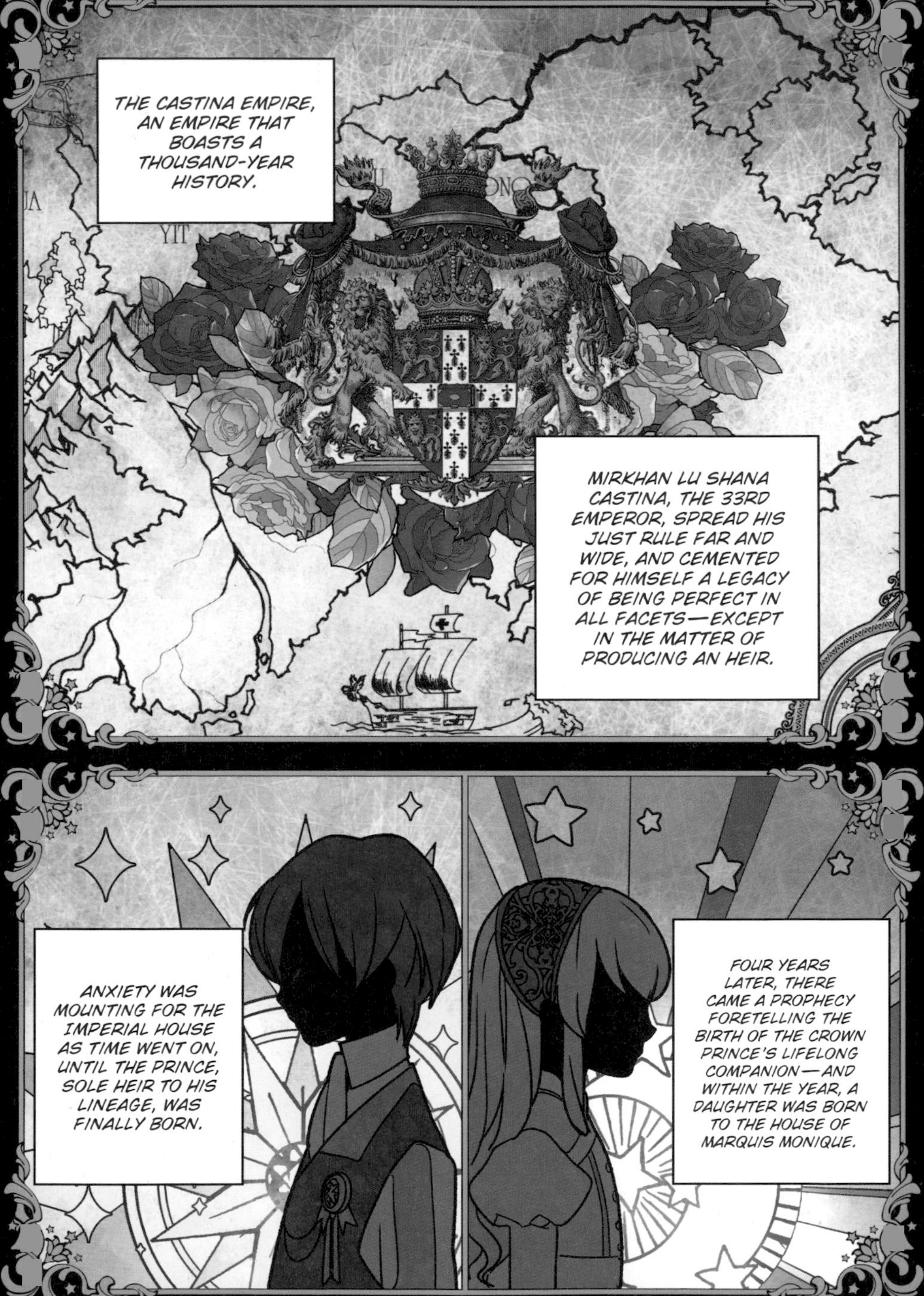
THE CASTINA EMPIRE, AN EMPIRE THAT BOASTS A THOUSAND-YEAR HISTORY.
MIRKHAN LU SHANA CASTINA, THE 33RD EMPEROR, SPREAD HIS JUST RULE FAR AND WIDE, AND CEMENTED FOR HIMSELF A LEGACY OF BEING PERFECT IN ALL FACETS—EXCEPT IN THE MATTER OF PRODUCING AN HEIR.
ANXIETY WAS MOUNTING FOR THE IMPERIAL HOUSE AS TIME WENT ON, UNTIL THE PRINCE, SOLE HEIR TO HIS LINEAGE, WAS FINALLY BORN.
FOUR YEARS LATER, THERE CAME A PROPHECY FORETELLING THE BIRTH OF THE CROWN PRINCE'S LIFELONG COMPANION—AND WITHIN THE YEAR, A DAUGHTER WAS BORN TO THE HOUSE OF MARQUIS MONIQUE.

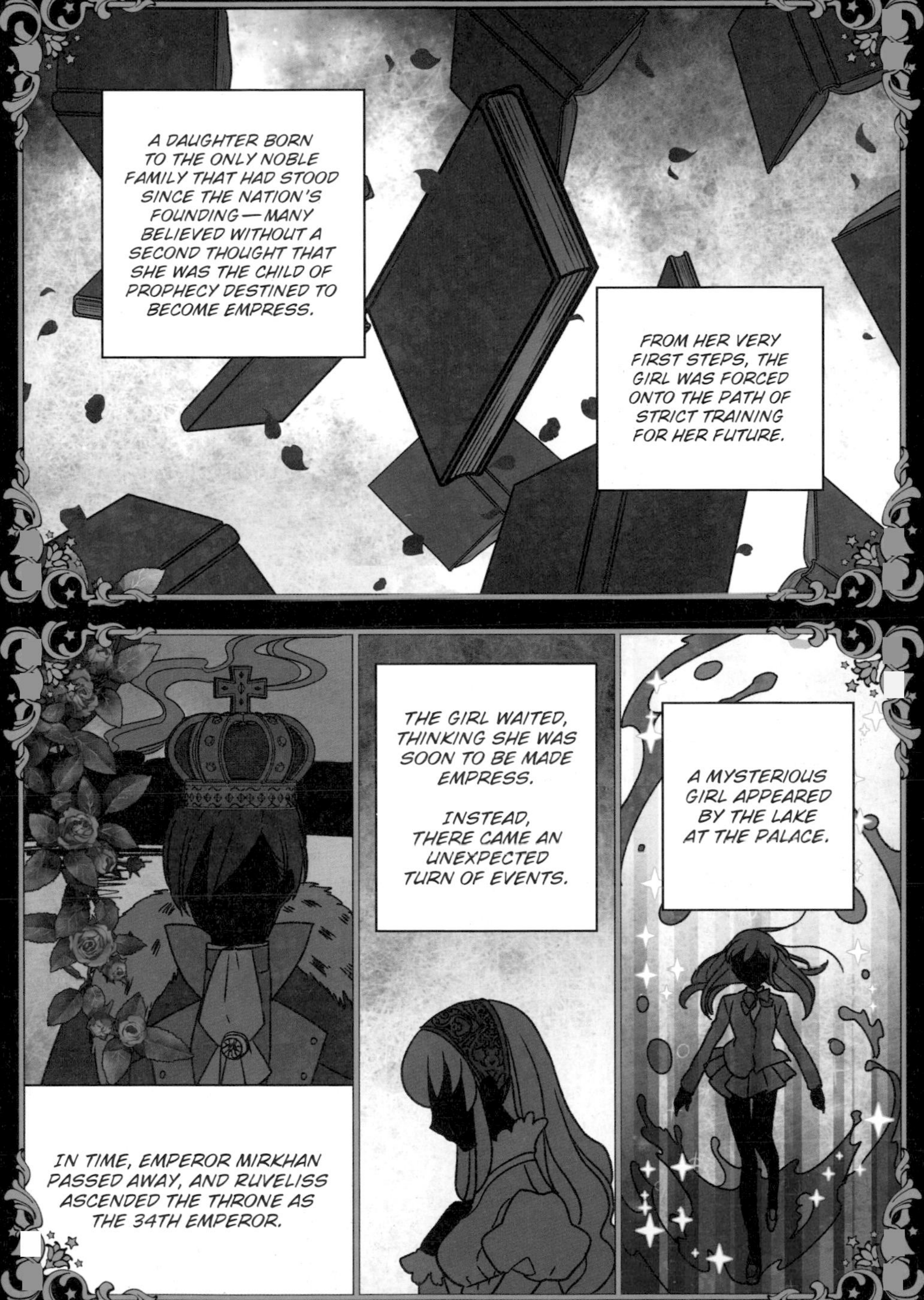
A DAUGHTER BORN TO THE ONLY NOBLE FAMILY THAT HAD STOOD SINCE THE NATION'S FOUNDING—MANY BELIEVED WITHOUT A SECOND THOUGHT THAT SHE WAS THE CHILD OF PROPHECY DESTINED TO BECOME EMPRESS.
FROM HER VERY FIRST STEPS, THE GIRL WAS FORCED ONTO THE PATH OF STRICT TRAINING FOR HER FUTURE.
IN TIME, EMPEROR MIRKHAN PASSED AWAY, AND RUVELISS ASCENDED THE THRONE AS THE 34TH EMPEROR.
THE GIRL WAITED, THINKING SHE WAS SOON TO BE MADE EMPRESS.
INSTEAD, THERE CAME AN UNEXPECTED TURN OF EVENTS.
A MYSTERIOUS GIRL APPEARED BY THE LAKE AT THE PALACE.

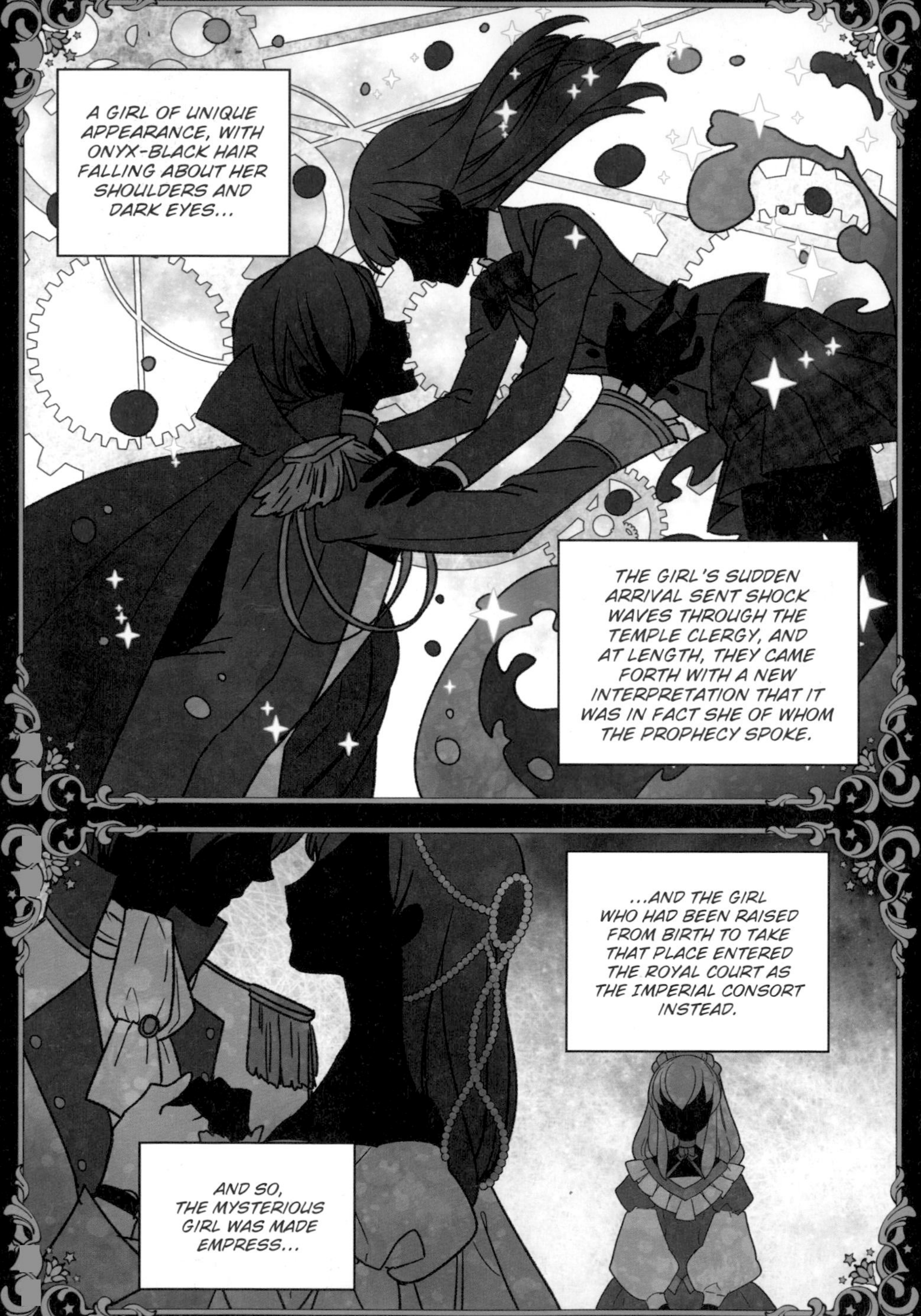
A GIRL OF UNIQUE APPEARANCE, WITH ONYX-BLACK HAIR FALLING ABOUT HER SHOULDERS AND DARK EYES...
THE GIRL'S SUDDEN ARRIVAL SENT SHOCK WAVES THROUGH THE TEMPLE CLERGY, AND AT LENGTH, THEY CAME FORTH WITH A NEW INTERPRETATION THAT IT WAS IN FACT SHE OF WHOM THE PROPHECY SPOKE.
AND SO, THE MYSTERIOUS GIRL WAS MADE EMPRESS...
...AND THE GIRL WHO HAD BEEN RAISED FROM BIRTH TO TAKE THAT PLACE ENTERED THE ROYAL COURT AS THE IMPERIAL CONSORT INSTEAD.

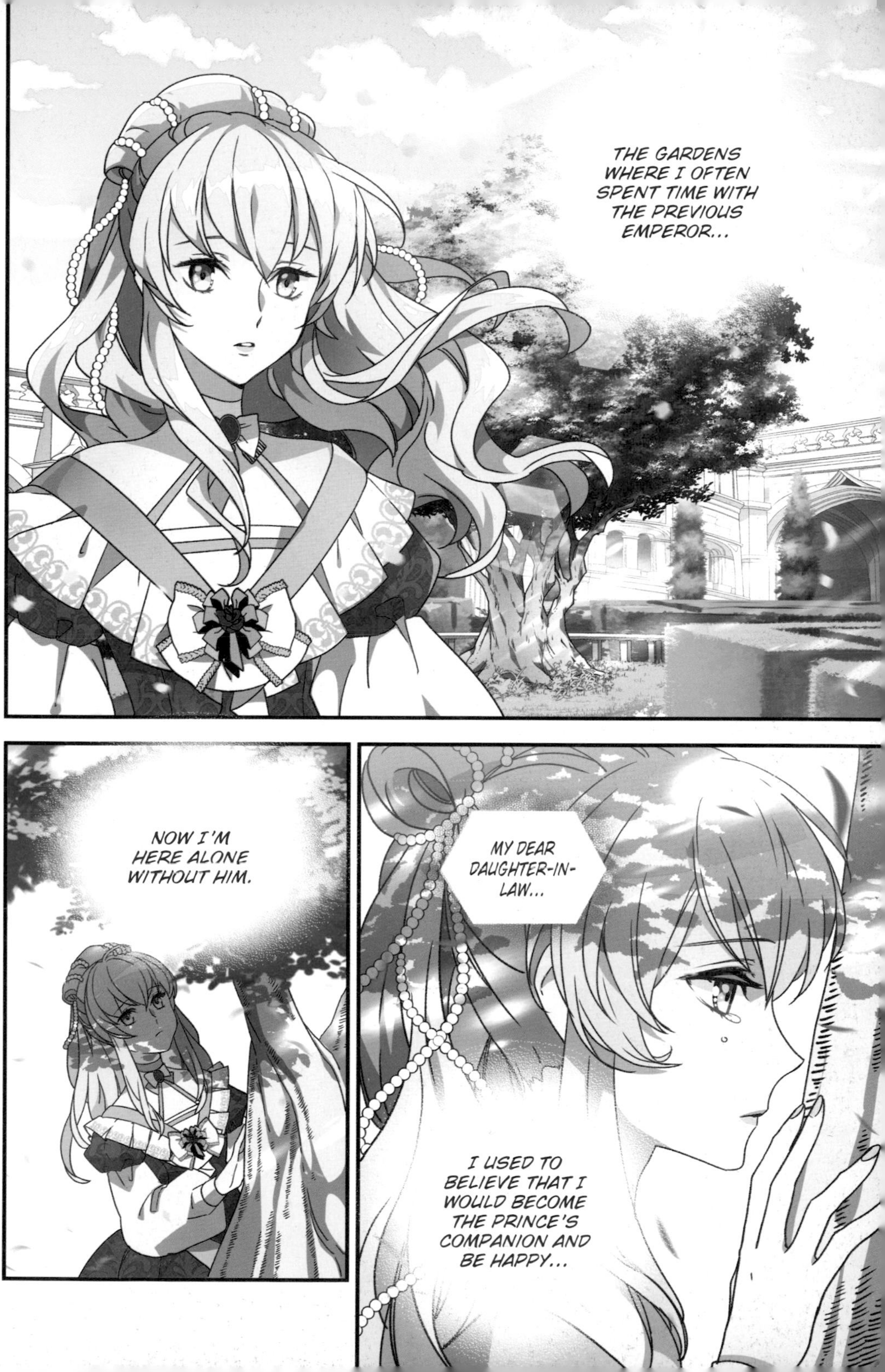
THE GARDENS WHERE I OFTEN SPENT TIME WITH THE PREVIOUS EMPEROR...
NOW I'M HERE ALONE WITHOUT HIM.
MY DEAR DAUGHTER-IN-LAW...
I USED TO BELIEVE THAT I WOULD BECOME THE PRINCE'S COMPANION AND BE HAPPY...

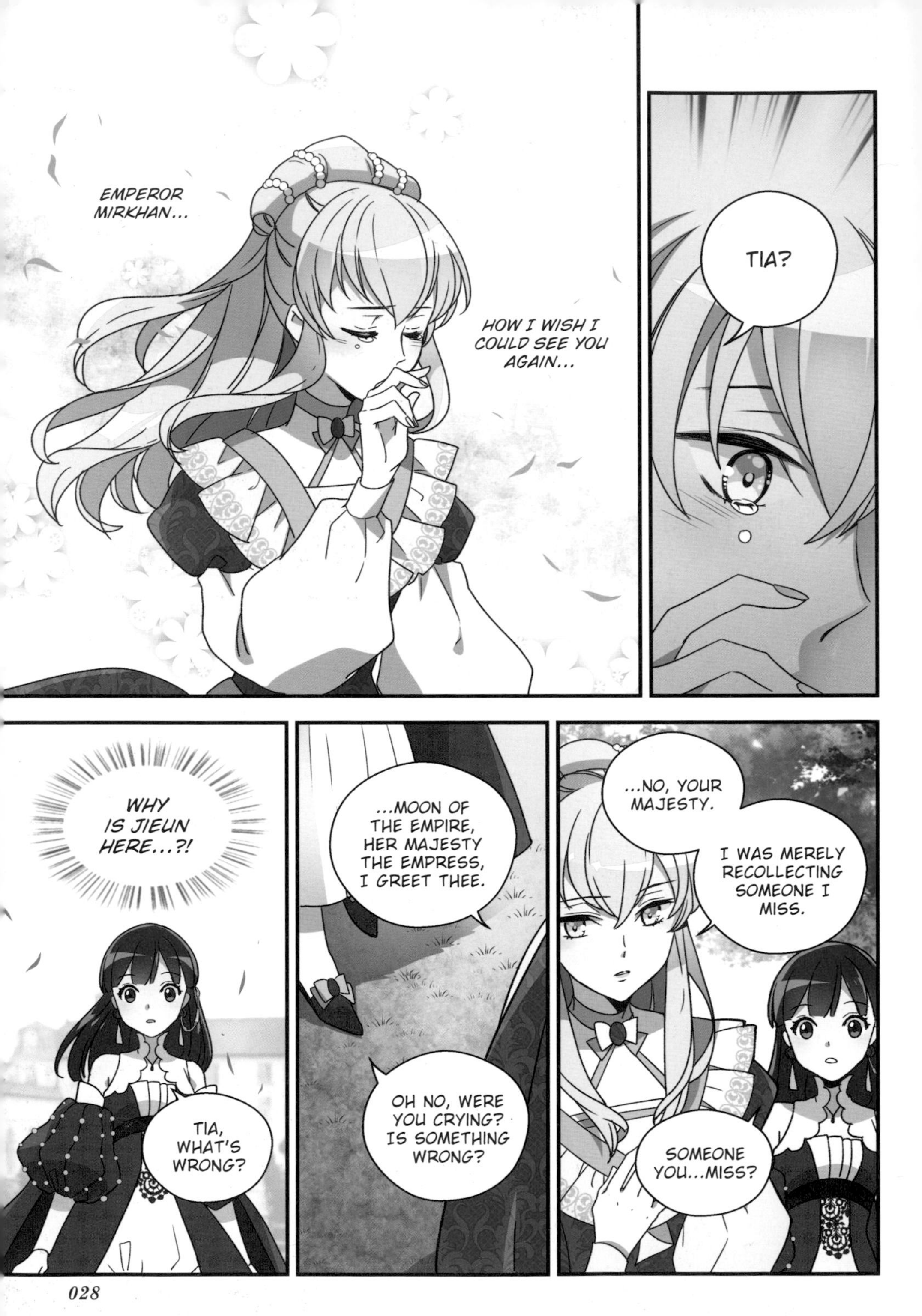
EMPEROR MIRKHAN...
HOW I WISH I COULD SEE YOU AGAIN...
TIA?
WHY IS JIEUN HERE...?!
TIA, WHAT'S WRONG?
...MOON OF THE EMPIRE, HER MAJESTY THE EMPRESS, I GREET THEE.
OH NO, WERE YOU CRYING? IS SOMETHING WRONG?
...NO, YOUR MAJESTY.
I WAS MERELY RECOLLECTING SOMEONE I MISS.
SOMEONE YOU...MISS?

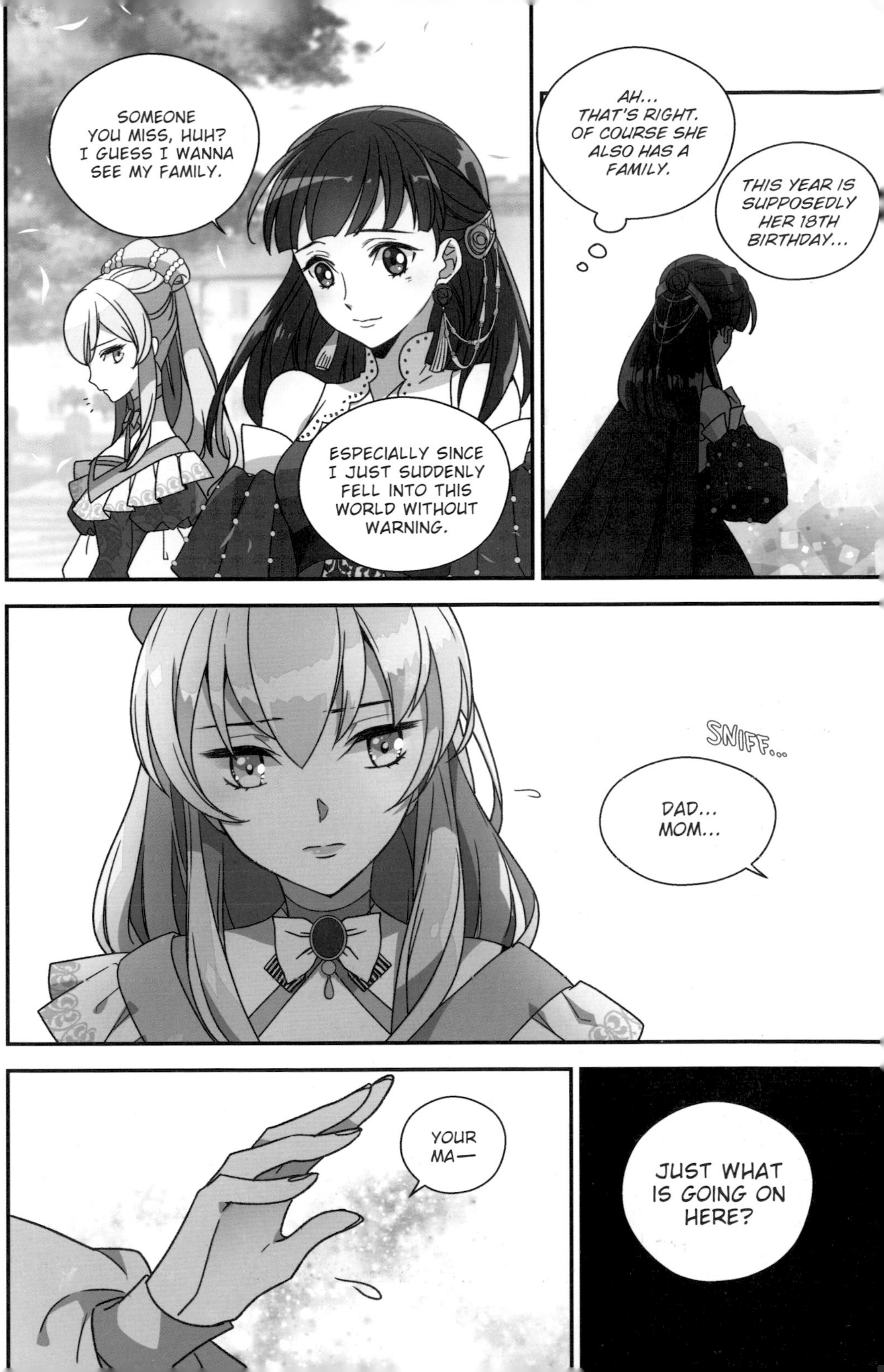
SOMEONE YOU MISS, HUH? I GUESS I WANNA SEE MY FAMILY.
ESPECIALLY SINCE I JUST SUDDENLY FELL INTO THIS WORLD WITHOUT WARNING.
AH... THAT'S RIGHT. OF COURSE SHE ALSO HAS A FAMILY.
THIS YEAR IS SUPPOSEDLY HER 18TH BIRTHDAY...
SNIFF...
DAD... MOM...
YOUR MA—
JUST WHAT IS GOING ON HERE?

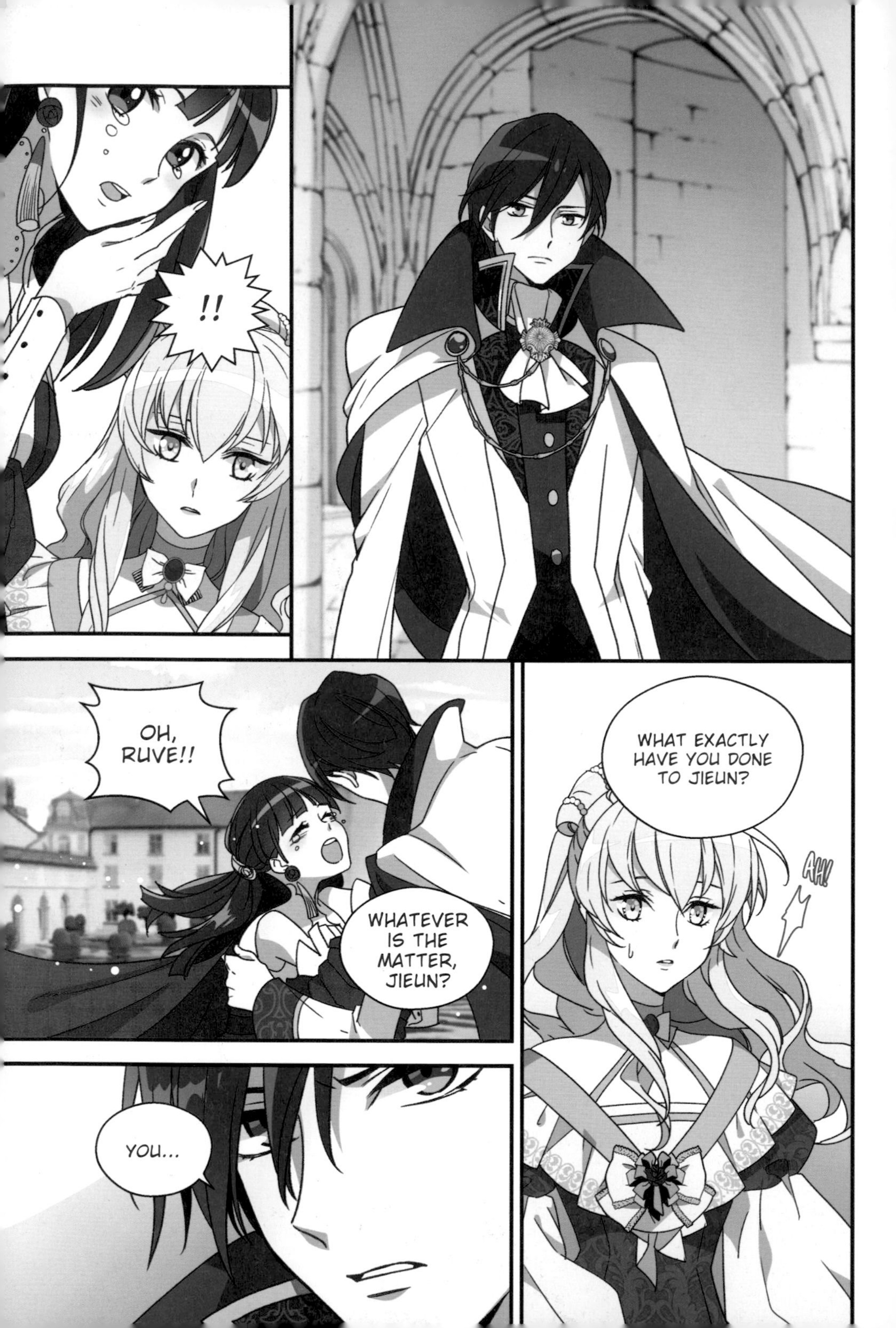
!!
OH, RUVE!!
WHATEVER IS THE MATTER, JIEUN?
WHAT EXACTLY HAVE YOU DONE TO JIEUN?
AH!
YOU...

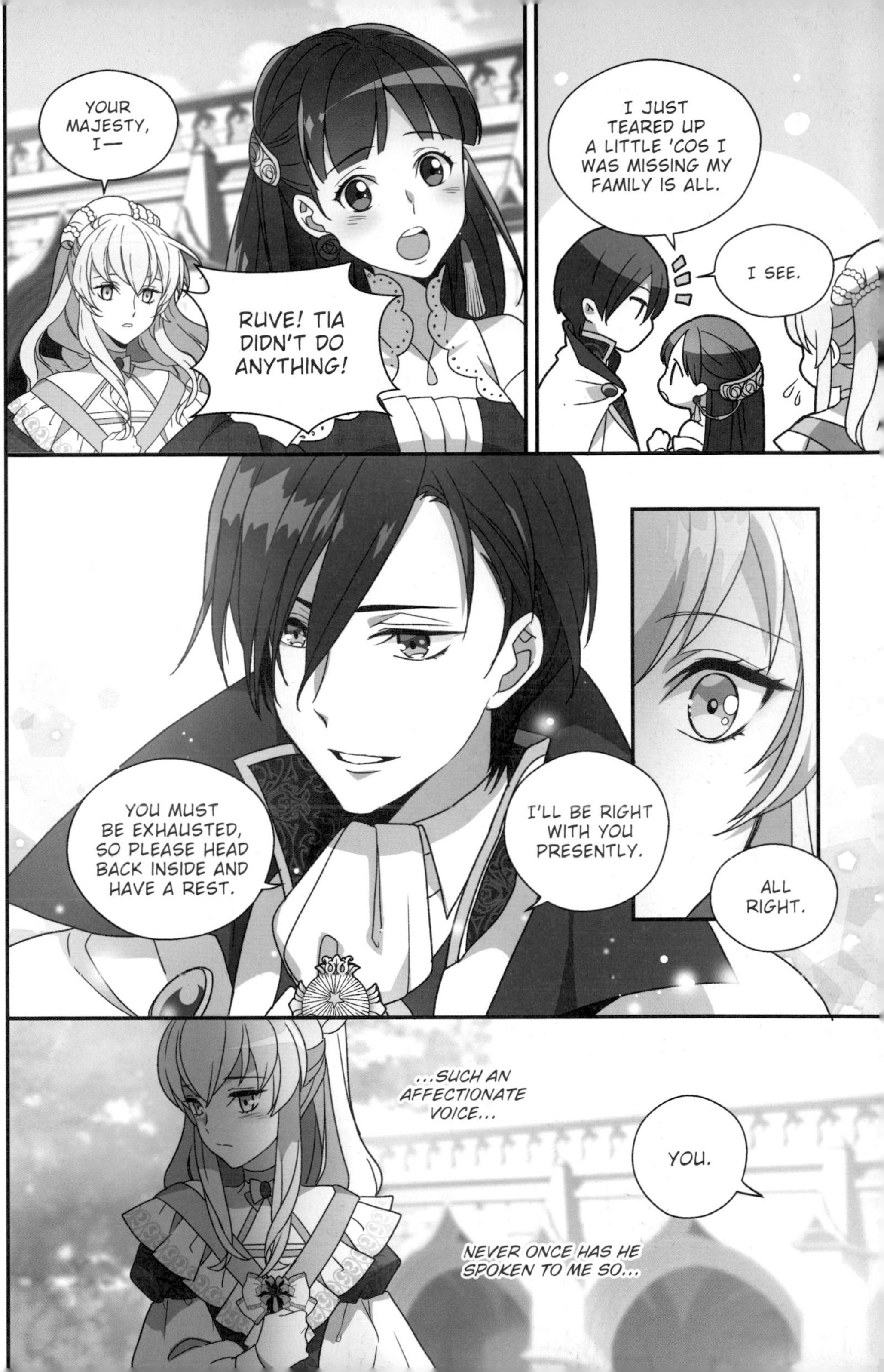
YOUR MAJESTY, I—
RUVE! TIA DIDN'T DO ANYTHING!
I JUST TEARED UP A LITTLE 'COS I WAS MISSING MY FAMILY IS ALL.
I SEE.
YOU MUST BE EXHAUSTED, SO PLEASE HEAD BACK INSIDE AND HAVE A REST.
I'LL BE RIGHT WITH YOU PRESENTLY.
ALL RIGHT.
...SUCH AN AFFECTIONATE VOICE...
YOU.
NEVER ONCE HAS HE SPOKEN TO ME SO...

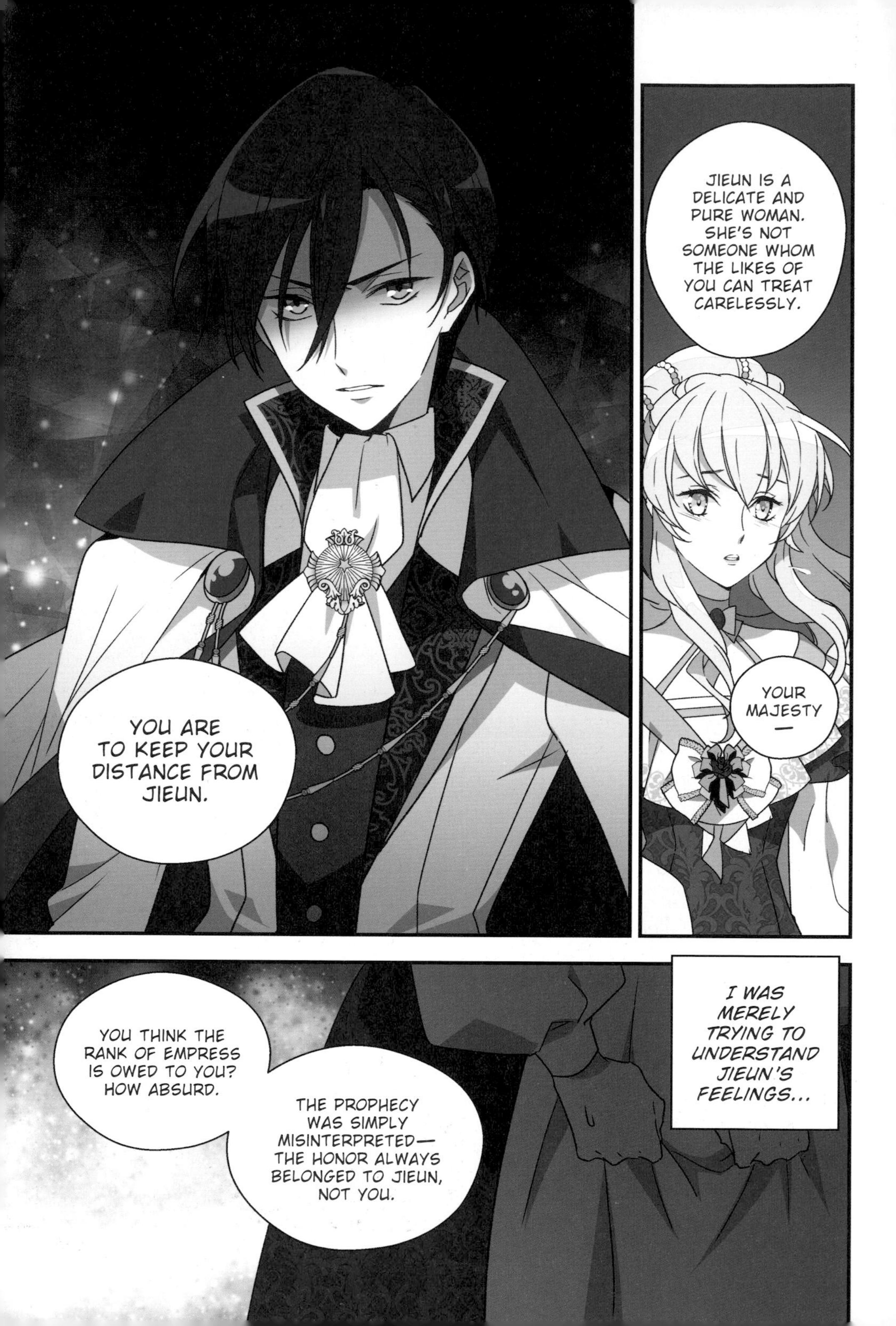
YOU ARE TO KEEP YOUR DISTANCE FROM JIEUN.
JIEUN IS A DELICATE AND PURE WOMAN. SHE'S NOT SOMEONE WHOM THE LIKES OF YOU CAN TREAT CARELESSLY.
YOUR MAJESTY—
YOU THINK THE RANK OF EMPRESS IS OWED TO YOU? HOW ABSURD.
THE PROPHECY WAS SIMPLY MISINTERPRETED—THE HONOR ALWAYS BELONGED TO JIEUN, NOT YOU.
I WAS MERELY TRYING TO UNDERSTAND JIEUN'S FEELINGS...

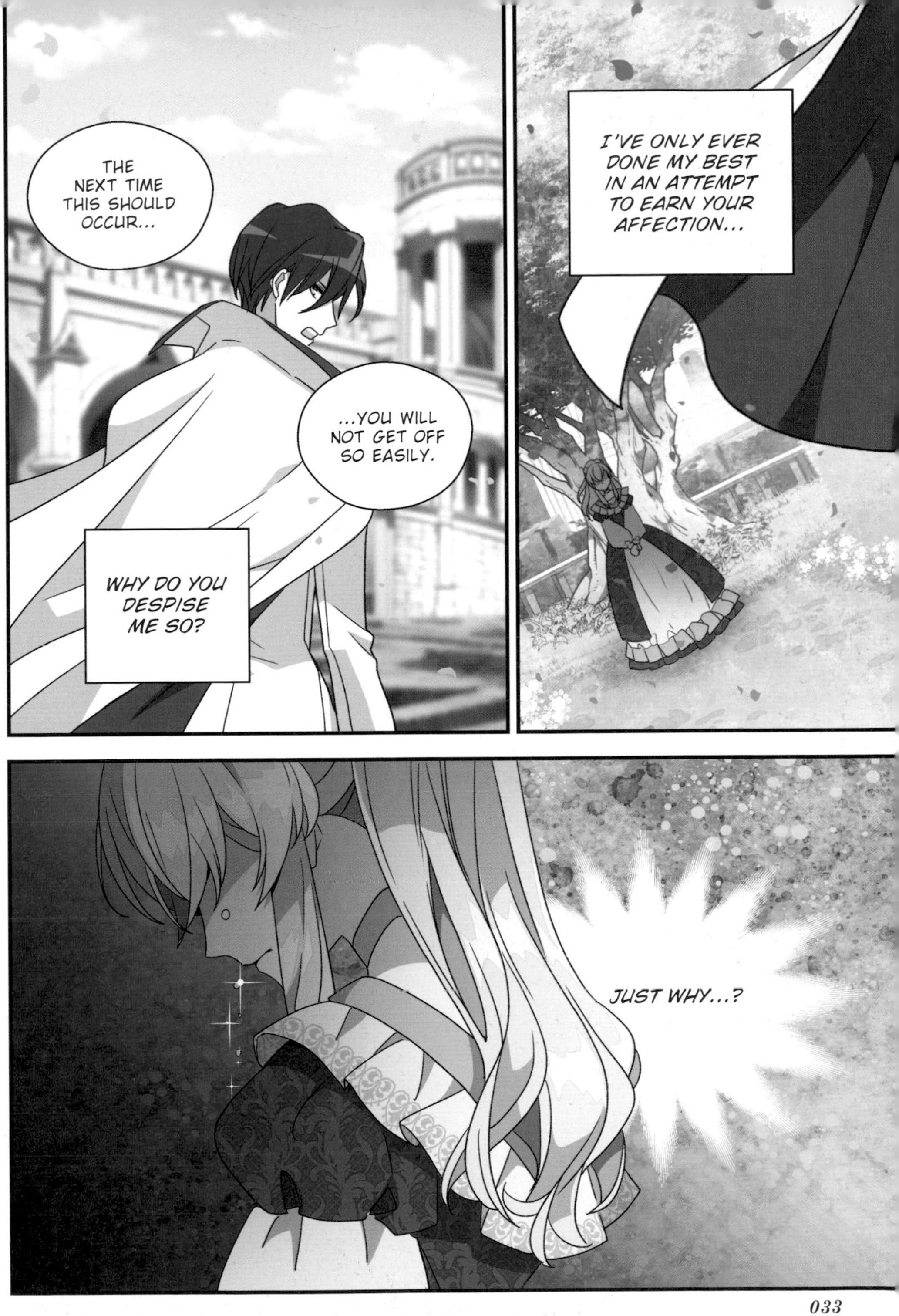
THE NEXT TIME THIS SHOULD OCCUR...
...YOU WILL NOT GET OFF SO EASILY.
WHY DO YOU DESPISE ME SO?
I'VE ONLY EVER DONE MY BEST IN AN ATTEMPT TO EARN YOUR AFFECTION...
JUST WHY...?

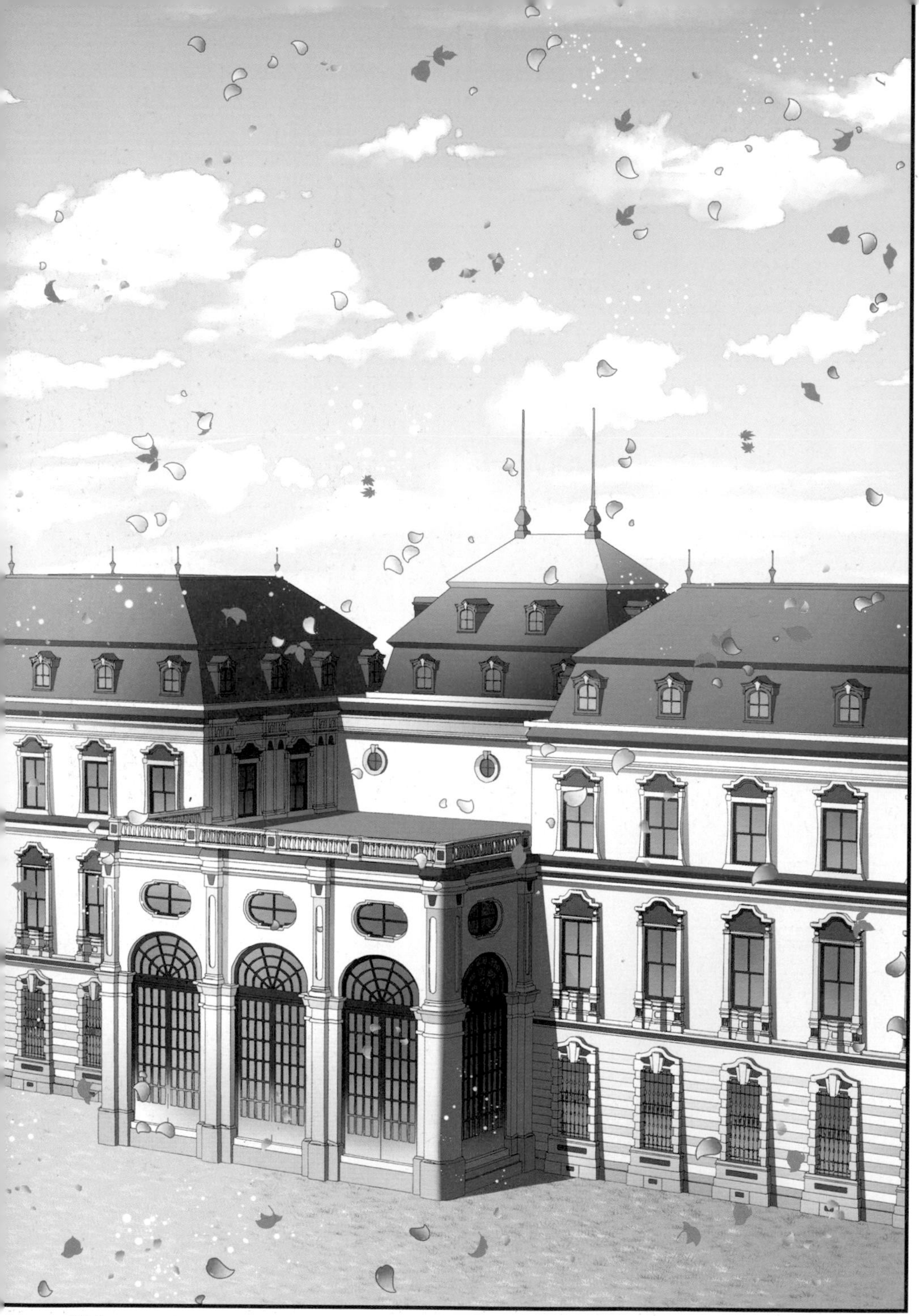

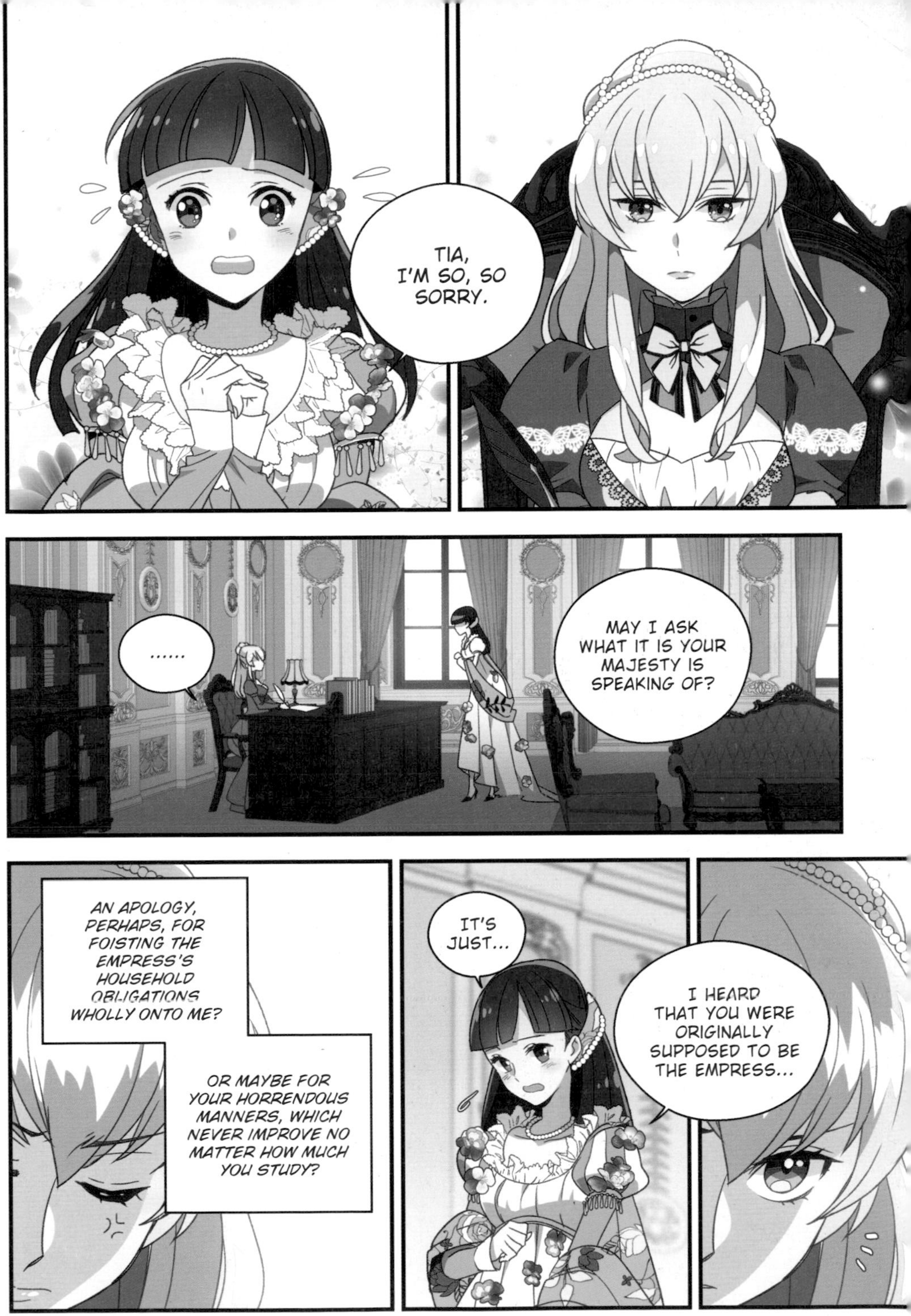
TIA, I'M SO, SO SORRY.
......
MAY I ASK WHAT IT IS YOUR MAJESTY IS SPEAKING OF?
AN APOLOGY, PERHAPS, FOR FOISTING THE EMPRESS'S HOUSEHOLD OBLIGATIONS WHOLLY ONTO ME?
OR MAYBE FOR YOUR HORRENDOUS MANNERS, WHICH NEVER IMPROVE NO MATTER HOW MUCH YOU STUDY?
IT'S JUST...
I HEARD THAT YOU WERE ORIGINALLY SUPPOSED TO BE THE EMPRESS...

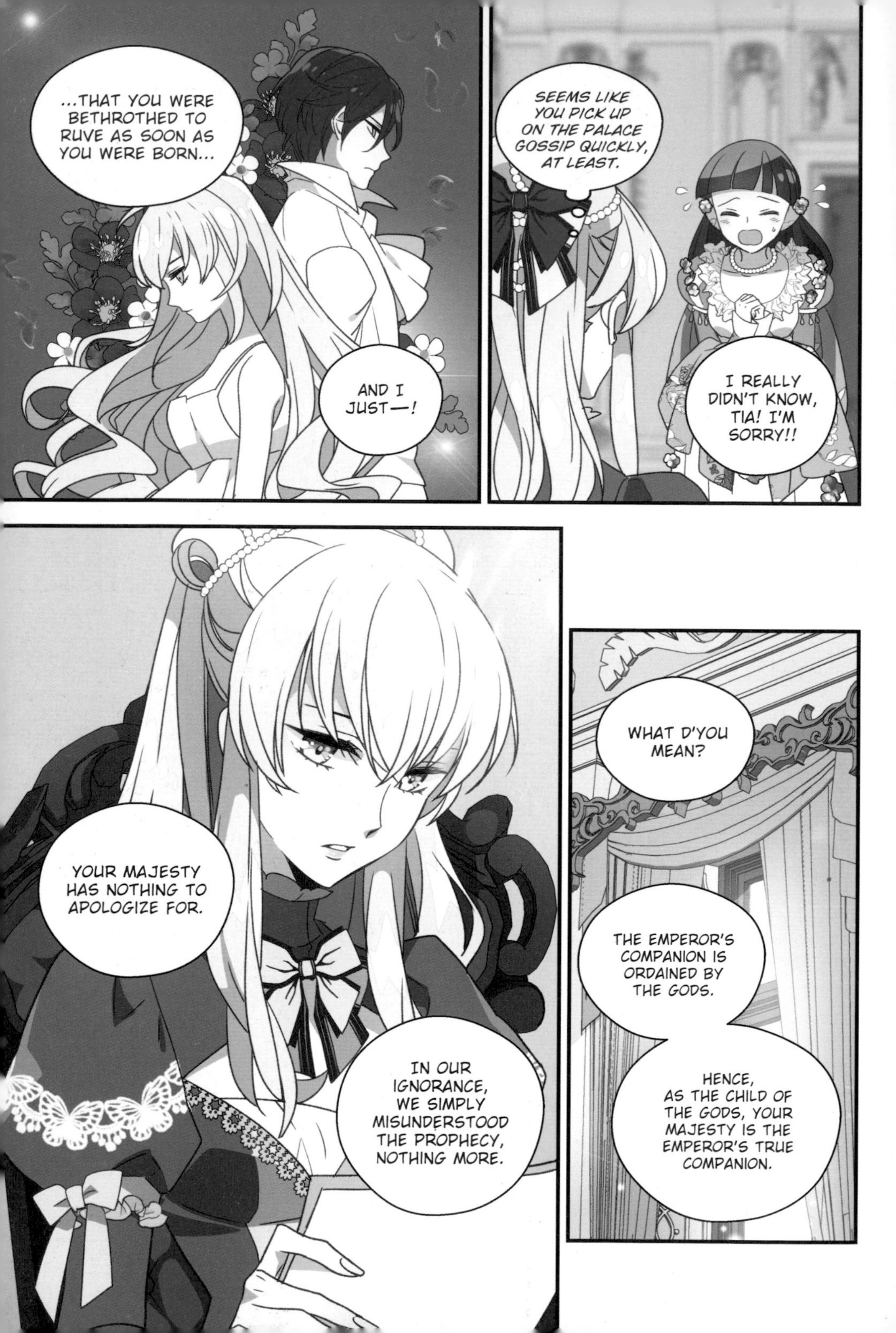
...THAT YOU WERE BETHROTHED TO RUVE AS SOON AS YOU WERE BORN...
AND I JUST—!
SEEMS LIKE YOU PICK UP ON THE PALACE GOSSIP QUICKLY, AT LEAST.
I REALLY DIDN'T KNOW, TIA! I'M SORRY!!
YOUR MAJESTY HAS NOTHING TO APOLOGIZE FOR.
IN OUR IGNORANCE, WE SIMPLY MISUNDERSTOOD THE PROPHECY, NOTHING MORE.
WHAT D'YOU MEAN?
THE EMPEROR'S COMPANION IS ORDAINED BY THE GODS.
HENCE, AS THE CHILD OF THE GODS, YOUR MAJESTY IS THE EMPEROR'S TRUE COMPANION.

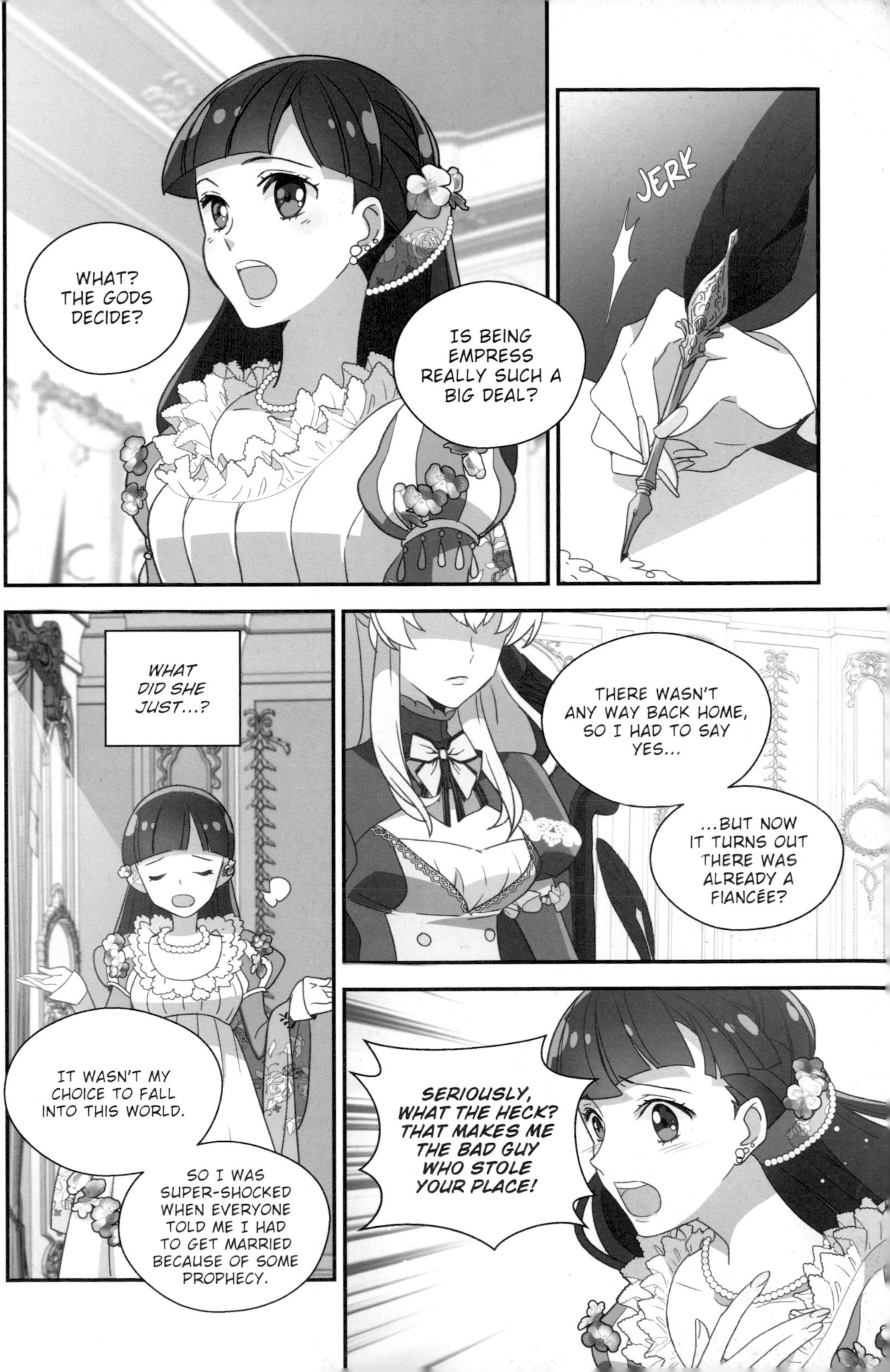
WHAT? THE GODS DECIDE?
IS BEING EMPRESS REALLY SUCH A BIG DEAL?
JERK
WHAT DID SHE JUST...?
THERE WASN'T ANY WAY BACK HOME, SO I HAD TO SAY YES...
...BUT NOW IT TURNS OUT THERE WAS ALREADY A FIANCÉE?
IT WASN'T MY CHOICE TO FALL INTO THIS WORLD.
SO I WAS SUPER-SHOCKED WHEN EVERYONE TOLD ME I HAD TO GET MARRIED BECAUSE OF SOME PROPHECY.
SERIOUSLY, WHAT THE HECK? THAT MAKES ME THE BAD GUY WHO STOLE YOUR PLACE!

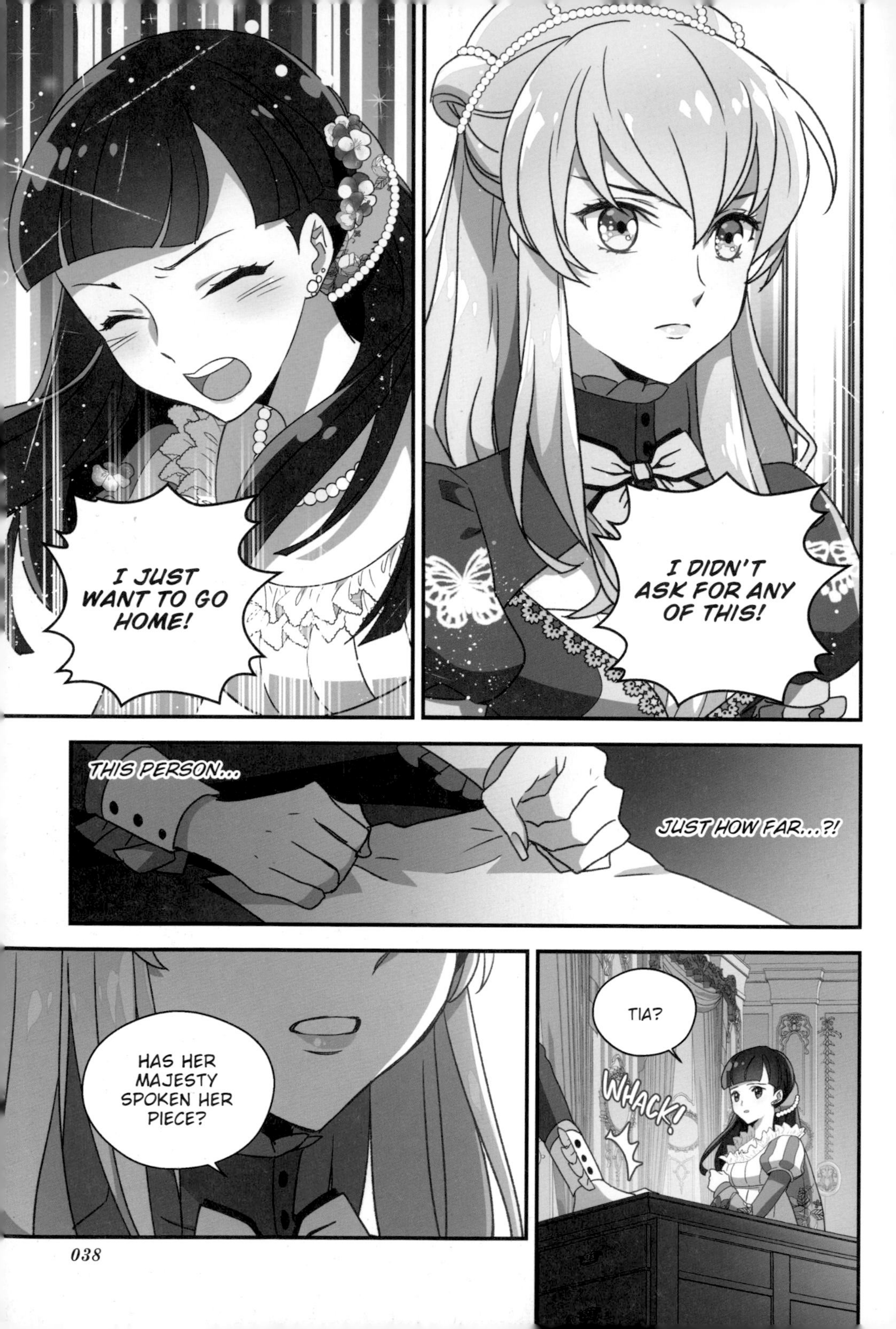

I DIDN'T ASK FOR ANY OF THIS!
I JUST WANT TO GO HOME!
THIS PERSON...
JUST HOW FAR...?!
TIA?
WHACK!
HAS HER MAJESTY SPOKEN HER PIECE?

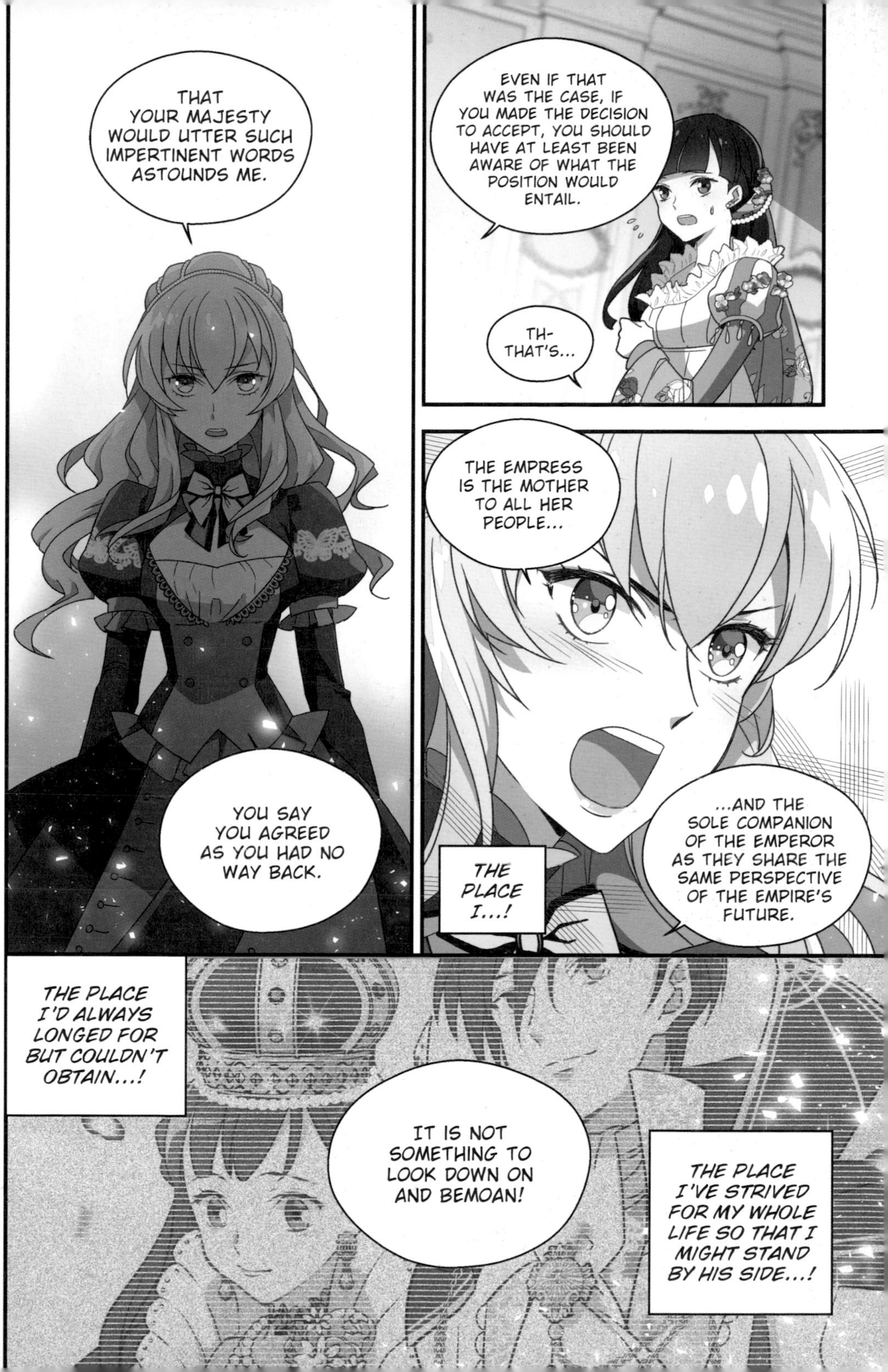
THAT YOUR MAJESTY WOULD UTTER SUCH IMPERTINENT WORDS ASTOUNDS ME.
YOU SAY YOU AGREED AS YOU HAD NO WAY BACK.
EVEN IF THAT WAS THE CASE, IF YOU MADE THE DECISION TO ACCEPT, YOU SHOULD HAVE AT LEAST BEEN AWARE OF WHAT THE POSITION WOULD ENTAIL.
TH- THAT'S...
THE EMPRESS IS THE MOTHER TO ALL HER PEOPLE...
...AND THE SOLE COMPANION OF THE EMPEROR AS THEY SHARE THE SAME PERSPECTIVE OF THE EMPIRE'S FUTURE.
THE PLACE I...!
THE PLACE I'D ALWAYS LONGED FOR BUT COULDN'T OBTAIN...!
IT IS NOT SOMETHING TO LOOK DOWN ON AND BEMOAN!
THE PLACE I'VE STRIVED FOR MY WHOLE LIFE SO THAT I MIGHT STAND BY HIS SIDE...!

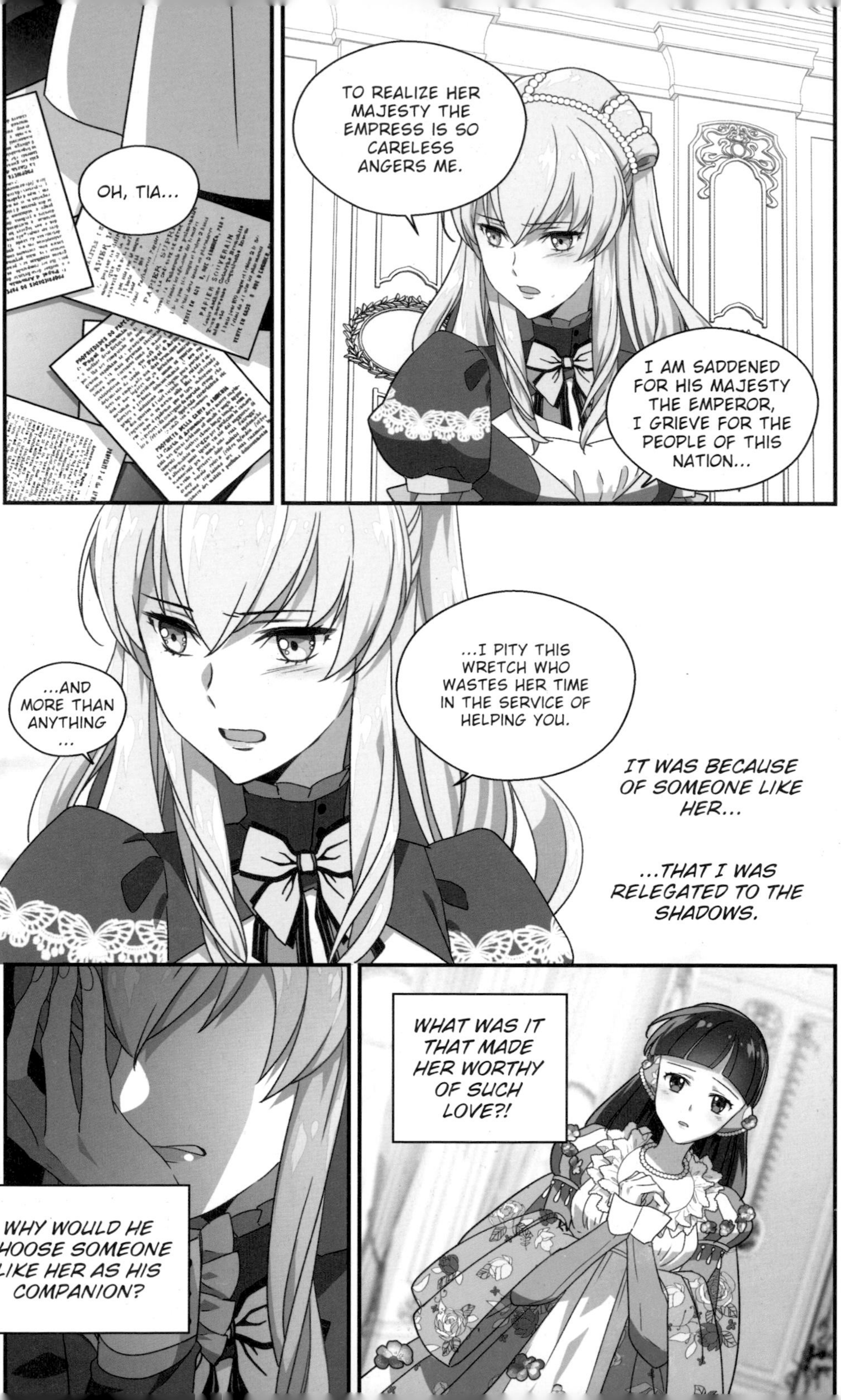
OH, TIA...
TO REALIZE HER MAJESTY THE EMPRESS IS SO CARELESS ANGERS ME.
I AM SADDENED FOR HIS MAJESTY THE EMPEROR, I GRIEVE FOR THE PEOPLE OF THIS NATION...
...AND MORE THAN ANYTHING...
...I PITY THIS WRETCH WHO WASTES HER TIME IN THE SERVICE OF HELPING YOU.
IT WAS BECAUSE OF SOMEONE LIKE HER...
...THAT I WAS RELEGATED TO THE SHADOWS.
WHY WOULD HE CHOOSE SOMEONE LIKE HER AS HIS COMPANION?
WHAT WAS IT THAT MADE HER WORTHY OF SUCH LOVE?!

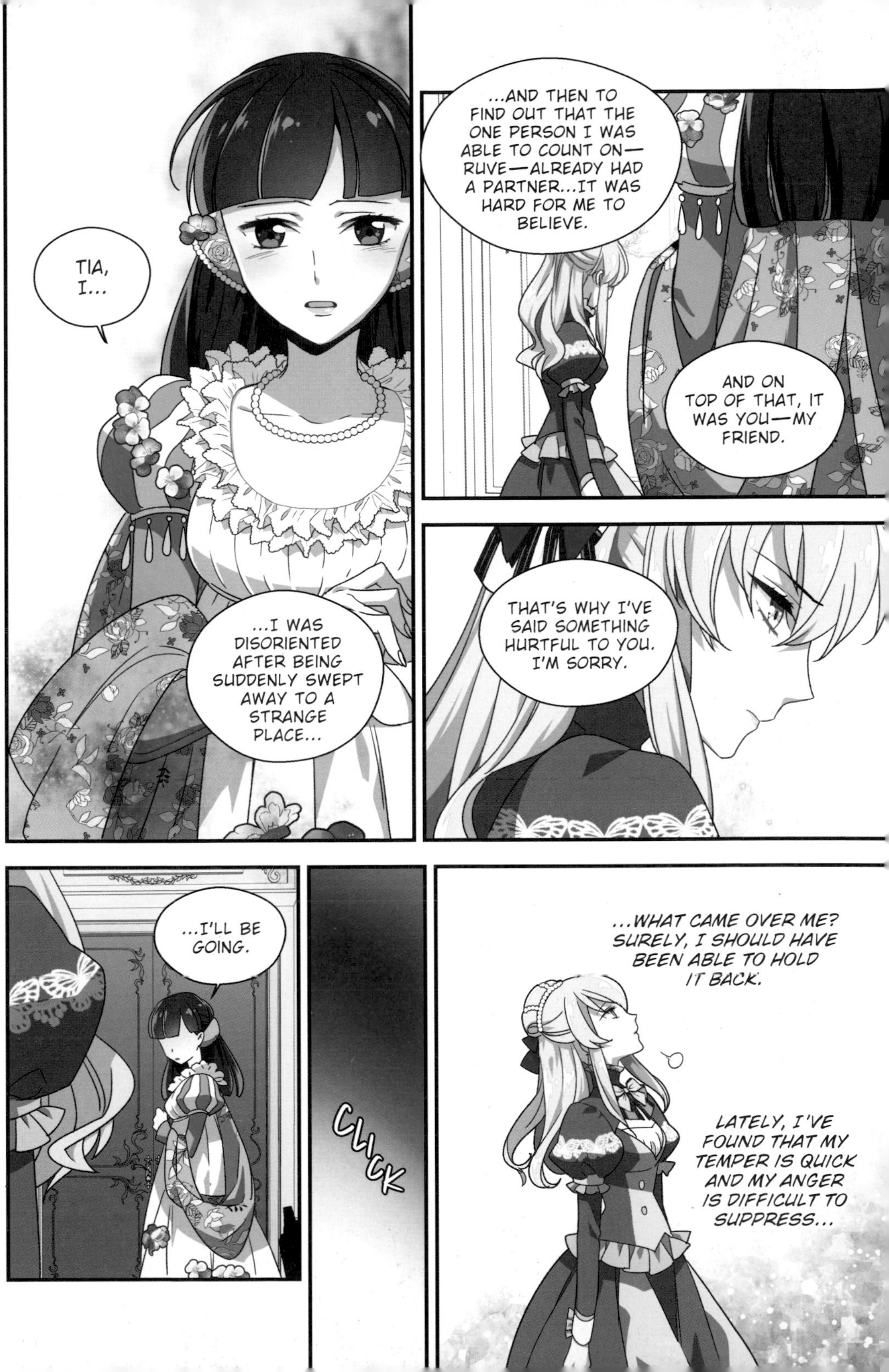
TIA, I...
...I WAS DISORIENTED AFTER BEING SUDDENLY SWEPT AWAY TO A STRANGE PLACE...
...AND THEN TO FIND OUT THAT THE ONE PERSON I WAS ABLE TO COUNT ON—RUVE—ALREADY HAD A PARTNER...IT WAS HARD FOR ME TO BELIEVE.
AND ON TOP OF THAT, IT WAS YOU—MY FRIEND.
THAT'S WHY I'VE SAID SOMETHING HURTFUL TO YOU. I'M SORRY.
...I'LL BE GOING.
CLICK
...WHAT CAME OVER ME? SURELY, I SHOULD HAVE BEEN ABLE TO HOLD IT BACK.
LATELY, I'VE FOUND THAT MY TEMPER IS QUICK AND MY ANGER IS DIFFICULT TO SUPPRESS...

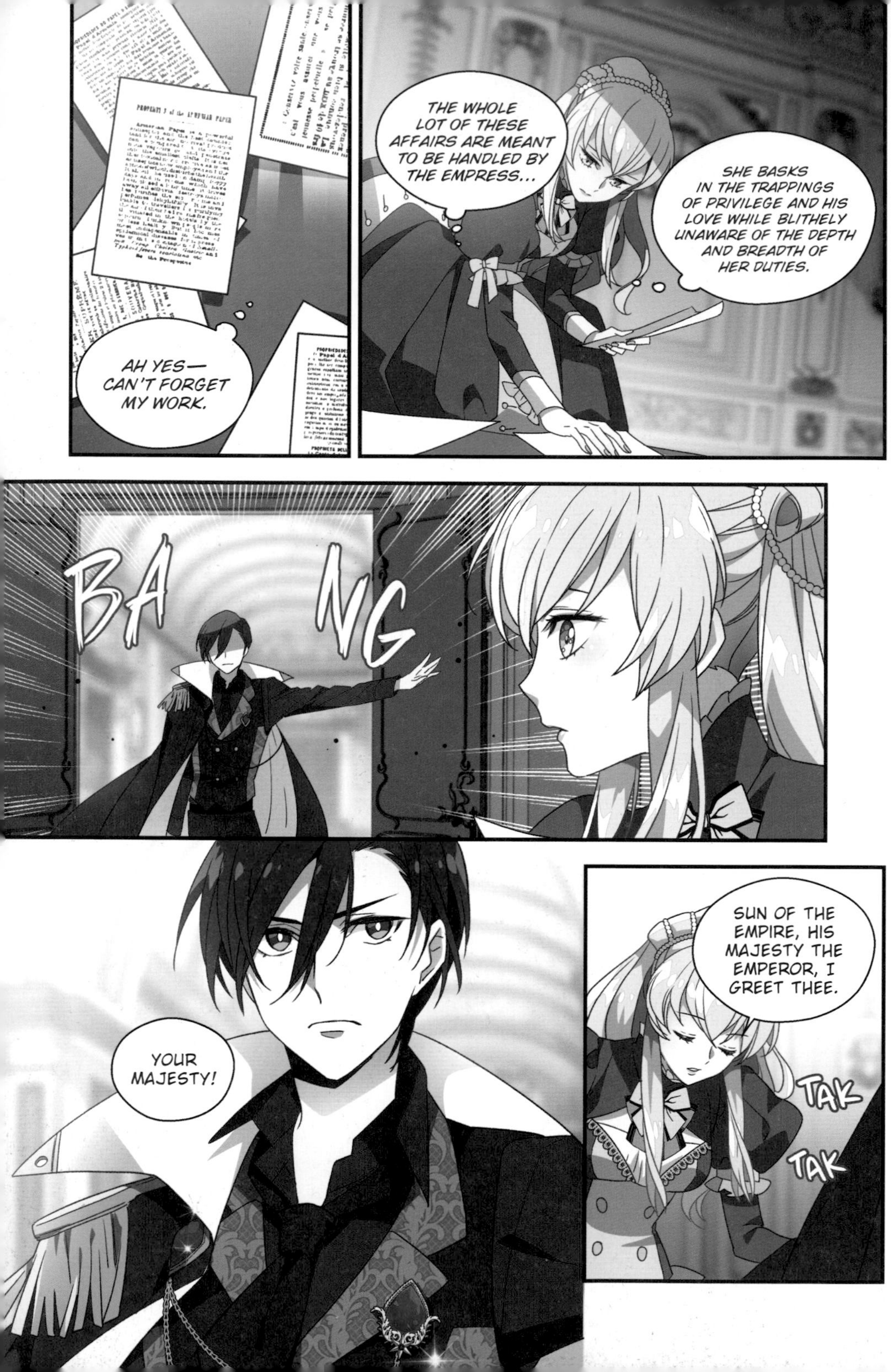
AH YES—
CAN'T FORGET
MY WORK.
THE WHOLE
LOT OF THESE
AFFAIRS ARE MEANT
TO BE HANDLED BY
THE EMPRESS...
SHE BASKS
IN THE TRAPPINGS
OF PRIVILEGE AND HIS
LOVE WHILE BLITHELY
UNAWARE OF THE DEPTH
AND BREADTH OF
HER DUTIES.
BANG
YOUR
MAJESTY!
SUN OF THE
EMPIRE, HIS
MAJESTY THE
EMPEROR, I
GREET THEE.
TAK
TAK

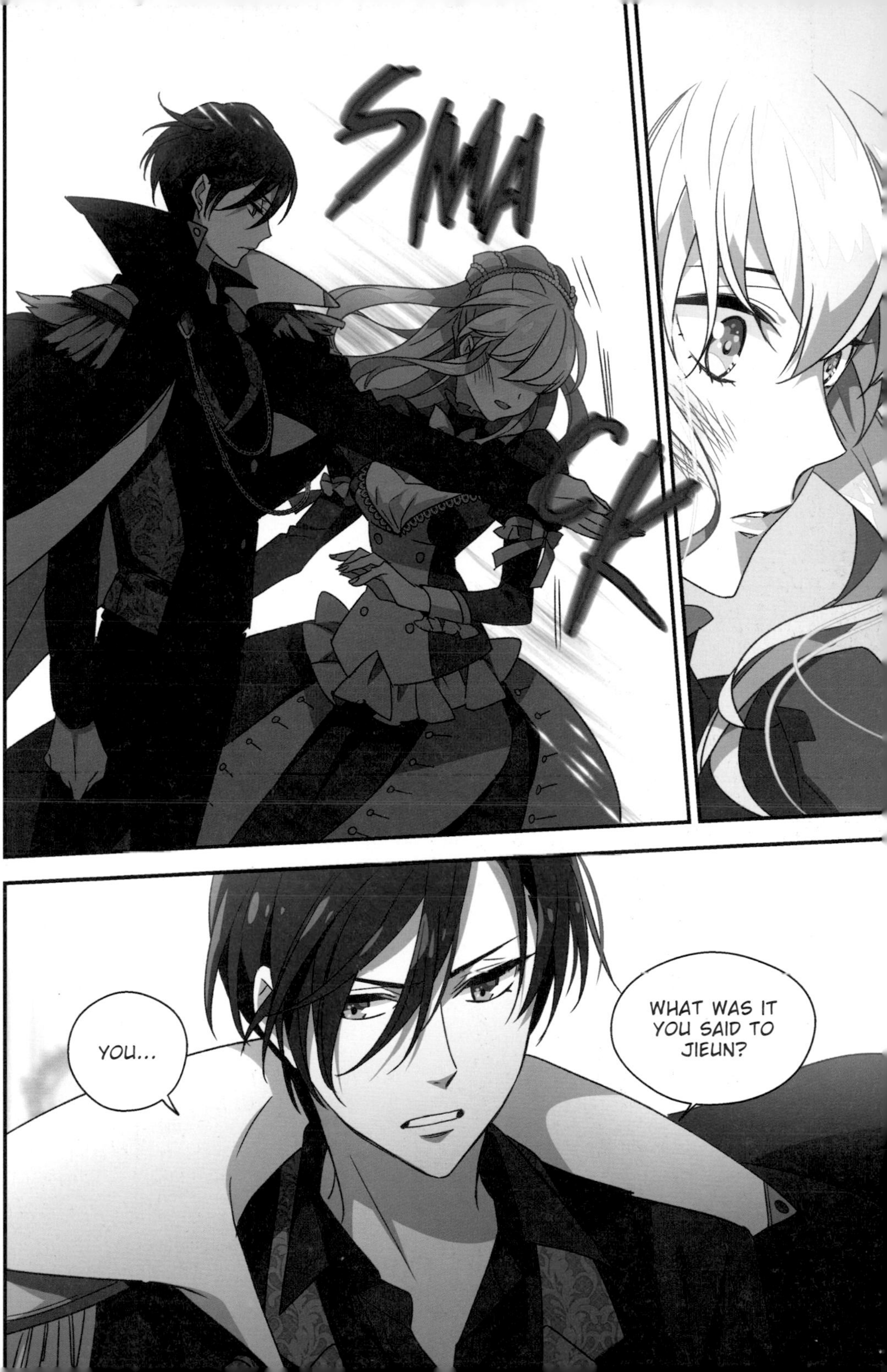
SMACK
YOU...
WHAT WAS IT YOU SAID TO JIEUN?

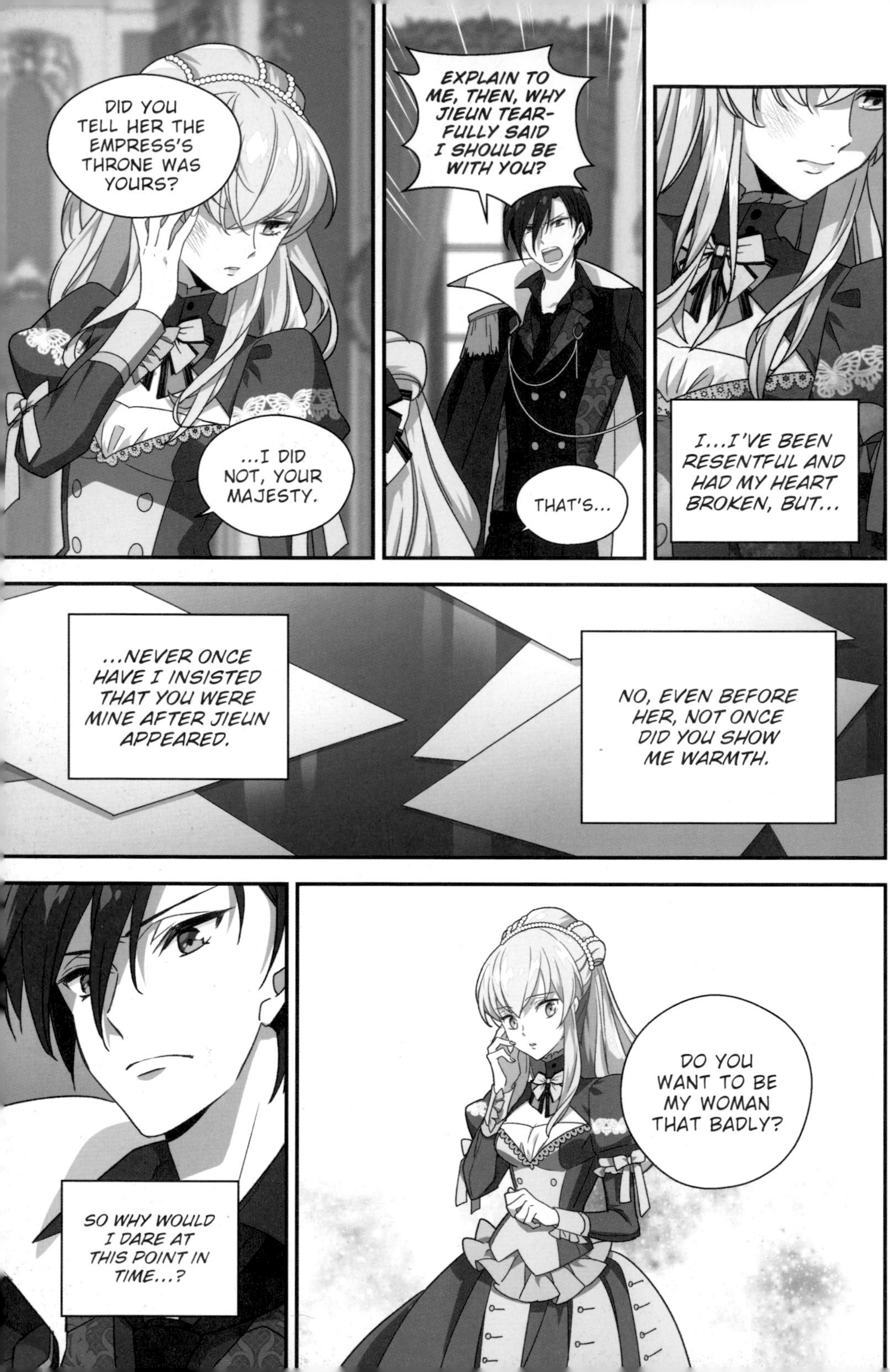
DID YOU TELL HER THE EMPRESS'S THRONE WAS YOURS?
...I DID NOT, YOUR MAJESTY.
EXPLAIN TO ME, THEN, WHY JIEUN TEAR-FULLY SAID I SHOULD BE WITH YOU?
THAT'S...
I...I'VE BEEN RESENTFUL AND HAD MY HEART BROKEN, BUT...
...NEVER ONCE HAVE I INSISTED THAT YOU WERE MINE AFTER JIEUN APPEARED.
NO, EVEN BEFORE HER, NOT ONCE DID YOU SHOW ME WARMTH.
SO WHY WOULD I DARE AT THIS POINT IN TIME...?
DO YOU WANT TO BE MY WOMAN THAT BADLY?

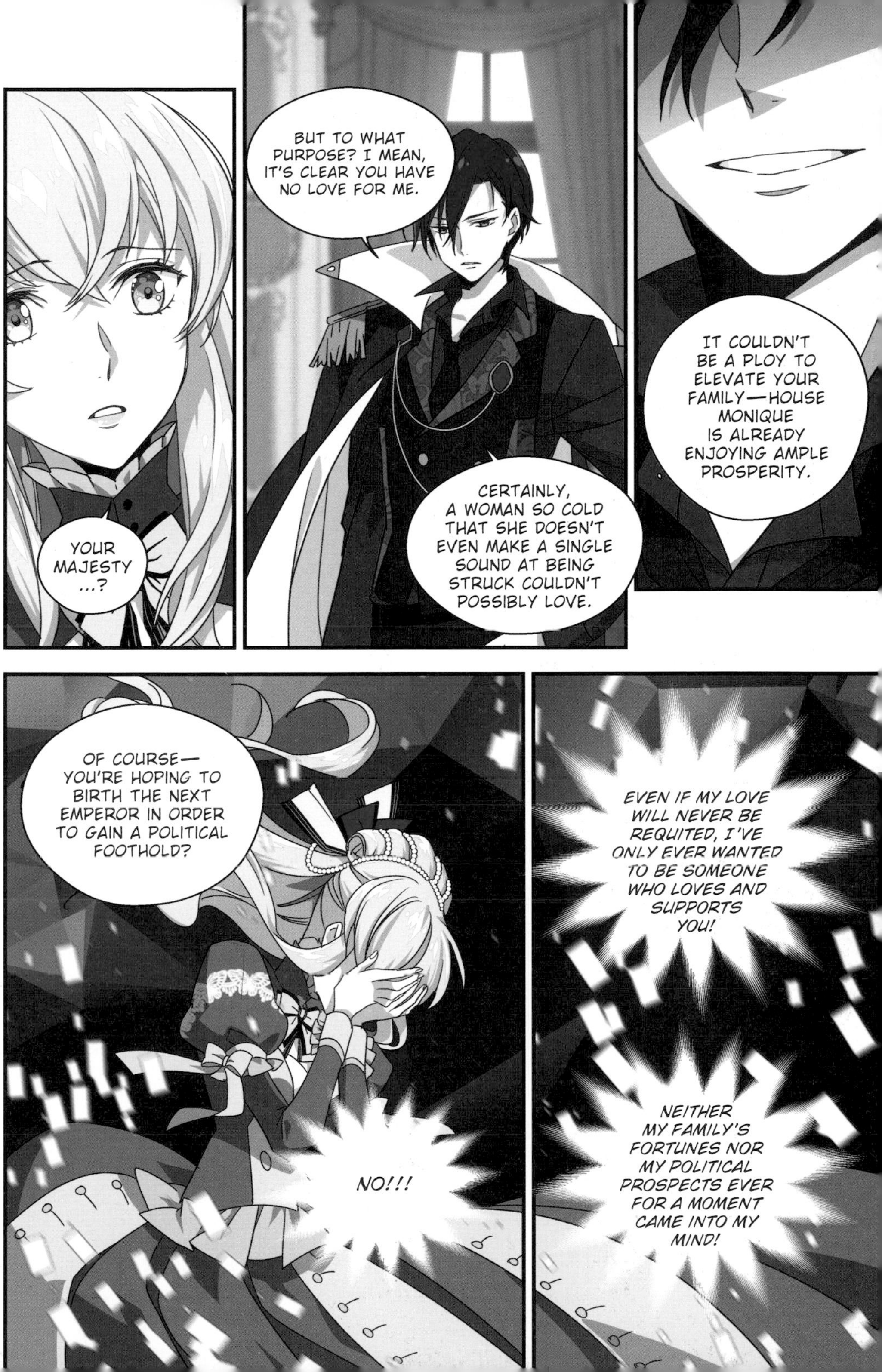
BUT TO WHAT PURPOSE? I MEAN, IT'S CLEAR YOU HAVE NO LOVE FOR ME.
IT COULDN'T BE A PLOY TO ELEVATE YOUR FAMILY—HOUSE MONIQUE IS ALREADY ENJOYING AMPLE PROSPERITY.
CERTAINLY, A WOMAN SO COLD THAT SHE DOESN'T EVEN MAKE A SINGLE SOUND AT BEING STRUCK COULDN'T POSSIBLY LOVE.
YOUR MAJESTY ...?
OF COURSE— YOU'RE HOPING TO BIRTH THE NEXT EMPEROR IN ORDER TO GAIN A POLITICAL FOOTHOLD?
NO!!!
EVEN IF MY LOVE WILL NEVER BE REQUITED, I'VE ONLY EVER WANTED TO BE SOMEONE WHO LOVES AND SUPPORTS YOU!
NEITHER MY FAMILY'S FORTUNES NOR MY POLITICAL PROSPECTS EVER FOR A MOMENT CAME INTO MY MIND!

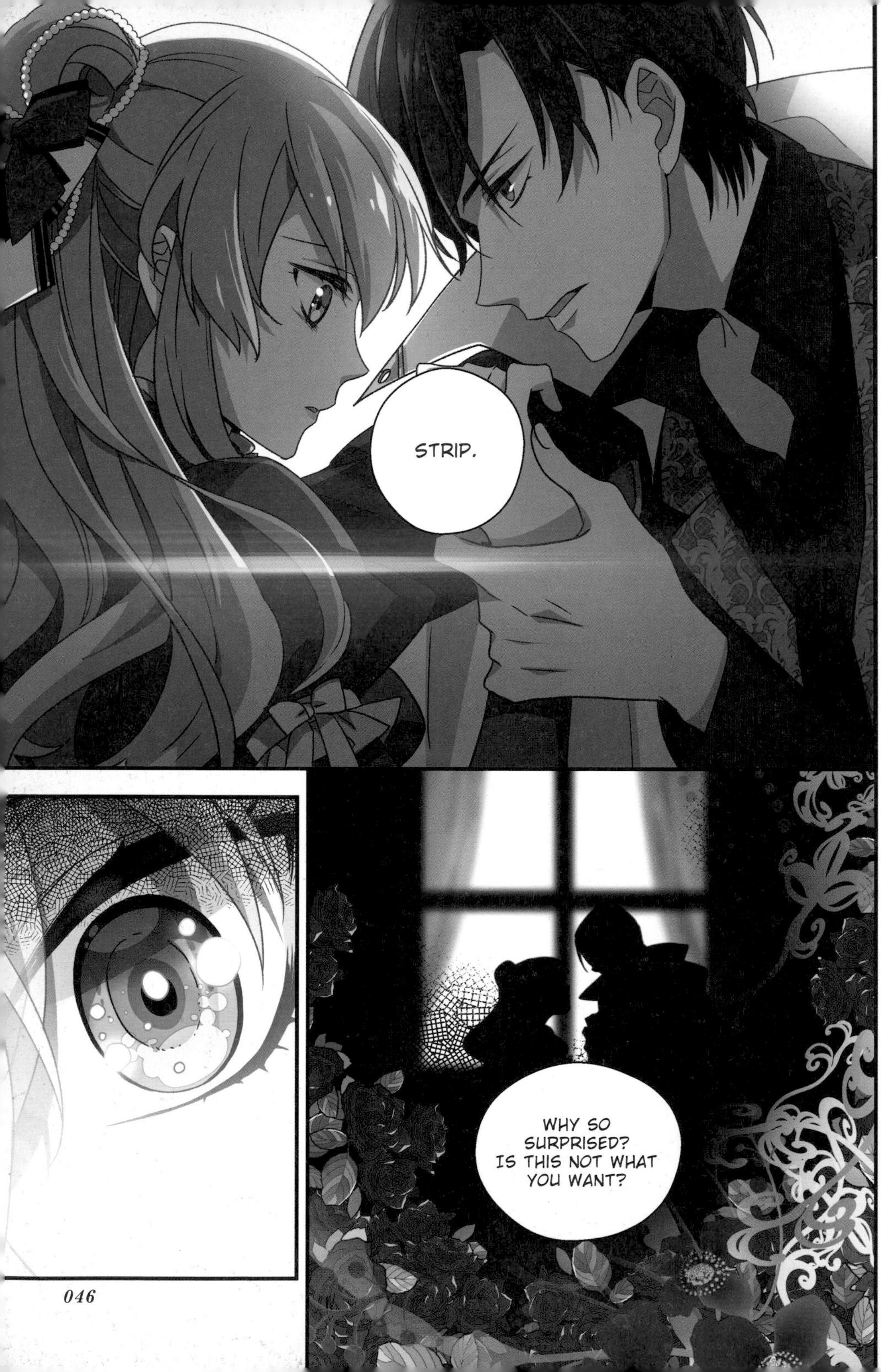
STRIP.
WHY SO SURPRISED? IS THIS NOT WHAT YOU WANT?

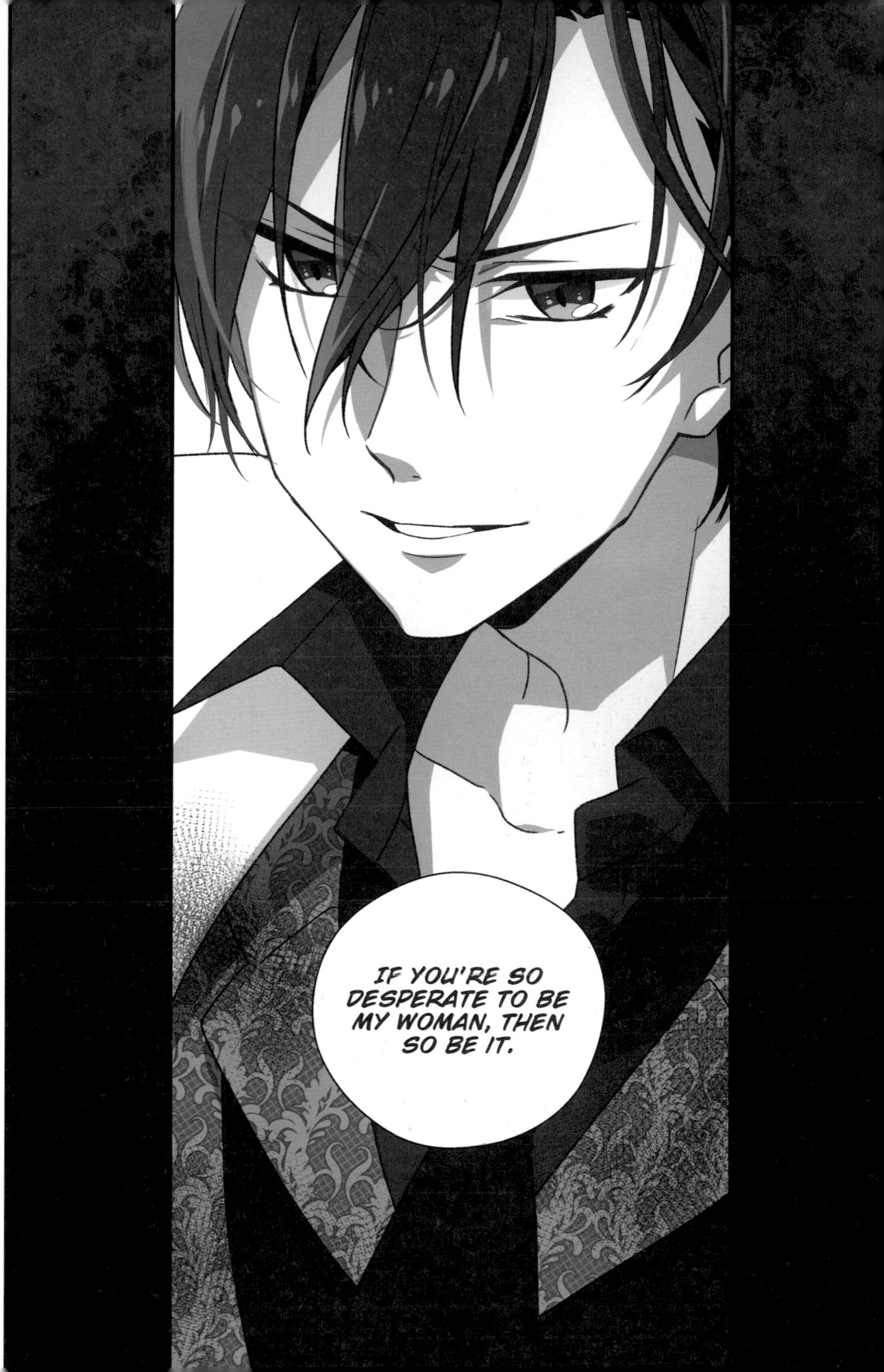
IF YOU'RE SO DESPERATE TO BE MY WOMAN, THEN SO BE IT.

# The Abandoned Empress

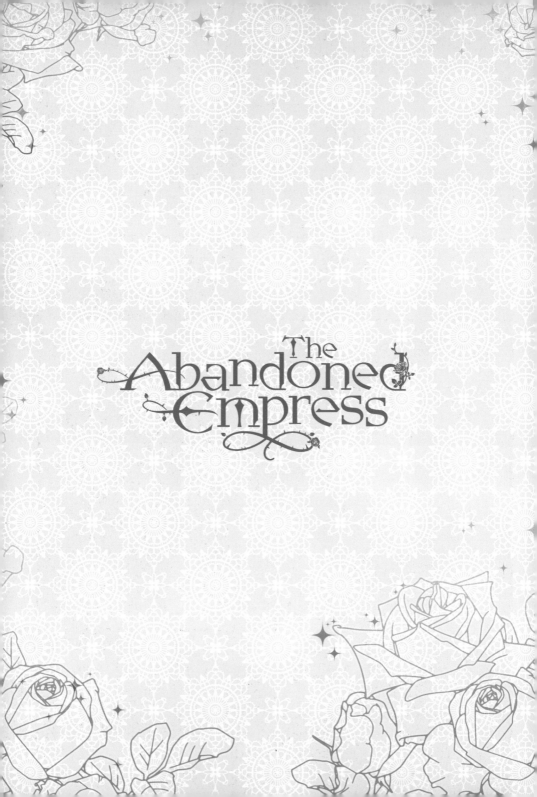

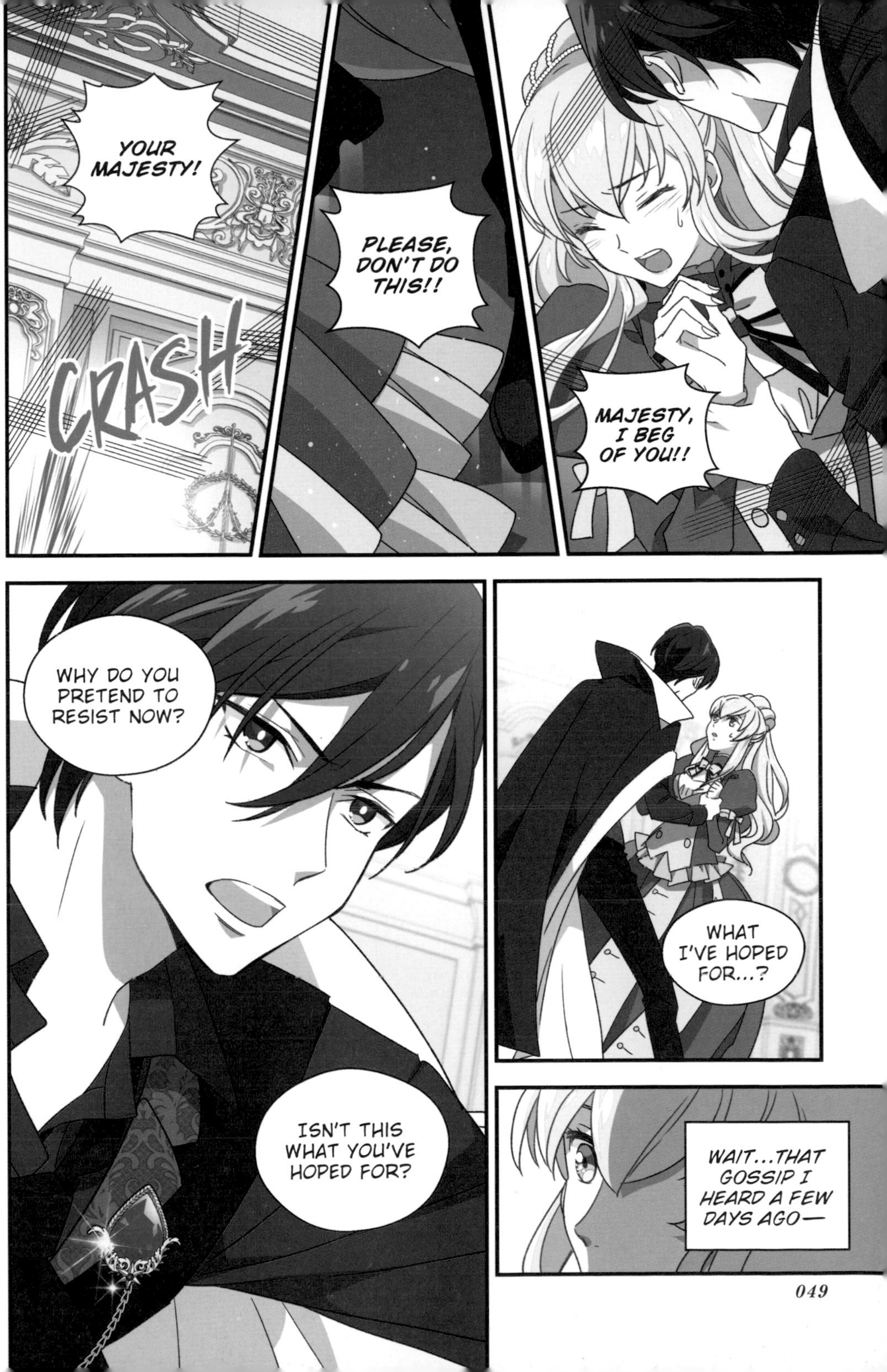
YOUR MAJESTY!
CRASH
PLEASE, DON'T DO THIS!!
MAJESTY, I BEG OF YOU!!
WHY DO YOU PRETEND TO RESIST NOW?
ISN'T THIS WHAT YOU'VE HOPED FOR?
WHAT I'VE HOPED FOR...?
WAIT...THAT GOSSIP I HEARD A FEW DAYS AGO—

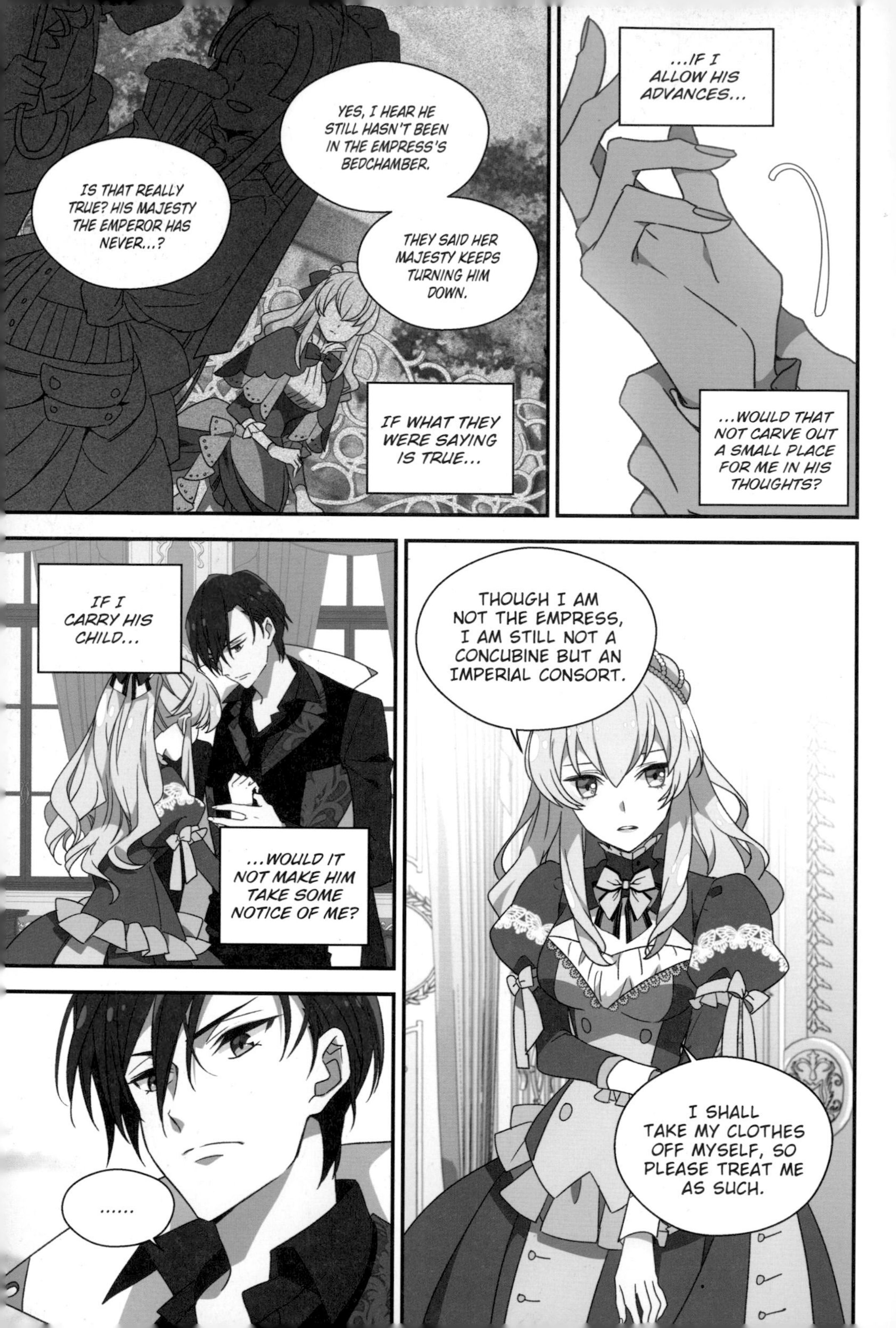
IS THAT REALLY TRUE? HIS MAJESTY THE EMPEROR HAS NEVER...?
YES, I HEAR HE STILL HASN'T BEEN IN THE EMPRESS'S BEDCHAMBER.
THEY SAID HER MAJESTY KEEPS TURNING HIM DOWN.
IF WHAT THEY WERE SAYING IS TRUE...
...IF I ALLOW HIS ADVANCES...
...WOULD THAT NOT CARVE OUT A SMALL PLACE FOR ME IN HIS THOUGHTS?
IF I CARRY HIS CHILD...
...WOULD IT NOT MAKE HIM TAKE SOME NOTICE OF ME?
THOUGH I AM NOT THE EMPRESS, I AM STILL NOT A CONCUBINE BUT AN IMPERIAL CONSORT.
I SHALL TAKE MY CLOTHES OFF MYSELF, SO PLEASE TREAT ME AS SUCH.
......

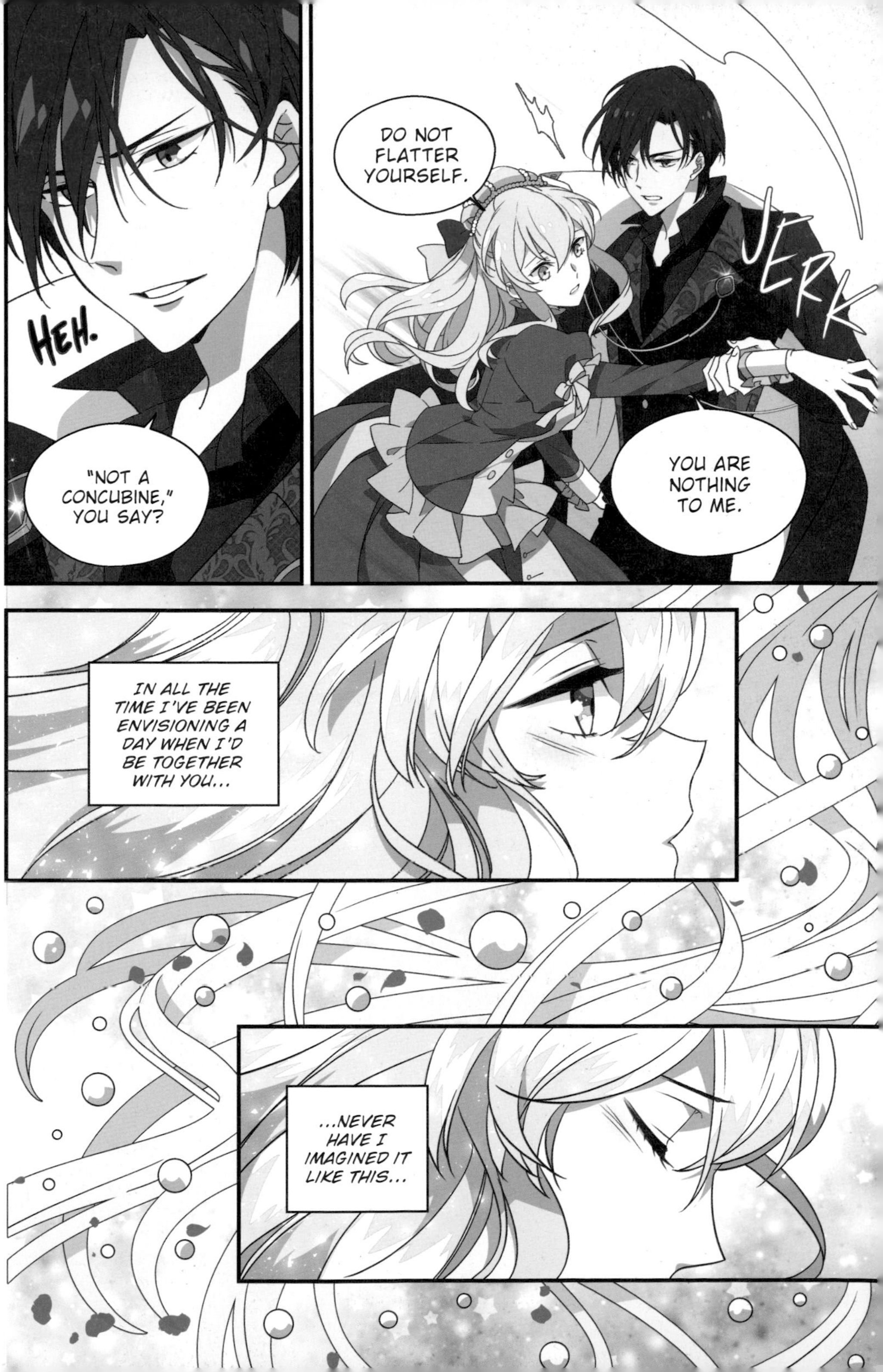
HEH.
"NOT A CONCUBINE," YOU SAY?
DO NOT FLATTER YOURSELF.
JERK
YOU ARE NOTHING TO ME.
IN ALL THE TIME I'VE BEEN ENVISIONING A DAY WHEN I'D BE TOGETHER WITH YOU...
...NEVER HAVE I IMAGINED IT LIKE THIS...

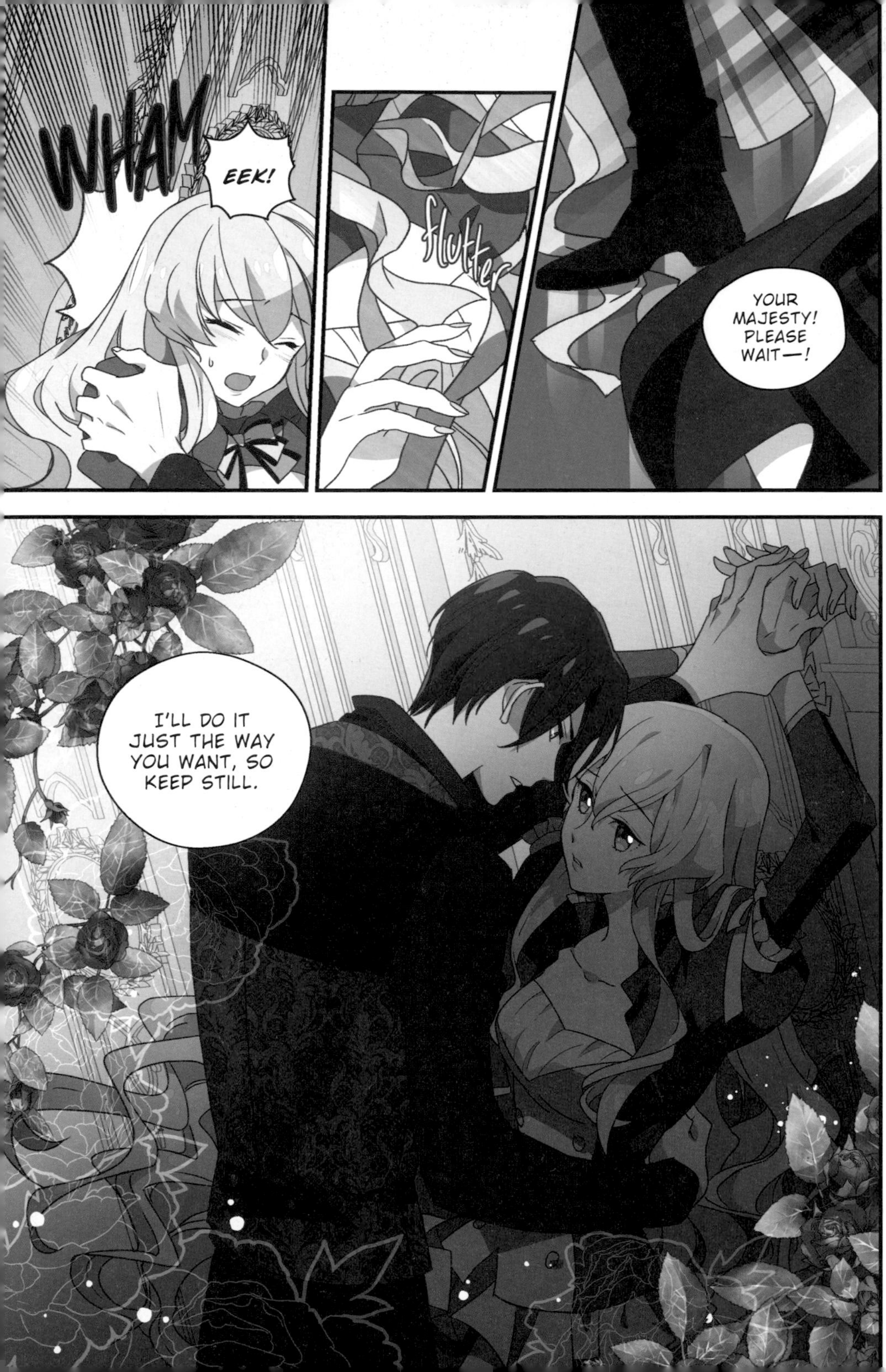
WHAM
EEK!
flutter
YOUR MAJESTY! PLEASE WAIT—!
I'LL DO IT JUST THE WAY YOU WANT, SO KEEP STILL.

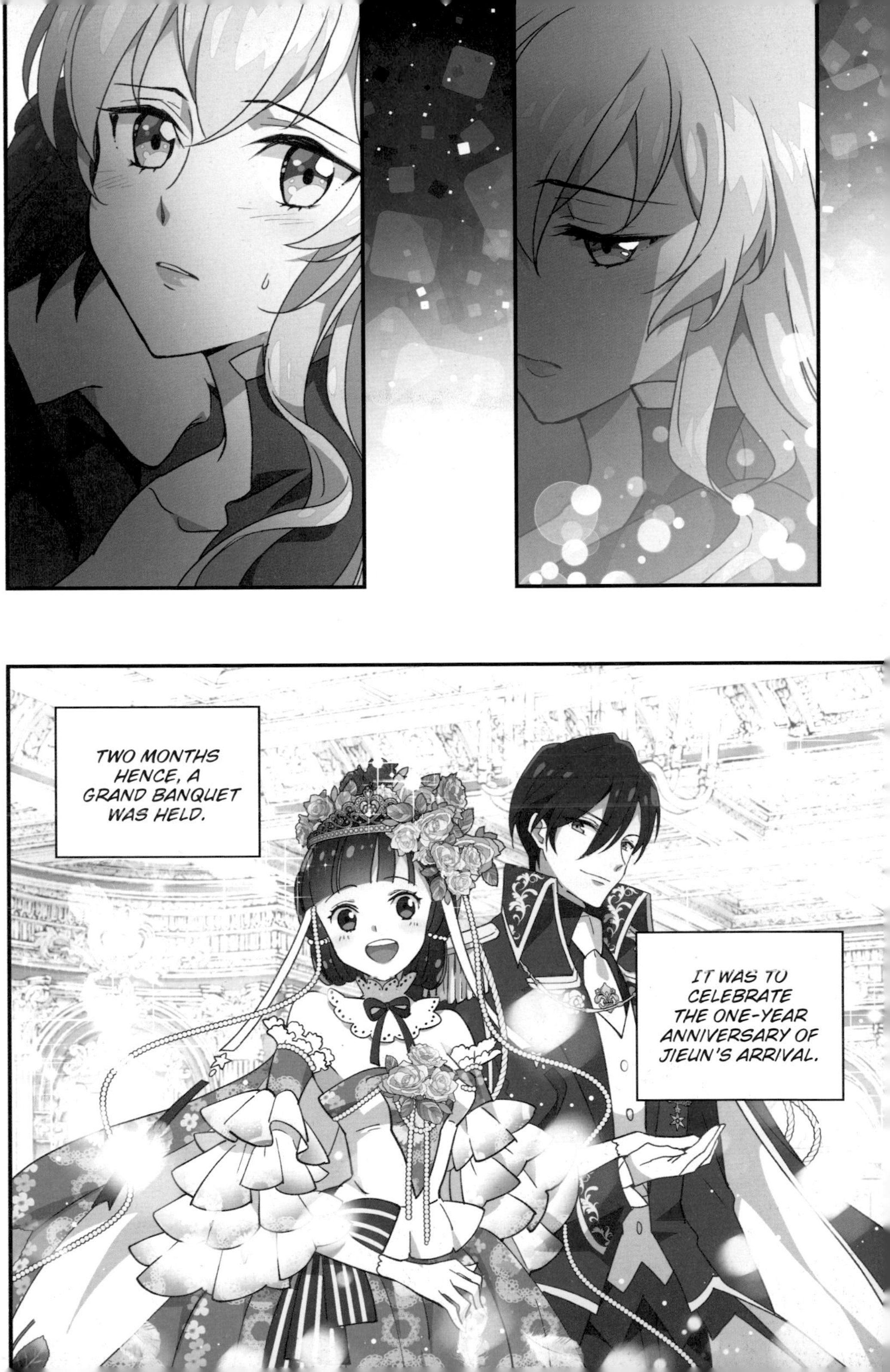
TWO MONTHS HENCE, A GRAND BANQUET WAS HELD.
IT WAS TO CELEBRATE THE ONE-YEAR ANNIVERSARY OF JIEUN'S ARRIVAL.

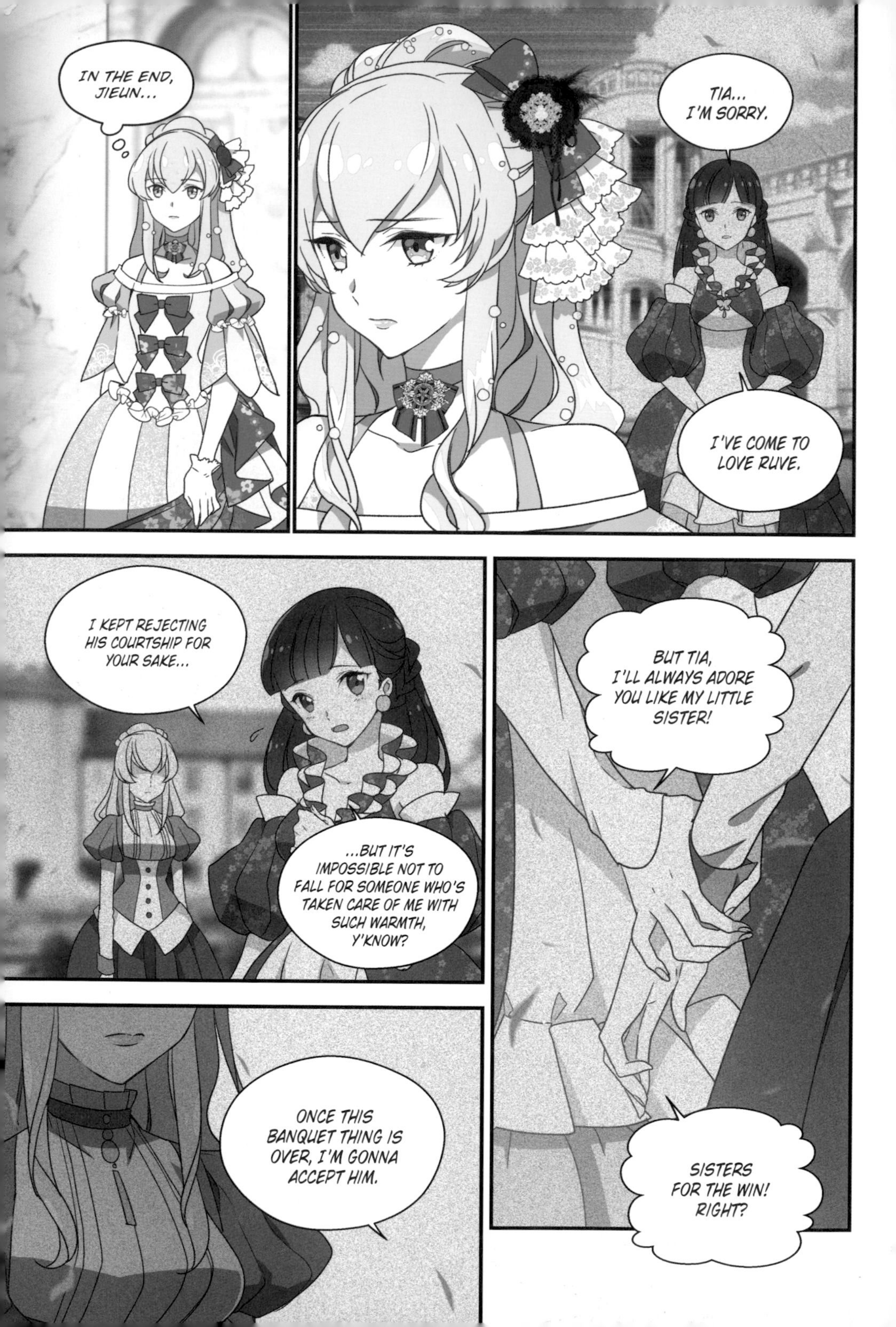
IN THE END, JIEUN...
TIA... I'M SORRY.
I'VE COME TO LOVE RUVE.
I KEPT REJECTING HIS COURTSHIP FOR YOUR SAKE...
...BUT IT'S IMPOSSIBLE NOT TO FALL FOR SOMEONE WHO'S TAKEN CARE OF ME WITH SUCH WARMTH, Y'KNOW?
BUT TIA, I'LL ALWAYS ADORE YOU LIKE MY LITTLE SISTER!
ONCE THIS BANQUET THING IS OVER, I'M GONNA ACCEPT HIM.
SISTERS FOR THE WIN! RIGHT?

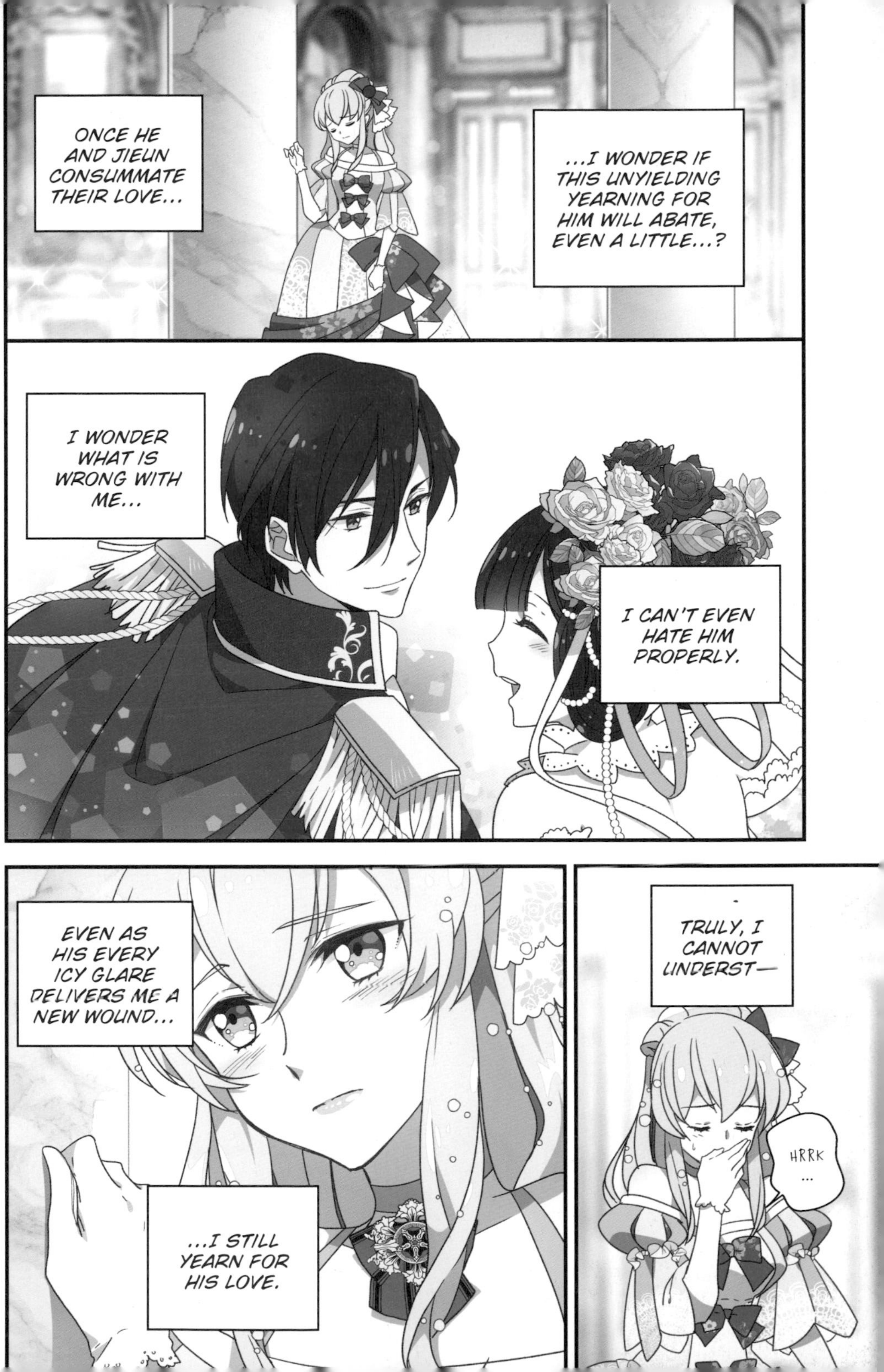
ONCE HE AND JIEUN CONSUMMATE THEIR LOVE...
...I WONDER IF THIS UNYIELDING YEARNING FOR HIM WILL ABATE, EVEN A LITTLE...?
I WONDER WHAT IS WRONG WITH ME...
I CAN'T EVEN HATE HIM PROPERLY.
EVEN AS HIS EVERY ICY GLARE DELIVERS ME A NEW WOUND...
...I STILL YEARN FOR HIS LOVE.
TRULY, I CANNOT UNDERST—
HRRK ...

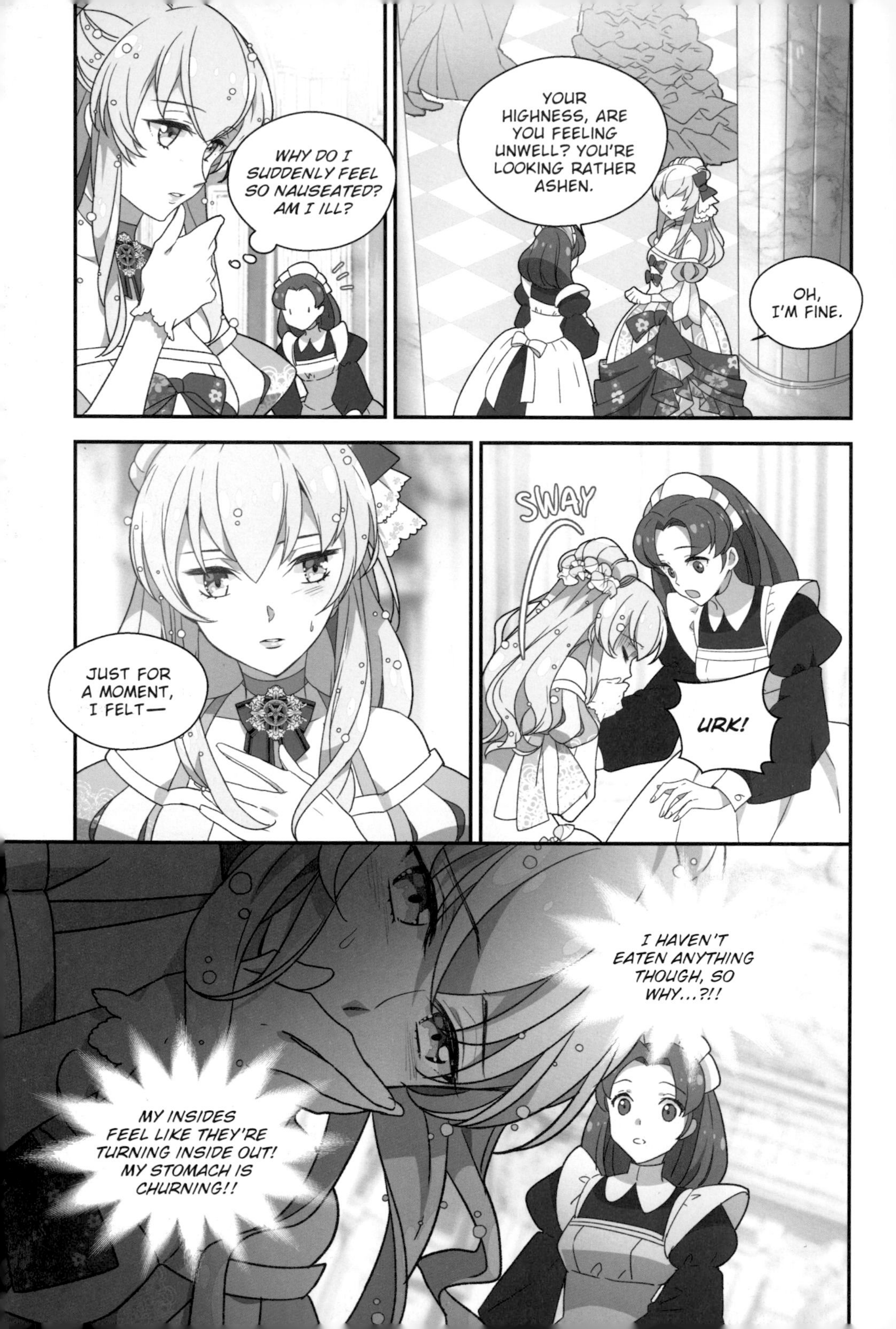
WHY DO I SUDDENLY FEEL SO NAUSEATED? AM I ILL?
YOUR HIGHNESS, ARE YOU FEELING UNWELL? YOU'RE LOOKING RATHER ASHEN.
OH, I'M FINE.
JUST FOR A MOMENT, I FELT—
SWAY
URK!
I HAVEN'T EATEN ANYTHING THOUGH, SO WHY...?!!
MY INSIDES FEEL LIKE THEY'RE TURNING INSIDE OUT! MY STOMACH IS CHURNING!!

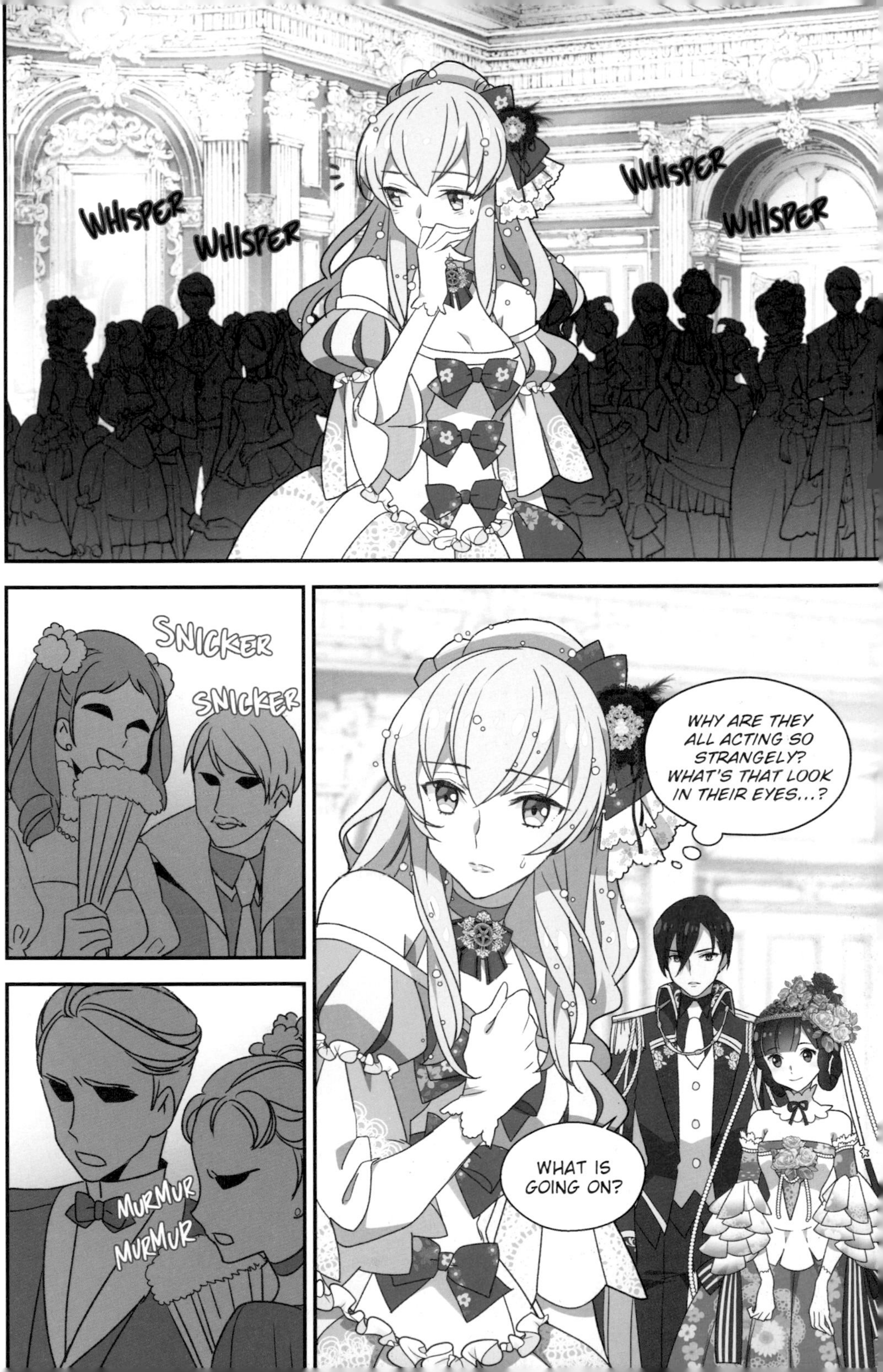
WHISPER
WHISPER
WHISPER
WHISPER
WHY ARE THEY ALL ACTING SO STRANGELY? WHAT'S THAT LOOK IN THEIR EYES...?
WHAT IS GOING ON?
SNICKER
SNICKER
MURMUR
MURMUR

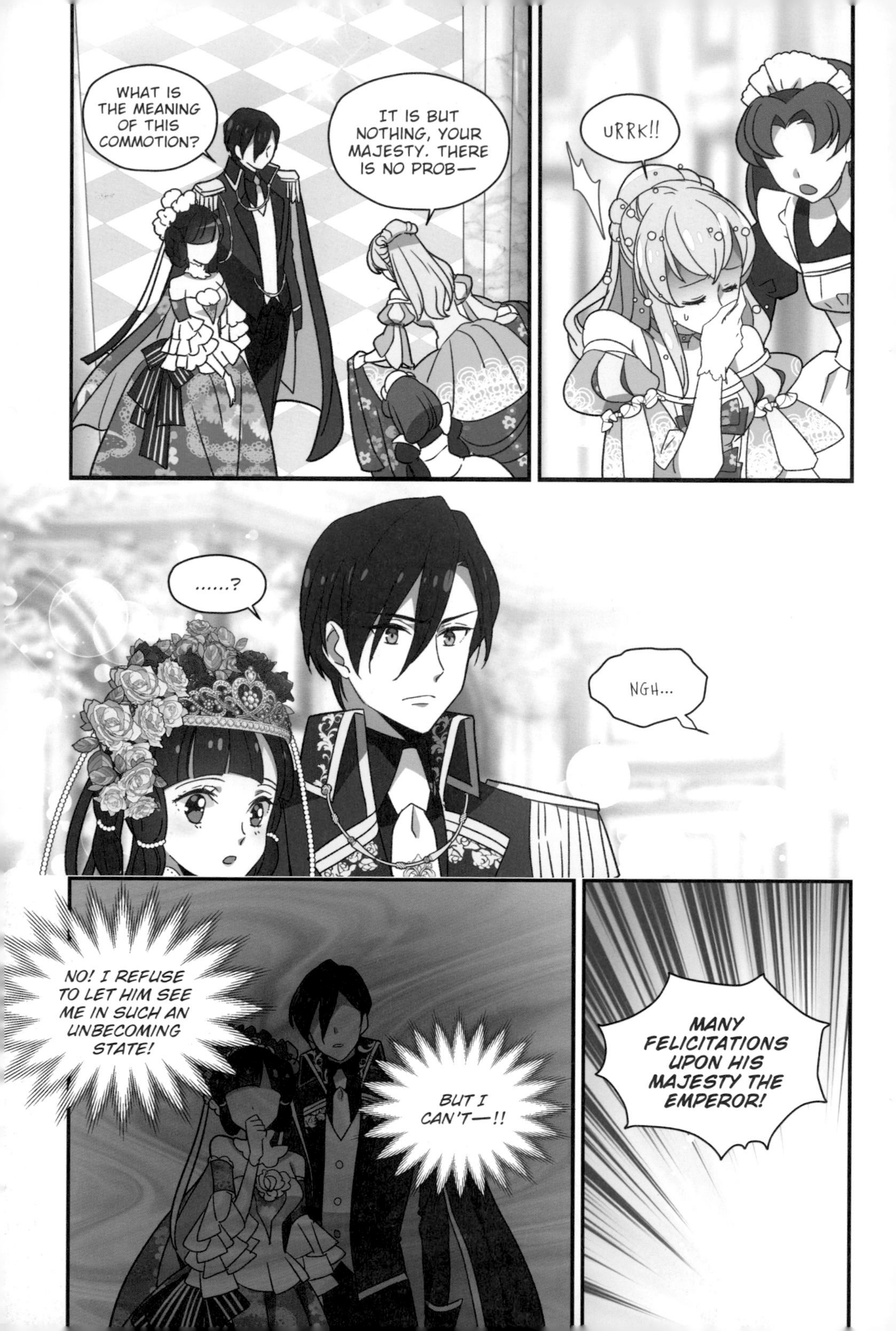
WHAT IS THE MEANING OF THIS COMMOTION?
IT IS BUT NOTHING, YOUR MAJESTY. THERE IS NO PROB—
URRK!!
......?
NGH...
NO! I REFUSE TO LET HIM SEE ME IN SUCH AN UNBECOMING STATE!
BUT I CAN'T—!!
MANY FELICITATIONS UPON HIS MAJESTY THE EMPEROR!

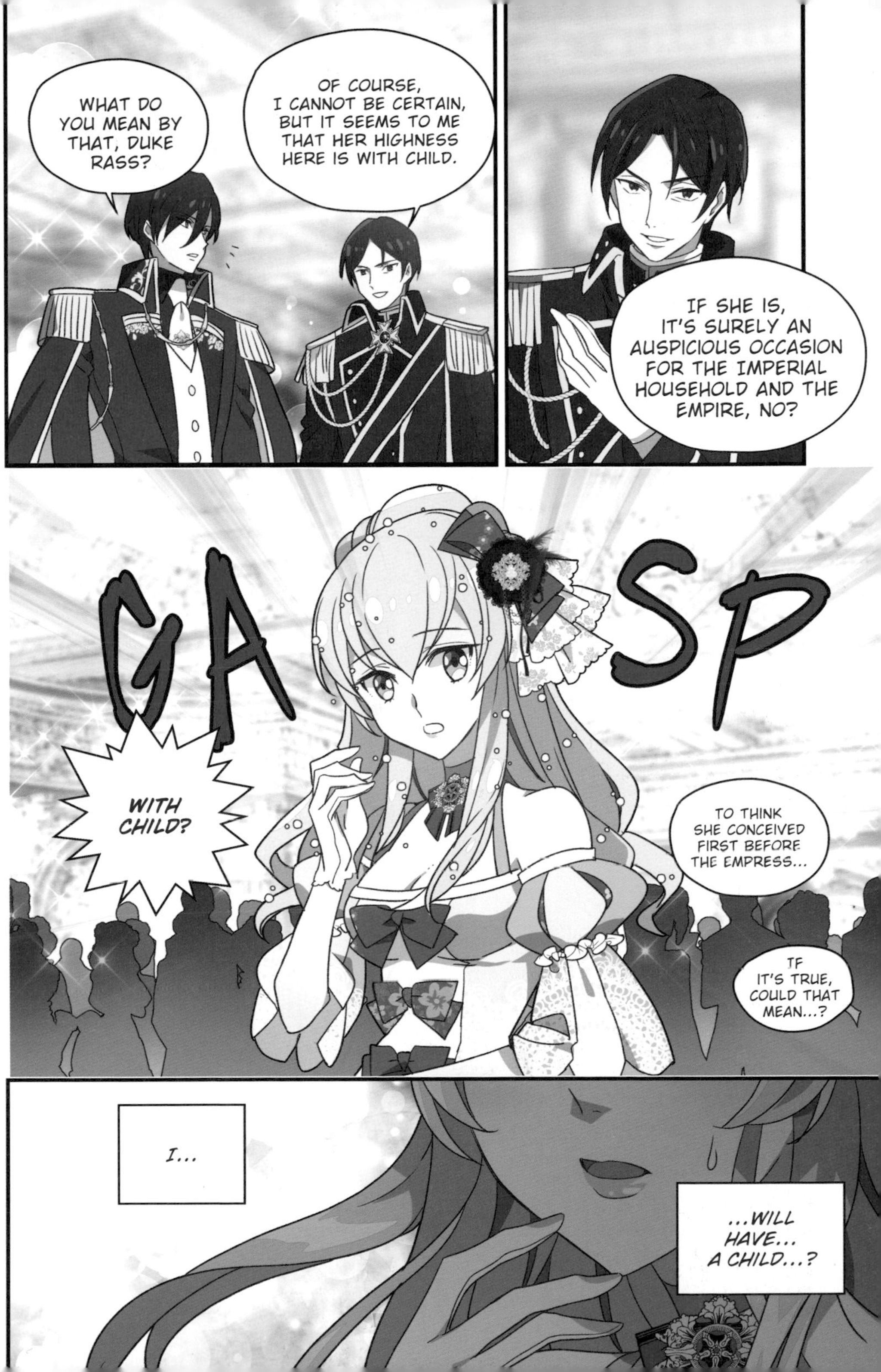
WHAT DO YOU MEAN BY THAT, DUKE RASS?
OF COURSE, I CANNOT BE CERTAIN, BUT IT SEEMS TO ME THAT HER HIGHNESS HERE IS WITH CHILD.
IF SHE IS, IT'S SURELY AN AUSPICIOUS OCCASION FOR THE IMPERIAL HOUSEHOLD AND THE EMPIRE, NO?
GASP
WITH CHILD?
TO THINK SHE CONCEIVED FIRST BEFORE THE EMPRESS...
IF IT'S TRUE, COULD THAT MEAN...?
I...
...WILL HAVE... A CHILD...?

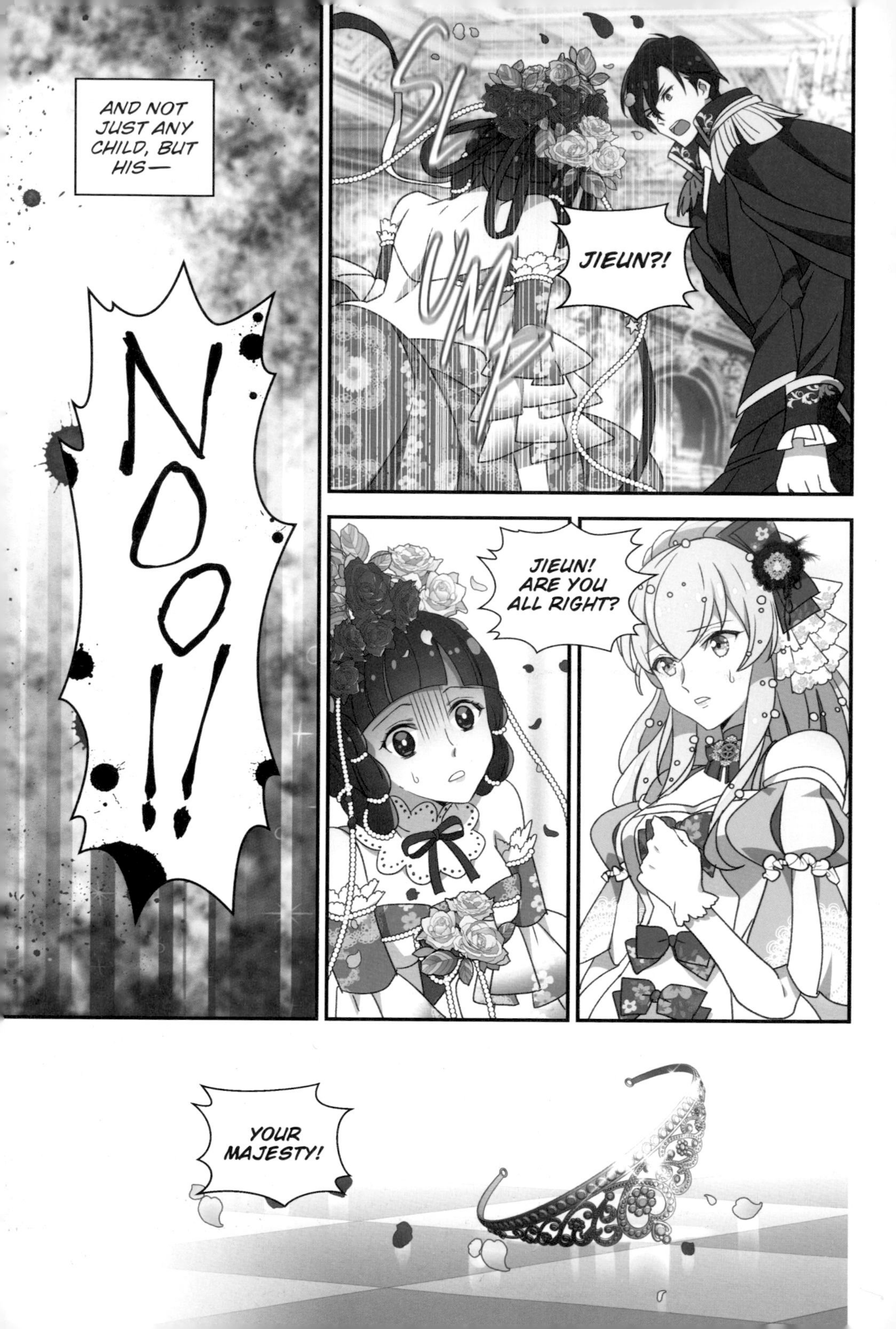
AND NOT JUST ANY CHILD, BUT HIS—
NO!!
SLUMP
JIEUN?!
JIEUN! ARE YOU ALL RIGHT?
YOUR MAJESTY!

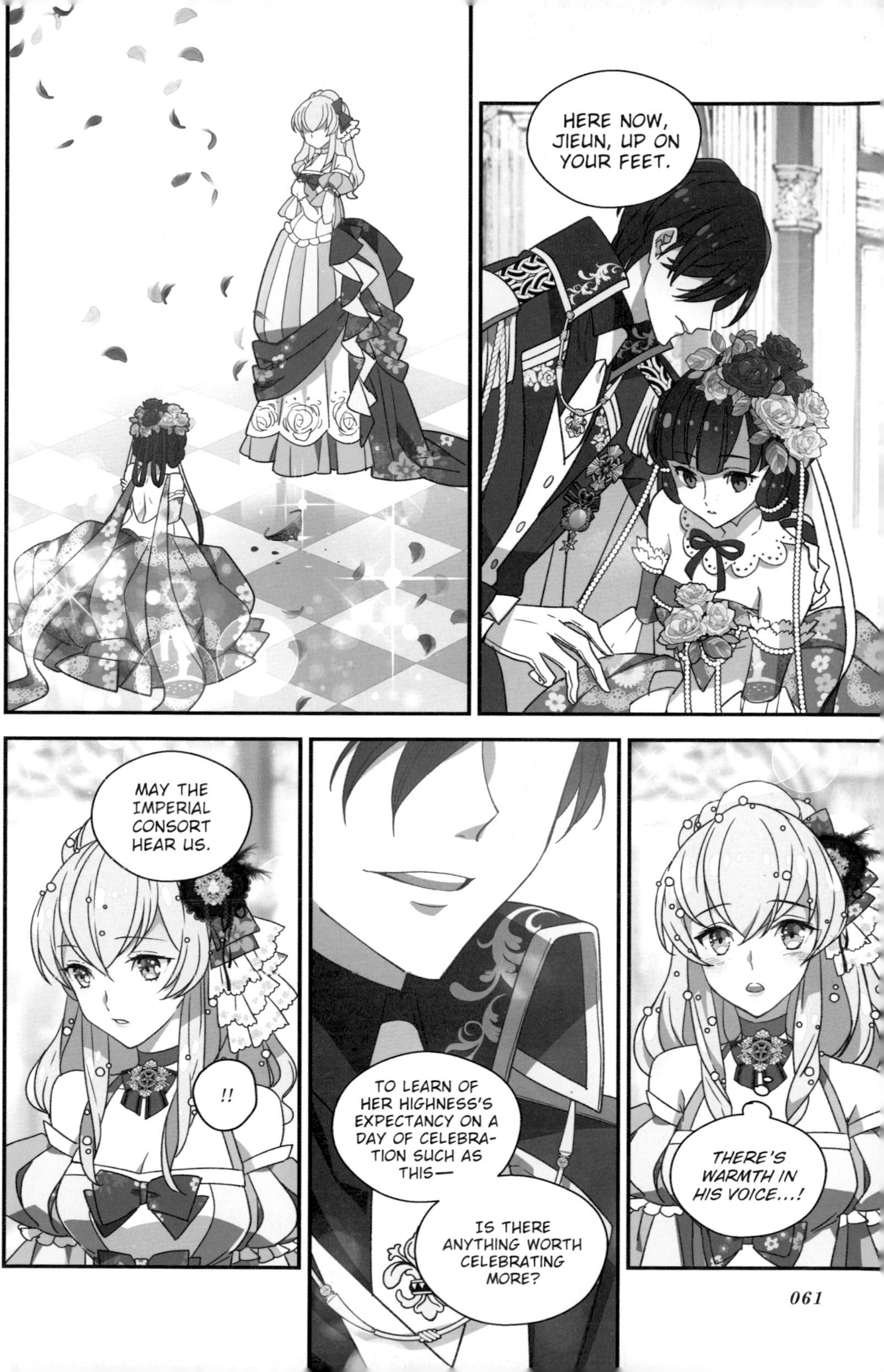
HERE NOW, JIEUN, UP ON YOUR FEET.
MAY THE IMPERIAL CONSORT HEAR US.
!!
TO LEARN OF HER HIGHNESS'S EXPECTANCY ON A DAY OF CELEBRATION SUCH AS THIS—
IS THERE ANYTHING WORTH CELEBRATING MORE?
THERE'S WARMTH IN HIS VOICE...!

WE ARE WELL PLEASED.

HE'S NOT IN THE LEAST SINCERE...! THAT ICY GLARE...!!

CONGRATULATIONS TO HIS MAJESTY THE EMPEROR!

CONGRATULATIONS TO HER HIGHNESS THE IMPERIAL CONSORT!

CONGRATULATIONS!

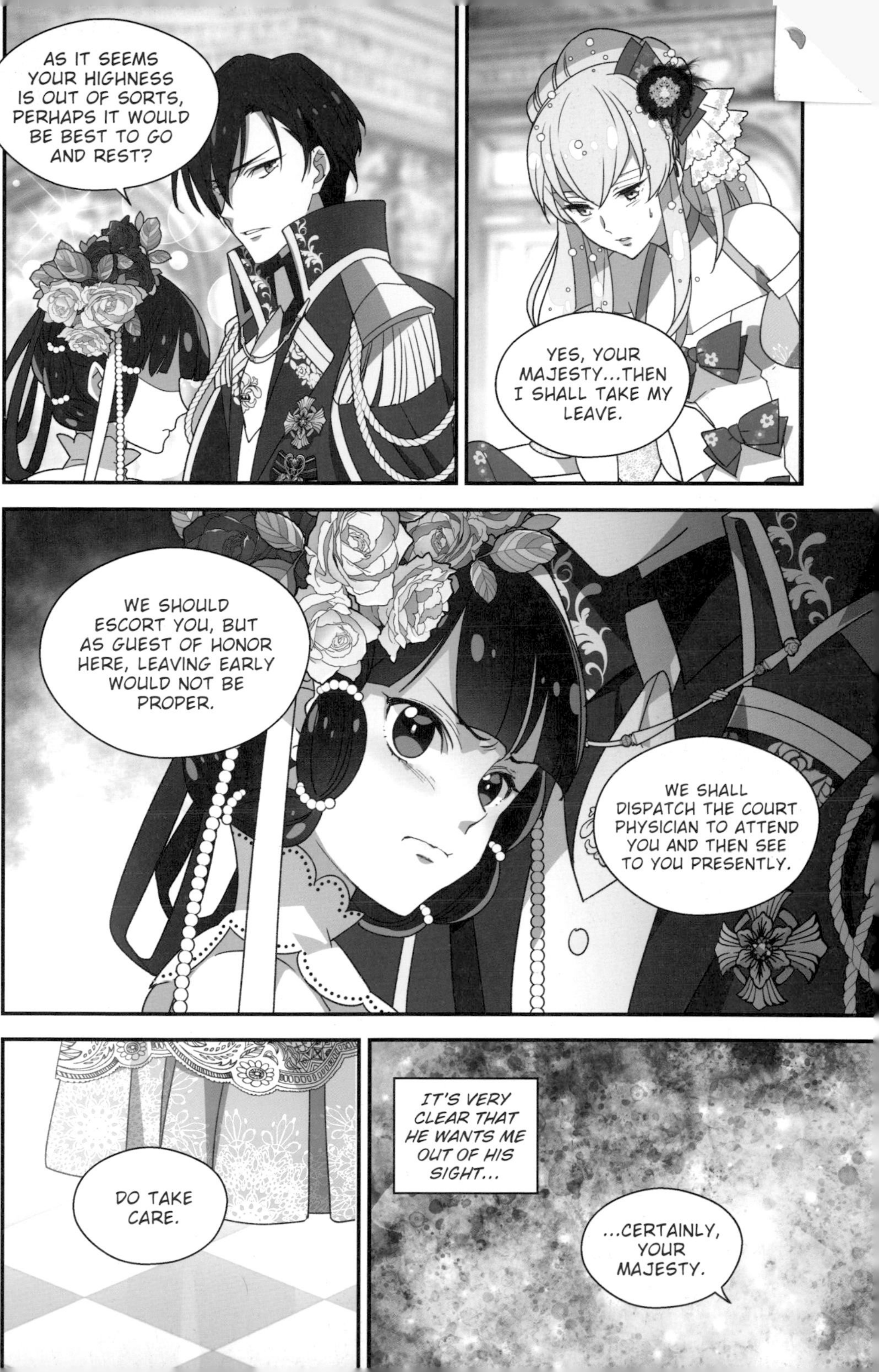
AS IT SEEMS YOUR HIGHNESS IS OUT OF SORTS, PERHAPS IT WOULD BE BEST TO GO AND REST?
YES, YOUR MAJESTY...THEN I SHALL TAKE MY LEAVE.
WE SHOULD ESCORT YOU, BUT AS GUEST OF HONOR HERE, LEAVING EARLY WOULD NOT BE PROPER.
WE SHALL DISPATCH THE COURT PHYSICIAN TO ATTEND YOU AND THEN SEE TO YOU PRESENTLY.
DO TAKE CARE.
IT'S VERY CLEAR THAT HE WANTS ME OUT OF HIS SIGHT...
...CERTAINLY, YOUR MAJESTY.

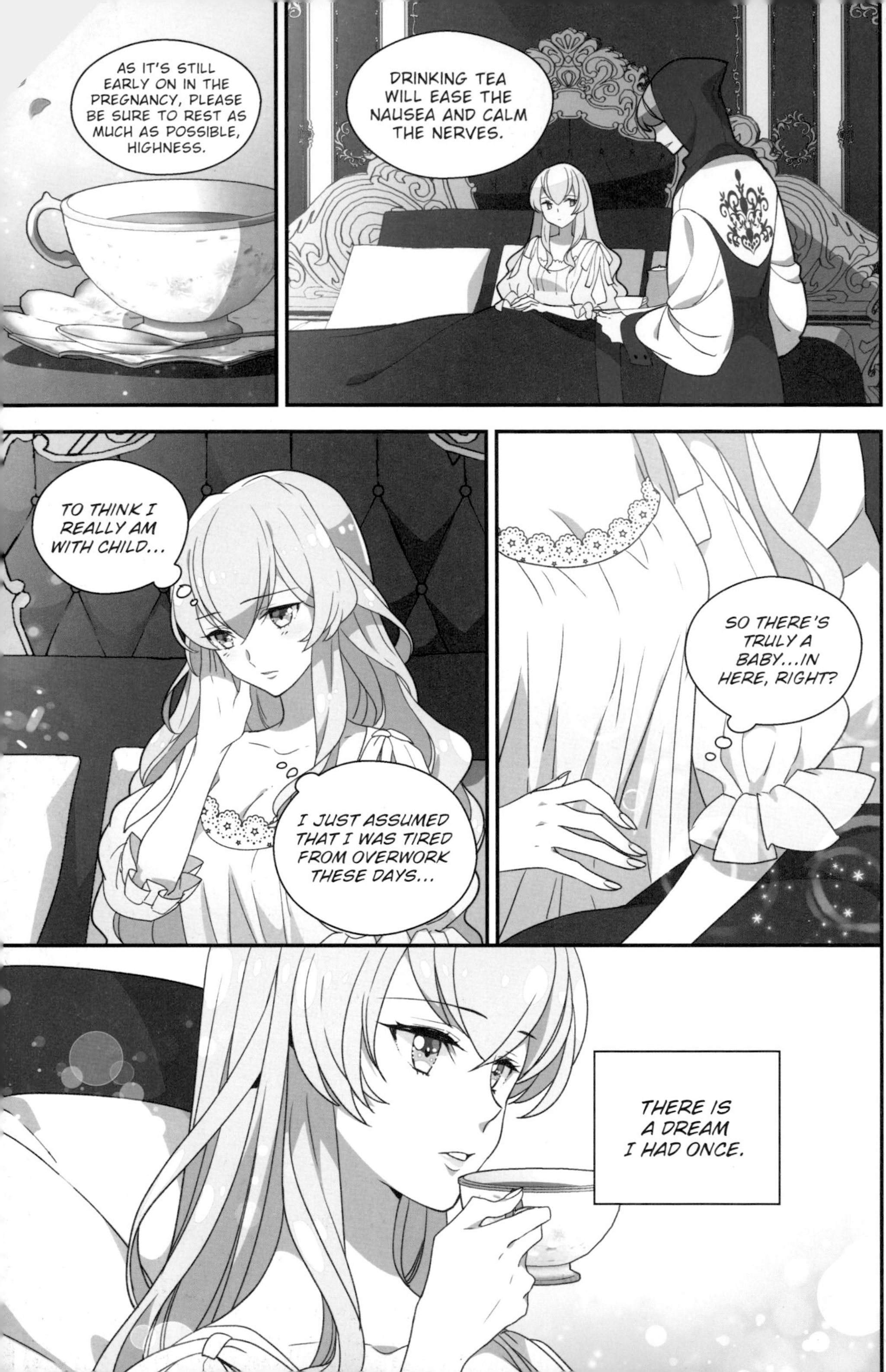
AS IT'S STILL EARLY ON IN THE PREGNANCY, PLEASE BE SURE TO REST AS MUCH AS POSSIBLE, HIGHNESS.
DRINKING TEA WILL EASE THE NAUSEA AND CALM THE NERVES.
TO THINK I REALLY AM WITH CHILD...
I JUST ASSUMED THAT I WAS TIRED FROM OVERWORK THESE DAYS...
SO THERE'S TRULY A BABY...IN HERE, RIGHT?
THERE IS A DREAM I HAD ONCE.

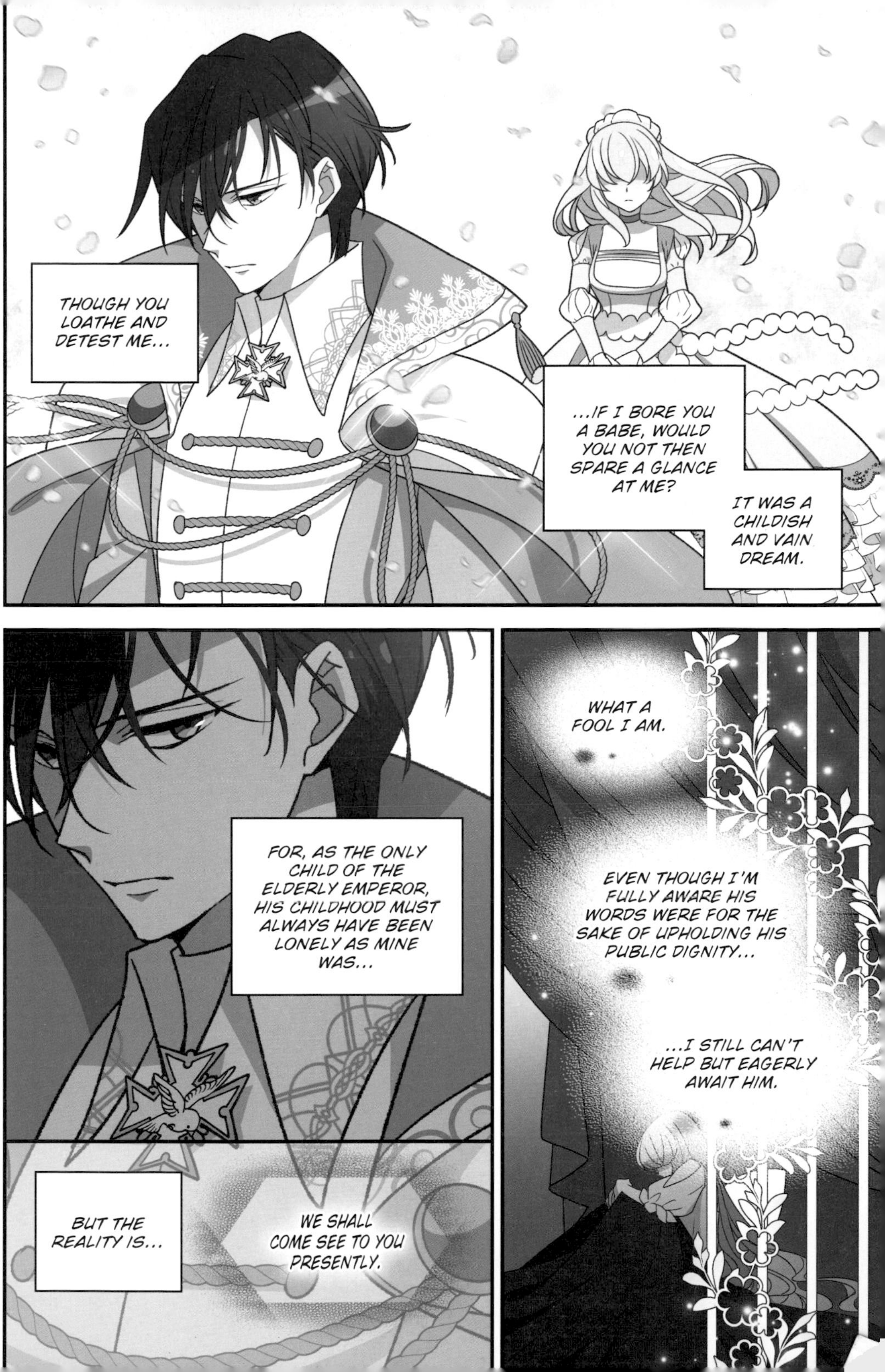
THOUGH YOU LOATHE AND DETEST ME...
...IF I BORE YOU A BABE, WOULD YOU NOT THEN SPARE A GLANCE AT ME?
IT WAS A CHILDISH AND VAIN DREAM.
WHAT A FOOL I AM.
FOR, AS THE ONLY CHILD OF THE ELDERLY EMPEROR, HIS CHILDHOOD MUST ALWAYS HAVE BEEN LONELY AS MINE WAS...
EVEN THOUGH I'M FULLY AWARE HIS WORDS WERE FOR THE SAKE OF UPHOLDING HIS PUBLIC DIGNITY...
...I STILL CAN'T HELP BUT EAGERLY AWAIT HIM.
BUT THE REALITY IS...
WE SHALL COME SEE TO YOU PRESENTLY.

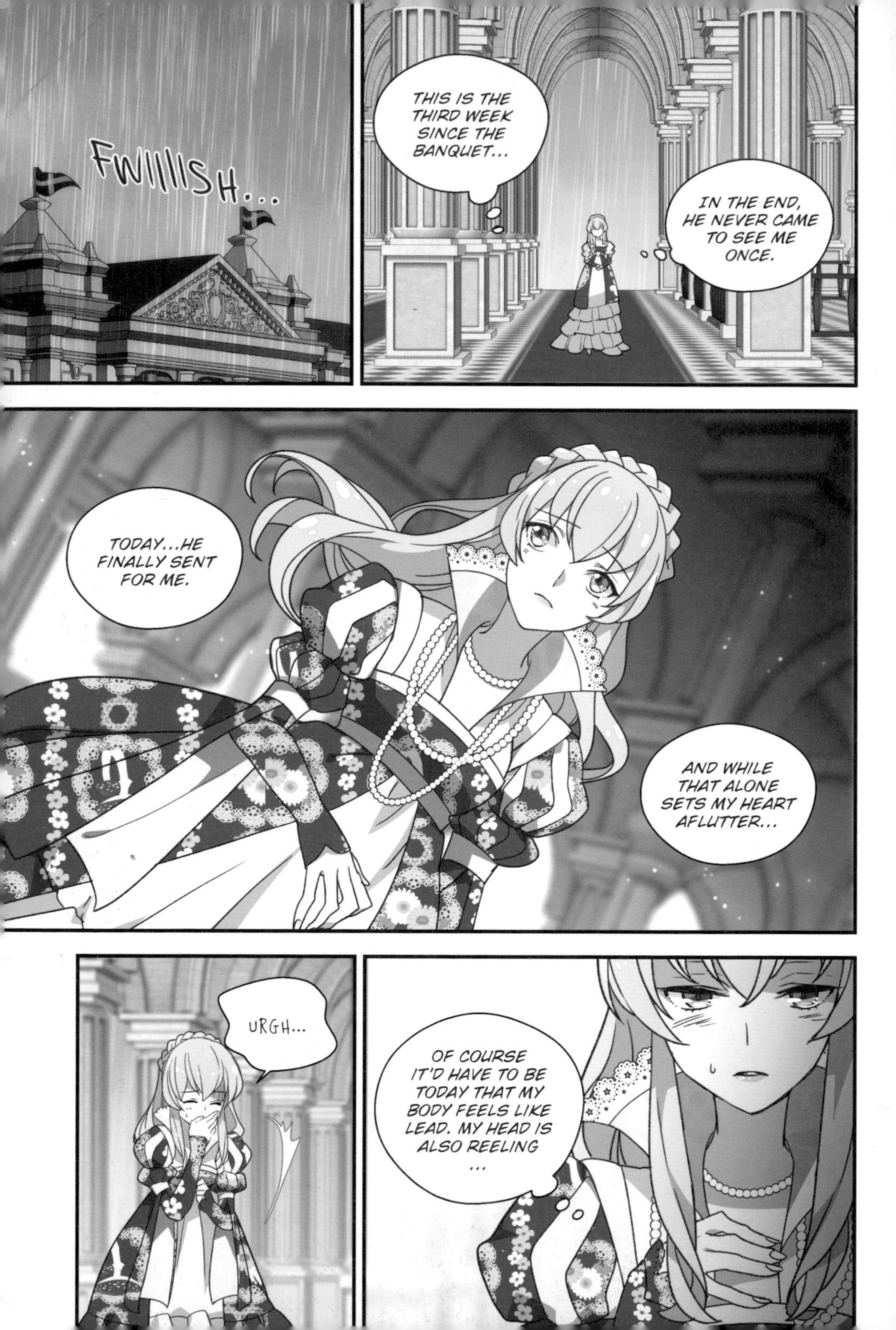
FWIIIISH...
THIS IS THE THIRD WEEK SINCE THE BANQUET...
IN THE END, HE NEVER CAME TO SEE ME ONCE.
TODAY...HE FINALLY SENT FOR ME.
AND WHILE THAT ALONE SETS MY HEART AFLUTTER...
URGH...
OF COURSE IT'D HAVE TO BE TODAY THAT MY BODY FEELS LIKE LEAD. MY HEAD IS ALSO REELING ...

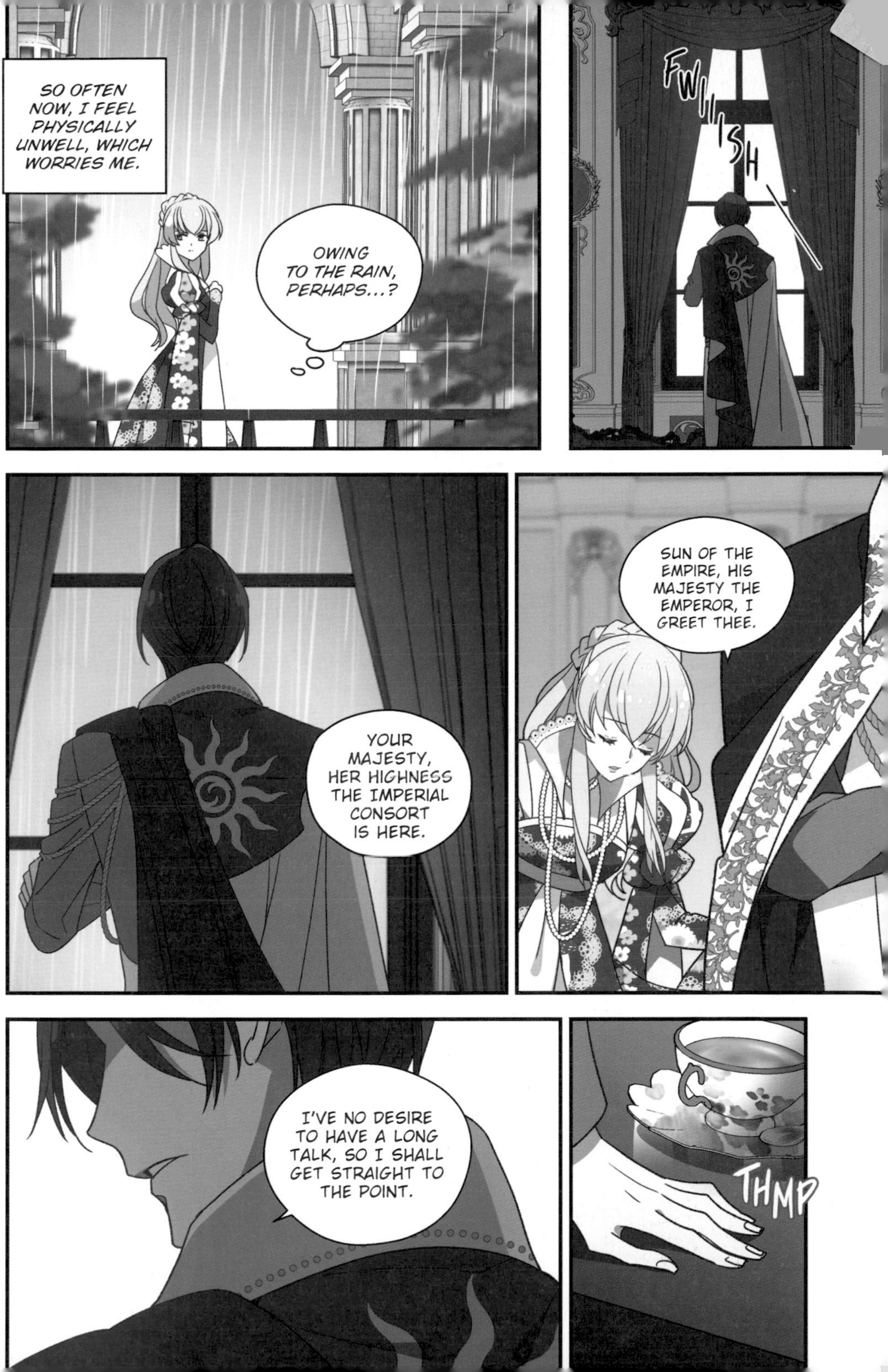
SO OFTEN NOW, I FEEL PHYSICALLY UNWELL, WHICH WORRIES ME.
OWING TO THE RAIN, PERHAPS...?
FWIIISH
YOUR MAJESTY, HER HIGHNESS THE IMPERIAL CONSORT IS HERE.
SUN OF THE EMPIRE, HIS MAJESTY THE EMPEROR, I GREET THEE.
I'VE NO DESIRE TO HAVE A LONG TALK, SO I SHALL GET STRAIGHT TO THE POINT.
THMP

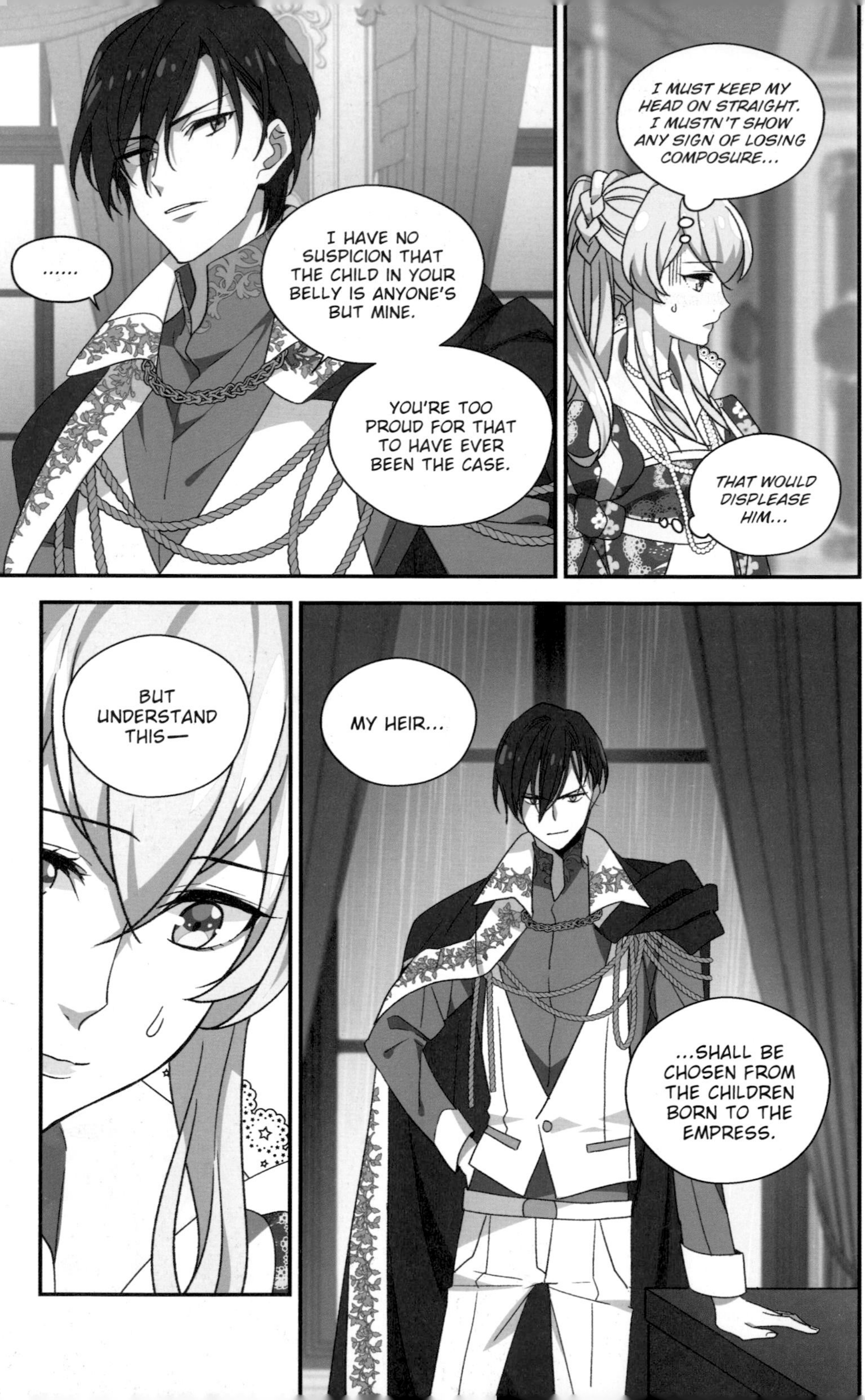
......
I HAVE NO SUSPICION THAT THE CHILD IN YOUR BELLY IS ANYONE'S BUT MINE.
YOU'RE TOO PROUD FOR THAT TO HAVE EVER BEEN THE CASE.
I MUST KEEP MY HEAD ON STRAIGHT. I MUSTN'T SHOW ANY SIGN OF LOSING COMPOSURE...
THAT WOULD DISPLEASE HIM...
BUT UNDERSTAND THIS—
MY HEIR...
...SHALL BE CHOSEN FROM THE CHILDREN BORN TO THE EMPRESS.

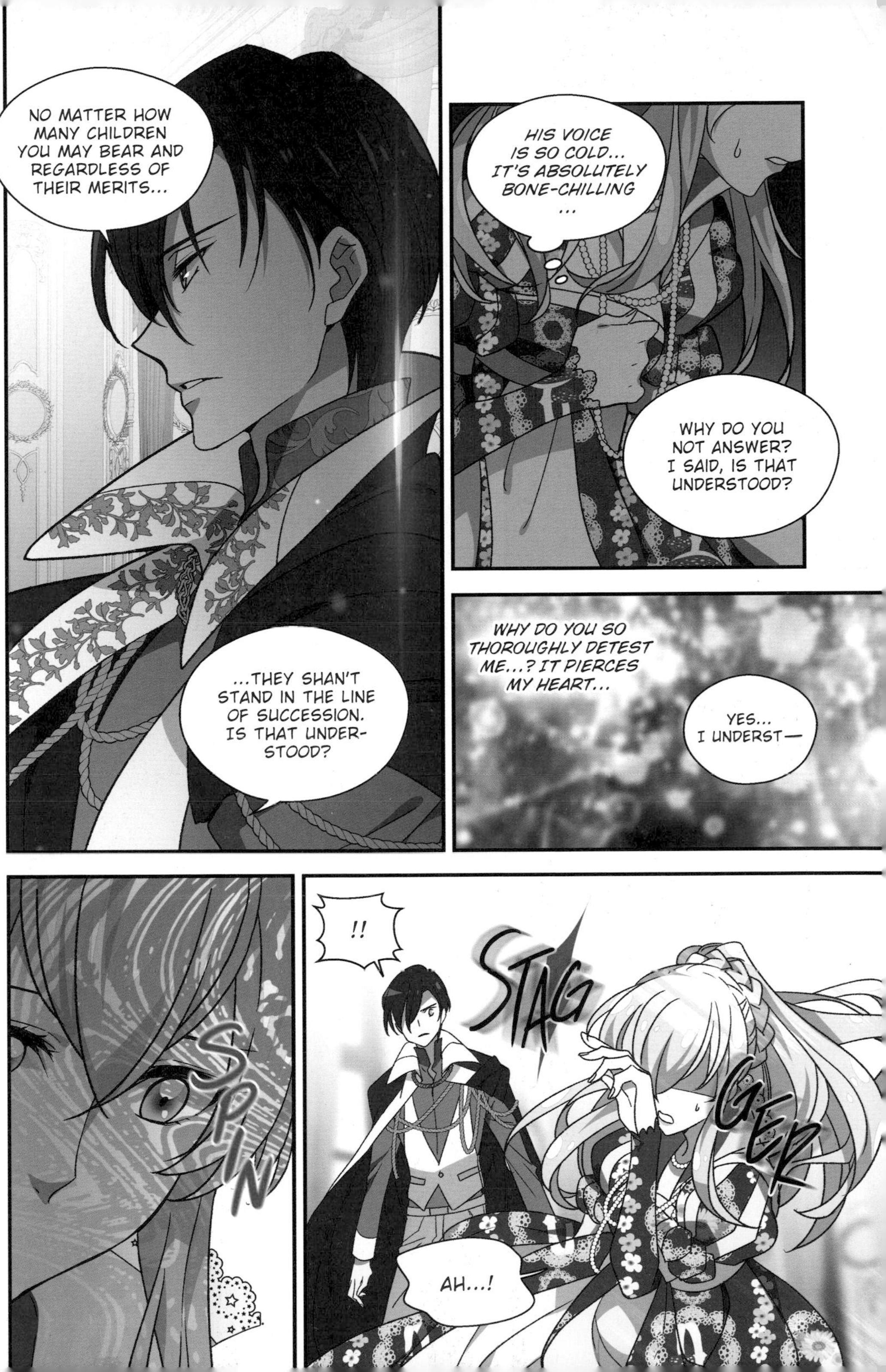
NO MATTER HOW MANY CHILDREN YOU MAY BEAR AND REGARDLESS OF THEIR MERITS...
HIS VOICE IS SO COLD... IT'S ABSOLUTELY BONE-CHILLING ...
WHY DO YOU NOT ANSWER? I SAID, IS THAT UNDERSTOOD?
...THEY SHAN'T STAND IN THE LINE OF SUCCESSION. IS THAT UNDER-STOOD?
WHY DO YOU SO THOROUGHLY DETEST ME...? IT PIERCES MY HEART...
YES... I UNDERST—
SPIN
!!
STAGGER
AH...!

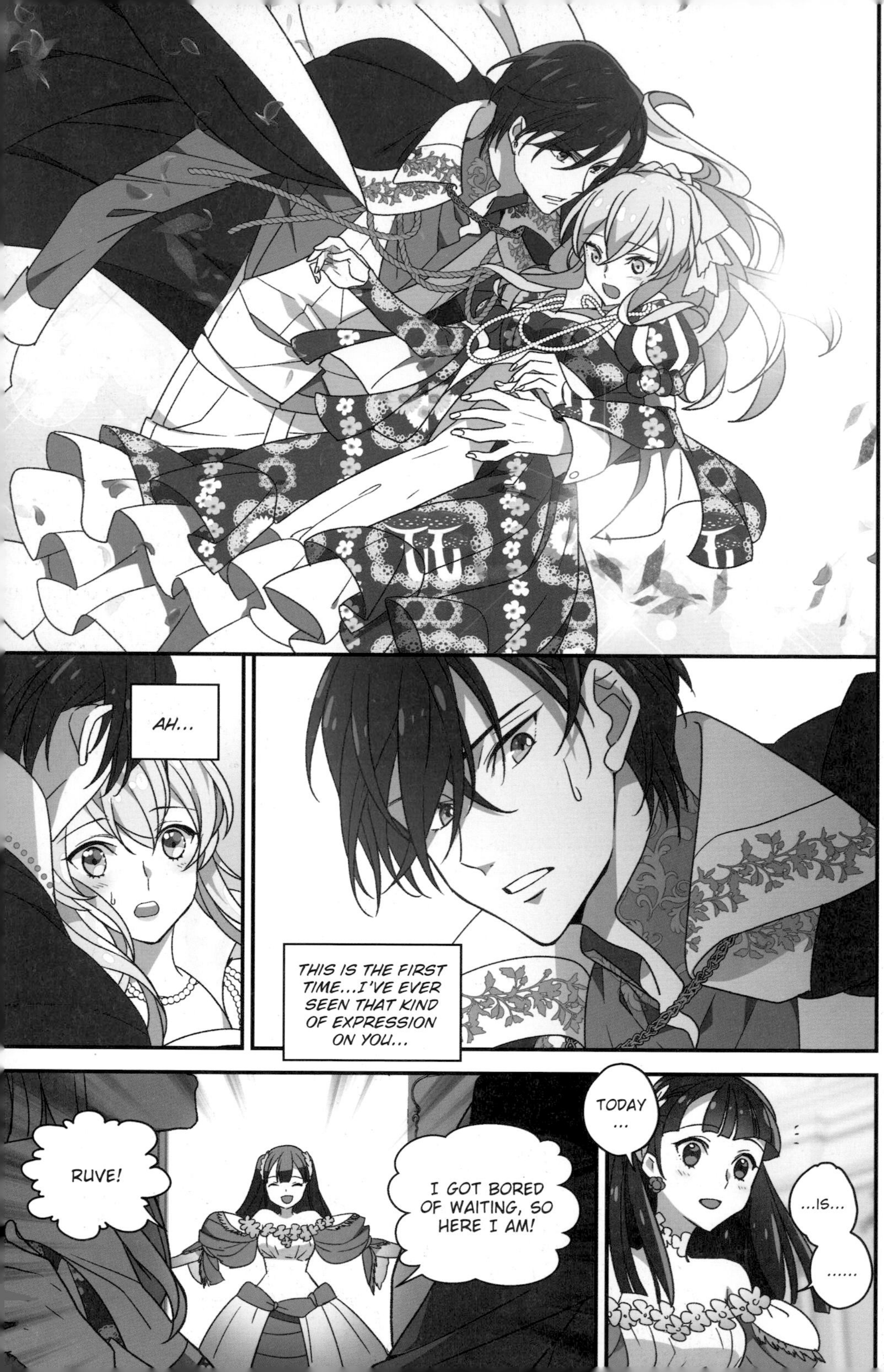
AH...
THIS IS THE FIRST TIME...I'VE EVER SEEN THAT KIND OF EXPRESSION ON YOU...
RUVE!
I GOT BORED OF WAITING, SO HERE I AM!
TODAY ...
...IS...
......

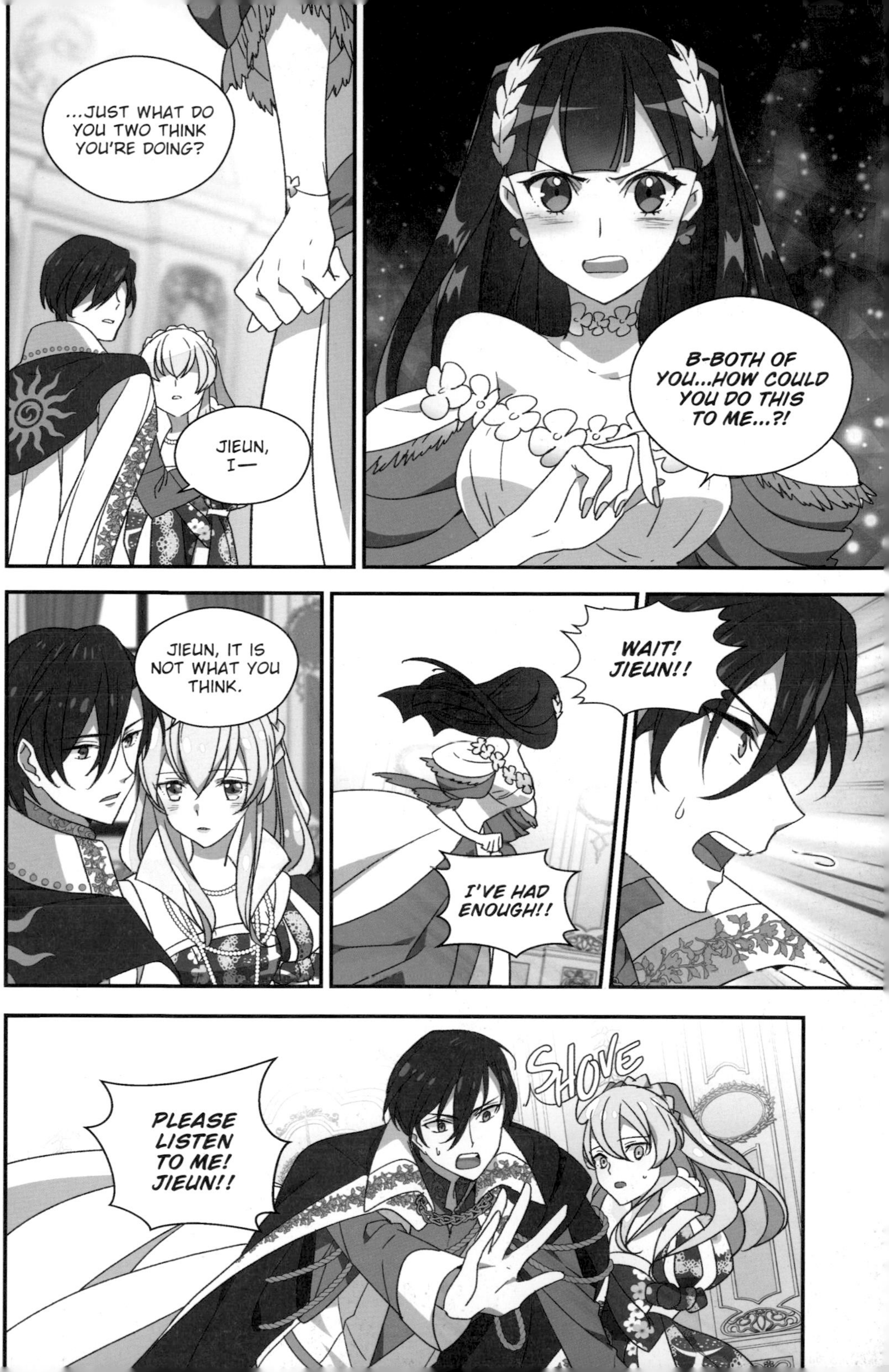
...JUST WHAT DO YOU TWO THINK YOU'RE DOING?
JIEUN, I—
B-BOTH OF YOU...HOW COULD YOU DO THIS TO ME...?!
JIEUN, IT IS NOT WHAT YOU THINK.
WAIT! JIEUN!!
I'VE HAD ENOUGH!!
SHOVE
PLEASE LISTEN TO ME! JIEUN!!

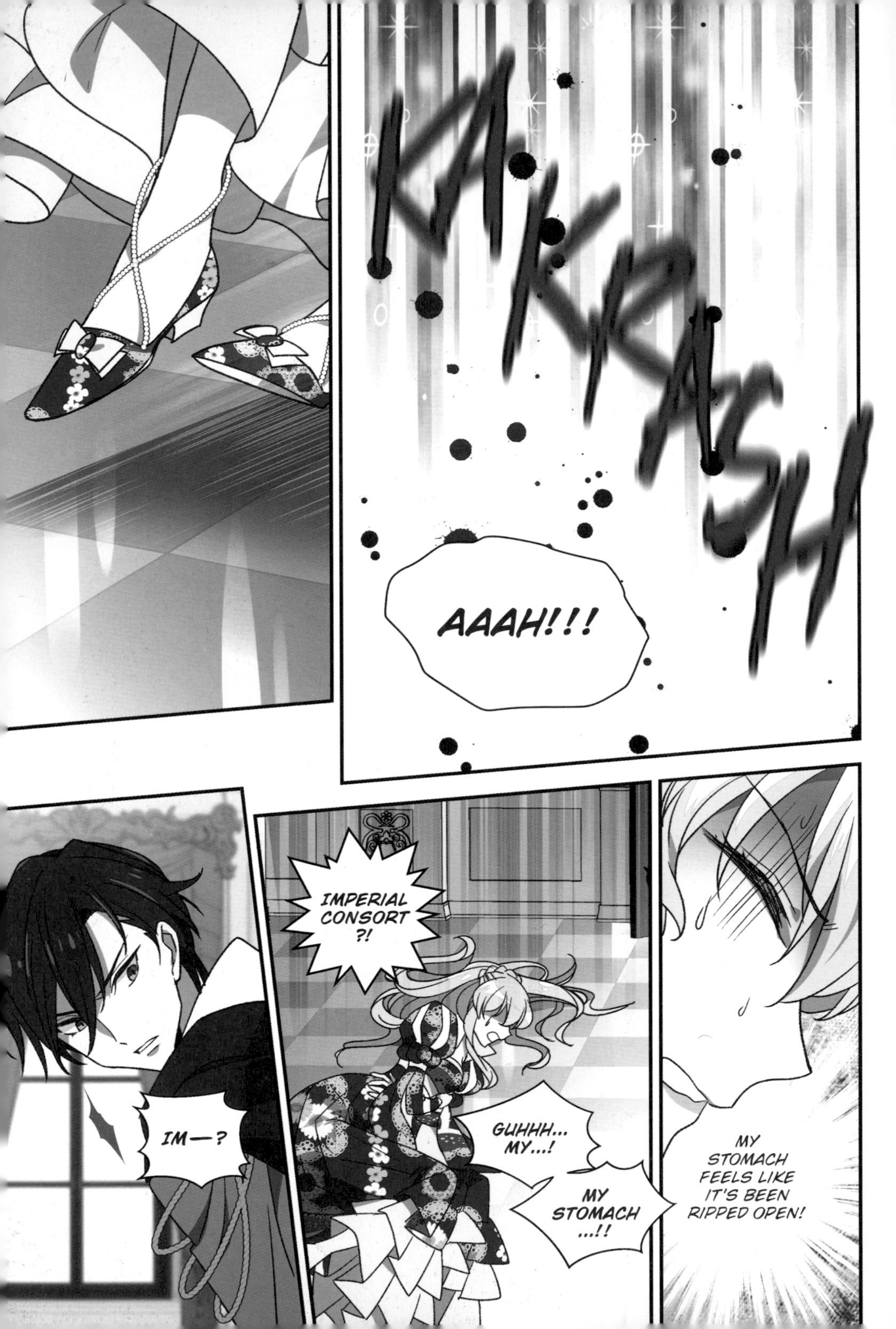
KAKRASH
AAAH!!!
IM—?
IMPERIAL CONSORT ?!
GUHHH... MY...!
MY STOMACH ...!!
MY STOMACH FEELS LIKE IT'S BEEN RIPPED OPEN!

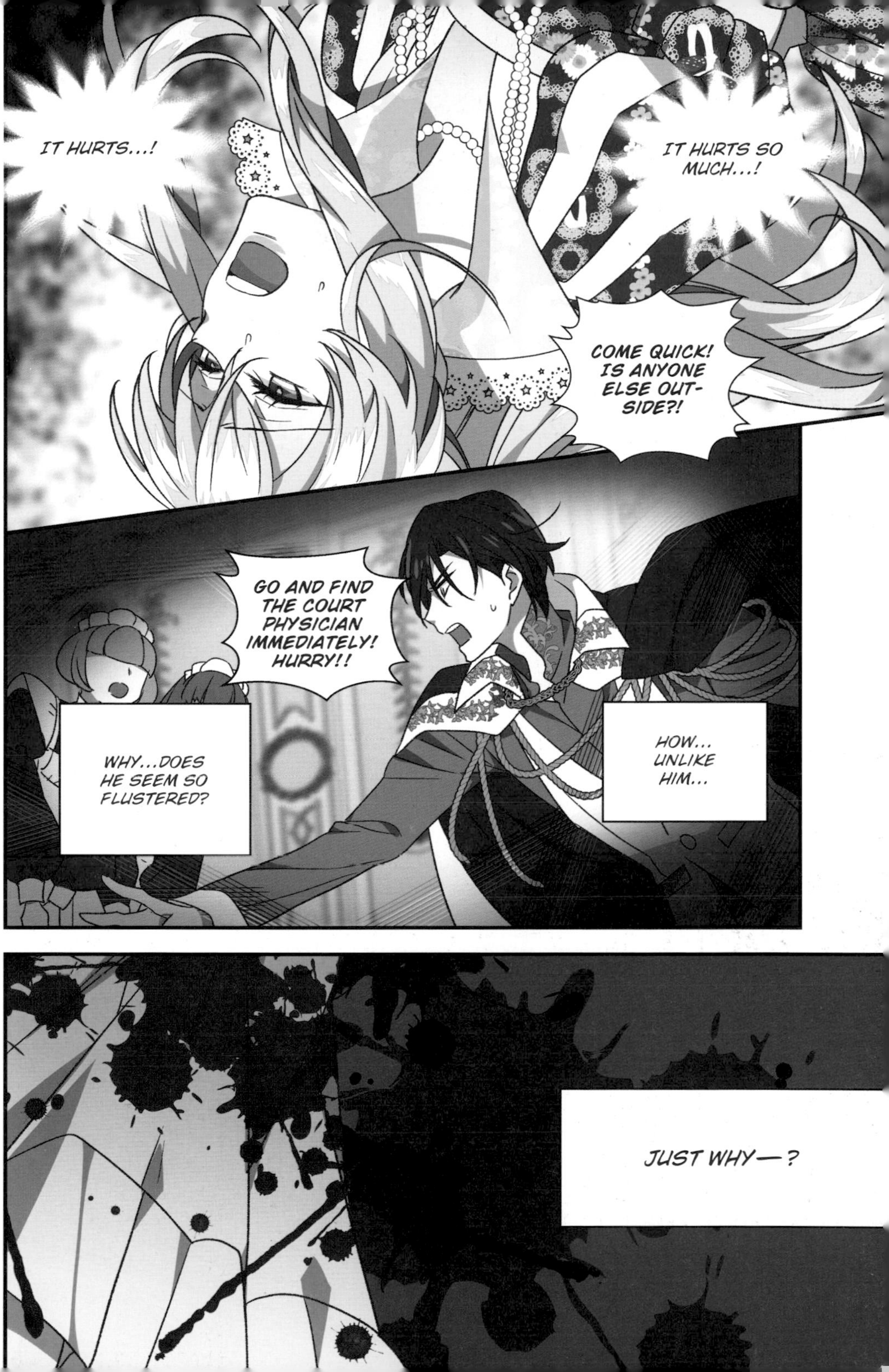
IT HURTS SO MUCH...!
IT HURTS...!
COME QUICK! IS ANYONE ELSE OUT-SIDE?!
GO AND FIND THE COURT PHYSICIAN IMMEDIATELY! HURRY!!
HOW... UNLIKE HIM...
WHY...DOES HE SEEM SO FLUSTERED?
JUST WHY—?

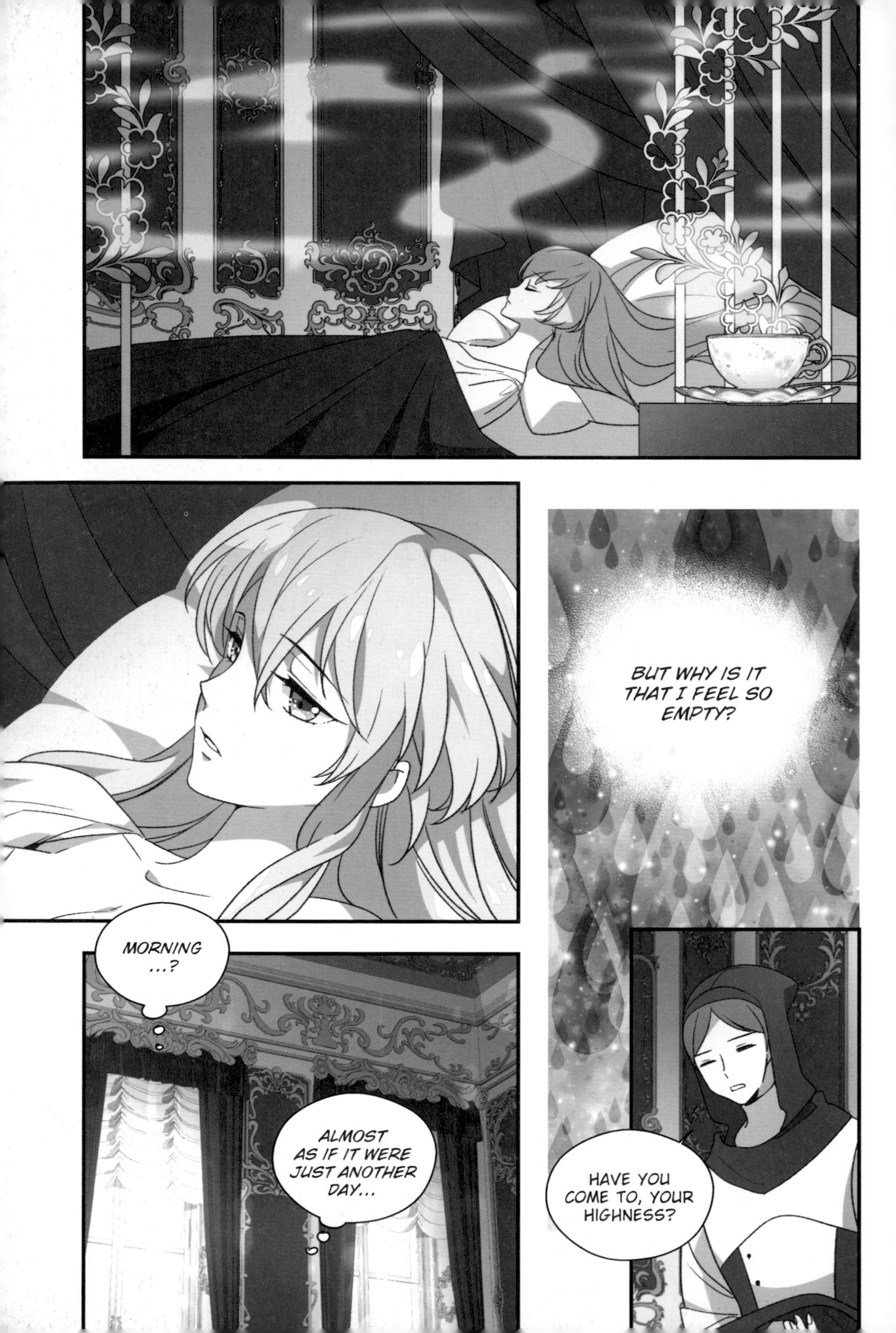
BUT WHY IS IT THAT I FEEL SO EMPTY?
MORNING ...?
ALMOST AS IF IT WERE JUST ANOTHER DAY...
HAVE YOU COME TO, YOUR HIGHNESS?

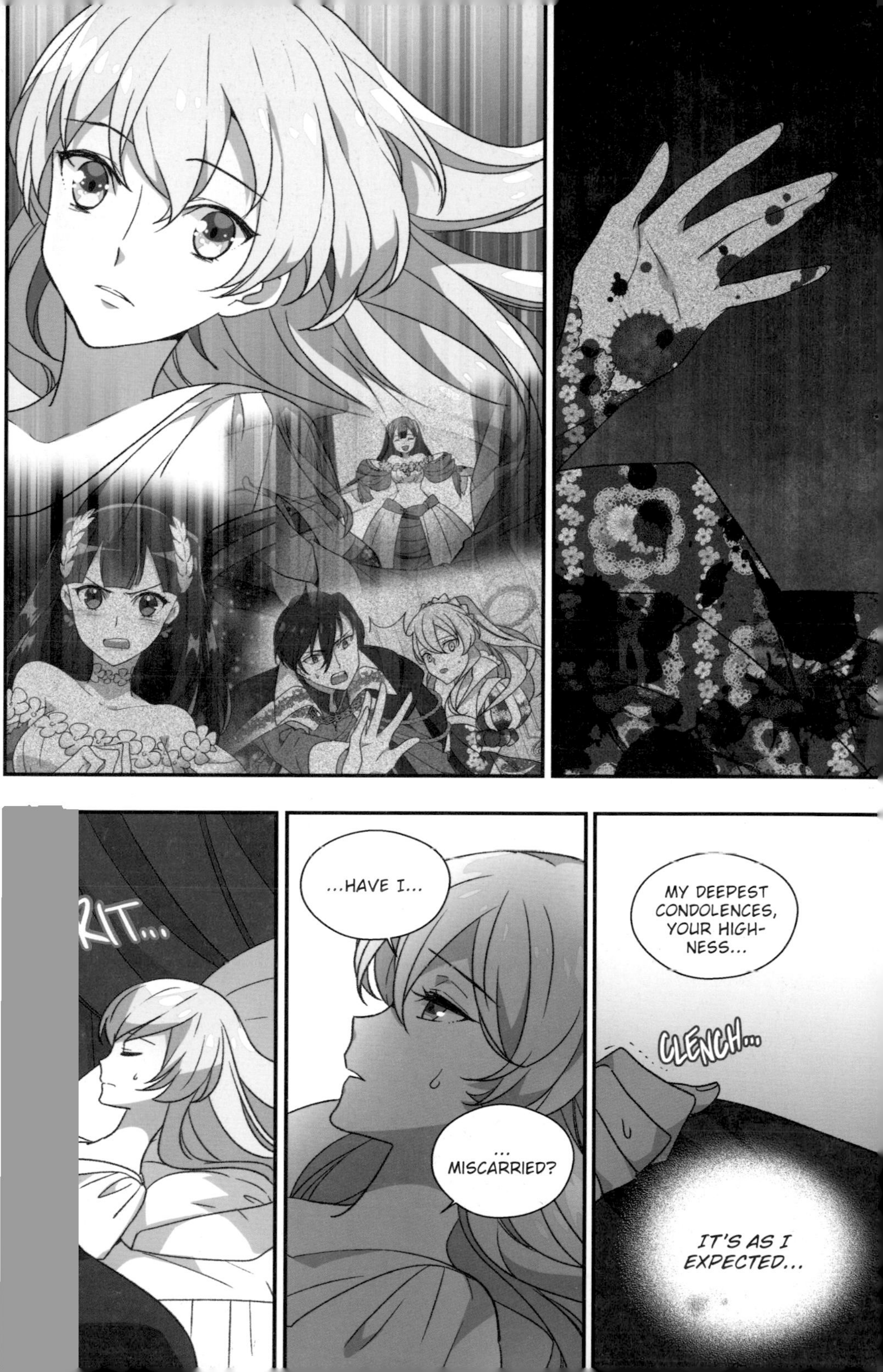

RIT...
...HAVE I...
...
MISCARRIED?
MY DEEPEST CONDOLENCES, YOUR HIGH-NESS...
CLENCH...
IT'S AS I EXPECTED...

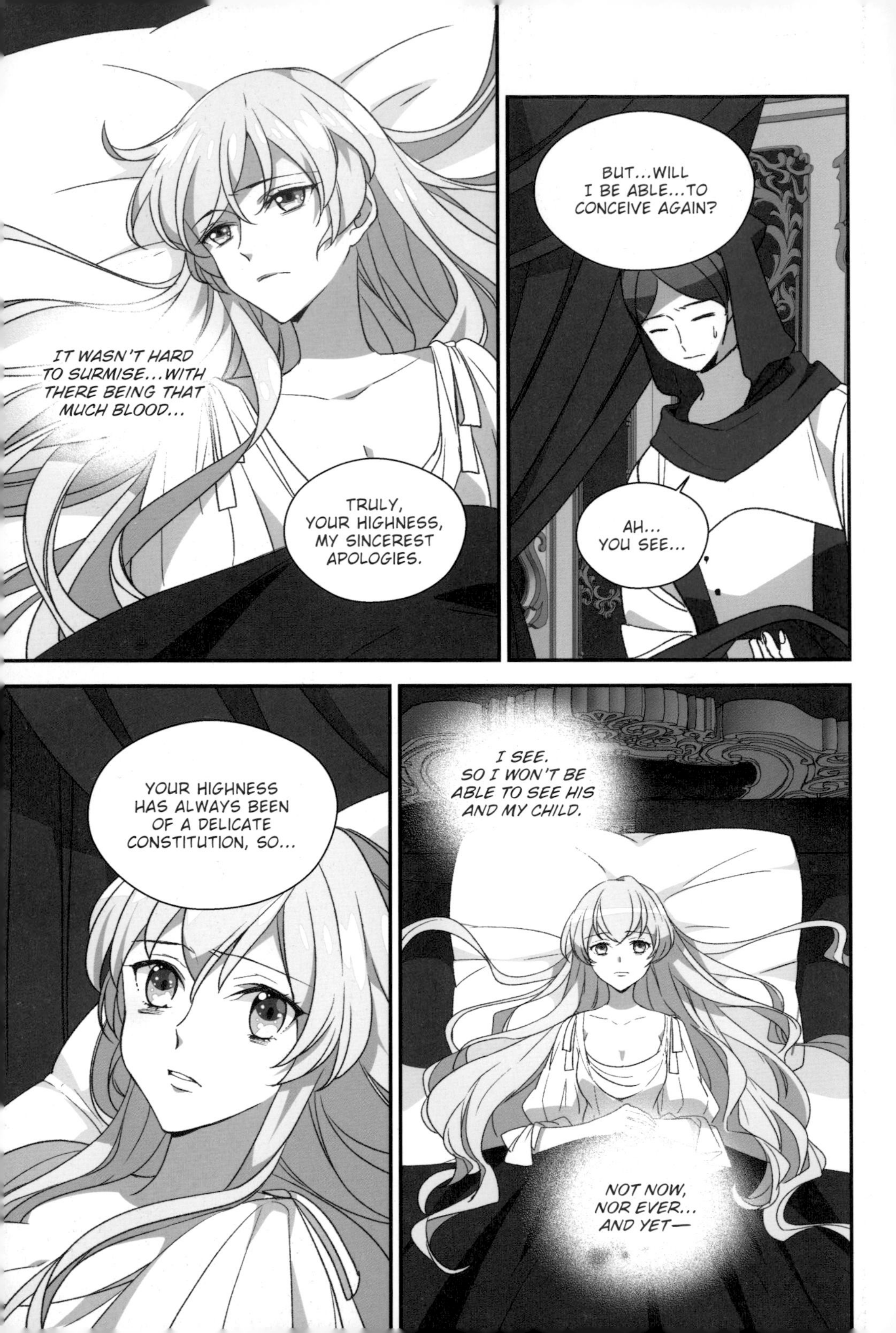
IT WASN'T HARD TO SURMISE...WITH THERE BEING THAT MUCH BLOOD...
TRULY, YOUR HIGHNESS, MY SINCEREST APOLOGIES.
BUT...WILL I BE ABLE...TO CONCEIVE AGAIN?
AH... YOU SEE...
YOUR HIGHNESS HAS ALWAYS BEEN OF A DELICATE CONSTITUTION, SO...
I SEE. SO I WON'T BE ABLE TO SEE HIS AND MY CHILD.
NOT NOW, NOR EVER... AND YET—

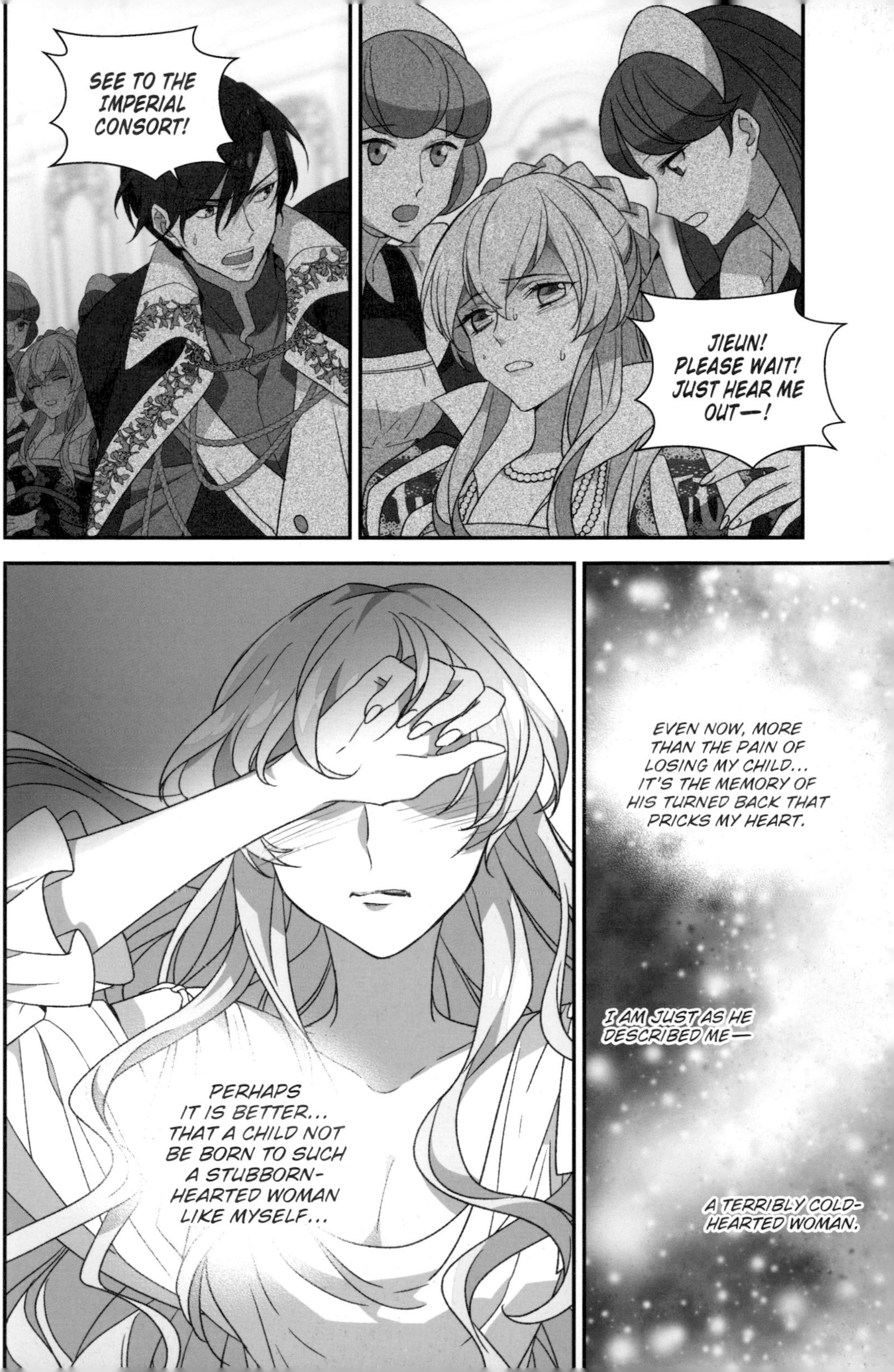
SEE TO THE IMPERIAL CONSORT!
JIEUN! PLEASE WAIT! JUST HEAR ME OUT—!
EVEN NOW, MORE THAN THE PAIN OF LOSING MY CHILD... IT'S THE MEMORY OF HIS TURNED BACK THAT PRICKS MY HEART.
I AM JUST AS HE DESCRIBED ME—
A TERRIBLY COLD-HEARTED WOMAN.
PERHAPS IT IS BETTER... THAT A CHILD NOT BE BORN TO SUCH A STUBBORN-HEARTED WOMAN LIKE MYSELF...

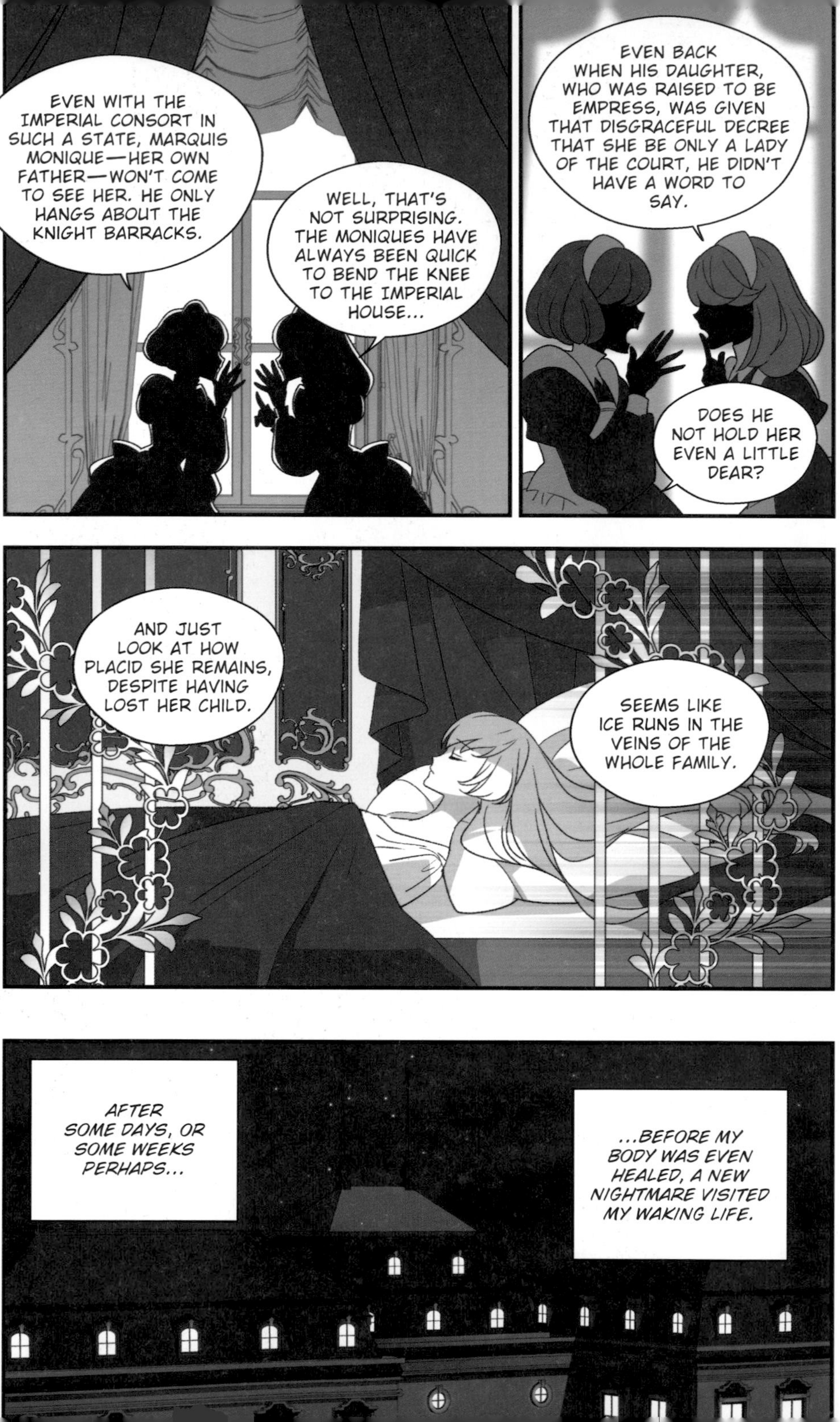

EVEN WITH THE IMPERIAL CONSORT IN SUCH A STATE, MARQUIS MONIQUE—HER OWN FATHER—WON'T COME TO SEE HER. HE ONLY HANGS ABOUT THE KNIGHT BARRACKS.
WELL, THAT'S NOT SURPRISING. THE MONIQUES HAVE ALWAYS BEEN QUICK TO BEND THE KNEE TO THE IMPERIAL HOUSE...
EVEN BACK WHEN HIS DAUGHTER, WHO WAS RAISED TO BE EMPRESS, WAS GIVEN THAT DISGRACEFUL DECREE THAT SHE BE ONLY A LADY OF THE COURT, HE DIDN'T HAVE A WORD TO SAY.
DOES HE NOT HOLD HER EVEN A LITTLE DEAR?
AND JUST LOOK AT HOW PLACID SHE REMAINS, DESPITE HAVING LOST HER CHILD.
SEEMS LIKE ICE RUNS IN THE VEINS OF THE WHOLE FAMILY.
AFTER SOME DAYS, OR SOME WEEKS PERHAPS...
...BEFORE MY BODY WAS EVEN HEALED, A NEW NIGHTMARE VISITED MY WAKING LIFE.

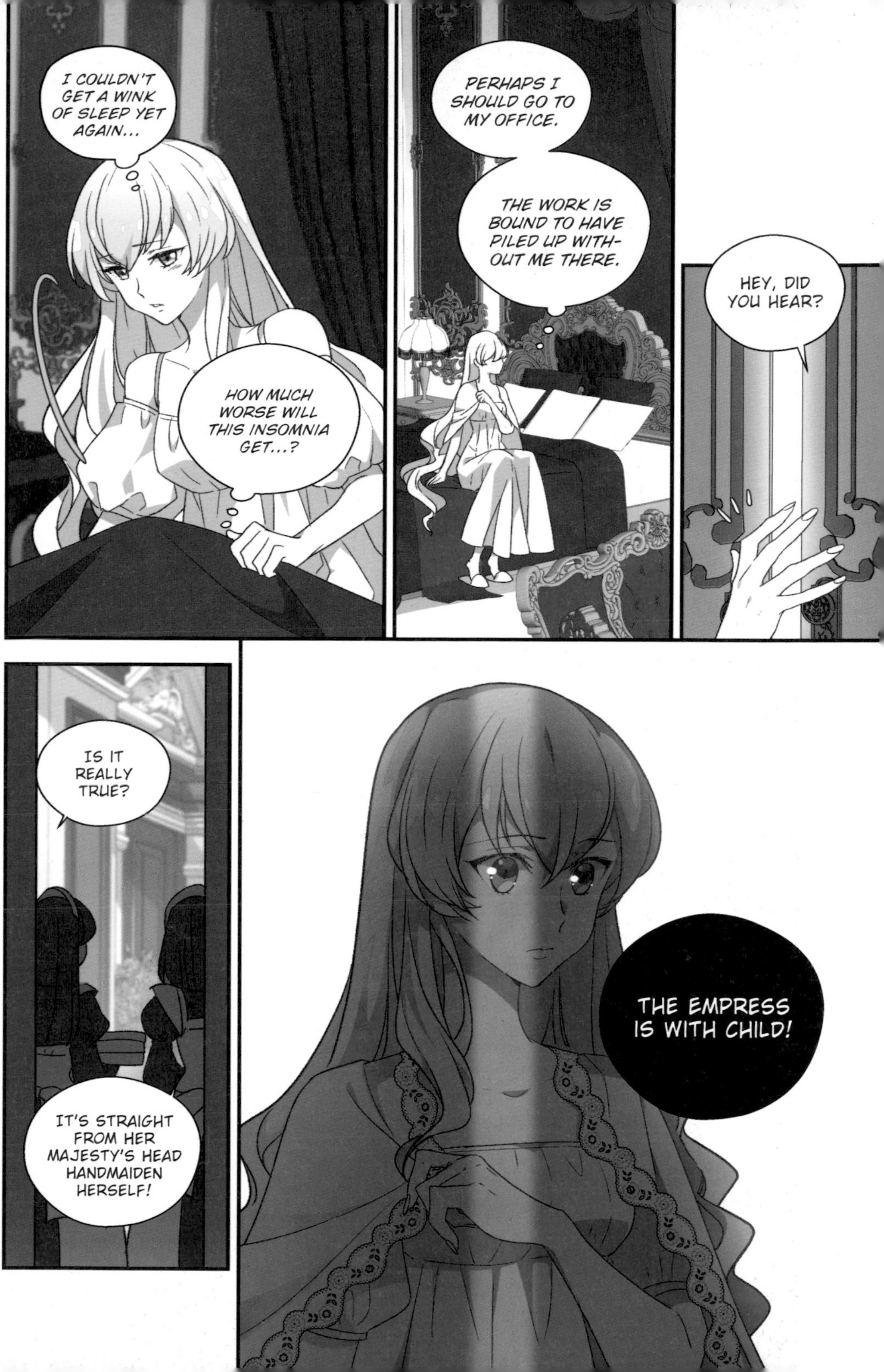
I COULDN'T GET A WINK OF SLEEP YET AGAIN...
HOW MUCH WORSE WILL THIS INSOMNIA GET...?
PERHAPS I SHOULD GO TO MY OFFICE.
THE WORK IS BOUND TO HAVE PILED UP WITH-OUT ME THERE.
HEY, DID YOU HEAR?
IS IT REALLY TRUE?
IT'S STRAIGHT FROM HER MAJESTY'S HEAD HANDMAIDEN HERSELF!
THE EMPRESS IS WITH CHILD!

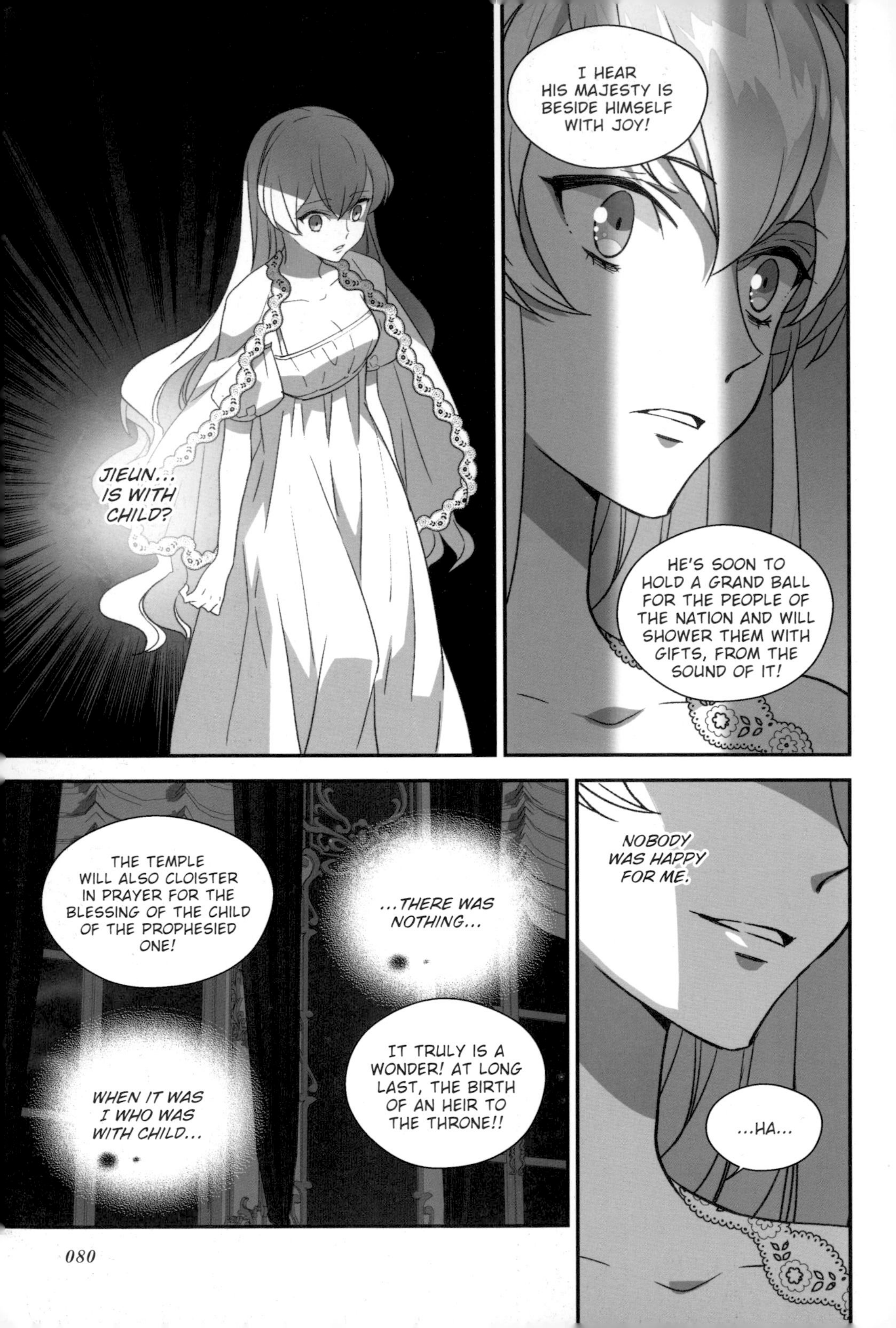
JIEUN... IS WITH CHILD?
I HEAR HIS MAJESTY IS BESIDE HIMSELF WITH JOY!
HE'S SOON TO HOLD A GRAND BALL FOR THE PEOPLE OF THE NATION AND WILL SHOWER THEM WITH GIFTS, FROM THE SOUND OF IT!
THE TEMPLE WILL ALSO CLOISTER IN PRAYER FOR THE BLESSING OF THE CHILD OF THE PROPHESIED ONE!
...THERE WAS NOTHING...
WHEN IT WAS I WHO WAS WITH CHILD...
IT TRULY IS A WONDER! AT LONG LAST, THE BIRTH OF AN HEIR TO THE THRONE!!
NOBODY WAS HAPPY FOR ME.
...HA...

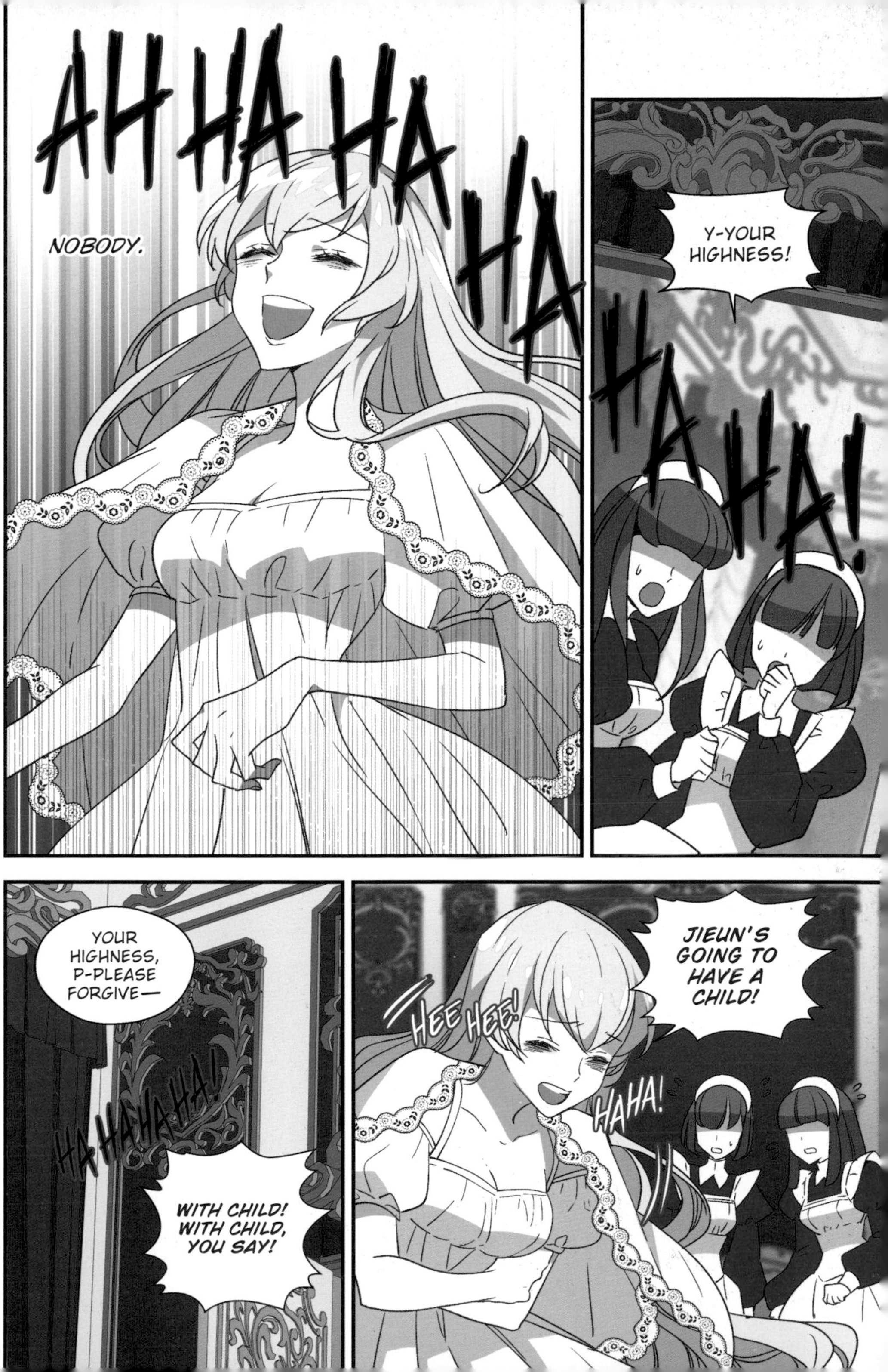
AH HA HA HA HA HA
NOBODY.
Y-YOUR HIGHNESS!
HA HA HA!
YOUR HIGHNESS, P-PLEASE FORGIVE—
HA HA HA HA HA!
WITH CHILD! WITH CHILD, YOU SAY!
JIEUN'S GOING TO HAVE A CHILD!
HEE HEE!
HAHA!

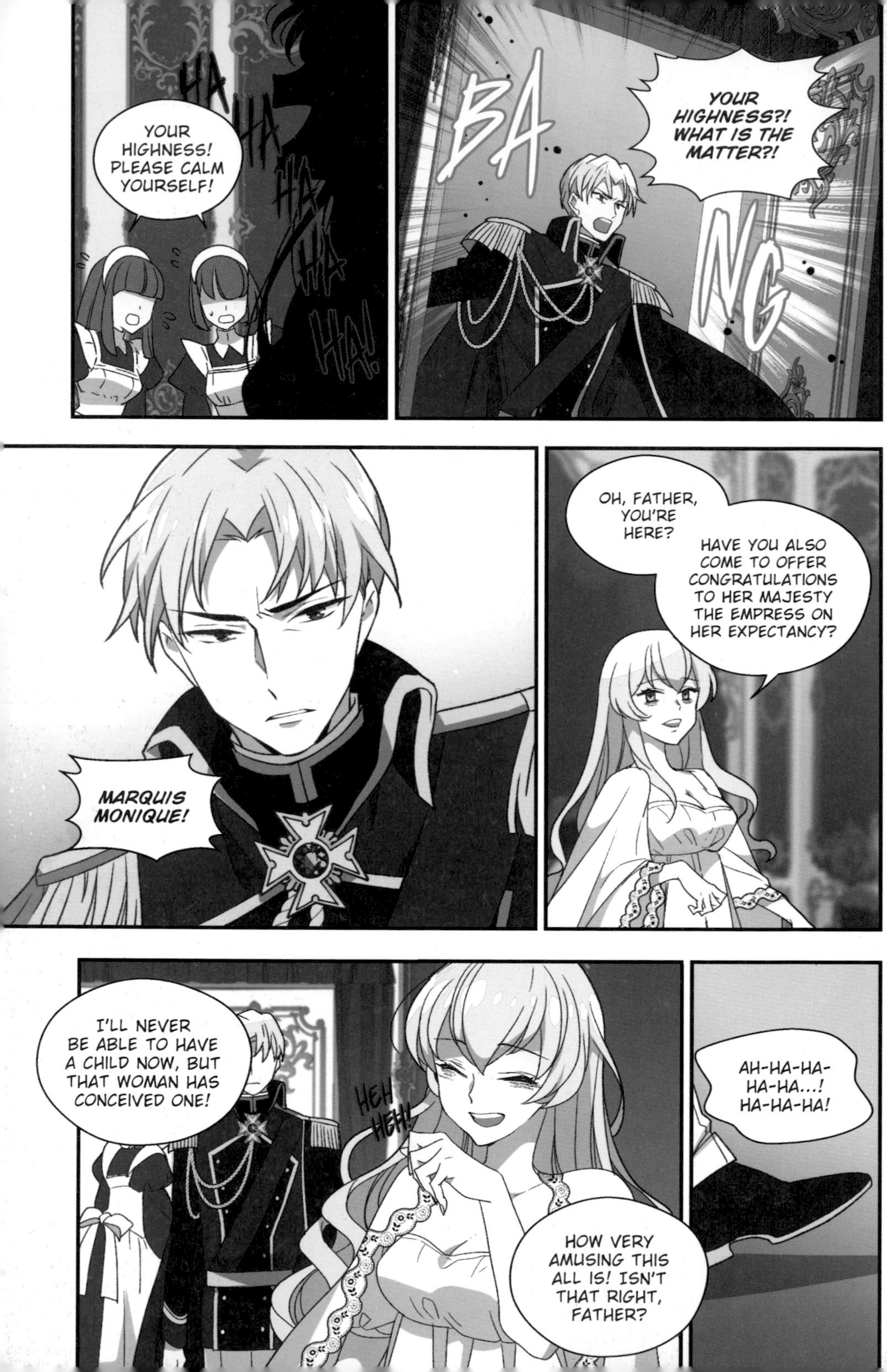
YOUR HIGHNESS! PLEASE CALM YOURSELF!
HA HA HA HA HA!
BANG
YOUR HIGHNESS?! WHAT IS THE MATTER?!
MARQUIS MONIQUE!
OH, FATHER, YOU'RE HERE?
HAVE YOU ALSO COME TO OFFER CONGRATULATIONS TO HER MAJESTY THE EMPRESS ON HER EXPECTANCY?
I'LL NEVER BE ABLE TO HAVE A CHILD NOW, BUT THAT WOMAN HAS CONCEIVED ONE!
HEH HEH!
HOW VERY AMUSING THIS ALL IS! ISN'T THAT RIGHT, FATHER?
AH-HA-HA-HA-HA...! HA-HA-HA!

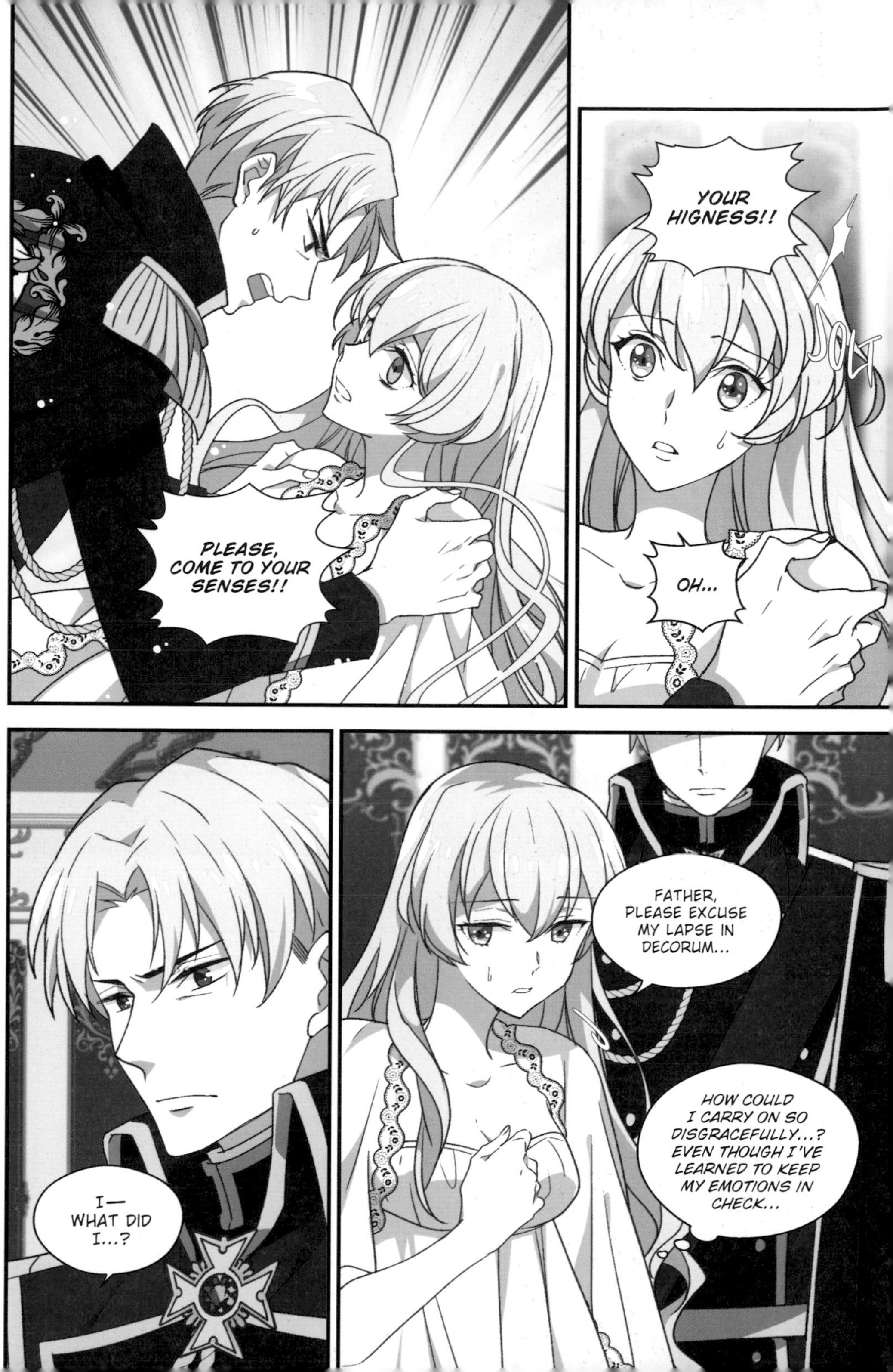
PLEASE, COME TO YOUR SENSES!!
YOUR HIGNESS!!
JOLT
OH...
I— WHAT DID I...?
FATHER, PLEASE EXCUSE MY LAPSE IN DECORUM...
HOW COULD I CARRY ON SO DISGRACEFULLY...? EVEN THOUGH I'VE LEARNED TO KEEP MY EMOTIONS IN CHECK...

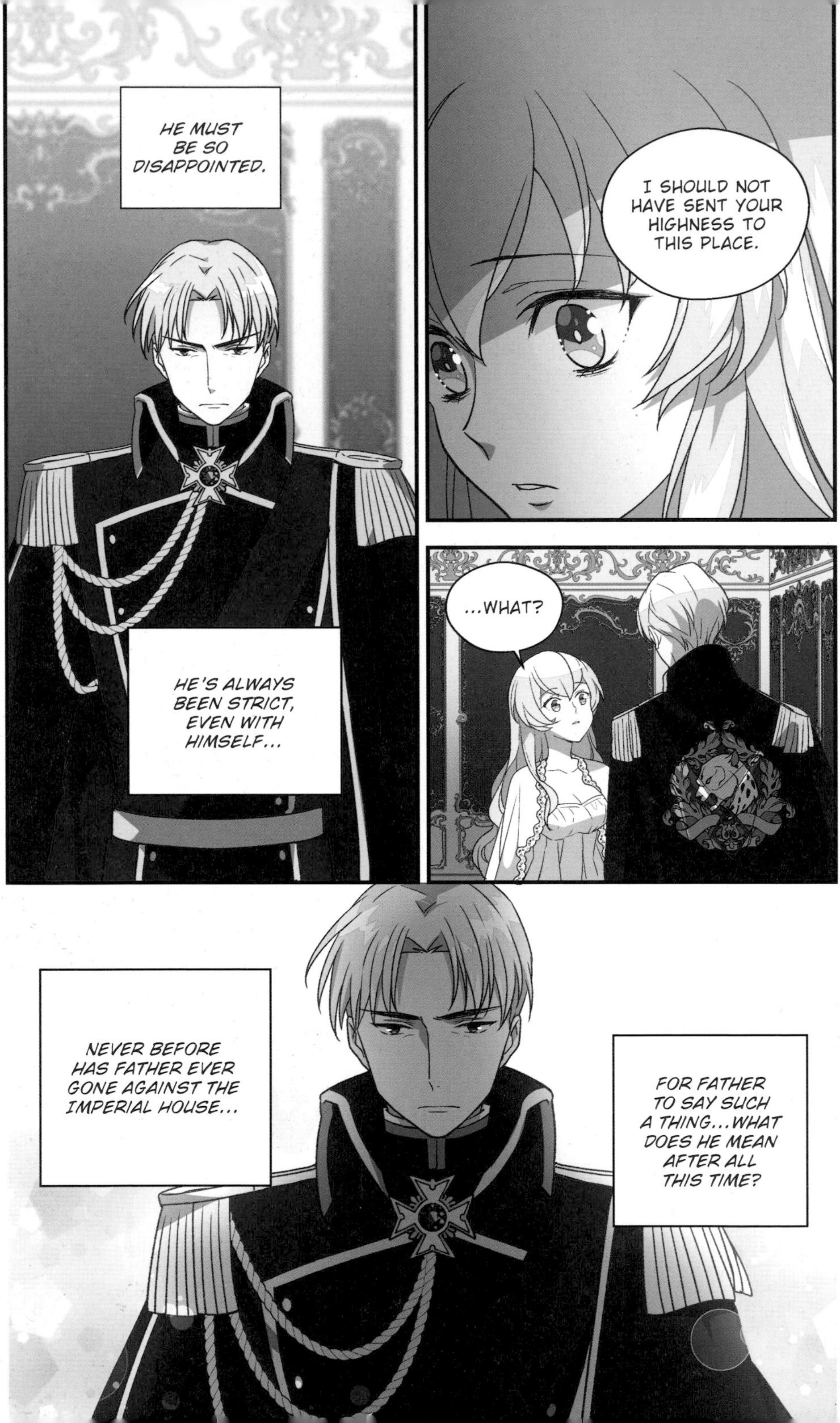
HE MUST BE SO DISAPPOINTED.
I SHOULD NOT HAVE SENT YOUR HIGHNESS TO THIS PLACE.
HE'S ALWAYS BEEN STRICT, EVEN WITH HIMSELF...
...WHAT?
NEVER BEFORE HAS FATHER EVER GONE AGAINST THE IMPERIAL HOUSE...
FOR FATHER TO SAY SUCH A THING...WHAT DOES HE MEAN AFTER ALL THIS TIME?

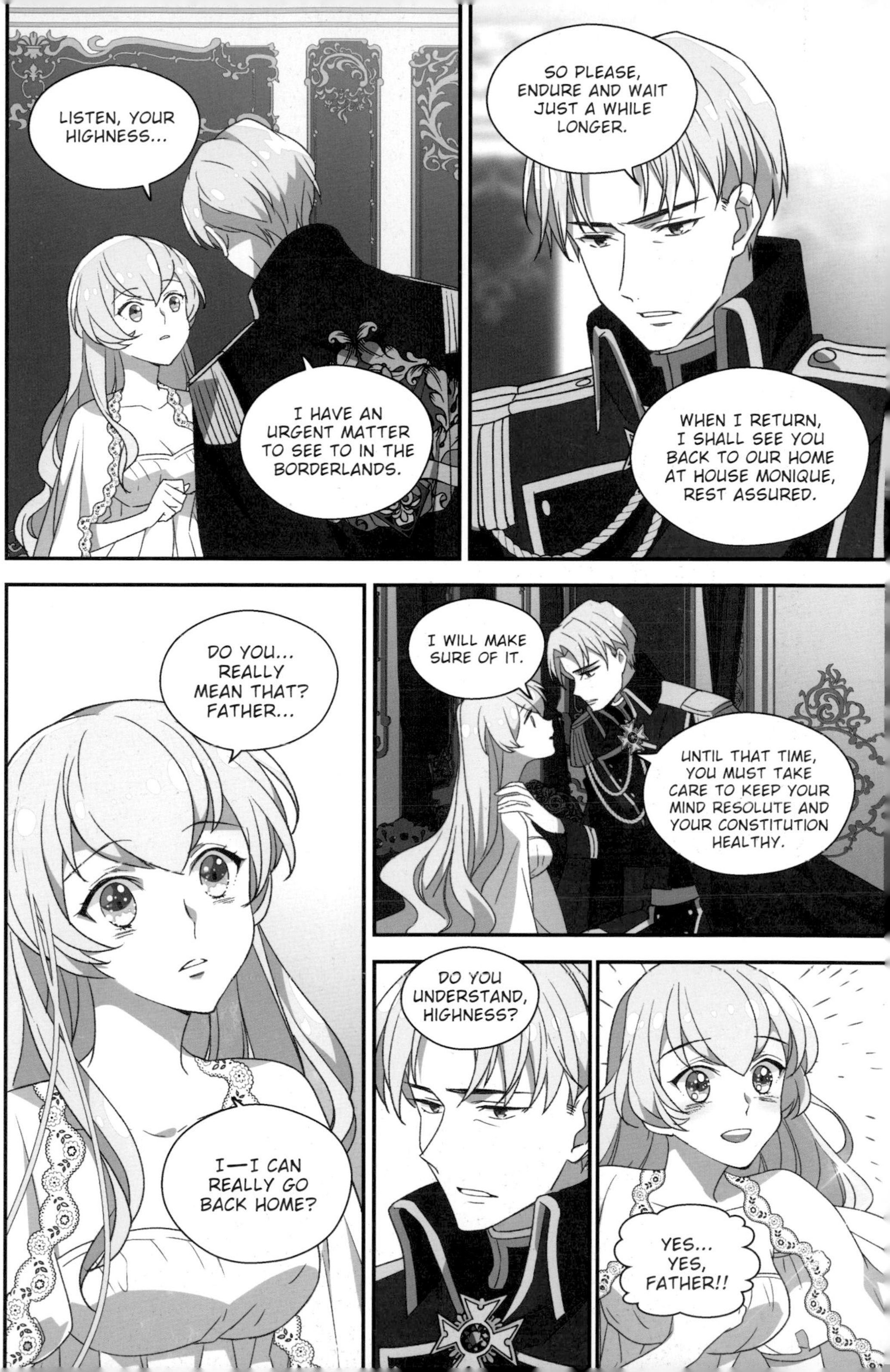
LISTEN, YOUR HIGHNESS...
I HAVE AN URGENT MATTER TO SEE TO IN THE BORDERLANDS.
SO PLEASE, ENDURE AND WAIT JUST A WHILE LONGER.
WHEN I RETURN, I SHALL SEE YOU BACK TO OUR HOME AT HOUSE MONIQUE, REST ASSURED.
DO YOU... REALLY MEAN THAT? FATHER...
I—I CAN REALLY GO BACK HOME?
I WILL MAKE SURE OF IT.
UNTIL THAT TIME, YOU MUST TAKE CARE TO KEEP YOUR MIND RESOLUTE AND YOUR CONSTITUTION HEALTHY.
DO YOU UNDERSTAND, HIGHNESS?
YES... YES, FATHER!!

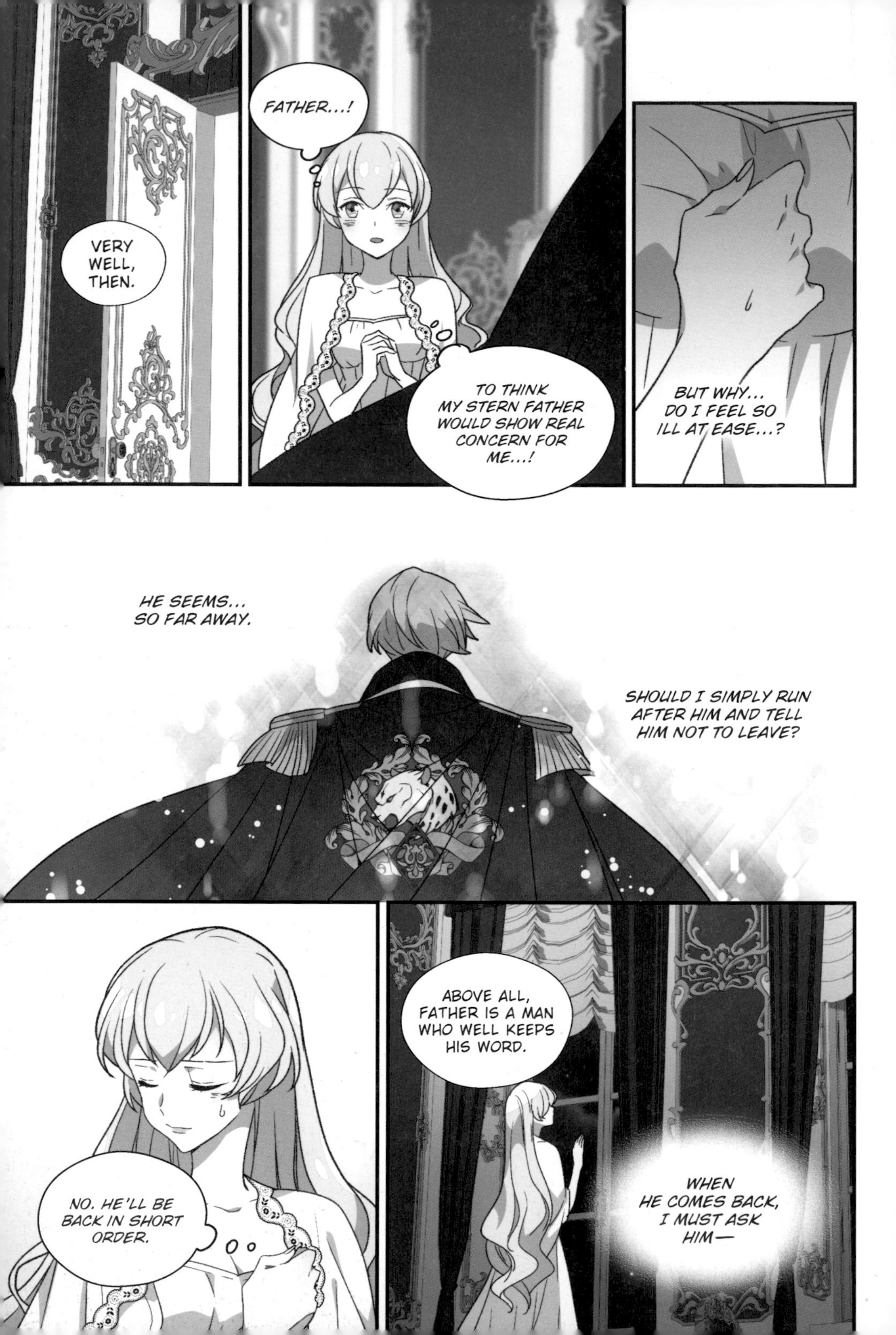
VERY WELL, THEN.
FATHER...!
TO THINK MY STERN FATHER WOULD SHOW REAL CONCERN FOR ME...!
BUT WHY... DO I FEEL SO ILL AT EASE...?
HE SEEMS... SO FAR AWAY.
SHOULD I SIMPLY RUN AFTER HIM AND TELL HIM NOT TO LEAVE?
NO. HE'LL BE BACK IN SHORT ORDER.
ABOVE ALL, FATHER IS A MAN WHO WELL KEEPS HIS WORD.
WHEN HE COMES BACK, I MUST ASK HIM—

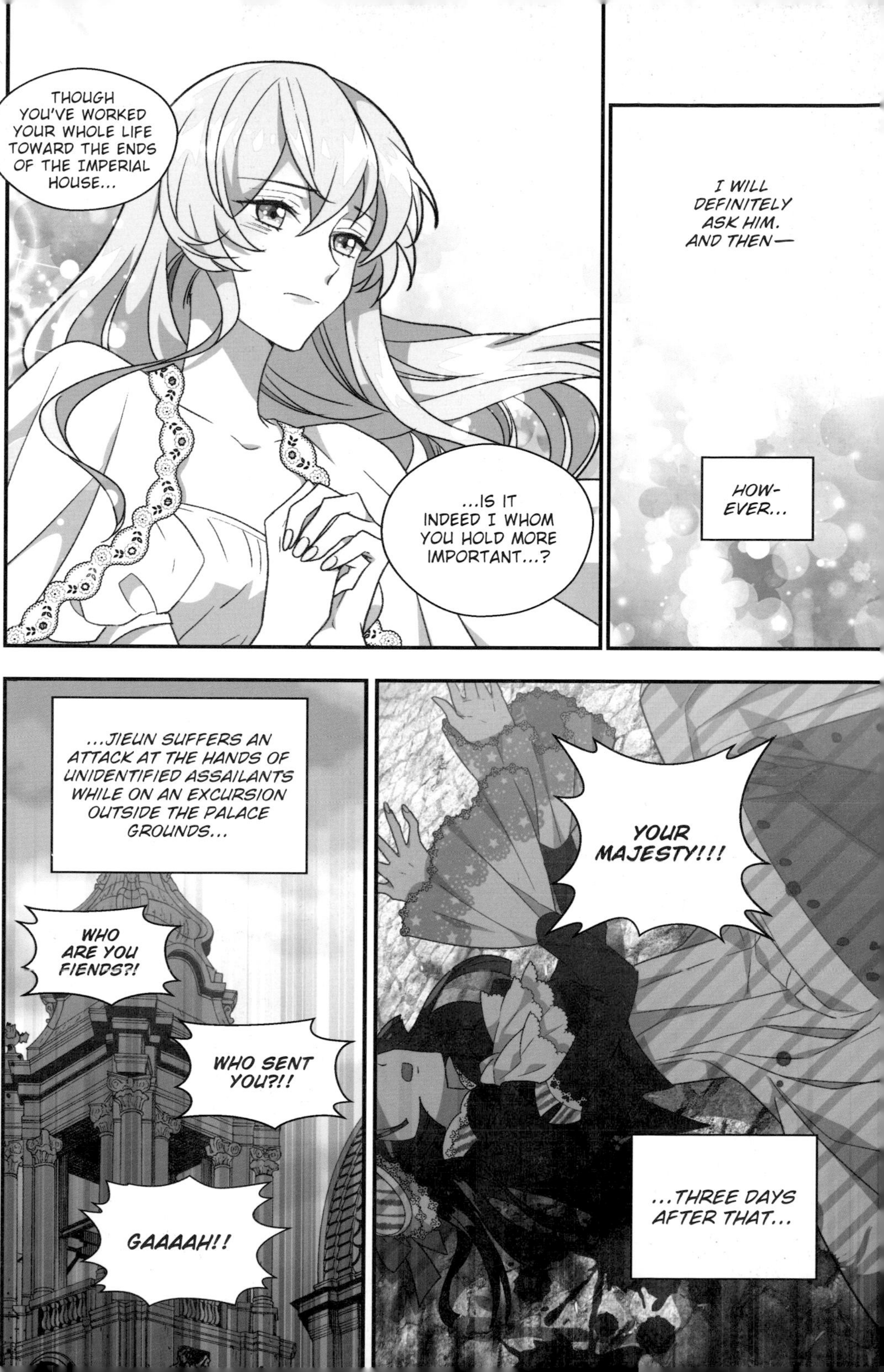
THOUGH YOU'VE WORKED YOUR WHOLE LIFE TOWARD THE ENDS OF THE IMPERIAL HOUSE...
...IS IT INDEED I WHOM YOU HOLD MORE IMPORTANT...?
I WILL DEFINITELY ASK HIM. AND THEN—
HOW-EVER...
...JIEUN SUFFERS AN ATTACK AT THE HANDS OF UNIDENTIFIED ASSAILANTS WHILE ON AN EXCURSION OUTSIDE THE PALACE GROUNDS...
WHO ARE YOU FIENDS?!
WHO SENT YOU?!!
GAAAAH!!
YOUR MAJESTY!!!
...THREE DAYS AFTER THAT...

# The Abandoned Empress

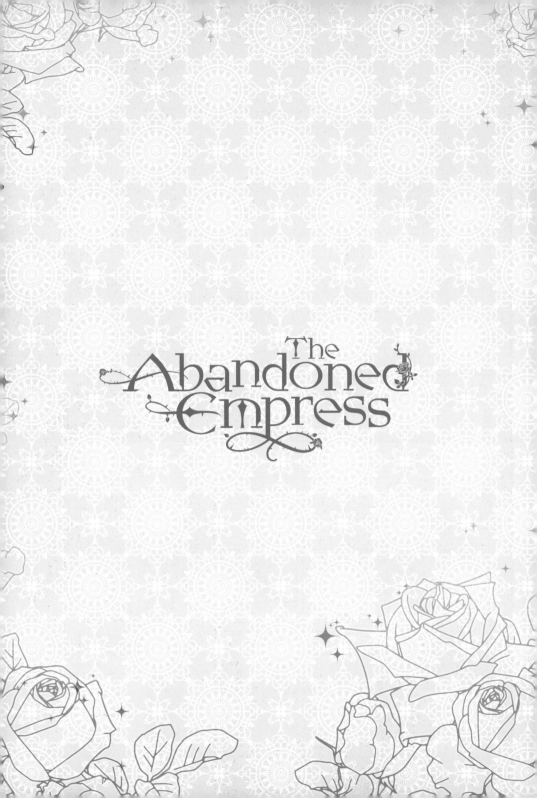

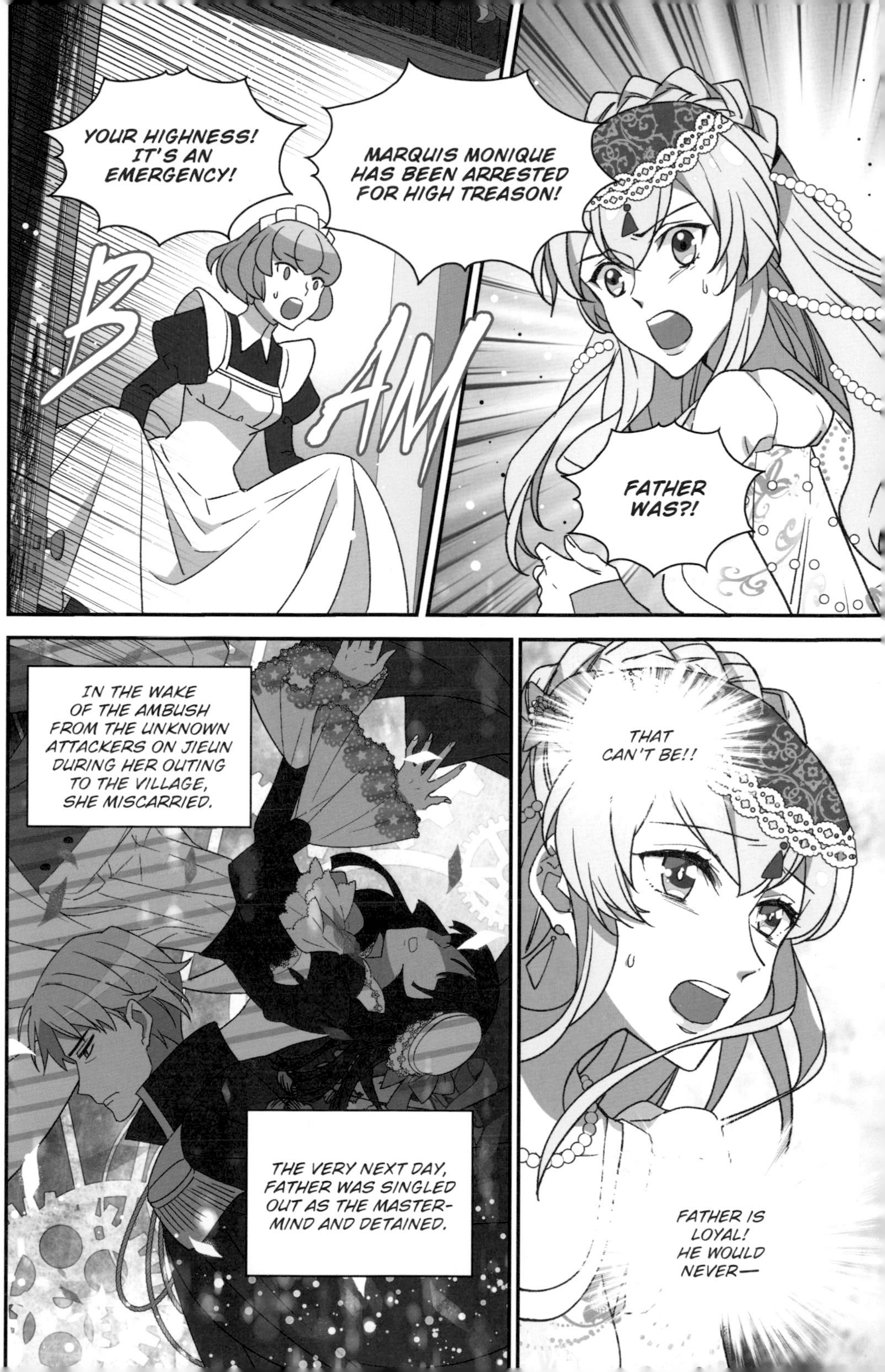
YOUR HIGHNESS! IT'S AN EMERGENCY!
MARQUIS MONIQUE HAS BEEN ARRESTED FOR HIGH TREASON!
BAM
FATHER WAS?!
IN THE WAKE OF THE AMBUSH FROM THE UNKNOWN ATTACKERS ON JIEUN DURING HER OUTING TO THE VILLAGE, SHE MISCARRIED.
THE VERY NEXT DAY, FATHER WAS SINGLED OUT AS THE MASTER-MIND AND DETAINED.
THAT CAN'T BE!!
FATHER IS LOYAL! HE WOULD NEVER—

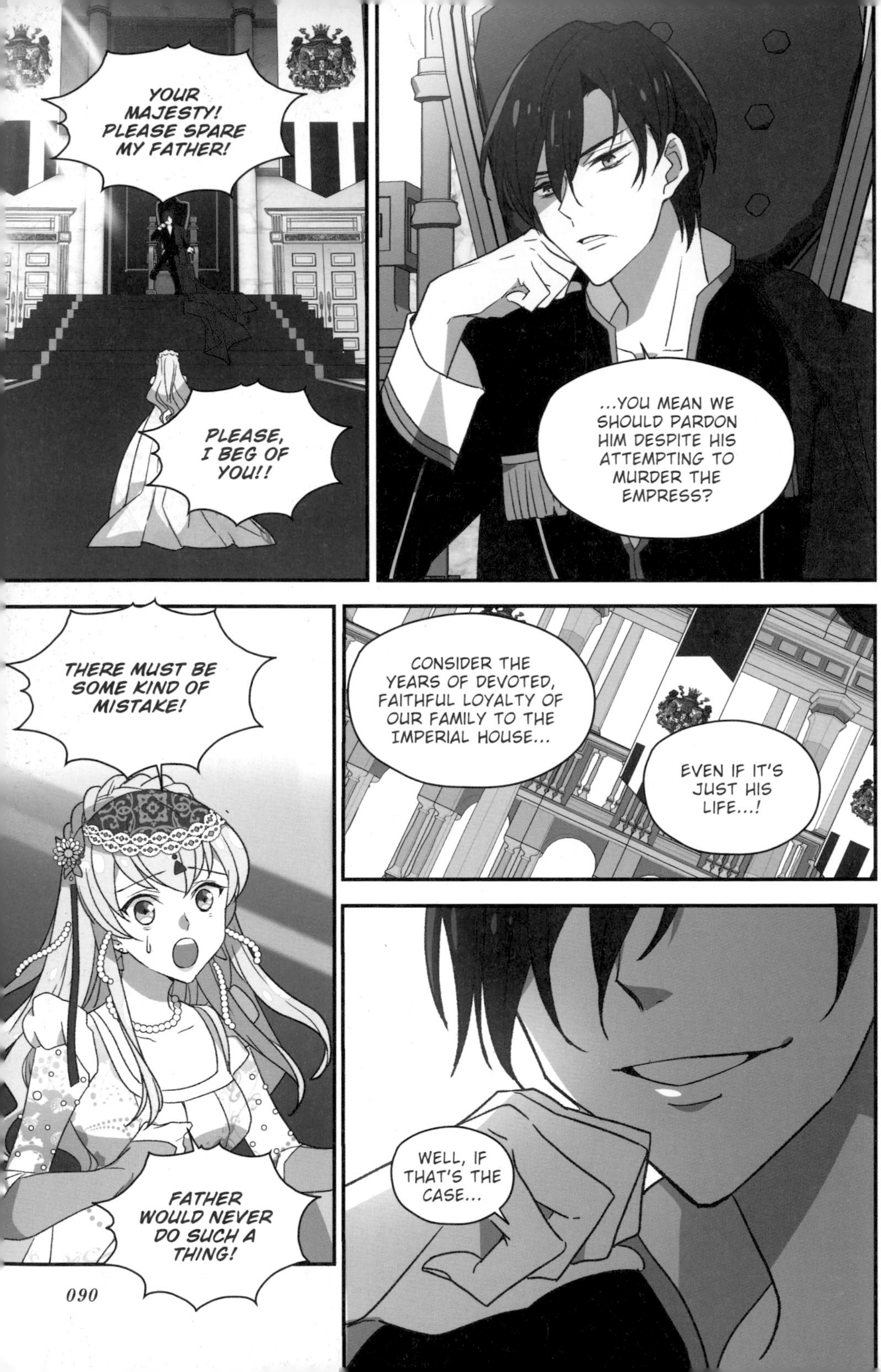
YOUR MAJESTY! PLEASE SPARE MY FATHER!
PLEASE, I BEG OF YOU!!
...YOU MEAN WE SHOULD PARDON HIM DESPITE HIS ATTEMPTING TO MURDER THE EMPRESS?
THERE MUST BE SOME KIND OF MISTAKE!
FATHER WOULD NEVER DO SUCH A THING!
CONSIDER THE YEARS OF DEVOTED, FAITHFUL LOYALTY OF OUR FAMILY TO THE IMPERIAL HOUSE...
EVEN IF IT'S JUST HIS LIFE...!
WELL, IF THAT'S THE CASE...

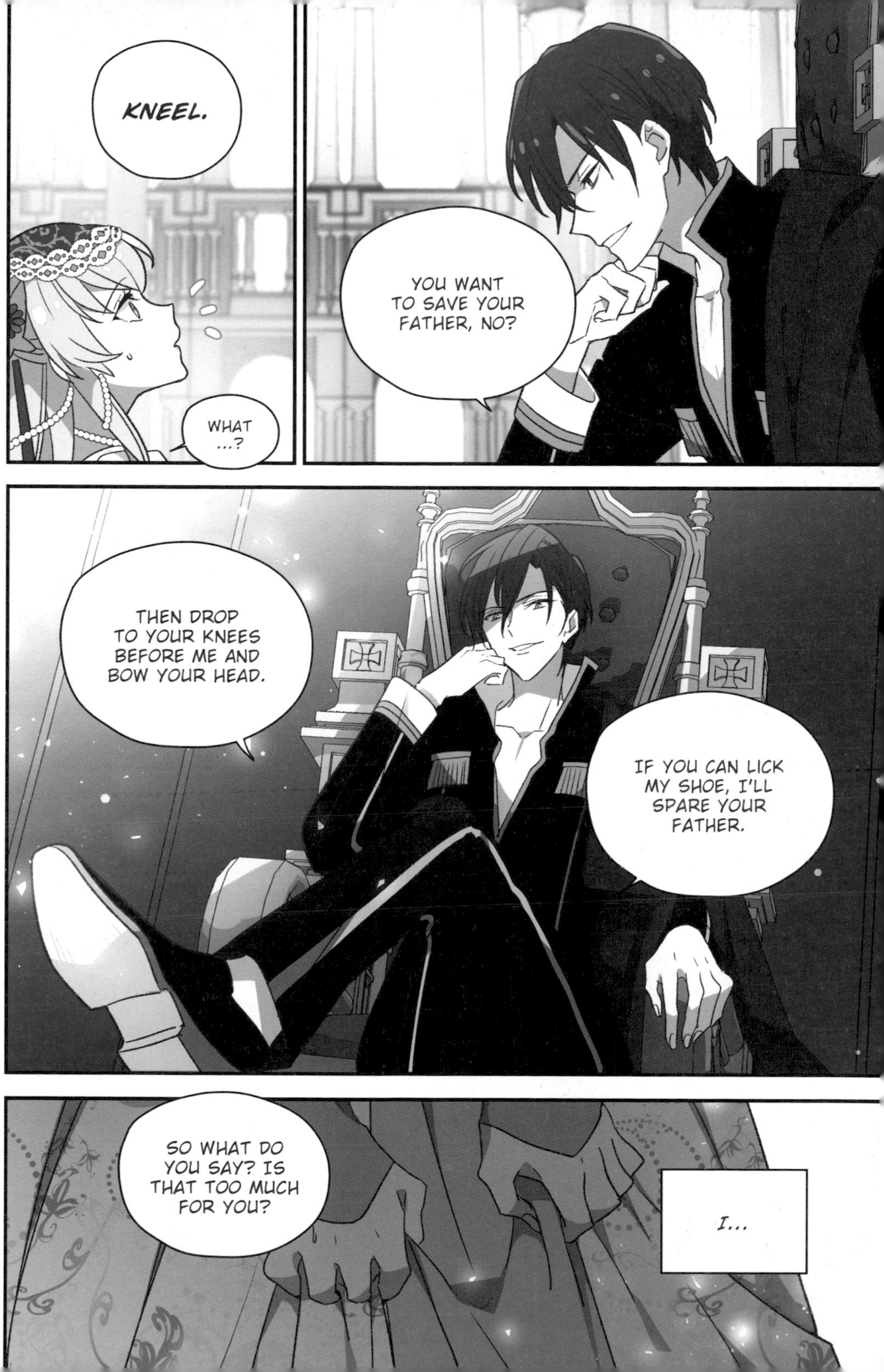
KNEEL.
WHAT ...?
YOU WANT TO SAVE YOUR FATHER, NO?
THEN DROP TO YOUR KNEES BEFORE ME AND BOW YOUR HEAD.
IF YOU CAN LICK MY SHOE, I'LL SPARE YOUR FATHER.
SO WHAT DO YOU SAY? IS THAT TOO MUCH FOR YOU?
I...

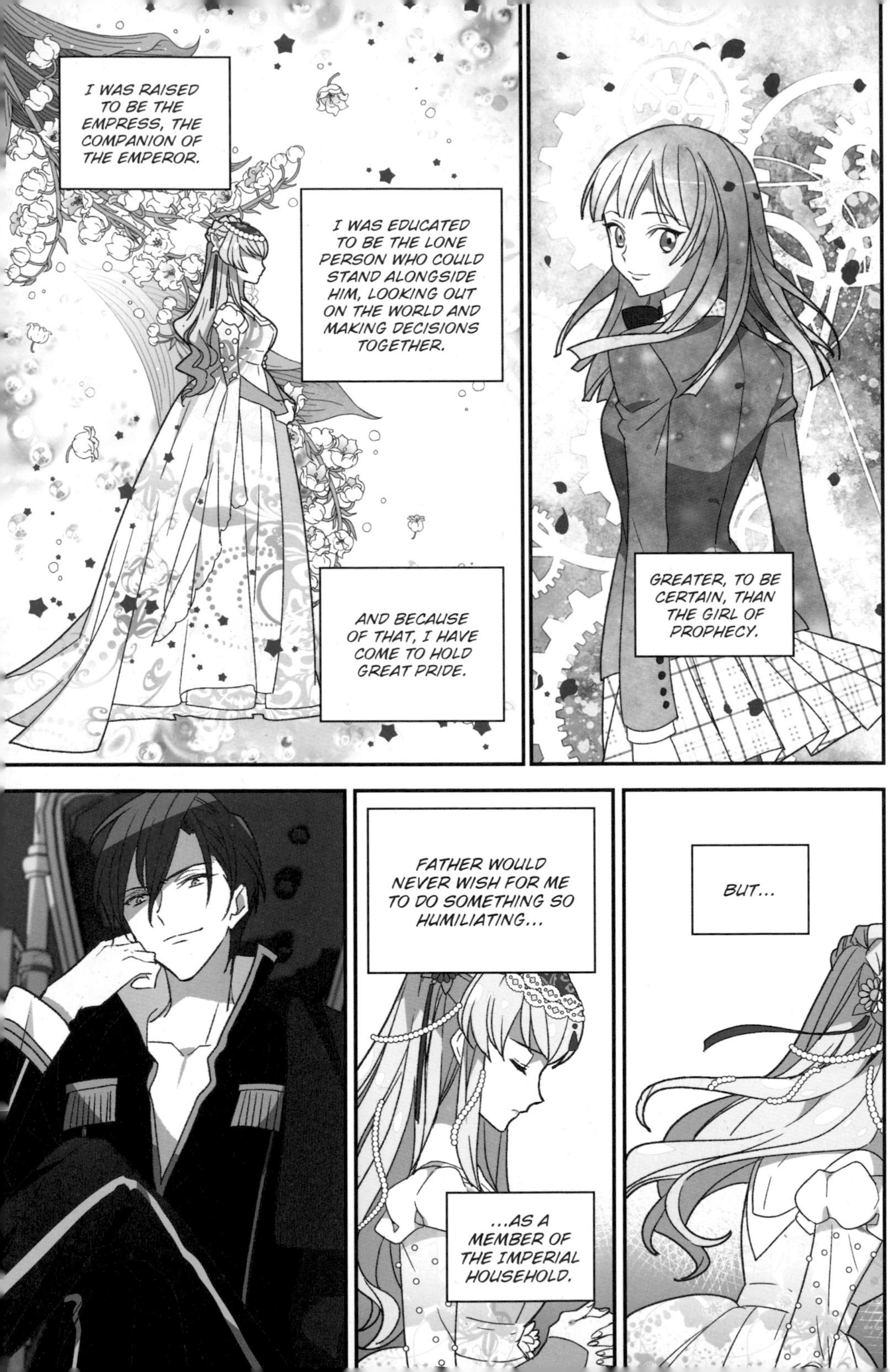
I WAS RAISED TO BE THE EMPRESS, THE COMPANION OF THE EMPEROR.
I WAS EDUCATED TO BE THE LONE PERSON WHO COULD STAND ALONGSIDE HIM, LOOKING OUT ON THE WORLD AND MAKING DECISIONS TOGETHER.
AND BECAUSE OF THAT, I HAVE COME TO HOLD GREAT PRIDE.
GREATER, TO BE CERTAIN, THAN THE GIRL OF PROPHECY.
FATHER WOULD NEVER WISH FOR ME TO DO SOMETHING SO HUMILIATING...
...AS A MEMBER OF THE IMPERIAL HOUSEHOLD.
BUT...

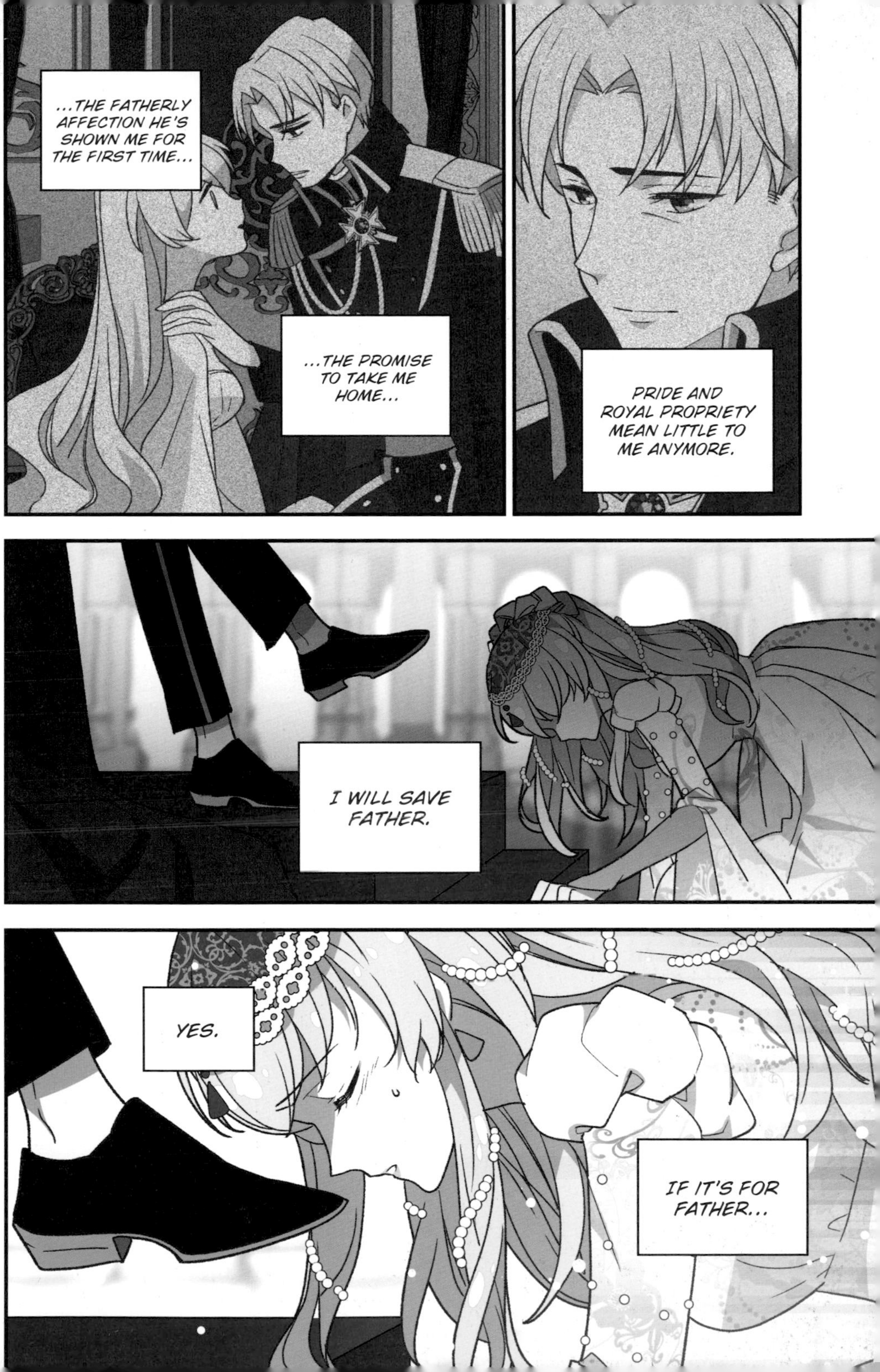
...THE FATHERLY AFFECTION HE'S SHOWN ME FOR THE FIRST TIME...
...THE PROMISE TO TAKE ME HOME...
PRIDE AND ROYAL PROPRIETY MEAN LITTLE TO ME ANYMORE.
I WILL SAVE FATHER.
YES.
IF IT'S FOR FATHER...

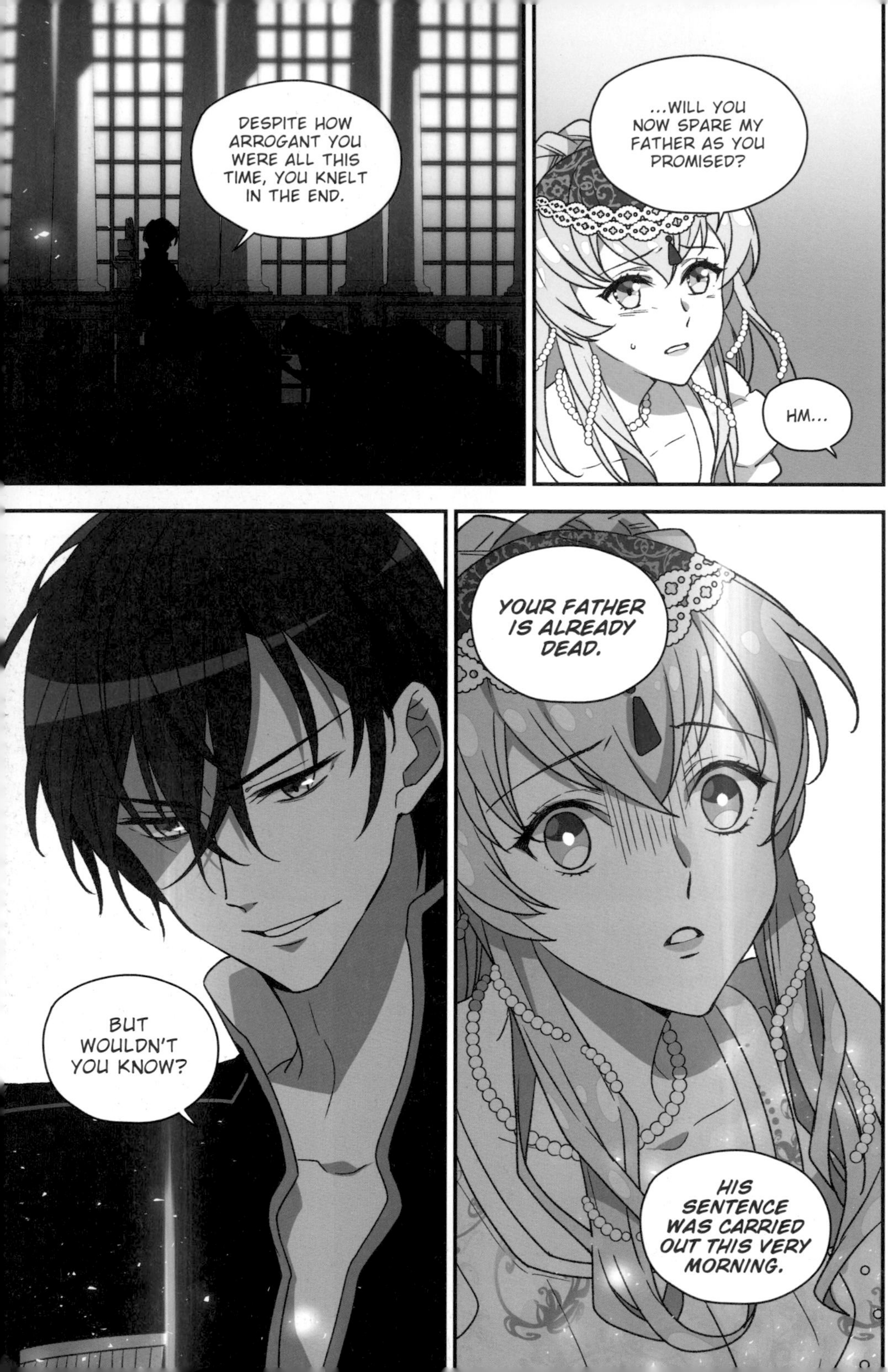
DESPITE HOW ARROGANT YOU WERE ALL THIS TIME, YOU KNELT IN THE END.
...WILL YOU NOW SPARE MY FATHER AS YOU PROMISED?
HM...
YOUR FATHER IS ALREADY DEAD.
BUT WOULDN'T YOU KNOW?
HIS SENTENCE WAS CARRIED OUT THIS VERY MORNING.

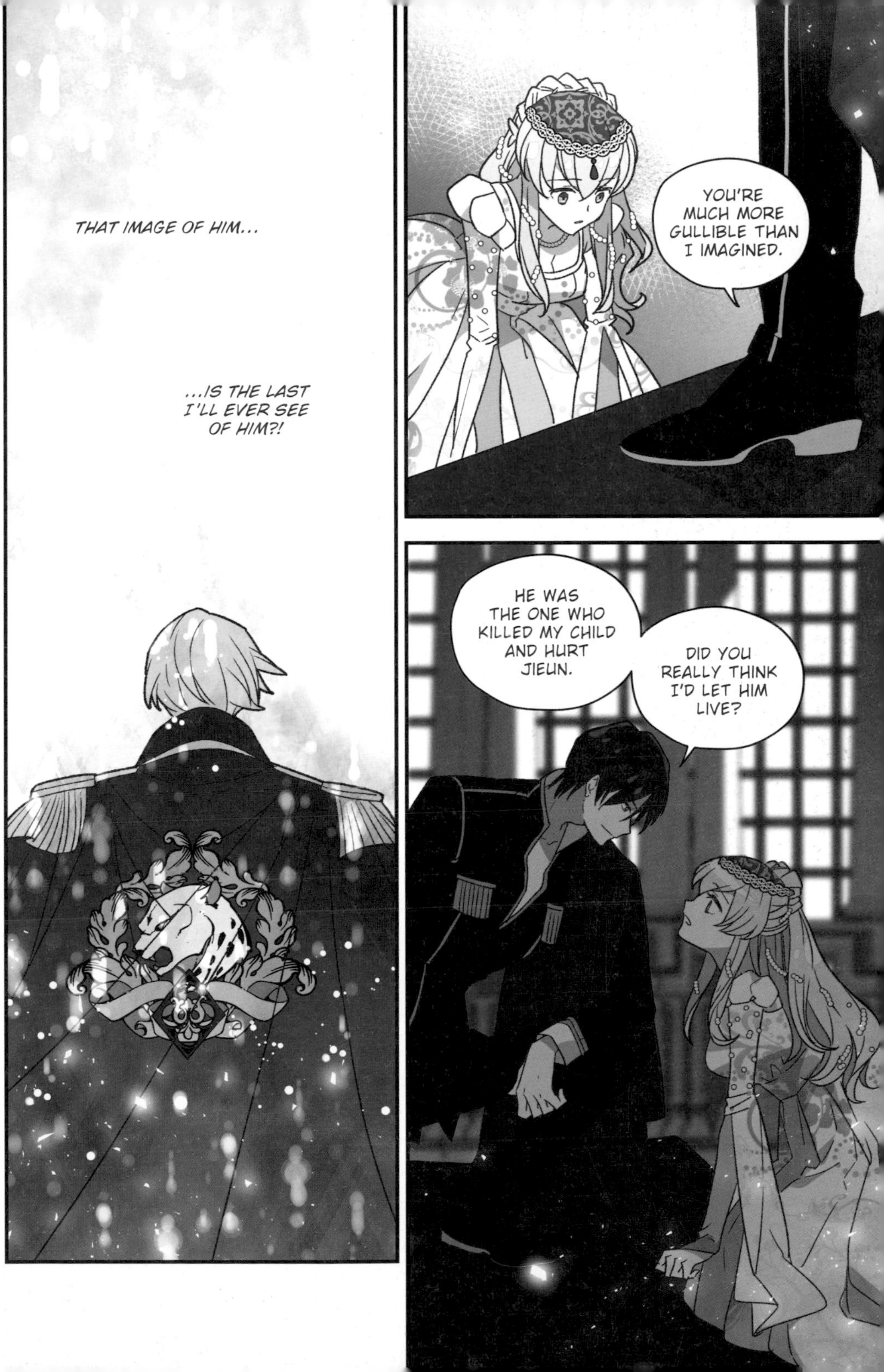
THAT IMAGE OF HIM...
...IS THE LAST I'LL EVER SEE OF HIM?!
YOU'RE MUCH MORE GULLIBLE THAN I IMAGINED.
HE WAS THE ONE WHO KILLED MY CHILD AND HURT JIEUN.
DID YOU REALLY THINK I'D LET HIM LIVE?

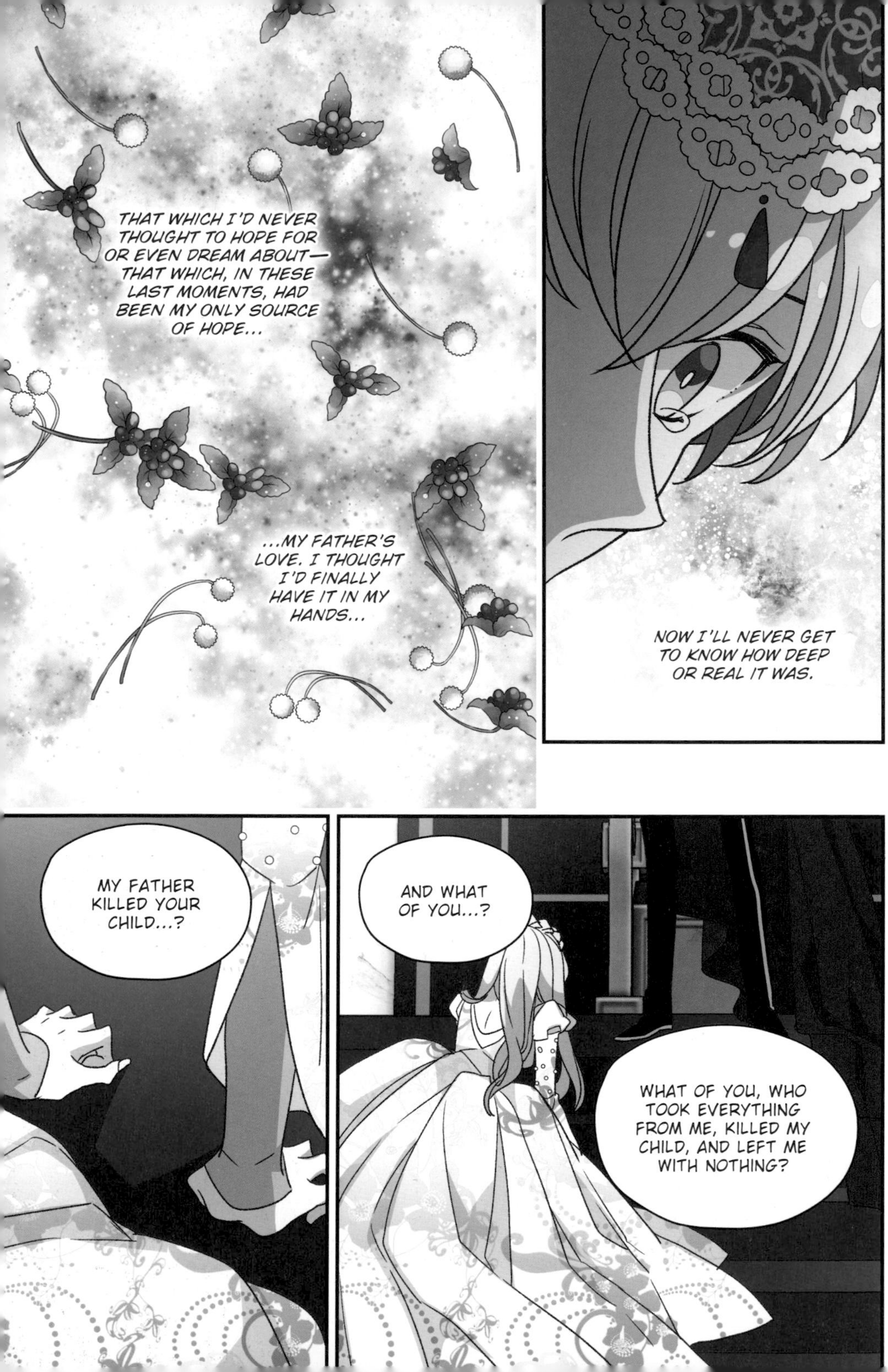

THAT WHICH I'D NEVER THOUGHT TO HOPE FOR OR EVEN DREAM ABOUT—THAT WHICH, IN THESE LAST MOMENTS, HAD BEEN MY ONLY SOURCE OF HOPE...
...MY FATHER'S LOVE. I THOUGHT I'D FINALLY HAVE IT IN MY HANDS...
NOW I'LL NEVER GET TO KNOW HOW DEEP OR REAL IT WAS.
MY FATHER KILLED YOUR CHILD...?
AND WHAT OF YOU...?
WHAT OF YOU, WHO TOOK EVERYTHING FROM ME, KILLED MY CHILD, AND LEFT ME WITH NOTHING?

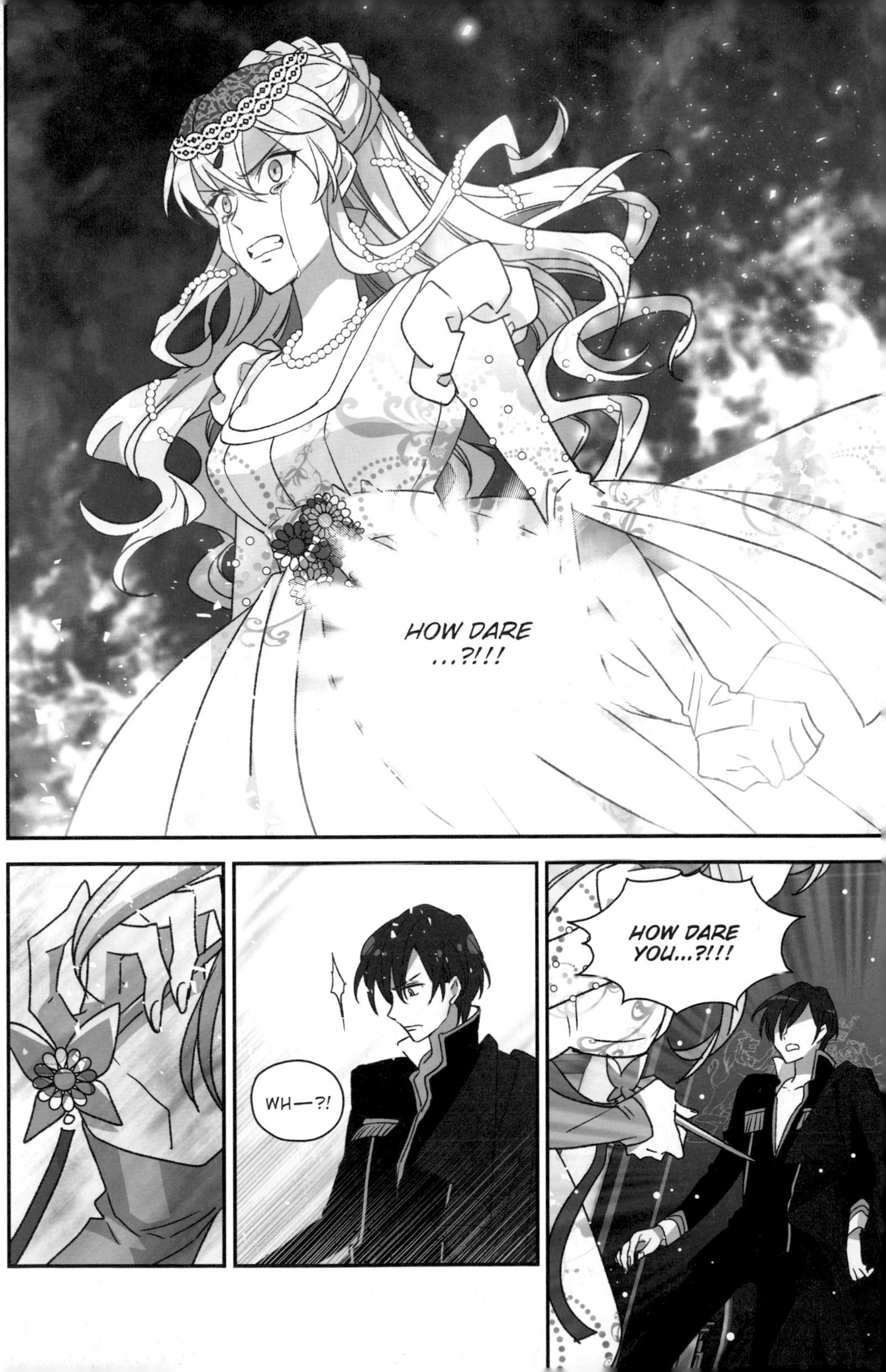
HOW DARE
...?!!!
WH—?!
HOW DARE
YOU...?!!!

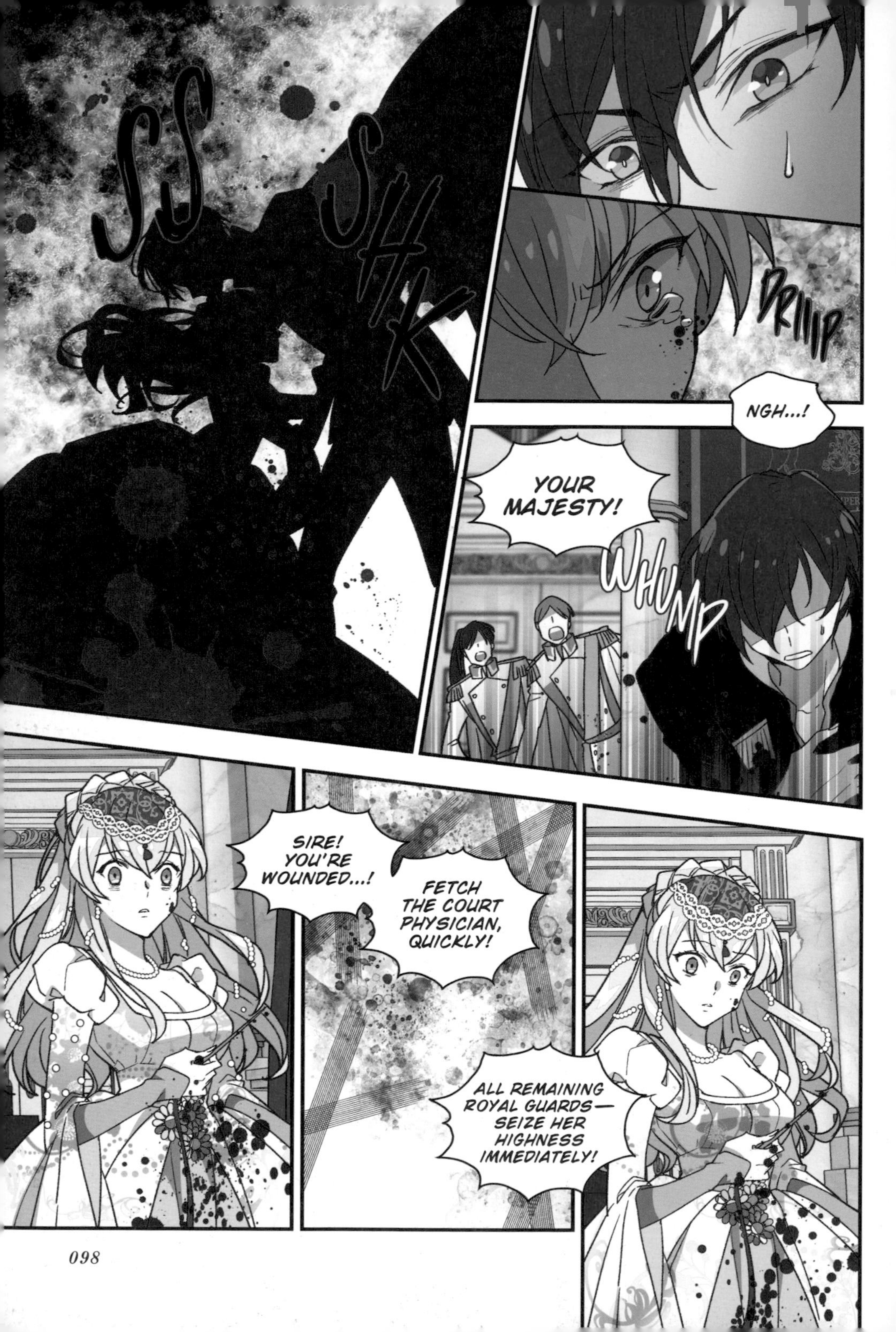
SS
SHK
DRIIIP
NGH...!
YOUR MAJESTY!
WHUMP
SIRE! YOU'RE WOUNDED...!
FETCH THE COURT PHYSICIAN, QUICKLY!
ALL REMAINING ROYAL GUARDS— SEIZE HER HIGHNESS IMMEDIATELY!

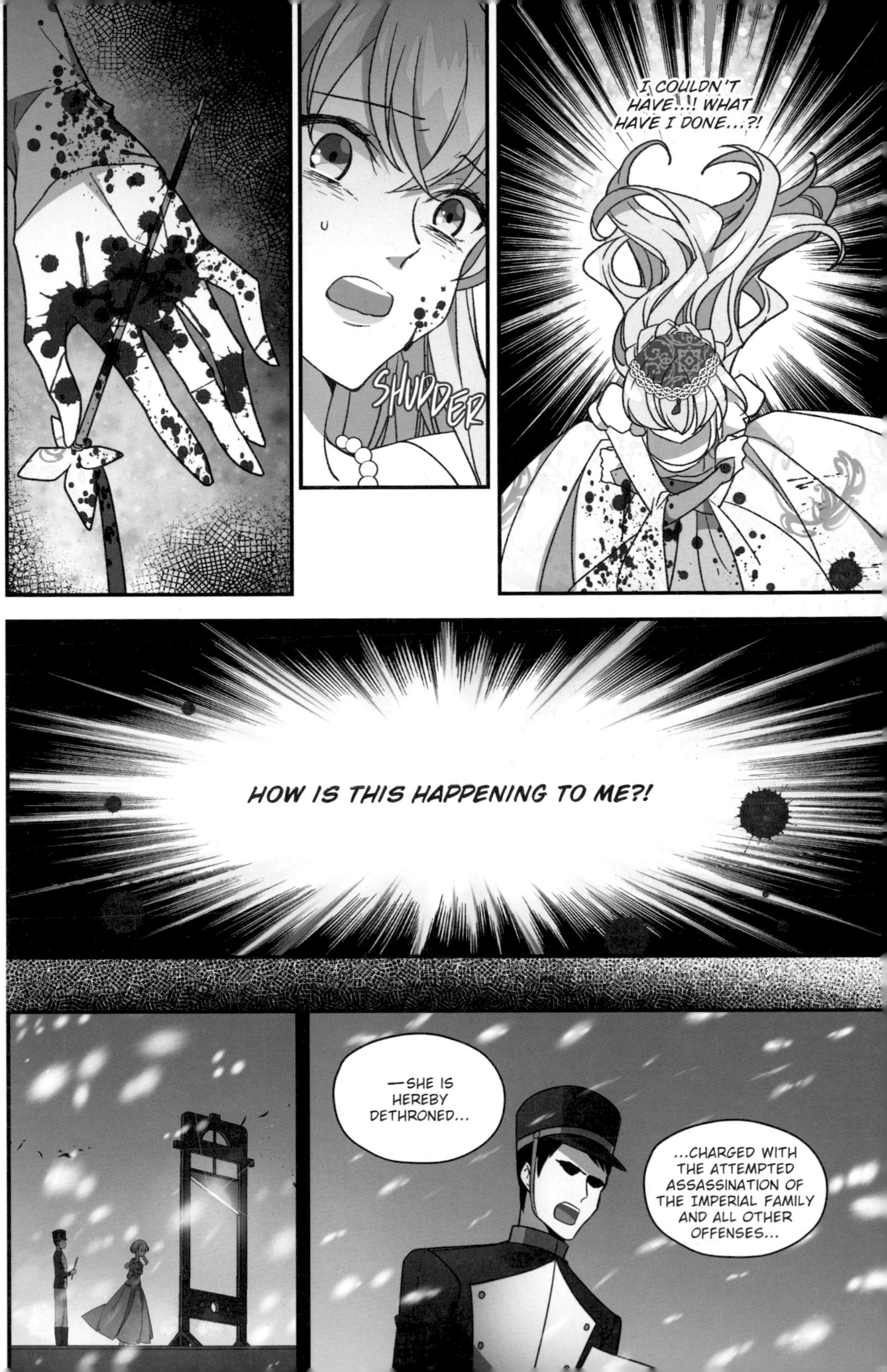
I COULDN'T HAVE...!! WHAT HAVE I DONE...?!
SHUDDER
HOW IS THIS HAPPENING TO ME?!
—SHE IS HEREBY DETHRONED...
...CHARGED WITH THE ATTEMPTED ASSASSINATION OF THE IMPERIAL FAMILY AND ALL OTHER OFFENSES...

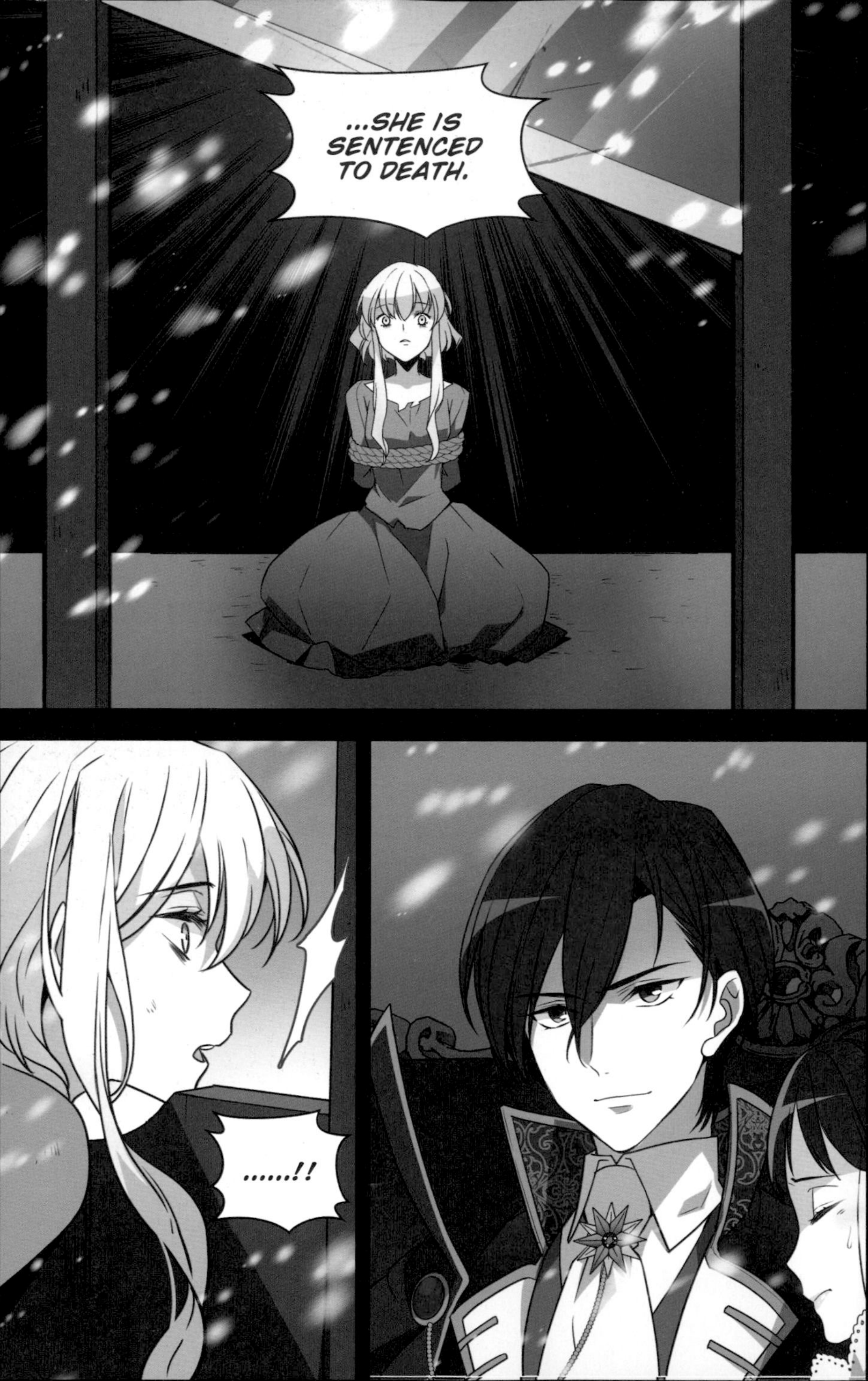
...SHE IS SENTENCED TO DEATH.
......!!

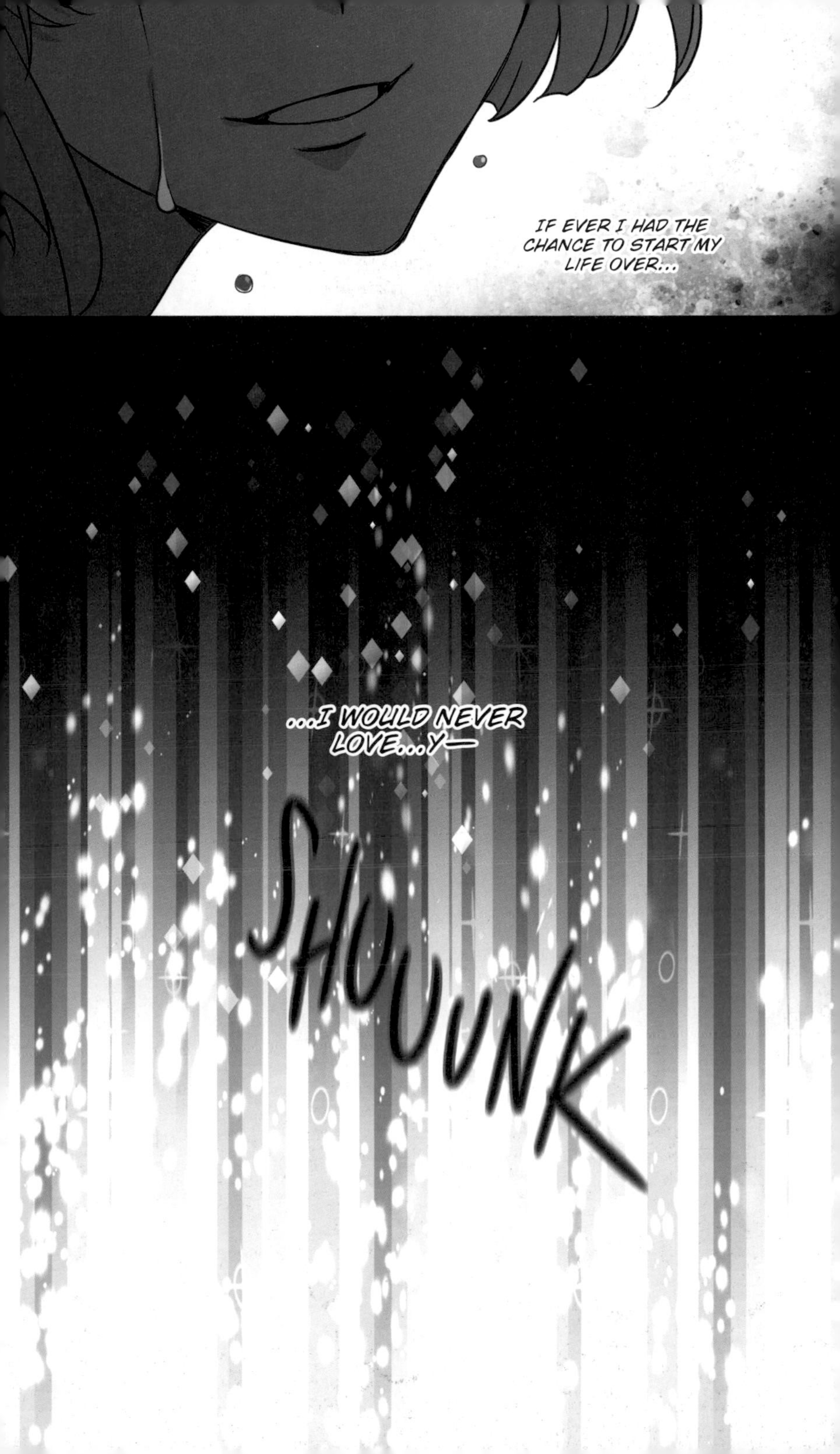
IF EVER I HAD THE CHANCE TO START MY LIFE OVER...
...I WOULD NEVER LOVE...Y—
SHOUUNK

# The Abandoned Empress

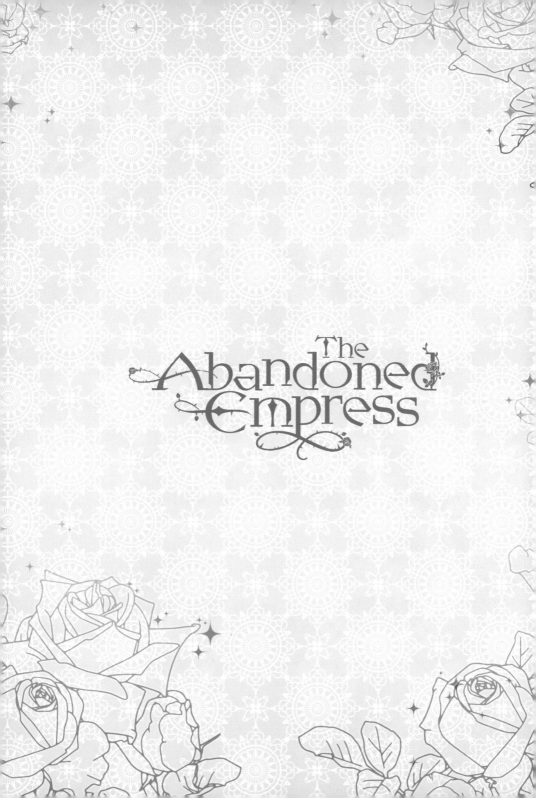

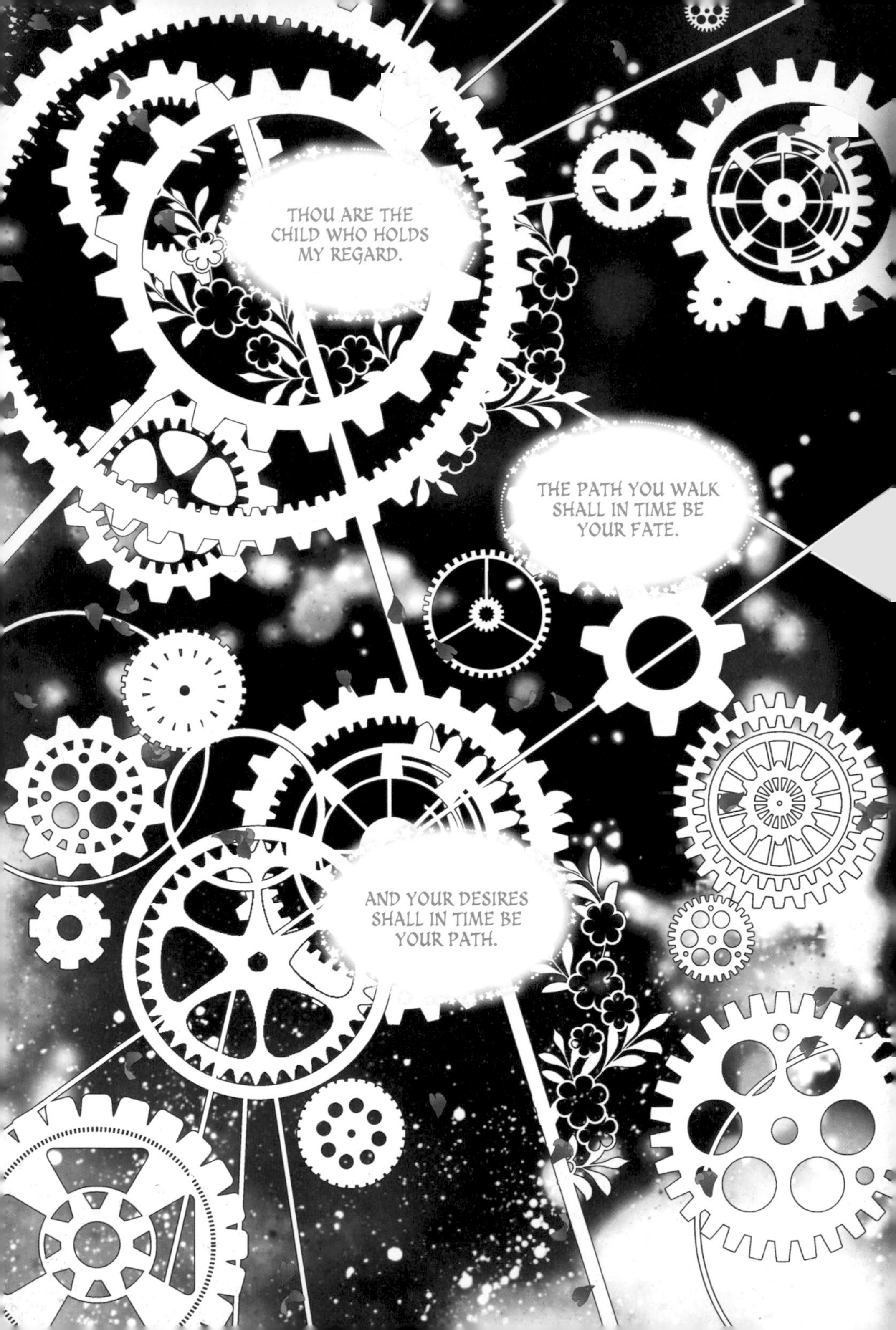
THOU ARE THE CHILD WHO HOLDS MY REGARD.
THE PATH YOU WALK SHALL IN TIME BE YOUR FATE.
AND YOUR DESIRES SHALL IN TIME BE YOUR PATH.

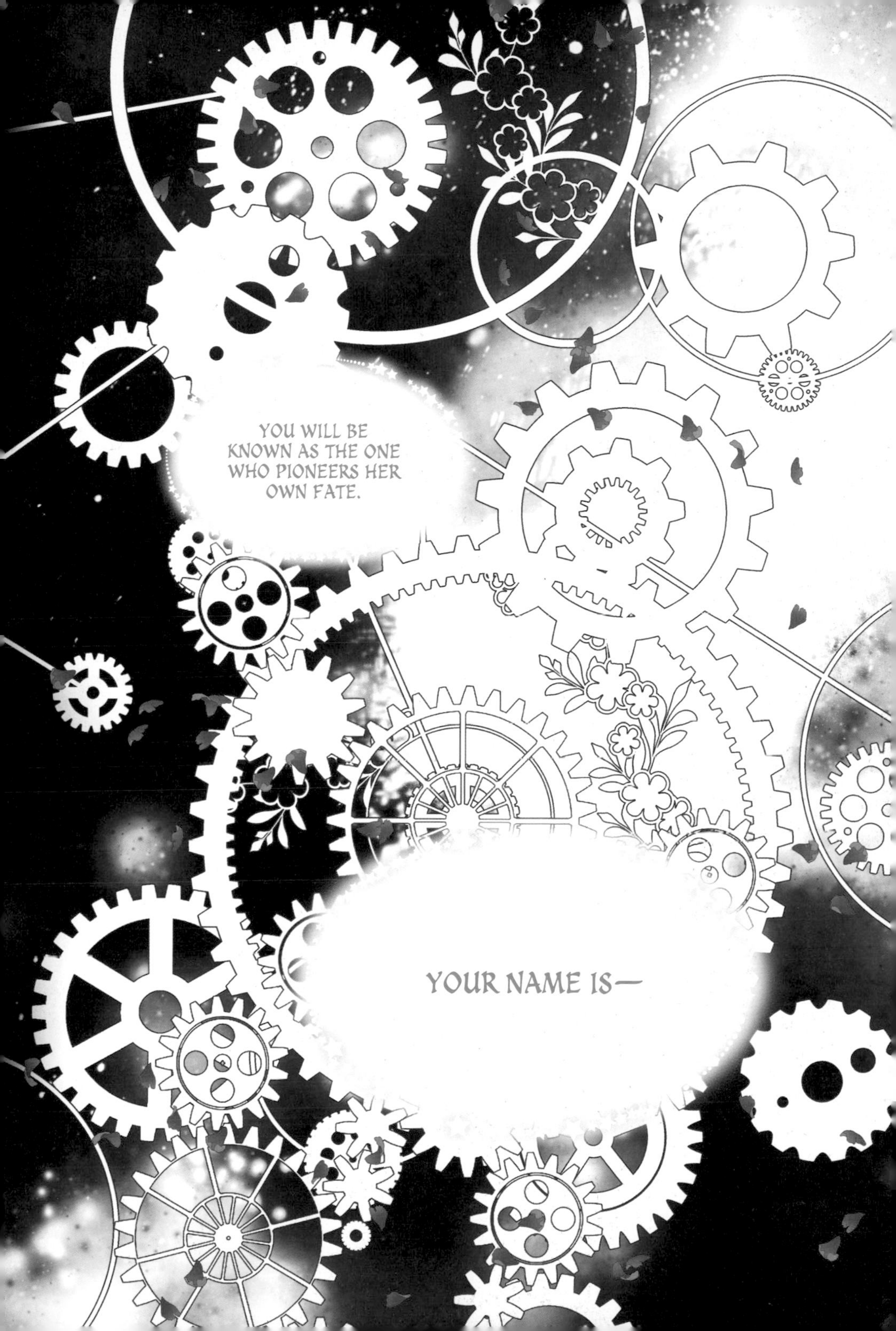
YOU WILL BE KNOWN AS THE ONE WHO PIONEERS HER OWN FATE.
YOUR NAME IS—

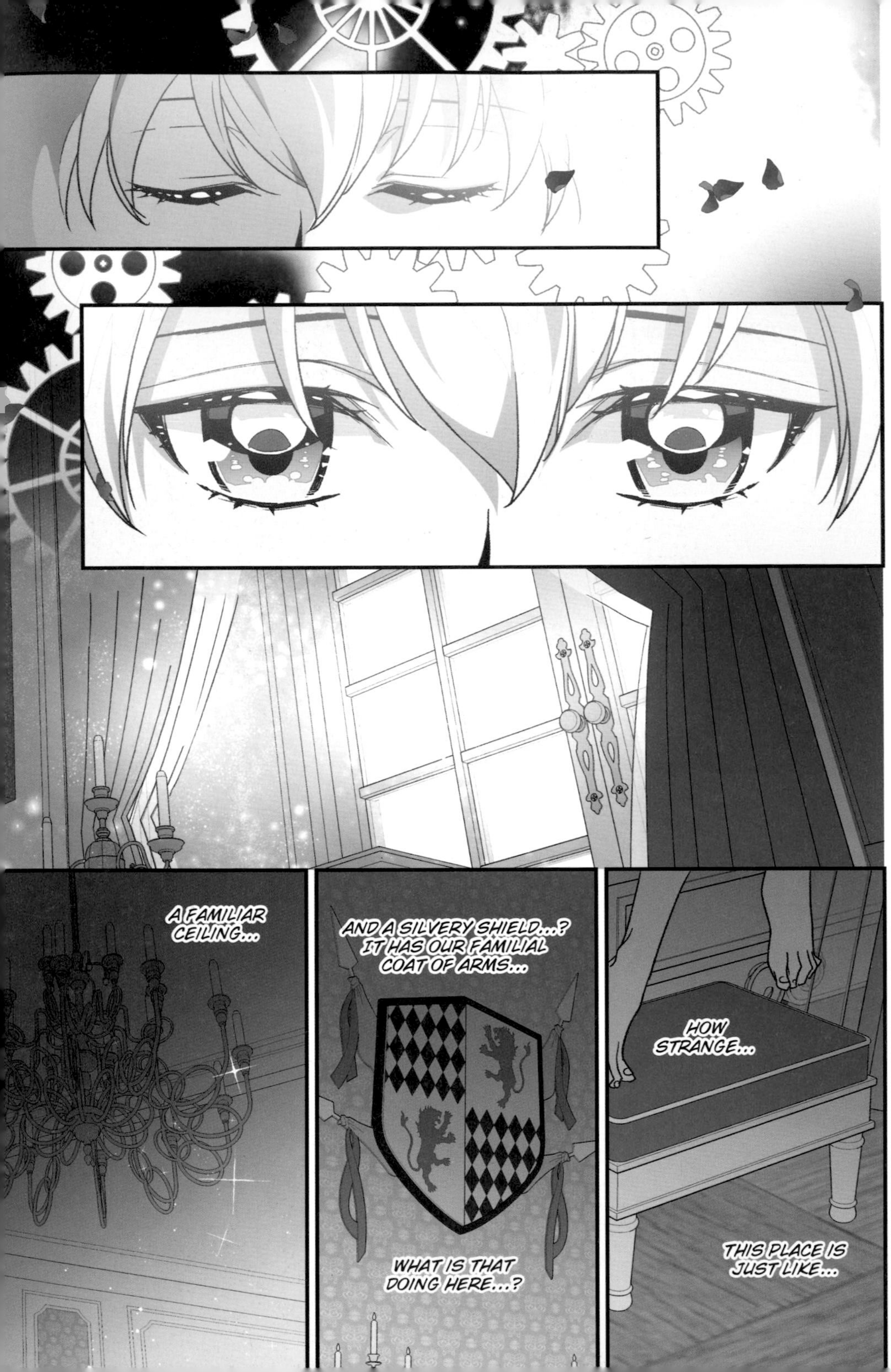
HOW STRANGE...
THIS PLACE IS JUST LIKE...
AND A SILVERY SHIELD...? IT HAS OUR FAMILIAL COAT OF ARMS...
WHAT IS THAT DOING HERE...?
A FAMILIAR CEILING...

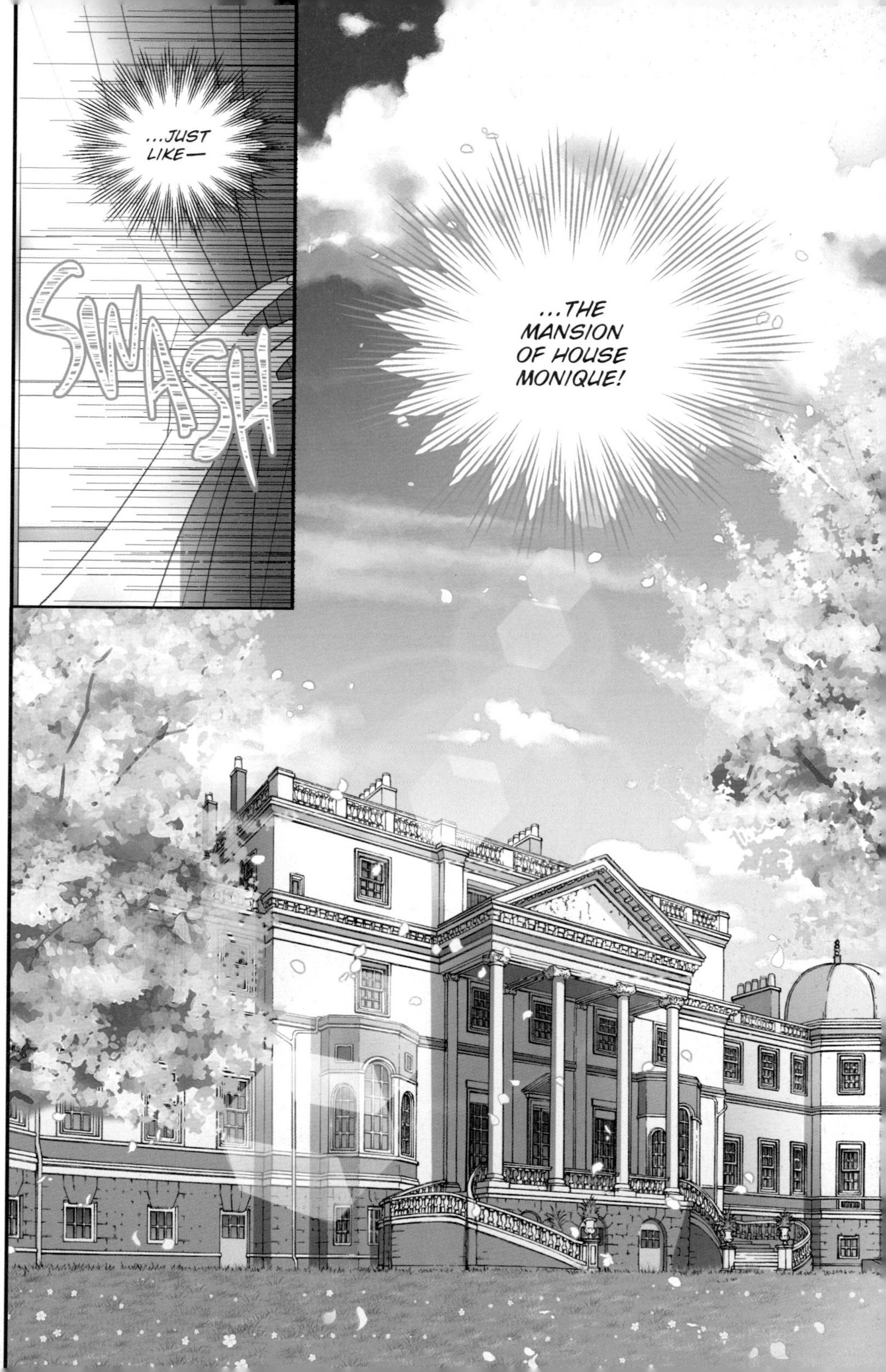
...JUST LIKE—
SWASH
...THE MANSION OF HOUSE MONIQUE!

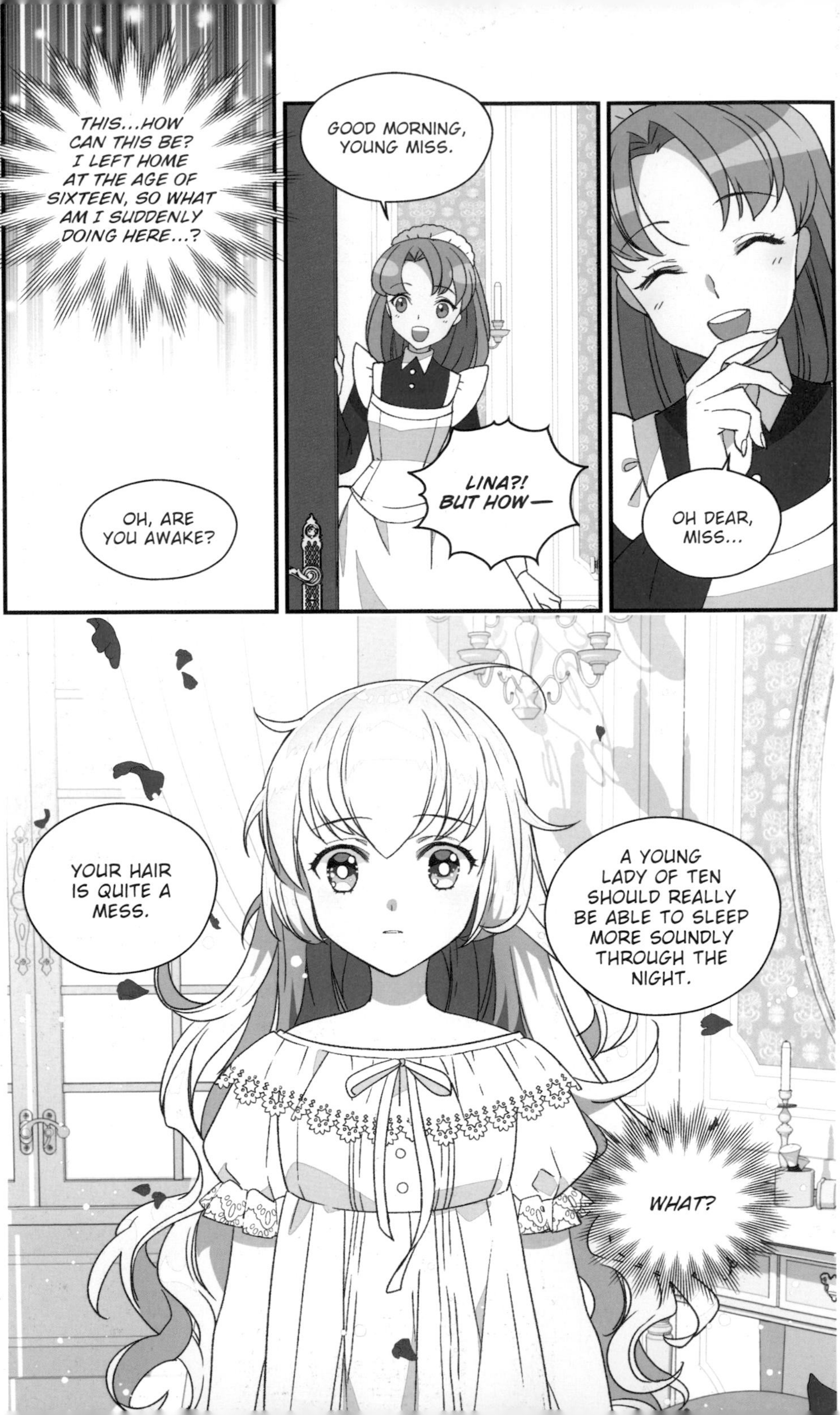
THIS...HOW CAN THIS BE? I LEFT HOME AT THE AGE OF SIXTEEN, SO WHAT AM I SUDDENLY DOING HERE...?
OH, ARE YOU AWAKE?
GOOD MORNING, YOUNG MISS.
LINA?! BUT HOW—
OH DEAR, MISS...
YOUR HAIR IS QUITE A MESS.
A YOUNG LADY OF TEN SHOULD REALLY BE ABLE TO SLEEP MORE SOUNDLY THROUGH THE NIGHT.
WHAT?

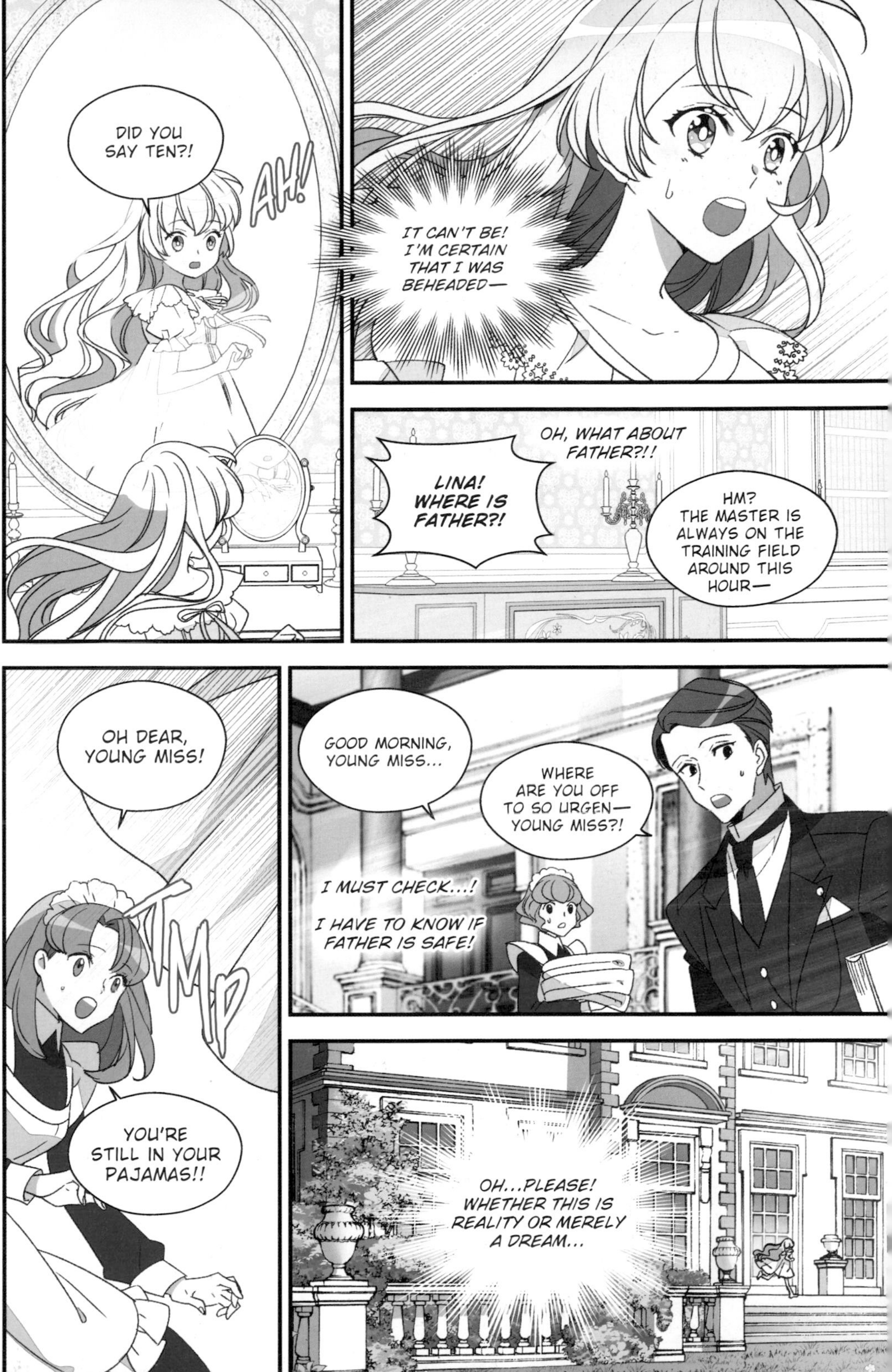
DID YOU SAY TEN?!
AH!
IT CAN'T BE! I'M CERTAIN THAT I WAS BEHEADED—
OH, WHAT ABOUT FATHER?!!
LINA! WHERE IS FATHER?!
HM? THE MASTER IS ALWAYS ON THE TRAINING FIELD AROUND THIS HOUR—
OH DEAR, YOUNG MISS!
TMP
YOU'RE STILL IN YOUR PAJAMAS!!
GOOD MORNING, YOUNG MISS...
WHERE ARE YOU OFF TO SO URGEN— YOUNG MISS?!
I MUST CHECK...!
I HAVE TO KNOW IF FATHER IS SAFE!
OH...PLEASE! WHETHER THIS IS REALITY OR MERELY A DREAM...

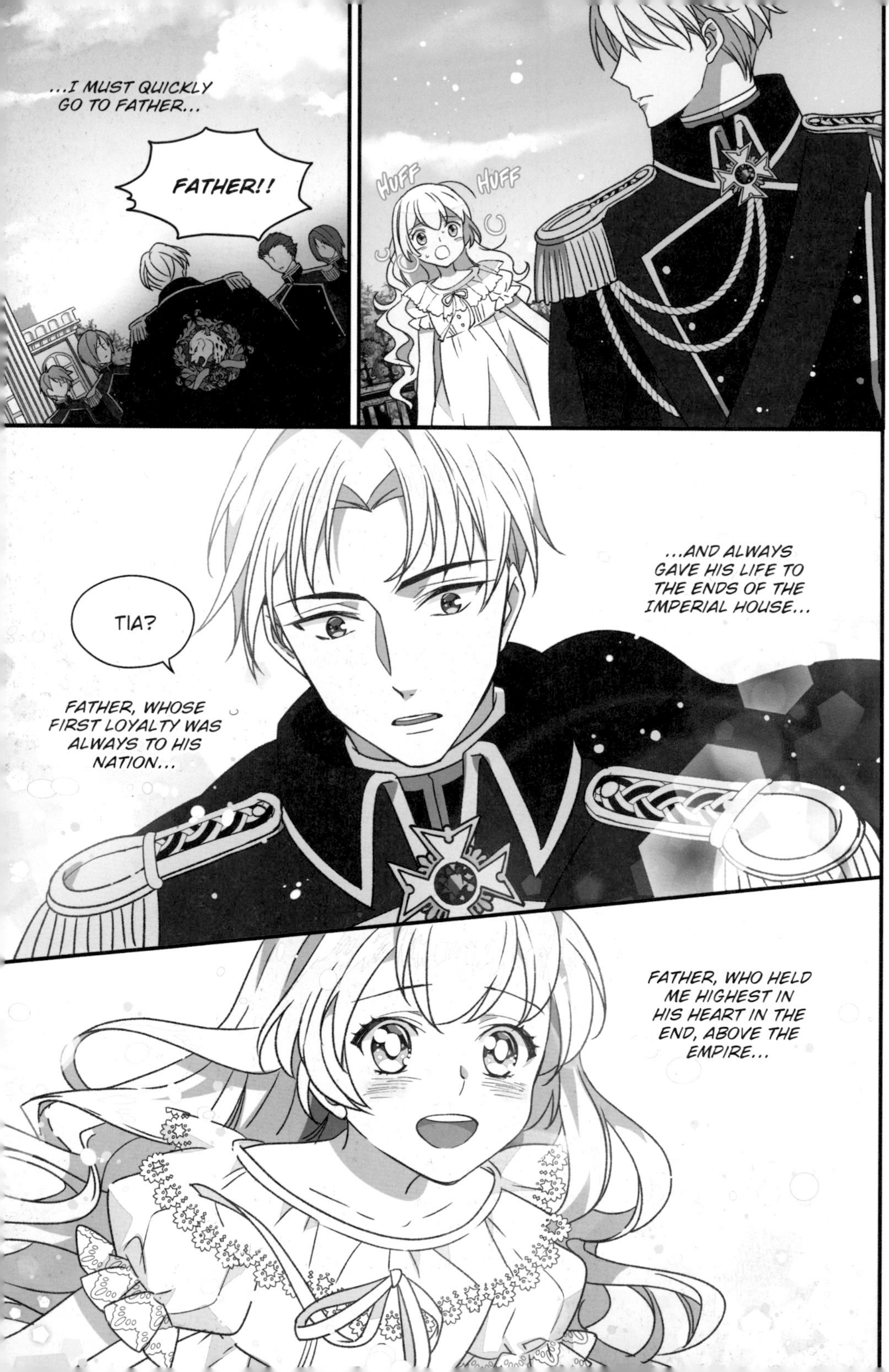
...I MUST QUICKLY GO TO FATHER...
FATHER!!
HUFF HUFF
TIA?
FATHER, WHOSE FIRST LOYALTY WAS ALWAYS TO HIS NATION...
...AND ALWAYS GAVE HIS LIFE TO THE ENDS OF THE IMPERIAL HOUSE...
FATHER, WHO HELD ME HIGHEST IN HIS HEART IN THE END, ABOVE THE EMPIRE...

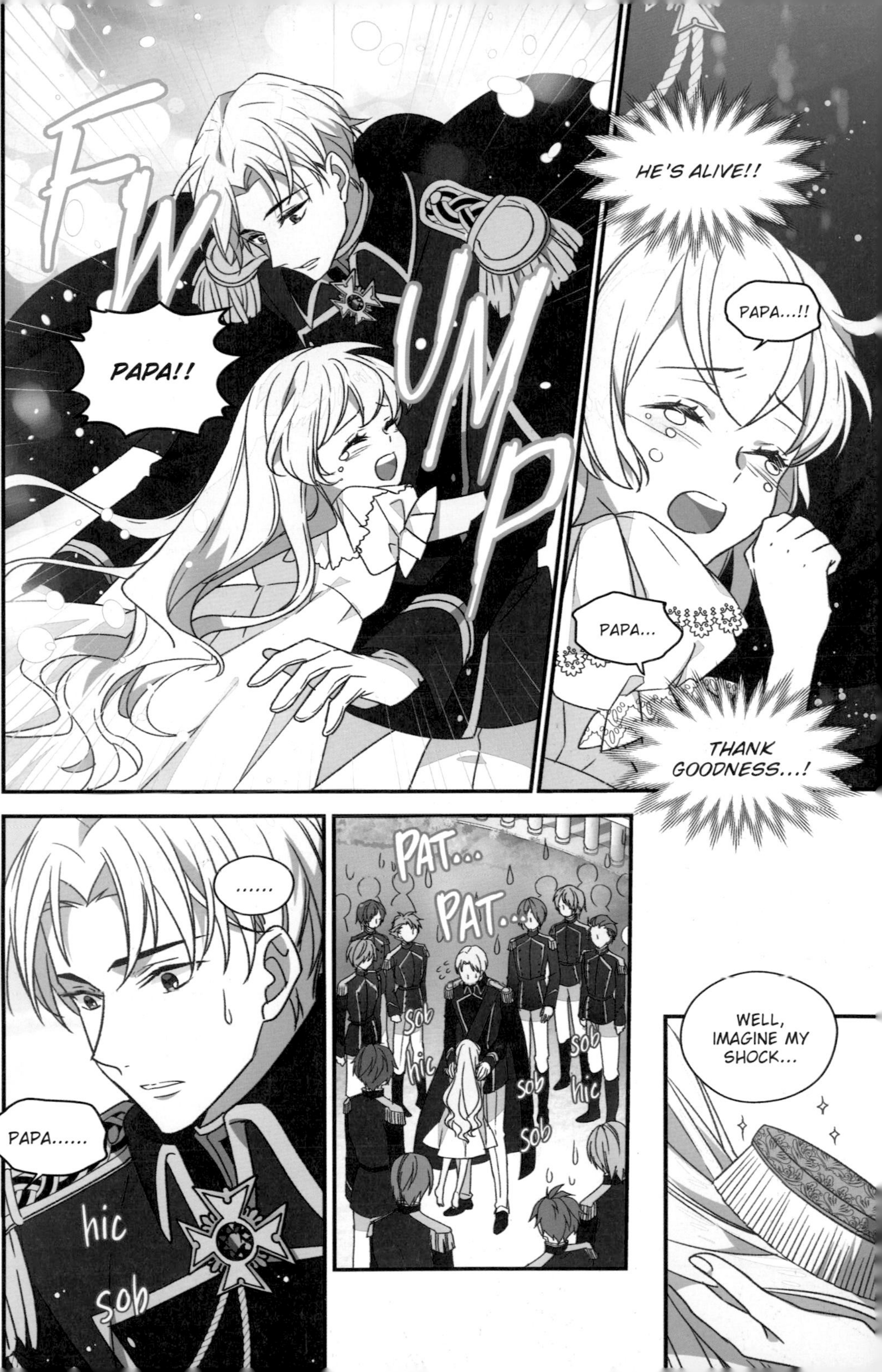
FWUMP
PAPA!!
HE'S ALIVE!!
PAPA...!!
PAPA...
THANK GOODNESS...!
......
PAPA......
hic
sob
PAT... PAT...
sob
hic
sob
hic
sob
sob
WELL, IMAGINE MY SHOCK...

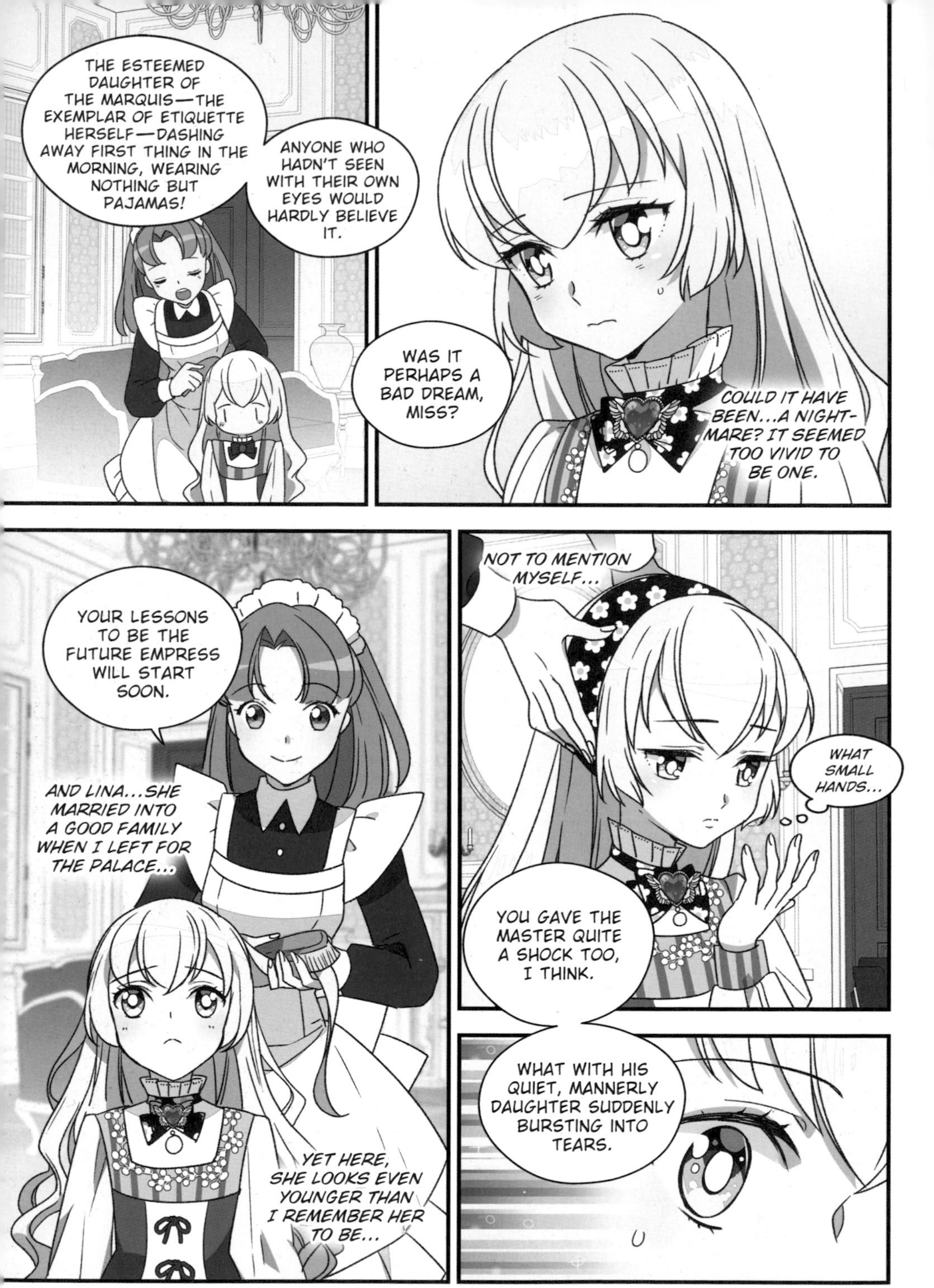
THE ESTEEMED DAUGHTER OF THE MARQUIS—THE EXEMPLAR OF ETIQUETTE HERSELF—DASHING AWAY FIRST THING IN THE MORNING, WEARING NOTHING BUT PAJAMAS!
ANYONE WHO HADN'T SEEN WITH THEIR OWN EYES WOULD HARDLY BELIEVE IT.
WAS IT PERHAPS A BAD DREAM, MISS?
COULD IT HAVE BEEN...A NIGHT-MARE? IT SEEMED TOO VIVID TO BE ONE.
YOUR LESSONS TO BE THE FUTURE EMPRESS WILL START SOON.
AND LINA...SHE MARRIED INTO A GOOD FAMILY WHEN I LEFT FOR THE PALACE...
YET HERE, SHE LOOKS EVEN YOUNGER THAN I REMEMBER HER TO BE...
NOT TO MENTION MYSELF...
WHAT SMALL HANDS...
YOU GAVE THE MASTER QUITE A SHOCK TOO, I THINK.
WHAT WITH HIS QUIET, MANNERLY DAUGHTER SUDDENLY BURSTING INTO TEARS.

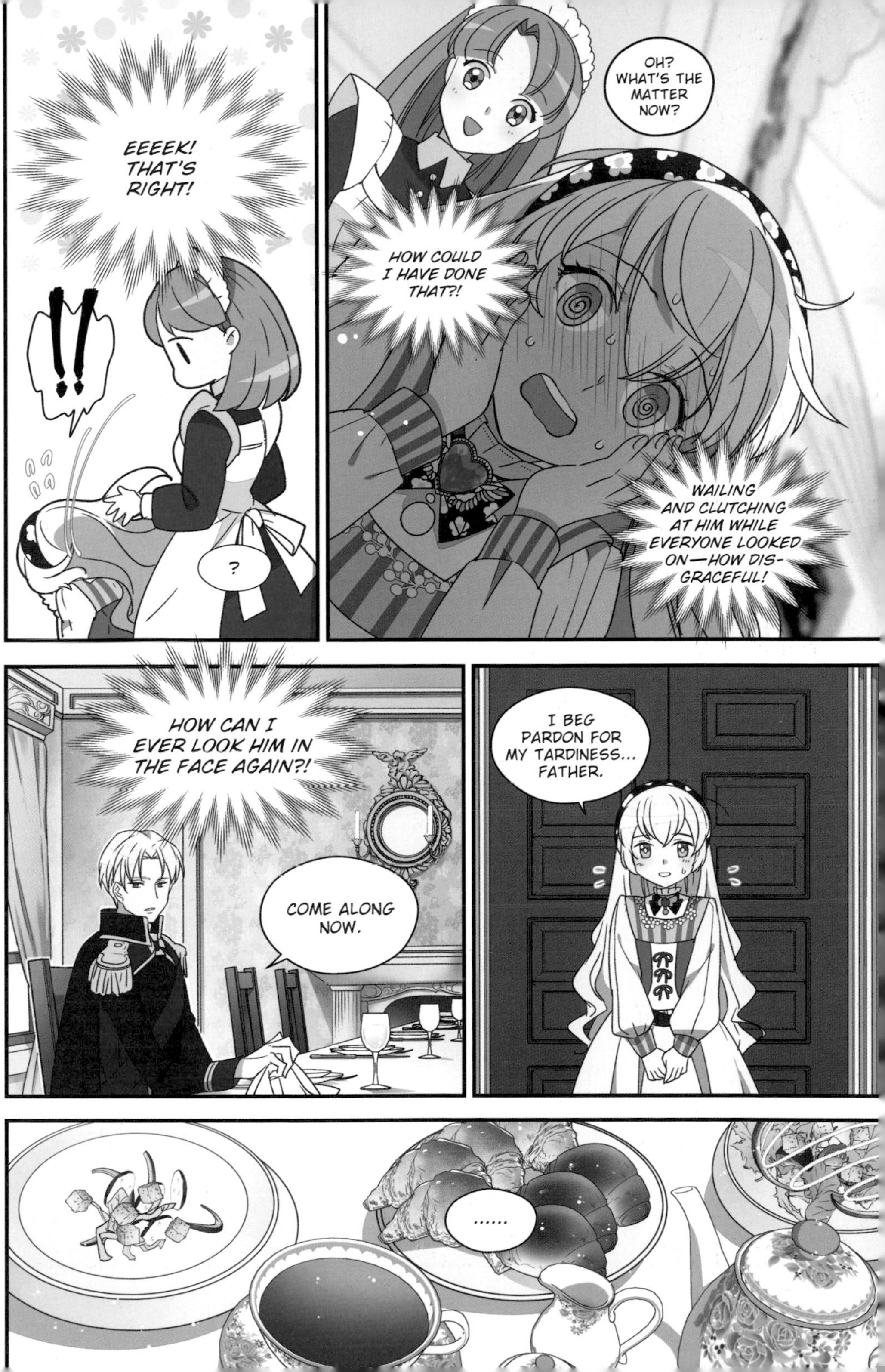
EEEEK! THAT'S RIGHT!
!!
?
OH? WHAT'S THE MATTER NOW?
HOW COULD I HAVE DONE THAT?!
WAILING AND CLUTCHING AT HIM WHILE EVERYONE LOOKED ON—HOW DIS-GRACEFUL!
HOW CAN I EVER LOOK HIM IN THE FACE AGAIN?!
COME ALONG NOW.
I BEG PARDON FOR MY TARDINESS... FATHER.
......

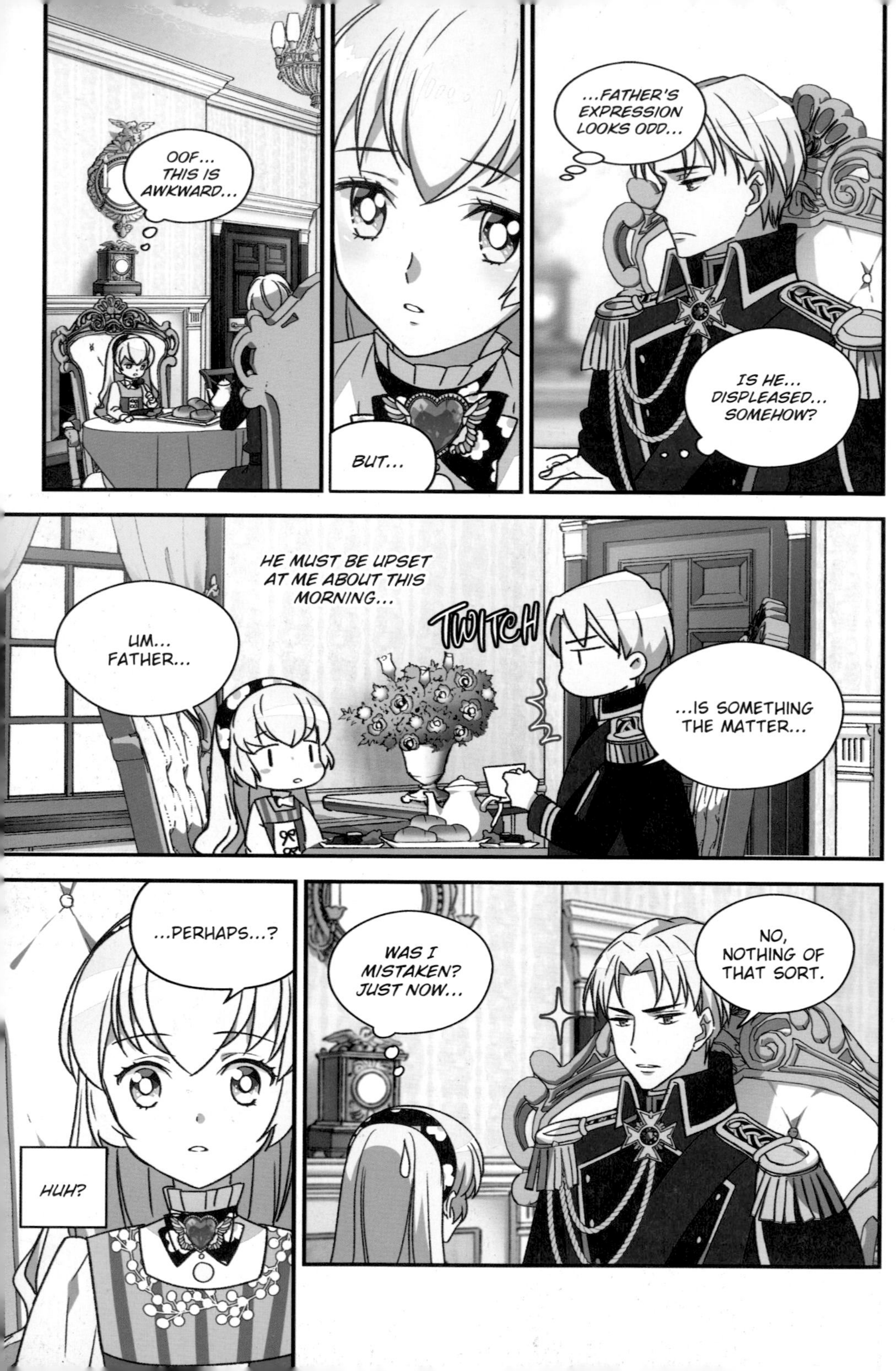
OOF... THIS IS AWKWARD...
BUT...
...FATHER'S EXPRESSION LOOKS ODD...
IS HE... DISPLEASED... SOMEHOW?
HE MUST BE UPSET AT ME ABOUT THIS MORNING...
UM... FATHER...
TWITCH
...IS SOMETHING THE MATTER...
...PERHAPS...?
HUH?
WAS I MISTAKEN? JUST NOW...
NO, NOTHING OF THAT SORT.

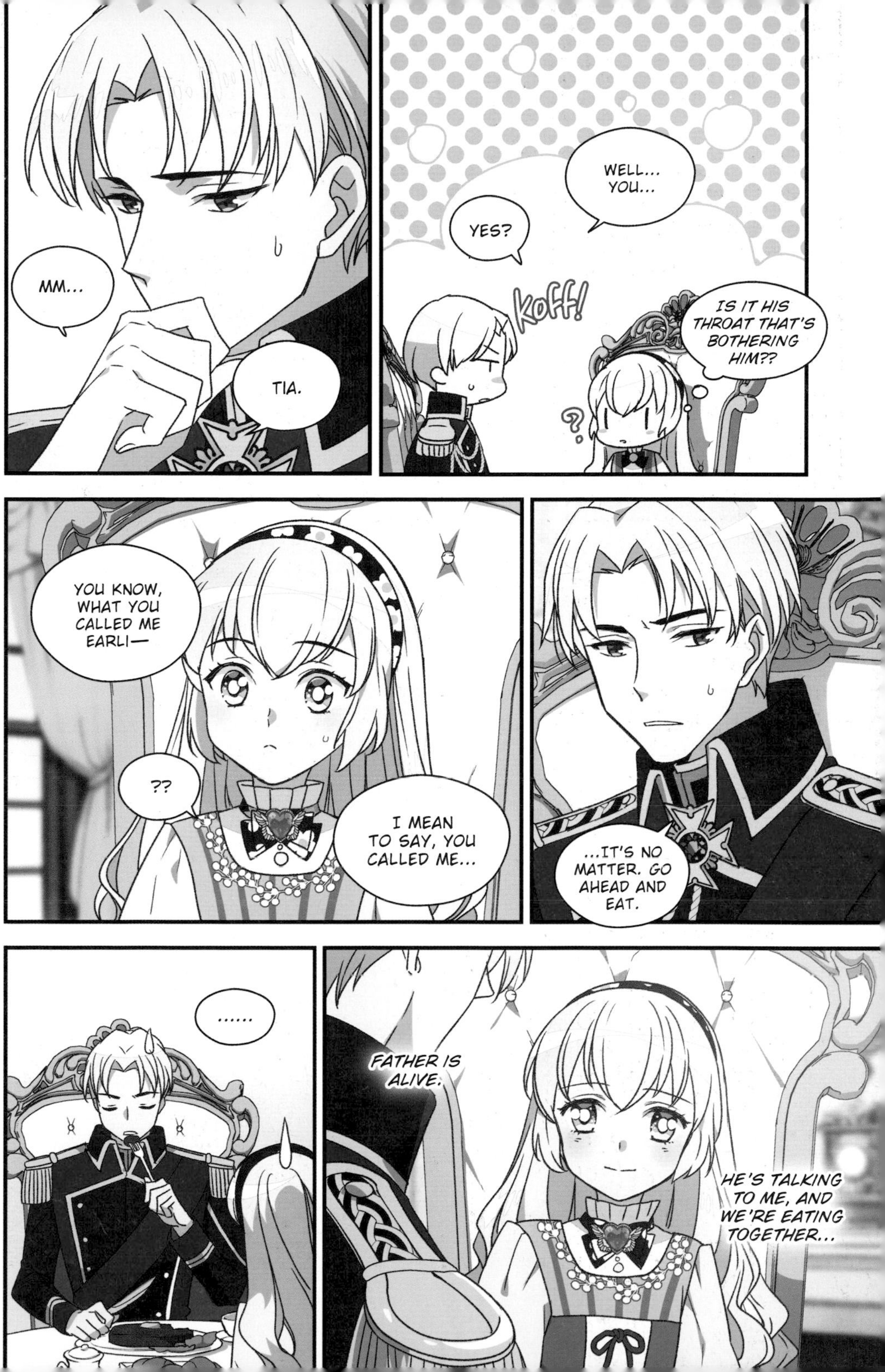
MM...
TIA.
YES?
WELL... YOU...
KOFF!
IS IT HIS THROAT THAT'S BOTHERING HIM??
?
YOU KNOW, WHAT YOU CALLED ME EARLI—
??
I MEAN TO SAY, YOU CALLED ME...
...IT'S NO MATTER. GO AHEAD AND EAT.
......
FATHER IS ALIVE.
HE'S TALKING TO ME, AND WE'RE EATING TOGETHER...

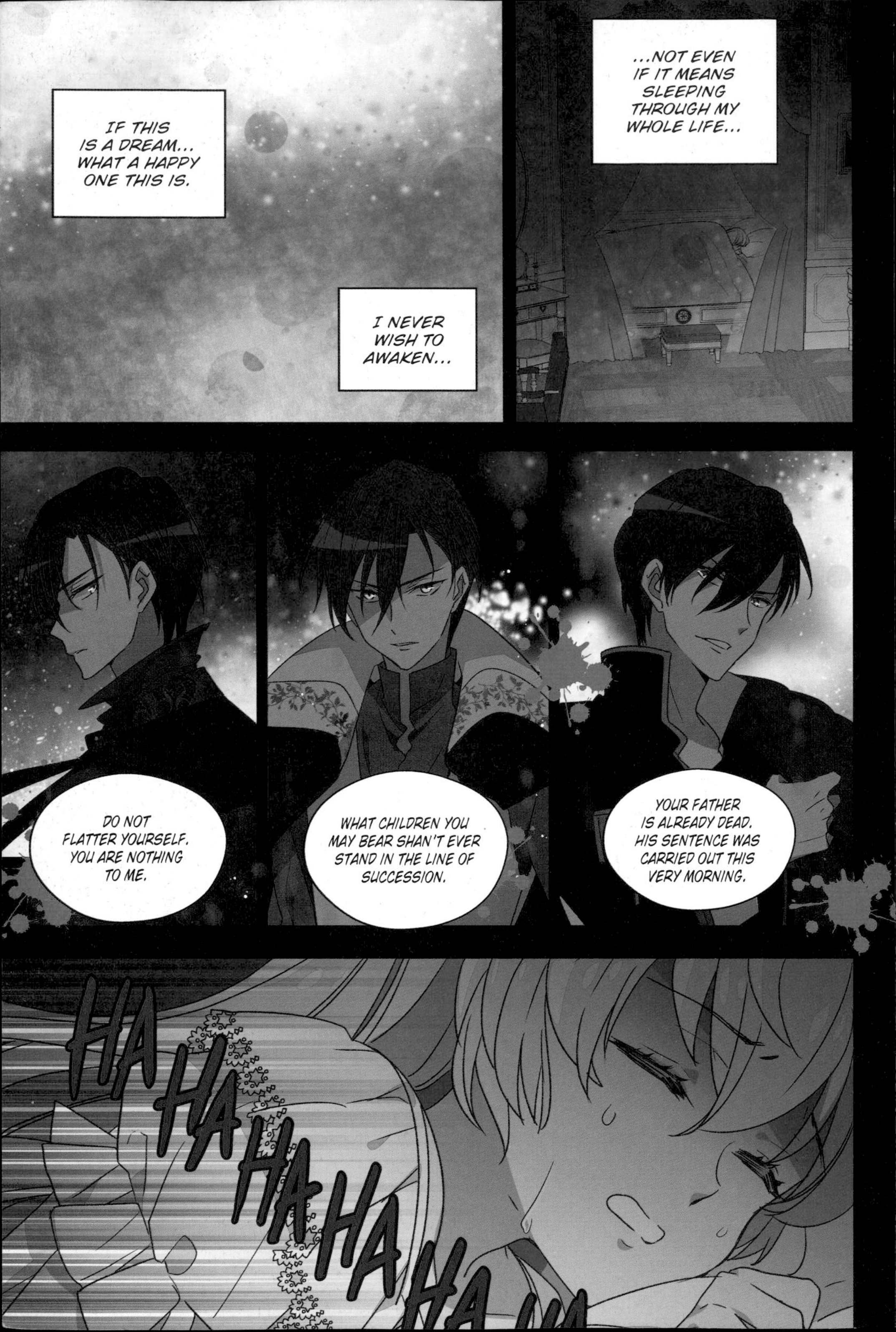
IF THIS IS A DREAM... WHAT A HAPPY ONE THIS IS.
I NEVER WISH TO AWAKEN...
...NOT EVEN IF IT MEANS SLEEPING THROUGH MY WHOLE LIFE...
DO NOT FLATTER YOURSELF. YOU ARE NOTHING TO ME.
WHAT CHILDREN YOU MAY BEAR SHAN'T EVER STAND IN THE LINE OF SUCCESSION.
YOUR FATHER IS ALREADY DEAD. HIS SENTENCE WAS CARRIED OUT THIS VERY MORNING.
HA HA HA HA HA HA HA HA

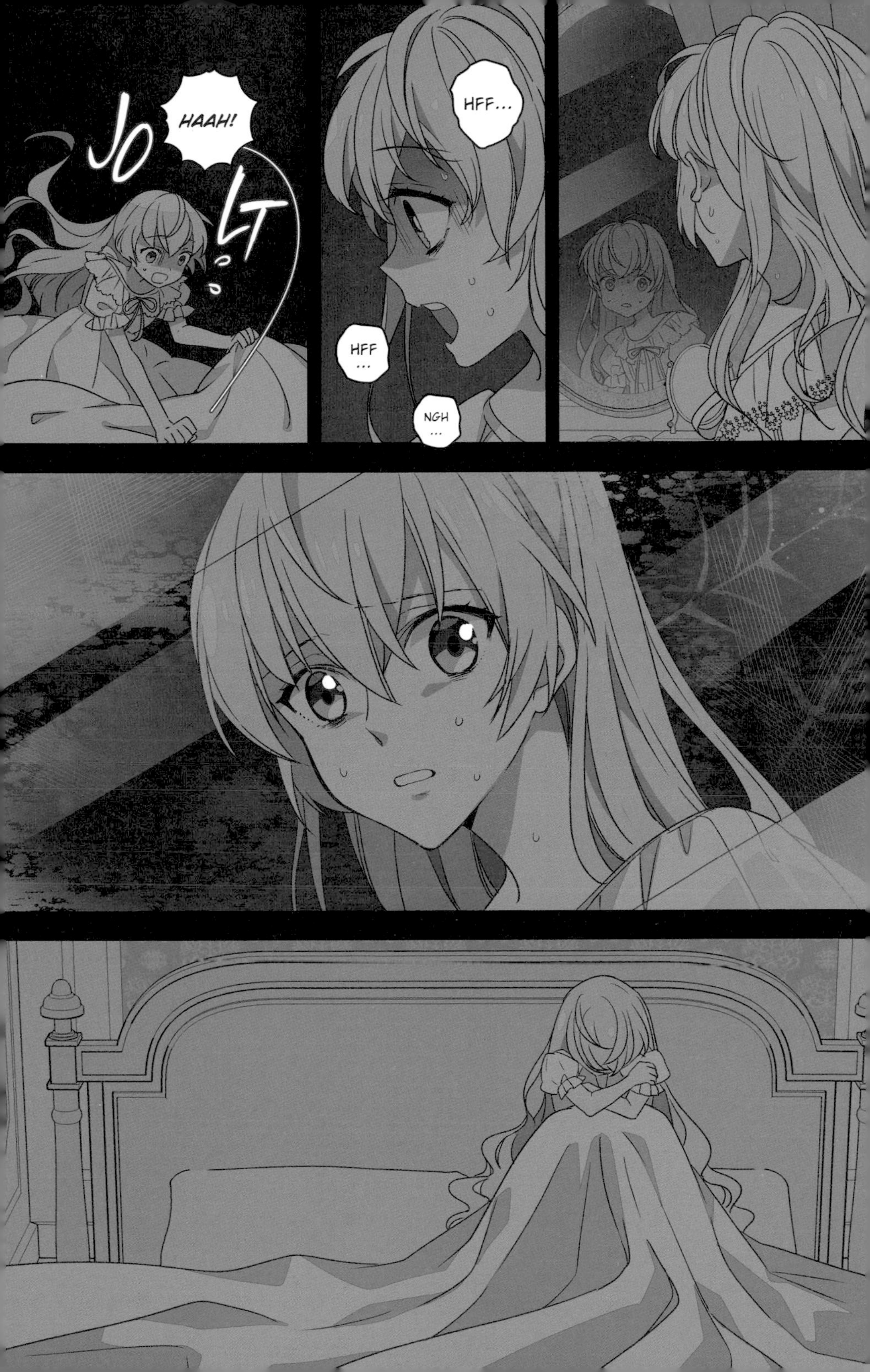
HAAH!
JOLT
HFF...
HFF...
NGH...

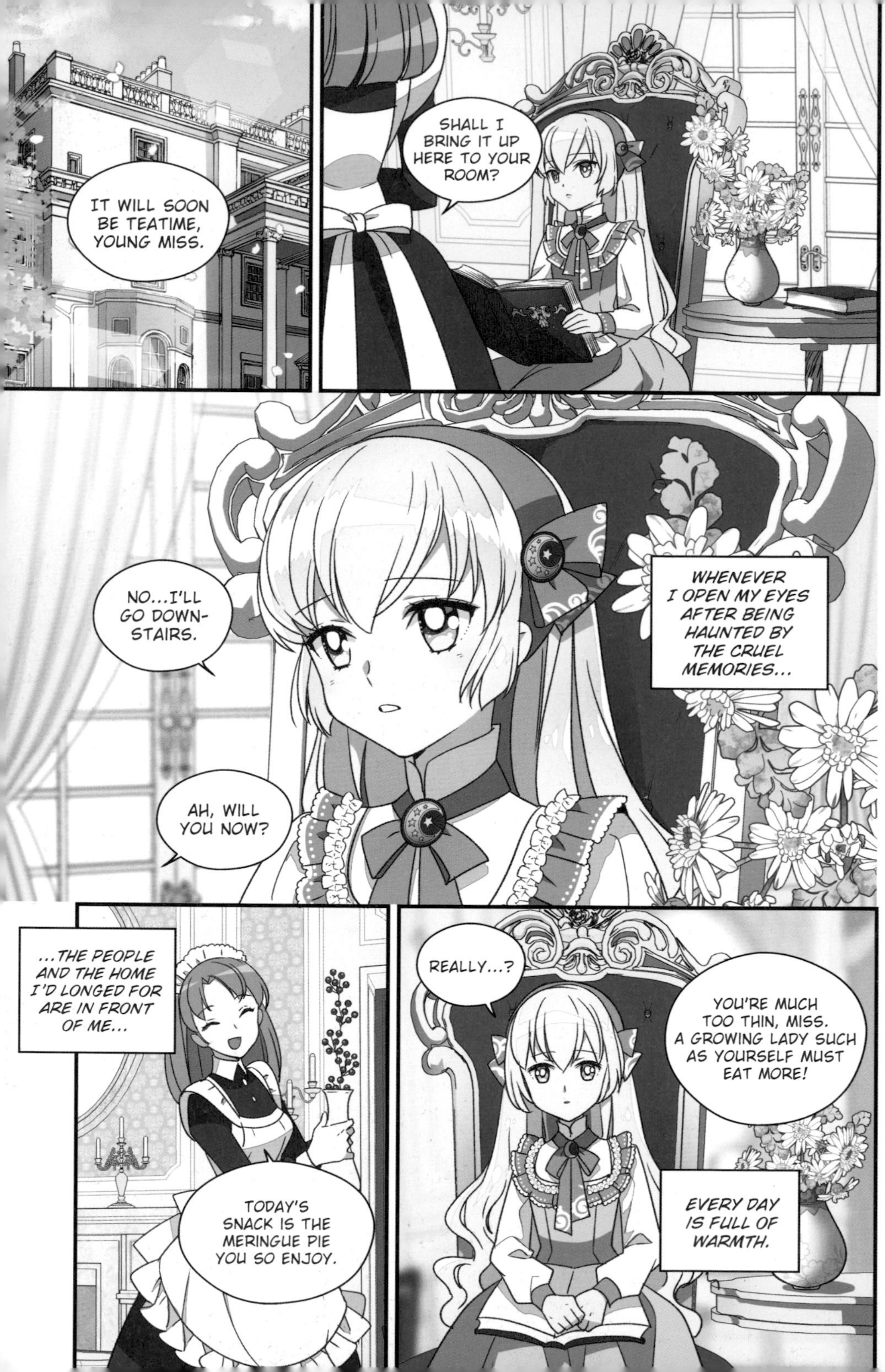
IT WILL SOON BE TEATIME, YOUNG MISS.
SHALL I BRING IT UP HERE TO YOUR ROOM?
NO...I'LL GO DOWN-STAIRS.
WHENEVER I OPEN MY EYES AFTER BEING HAUNTED BY THE CRUEL MEMORIES...
AH, WILL YOU NOW?
...THE PEOPLE AND THE HOME I'D LONGED FOR ARE IN FRONT OF ME...
TODAY'S SNACK IS THE MERINGUE PIE YOU SO ENJOY.
REALLY...?
YOU'RE MUCH TOO THIN, MISS. A GROWING LADY SUCH AS YOURSELF MUST EAT MORE!
EVERY DAY IS FULL OF WARMTH.

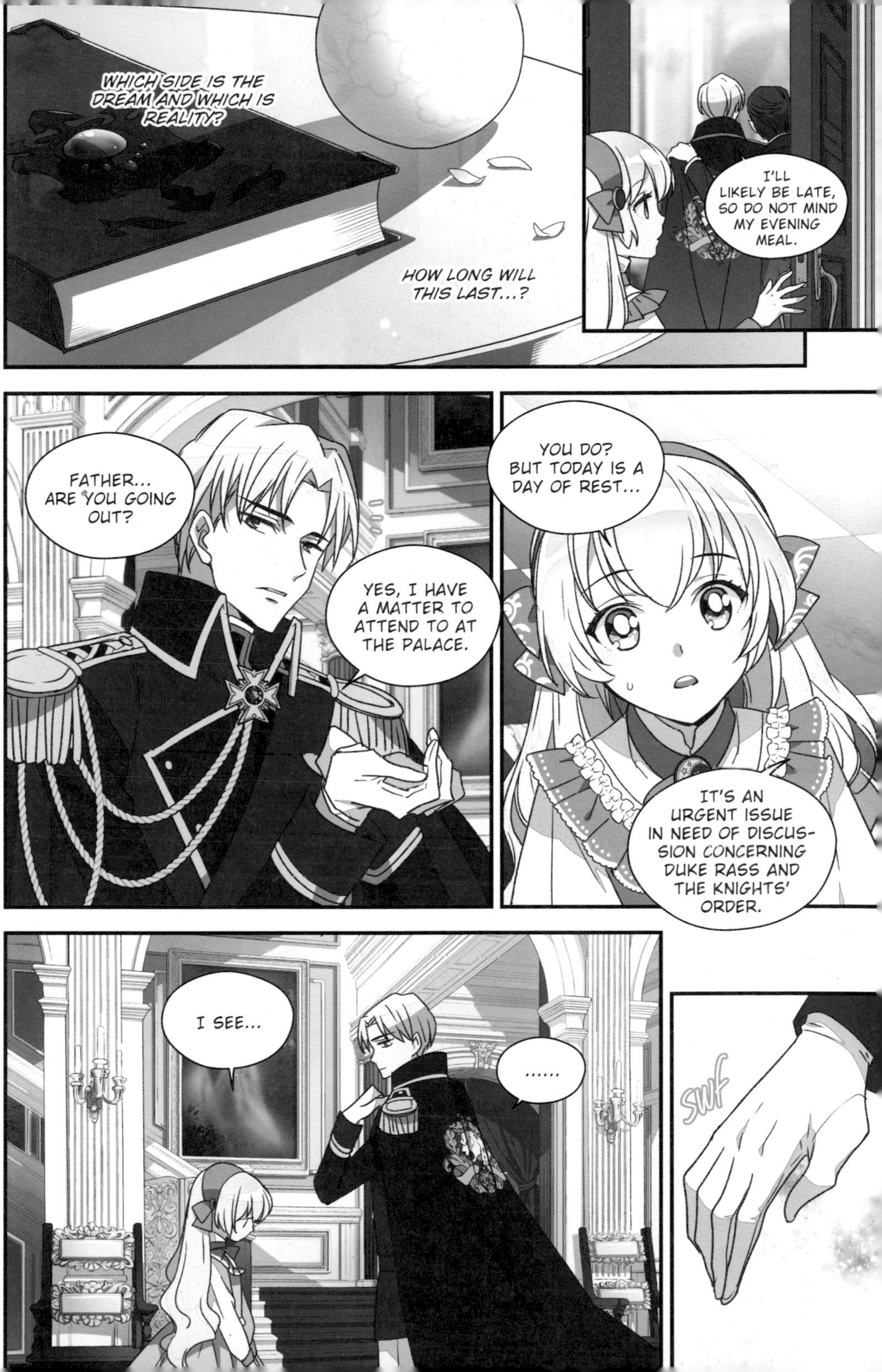
WHICH SIDE IS THE DREAM AND WHICH IS REALITY?
HOW LONG WILL THIS LAST...?
I'LL LIKELY BE LATE, SO DO NOT MIND MY EVENING MEAL.
FATHER... ARE YOU GOING OUT?
YES, I HAVE A MATTER TO ATTEND TO AT THE PALACE.
YOU DO? BUT TODAY IS A DAY OF REST...
IT'S AN URGENT ISSUE IN NEED OF DISCUS-SION CONCERNING DUKE RASS AND THE KNIGHTS' ORDER.
I SEE...
......
SWF

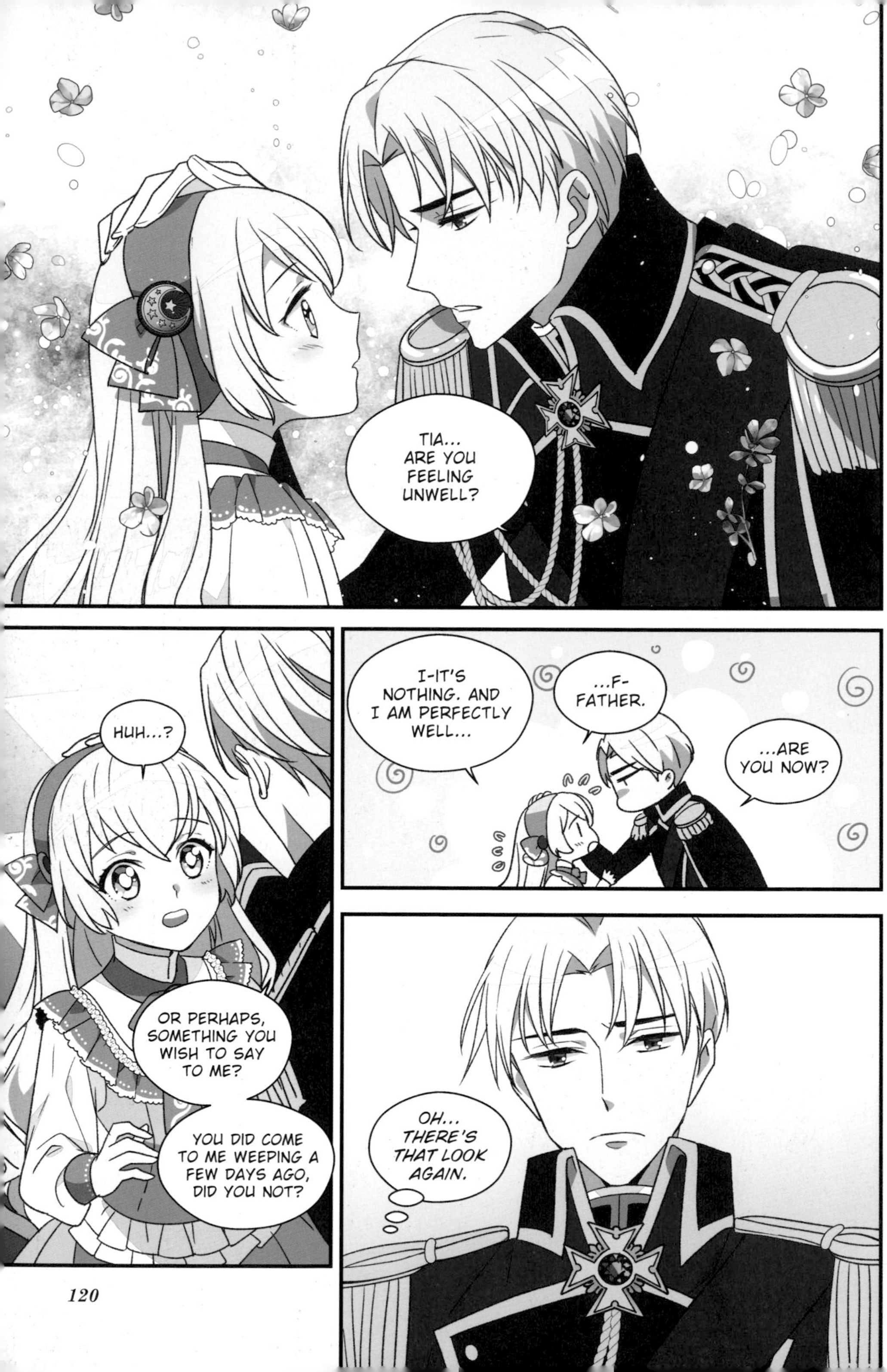
TIA... ARE YOU FEELING UNWELL?
HUH...?
OR PERHAPS, SOMETHING YOU WISH TO SAY TO ME?
YOU DID COME TO ME WEEPING A FEW DAYS AGO, DID YOU NOT?
I-IT'S NOTHING. AND I AM PERFECTLY WELL...
...F- FATHER.
...ARE YOU NOW?
OH... THERE'S THAT LOOK AGAIN.

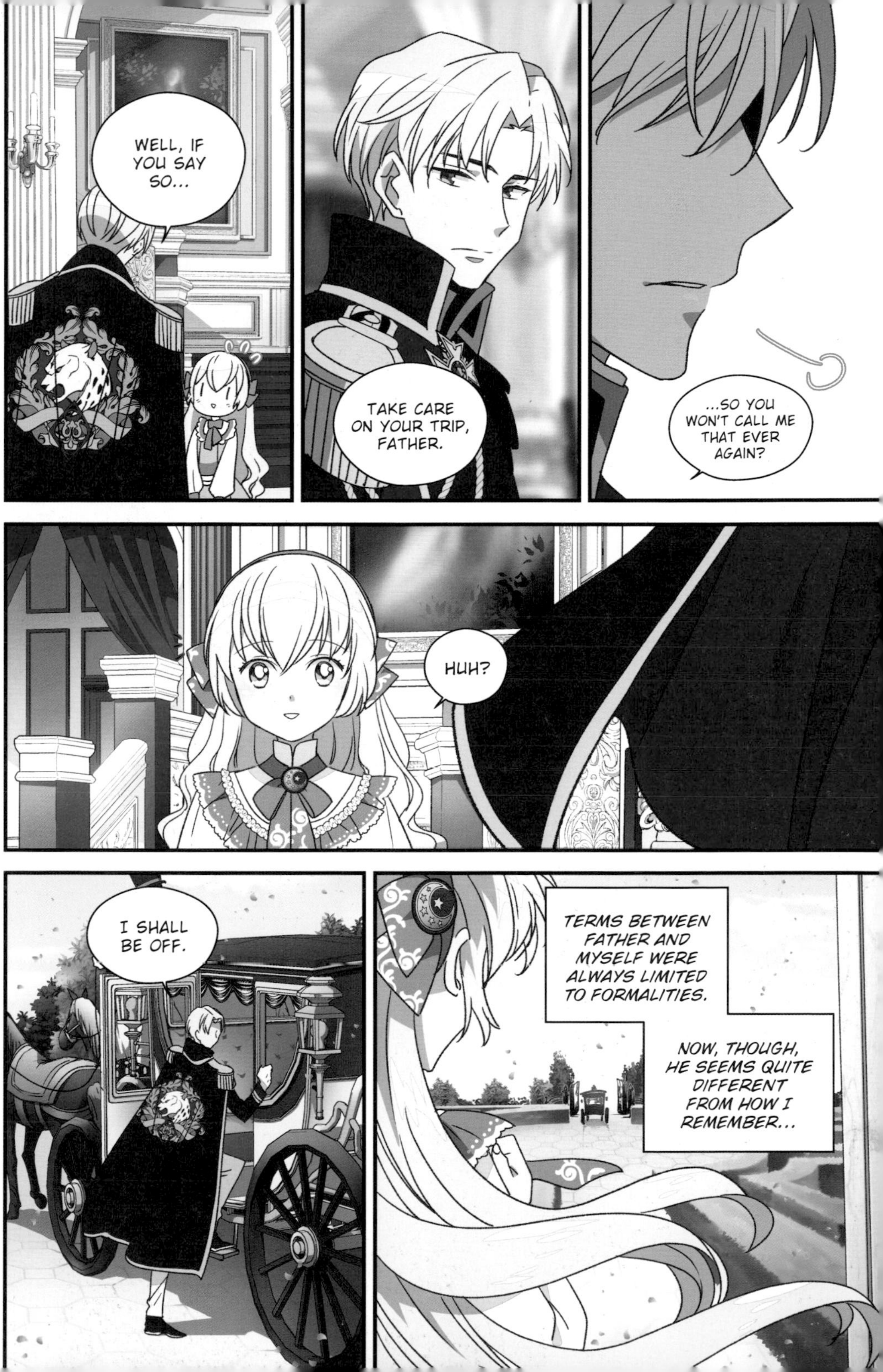
WELL, IF YOU SAY SO...
TAKE CARE ON YOUR TRIP, FATHER.
...SO YOU WON'T CALL ME THAT EVER AGAIN?
HUH?
I SHALL BE OFF.
TERMS BETWEEN FATHER AND MYSELF WERE ALWAYS LIMITED TO FORMALITIES.
NOW, THOUGH, HE SEEMS QUITE DIFFERENT FROM HOW I REMEMBER...

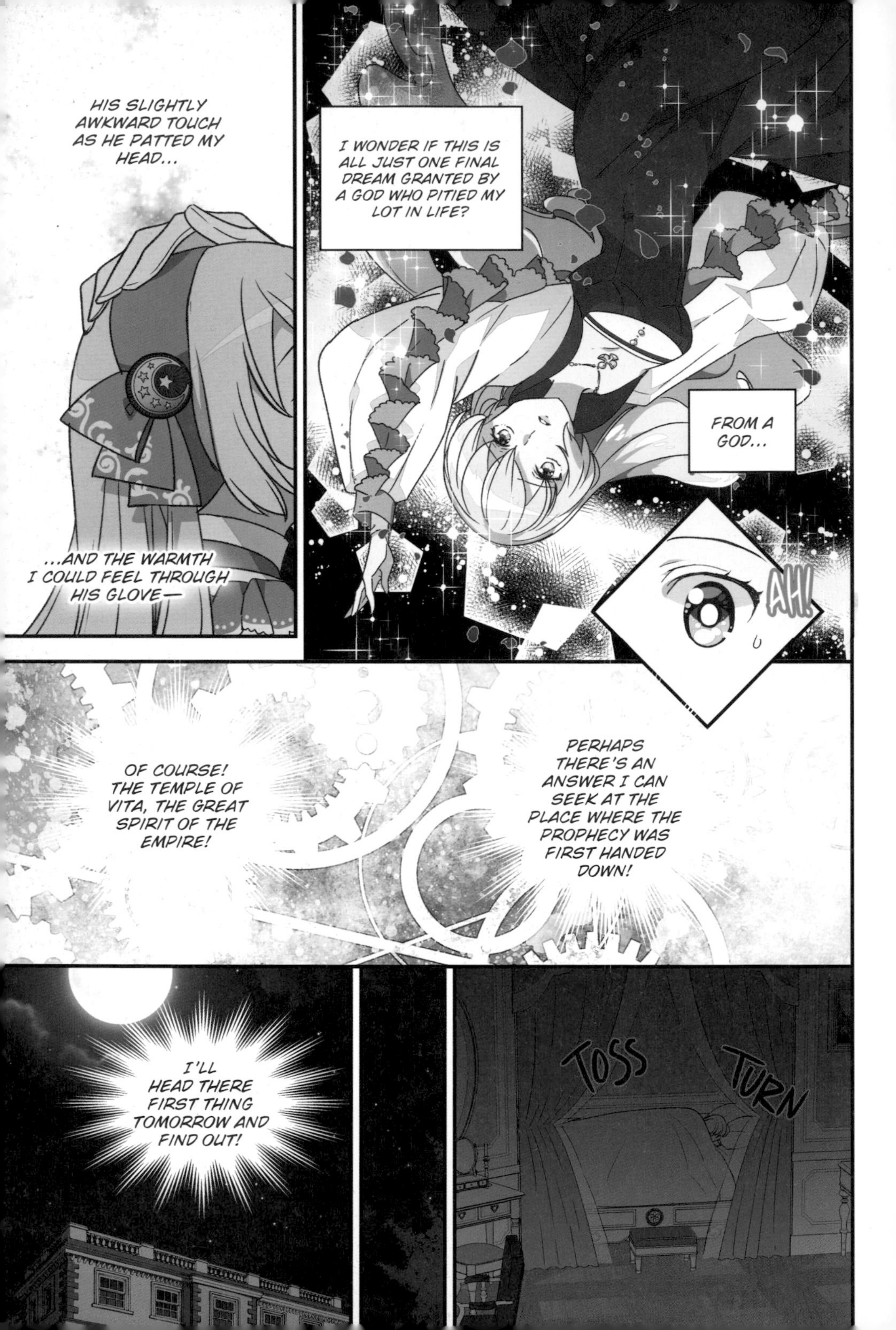
HIS SLIGHTLY AWKWARD TOUCH AS HE PATTED MY HEAD...
...AND THE WARMTH I COULD FEEL THROUGH HIS GLOVE—
I WONDER IF THIS IS ALL JUST ONE FINAL DREAM GRANTED BY A GOD WHO PITIED MY LOT IN LIFE?
FROM A GOD...
AH!
OF COURSE! THE TEMPLE OF VITA, THE GREAT SPIRIT OF THE EMPIRE!
PERHAPS THERE'S AN ANSWER I CAN SEEK AT THE PLACE WHERE THE PROPHECY WAS FIRST HANDED DOWN!
I'LL HEAD THERE FIRST THING TOMORROW AND FIND OUT!
TOSS
TURN

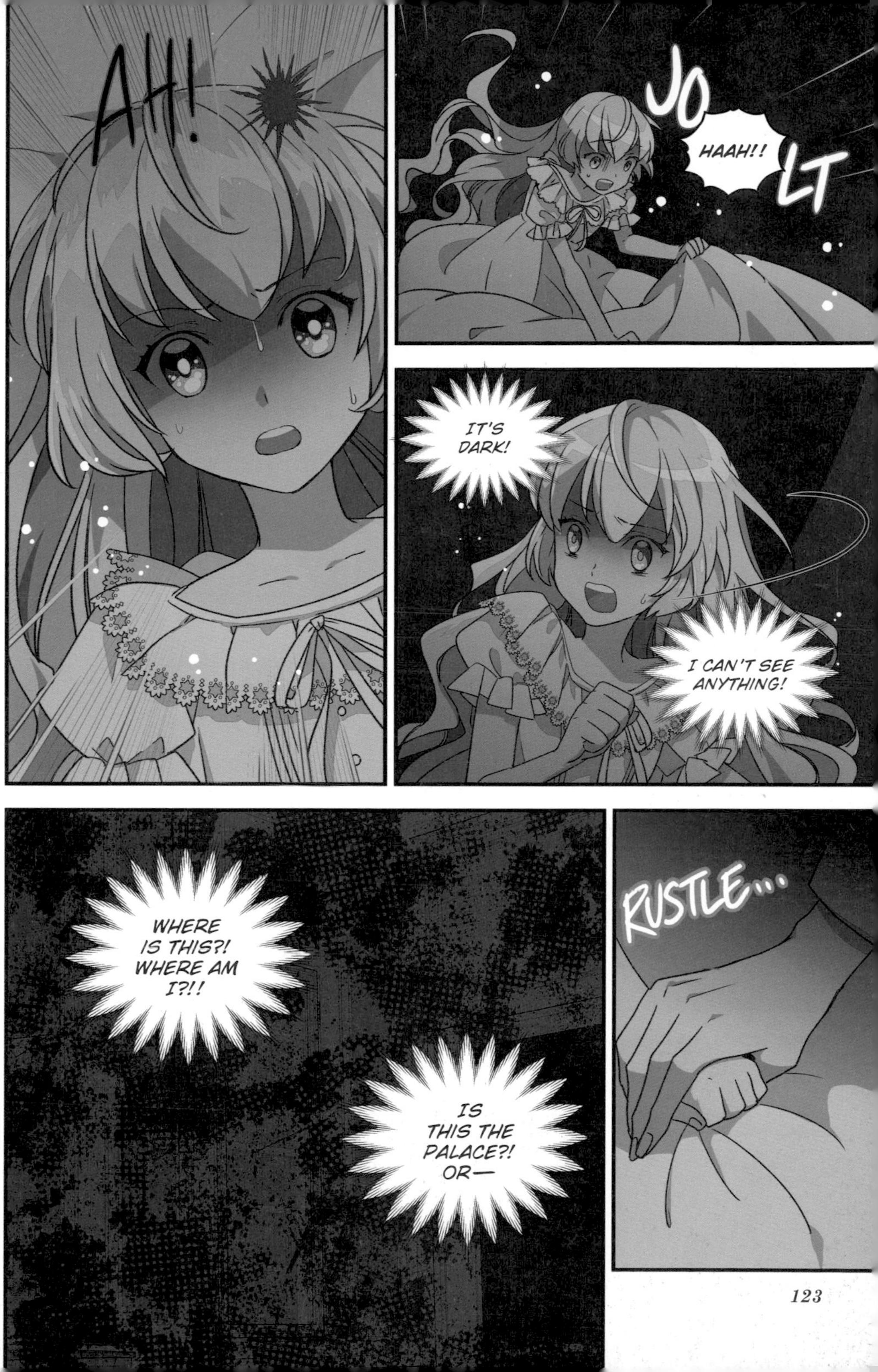
AH!
JOLT
HAAH!!
IT'S DARK!
I CAN'T SEE ANYTHING!
WHERE IS THIS?! WHERE AM I?!!
IS THIS THE PALACE?! OR—
RUSTLE...

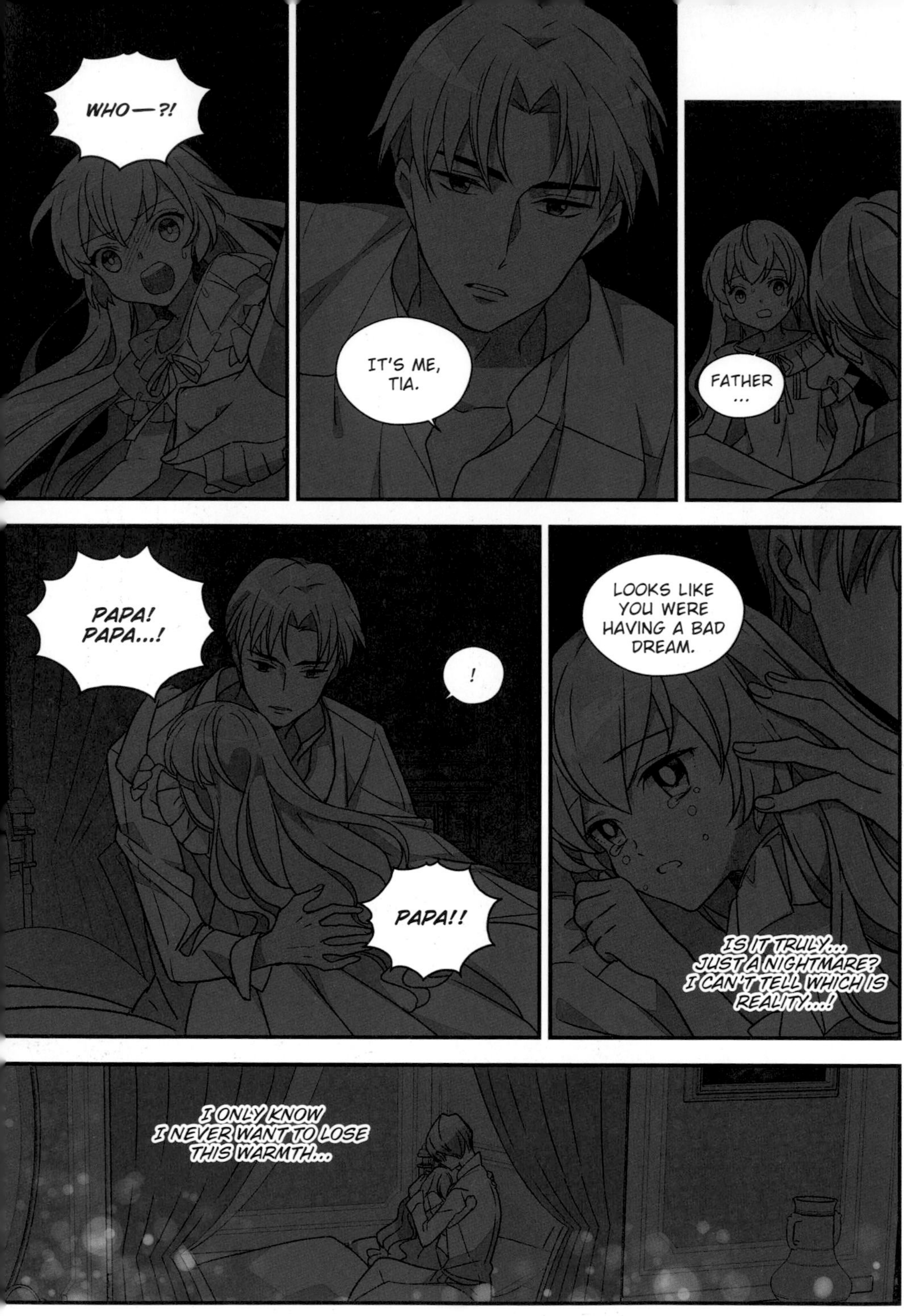
WHO—?!
IT'S ME, TIA.
FATHER...
PAPA! PAPA...!
!
PAPA!!
LOOKS LIKE YOU WERE HAVING A BAD DREAM.
IS IT TRULY... JUST A NIGHTMARE? I CAN'T TELL WHICH IS REALITY...!
I ONLY KNOW I NEVER WANT TO LOSE THIS WARMTH...

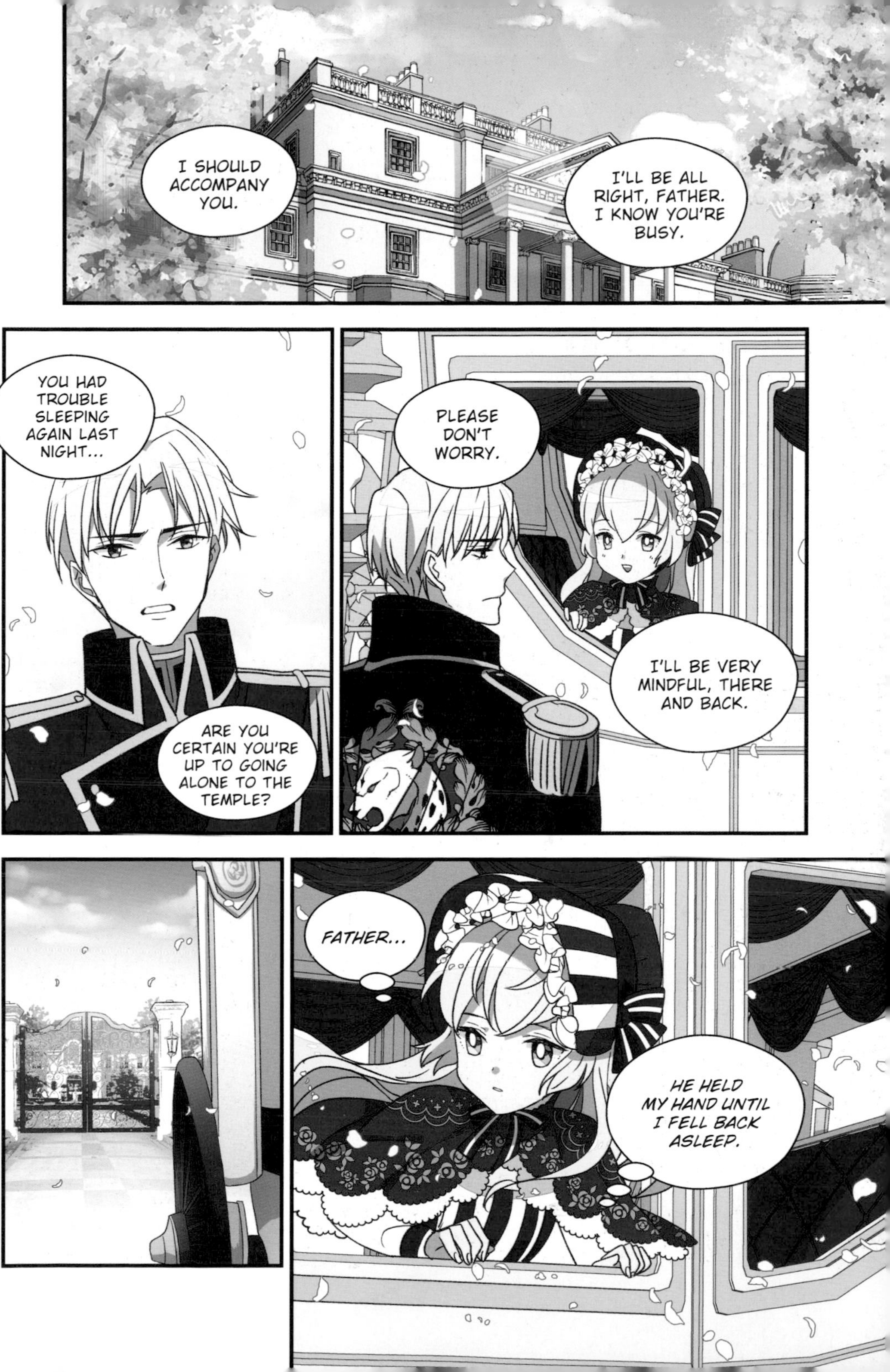
I SHOULD ACCOMPANY YOU.
I'LL BE ALL RIGHT, FATHER. I KNOW YOU'RE BUSY.
YOU HAD TROUBLE SLEEPING AGAIN LAST NIGHT...
ARE YOU CERTAIN YOU'RE UP TO GOING ALONE TO THE TEMPLE?
PLEASE DON'T WORRY.
I'LL BE VERY MINDFUL, THERE AND BACK.
FATHER...
HE HELD MY HAND UNTIL I FELL BACK ASLEEP.

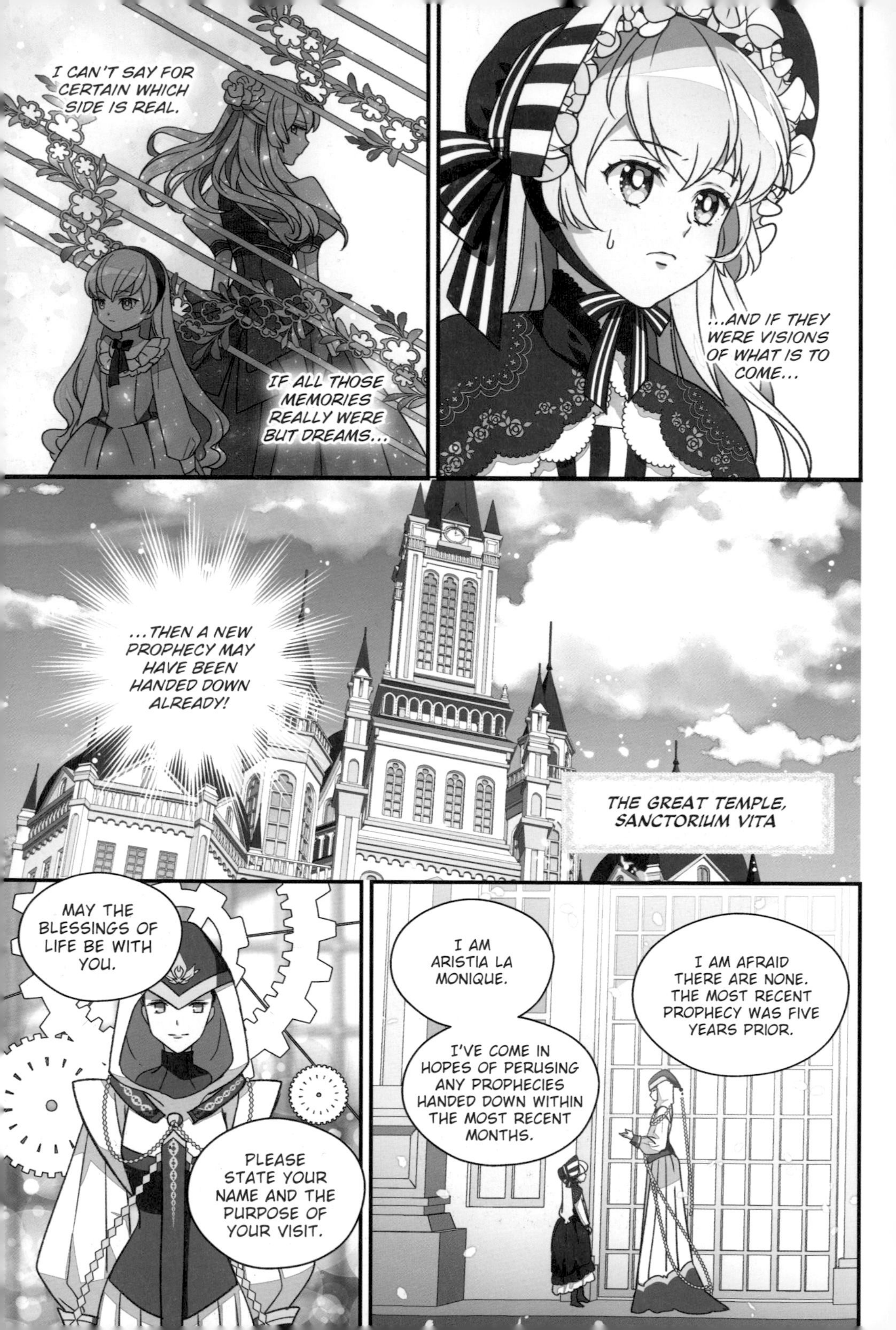
I CAN'T SAY FOR CERTAIN WHICH SIDE IS REAL.
IF ALL THOSE MEMORIES REALLY WERE BUT DREAMS...
...AND IF THEY WERE VISIONS OF WHAT IS TO COME...
...THEN A NEW PROPHECY MAY HAVE BEEN HANDED DOWN ALREADY!
THE GREAT TEMPLE, SANCTORIUM VITA
MAY THE BLESSINGS OF LIFE BE WITH YOU.
PLEASE STATE YOUR NAME AND THE PURPOSE OF YOUR VISIT.
I AM ARISTIA LA MONIQUE.
I'VE COME IN HOPES OF PERUSING ANY PROPHECIES HANDED DOWN WITHIN THE MOST RECENT MONTHS.
I AM AFRAID THERE ARE NONE. THE MOST RECENT PROPHECY WAS FIVE YEARS PRIOR.

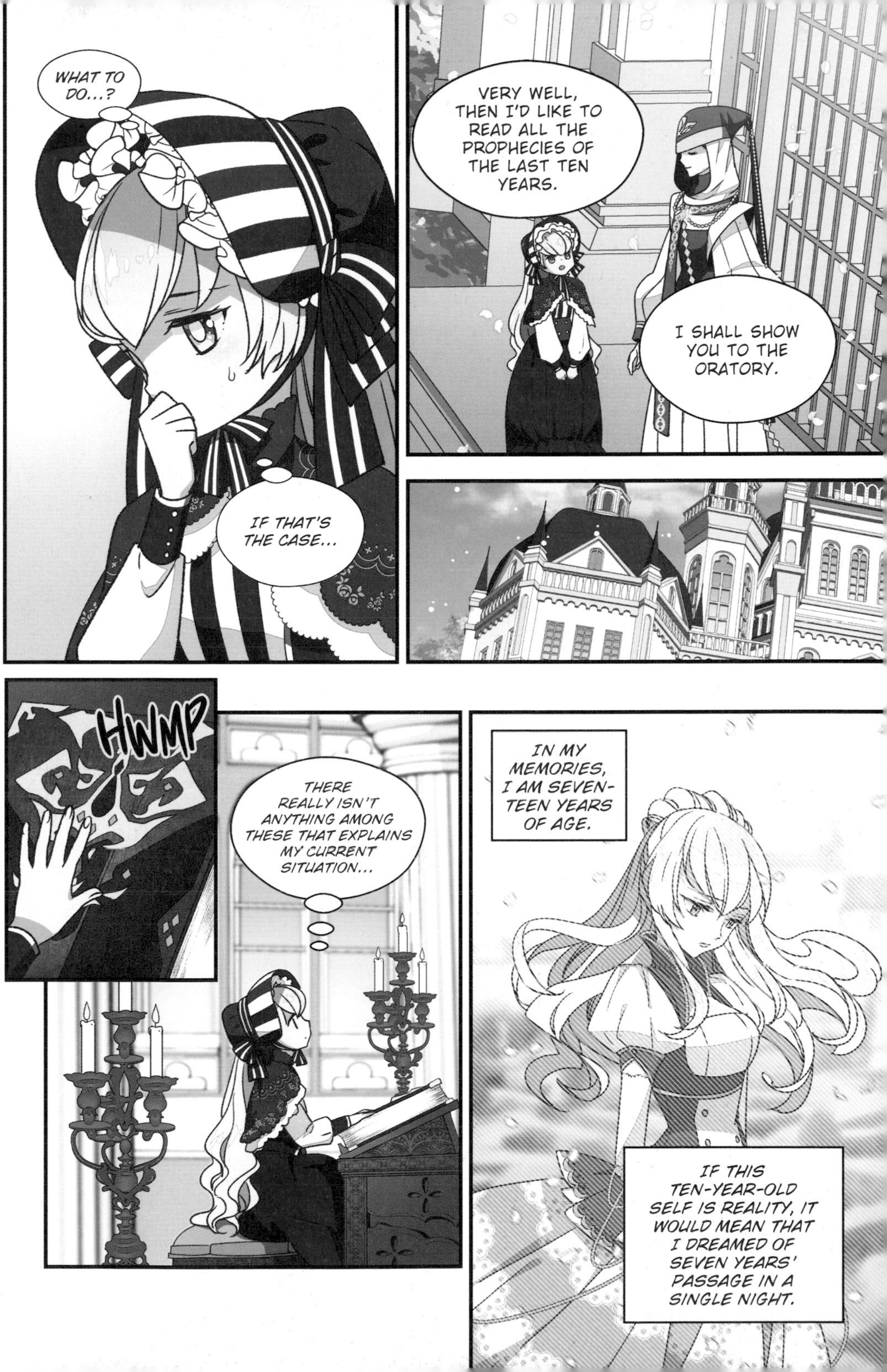

WHAT TO DO...?
IF THAT'S THE CASE...
VERY WELL, THEN I'D LIKE TO READ ALL THE PROPHECIES OF THE LAST TEN YEARS.
I SHALL SHOW YOU TO THE ORATORY.
HWMP
THERE REALLY ISN'T ANYTHING AMONG THESE THAT EXPLAINS MY CURRENT SITUATION...
IN MY MEMORIES, I AM SEVEN-TEEN YEARS OF AGE.
IF THIS TEN-YEAR-OLD SELF IS REALITY, IT WOULD MEAN THAT I DREAMED OF SEVEN YEARS' PASSAGE IN A SINGLE NIGHT.

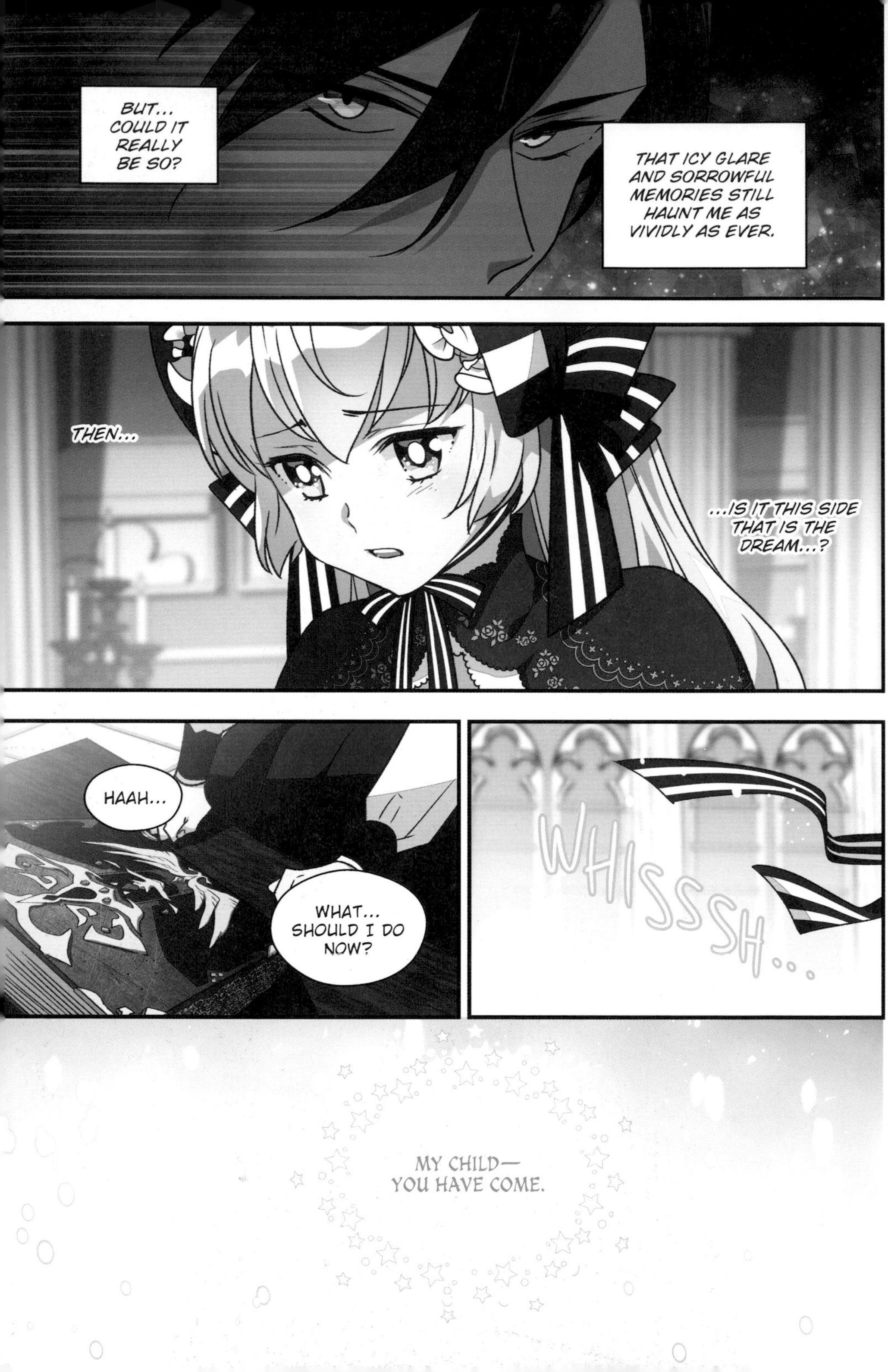
BUT... COULD IT REALLY BE SO?
THAT ICY GLARE AND SORROWFUL MEMORIES STILL HAUNT ME AS VIVIDLY AS EVER.
THEN...
...IS IT THIS SIDE THAT IS THE DREAM...?
HAAH...
WHAT... SHOULD I DO NOW?
WHISSSH...
MY CHILD—
YOU HAVE COME.

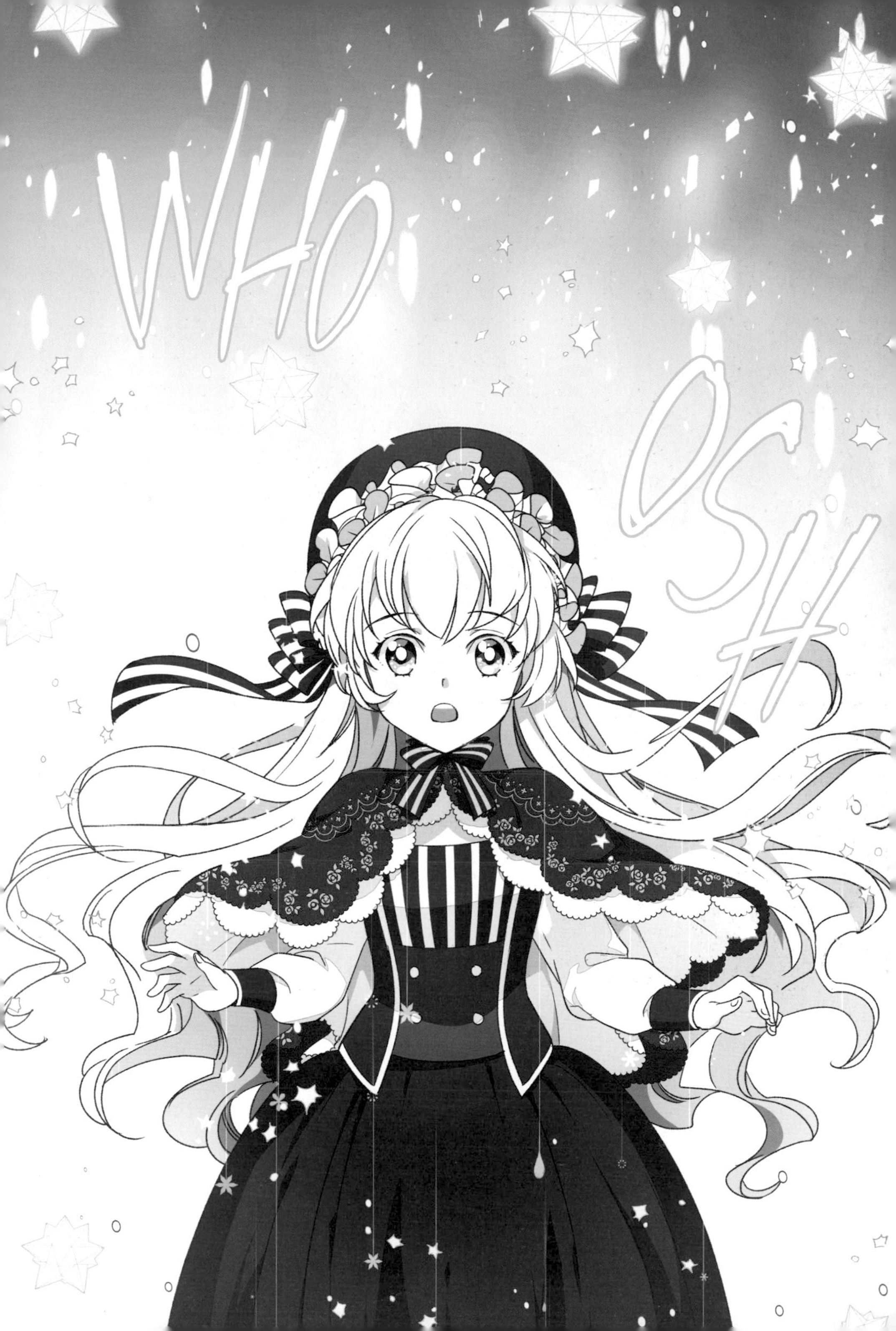
WHO
OSH

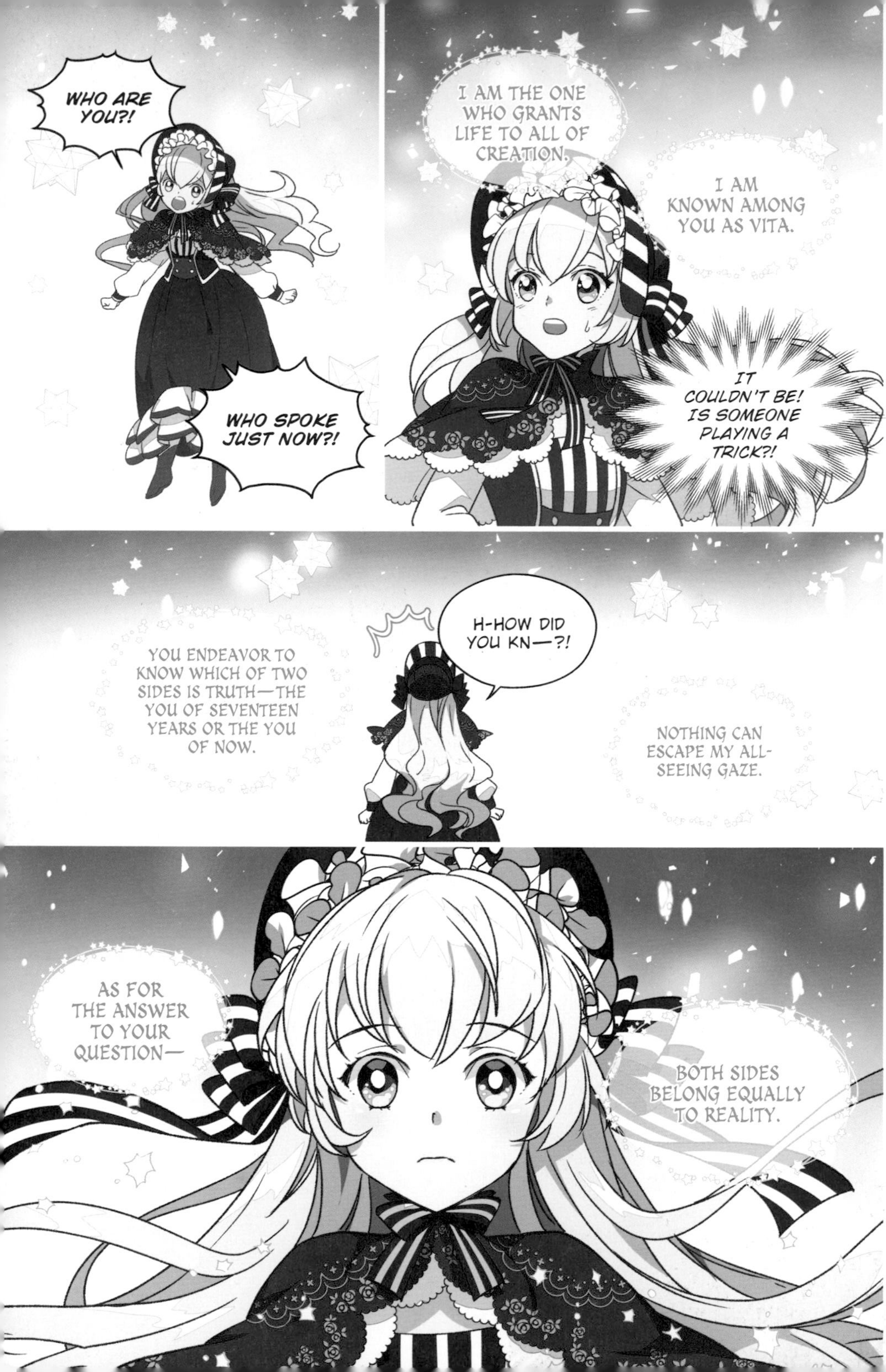
WHO ARE YOU?!
WHO SPOKE JUST NOW?!
I AM THE ONE WHO GRANTS LIFE TO ALL OF CREATION.
I AM KNOWN AMONG YOU AS VITA.
IT COULDN'T BE! IS SOMEONE PLAYING A TRICK?!
YOU ENDEAVOR TO KNOW WHICH OF TWO SIDES IS TRUTH—THE YOU OF SEVENTEEN YEARS OR THE YOU OF NOW.
H-HOW DID YOU KN—?!
NOTHING CAN ESCAPE MY ALL-SEEING GAZE.
AS FOR THE ANSWER TO YOUR QUESTION—
BOTH SIDES BELONG EQUALLY TO REALITY.

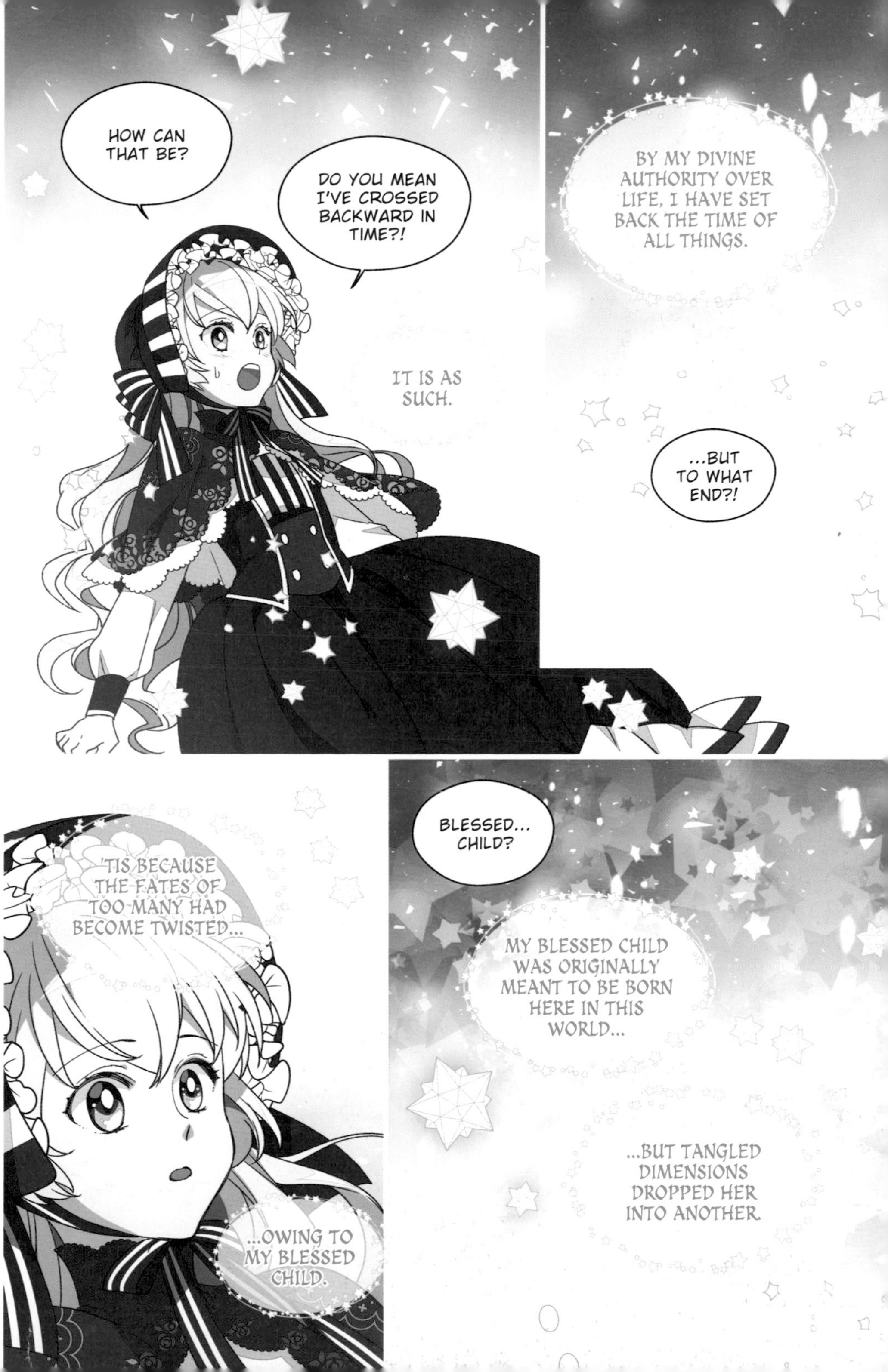
HOW CAN THAT BE?
DO YOU MEAN I'VE CROSSED BACKWARD IN TIME?!
BY MY DIVINE AUTHORITY OVER LIFE, I HAVE SET BACK THE TIME OF ALL THINGS.
IT IS AS SUCH.
...BUT TO WHAT END?!
'TIS BECAUSE THE FATES OF TOO MANY HAD BECOME TWISTED...
...OWING TO MY BLESSED CHILD.
BLESSED... CHILD?
MY BLESSED CHILD WAS ORIGINALLY MEANT TO BE BORN HERE IN THIS WORLD...
...BUT TANGLED DIMENSIONS DROPPED HER INTO ANOTHER.

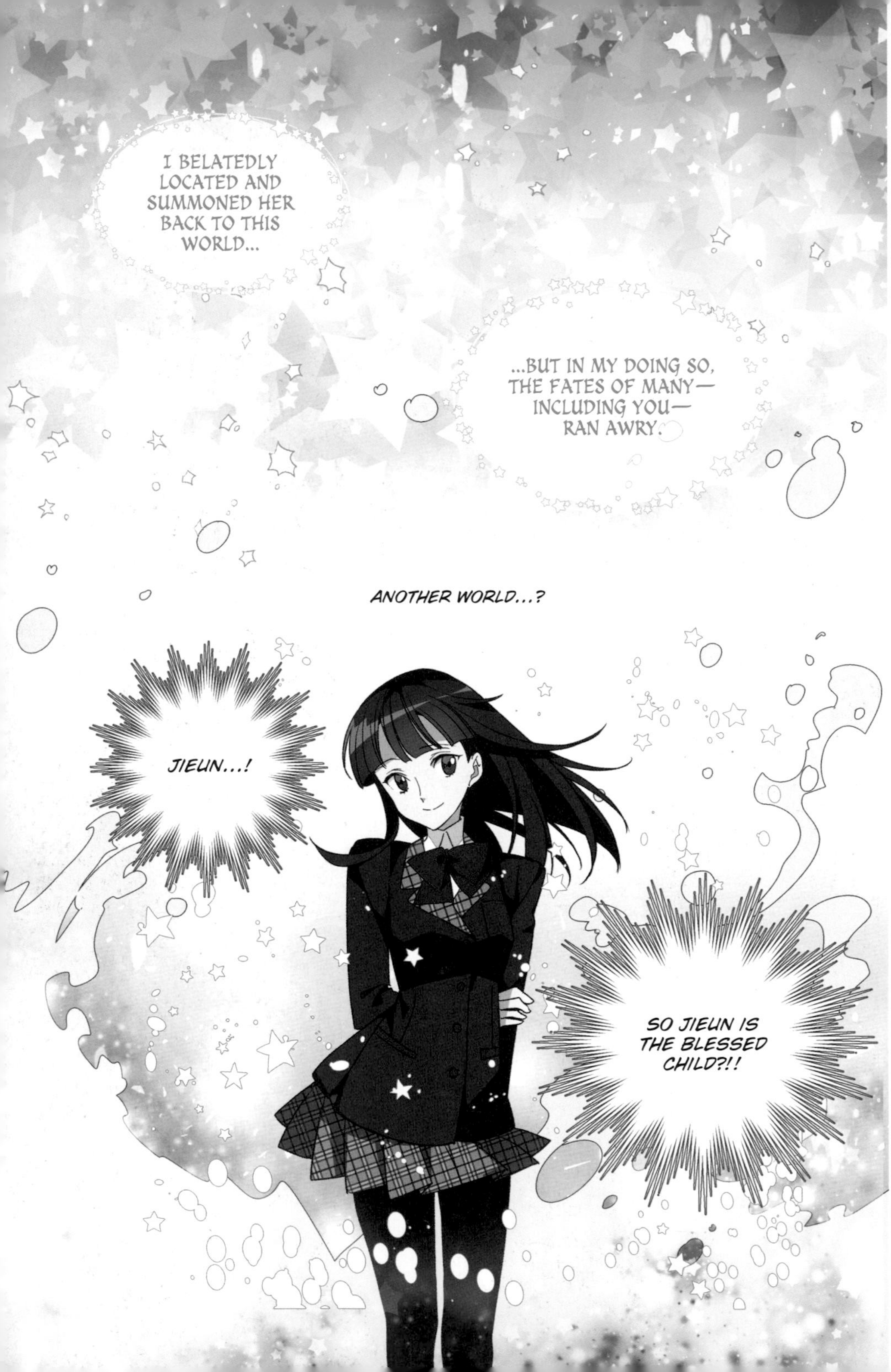
I BELATEDLY LOCATED AND SUMMONED HER BACK TO THIS WORLD...
...BUT IN MY DOING SO, THE FATES OF MANY— INCLUDING YOU— RAN AWRY.
ANOTHER WORLD...?
JIEUN...!
SO JIEUN IS THE BLESSED CHILD?!!

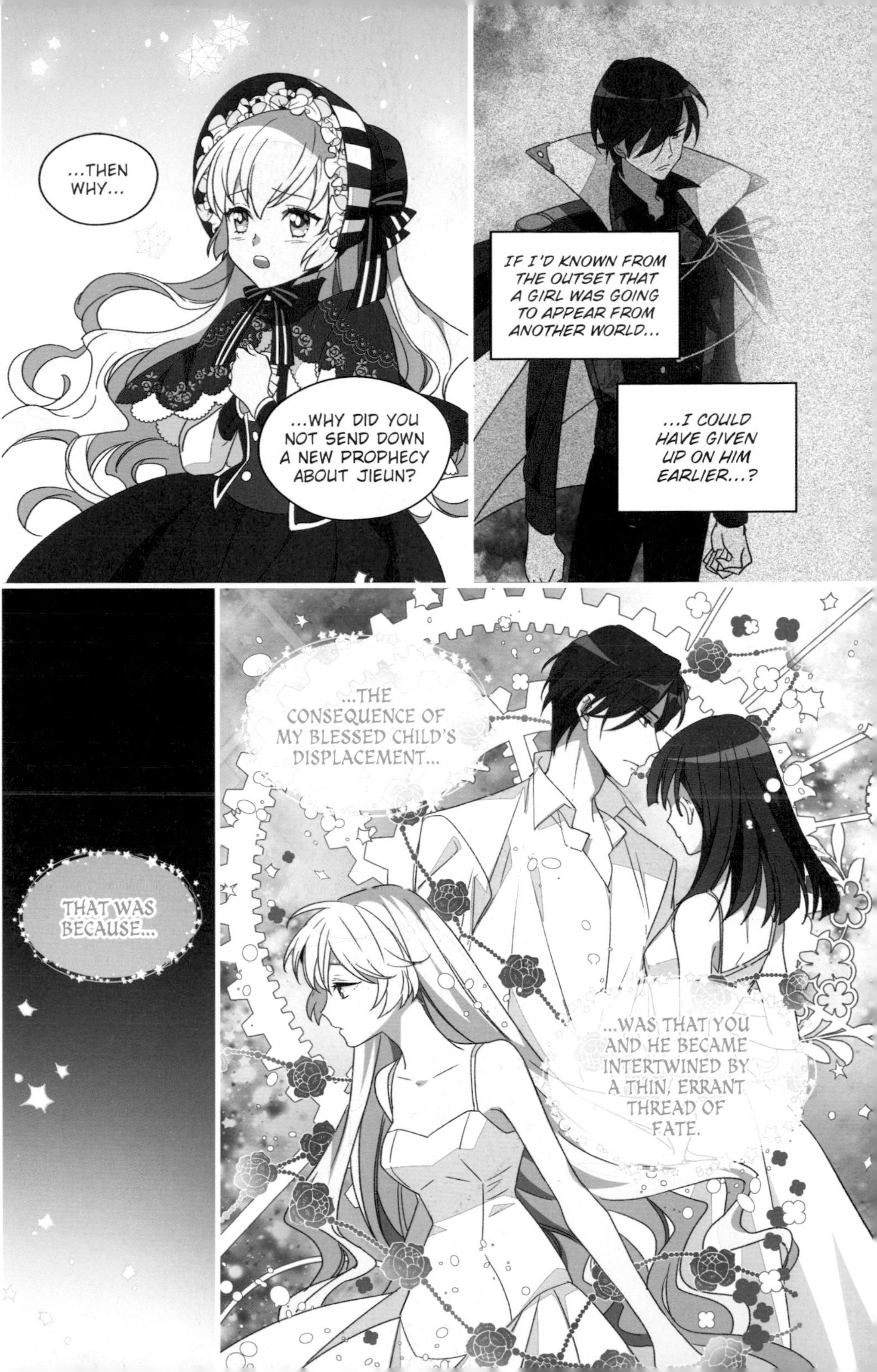
...THEN WHY...
...WHY DID YOU NOT SEND DOWN A NEW PROPHECY ABOUT JIEUN?
IF I'D KNOWN FROM THE OUTSET THAT A GIRL WAS GOING TO APPEAR FROM ANOTHER WORLD...
...I COULD HAVE GIVEN UP ON HIM EARLIER...?
THAT WAS BECAUSE...
...THE CONSEQUENCE OF MY BLESSED CHILD'S DISPLACEMENT...
...WAS THAT YOU AND HE BECAME INTERTWINED BY A THIN, ERRANT THREAD OF FATE.

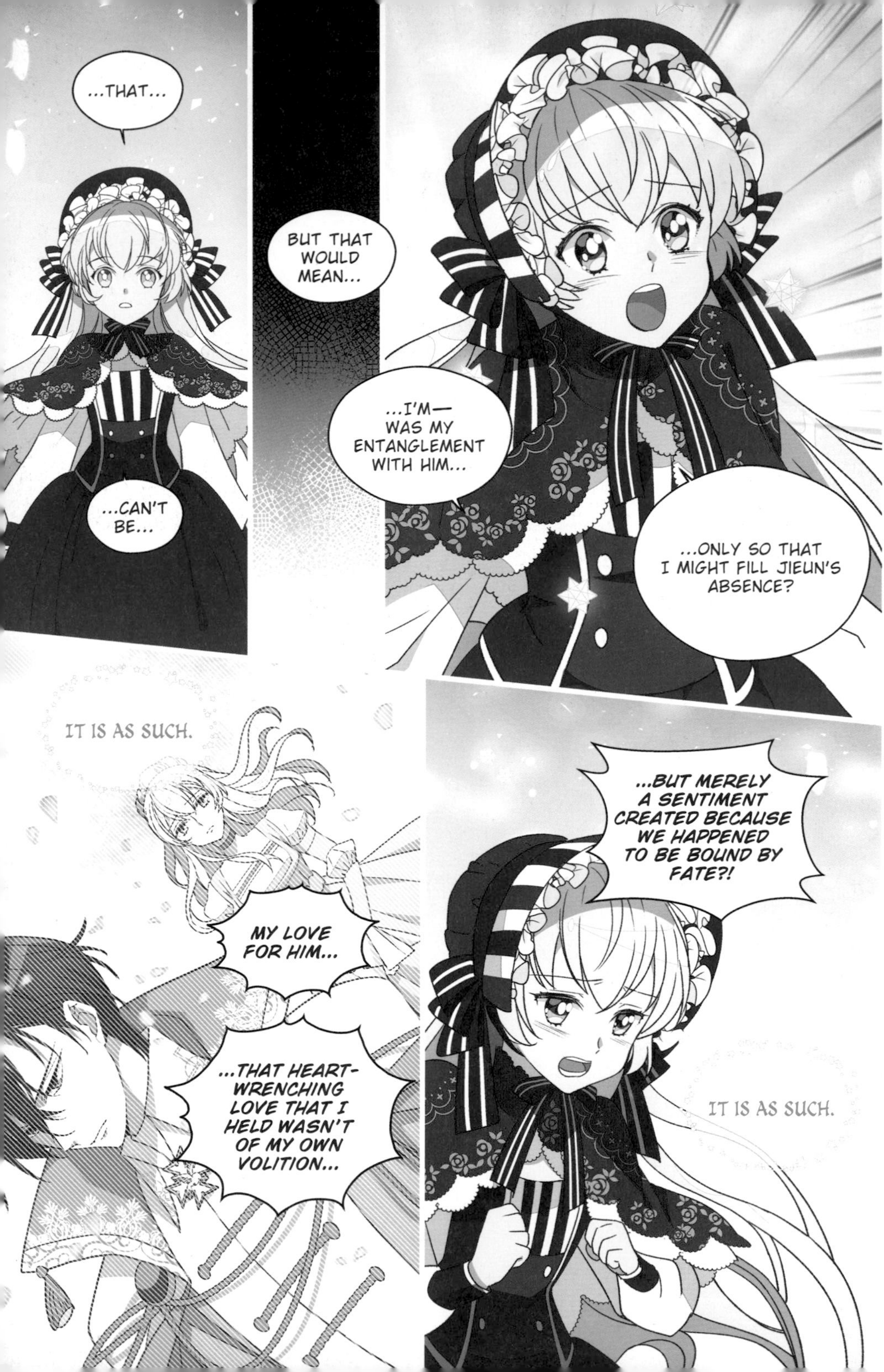
...THAT...
...CAN'T BE...
BUT THAT WOULD MEAN...
...I'M— WAS MY ENTANGLEMENT WITH HIM...
...ONLY SO THAT I MIGHT FILL JIEUN'S ABSENCE?
IT IS AS SUCH.
MY LOVE FOR HIM...
...THAT HEART-WRENCHING LOVE THAT I HELD WASN'T OF MY OWN VOLITION...
...BUT MERELY A SENTIMENT CREATED BECAUSE WE HAPPENED TO BE BOUND BY FATE?!
IT IS AS SUCH.

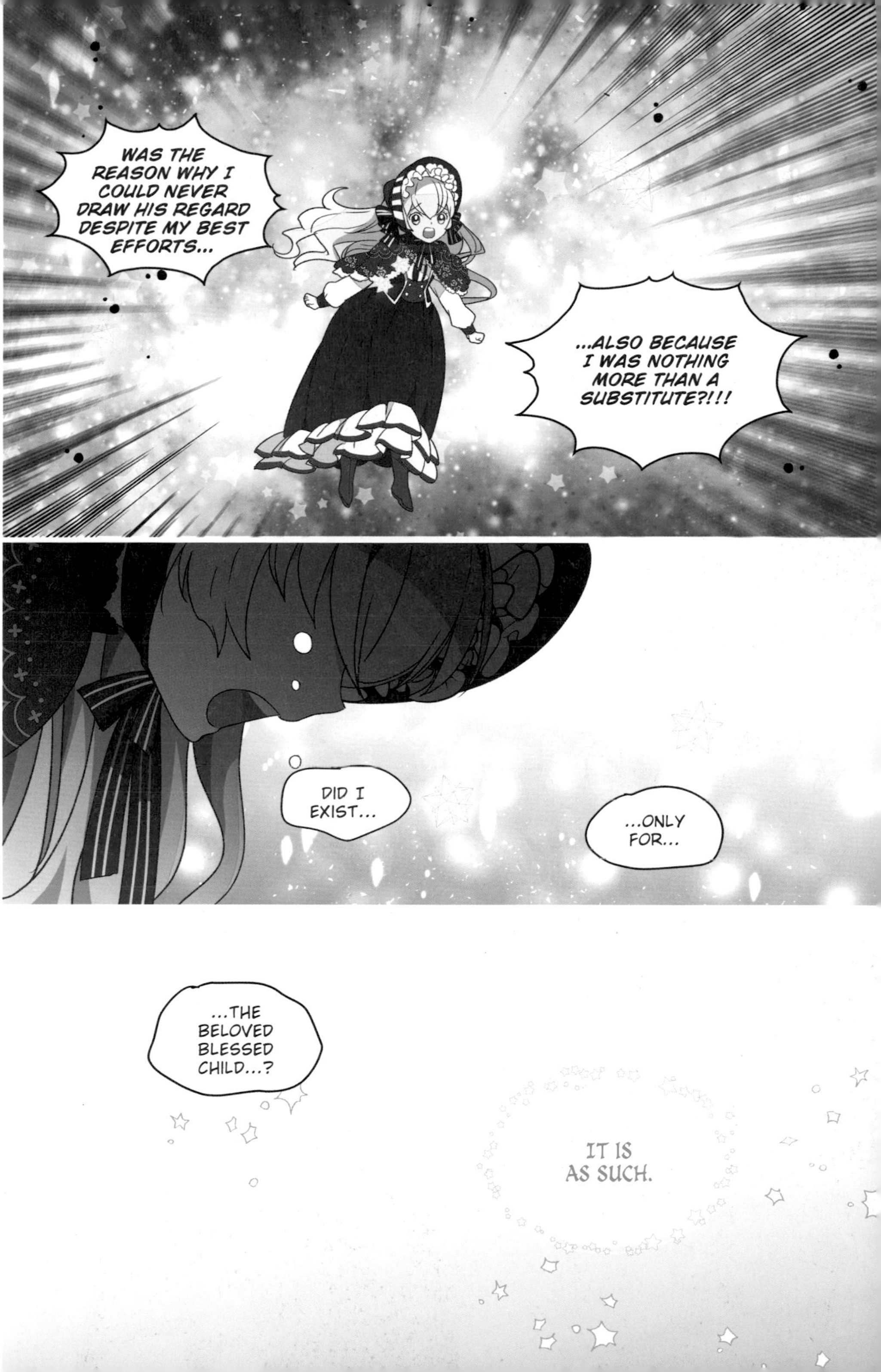
WAS THE REASON WHY I COULD NEVER DRAW HIS REGARD DESPITE MY BEST EFFORTS...
...ALSO BECAUSE I WAS NOTHING MORE THAN A SUBSTITUTE?!!!
DID I EXIST...
...ONLY FOR...
...THE BELOVED BLESSED CHILD...?
IT IS AS SUCH.

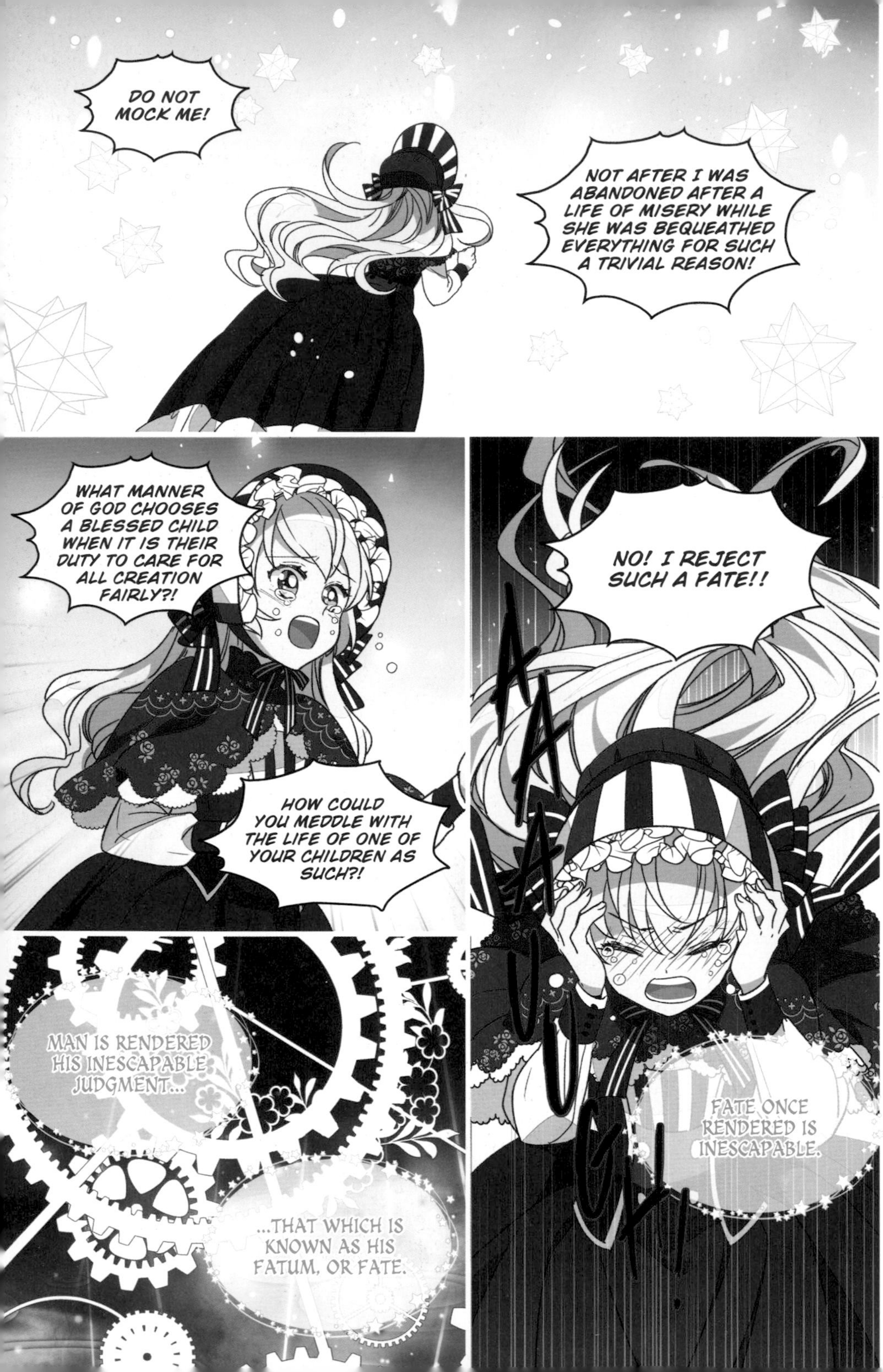
DO NOT MOCK ME!
NOT AFTER I WAS ABANDONED AFTER A LIFE OF MISERY WHILE SHE WAS BEQUEATHED EVERYTHING FOR SUCH A TRIVIAL REASON!
WHAT MANNER OF GOD CHOOSES A BLESSED CHILD WHEN IT IS THEIR DUTY TO CARE FOR ALL CREATION FAIRLY?!
HOW COULD YOU MEDDLE WITH THE LIFE OF ONE OF YOUR CHILDREN AS SUCH?!
NO! I REJECT SUCH A FATE!!
AAAUUGH!
MAN IS RENDERED HIS INESCAPABLE JUDGMENT...
...THAT WHICH IS KNOWN AS HIS FATUM, OR FATE.
FATE ONCE RENDERED IS INESCAPABLE.

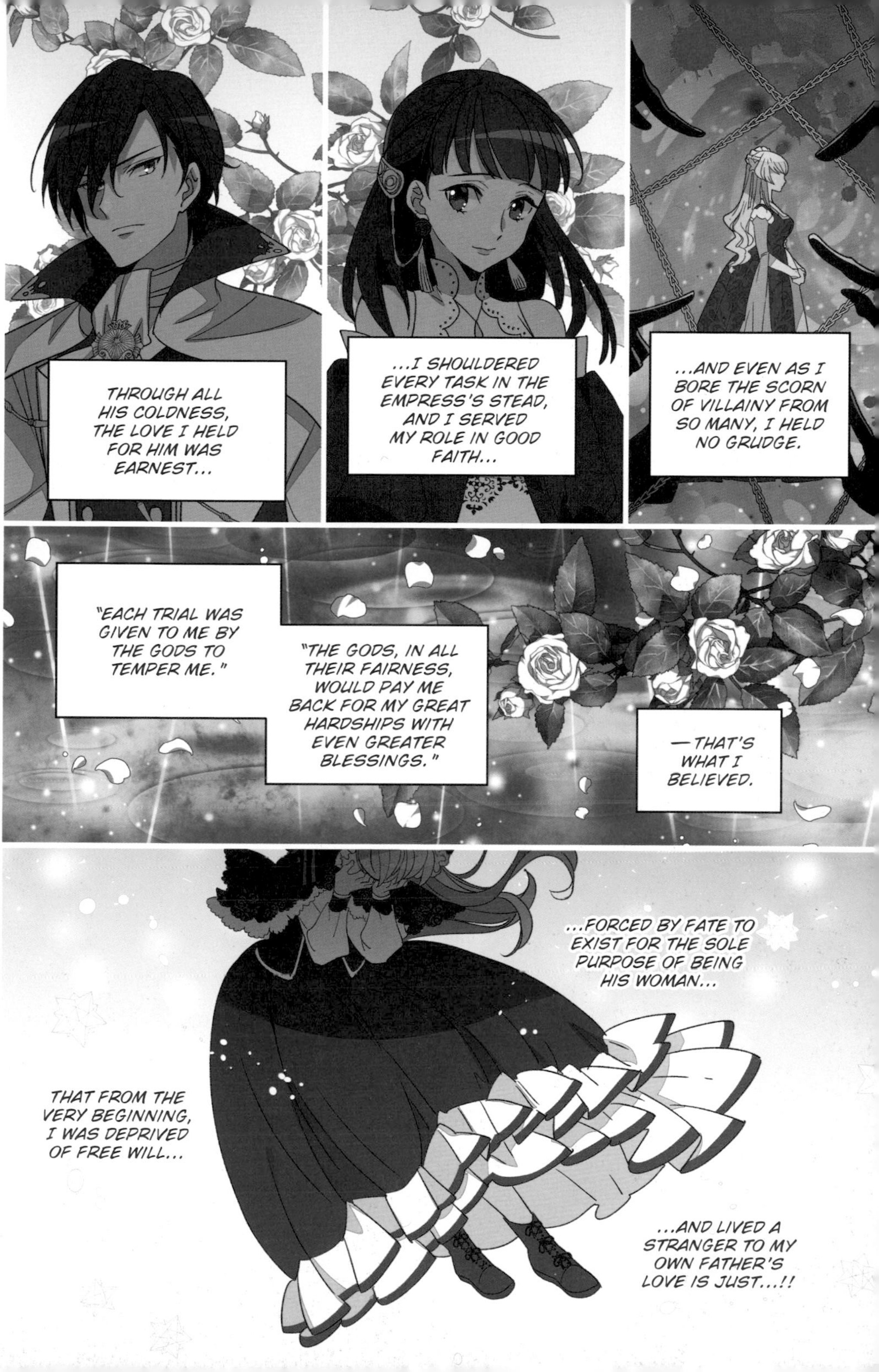
THROUGH ALL HIS COLDNESS, THE LOVE I HELD FOR HIM WAS EARNEST...
...I SHOULDERED EVERY TASK IN THE EMPRESS'S STEAD, AND I SERVED MY ROLE IN GOOD FAITH...
...AND EVEN AS I BORE THE SCORN OF VILLAINY FROM SO MANY, I HELD NO GRUDGE.
"EACH TRIAL WAS GIVEN TO ME BY THE GODS TO TEMPER ME."
"THE GODS, IN ALL THEIR FAIRNESS, WOULD PAY ME BACK FOR MY GREAT HARDSHIPS WITH EVEN GREATER BLESSINGS."
—THAT'S WHAT I BELIEVED.
...FORCED BY FATE TO EXIST FOR THE SOLE PURPOSE OF BEING HIS WOMAN...
THAT FROM THE VERY BEGINNING, I WAS DEPRIVED OF FREE WILL...
...AND LIVED A STRANGER TO MY OWN FATHER'S LOVE IS JUST...!!

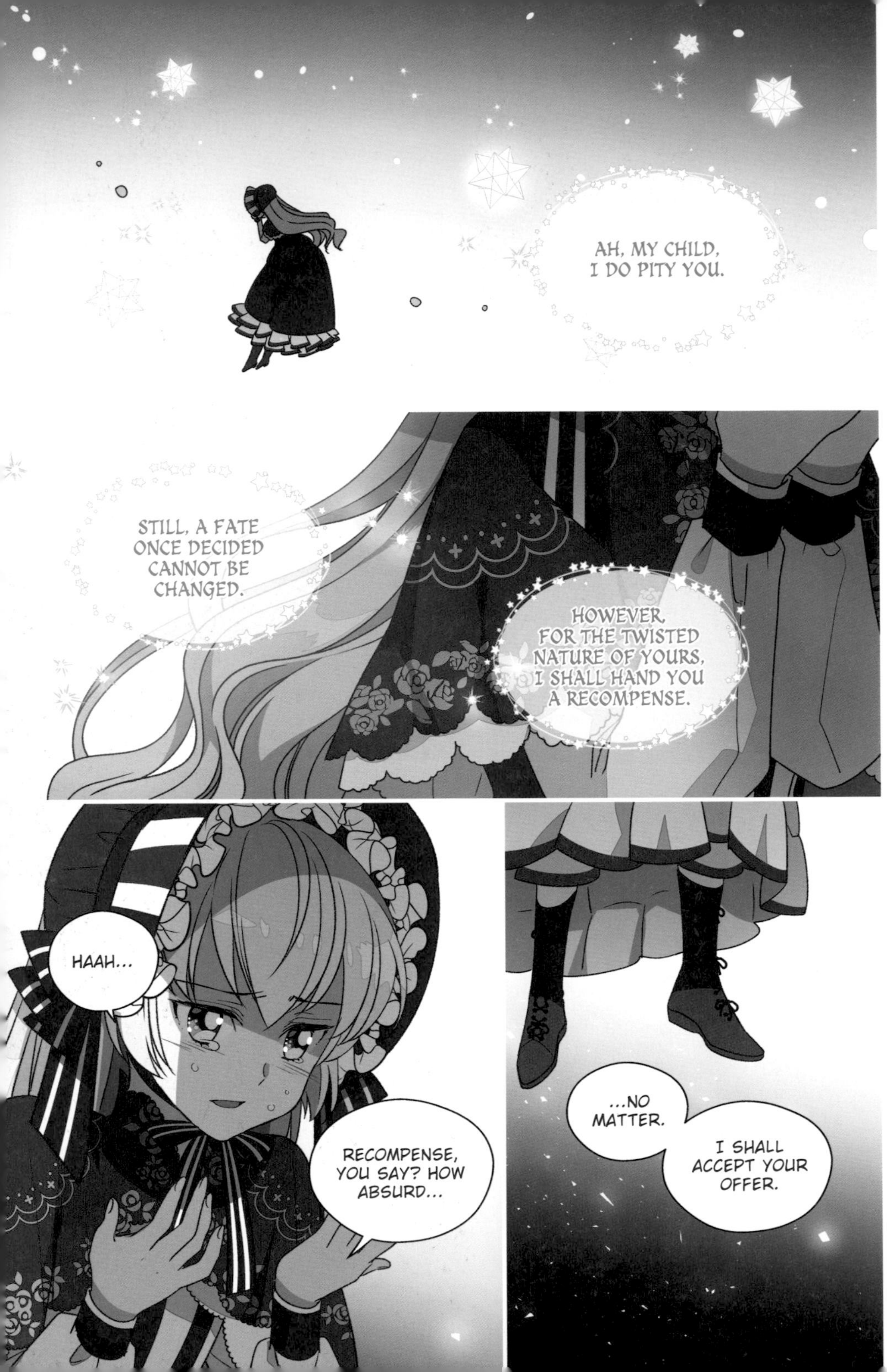
AH, MY CHILD, I DO PITY YOU.
STILL, A FATE ONCE DECIDED CANNOT BE CHANGED.
HOWEVER, FOR THE TWISTED NATURE OF YOURS, I SHALL HAND YOU A RECOMPENSE.
HAAH...
RECOMPENSE, YOU SAY? HOW ABSURD...
...NO MATTER.
I SHALL ACCEPT YOUR OFFER.

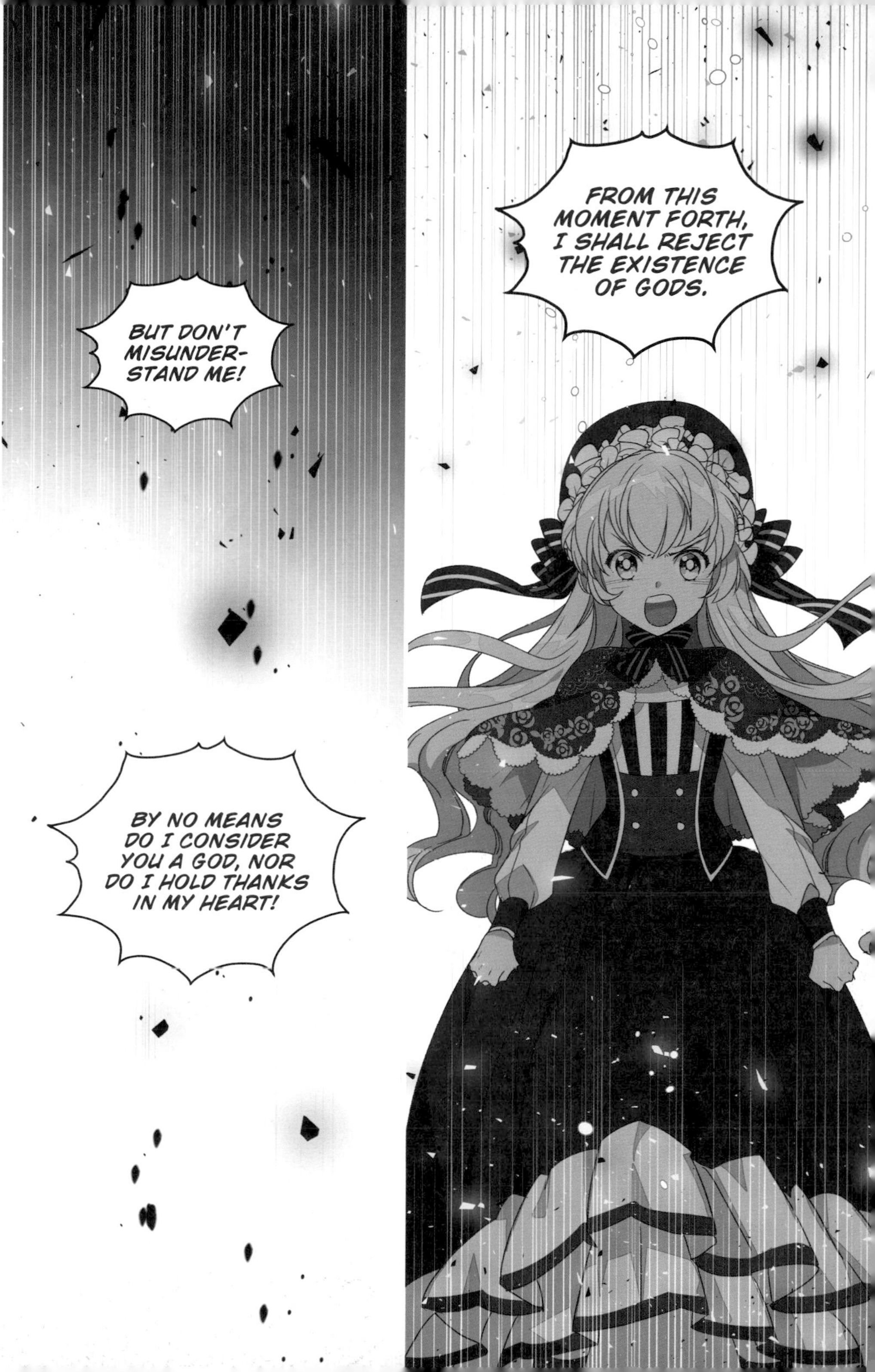
FROM THIS MOMENT FORTH, I SHALL REJECT THE EXISTENCE OF GODS.
BUT DON'T MISUNDER-STAND ME!
BY NO MEANS DO I CONSIDER YOU A GOD, NOR DO I HOLD THANKS IN MY HEART!

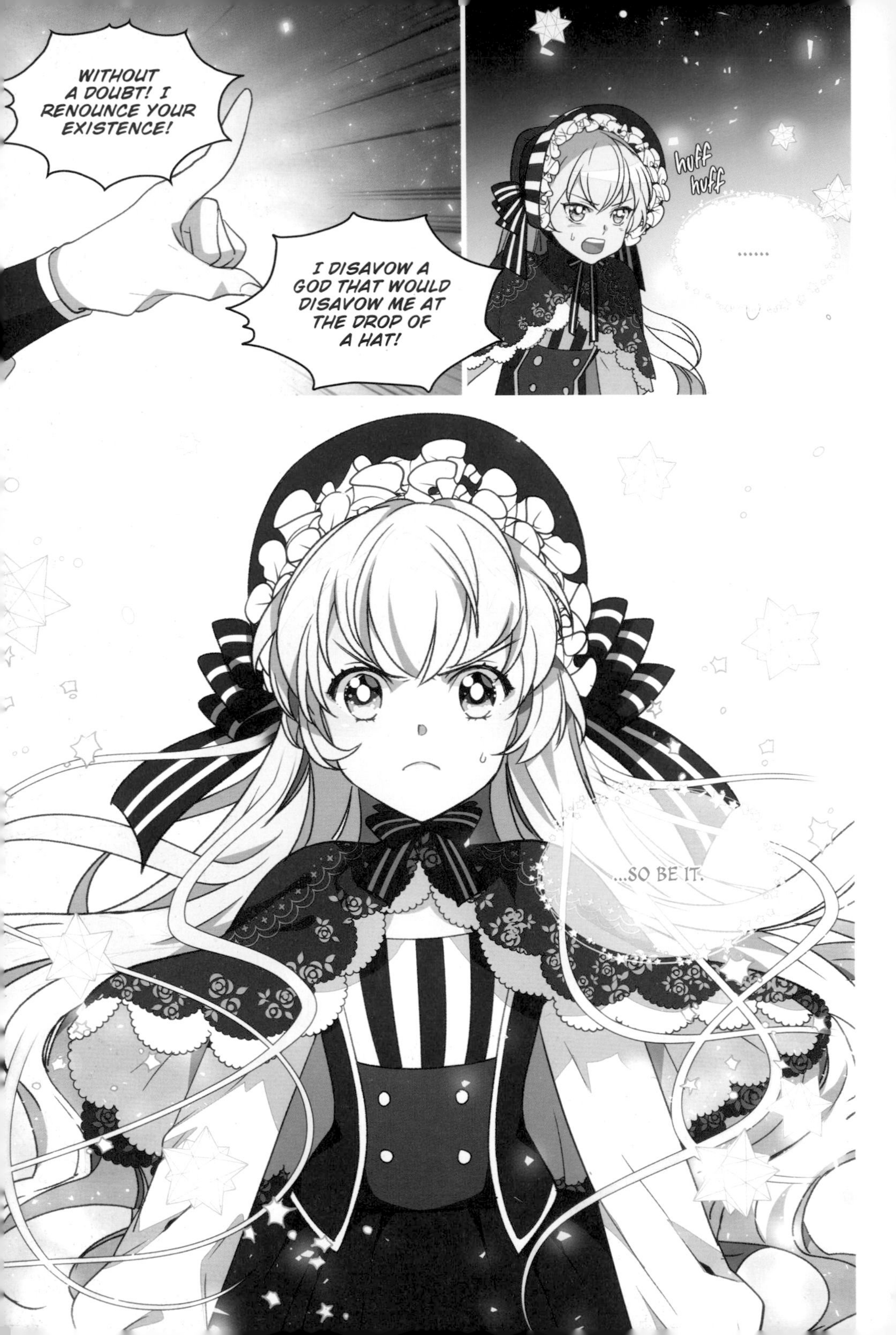
WITHOUT A DOUBT! I RENOUNCE YOUR EXISTENCE!
I DISAVOW A GOD THAT WOULD DISAVOW ME AT THE DROP OF A HAT!
huff huff
......
...SO BE IT.

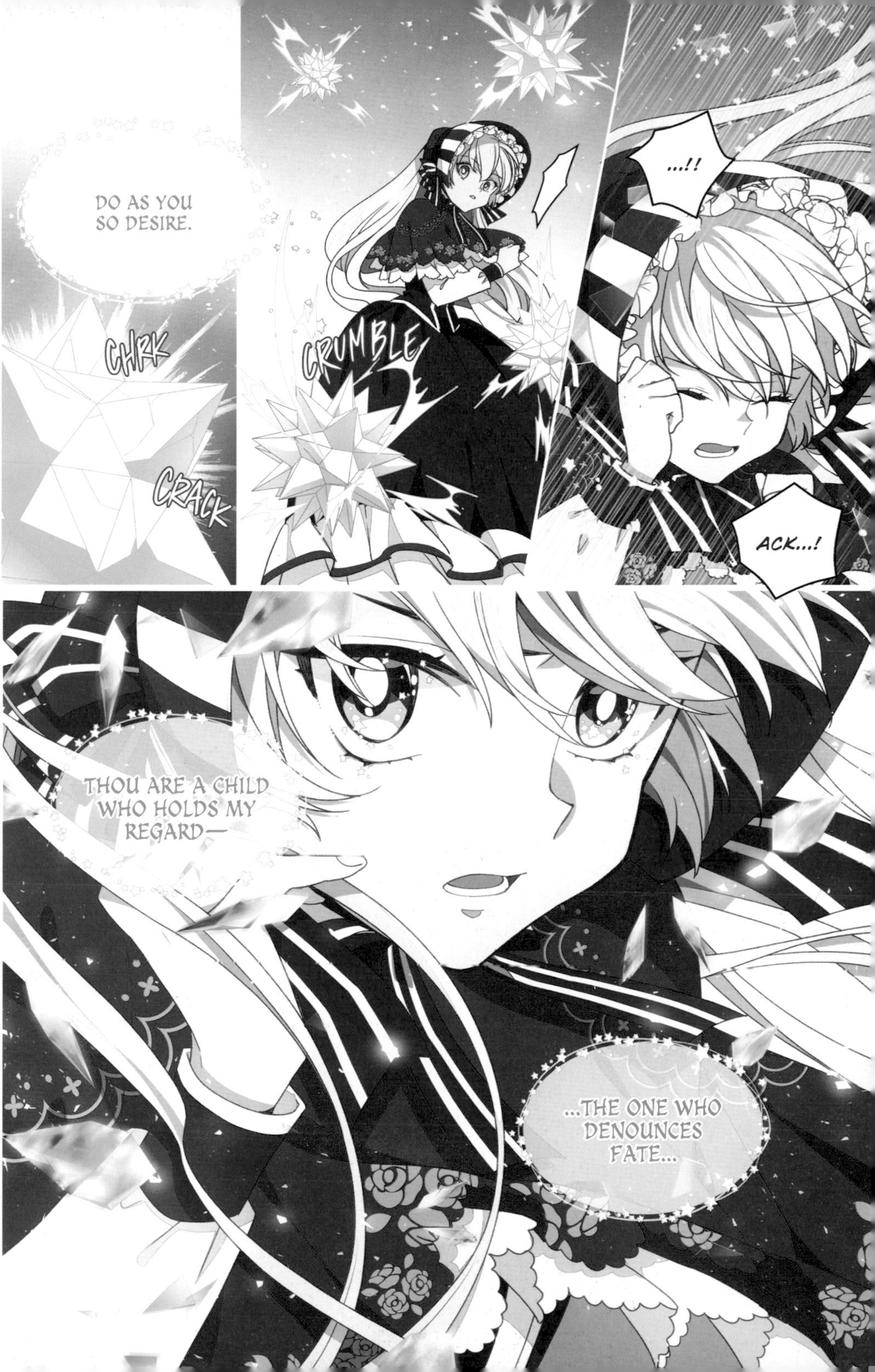
...!!
ACK...!
!
CRUMBLE
DO AS YOU SO DESIRE.
CHRK
CRACK
THOU ARE A CHILD WHO HOLDS MY REGARD—
...THE ONE WHO DENOUNCES FATE...

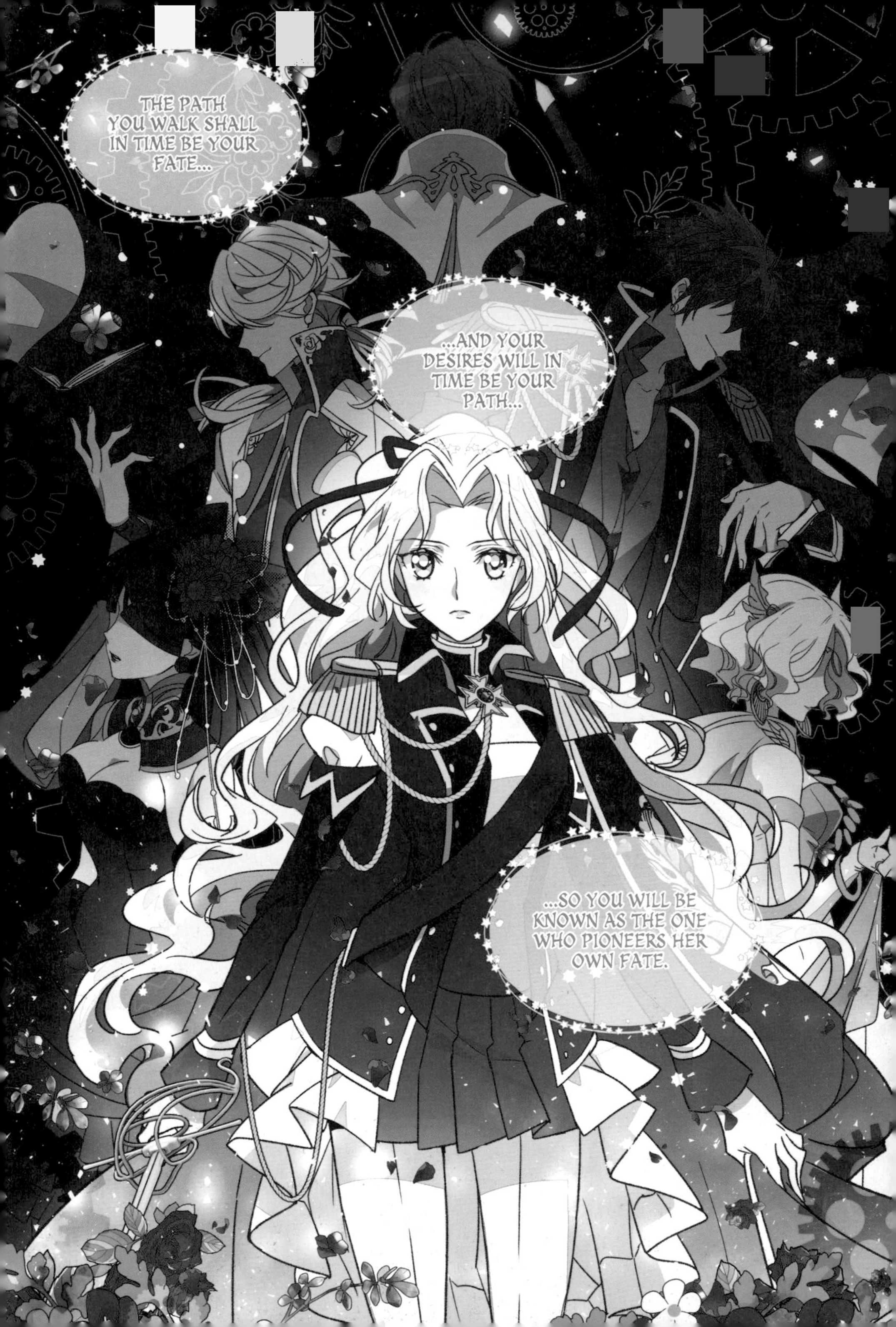
THE PATH YOU WALK SHALL IN TIME BE YOUR FATE...
...AND YOUR DESIRES WILL IN TIME BE YOUR PATH...
...SO YOU WILL BE KNOWN AS THE ONE WHO PIONEERS HER OWN FATE.

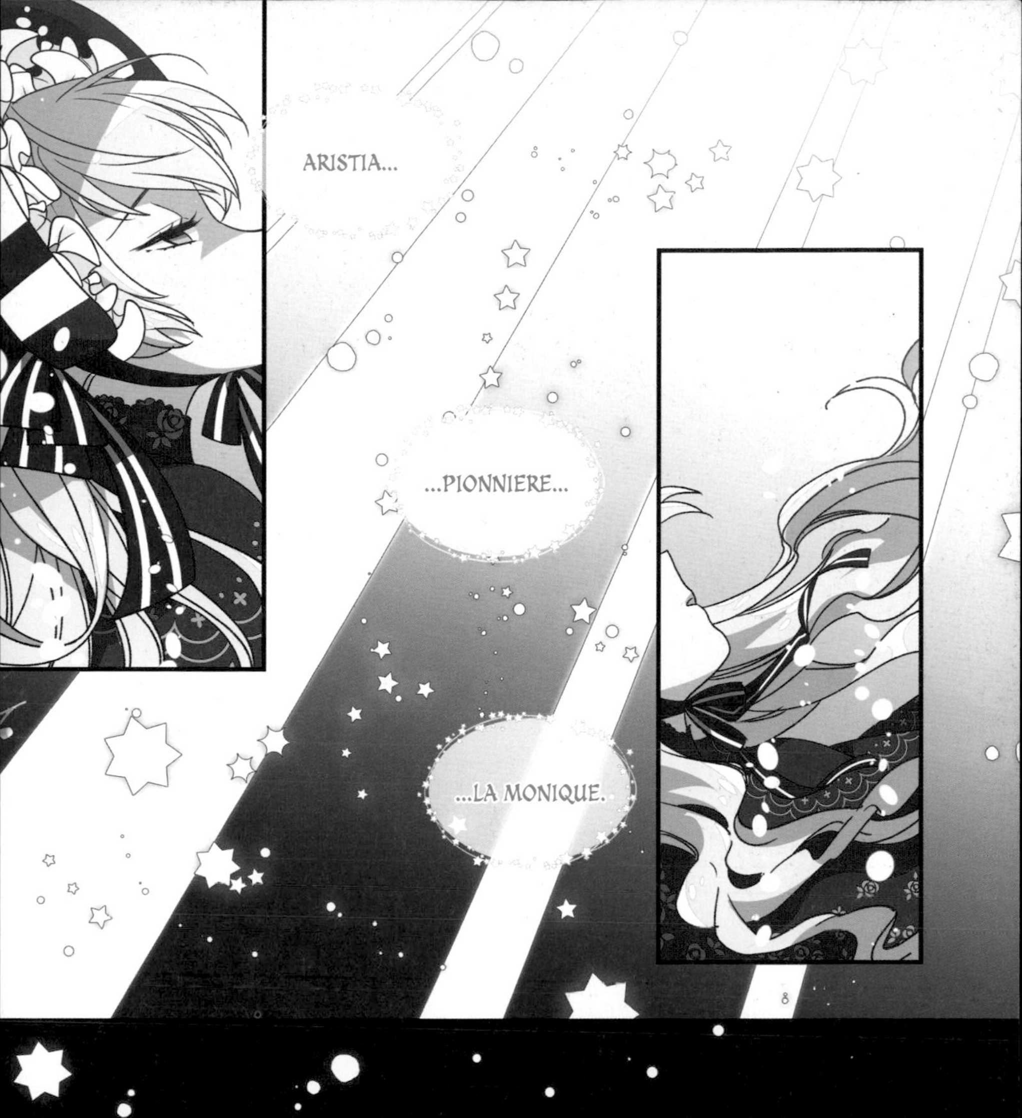
ARISTIA...
...PIONNIERE...
...LA MONIQUE.

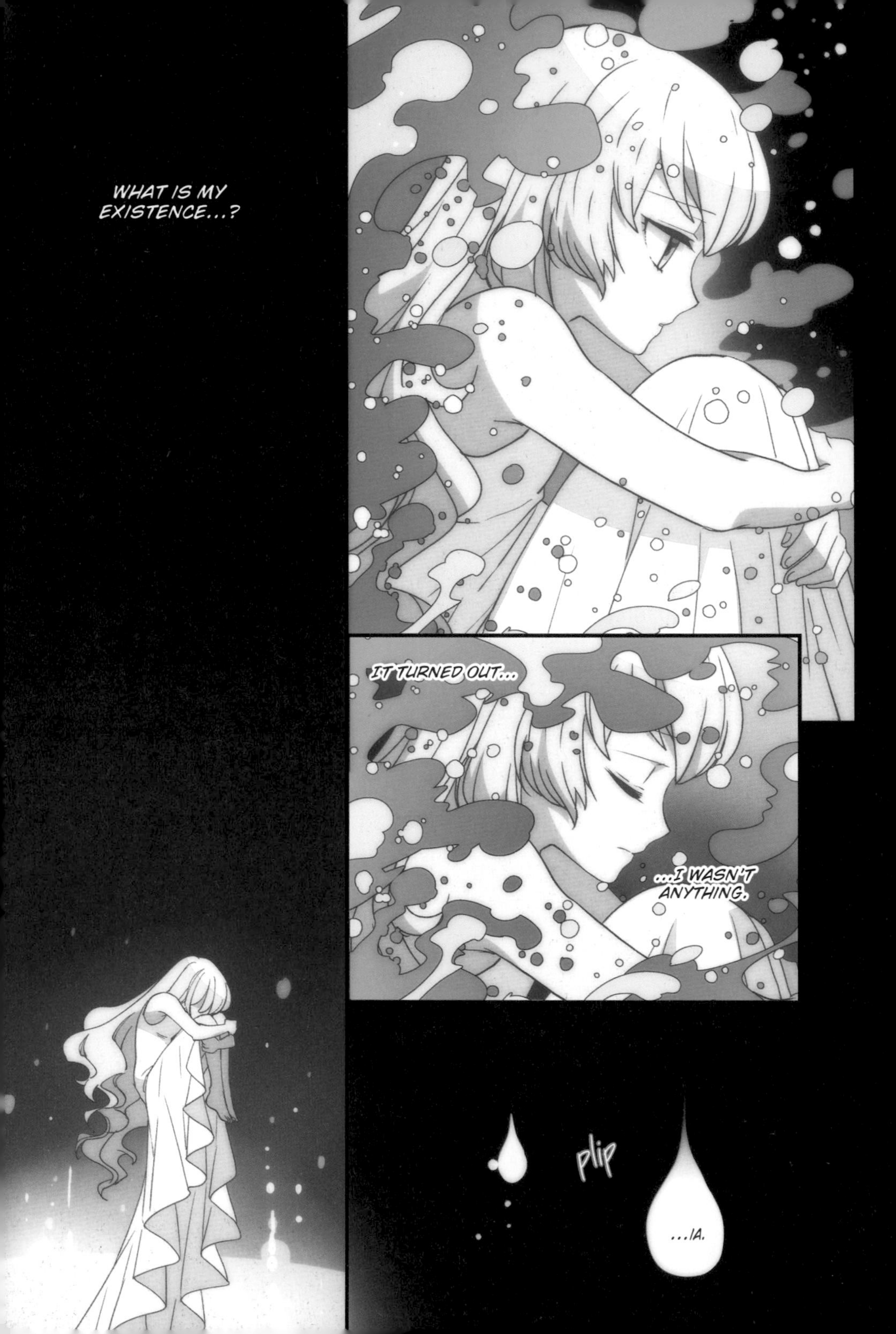
WHAT IS MY EXISTENCE...?
IT TURNED OUT...
...I WASN'T ANYTHING.
plip
...IA.

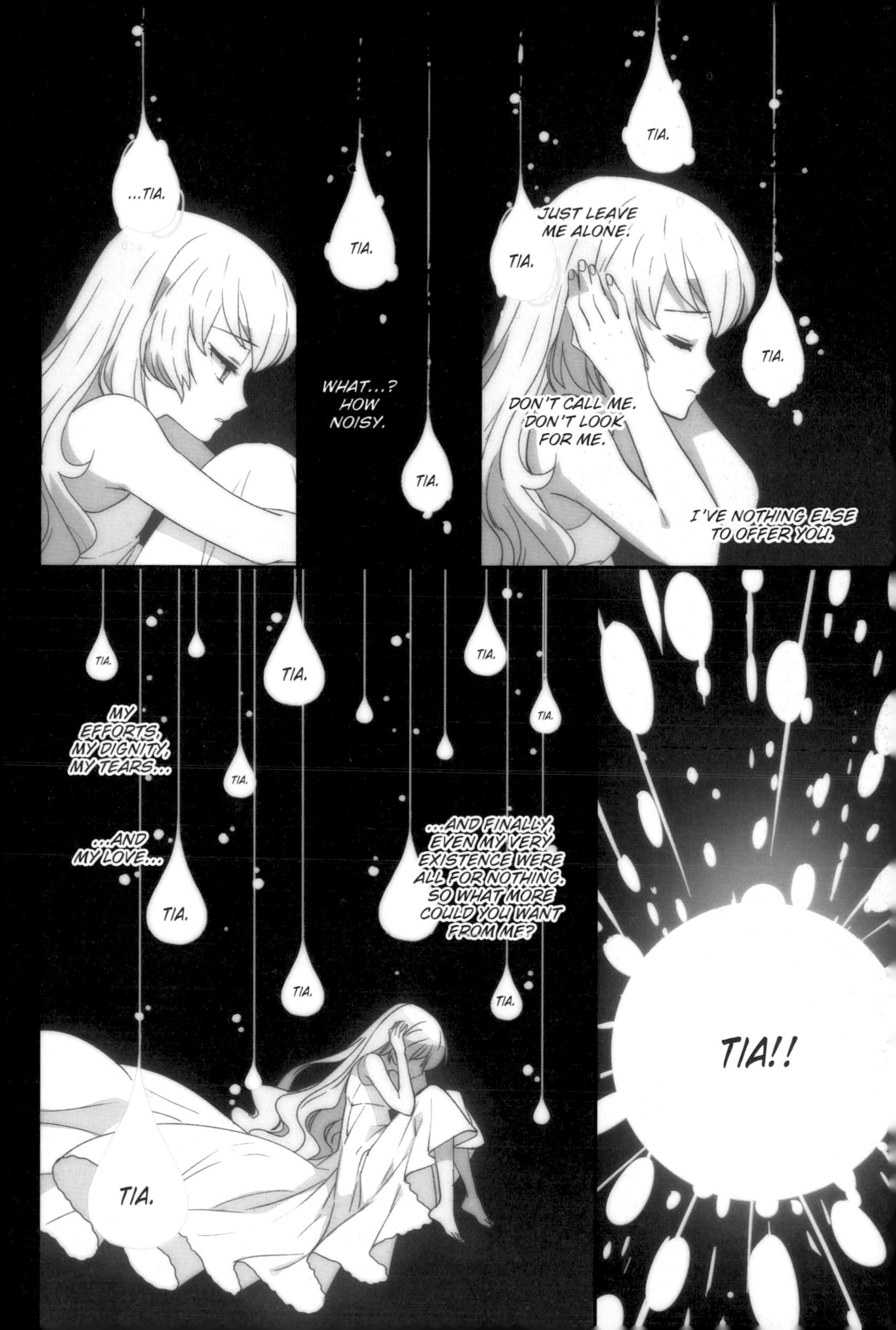
TIA.
JUST LEAVE ME ALONE.
TIA.
TIA.
DON'T CALL ME. DON'T LOOK FOR ME.
I'VE NOTHING ELSE TO OFFER YOU.
TIA.
WHAT...? HOW NOISY.
TIA.
...TIA.
TIA.
TIA.
TIA.
TIA.
MY EFFORTS, MY DIGNITY, MY TEARS...
TIA.
...AND MY LOVE...
TIA.
...AND FINALLY, EVEN MY VERY EXISTENCE WERE ALL FOR NOTHING. SO WHAT MORE COULD YOU WANT FROM ME?
TIA.
TIA.
TIA.
TIA!!

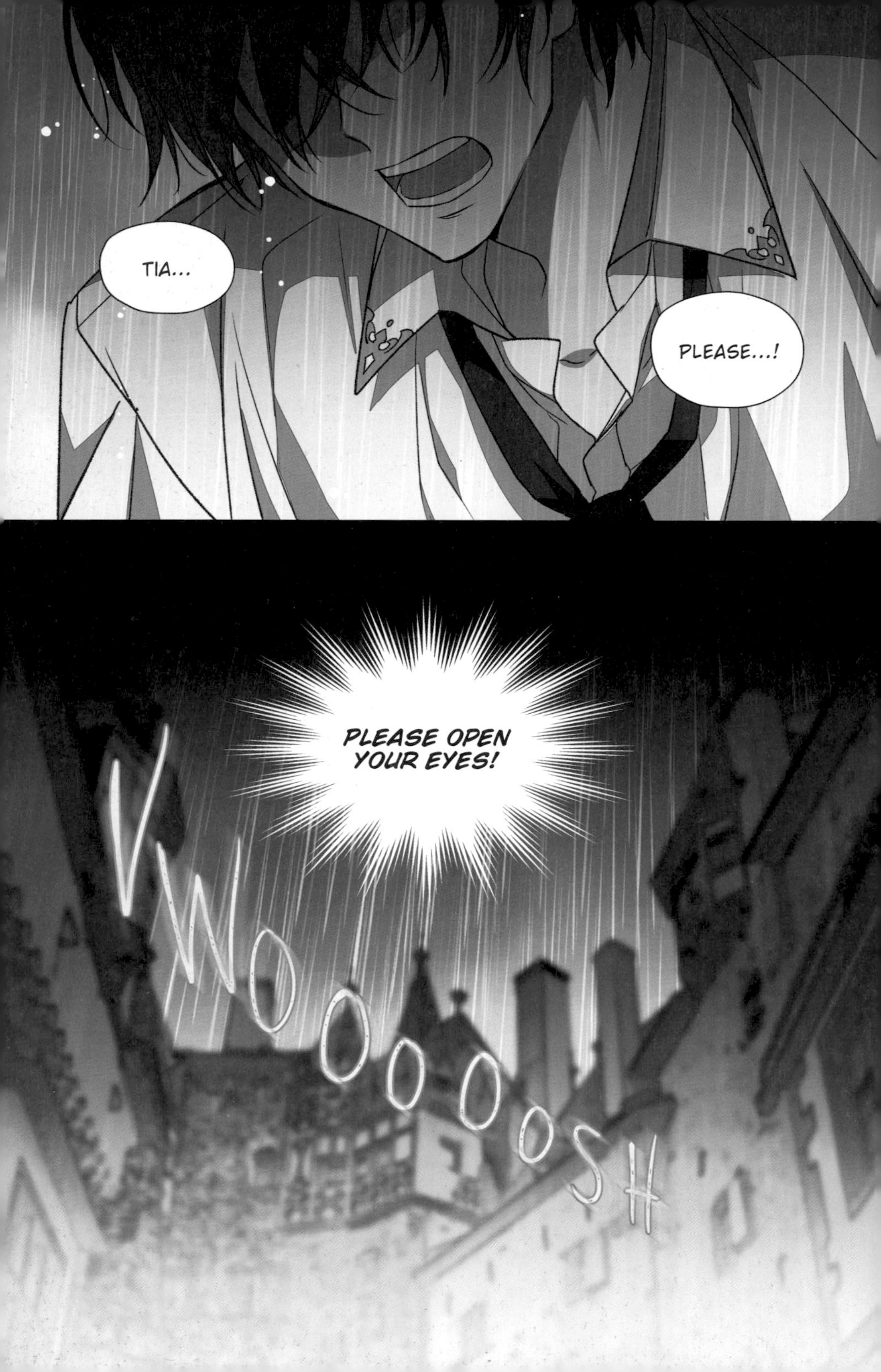
TIA...
PLEASE...!
PLEASE OPEN YOUR EYES!
VWOOOOOOOSH

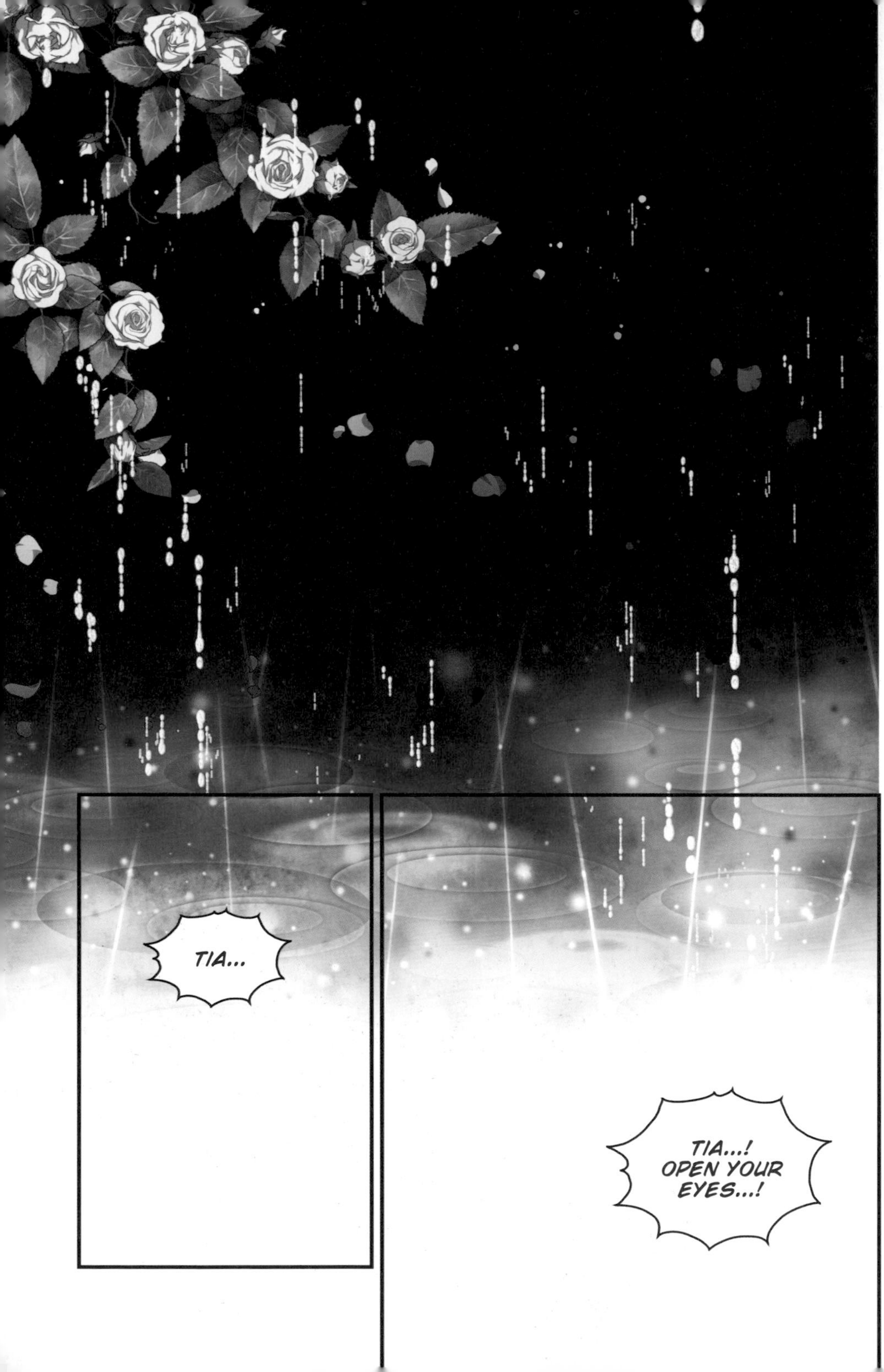
TIA...
TIA...! OPEN YOUR EYES...!

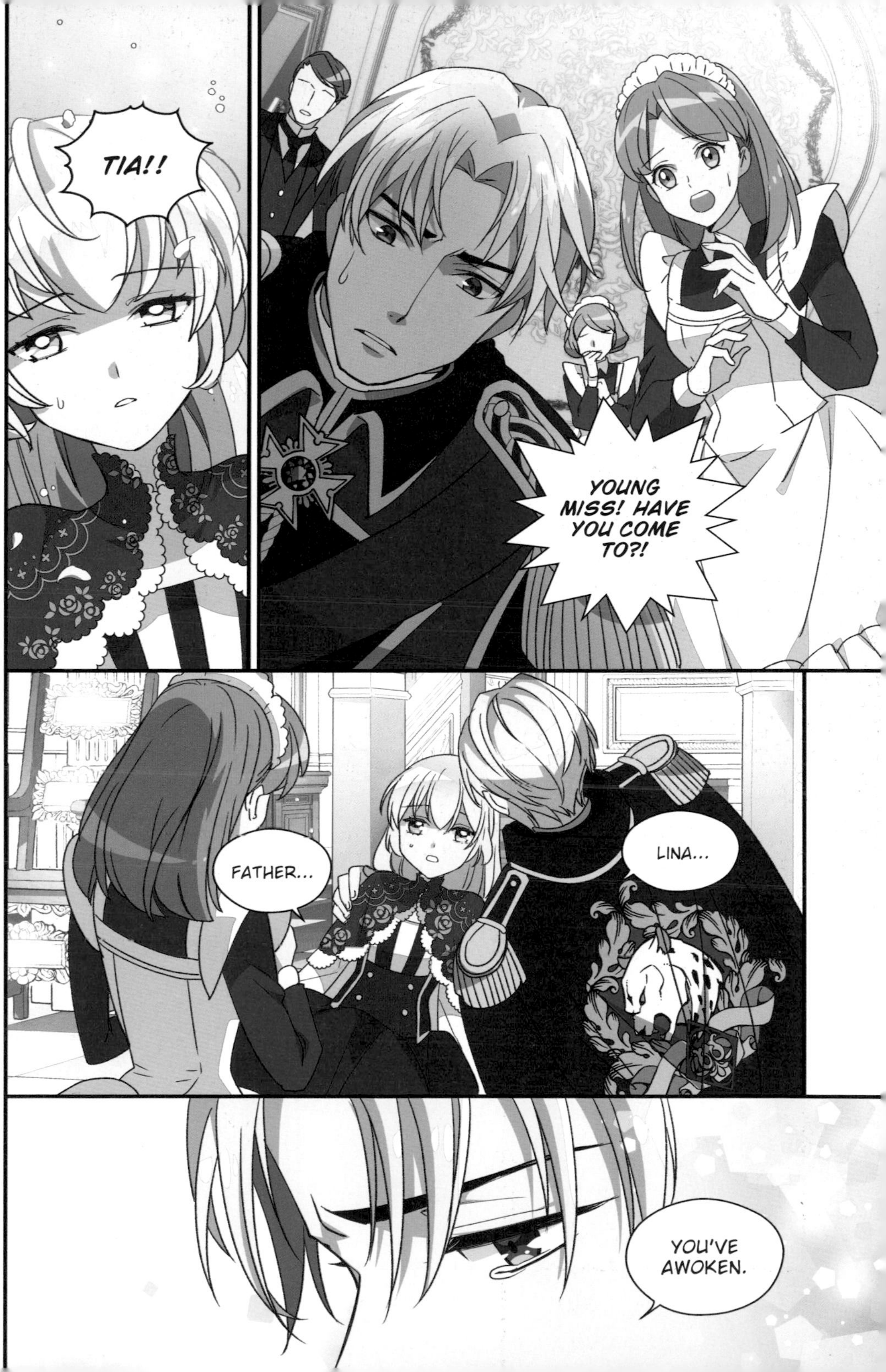
TIA!!
YOUNG MISS! HAVE YOU COME TO?!
FATHER...
LINA...
YOU'VE AWOKEN.

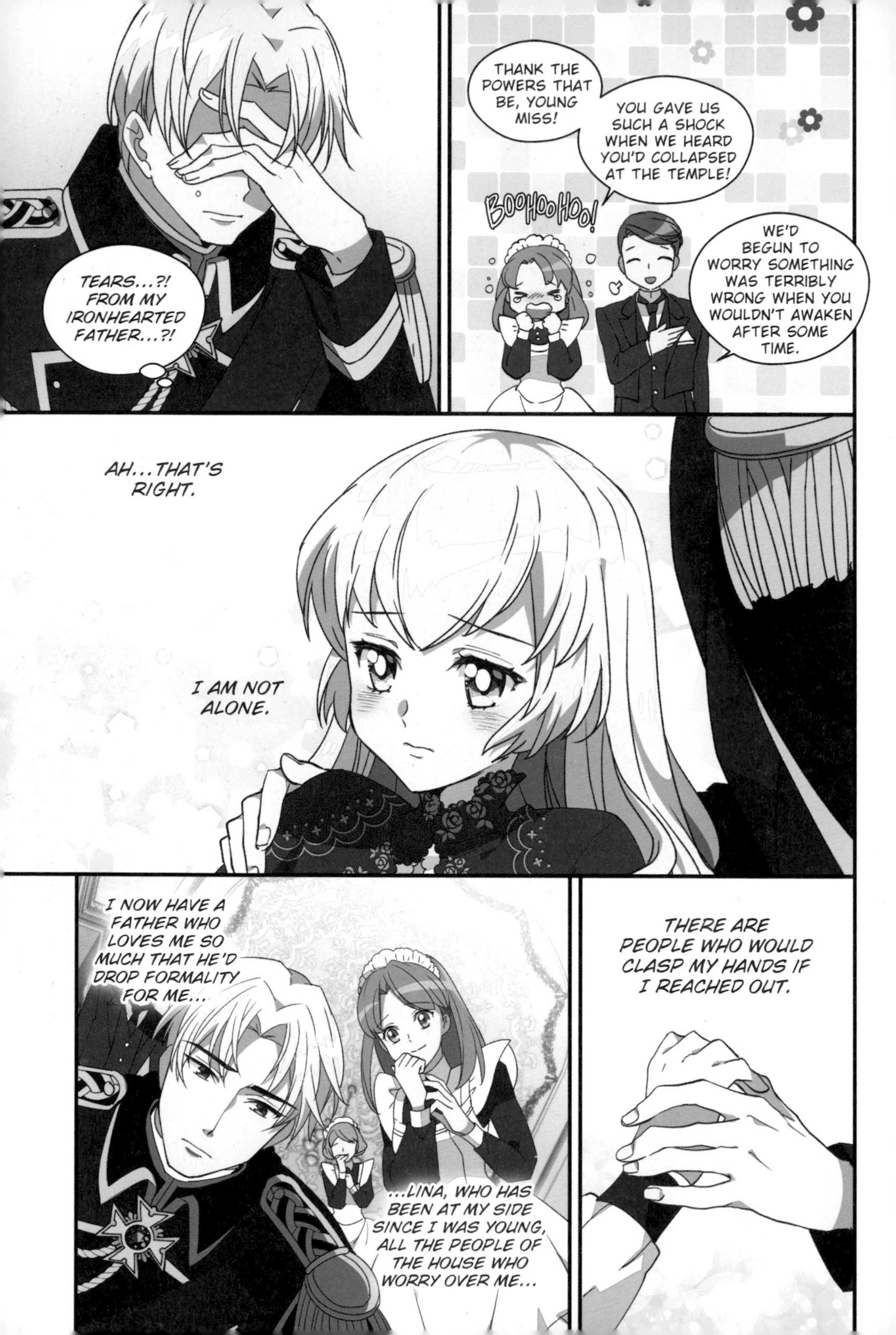
TEARS...?! FROM MY IRONHEARTED FATHER...?!
THANK THE POWERS THAT BE, YOUNG MISS!
YOU GAVE US SUCH A SHOCK WHEN WE HEARD YOU'D COLLAPSED AT THE TEMPLE!
BOOHOOHOO!
WE'D BEGUN TO WORRY SOMETHING WAS TERRIBLY WRONG WHEN YOU WOULDN'T AWAKEN AFTER SOME TIME.
AH...THAT'S RIGHT.
I AM NOT ALONE.
I NOW HAVE A FATHER WHO LOVES ME SO MUCH THAT HE'D DROP FORMALITY FOR ME...
...LINA, WHO HAS BEEN AT MY SIDE SINCE I WAS YOUNG, ALL THE PEOPLE OF THE HOUSE WHO WORRY OVER ME...
THERE ARE PEOPLE WHO WOULD CLASP MY HANDS IF I REACHED OUT.

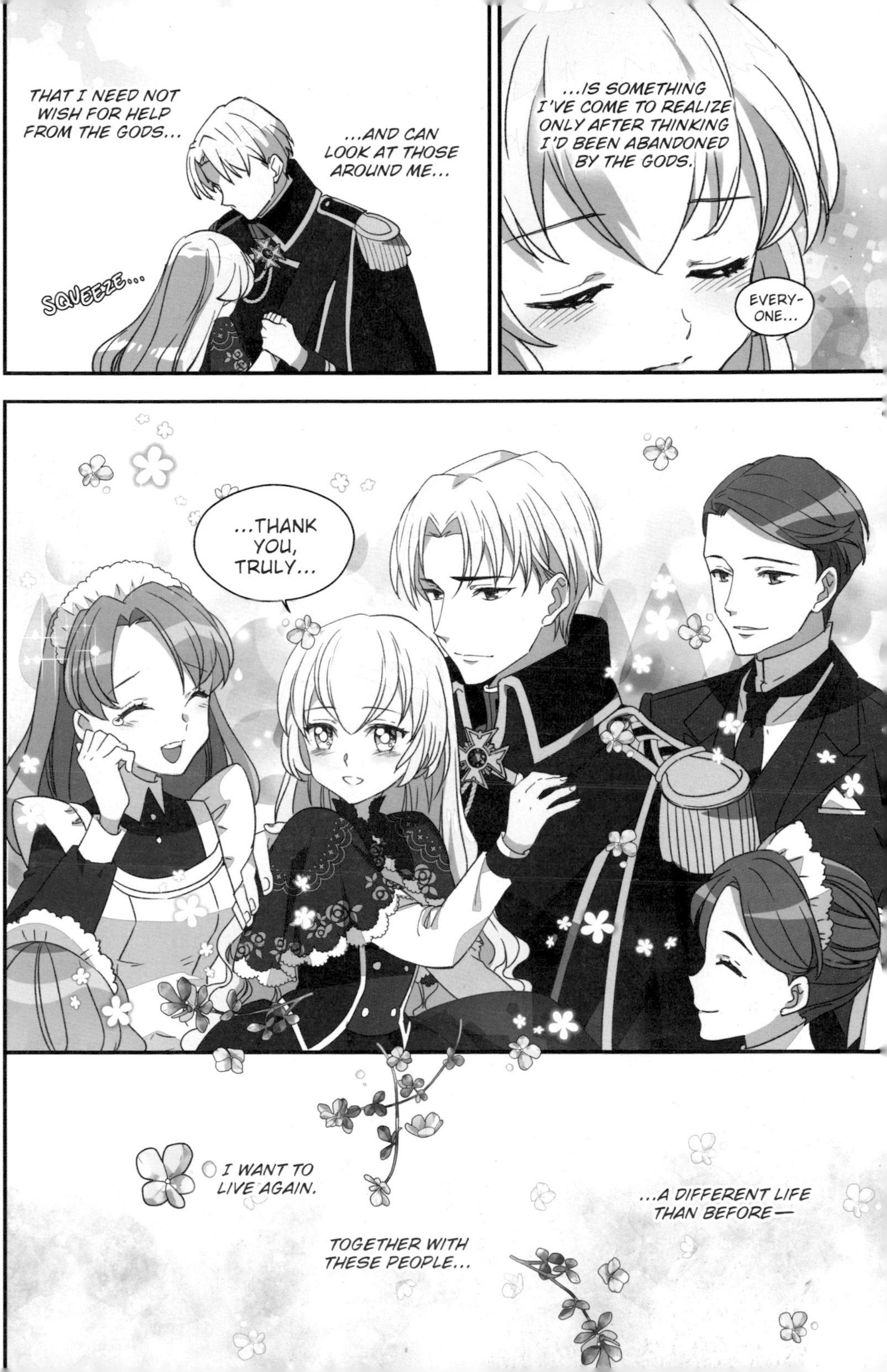
THAT I NEED NOT WISH FOR HELP FROM THE GODS...
...AND CAN LOOK AT THOSE AROUND ME...
SQUEEZE...
...IS SOMETHING I'VE COME TO REALIZE ONLY AFTER THINKING I'D BEEN ABANDONED BY THE GODS.
EVERY-ONE...
...THANK YOU, TRULY...
I WANT TO LIVE AGAIN.
TOGETHER WITH THESE PEOPLE...
...A DIFFERENT LIFE THAN BEFORE—

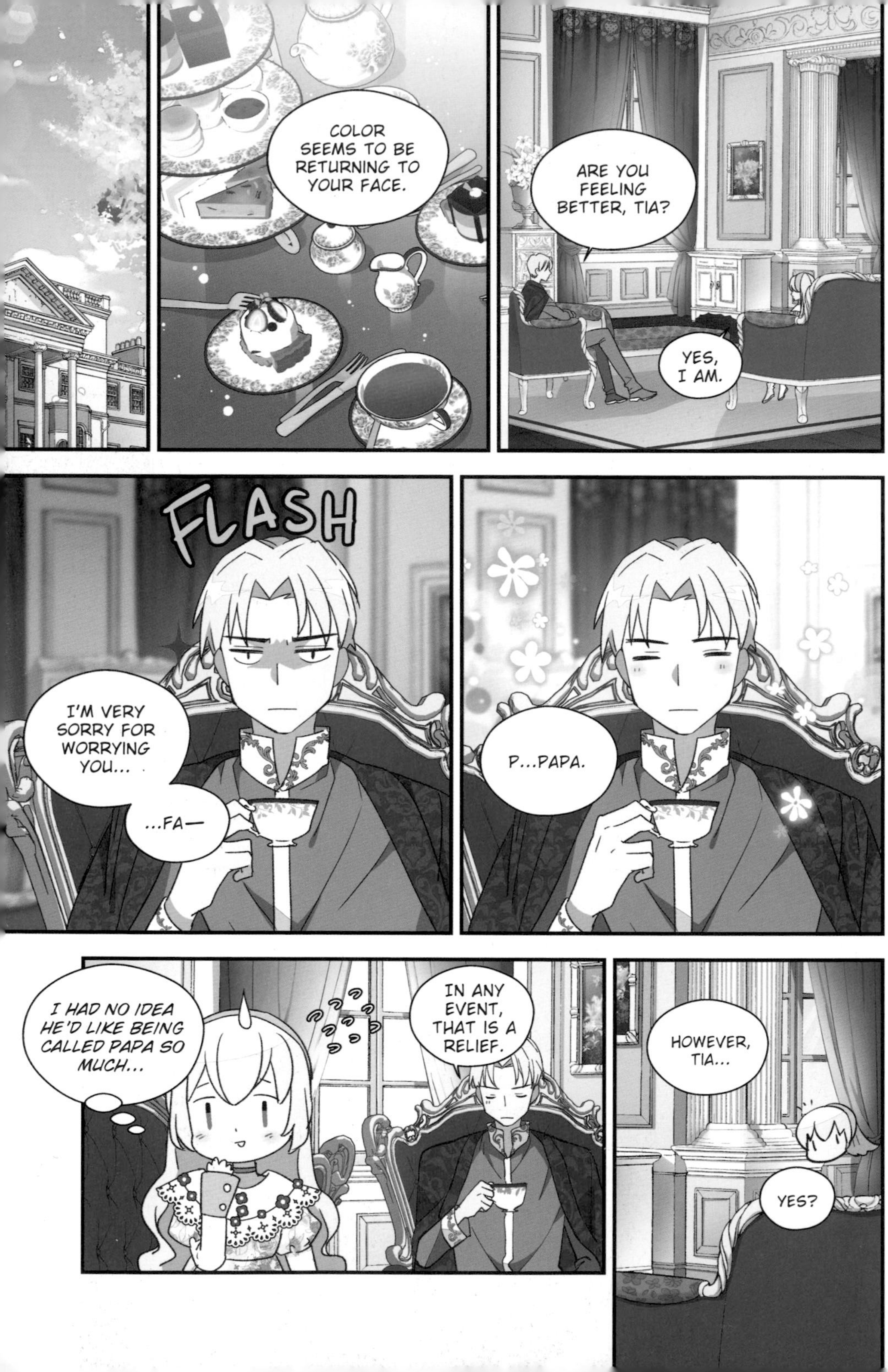
COLOR SEEMS TO BE RETURNING TO YOUR FACE.
ARE YOU FEELING BETTER, TIA?
YES, I AM.
FLASH
I'M VERY SORRY FOR WORRYING YOU...
...FA—
P...PAPA.
I HAD NO IDEA HE'D LIKE BEING CALLED PAPA SO MUCH...
IN ANY EVENT, THAT IS A RELIEF.
HOWEVER, TIA...
YES?

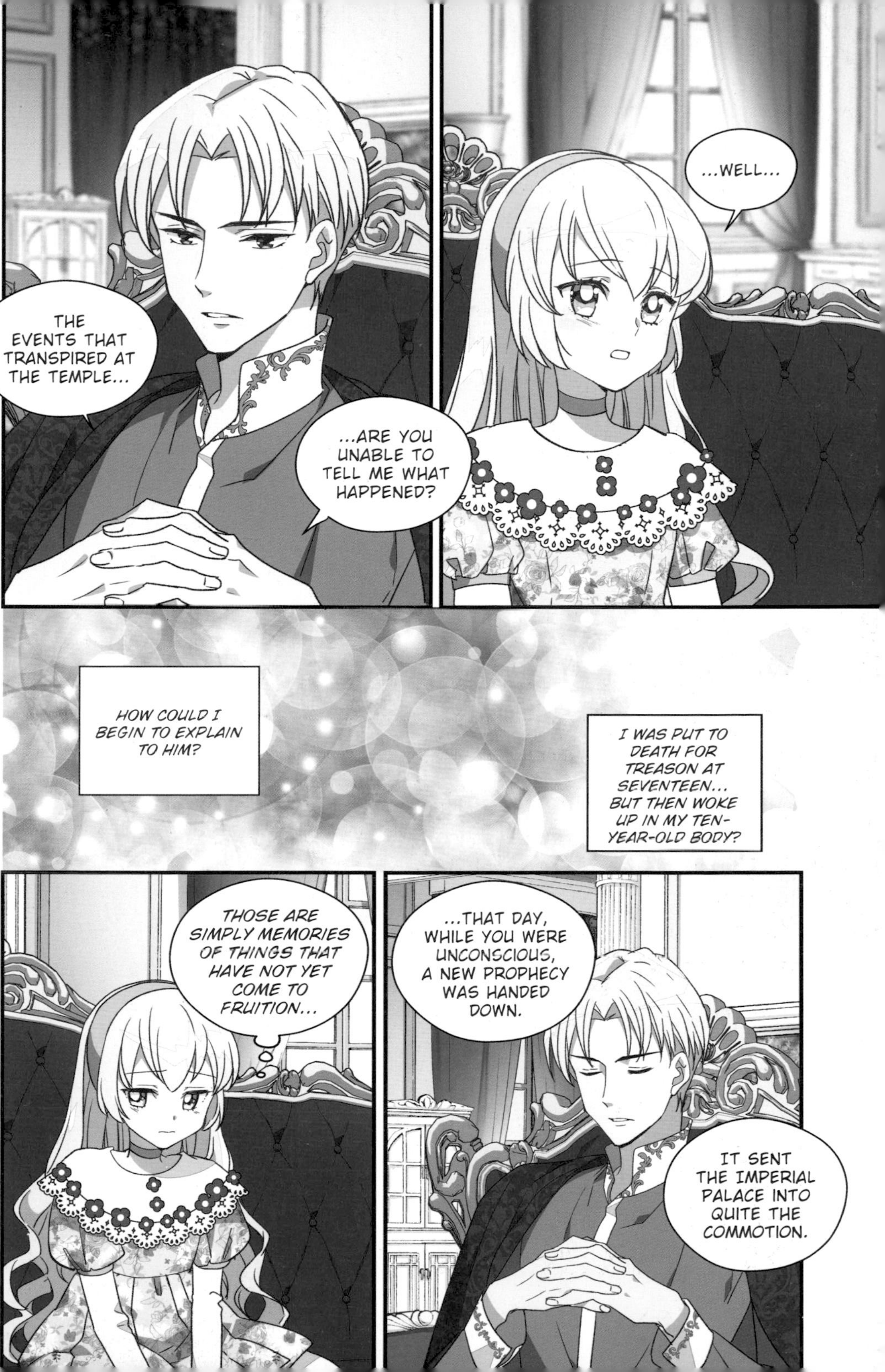
THE EVENTS THAT TRANSPIRED AT THE TEMPLE...
...ARE YOU UNABLE TO TELL ME WHAT HAPPENED?
...WELL...
HOW COULD I BEGIN TO EXPLAIN TO HIM?
I WAS PUT TO DEATH FOR TREASON AT SEVENTEEN... BUT THEN WOKE UP IN MY TEN-YEAR-OLD BODY?
THOSE ARE SIMPLY MEMORIES OF THINGS THAT HAVE NOT YET COME TO FRUITION...
...THAT DAY, WHILE YOU WERE UNCONSCIOUS, A NEW PROPHECY WAS HANDED DOWN.
IT SENT THE IMPERIAL PALACE INTO QUITE THE COMMOTION.

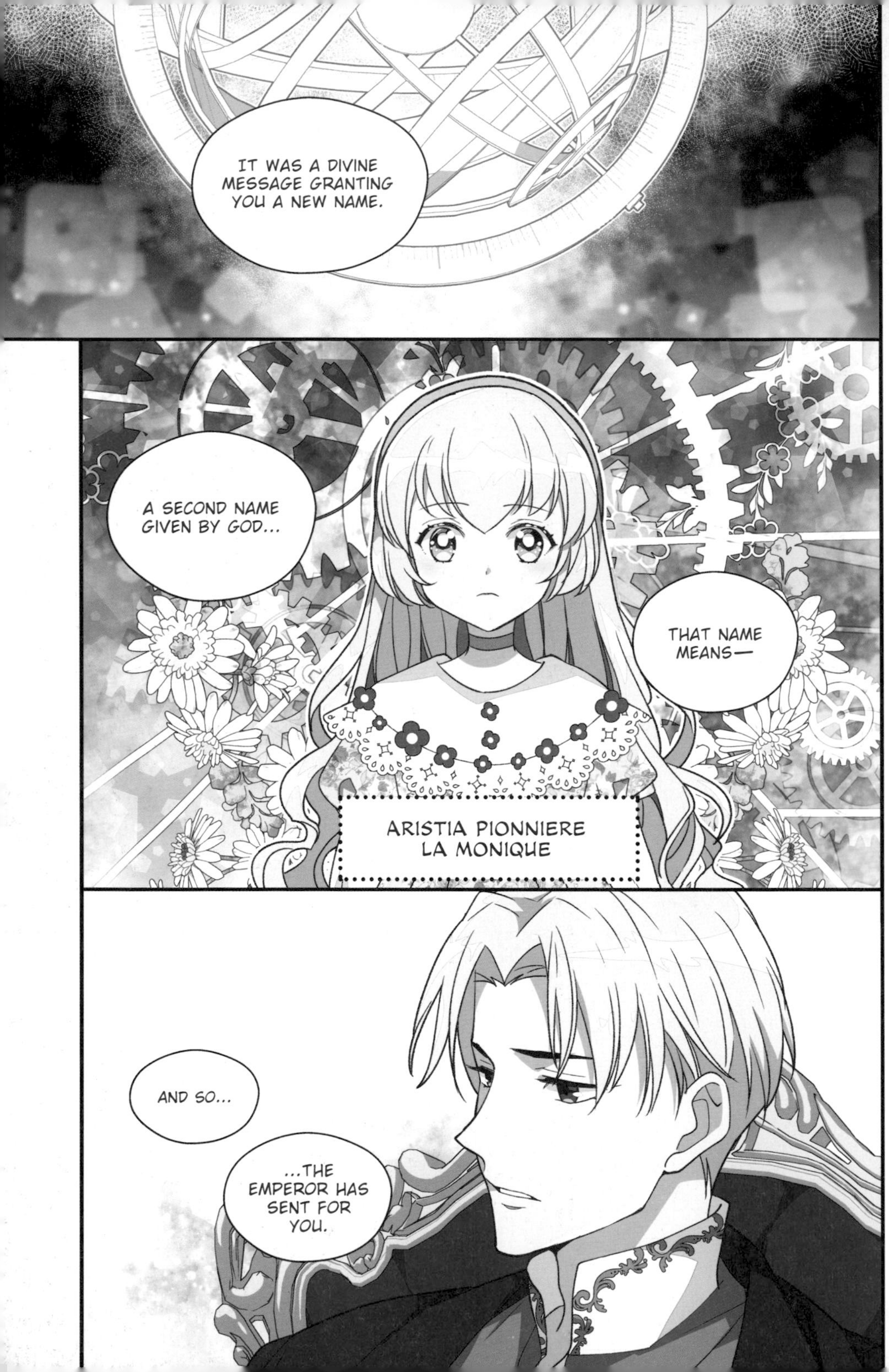
IT WAS A DIVINE MESSAGE GRANTING YOU A NEW NAME.
A SECOND NAME GIVEN BY GOD...
THAT NAME MEANS—
ARISTIA PIONNIERE LA MONIQUE
AND SO...
...THE EMPEROR HAS SENT FOR YOU.

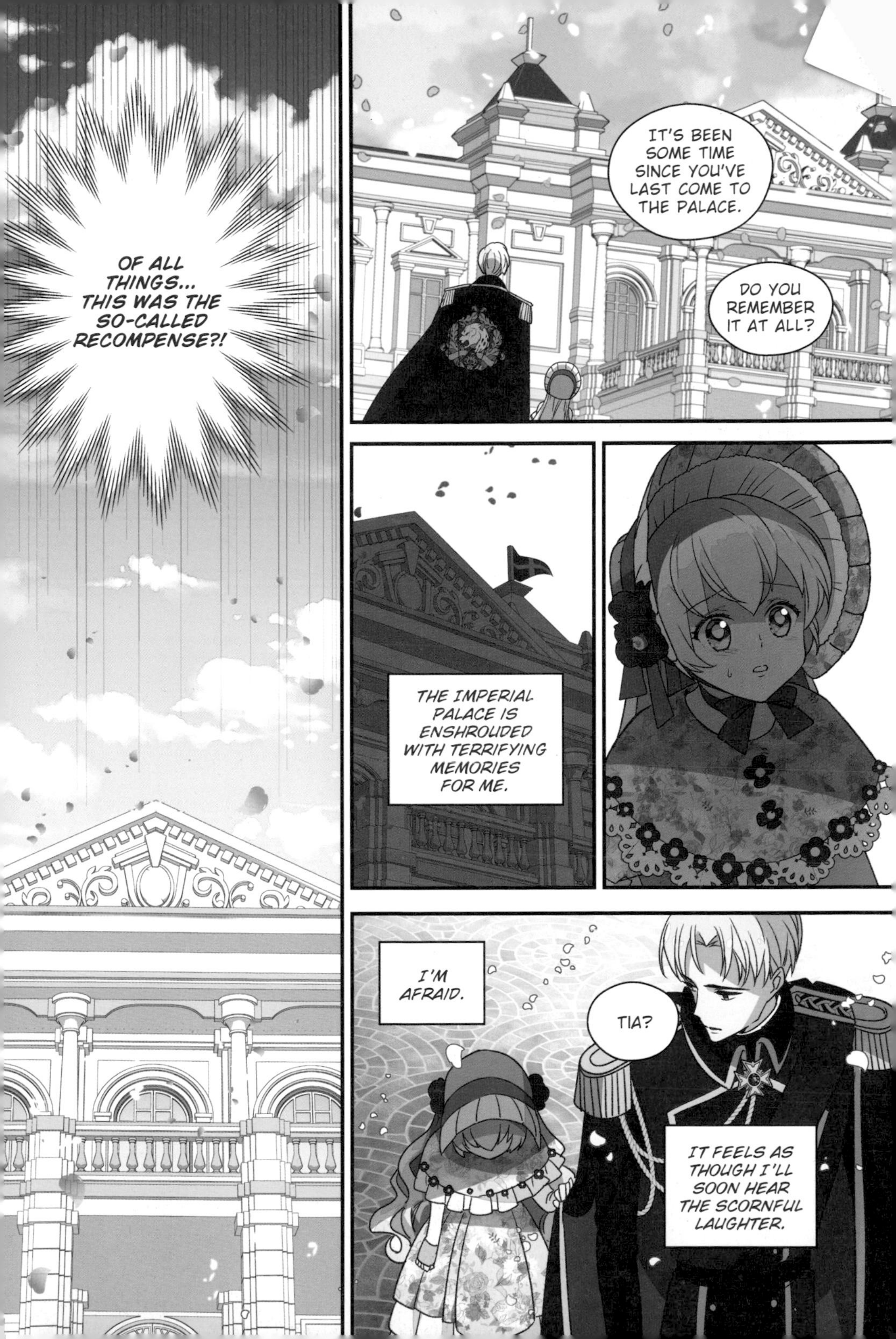
OF ALL THINGS... THIS WAS THE SO-CALLED RECOMPENSE?!
IT'S BEEN SOME TIME SINCE YOU'VE LAST COME TO THE PALACE.
DO YOU REMEMBER IT AT ALL?
THE IMPERIAL PALACE IS ENSHROUDED WITH TERRIFYING MEMORIES FOR ME.
I'M AFRAID.
TIA?
IT FEELS AS THOUGH I'LL SOON HEAR THE SCORNFUL LAUGHTER.

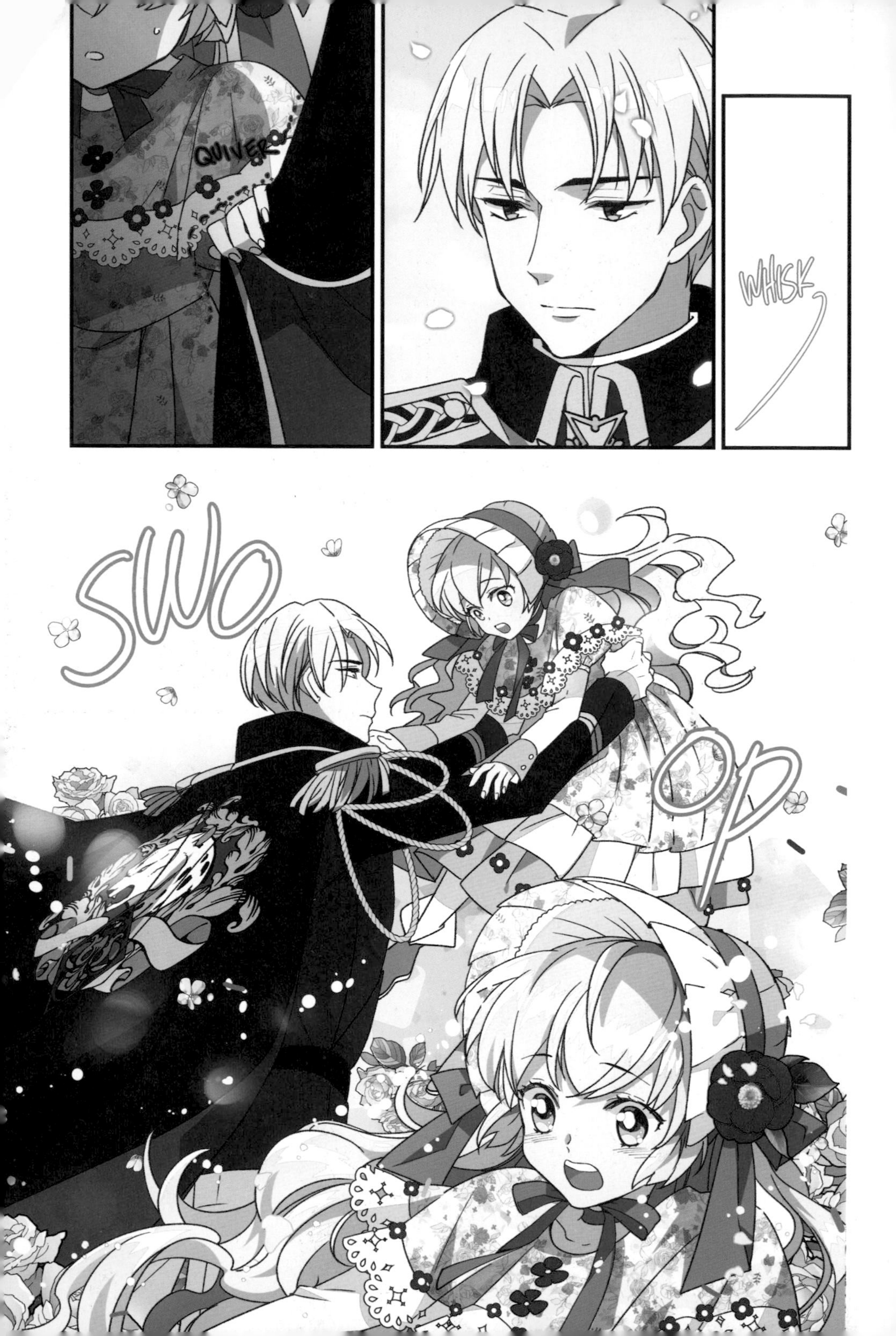
QUIVER
WHISK
SWOOP

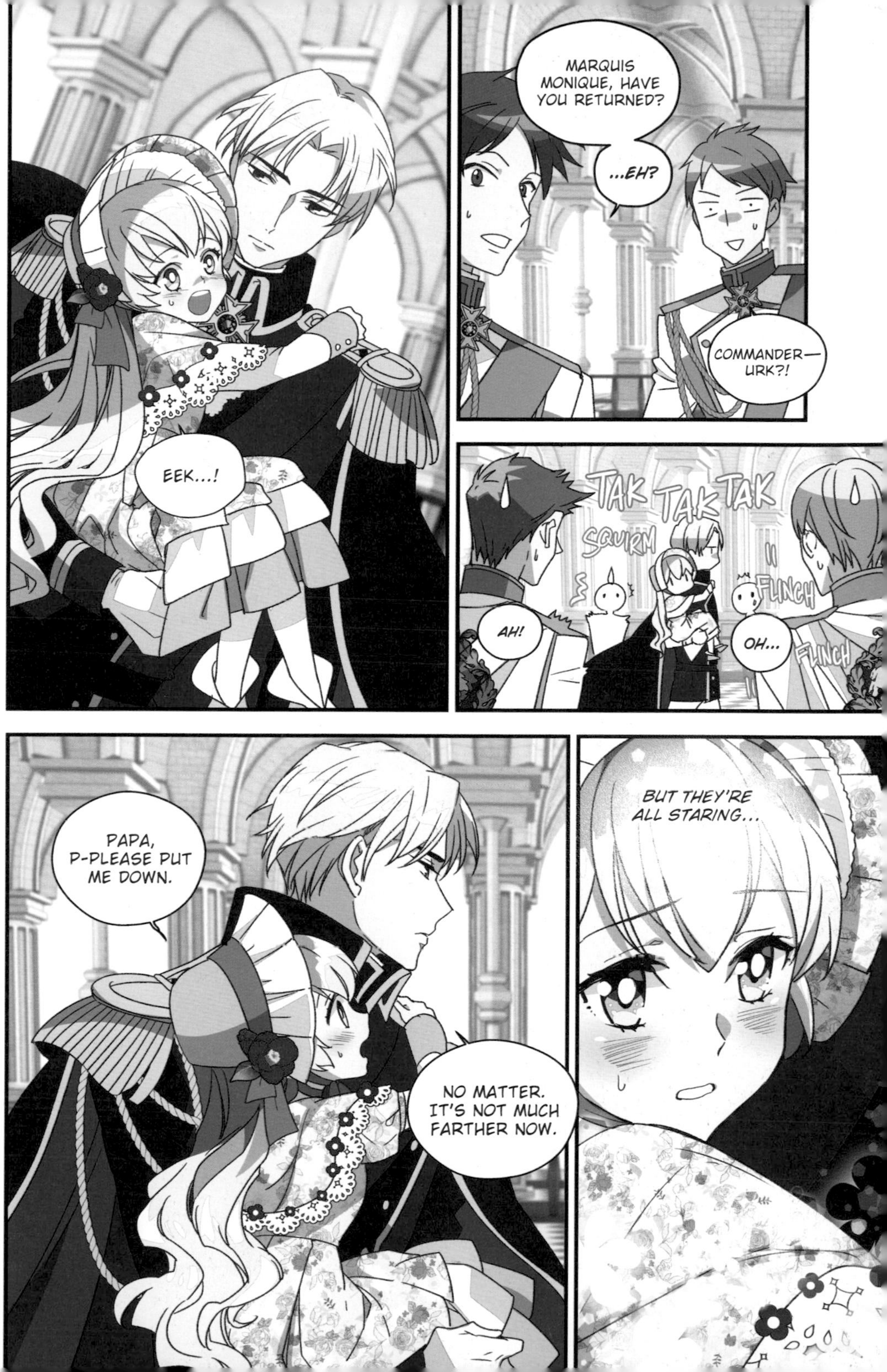
EEK...!
MARQUIS MONIQUE, HAVE YOU RETURNED?
...EH?
COMMANDER—URK?!
TAK TAK TAK
SQUIRM
FLINCH
AH!
OH...
FLINCH
PAPA, P-PLEASE PUT ME DOWN.
NO MATTER. IT'S NOT MUCH FARTHER NOW.
BUT THEY'RE ALL STARING...

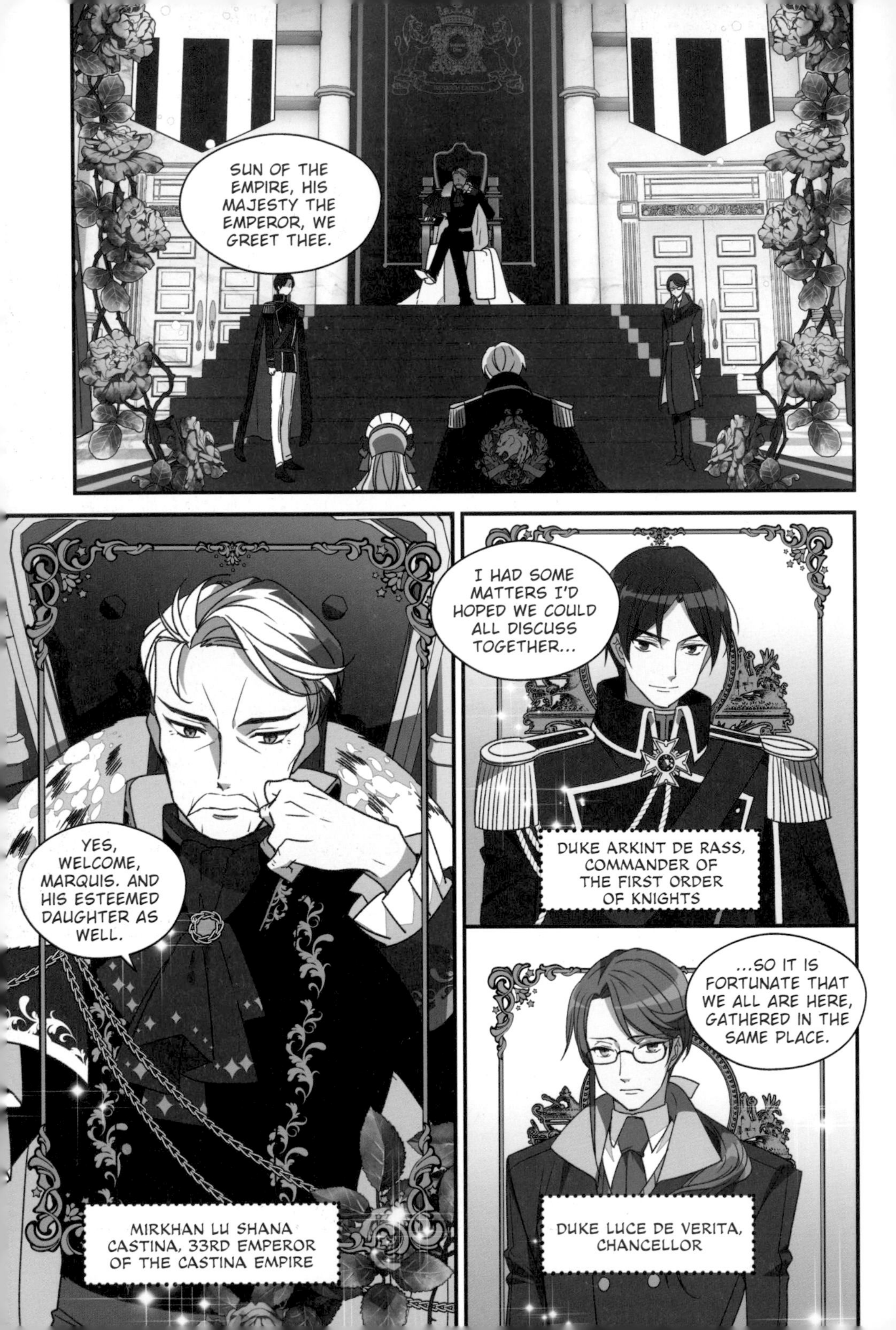
SUN OF THE EMPIRE, HIS MAJESTY THE EMPEROR, WE GREET THEE.
MIRKHAN LU SHANA CASTINA, 33RD EMPEROR OF THE CASTINA EMPIRE
YES, WELCOME, MARQUIS. AND HIS ESTEEMED DAUGHTER AS WELL.
I HAD SOME MATTERS I'D HOPED WE COULD ALL DISCUSS TOGETHER...
DUKE ARKINT DE RASS, COMMANDER OF THE FIRST ORDER OF KNIGHTS
...SO IT IS FORTUNATE THAT WE ALL ARE HERE, GATHERED IN THE SAME PLACE.
DUKE LUCE DE VERITA, CHANCELLOR

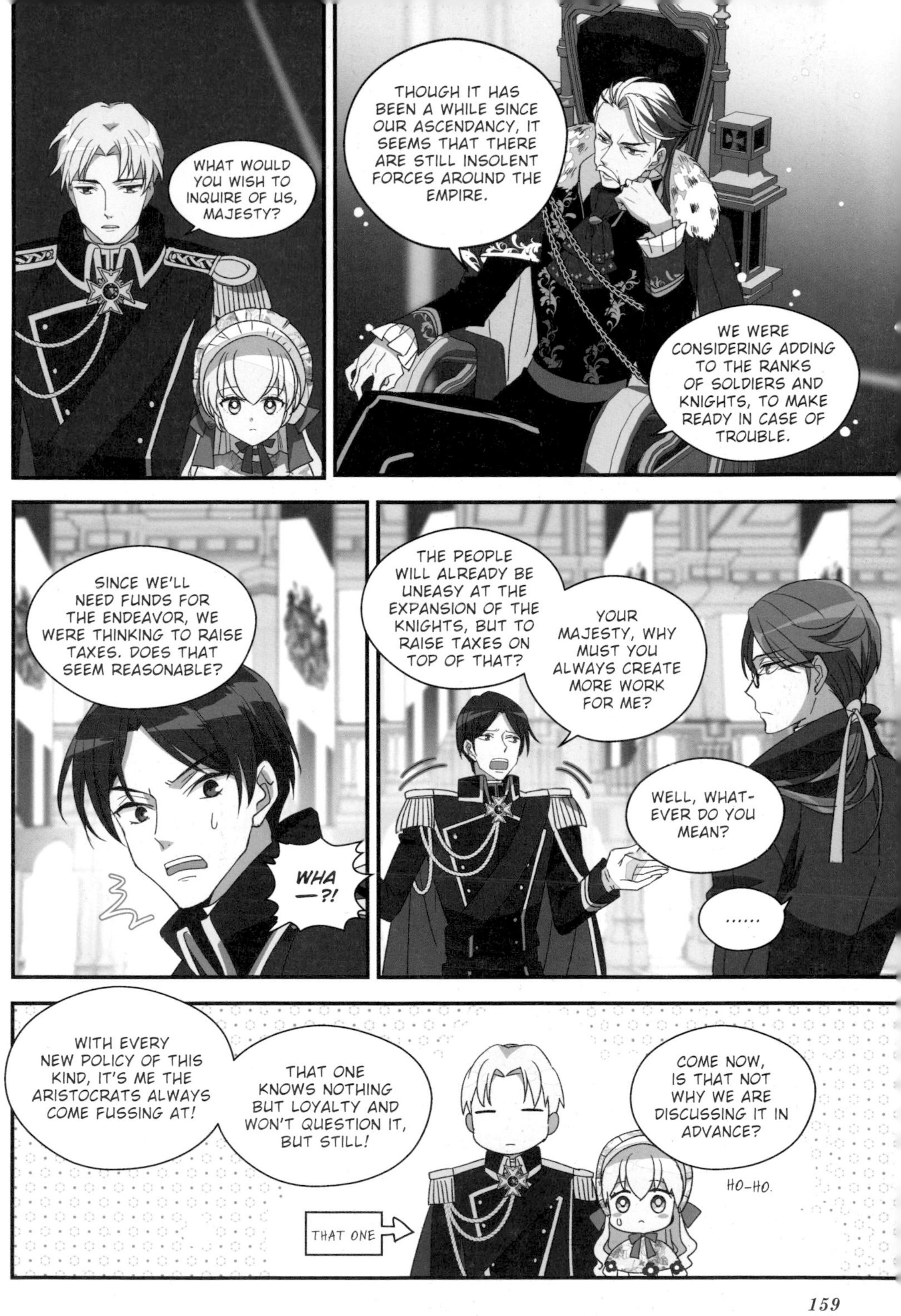
WHAT WOULD YOU WISH TO INQUIRE OF US, MAJESTY?
THOUGH IT HAS BEEN A WHILE SINCE OUR ASCENDANCY, IT SEEMS THAT THERE ARE STILL INSOLENT FORCES AROUND THE EMPIRE.
WE WERE CONSIDERING ADDING TO THE RANKS OF SOLDIERS AND KNIGHTS, TO MAKE READY IN CASE OF TROUBLE.
SINCE WE'LL NEED FUNDS FOR THE ENDEAVOR, WE WERE THINKING TO RAISE TAXES. DOES THAT SEEM REASONABLE?
WHA—?!
THE PEOPLE WILL ALREADY BE UNEASY AT THE EXPANSION OF THE KNIGHTS, BUT TO RAISE TAXES ON TOP OF THAT?
YOUR MAJESTY, WHY MUST YOU ALWAYS CREATE MORE WORK FOR ME?
WELL, WHAT-EVER DO YOU MEAN?
......
WITH EVERY NEW POLICY OF THIS KIND, IT'S ME THE ARISTOCRATS ALWAYS COME FUSSING AT!
THAT ONE KNOWS NOTHING BUT LOYALTY AND WON'T QUESTION IT, BUT STILL!
COME NOW, IS THAT NOT WHY WE ARE DISCUSSING IT IN ADVANCE?
HO-HO.
THAT ONE

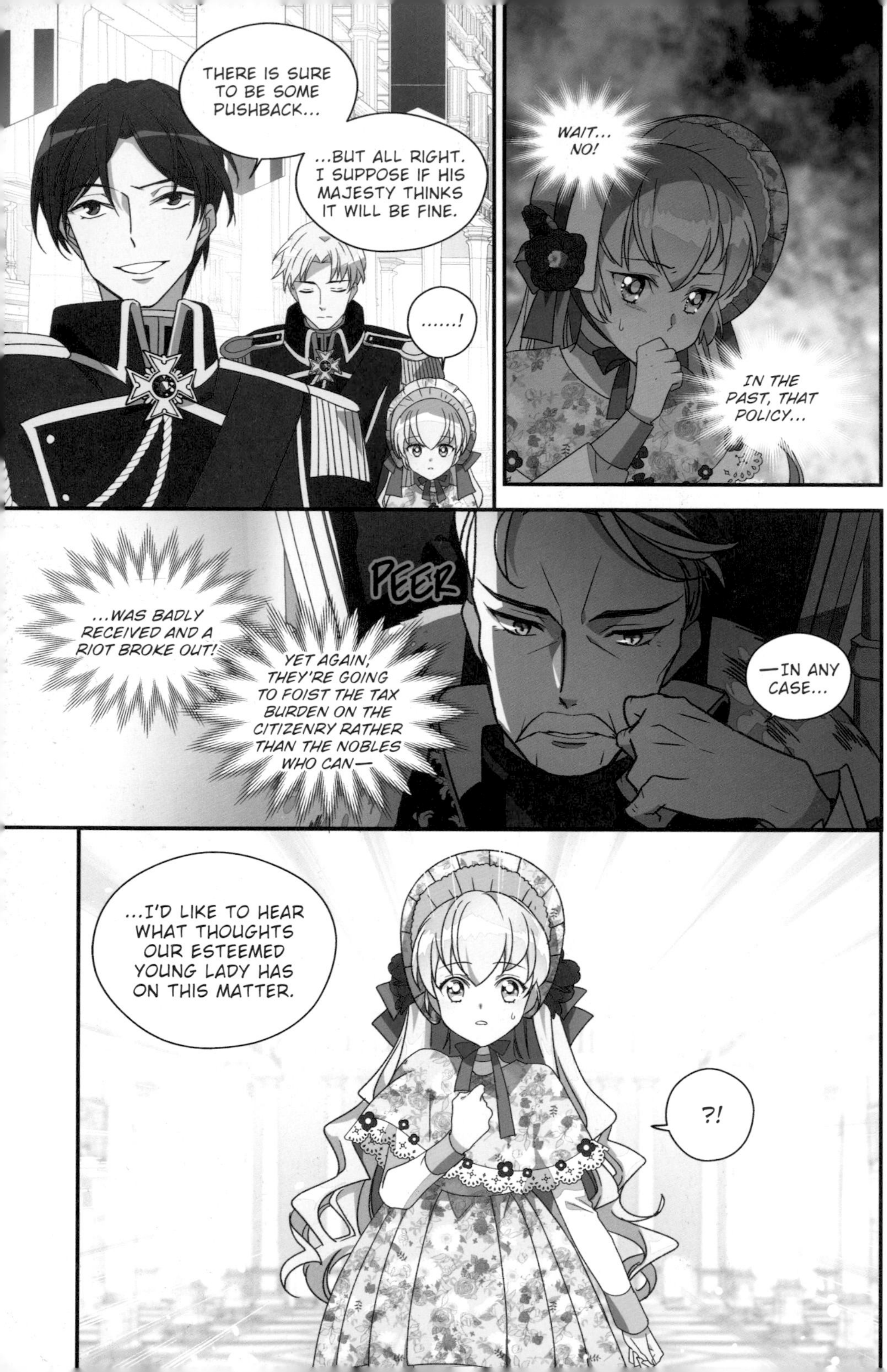
THERE IS SURE TO BE SOME PUSHBACK...
...BUT ALL RIGHT. I SUPPOSE IF HIS MAJESTY THINKS IT WILL BE FINE.
......!
WAIT... NO!
IN THE PAST, THAT POLICY...
...WAS BADLY RECEIVED AND A RIOT BROKE OUT!
YET AGAIN, THEY'RE GOING TO FOIST THE TAX BURDEN ON THE CITIZENRY RATHER THAN THE NOBLES WHO CAN—
PEER
—IN ANY CASE...
...I'D LIKE TO HEAR WHAT THOUGHTS OUR ESTEEMED YOUNG LADY HAS ON THIS MATTER.
?!

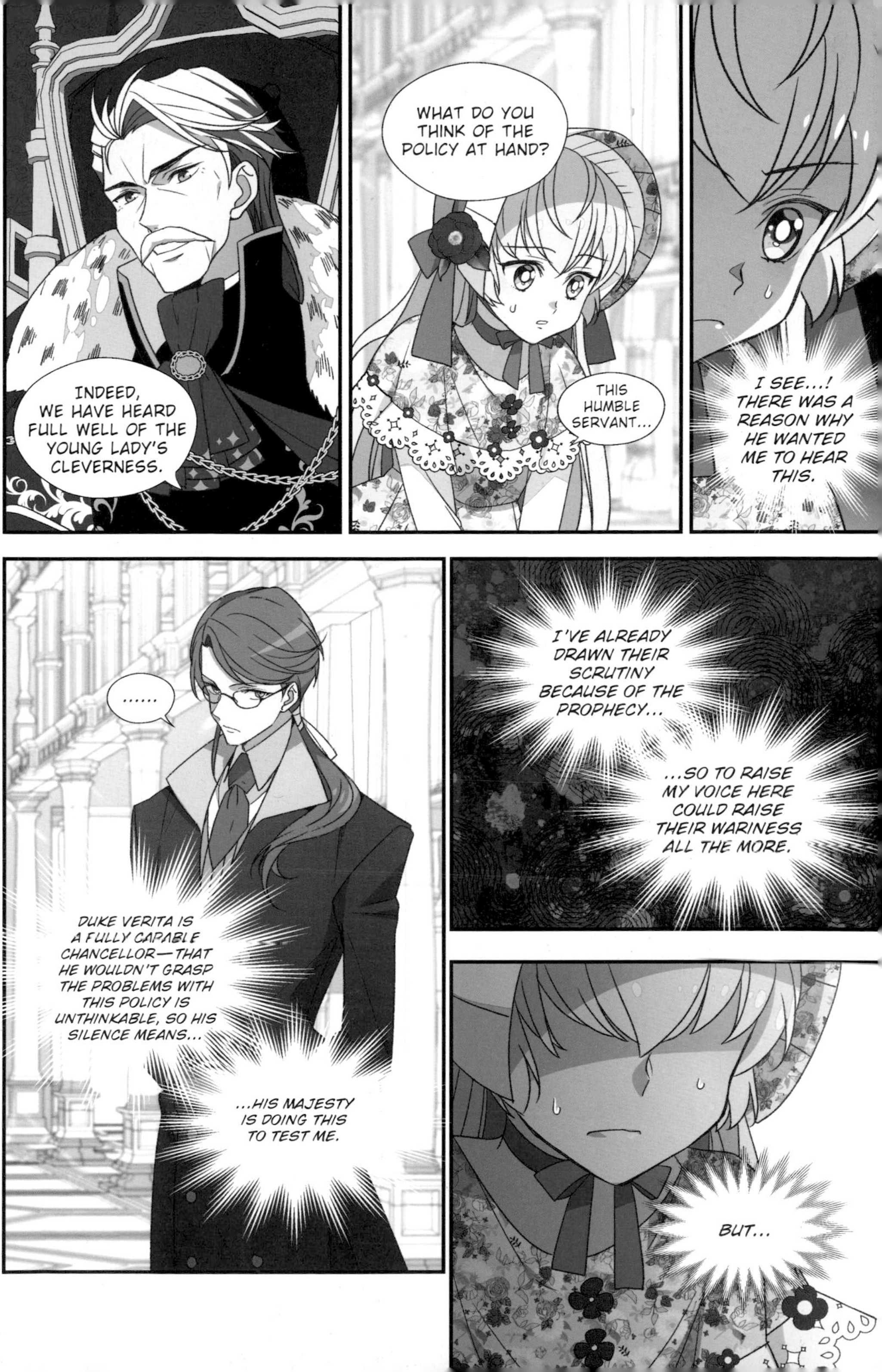
INDEED, WE HAVE HEARD FULL WELL OF THE YOUNG LADY'S CLEVERNESS.
WHAT DO YOU THINK OF THE POLICY AT HAND?
THIS HUMBLE SERVANT...
I SEE...! THERE WAS A REASON WHY HE WANTED ME TO HEAR THIS.
......
DUKE VERITA IS A FULLY CAPABLE CHANCELLOR—THAT HE WOULDN'T GRASP THE PROBLEMS WITH THIS POLICY IS UNTHINKABLE, SO HIS SILENCE MEANS...
...HIS MAJESTY IS DOING THIS TO TEST ME.
I'VE ALREADY DRAWN THEIR SCRUTINY BECAUSE OF THE PROPHECY...
...SO TO RAISE MY VOICE HERE COULD RAISE THEIR WARINESS ALL THE MORE.
BUT...

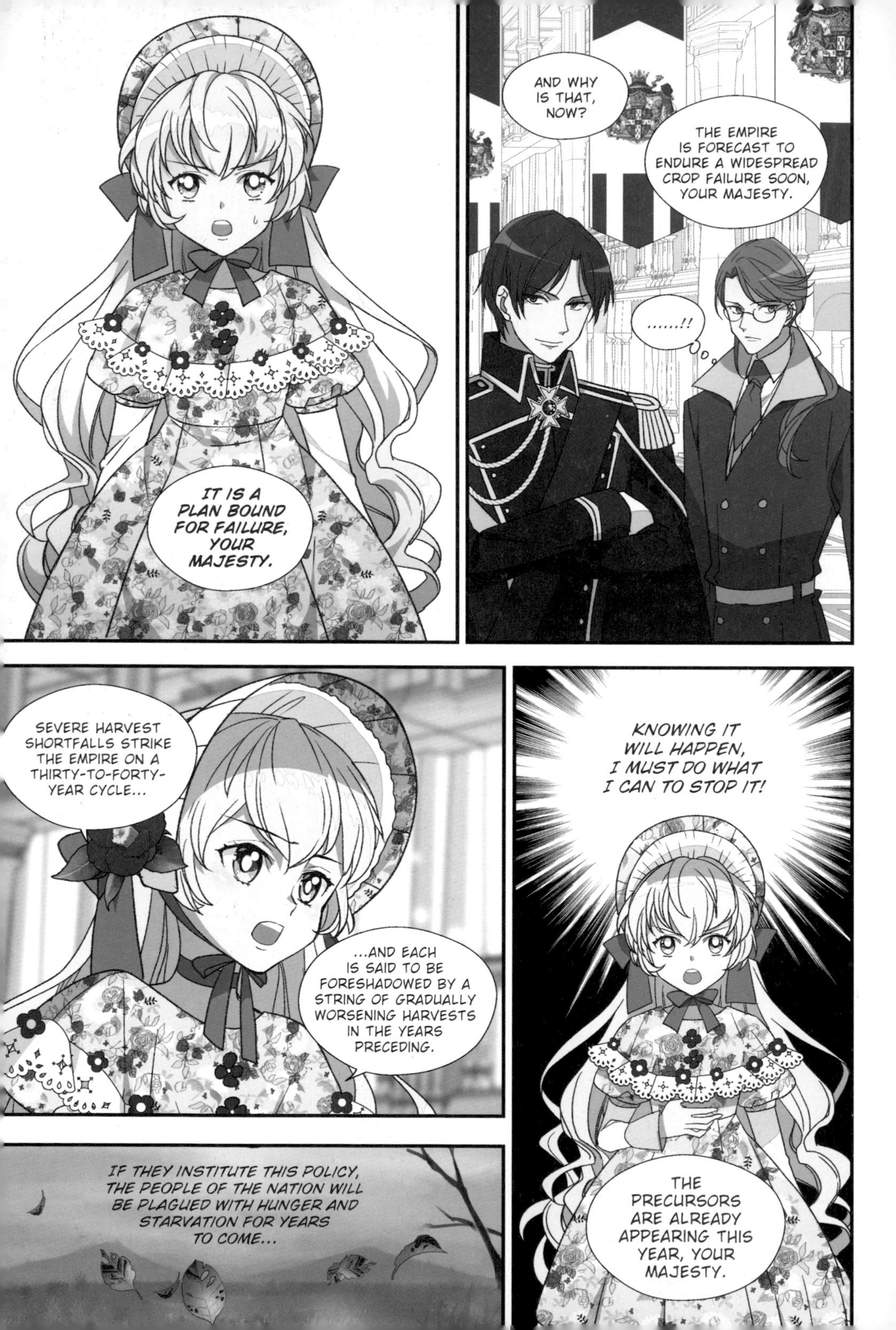
IT IS A PLAN BOUND FOR FAILURE, YOUR MAJESTY.
AND WHY IS THAT, NOW?
THE EMPIRE IS FORECAST TO ENDURE A WIDESPREAD CROP FAILURE SOON, YOUR MAJESTY.
......!!
SEVERE HARVEST SHORTFALLS STRIKE THE EMPIRE ON A THIRTY-TO-FORTY-YEAR CYCLE...
...AND EACH IS SAID TO BE FORESHADOWED BY A STRING OF GRADUALLY WORSENING HARVESTS IN THE YEARS PRECEDING.
IF THEY INSTITUTE THIS POLICY, THE PEOPLE OF THE NATION WILL BE PLAGUED WITH HUNGER AND STARVATION FOR YEARS TO COME...
KNOWING IT WILL HAPPEN, I MUST DO WHAT I CAN TO STOP IT!
THE PRECURSORS ARE ALREADY APPEARING THIS YEAR, YOUR MAJESTY.

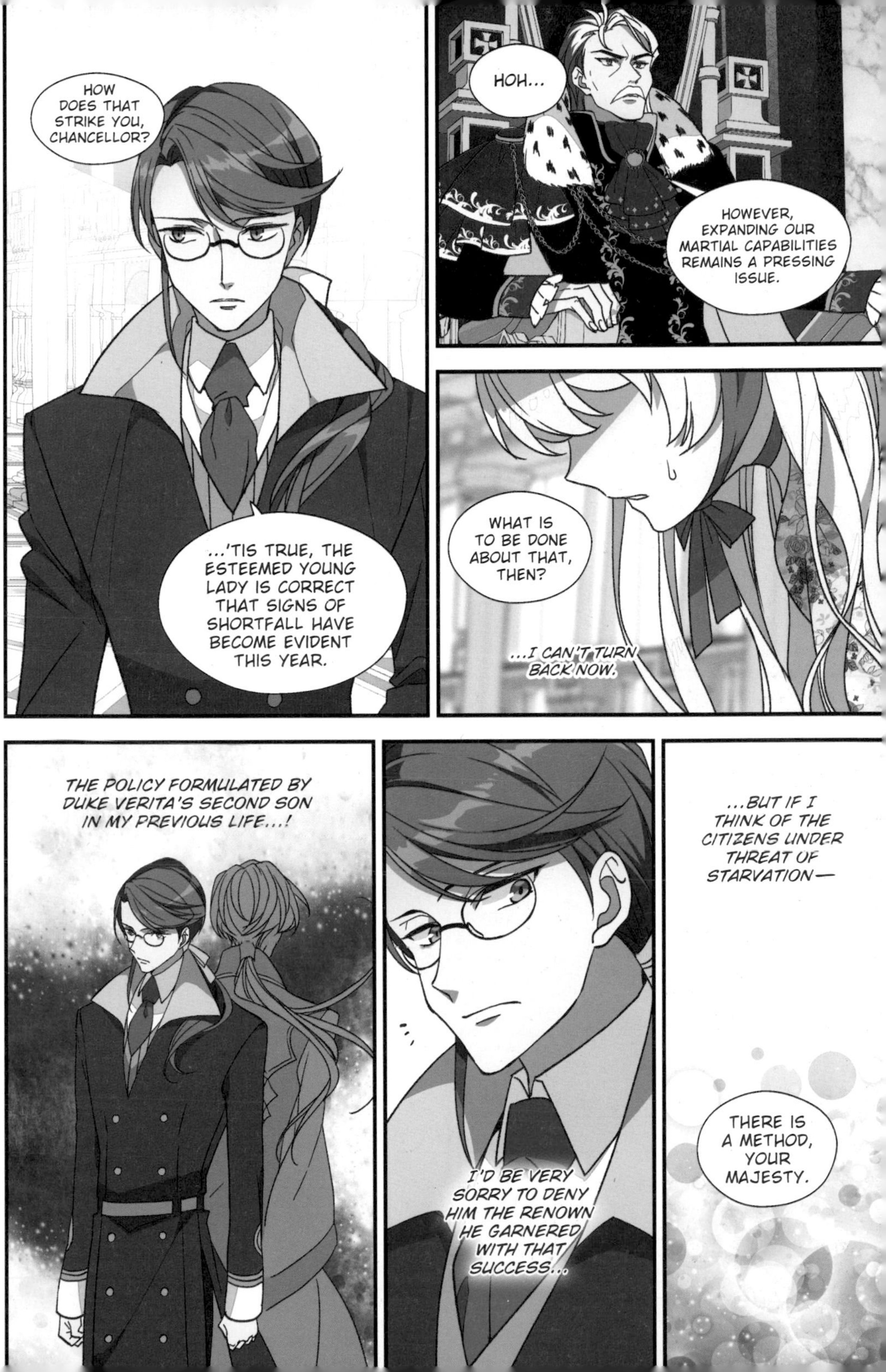
HOW DOES THAT STRIKE YOU, CHANCELLOR?
HOH...
HOWEVER, EXPANDING OUR MARTIAL CAPABILITIES REMAINS A PRESSING ISSUE.
...'TIS TRUE, THE ESTEEMED YOUNG LADY IS CORRECT THAT SIGNS OF SHORTFALL HAVE BECOME EVIDENT THIS YEAR.
WHAT IS TO BE DONE ABOUT THAT, THEN?
...I CAN'T TURN BACK NOW.
THE POLICY FORMULATED BY DUKE VERITA'S SECOND SON IN MY PREVIOUS LIFE...!
...
I'D BE VERY SORRY TO DENY HIM THE RENOWN HE GARNERED WITH THAT SUCCESS...
...BUT IF I THINK OF THE CITIZENS UNDER THREAT OF STARVATION—
THERE IS A METHOD, YOUR MAJESTY.

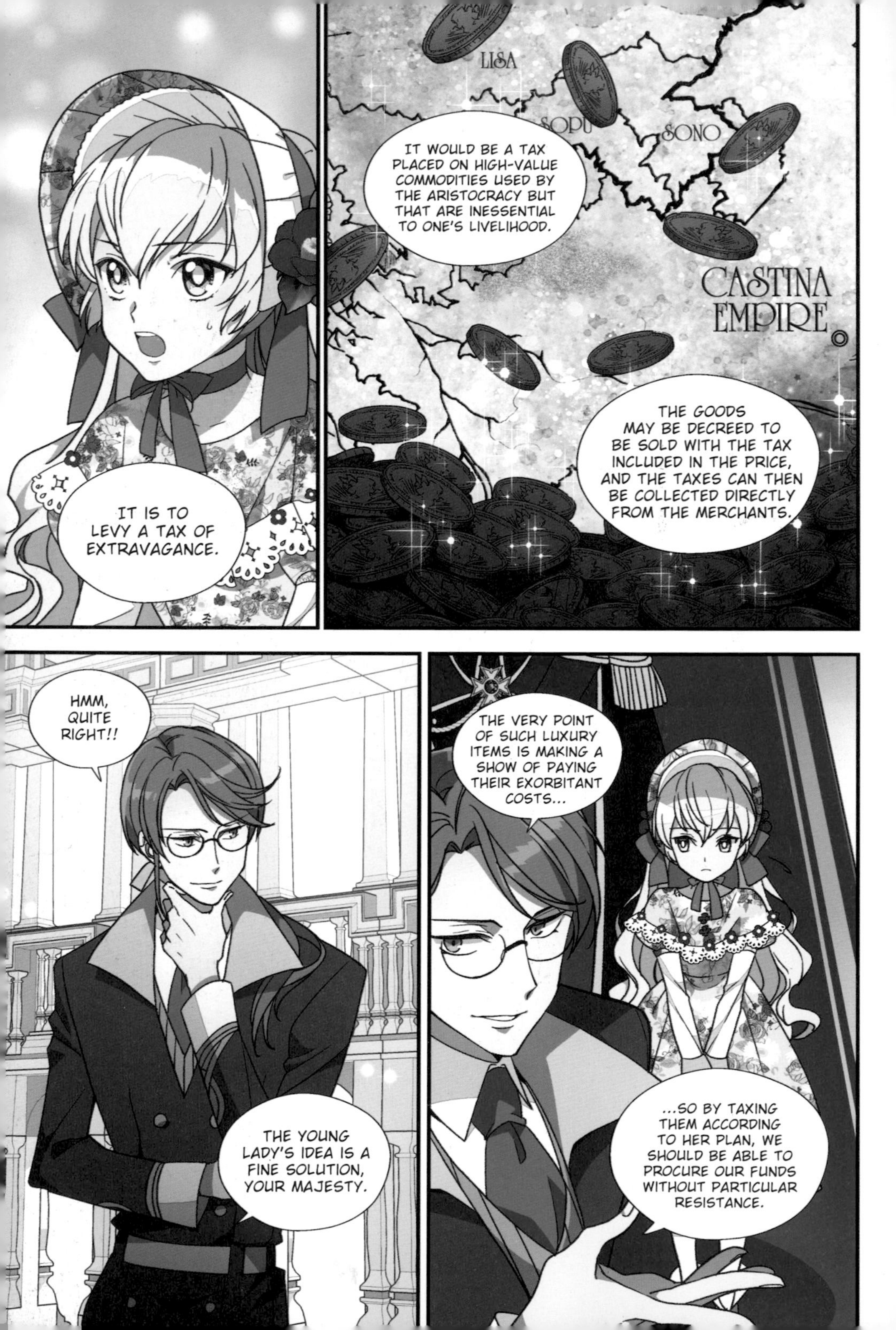
IT IS TO LEVY A TAX OF EXTRAVAGANCE.
LISA
SOPU
SONO
CASTINA EMPIRE
IT WOULD BE A TAX PLACED ON HIGH-VALUE COMMODITIES USED BY THE ARISTOCRACY BUT THAT ARE INESSENTIAL TO ONE'S LIVELIHOOD.
THE GOODS MAY BE DECREED TO BE SOLD WITH THE TAX INCLUDED IN THE PRICE, AND THE TAXES CAN THEN BE COLLECTED DIRECTLY FROM THE MERCHANTS.
HMM, QUITE RIGHT!!
THE YOUNG LADY'S IDEA IS A FINE SOLUTION, YOUR MAJESTY.
THE VERY POINT OF SUCH LUXURY ITEMS IS MAKING A SHOW OF PAYING THEIR EXORBITANT COSTS...
...SO BY TAXING THEM ACCORDING TO HER PLAN, WE SHOULD BE ABLE TO PROCURE OUR FUNDS WITHOUT PARTICULAR RESISTANCE.

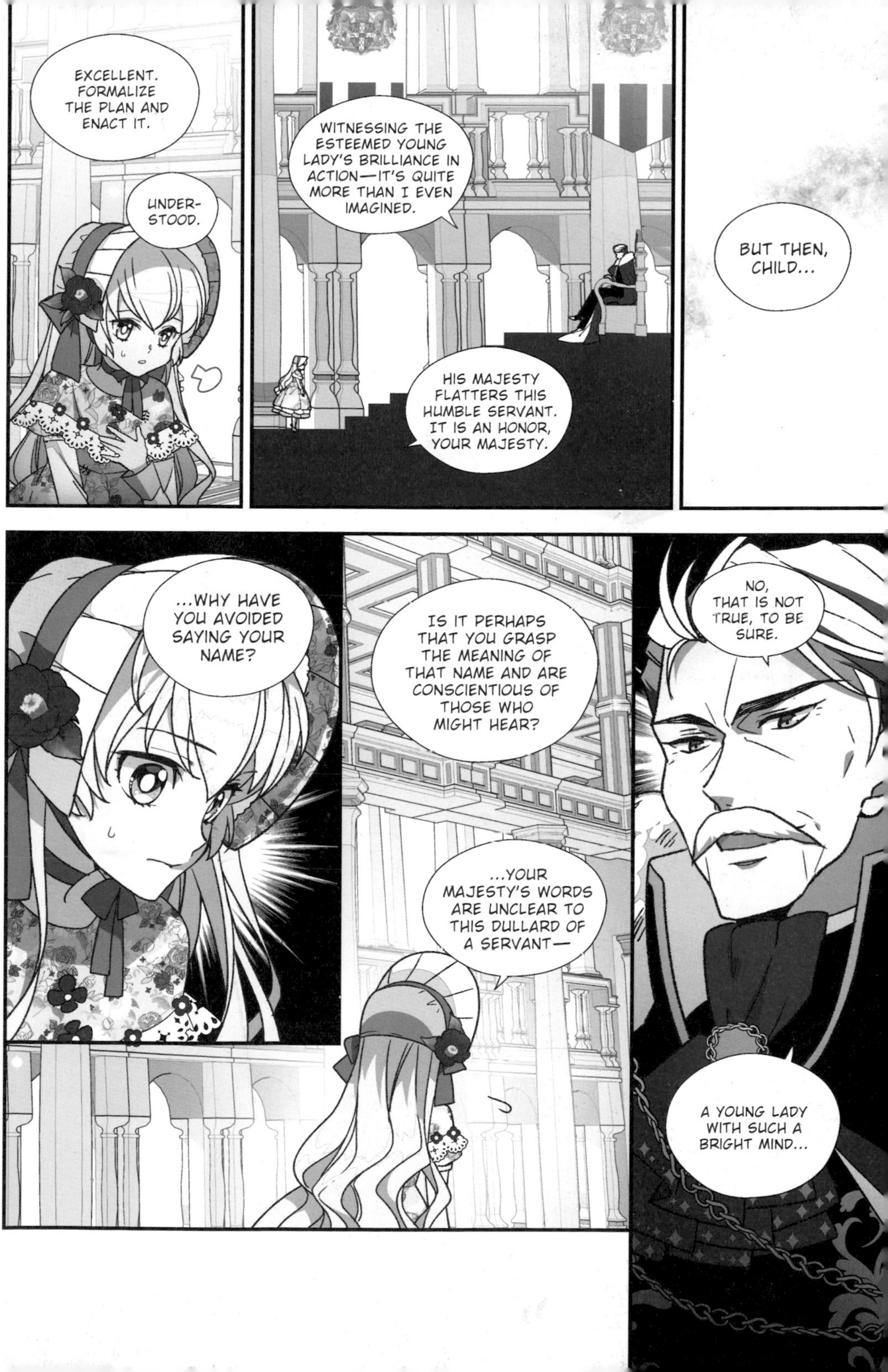
EXCELLENT. FORMALIZE THE PLAN AND ENACT IT.
UNDER-STOOD.
WITNESSING THE ESTEEMED YOUNG LADY'S BRILLIANCE IN ACTION—IT'S QUITE MORE THAN I EVEN IMAGINED.
HIS MAJESTY FLATTERS THIS HUMBLE SERVANT. IT IS AN HONOR, YOUR MAJESTY.
BUT THEN, CHILD...
...WHY HAVE YOU AVOIDED SAYING YOUR NAME?
IS IT PERHAPS THAT YOU GRASP THE MEANING OF THAT NAME AND ARE CONSCIENTIOUS OF THOSE WHO MIGHT HEAR?
...YOUR MAJESTY'S WORDS ARE UNCLEAR TO THIS DULLARD OF A SERVANT—
NO, THAT IS NOT TRUE, TO BE SURE.
A YOUNG LADY WITH SUCH A BRIGHT MIND...

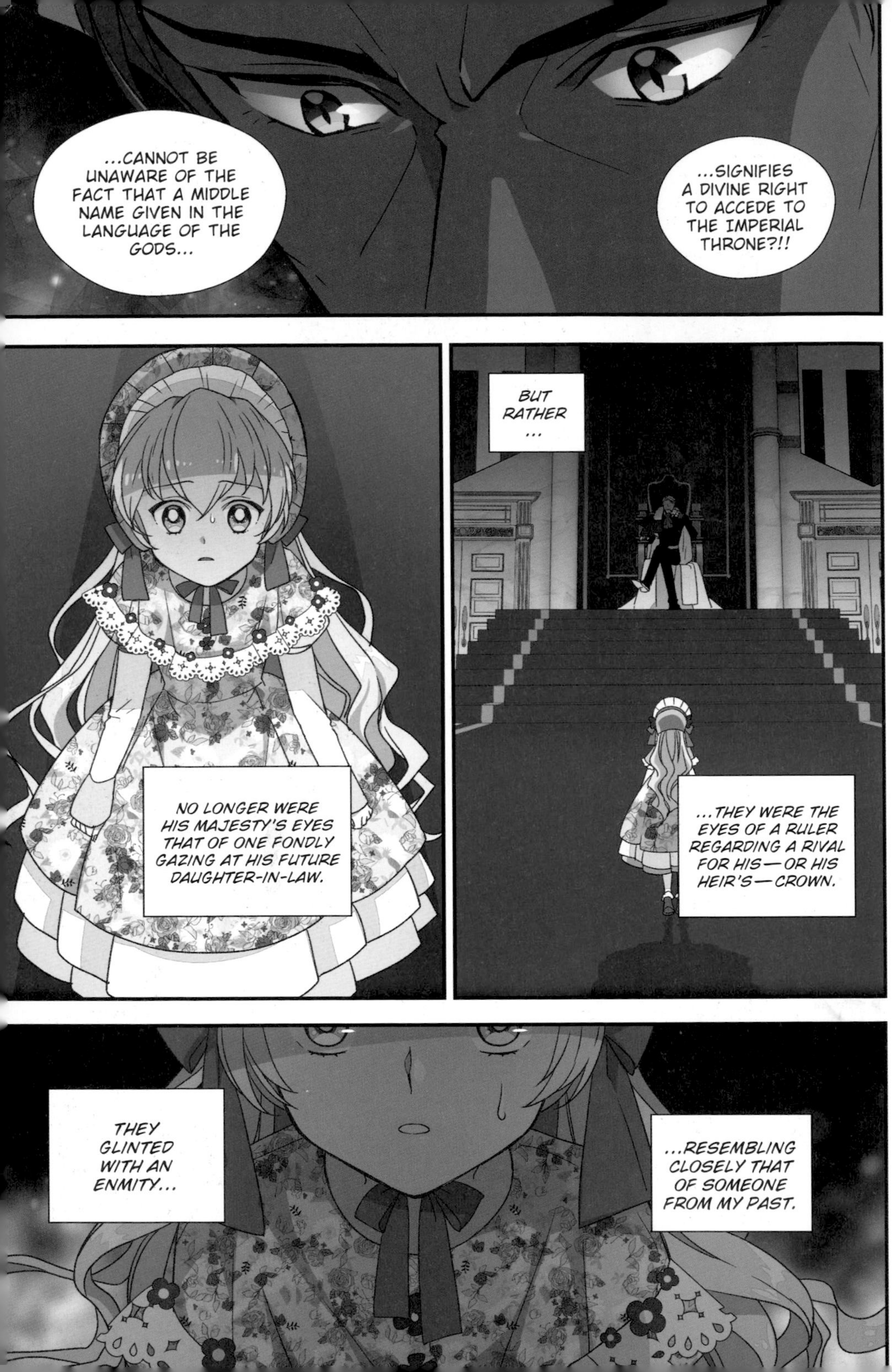
...CANNOT BE UNAWARE OF THE FACT THAT A MIDDLE NAME GIVEN IN THE LANGUAGE OF THE GODS...
...SIGNIFIES A DIVINE RIGHT TO ACCEDE TO THE IMPERIAL THRONE?!!
BUT RATHER ...
NO LONGER WERE HIS MAJESTY'S EYES THAT OF ONE FONDLY GAZING AT HIS FUTURE DAUGHTER-IN-LAW.
...THEY WERE THE EYES OF A RULER REGARDING A RIVAL FOR HIS—OR HIS HEIR'S—CROWN.
THEY GLINTED WITH AN ENMITY...
...RESEMBLING CLOSELY THAT OF SOMEONE FROM MY PAST.

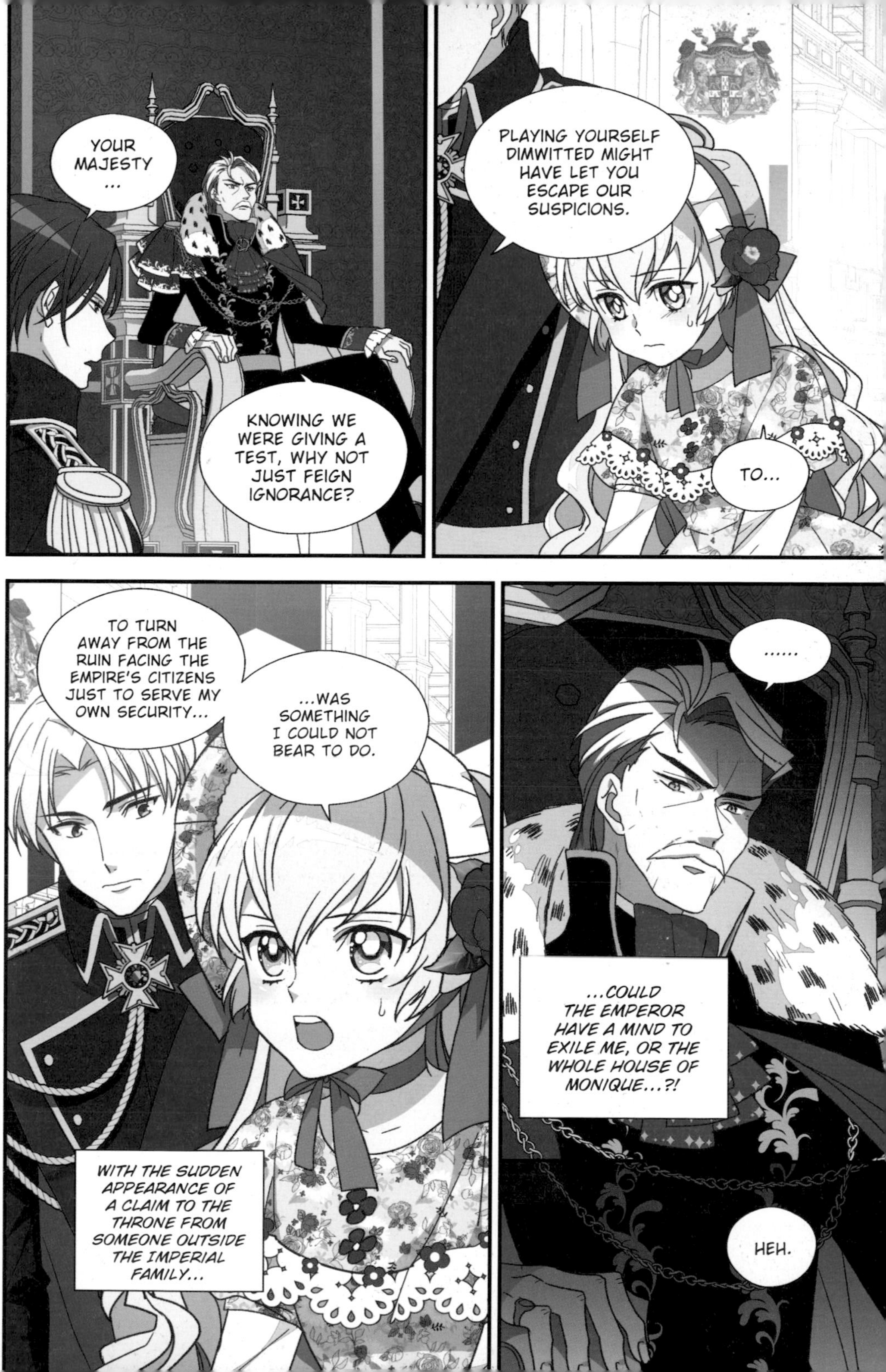
YOUR MAJESTY ...
KNOWING WE WERE GIVING A TEST, WHY NOT JUST FEIGN IGNORANCE?
PLAYING YOURSELF DIMWITTED MIGHT HAVE LET YOU ESCAPE OUR SUSPICIONS.
TO...
TO TURN AWAY FROM THE RUIN FACING THE EMPIRE'S CITIZENS JUST TO SERVE MY OWN SECURITY...
...WAS SOMETHING I COULD NOT BEAR TO DO.
WITH THE SUDDEN APPEARANCE OF A CLAIM TO THE THRONE FROM SOMEONE OUTSIDE THE IMPERIAL FAMILY...
......
...COULD THE EMPEROR HAVE A MIND TO EXILE ME, OR THE WHOLE HOUSE OF MONIQUE...?!
HEH.

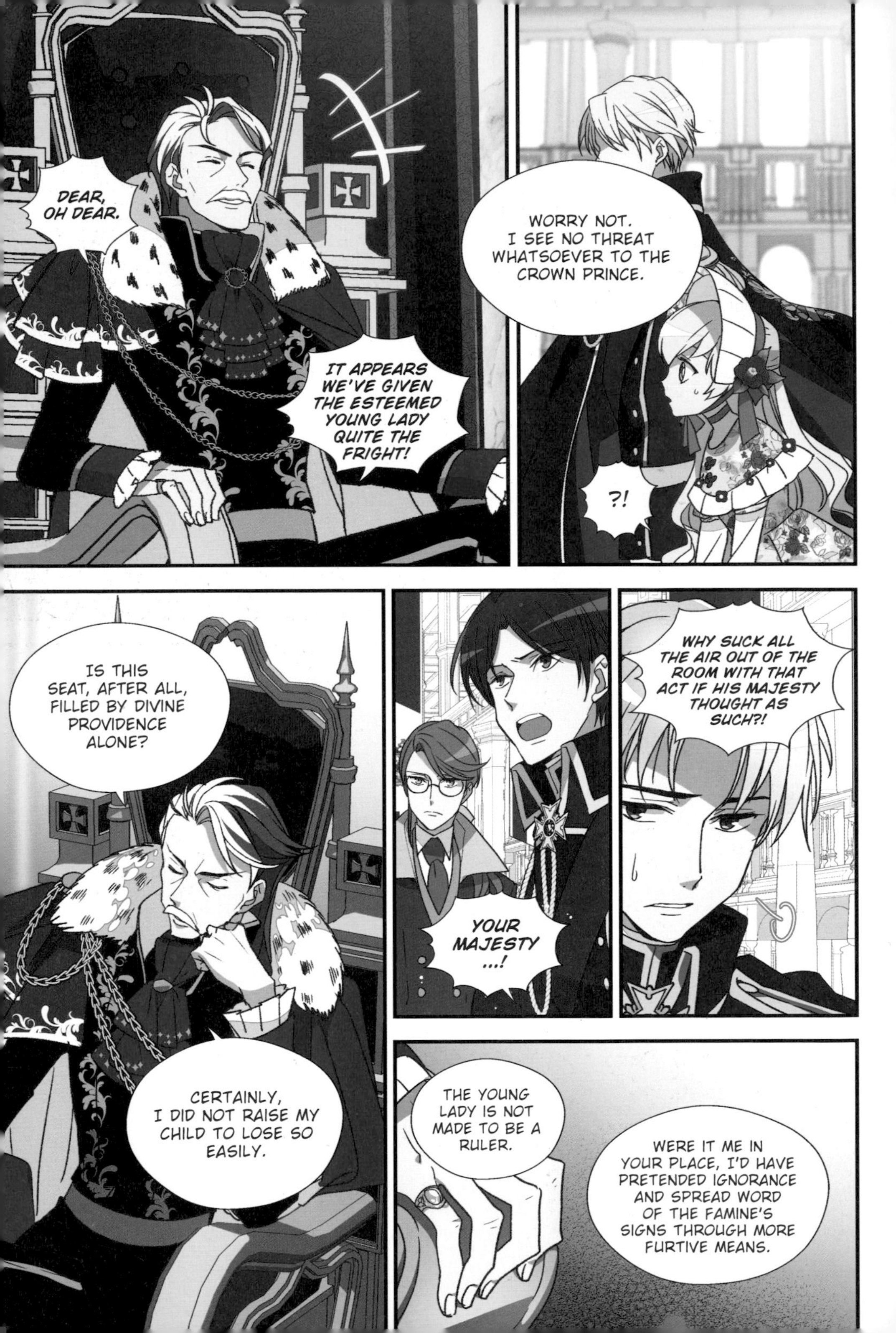
DEAR, OH DEAR.
IT APPEARS WE'VE GIVEN THE ESTEEMED YOUNG LADY QUITE THE FRIGHT!
WORRY NOT. I SEE NO THREAT WHATSOEVER TO THE CROWN PRINCE.
?!
IS THIS SEAT, AFTER ALL, FILLED BY DIVINE PROVIDENCE ALONE?
CERTAINLY, I DID NOT RAISE MY CHILD TO LOSE SO EASILY.
YOUR MAJESTY ...!
WHY SUCK ALL THE AIR OUT OF THE ROOM WITH THAT ACT IF HIS MAJESTY THOUGHT AS SUCH?!
THE YOUNG LADY IS NOT MADE TO BE A RULER.
WERE IT ME IN YOUR PLACE, I'D HAVE PRETENDED IGNORANCE AND SPREAD WORD OF THE FAMINE'S SIGNS THROUGH MORE FURTIVE MEANS.

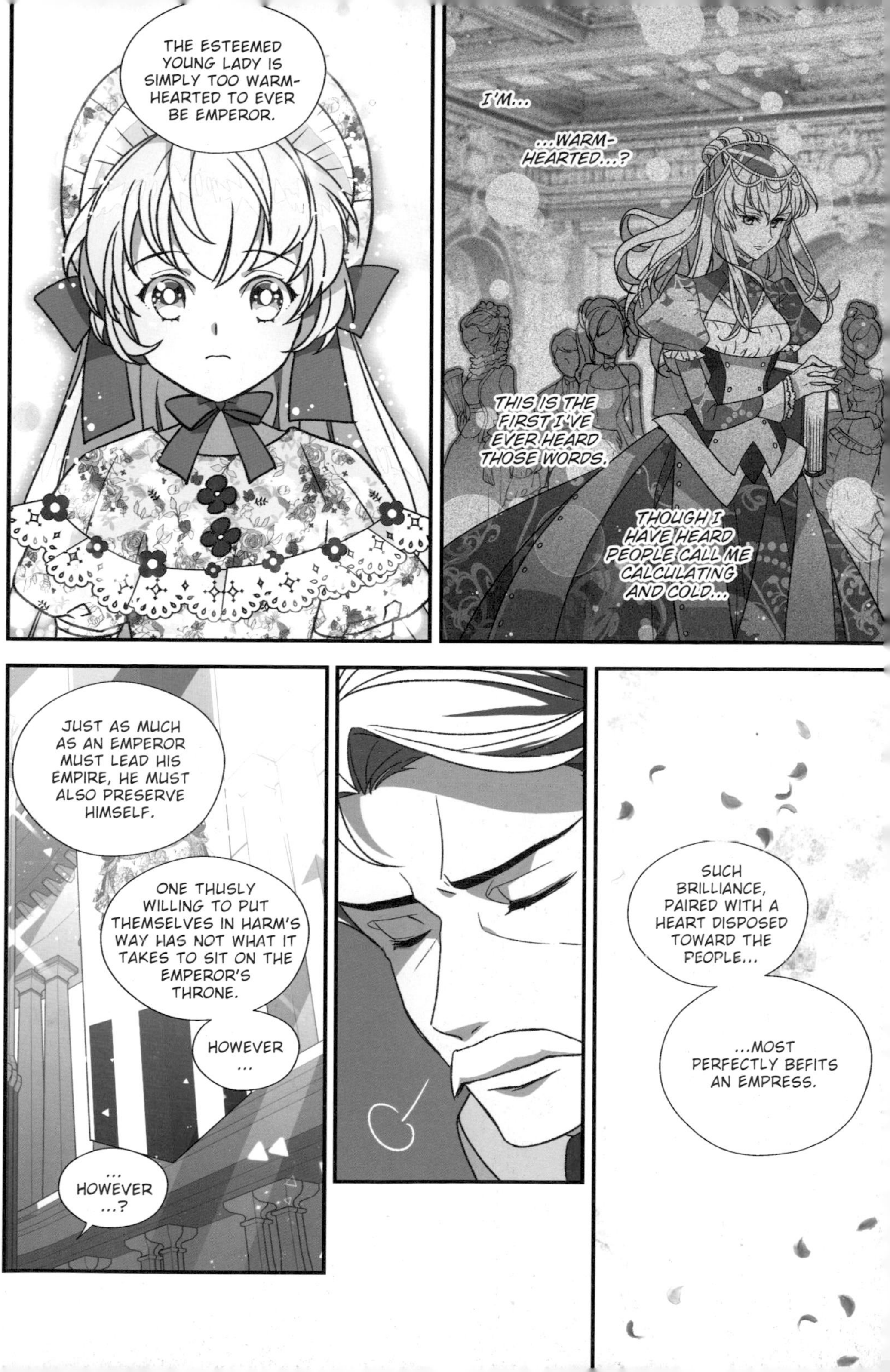
THE ESTEEMED YOUNG LADY IS SIMPLY TOO WARM-HEARTED TO EVER BE EMPEROR.
I'M...
...WARM-HEARTED...?
THIS IS THE FIRST I'VE EVER HEARD THOSE WORDS.
THOUGH I HAVE HEARD PEOPLE CALL ME CALCULATING AND COLD...
JUST AS MUCH AS AN EMPEROR MUST LEAD HIS EMPIRE, HE MUST ALSO PRESERVE HIMSELF.
ONE THUSLY WILLING TO PUT THEMSELVES IN HARM'S WAY HAS NOT WHAT IT TAKES TO SIT ON THE EMPEROR'S THRONE.
HOWEVER ...
... HOWEVER ...?
SUCH BRILLIANCE, PAIRED WITH A HEART DISPOSED TOWARD THE PEOPLE...
...MOST PERFECTLY BEFITS AN EMPRESS.

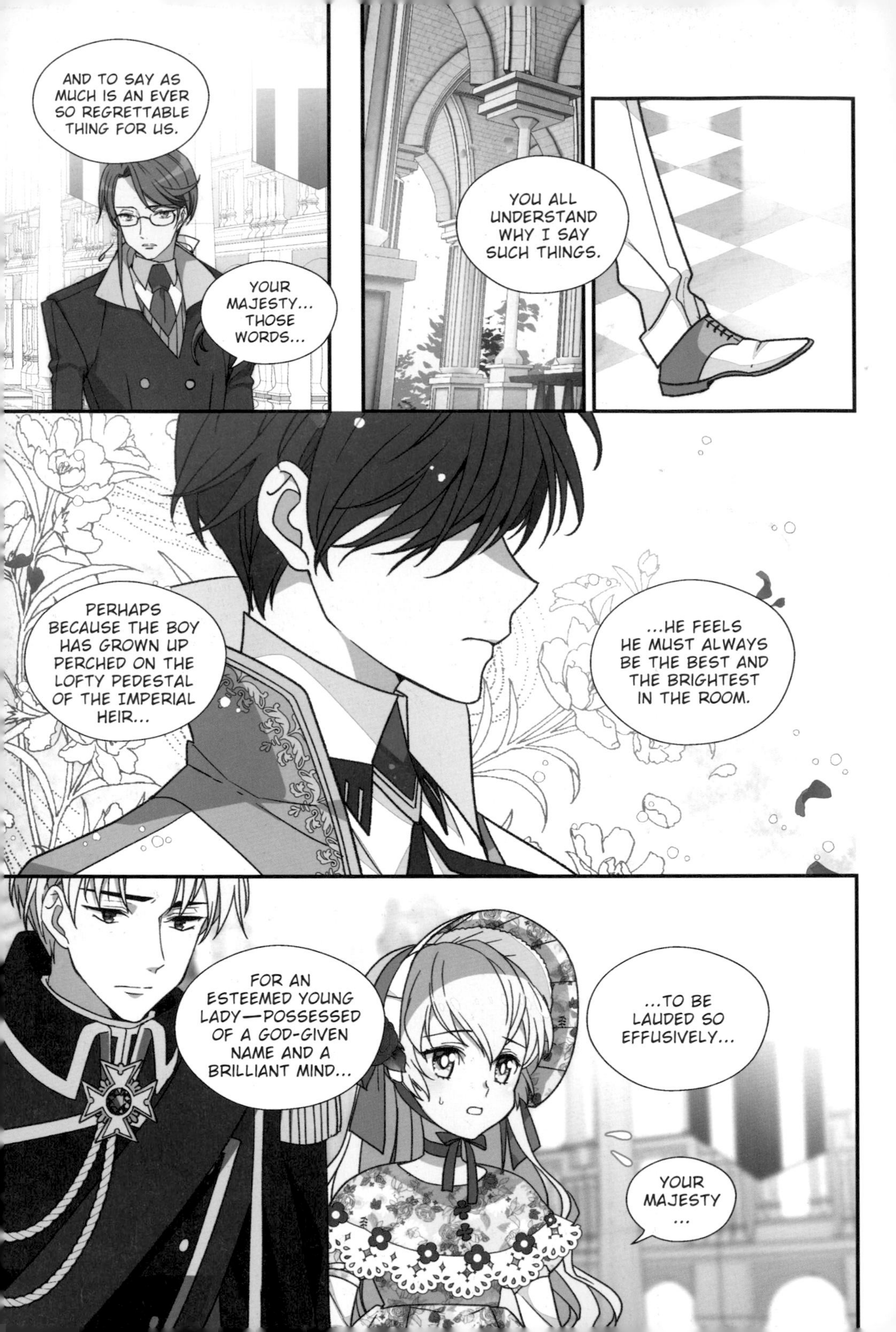
AND TO SAY AS MUCH IS AN EVER SO REGRETTABLE THING FOR US.
YOUR MAJESTY... THOSE WORDS...
YOU ALL UNDERSTAND WHY I SAY SUCH THINGS.
PERHAPS BECAUSE THE BOY HAS GROWN UP PERCHED ON THE LOFTY PEDESTAL OF THE IMPERIAL HEIR...
...HE FEELS HE MUST ALWAYS BE THE BEST AND THE BRIGHTEST IN THE ROOM.
FOR AN ESTEEMED YOUNG LADY—POSSESSED OF A GOD-GIVEN NAME AND A BRILLIANT MIND...
...TO BE LAUDED SO EFFUSIVELY...
YOUR MAJESTY ...

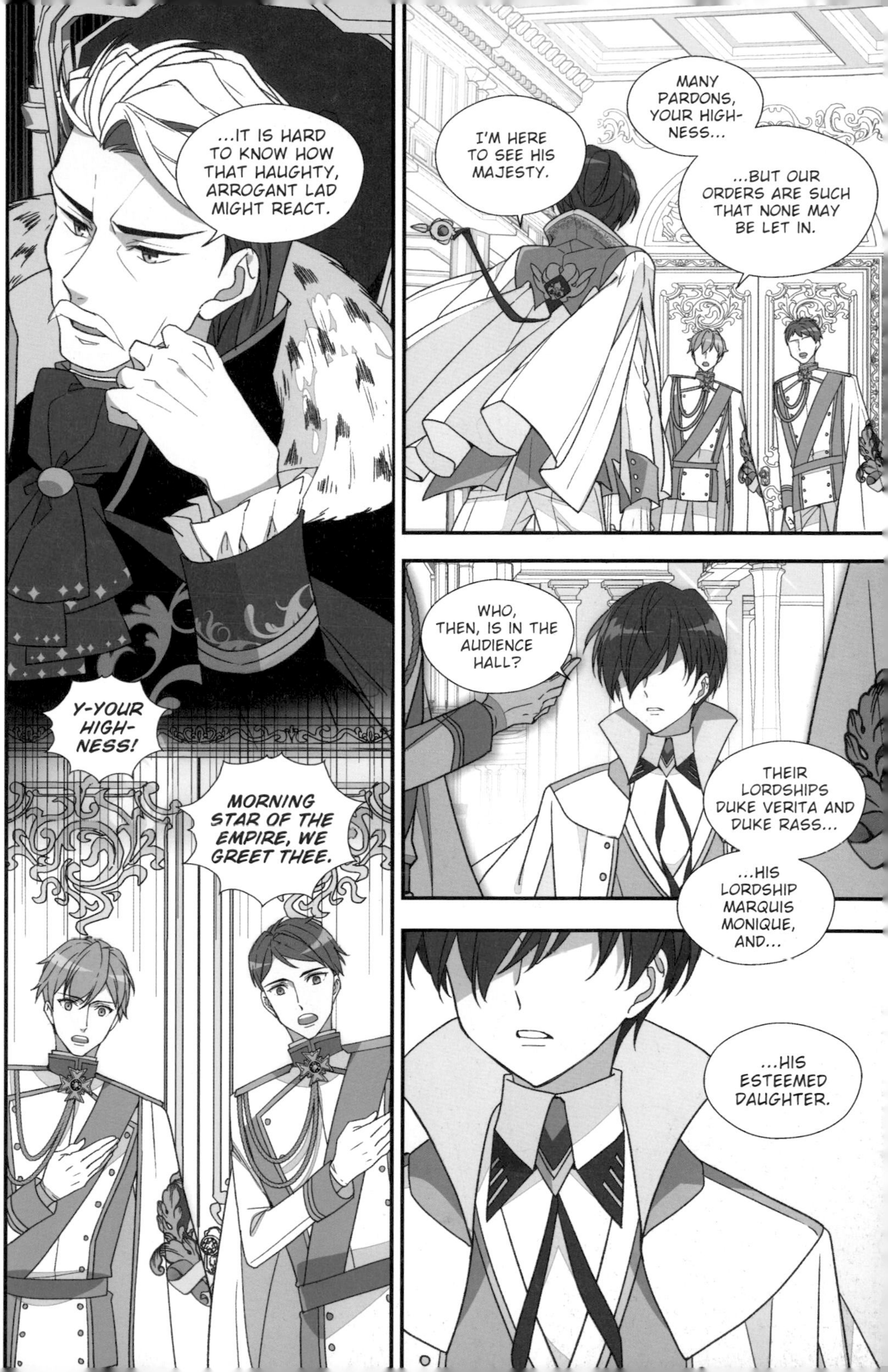
...IT IS HARD TO KNOW HOW THAT HAUGHTY, ARROGANT LAD MIGHT REACT.
Y-YOUR HIGH-NESS!
MORNING STAR OF THE EMPIRE, WE GREET THEE.
I'M HERE TO SEE HIS MAJESTY.
MANY PARDONS, YOUR HIGH-NESS...
...BUT OUR ORDERS ARE SUCH THAT NONE MAY BE LET IN.
WHO, THEN, IS IN THE AUDIENCE HALL?
THEIR LORDSHIPS DUKE VERITA AND DUKE RASS...
...HIS LORDSHIP MARQUIS MONIQUE, AND...
...HIS ESTEEMED DAUGHTER.

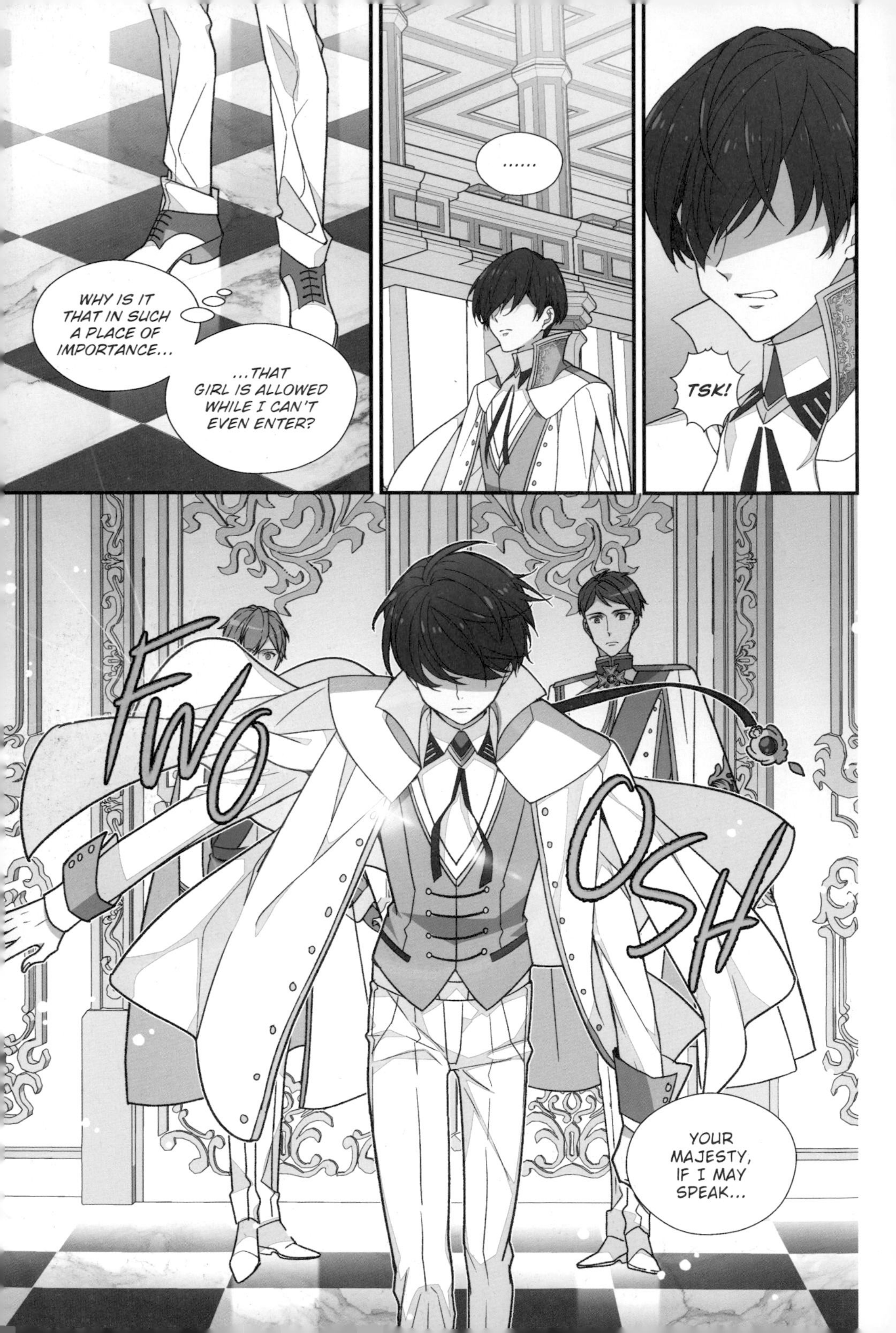
WHY IS IT THAT IN SUCH A PLACE OF IMPORTANCE...
...THAT GIRL IS ALLOWED WHILE I CAN'T EVEN ENTER?
......
TSK!
FWOOSH
YOUR MAJESTY, IF I MAY SPEAK...

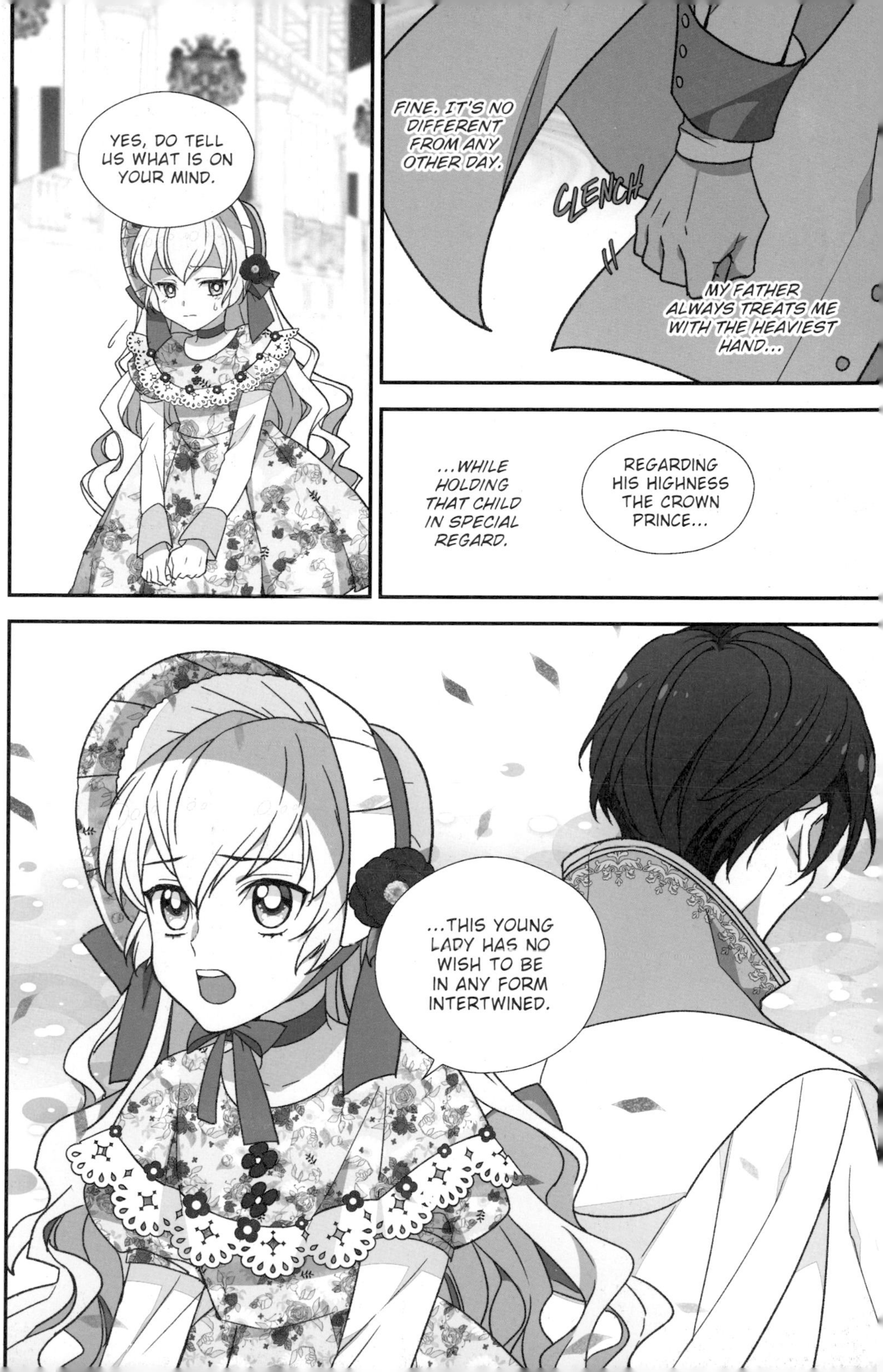
YES, DO TELL US WHAT IS ON YOUR MIND.
FINE. IT'S NO DIFFERENT FROM ANY OTHER DAY.
CLENCH
MY FATHER ALWAYS TREATS ME WITH THE HEAVIEST HAND...
...WHILE HOLDING THAT CHILD IN SPECIAL REGARD.
REGARDING HIS HIGHNESS THE CROWN PRINCE...
...THIS YOUNG LADY HAS NO WISH TO BE IN ANY FORM INTERTWINED.

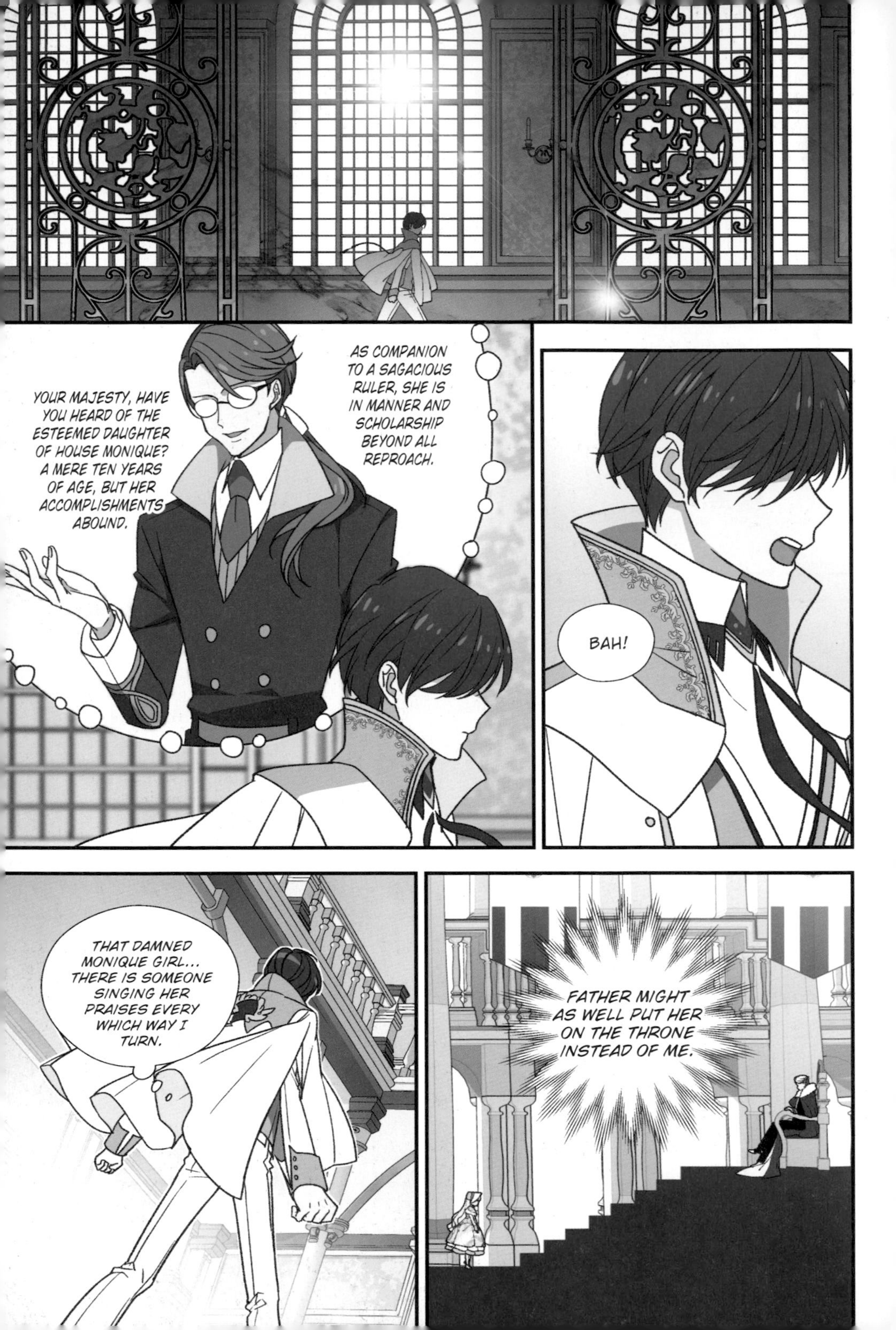
YOUR MAJESTY, HAVE YOU HEARD OF THE ESTEEMED DAUGHTER OF HOUSE MONIQUE? A MERE TEN YEARS OF AGE, BUT HER ACCOMPLISHMENTS ABOUND.
AS COMPANION TO A SAGACIOUS RULER, SHE IS IN MANNER AND SCHOLARSHIP BEYOND ALL REPROACH.
BAH!
THAT DAMNED MONIQUE GIRL... THERE IS SOMEONE SINGING HER PRAISES EVERY WHICH WAY I TURN.
FATHER MIGHT AS WELL PUT HER ON THE THRONE INSTEAD OF ME.

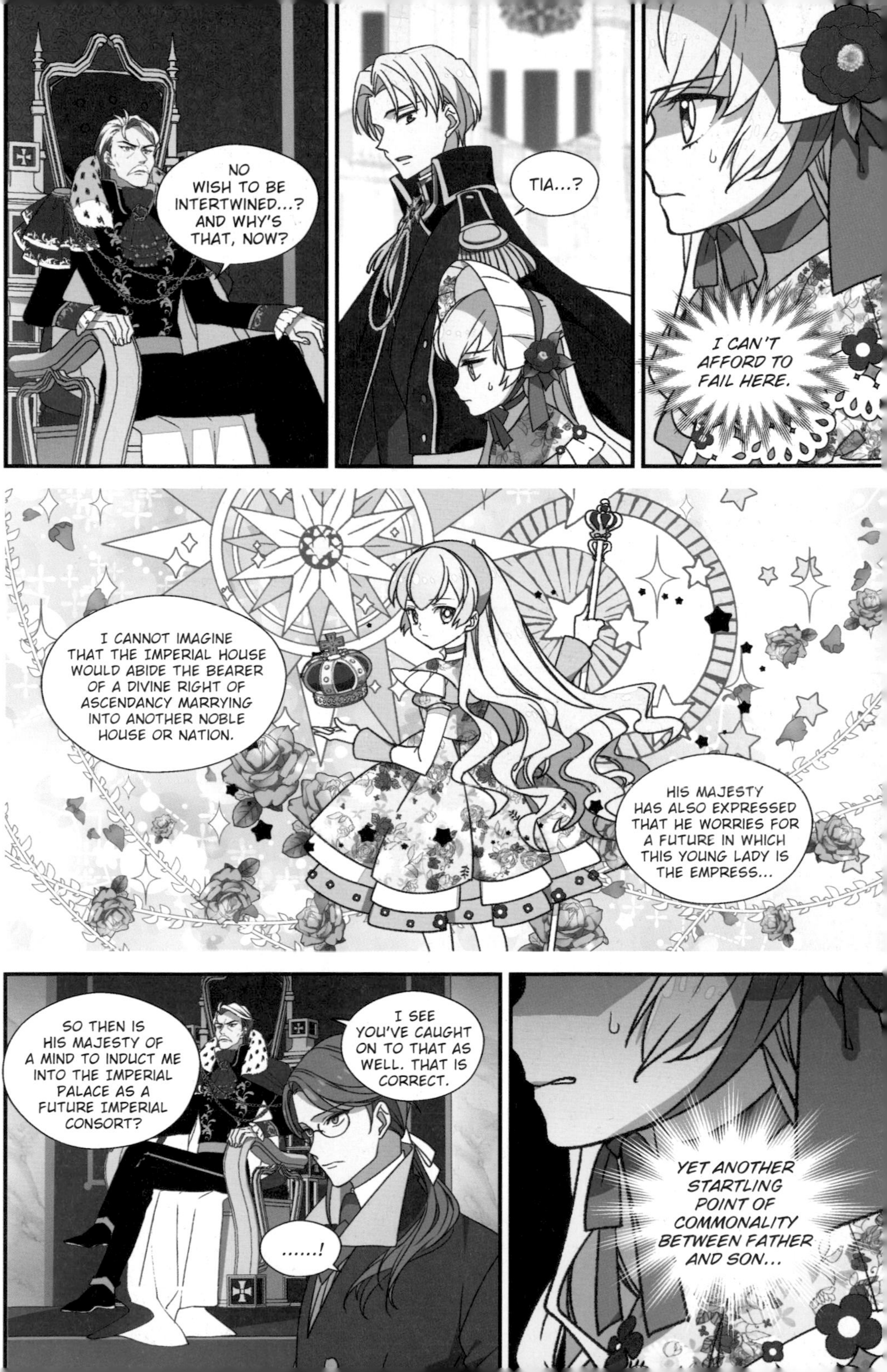
NO WISH TO BE INTERTWINED...? AND WHY'S THAT, NOW?
TIA...?
I CAN'T AFFORD TO FAIL HERE.
I CANNOT IMAGINE THAT THE IMPERIAL HOUSE WOULD ABIDE THE BEARER OF A DIVINE RIGHT OF ASCENDANCY MARRYING INTO ANOTHER NOBLE HOUSE OR NATION.
HIS MAJESTY HAS ALSO EXPRESSED THAT HE WORRIES FOR A FUTURE IN WHICH THIS YOUNG LADY IS THE EMPRESS...
SO THEN IS HIS MAJESTY OF A MIND TO INDUCT ME INTO THE IMPERIAL PALACE AS A FUTURE IMPERIAL CONSORT?
I SEE YOU'VE CAUGHT ON TO THAT AS WELL. THAT IS CORRECT.
......!
YET ANOTHER STARTLING POINT OF COMMONALITY BETWEEN FATHER AND SON...

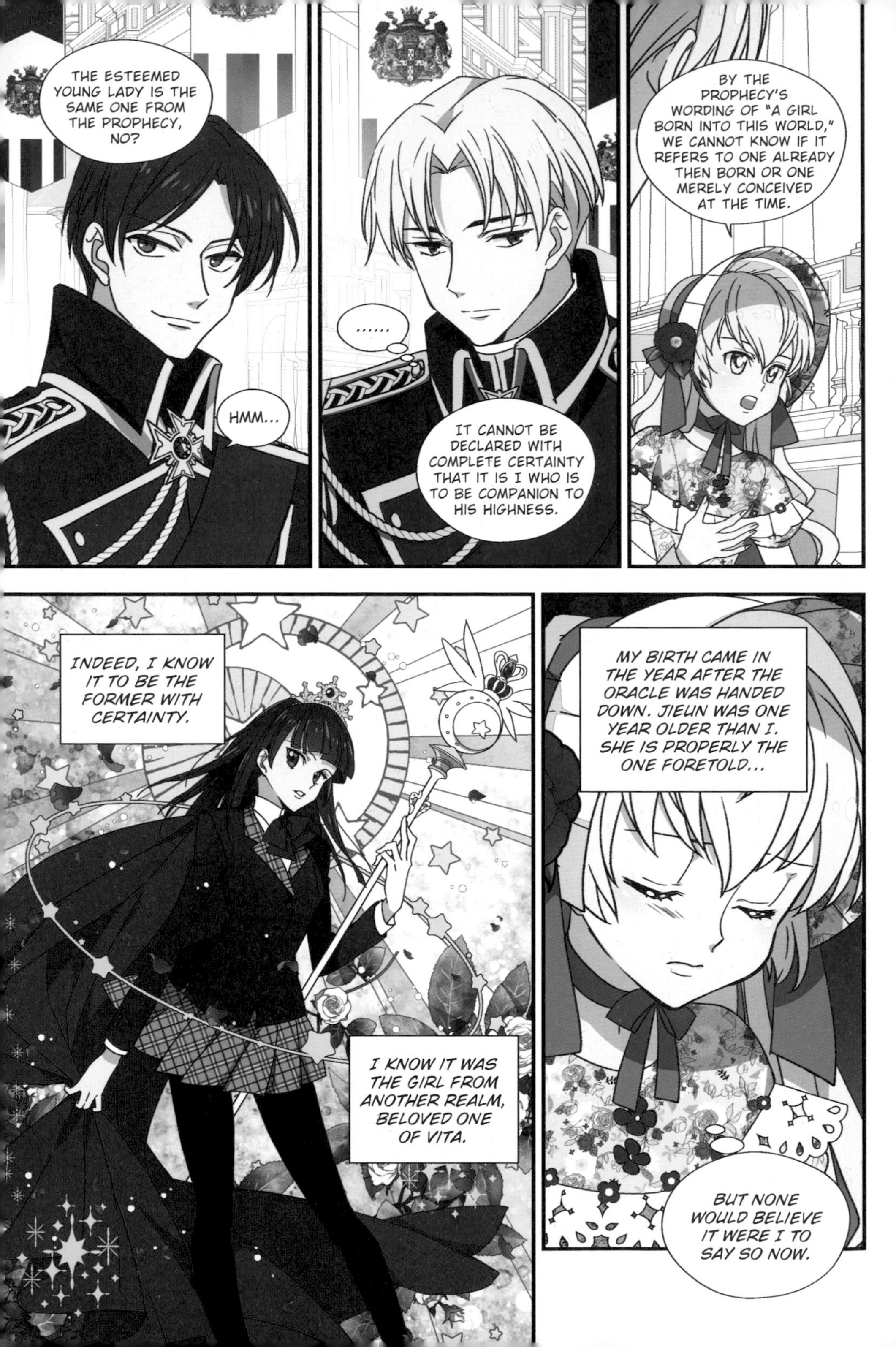
THE ESTEEMED YOUNG LADY IS THE SAME ONE FROM THE PROPHECY, NO?
HMM...
......
IT CANNOT BE DECLARED WITH COMPLETE CERTAINTY THAT IT IS I WHO IS TO BE COMPANION TO HIS HIGHNESS.
BY THE PROPHECY'S WORDING OF "A GIRL BORN INTO THIS WORLD," WE CANNOT KNOW IF IT REFERS TO ONE ALREADY THEN BORN OR ONE MERELY CONCEIVED AT THE TIME.
INDEED, I KNOW IT TO BE THE FORMER WITH CERTAINTY.
I KNOW IT WAS THE GIRL FROM ANOTHER REALM, BELOVED ONE OF VITA.
MY BIRTH CAME IN THE YEAR AFTER THE ORACLE WAS HANDED DOWN. JIEUN WAS ONE YEAR OLDER THAN I. SHE IS PROPERLY THE ONE FORETOLD...
BUT NONE WOULD BELIEVE IT WERE I TO SAY SO NOW.

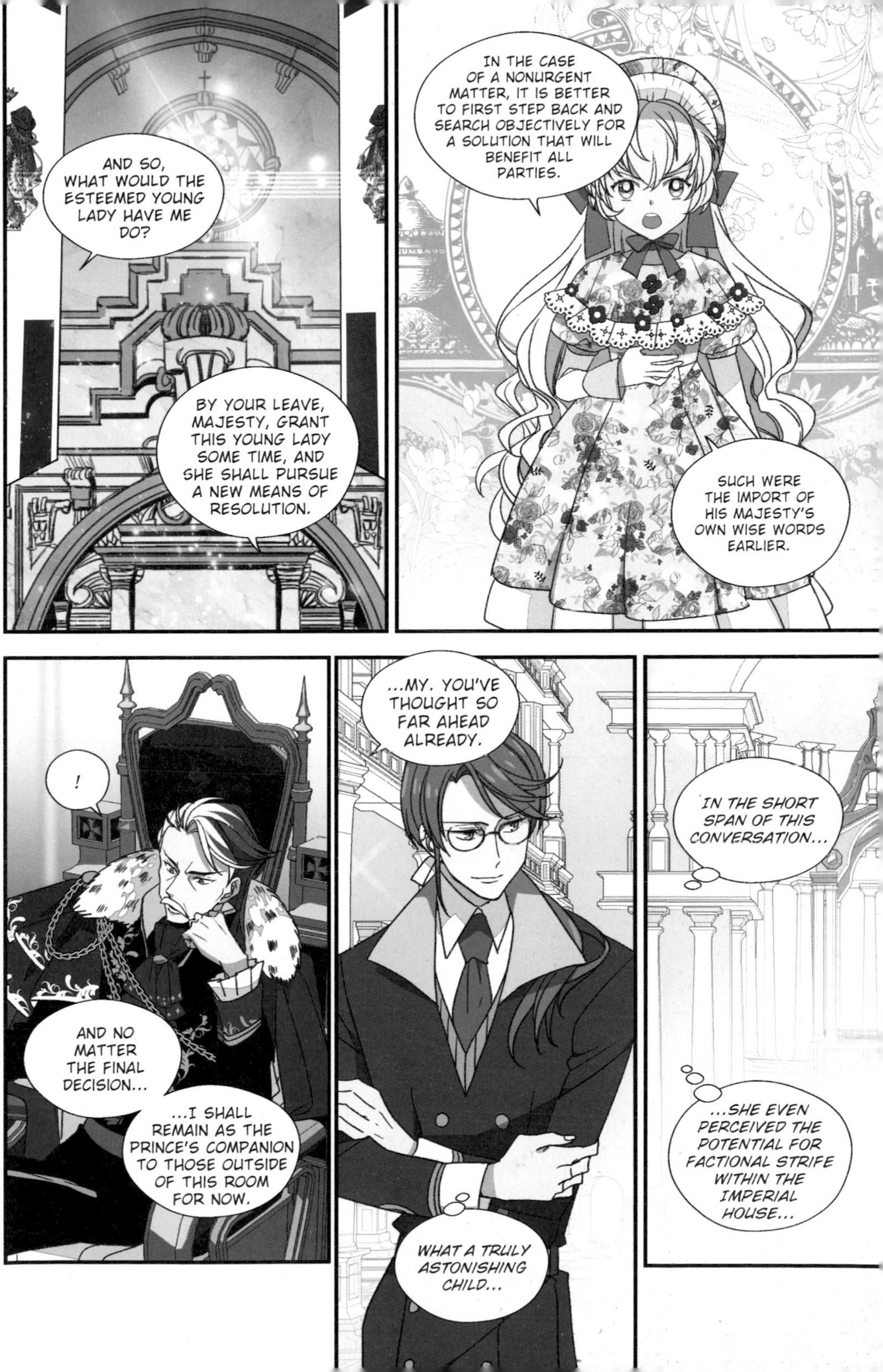
AND SO, WHAT WOULD THE ESTEEMED YOUNG LADY HAVE ME DO?
BY YOUR LEAVE, MAJESTY, GRANT THIS YOUNG LADY SOME TIME, AND SHE SHALL PURSUE A NEW MEANS OF RESOLUTION.
IN THE CASE OF A NONURGENT MATTER, IT IS BETTER TO FIRST STEP BACK AND SEARCH OBJECTIVELY FOR A SOLUTION THAT WILL BENEFIT ALL PARTIES.
SUCH WERE THE IMPORT OF HIS MAJESTY'S OWN WISE WORDS EARLIER.
!
AND NO MATTER THE FINAL DECISION...
...I SHALL REMAIN AS THE PRINCE'S COMPANION TO THOSE OUTSIDE OF THIS ROOM FOR NOW.
...MY. YOU'VE THOUGHT SO FAR AHEAD ALREADY.
WHAT A TRULY ASTONISHING CHILD...
IN THE SHORT SPAN OF THIS CONVERSATION...
...SHE EVEN PERCEIVED THE POTENTIAL FOR FACTIONAL STRIFE WITHIN THE IMPERIAL HOUSE...

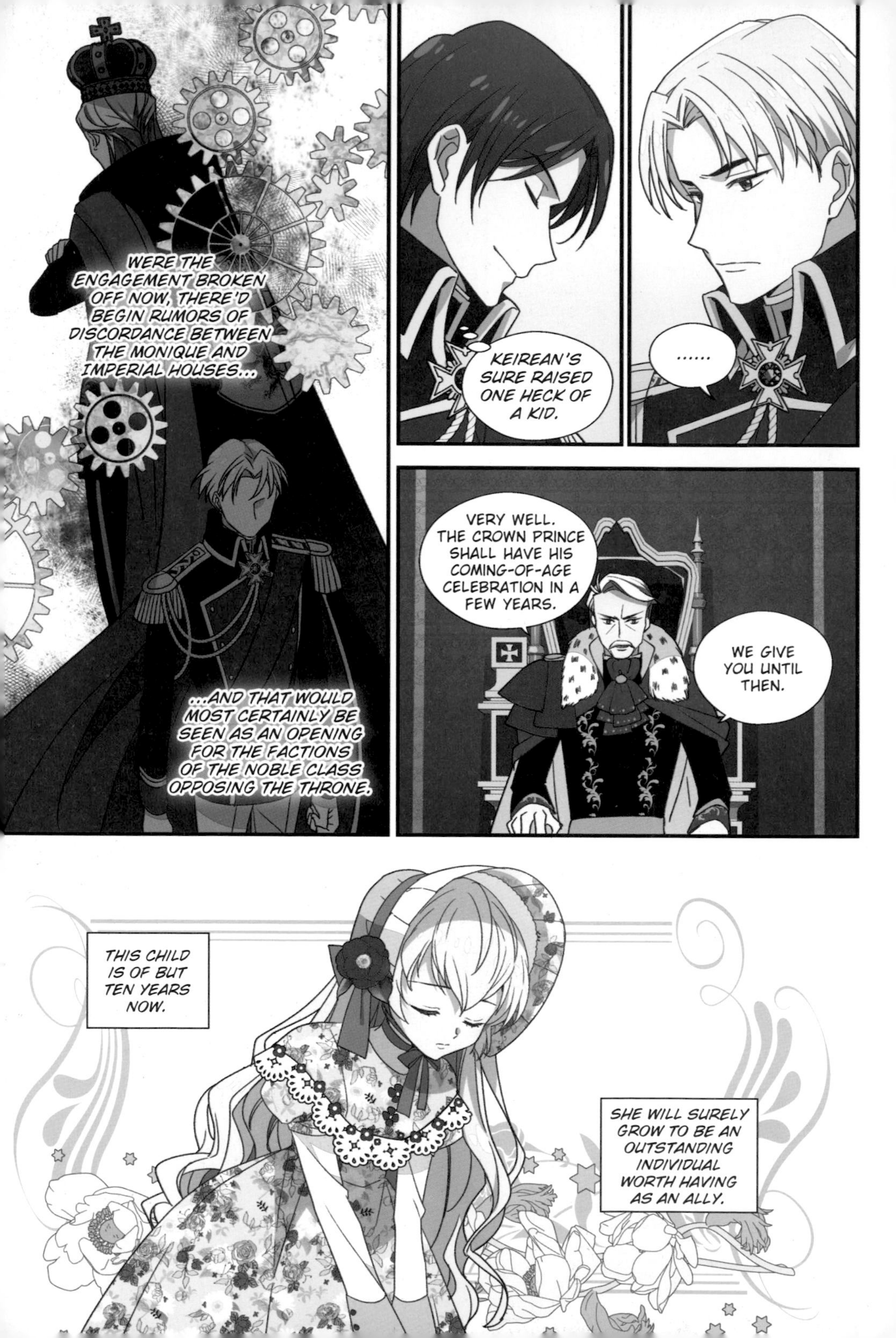
WERE THE ENGAGEMENT BROKEN OFF NOW, THERE'D BEGIN RUMORS OF DISCORDANCE BETWEEN THE MONIQUE AND IMPERIAL HOUSES...
...AND THAT WOULD MOST CERTAINLY BE SEEN AS AN OPENING FOR THE FACTIONS OF THE NOBLE CLASS OPPOSING THE THRONE.
KEIREAN'S SURE RAISED ONE HECK OF A KID.
......
VERY WELL. THE CROWN PRINCE SHALL HAVE HIS COMING-OF-AGE CELEBRATION IN A FEW YEARS.
WE GIVE YOU UNTIL THEN.
THIS CHILD IS OF BUT TEN YEARS NOW.
SHE WILL SURELY GROW TO BE AN OUTSTANDING INDIVIDUAL WORTH HAVING AS AN ALLY.

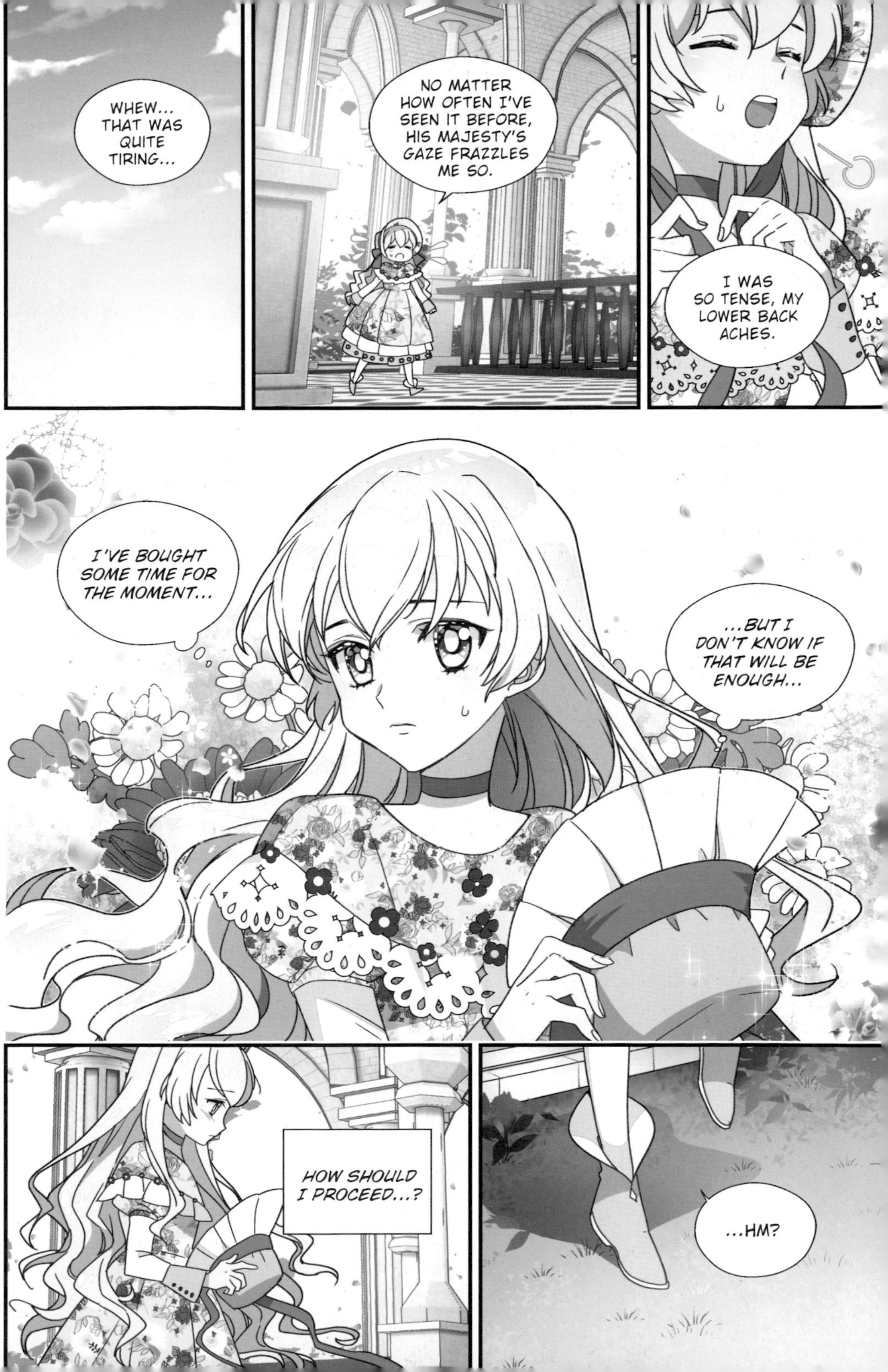
WHEW... THAT WAS QUITE TIRING...
NO MATTER HOW OFTEN I'VE SEEN IT BEFORE, HIS MAJESTY'S GAZE FRAZZLES ME SO.
I WAS SO TENSE, MY LOWER BACK ACHES.
I'VE BOUGHT SOME TIME FOR THE MOMENT...
...BUT I DON'T KNOW IF THAT WILL BE ENOUGH...
HOW SHOULD I PROCEED...?
...HM?

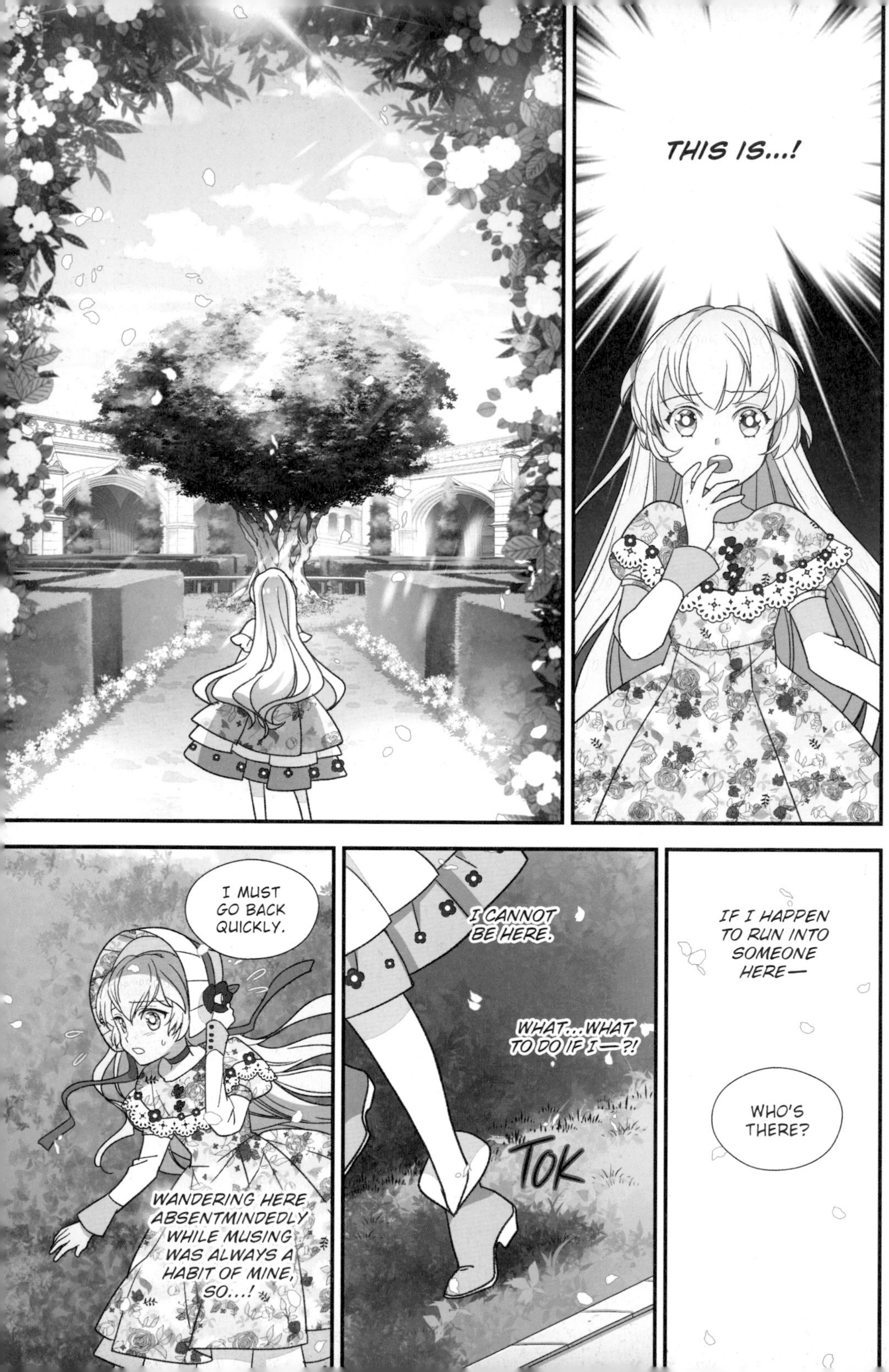
THIS IS...!
I MUST GO BACK QUICKLY.
WANDERING HERE ABSENTMINDEDLY WHILE MUSING WAS ALWAYS A HABIT OF MINE, SO...!
I CANNOT BE HERE.
WHAT...WHAT TO DO IF I—?!
TOK
IF I HAPPEN TO RUN INTO SOMEONE HERE—
WHO'S THERE?

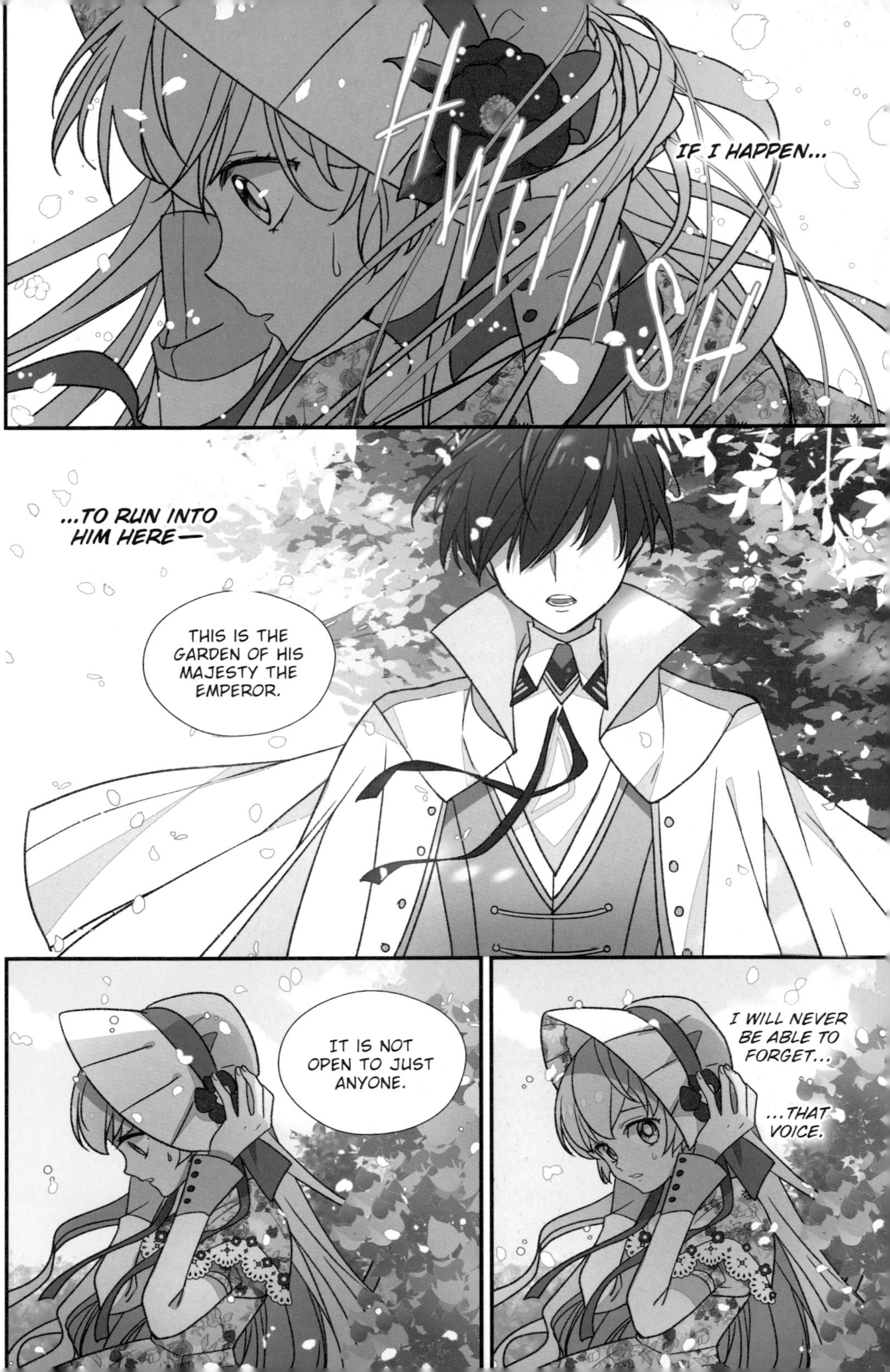
HWIIISH
IF I HAPPEN...
...TO RUN INTO HIM HERE—
THIS IS THE GARDEN OF HIS MAJESTY THE EMPEROR.
IT IS NOT OPEN TO JUST ANYONE.
I WILL NEVER BE ABLE TO FORGET...
...THAT VOICE.

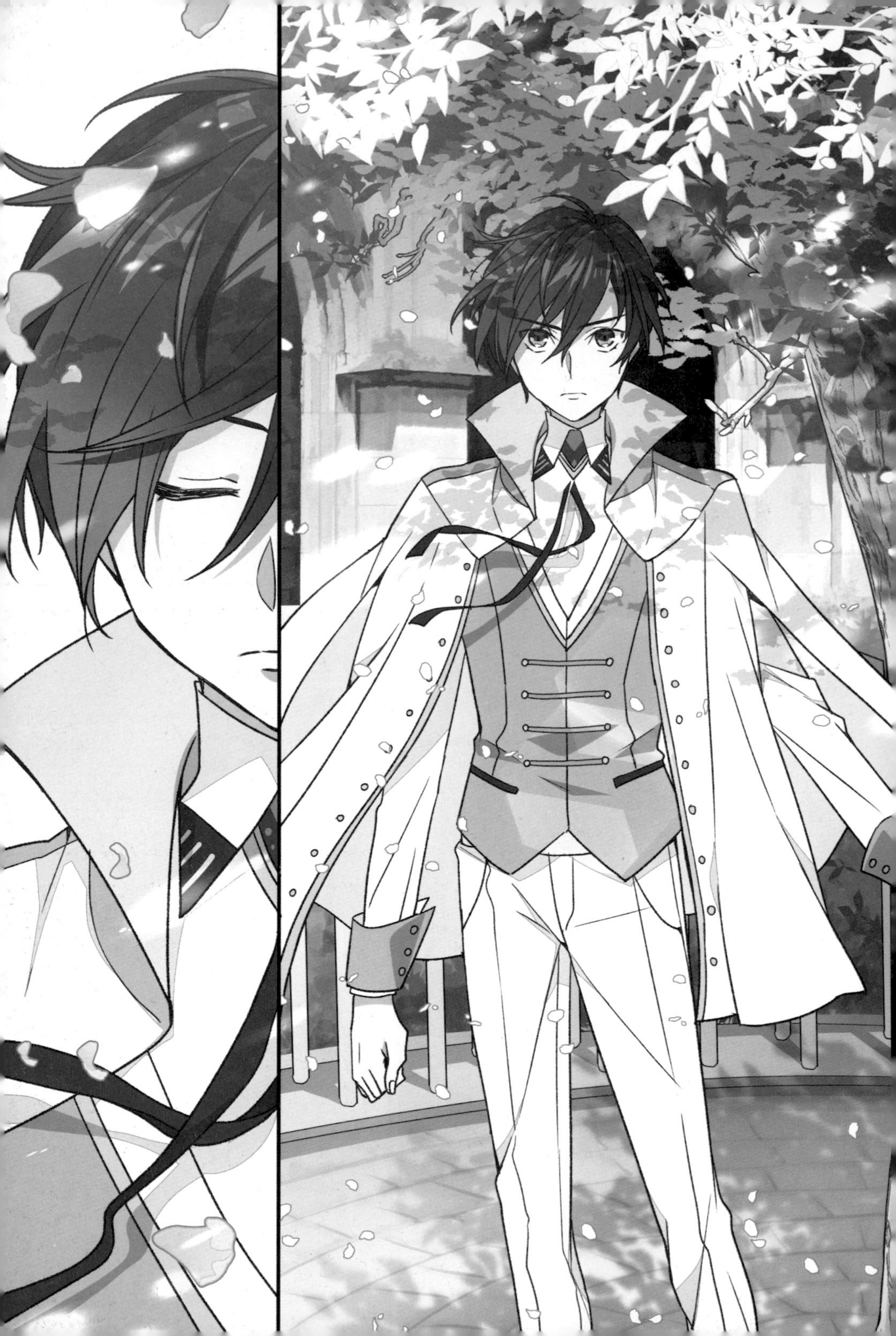

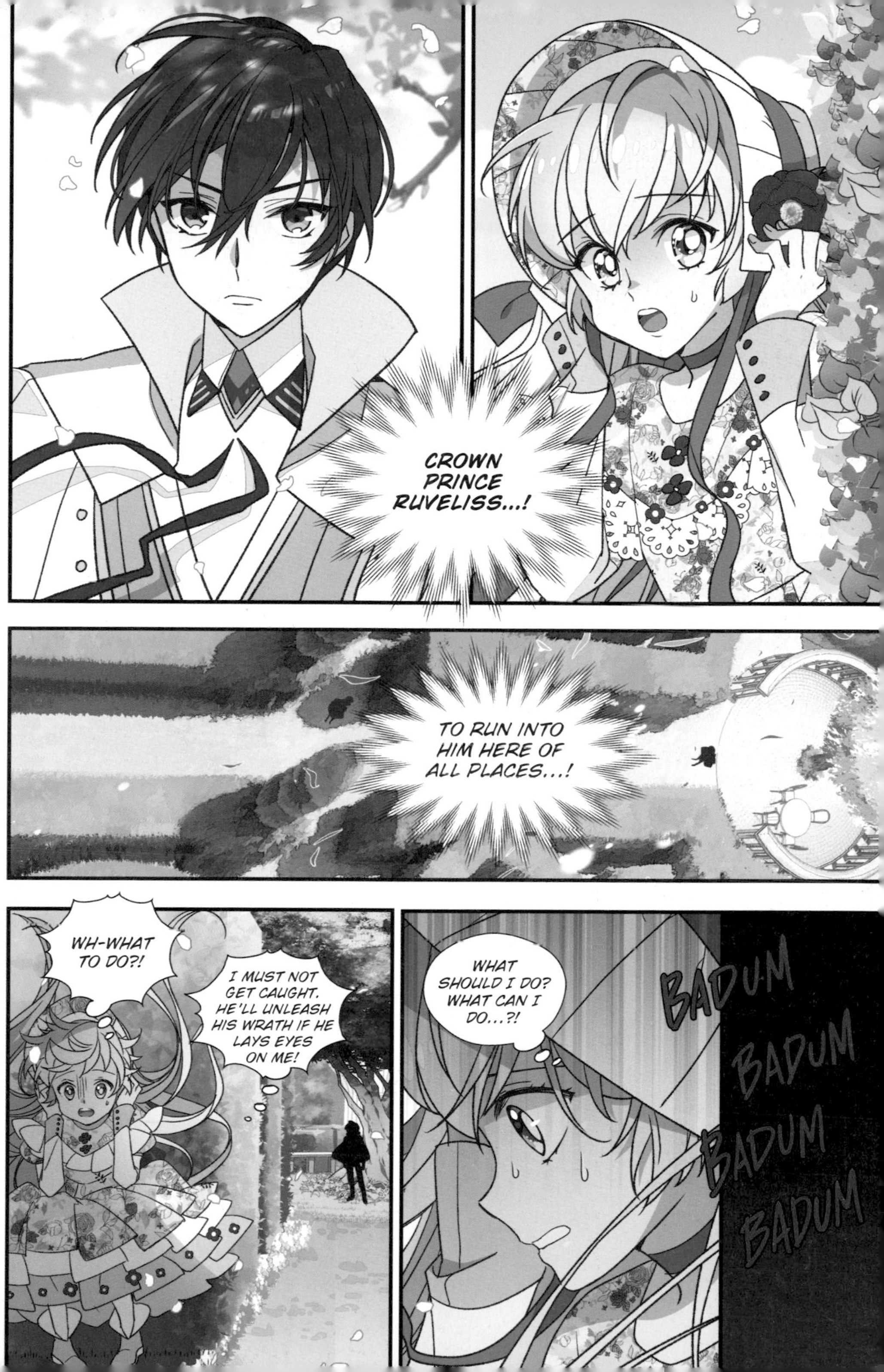
CROWN PRINCE RUVELISS...!
TO RUN INTO HIM HERE OF ALL PLACES...!
WH-WHAT TO DO?!
I MUST NOT GET CAUGHT. HE'LL UNLEASH HIS WRATH IF HE LAYS EYES ON ME!
WHAT SHOULD I DO? WHAT CAN I DO...?!
BADUM
BADUM
BADUM
BADUM

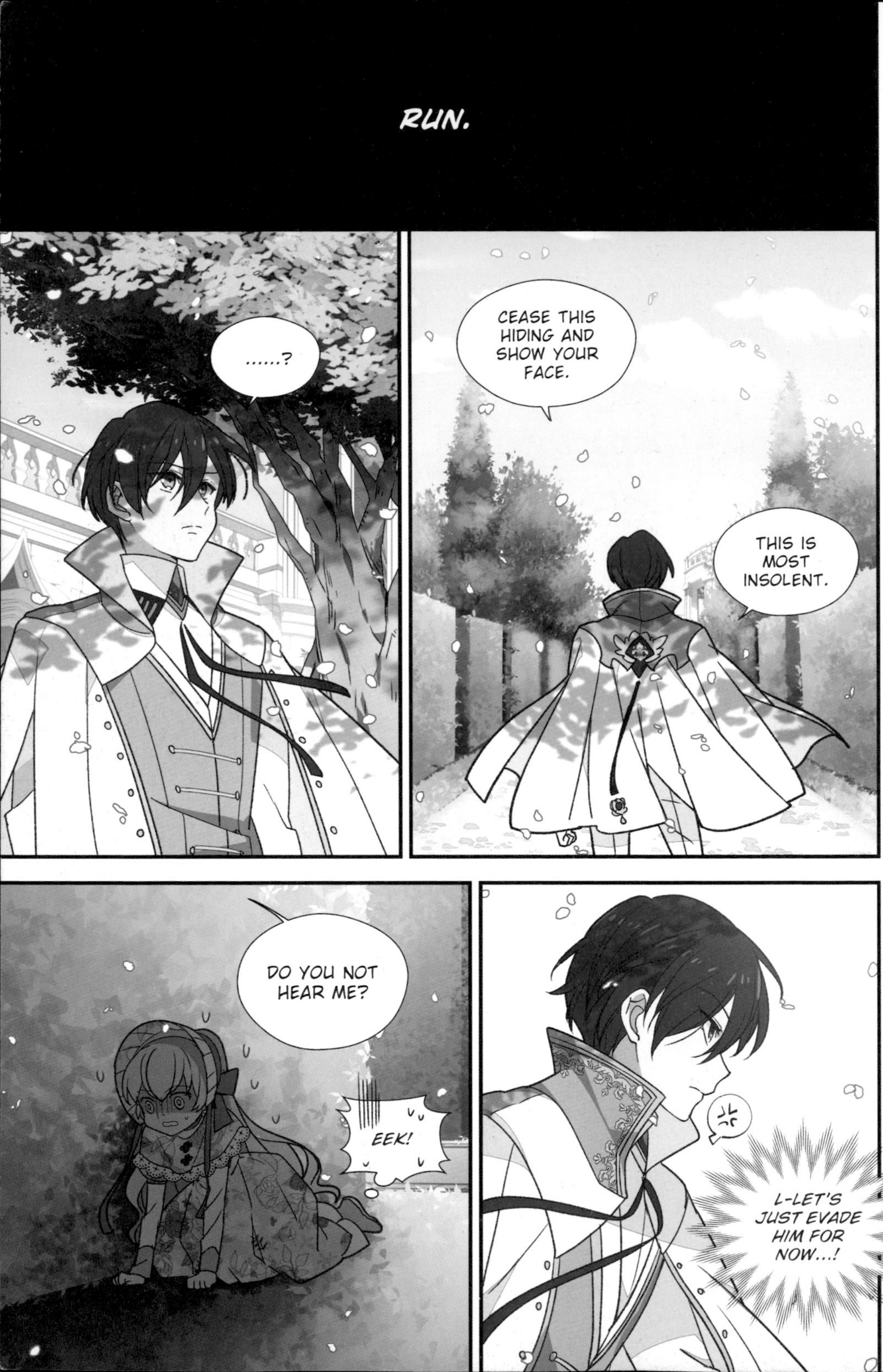
RUN.
......?
CEASE THIS HIDING AND SHOW YOUR FACE.
THIS IS MOST INSOLENT.
DO YOU NOT HEAR ME?
EEK!
L-LET'S JUST EVADE HIM FOR NOW...!

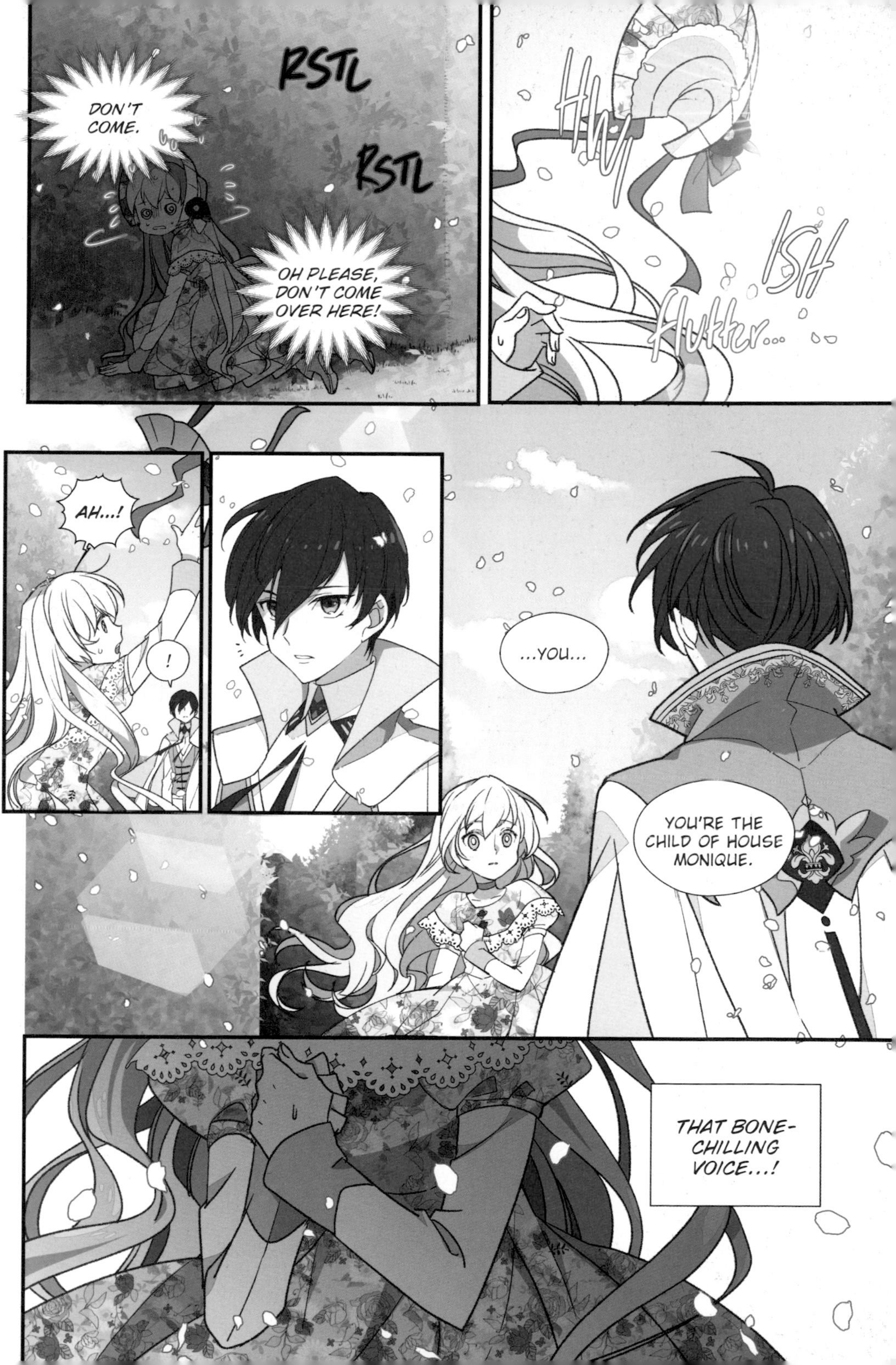
DON'T COME.
RSTL
RSTL
OH PLEASE, DON'T COME OVER HERE!
HWISH
flutter...
AH...!
!
...YOU...
YOU'RE THE CHILD OF HOUSE MONIQUE.
THAT BONE-CHILLING VOICE...!

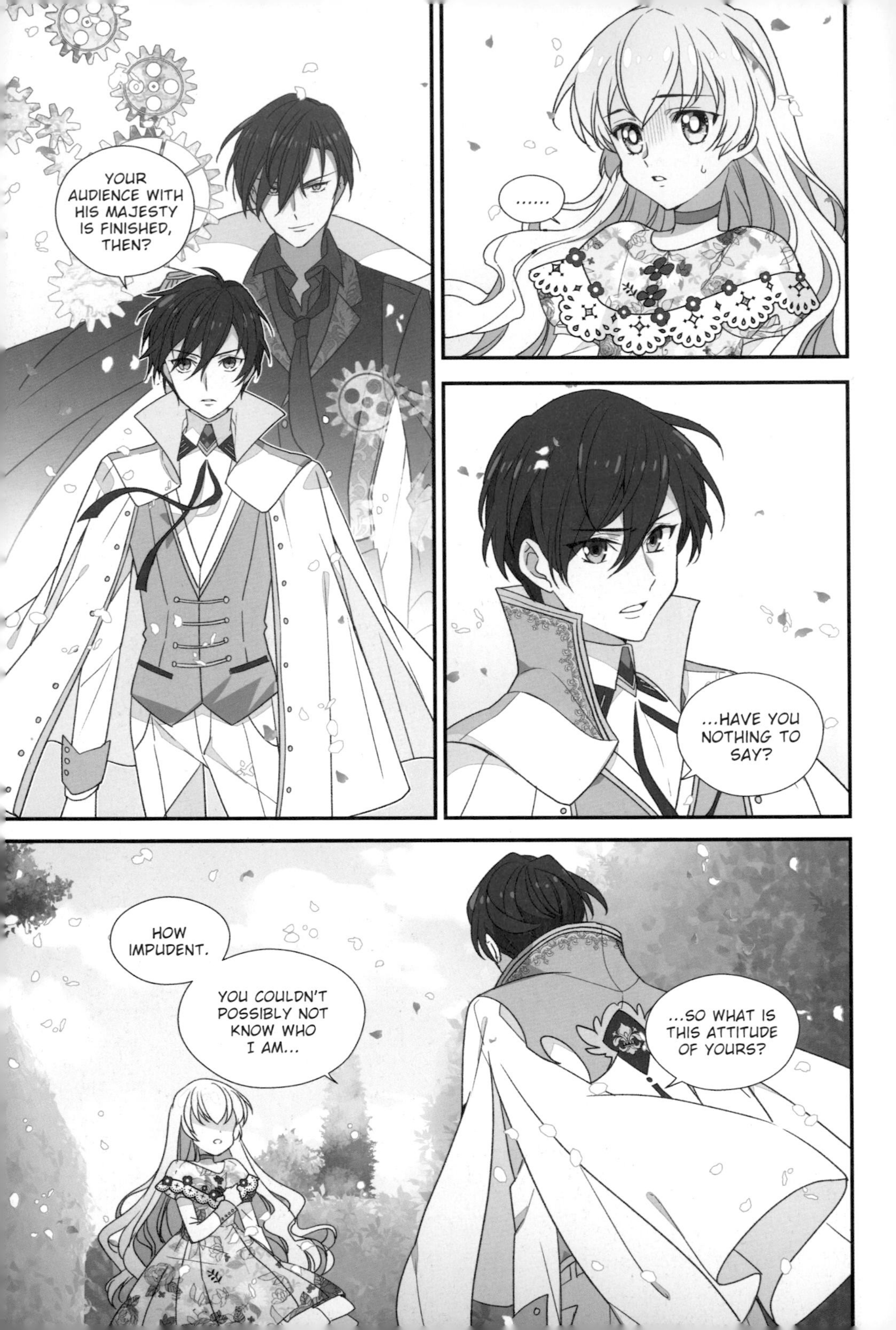

YOUR AUDIENCE WITH HIS MAJESTY IS FINISHED, THEN?
......
...HAVE YOU NOTHING TO SAY?
HOW IMPUDENT.
YOU COULDN'T POSSIBLY NOT KNOW WHO I AM...
...SO WHAT IS THIS ATTITUDE OF YOURS?

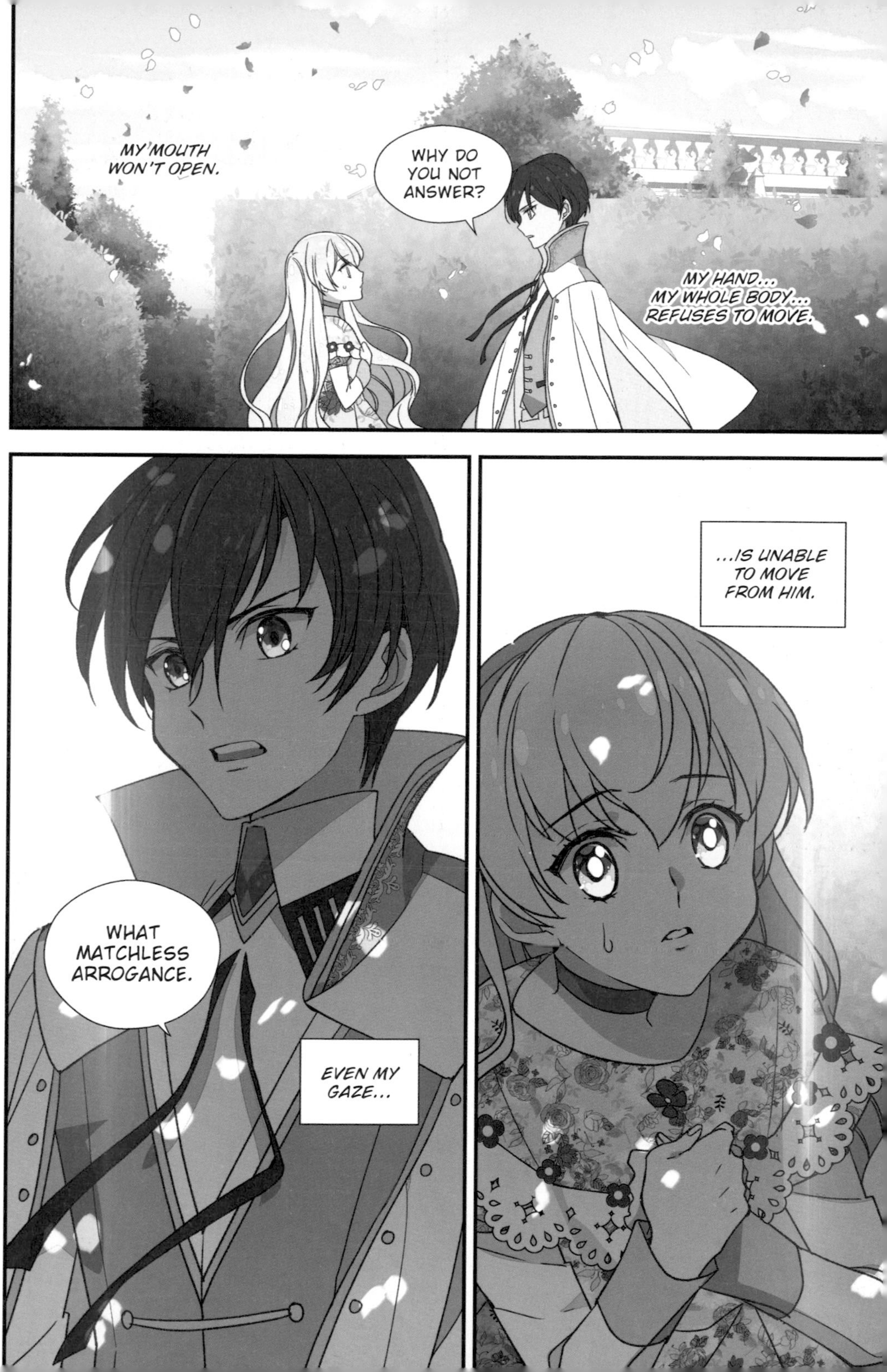
MY MOUTH WON'T OPEN.
WHY DO YOU NOT ANSWER?
MY HAND... MY WHOLE BODY... REFUSES TO MOVE.
WHAT MATCHLESS ARROGANCE.
EVEN MY GAZE...
...IS UNABLE TO MOVE FROM HIM.

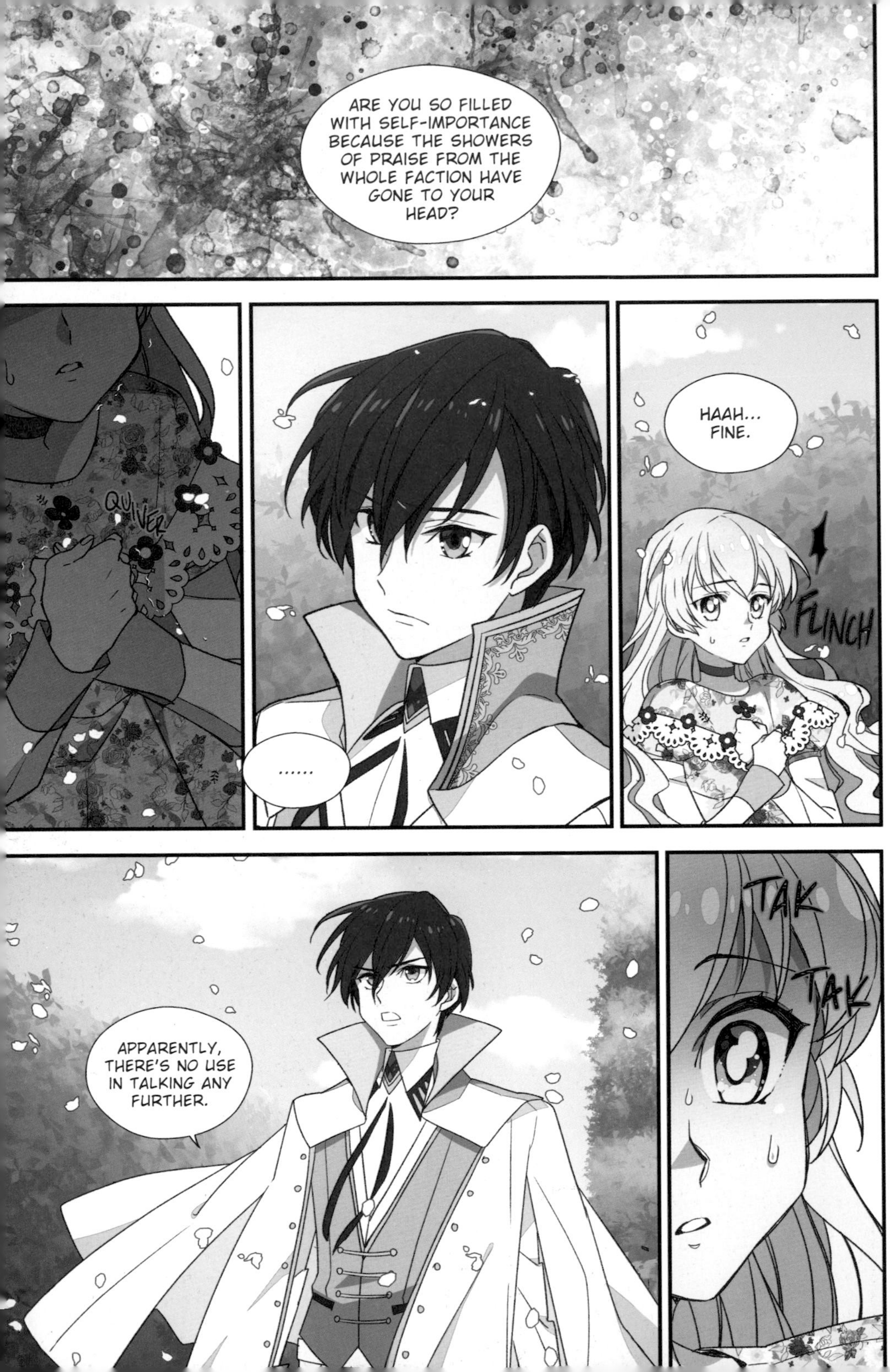
ARE YOU SO FILLED WITH SELF-IMPORTANCE BECAUSE THE SHOWERS OF PRAISE FROM THE WHOLE FACTION HAVE GONE TO YOUR HEAD?
QUIVER
......
HAAH... FINE.
FLINCH
APPARENTLY, THERE'S NO USE IN TALKING ANY FURTHER.
TAK
TAK

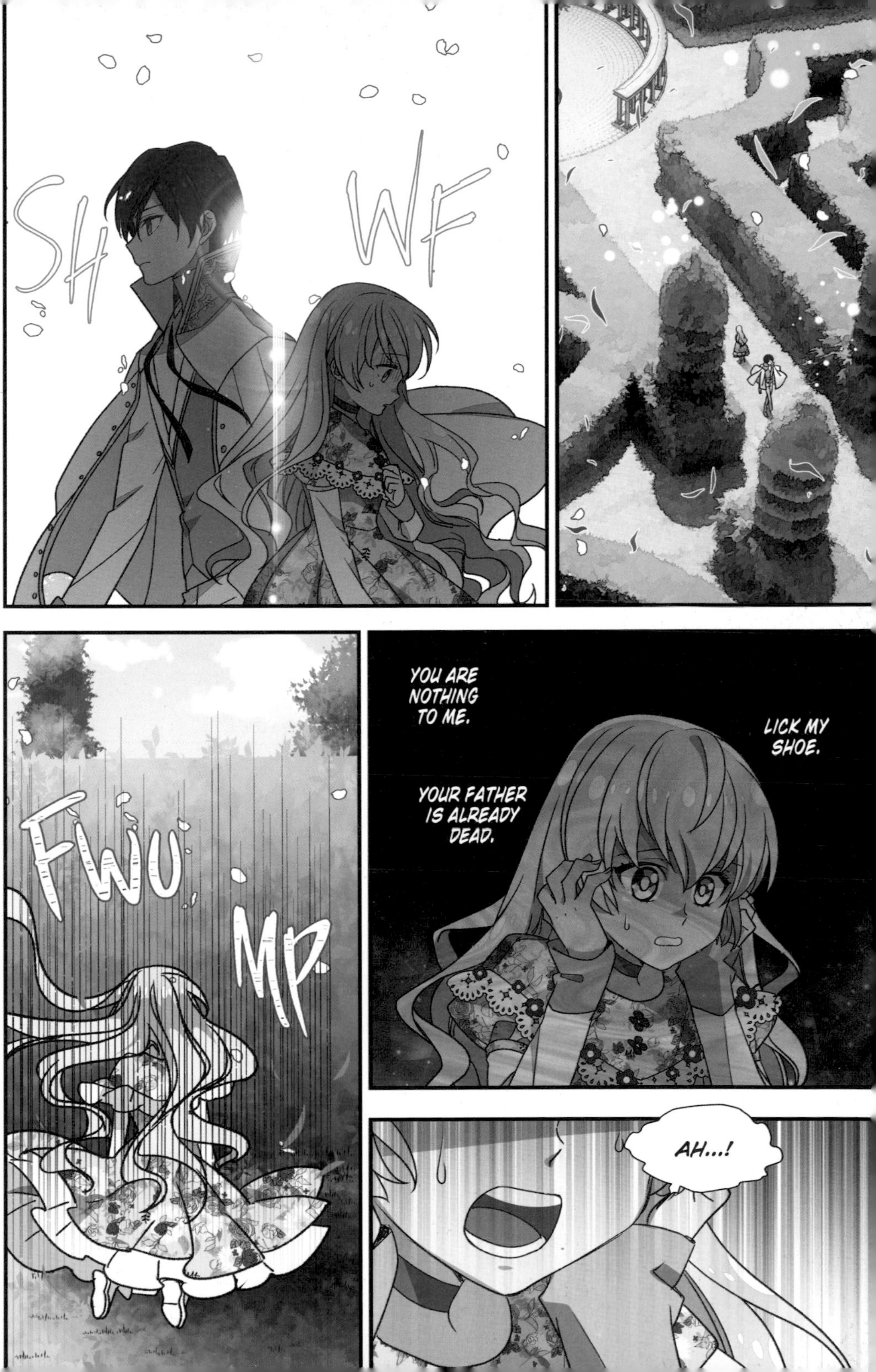
SHWF
FWUMP
YOU ARE NOTHING TO ME.
YOUR FATHER IS ALREADY DEAD.
LICK MY SHOE.
AH...!

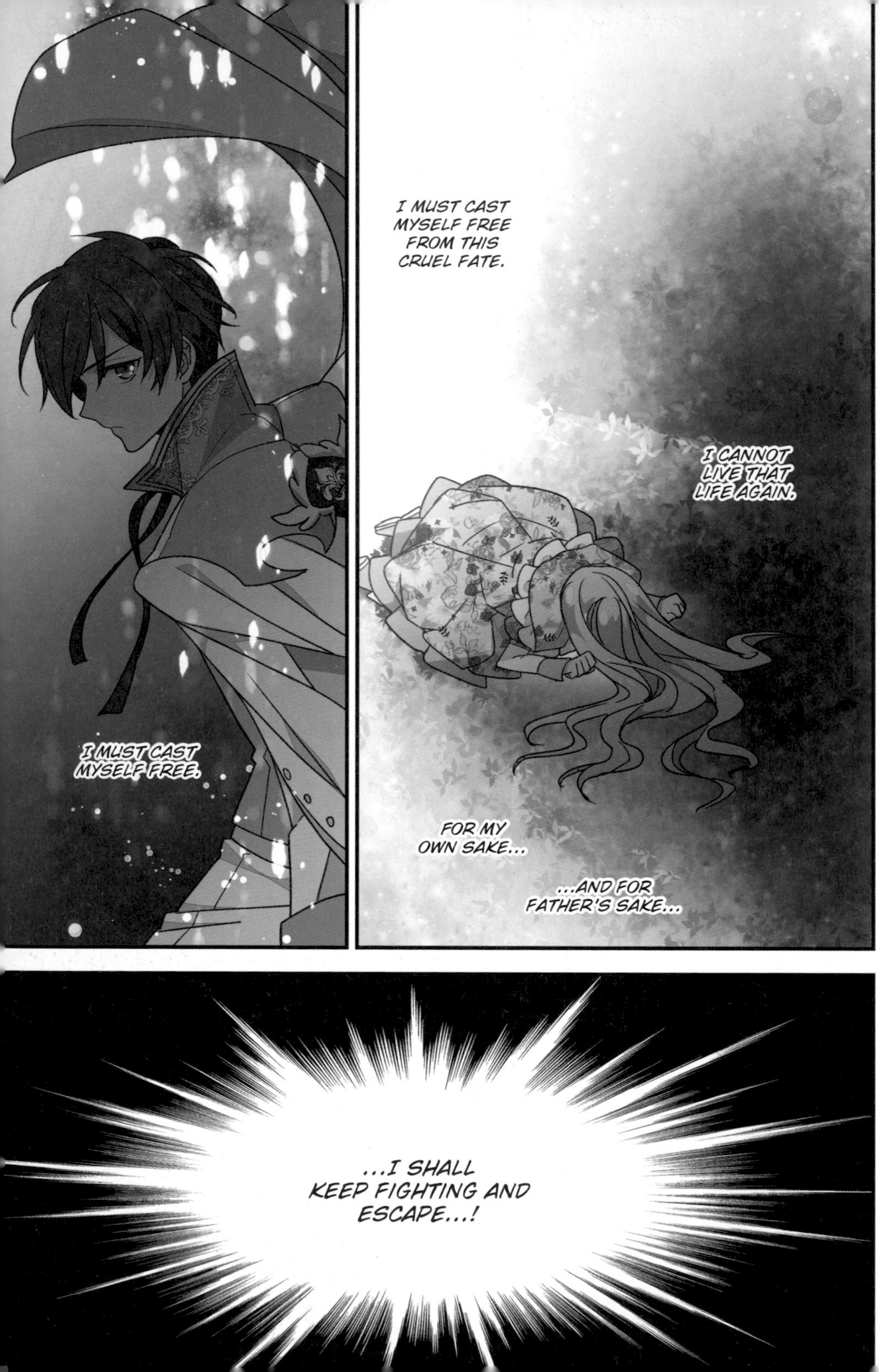
I MUST CAST MYSELF FREE FROM THIS CRUEL FATE.
I CANNOT LIVE THAT LIFE AGAIN.
FOR MY OWN SAKE...
...AND FOR FATHER'S SAKE...
I MUST CAST MYSELF FREE.
...I SHALL KEEP FIGHTING AND ESCAPE...!

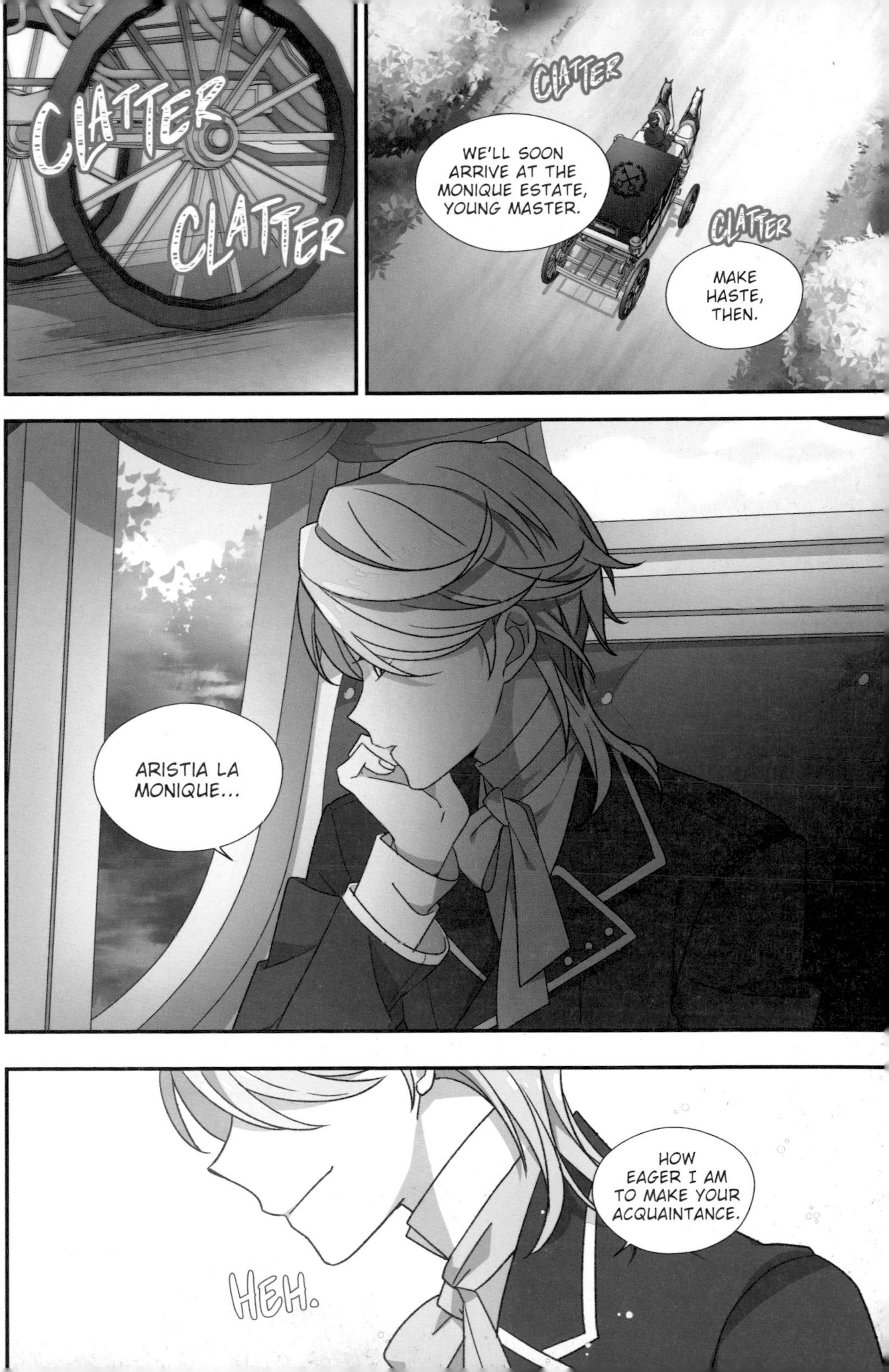
CLATTER
CLATTER
CLATTER
WE'LL SOON ARRIVE AT THE MONIQUE ESTATE, YOUNG MASTER.
CLATTER
MAKE HASTE, THEN.
ARISTIA LA MONIQUE...
HOW EAGER I AM TO MAKE YOUR ACQUAINTANCE.
HEH.

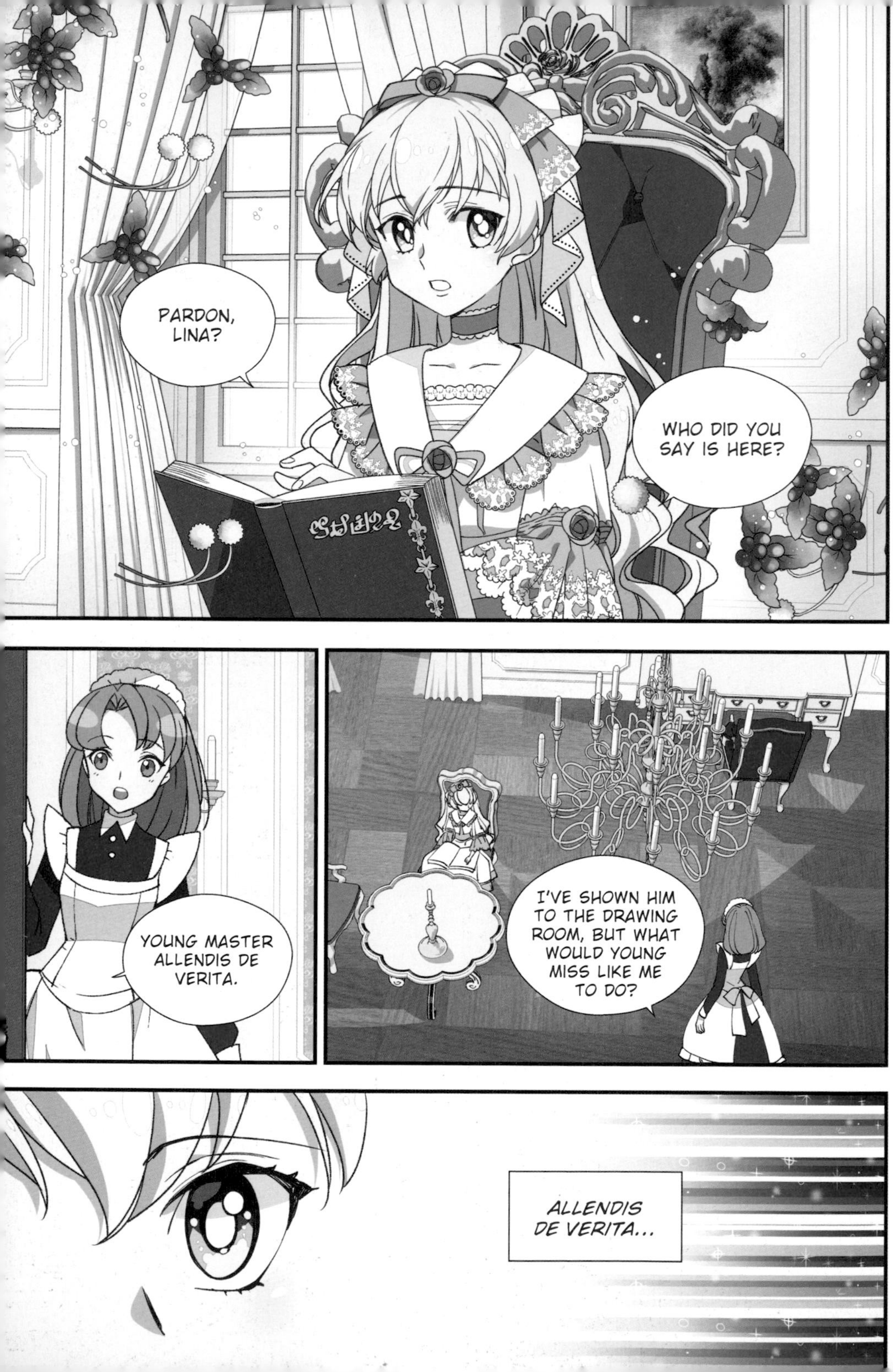
PARDON, LINA?
WHO DID YOU SAY IS HERE?
YOUNG MASTER ALLENDIS DE VERITA.
I'VE SHOWN HIM TO THE DRAWING ROOM, BUT WHAT WOULD YOUNG MISS LIKE ME TO DO?
ALLENDIS DE VERITA...

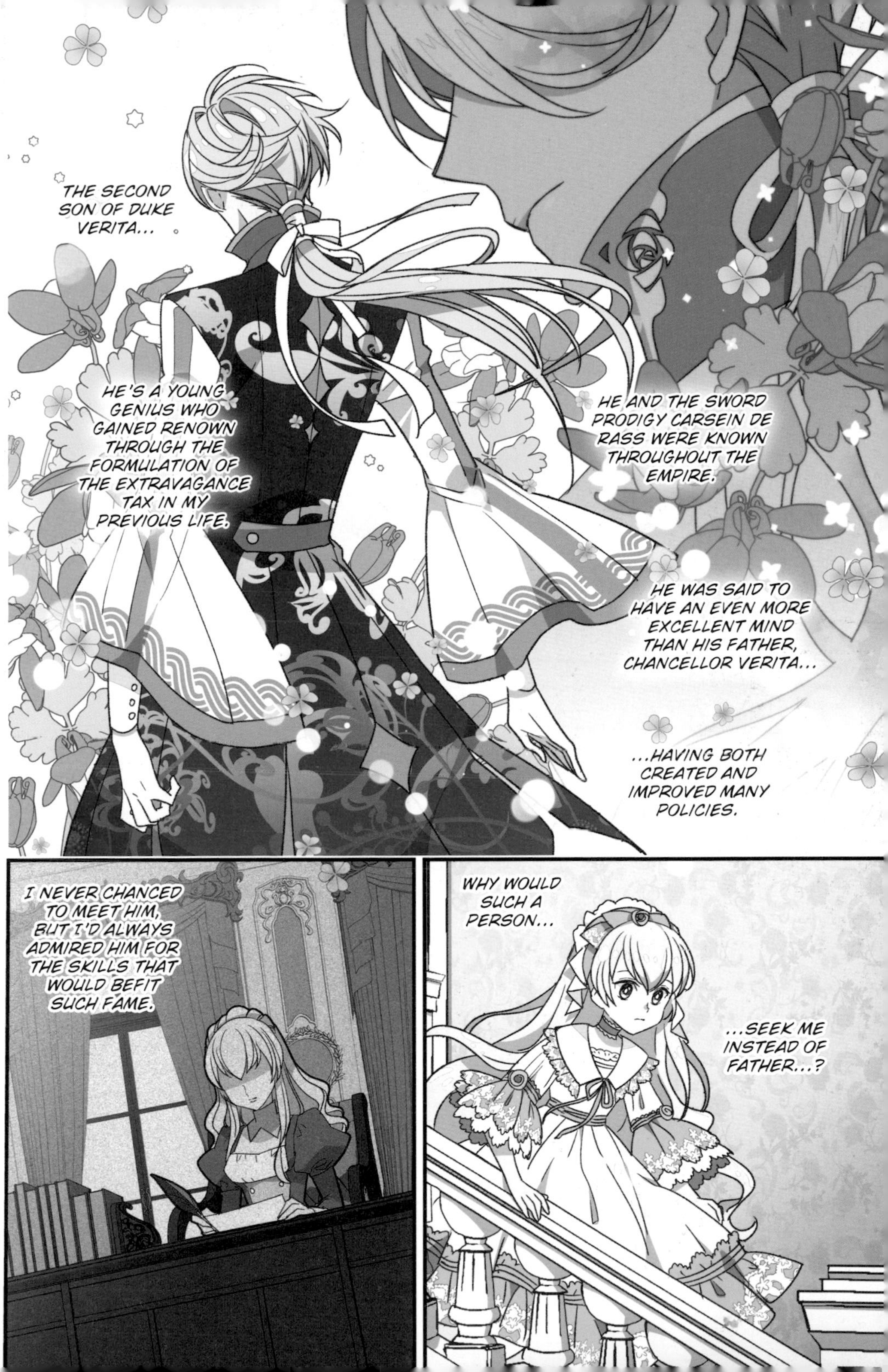
THE SECOND SON OF DUKE VERITA...
HE'S A YOUNG GENIUS WHO GAINED RENOWN THROUGH THE FORMULATION OF THE EXTRAVAGANCE TAX IN MY PREVIOUS LIFE.
HE AND THE SWORD PRODIGY CARSEIN DE RASS WERE KNOWN THROUGHOUT THE EMPIRE.
HE WAS SAID TO HAVE AN EVEN MORE EXCELLENT MIND THAN HIS FATHER, CHANCELLOR VERITA...
...HAVING BOTH CREATED AND IMPROVED MANY POLICIES.
I NEVER CHANCED TO MEET HIM, BUT I'D ALWAYS ADMIRED HIM FOR THE SKILLS THAT WOULD BEFIT SUCH FAME.
WHY WOULD SUCH A PERSON...
...SEEK ME INSTEAD OF FATHER...?

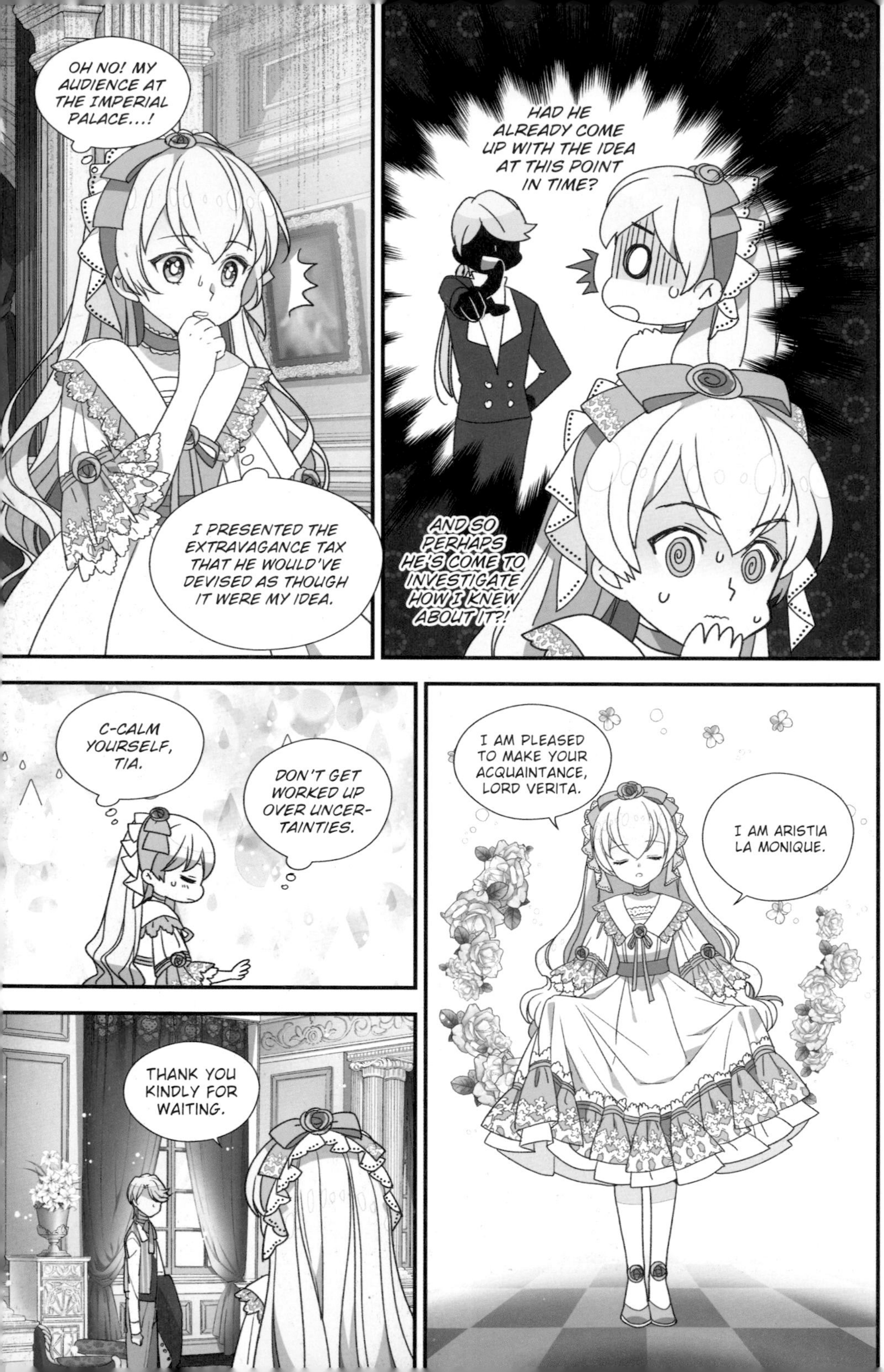
OH NO! MY AUDIENCE AT THE IMPERIAL PALACE...!
I PRESENTED THE EXTRAVAGANCE TAX THAT HE WOULD'VE DEVISED AS THOUGH IT WERE MY IDEA.
HAD HE ALREADY COME UP WITH THE IDEA AT THIS POINT IN TIME?
AND SO PERHAPS HE'S COME TO INVESTIGATE HOW I KNEW ABOUT IT?!
C-CALM YOURSELF, TIA.
DON'T GET WORKED UP OVER UNCER-TAINTIES.
THANK YOU KINDLY FOR WAITING.
I AM PLEASED TO MAKE YOUR ACQUAINTANCE, LORD VERITA.
I AM ARISTIA LA MONIQUE.

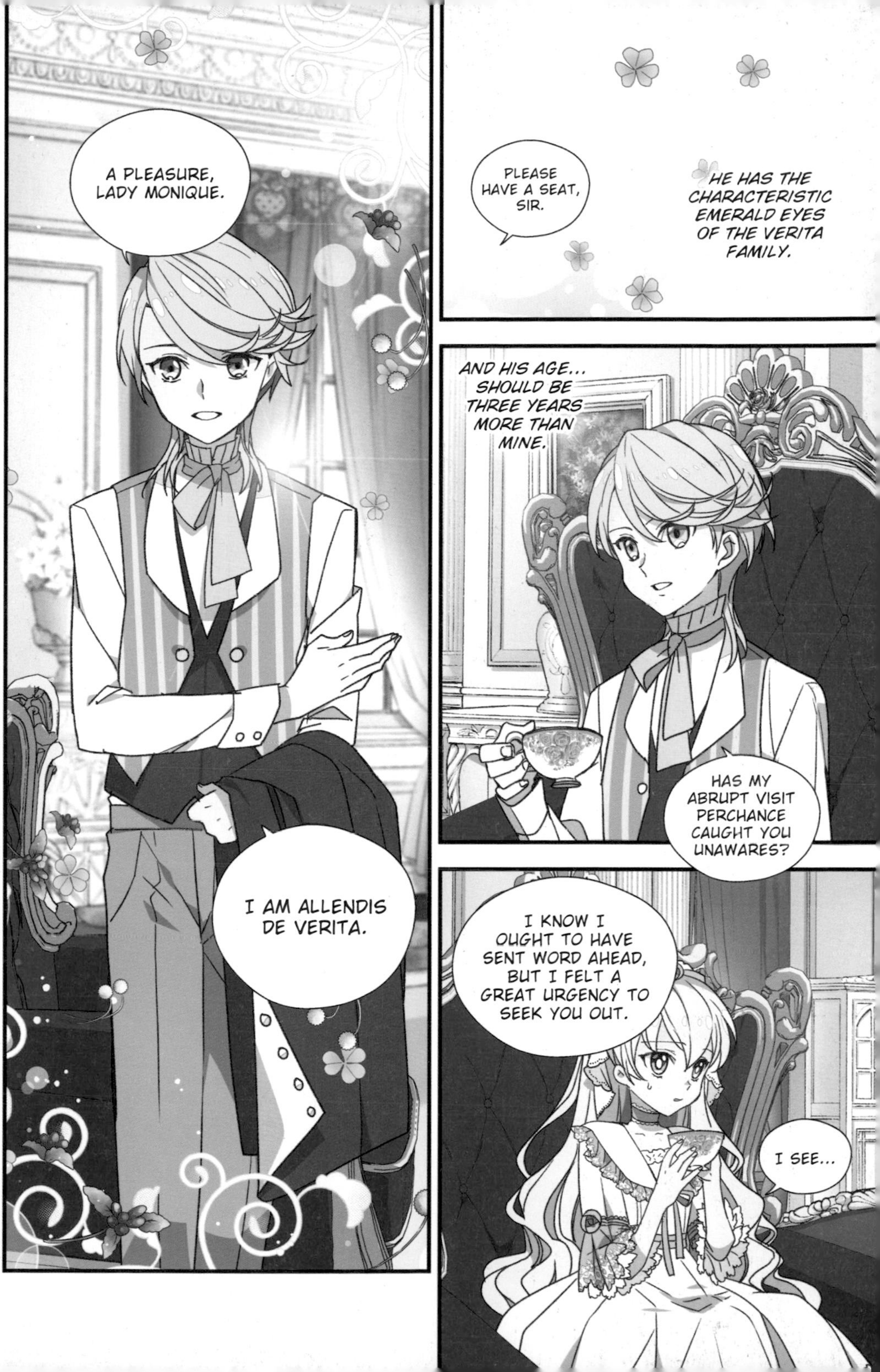
A PLEASURE, LADY MONIQUE.
I AM ALLENDIS DE VERITA.
PLEASE HAVE A SEAT, SIR.
HE HAS THE CHARACTERISTIC EMERALD EYES OF THE VERITA FAMILY.
AND HIS AGE... SHOULD BE THREE YEARS MORE THAN MINE.
HAS MY ABRUPT VISIT PERCHANCE CAUGHT YOU UNAWARES?
I KNOW I OUGHT TO HAVE SENT WORD AHEAD, BUT I FELT A GREAT URGENCY TO SEEK YOU OUT.
I SEE...

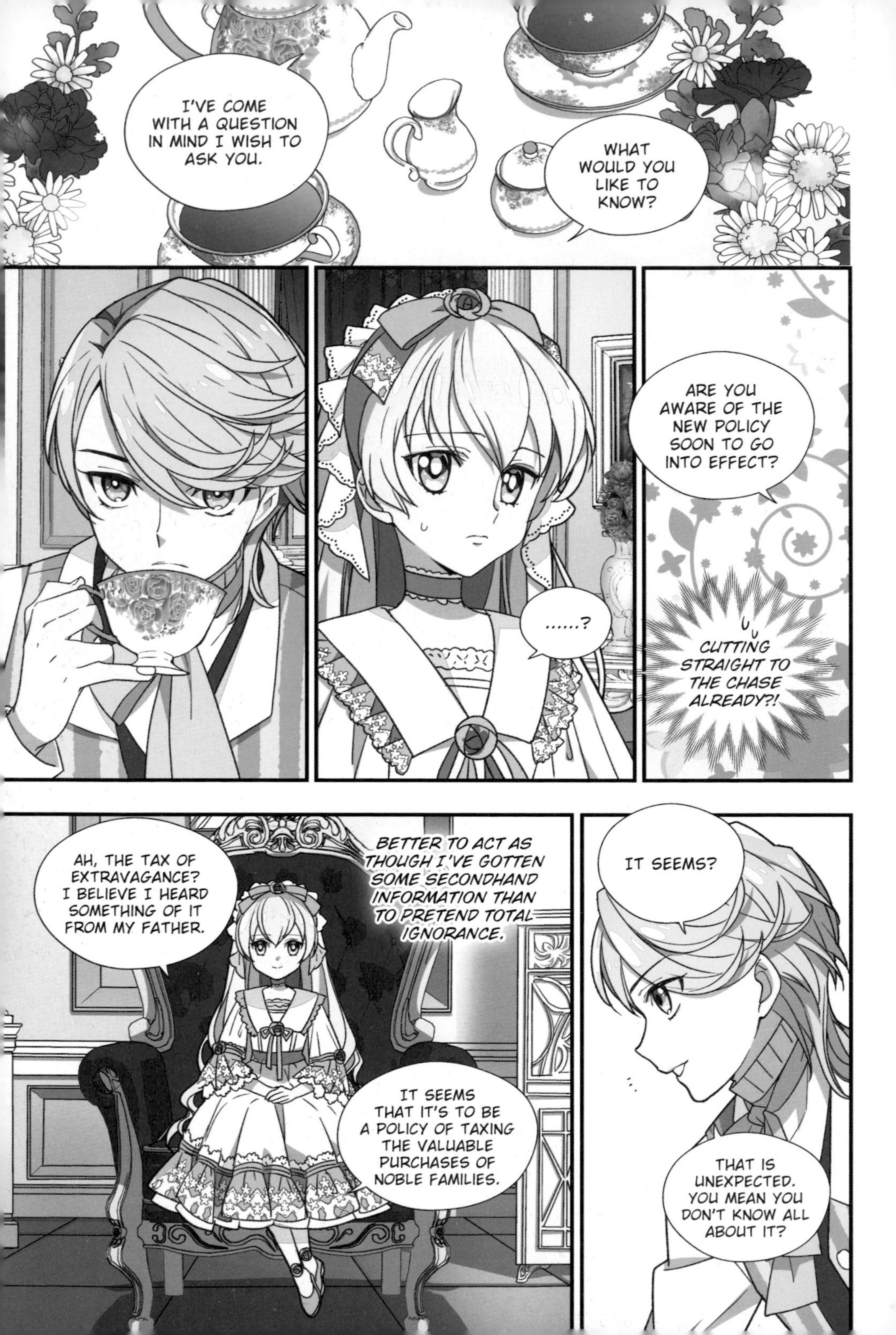
I'VE COME WITH A QUESTION IN MIND I WISH TO ASK YOU.
WHAT WOULD YOU LIKE TO KNOW?
ARE YOU AWARE OF THE NEW POLICY SOON TO GO INTO EFFECT?
......?
CUTTING STRAIGHT TO THE CHASE ALREADY?!
AH, THE TAX OF EXTRAVAGANCE? I BELIEVE I HEARD SOMETHING OF IT FROM MY FATHER.
BETTER TO ACT AS THOUGH I'VE GOTTEN SOME SECONDHAND INFORMATION THAN TO PRETEND TOTAL IGNORANCE.
IT SEEMS THAT IT'S TO BE A POLICY OF TAXING THE VALUABLE PURCHASES OF NOBLE FAMILIES.
IT SEEMS?
THAT IS UNEXPECTED. YOU MEAN YOU DON'T KNOW ALL ABOUT IT?

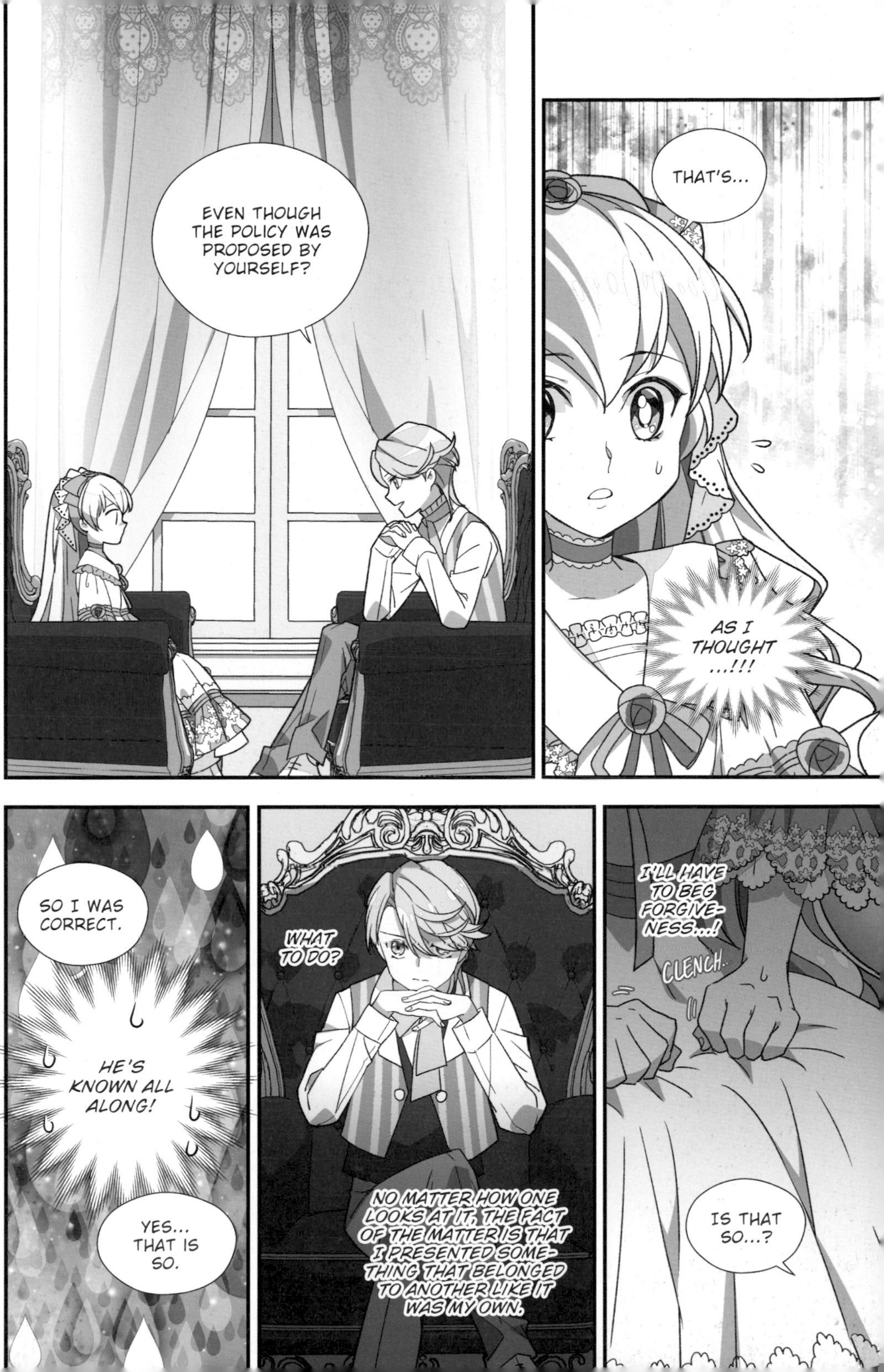
EVEN THOUGH THE POLICY WAS PROPOSED BY YOURSELF?
THAT'S...
AS I THOUGHT ...!!!
SO I WAS CORRECT.
HE'S KNOWN ALL ALONG!
YES... THAT IS SO.
WHAT TO DO?
NO MATTER HOW ONE LOOKS AT IT, THE FACT OF THE MATTER IS THAT I PRESENTED SOME-THING THAT BELONGED TO ANOTHER LIKE IT WAS MY OWN.
I'LL HAVE TO BEG FORGIVE-NESS...!
CLENCH...
IS THAT SO...?

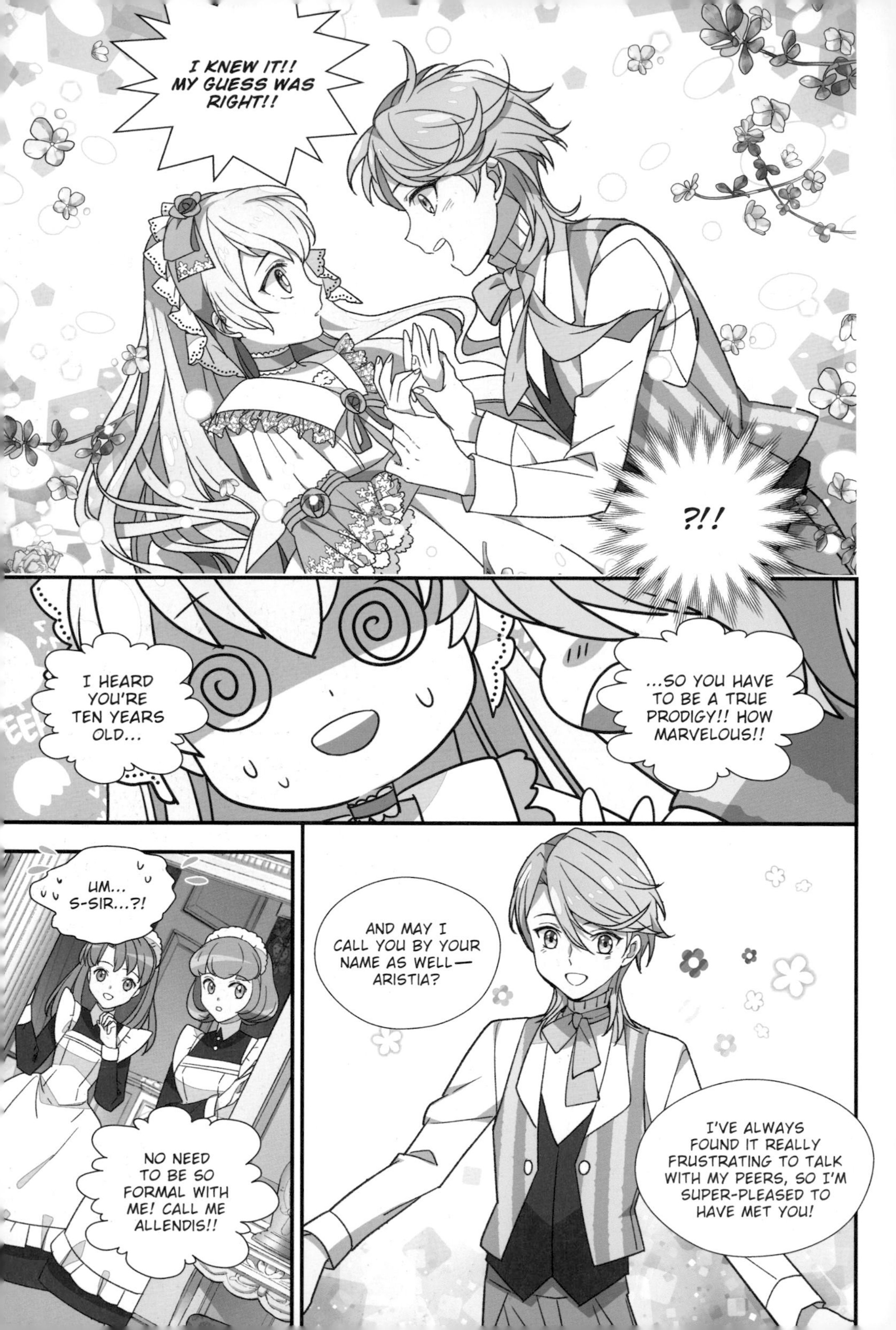
I KNEW IT!! MY GUESS WAS RIGHT!!
?!!
I HEARD YOU'RE TEN YEARS OLD...
...SO YOU HAVE TO BE A TRUE PRODIGY!! HOW MARVELOUS!!
UM... S-SIR...?!
NO NEED TO BE SO FORMAL WITH ME! CALL ME ALLENDIS!!
AND MAY I CALL YOU BY YOUR NAME AS WELL—ARISTIA?
I'VE ALWAYS FOUND IT REALLY FRUSTRATING TO TALK WITH MY PEERS, SO I'M SUPER-PLEASED TO HAVE MET YOU!

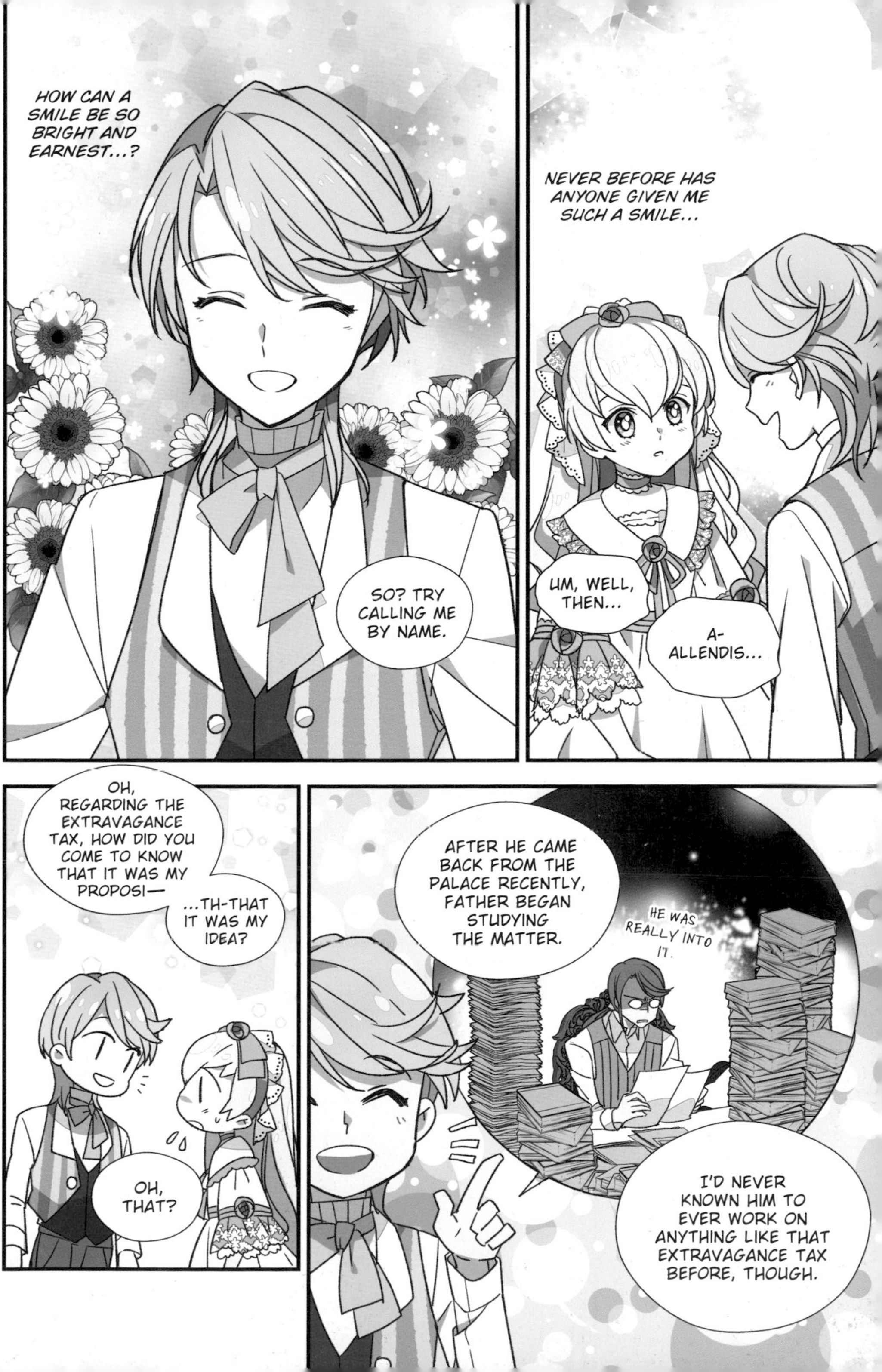
HOW CAN A SMILE BE SO BRIGHT AND EARNEST...?
SO? TRY CALLING ME BY NAME.
NEVER BEFORE HAS ANYONE GIVEN ME SUCH A SMILE...
UM, WELL, THEN...
A-ALLENDIS...
OH, REGARDING THE EXTRAVAGANCE TAX, HOW DID YOU COME TO KNOW THAT IT WAS MY PROPOSI—
...TH-THAT IT WAS MY IDEA?
OH, THAT?
AFTER HE CAME BACK FROM THE PALACE RECENTLY, FATHER BEGAN STUDYING THE MATTER.
HE WAS REALLY INTO IT.
I'D NEVER KNOWN HIM TO EVER WORK ON ANYTHING LIKE THAT EXTRAVAGANCE TAX BEFORE, THOUGH.

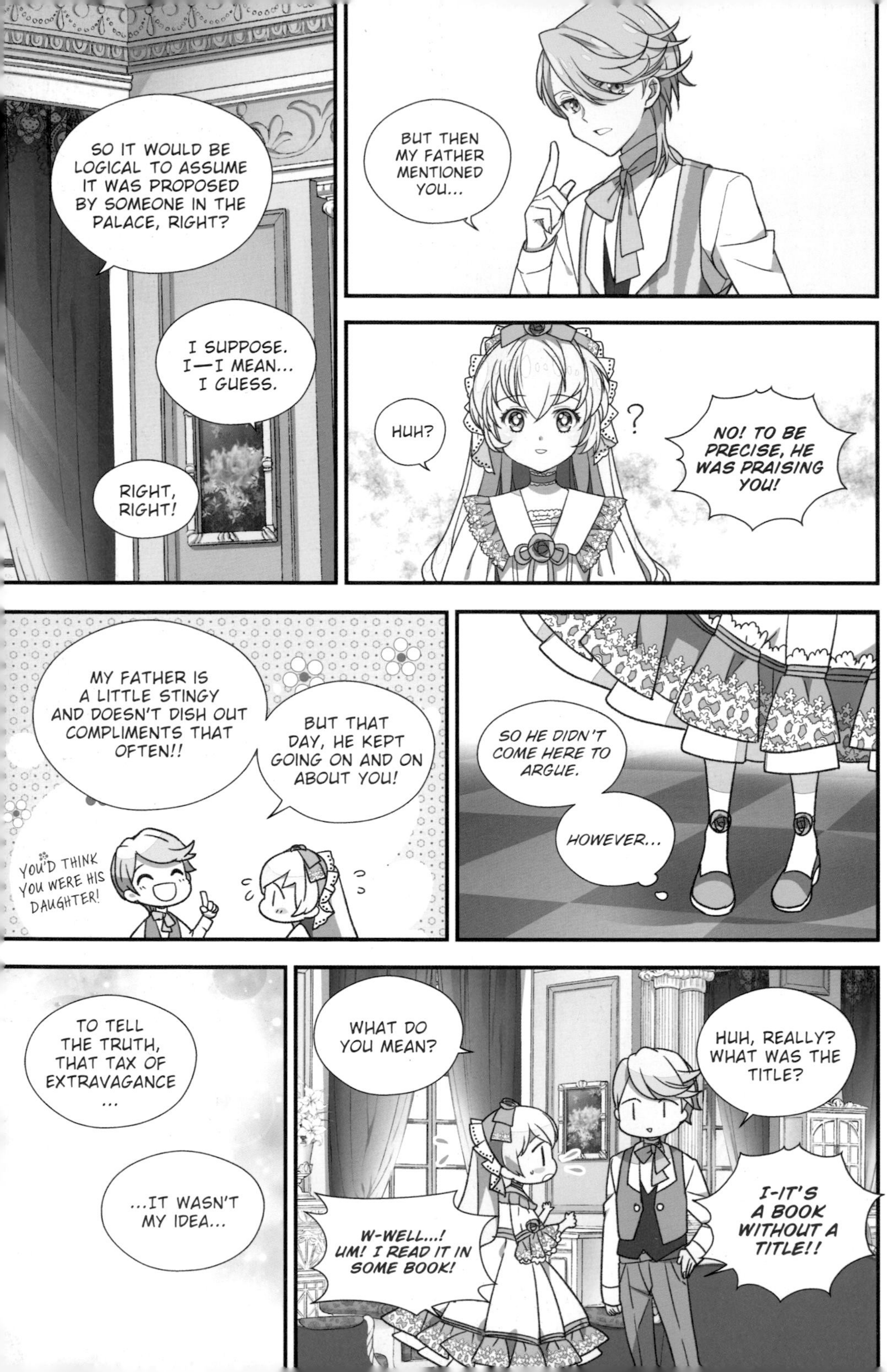
SO IT WOULD BE LOGICAL TO ASSUME IT WAS PROPOSED BY SOMEONE IN THE PALACE, RIGHT?
BUT THEN MY FATHER MENTIONED YOU...
I SUPPOSE. I—I MEAN... I GUESS.
RIGHT, RIGHT!
HUH?
NO! TO BE PRECISE, HE WAS PRAISING YOU!
MY FATHER IS A LITTLE STINGY AND DOESN'T DISH OUT COMPLIMENTS THAT OFTEN!!
BUT THAT DAY, HE KEPT GOING ON AND ON ABOUT YOU!
YOU'D THINK YOU WERE HIS DAUGHTER!
SO HE DIDN'T COME HERE TO ARGUE.
HOWEVER...
TO TELL THE TRUTH, THAT TAX OF EXTRAVAGANCE ...
...IT WASN'T MY IDEA...
WHAT DO YOU MEAN?
HUH, REALLY? WHAT WAS THE TITLE?
W-WELL...! UM! I READ IT IN SOME BOOK!
I-IT'S A BOOK WITHOUT A TITLE!!

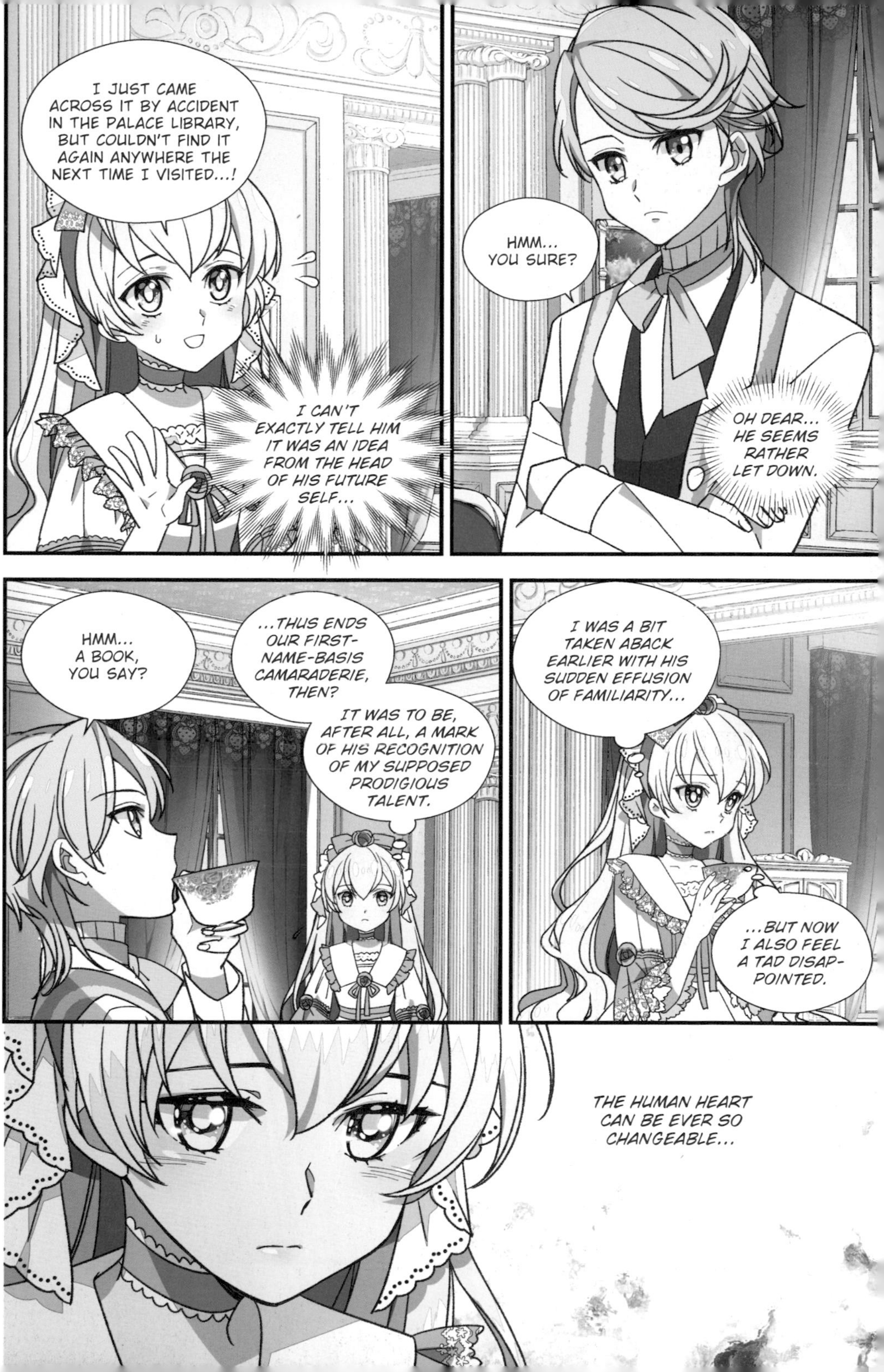
I JUST CAME ACROSS IT BY ACCIDENT IN THE PALACE LIBRARY, BUT COULDN'T FIND IT AGAIN ANYWHERE THE NEXT TIME I VISITED...!
HMM... YOU SURE?
I CAN'T EXACTLY TELL HIM IT WAS AN IDEA FROM THE HEAD OF HIS FUTURE SELF...
OH DEAR... HE SEEMS RATHER LET DOWN.
HMM... A BOOK, YOU SAY?
...THUS ENDS OUR FIRST-NAME-BASIS CAMARADERIE, THEN?
IT WAS TO BE, AFTER ALL, A MARK OF HIS RECOGNITION OF MY SUPPOSED PRODIGIOUS TALENT.
I WAS A BIT TAKEN ABACK EARLIER WITH HIS SUDDEN EFFUSION OF FAMILIARITY...
...BUT NOW I ALSO FEEL A TAD DISAPPOINTED.
THE HUMAN HEART CAN BE EVER SO CHANGEABLE...

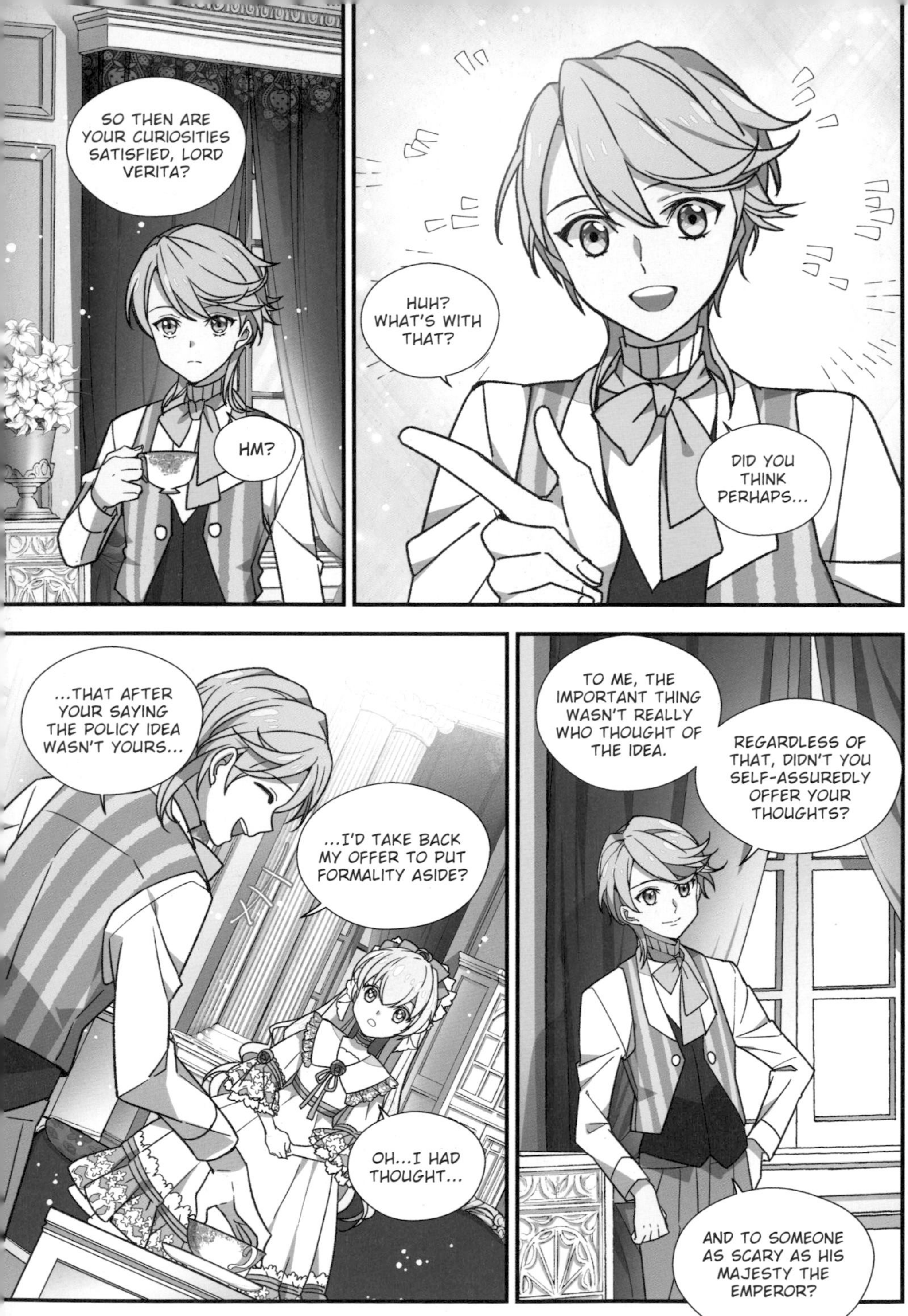
SO THEN ARE YOUR CURIOSITIES SATISFIED, LORD VERITA?
HM?
HUH? WHAT'S WITH THAT?
DID YOU THINK PERHAPS...
...THAT AFTER YOUR SAYING THE POLICY IDEA WASN'T YOURS...
...I'D TAKE BACK MY OFFER TO PUT FORMALITY ASIDE?
OH...I HAD THOUGHT...
TO ME, THE IMPORTANT THING WASN'T REALLY WHO THOUGHT OF THE IDEA.
REGARDLESS OF THAT, DIDN'T YOU SELF-ASSUREDLY OFFER YOUR THOUGHTS?
AND TO SOMEONE AS SCARY AS HIS MAJESTY THE EMPEROR?

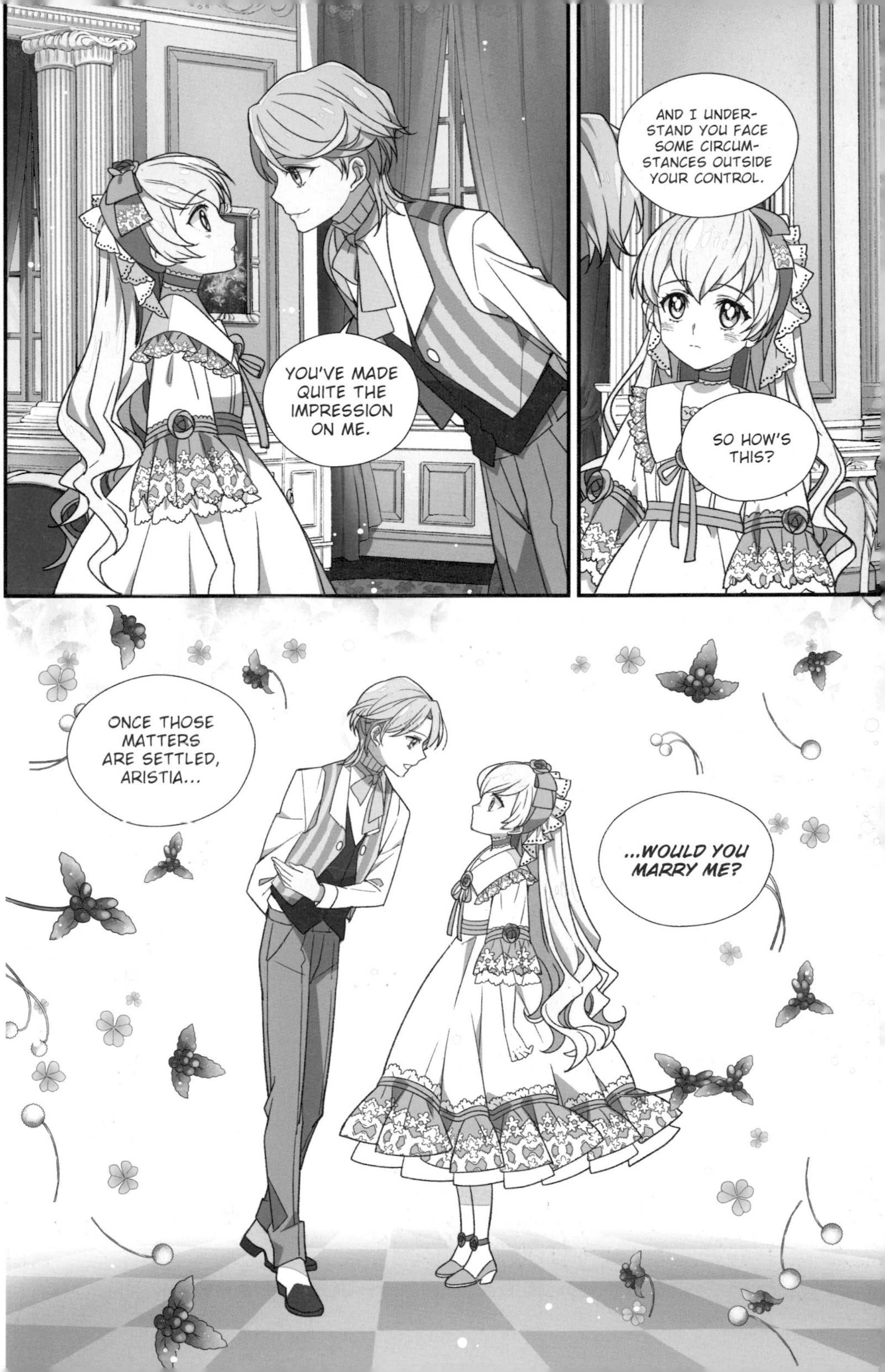
YOU'VE MADE QUITE THE IMPRESSION ON ME.
AND I UNDERSTAND YOU FACE SOME CIRCUMSTANCES OUTSIDE YOUR CONTROL.
SO HOW'S THIS?
ONCE THOSE MATTERS ARE SETTLED, ARISTIA...
...WOULD YOU MARRY ME?

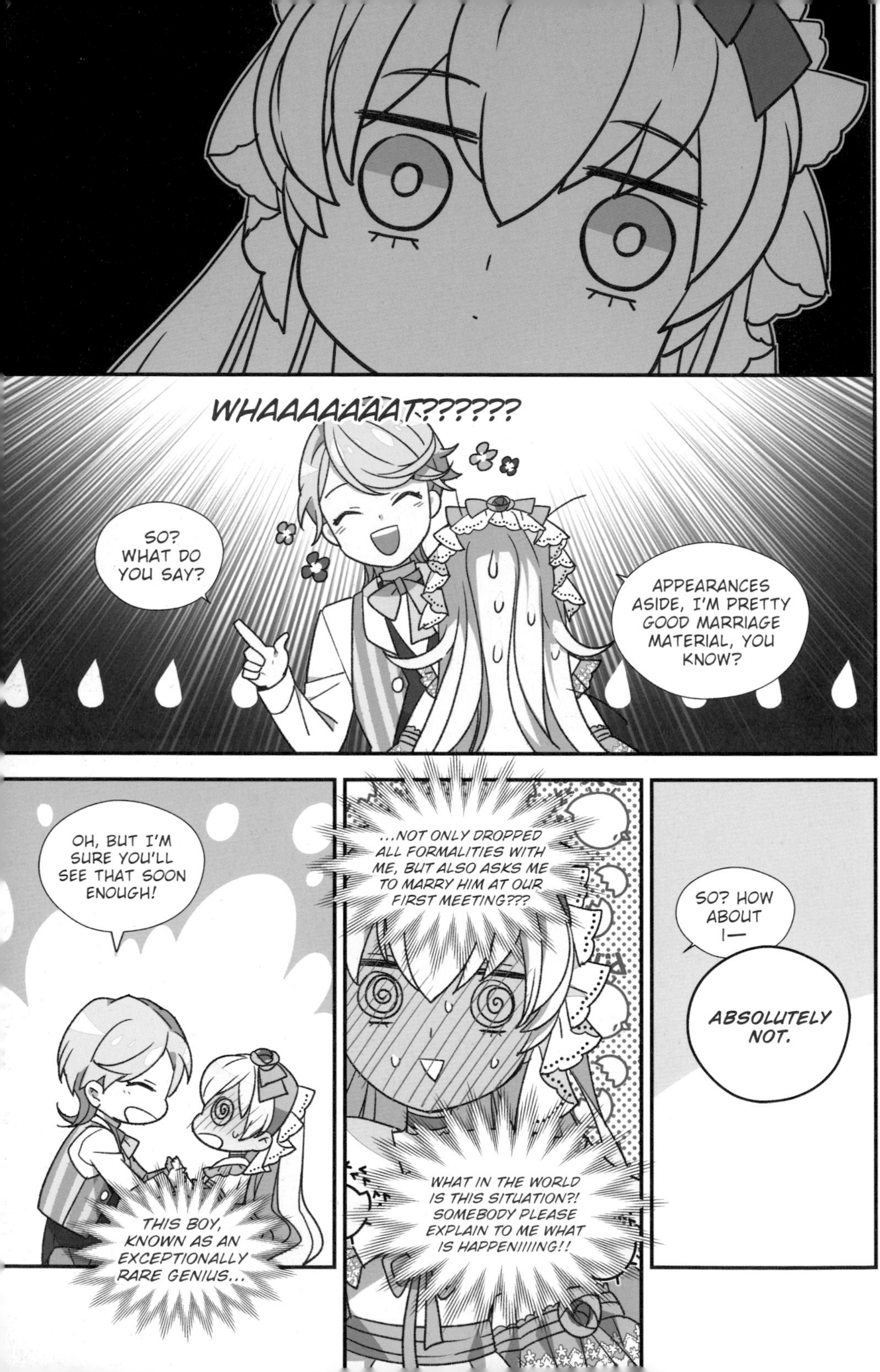
WHAAAAAAAT??????
SO? WHAT DO YOU SAY?
APPEARANCES ASIDE, I'M PRETTY GOOD MARRIAGE MATERIAL, YOU KNOW?
OH, BUT I'M SURE YOU'LL SEE THAT SOON ENOUGH!
THIS BOY, KNOWN AS AN EXCEPTIONALLY RARE GENIUS...
...NOT ONLY DROPPED ALL FORMALITIES WITH ME, BUT ALSO ASKS ME TO MARRY HIM AT OUR FIRST MEETING???
WHAT IN THE WORLD IS THIS SITUATION?! SOMEBODY PLEASE EXPLAIN TO ME WHAT IS HAPPENIIIING!!
SO? HOW ABOUT I—
ABSOLUTELY NOT.

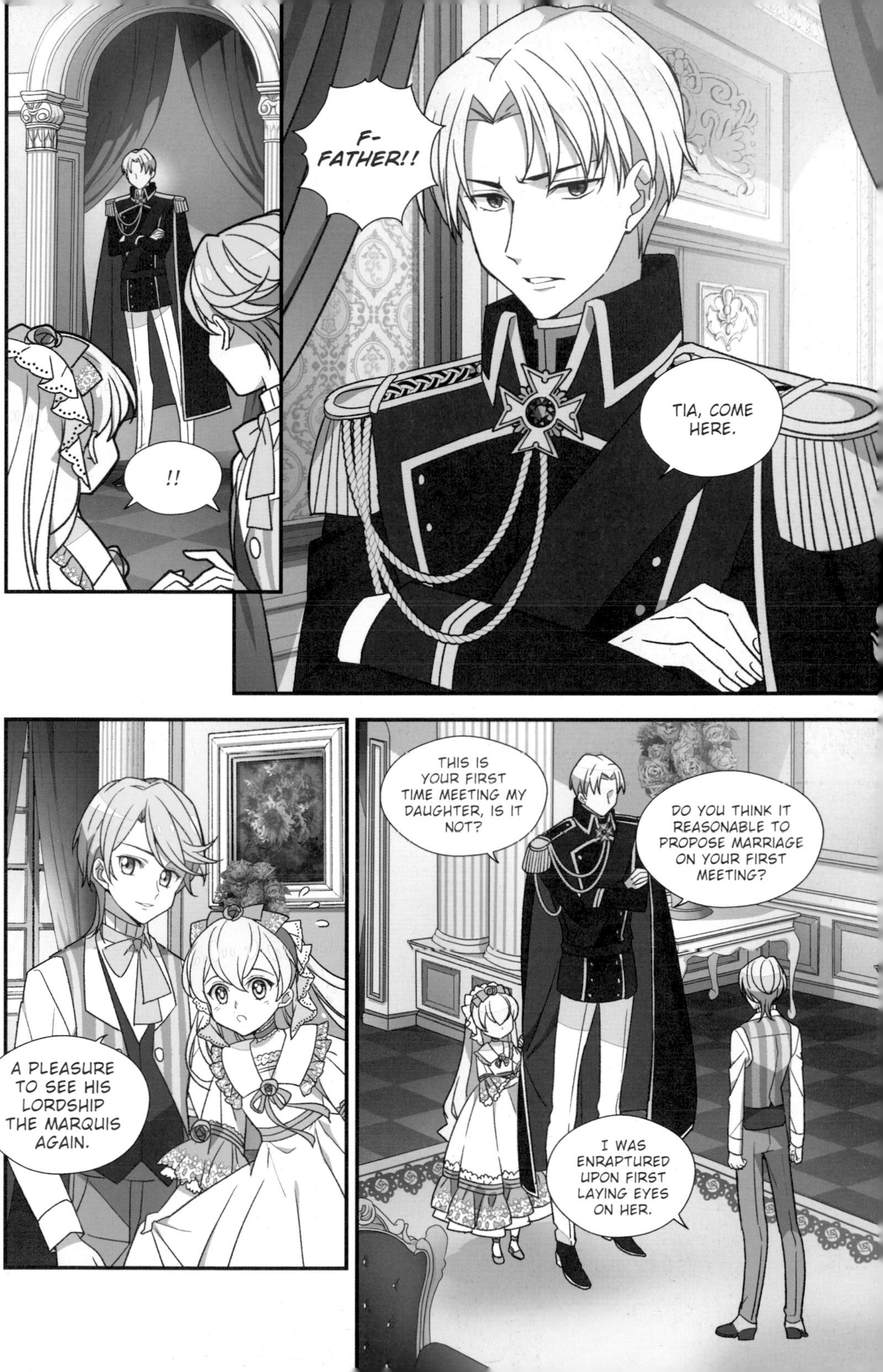
!!
F-FATHER!!
TIA, COME HERE.
A PLEASURE TO SEE HIS LORDSHIP THE MARQUIS AGAIN.
THIS IS YOUR FIRST TIME MEETING MY DAUGHTER, IS IT NOT?
DO YOU THINK IT REASONABLE TO PROPOSE MARRIAGE ON YOUR FIRST MEETING?
I WAS ENRAPTURED UPON FIRST LAYING EYES ON HER.

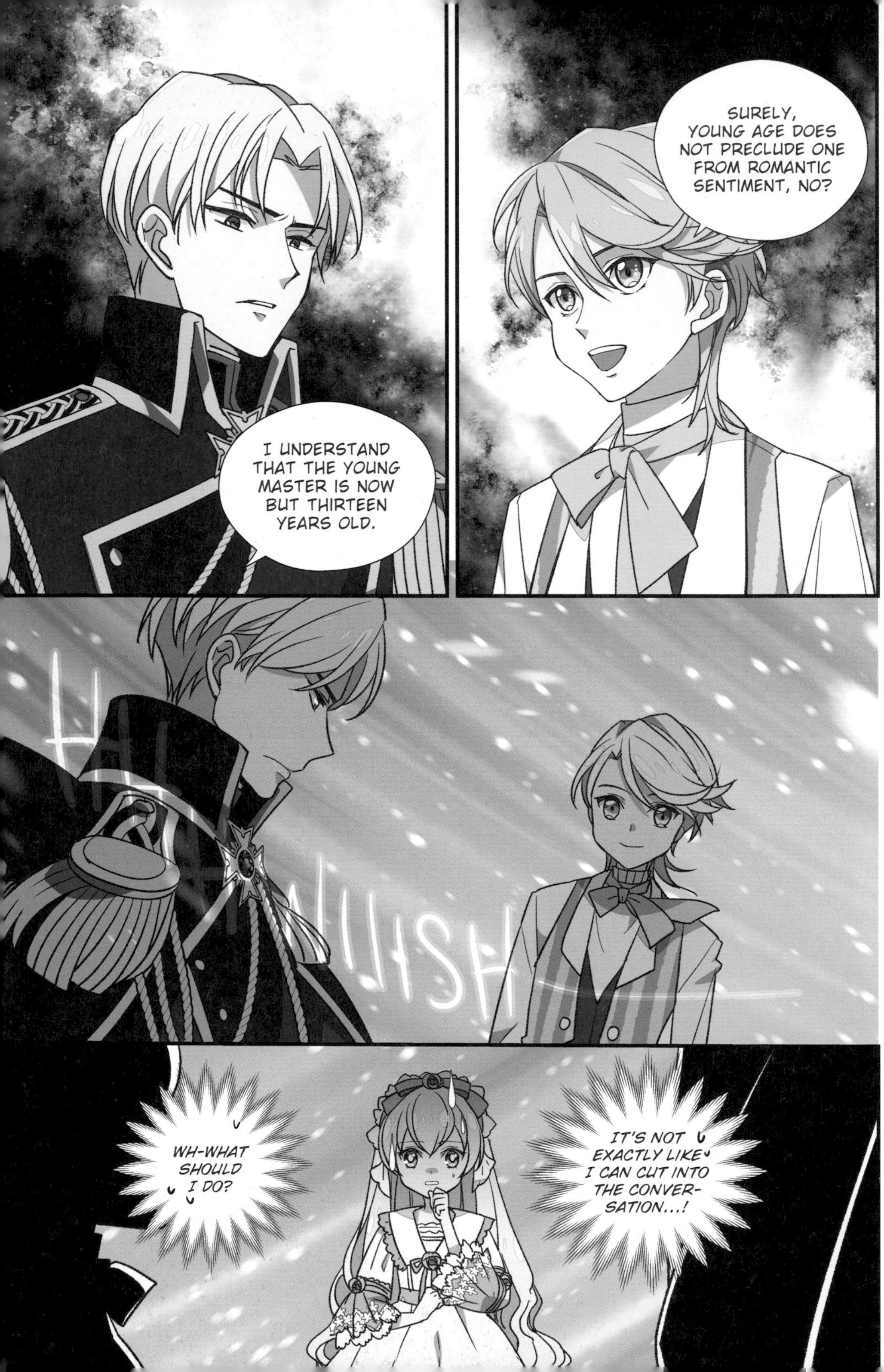
I UNDERSTAND THAT THE YOUNG MASTER IS NOW BUT THIRTEEN YEARS OLD.
SURELY, YOUNG AGE DOES NOT PRECLUDE ONE FROM ROMANTIC SENTIMENT, NO?
WH-WHAT SHOULD I DO?
IT'S NOT EXACTLY LIKE I CAN CUT INTO THE CONVER-SATION...!

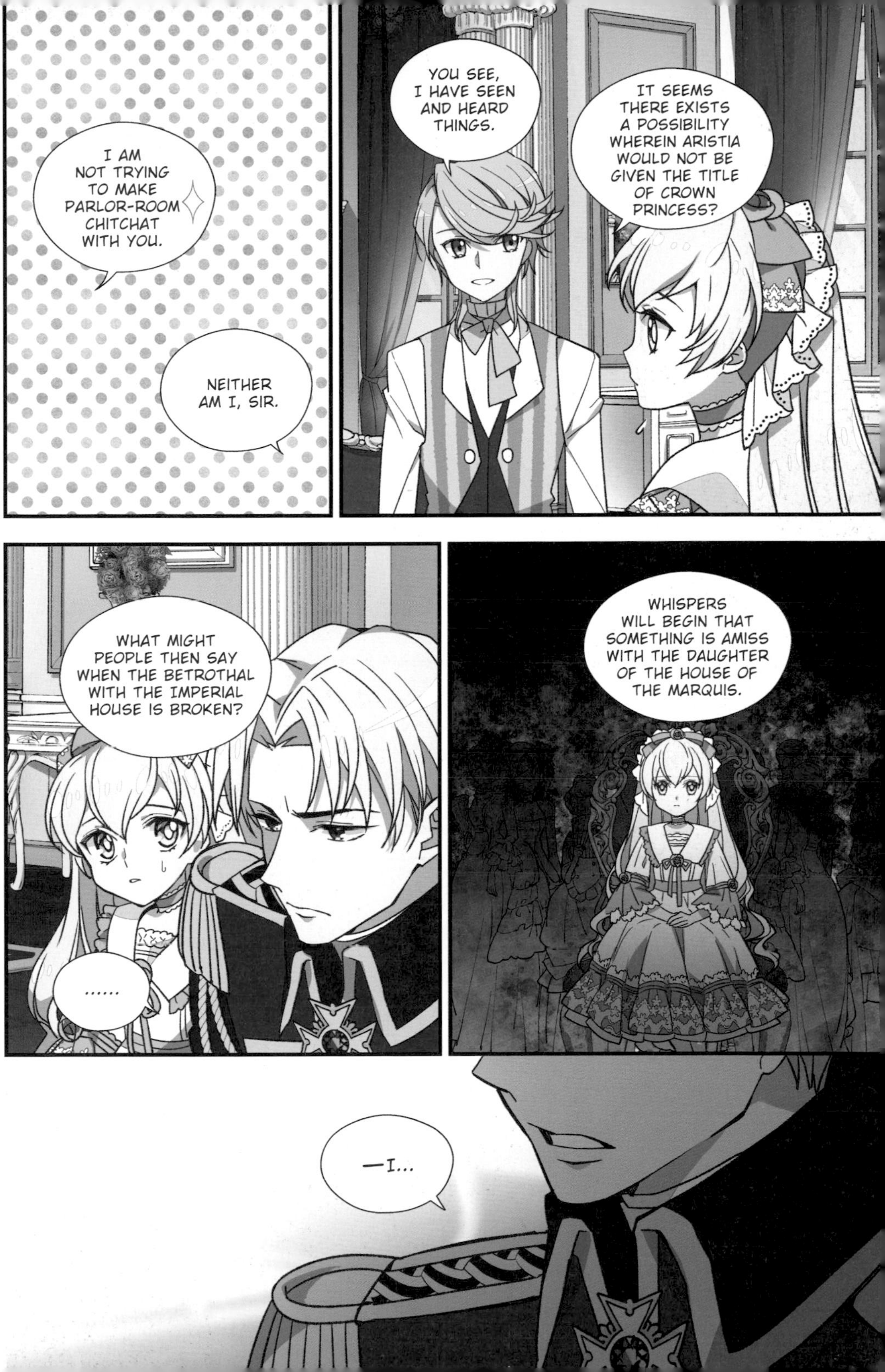
I AM NOT TRYING TO MAKE PARLOR-ROOM CHITCHAT WITH YOU.
NEITHER AM I, SIR.
YOU SEE, I HAVE SEEN AND HEARD THINGS.
IT SEEMS THERE EXISTS A POSSIBILITY WHEREIN ARISTIA WOULD NOT BE GIVEN THE TITLE OF CROWN PRINCESS?
WHAT MIGHT PEOPLE THEN SAY WHEN THE BETROTHAL WITH THE IMPERIAL HOUSE IS BROKEN?
......
WHISPERS WILL BEGIN THAT SOMETHING IS AMISS WITH THE DAUGHTER OF THE HOUSE OF THE MARQUIS.
—I...

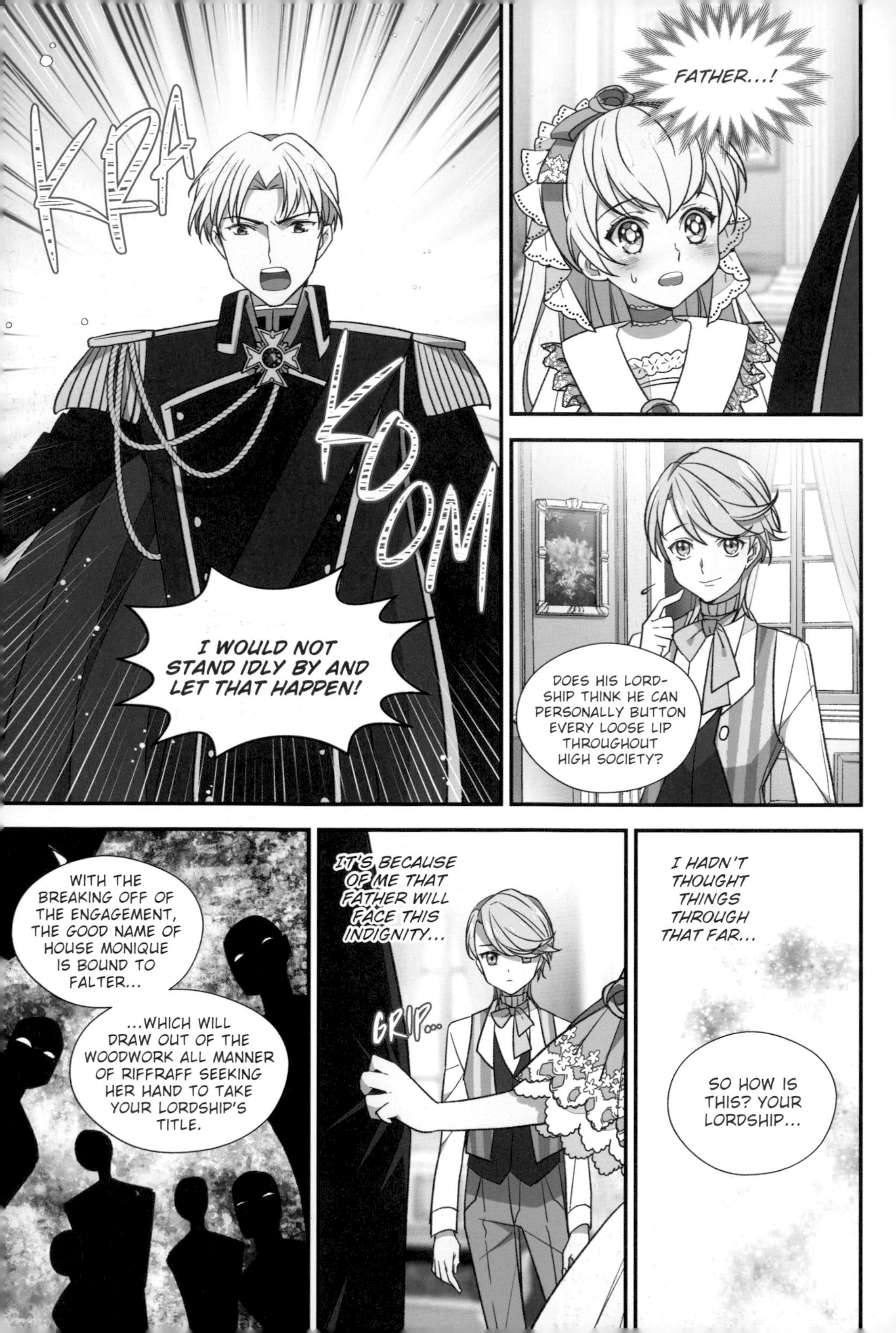
KIRA
FATHER...!
KOOM
I WOULD NOT STAND IDLY BY AND LET THAT HAPPEN!
DOES HIS LORDSHIP THINK HE CAN PERSONALLY BUTTON EVERY LOOSE LIP THROUGHOUT HIGH SOCIETY?
WITH THE BREAKING OFF OF THE ENGAGEMENT, THE GOOD NAME OF HOUSE MONIQUE IS BOUND TO FALTER...
...WHICH WILL DRAW OUT OF THE WOODWORK ALL MANNER OF RIFFRAFF SEEKING HER HAND TO TAKE YOUR LORDSHIP'S TITLE.
IT'S BECAUSE OF ME THAT FATHER WILL FACE THIS INDIGNITY...
GRIP...
I HADN'T THOUGHT THINGS THROUGH THAT FAR...
SO HOW IS THIS? YOUR LORDSHIP...

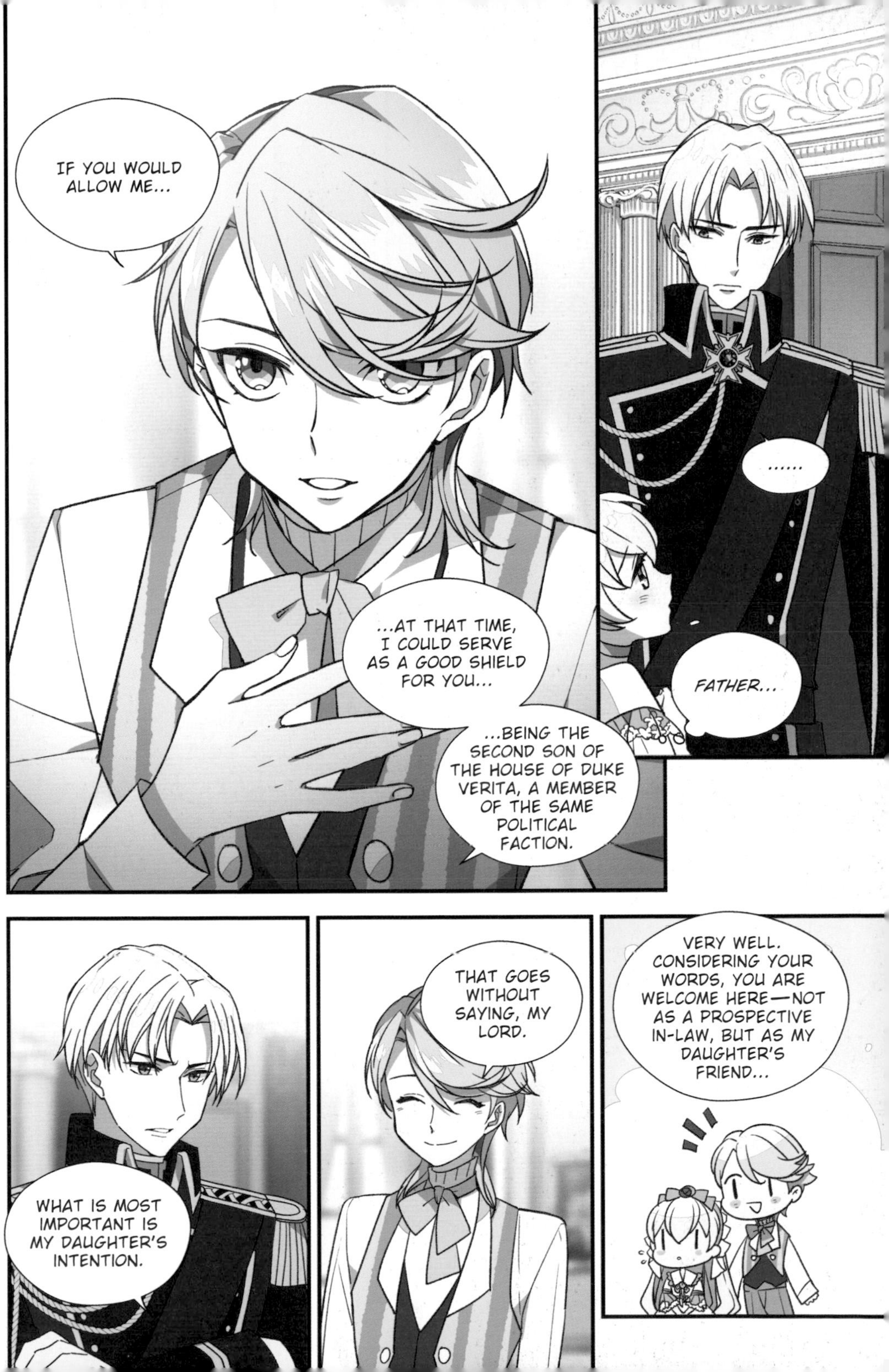
IF YOU WOULD ALLOW ME...
......
FATHER...
...AT THAT TIME, I COULD SERVE AS A GOOD SHIELD FOR YOU...
...BEING THE SECOND SON OF THE HOUSE OF DUKE VERITA, A MEMBER OF THE SAME POLITICAL FACTION.
WHAT IS MOST IMPORTANT IS MY DAUGHTER'S INTENTION.
THAT GOES WITHOUT SAYING, MY LORD.
VERY WELL. CONSIDERING YOUR WORDS, YOU ARE WELCOME HERE—NOT AS A PROSPECTIVE IN-LAW, BUT AS MY DAUGHTER'S FRIEND...

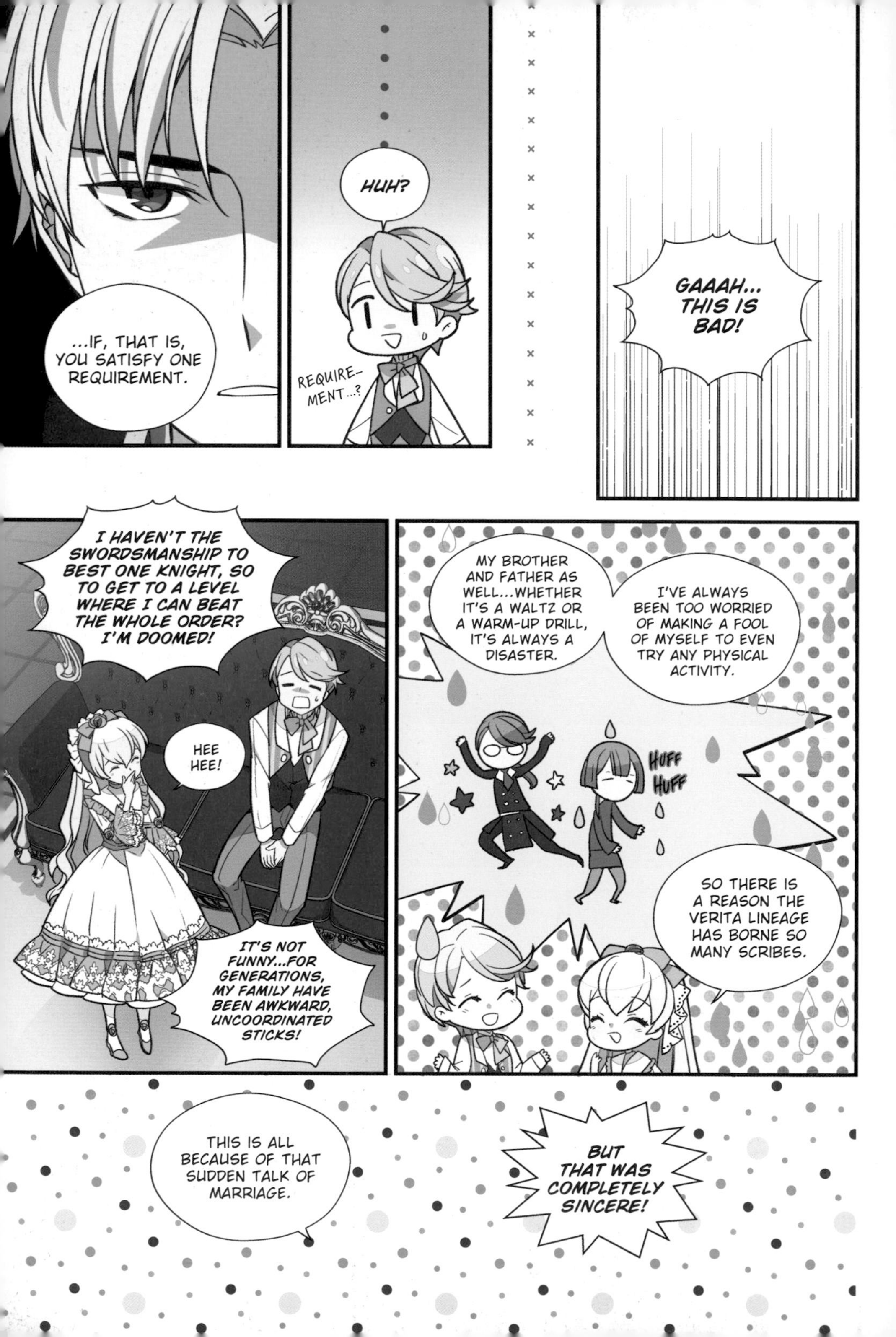
...IF, THAT IS, YOU SATISFY ONE REQUIREMENT.
HUH?
REQUIRE-MENT...?
GAAAH... THIS IS BAD!
I HAVEN'T THE SWORDSMANSHIP TO BEST ONE KNIGHT, SO TO GET TO A LEVEL WHERE I CAN BEAT THE WHOLE ORDER? I'M DOOMED!
HEE HEE!
IT'S NOT FUNNY...FOR GENERATIONS, MY FAMILY HAVE BEEN AWKWARD, UNCOORDINATED STICKS!
MY BROTHER AND FATHER AS WELL...WHETHER IT'S A WALTZ OR A WARM-UP DRILL, IT'S ALWAYS A DISASTER.
I'VE ALWAYS BEEN TOO WORRIED OF MAKING A FOOL OF MYSELF TO EVEN TRY ANY PHYSICAL ACTIVITY.
HUFF HUFF
SO THERE IS A REASON THE VERITA LINEAGE HAS BORNE SO MANY SCRIBES.
THIS IS ALL BECAUSE OF THAT SUDDEN TALK OF MARRIAGE.
BUT THAT WAS COMPLETELY SINCERE!

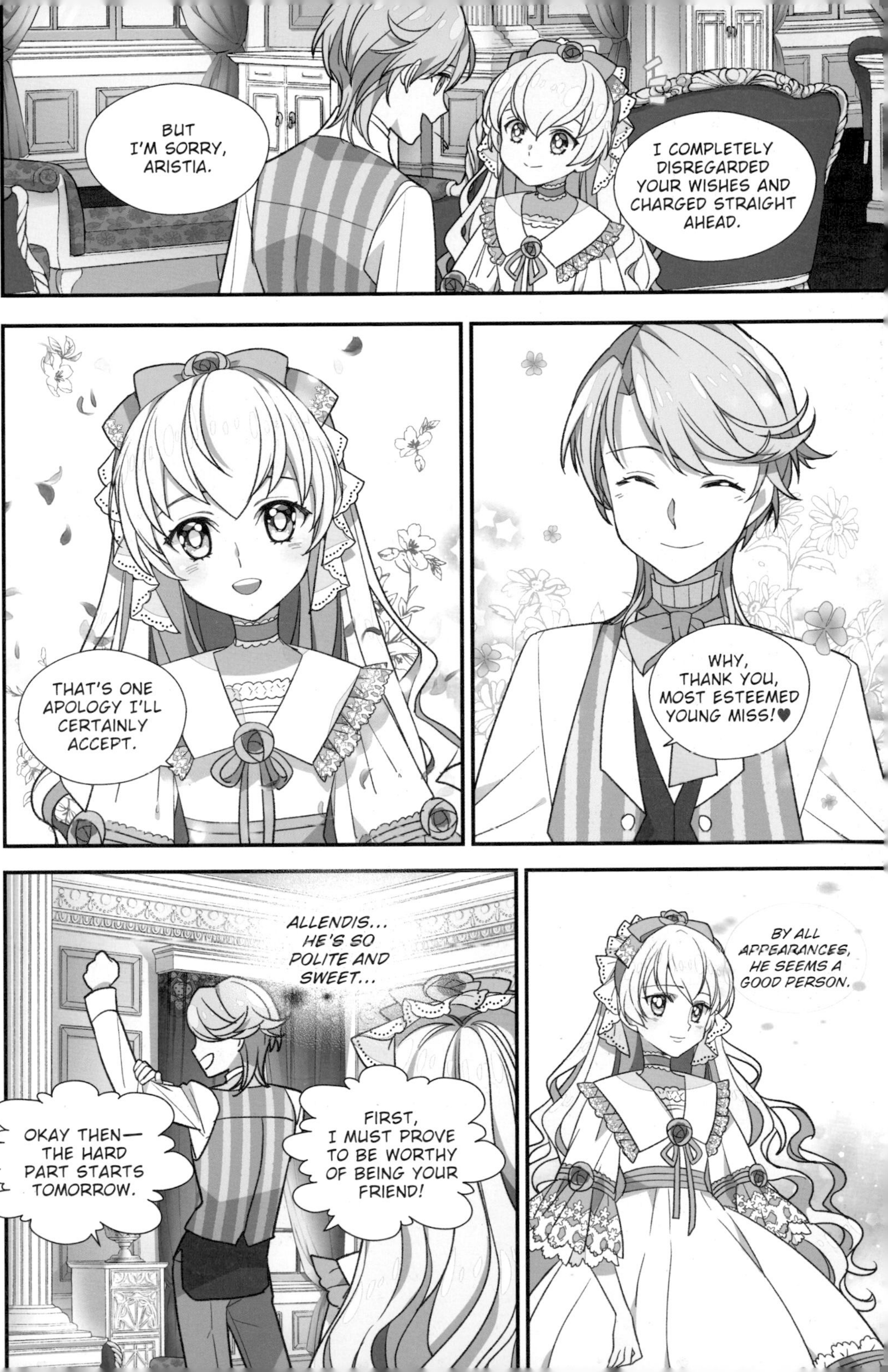
BUT I'M SORRY, ARISTIA.
I COMPLETELY DISREGARDED YOUR WISHES AND CHARGED STRAIGHT AHEAD.
THAT'S ONE APOLOGY I'LL CERTAINLY ACCEPT.
WHY, THANK YOU, MOST ESTEEMED YOUNG MISS!♥
ALLENDIS... HE'S SO POLITE AND SWEET...
BY ALL APPEARANCES, HE SEEMS A GOOD PERSON.
OKAY THEN— THE HARD PART STARTS TOMORROW.
FIRST, I MUST PROVE TO BE WORTHY OF BEING YOUR FRIEND!

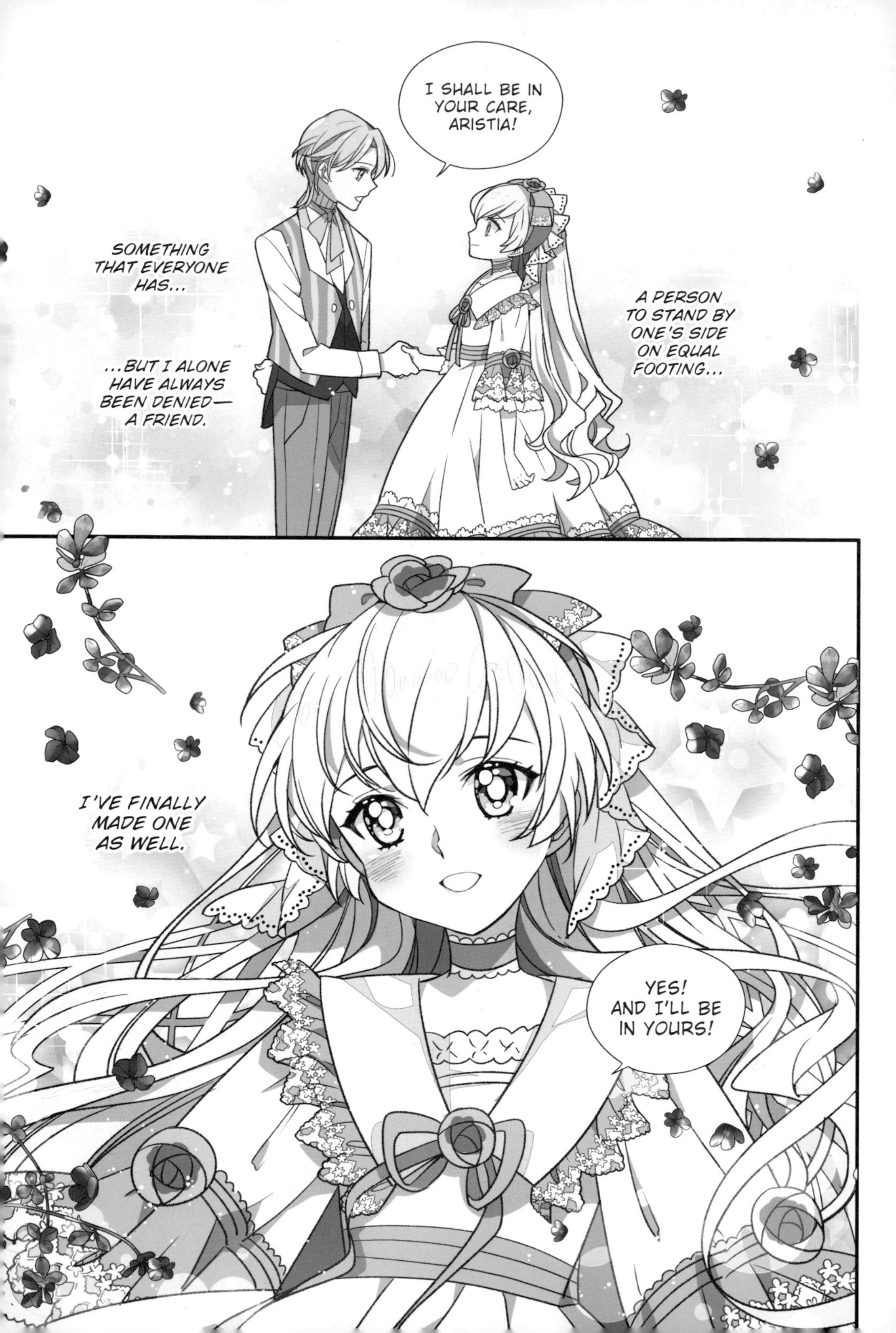
I SHALL BE IN YOUR CARE, ARISTIA!
SOMETHING THAT EVERYONE HAS...
...BUT I ALONE HAVE ALWAYS BEEN DENIED— A FRIEND.
A PERSON TO STAND BY ONE'S SIDE ON EQUAL FOOTING...
I'VE FINALLY MADE ONE AS WELL.
YES! AND I'LL BE IN YOURS!

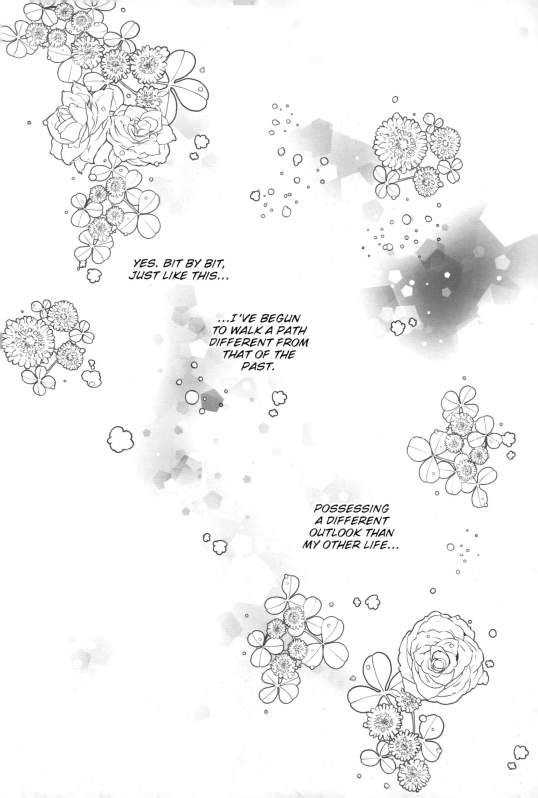

YES. BIT BY BIT,
JUST LIKE THIS...

...I'VE BEGUN
TO WALK A PATH
DIFFERENT FROM
THAT OF THE
PAST.

POSSESSING
A DIFFERENT
OUTLOOK THAN
MY OTHER LIFE...

# The Abandoned Empress

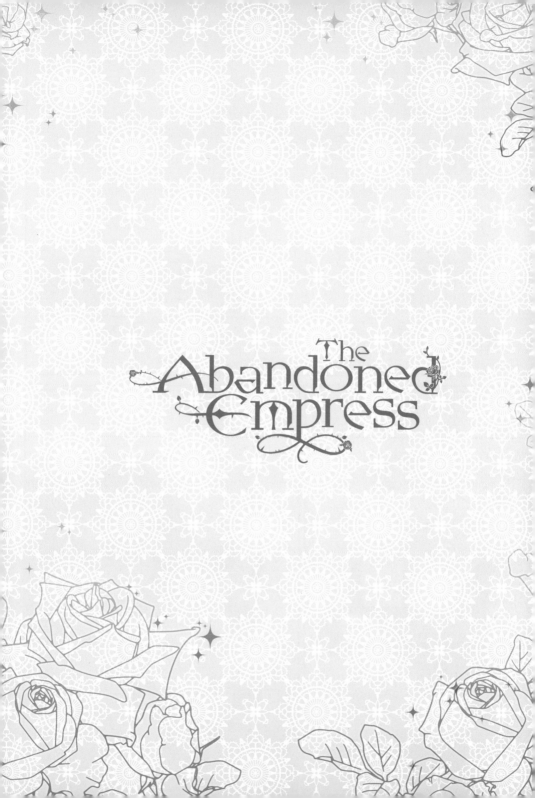

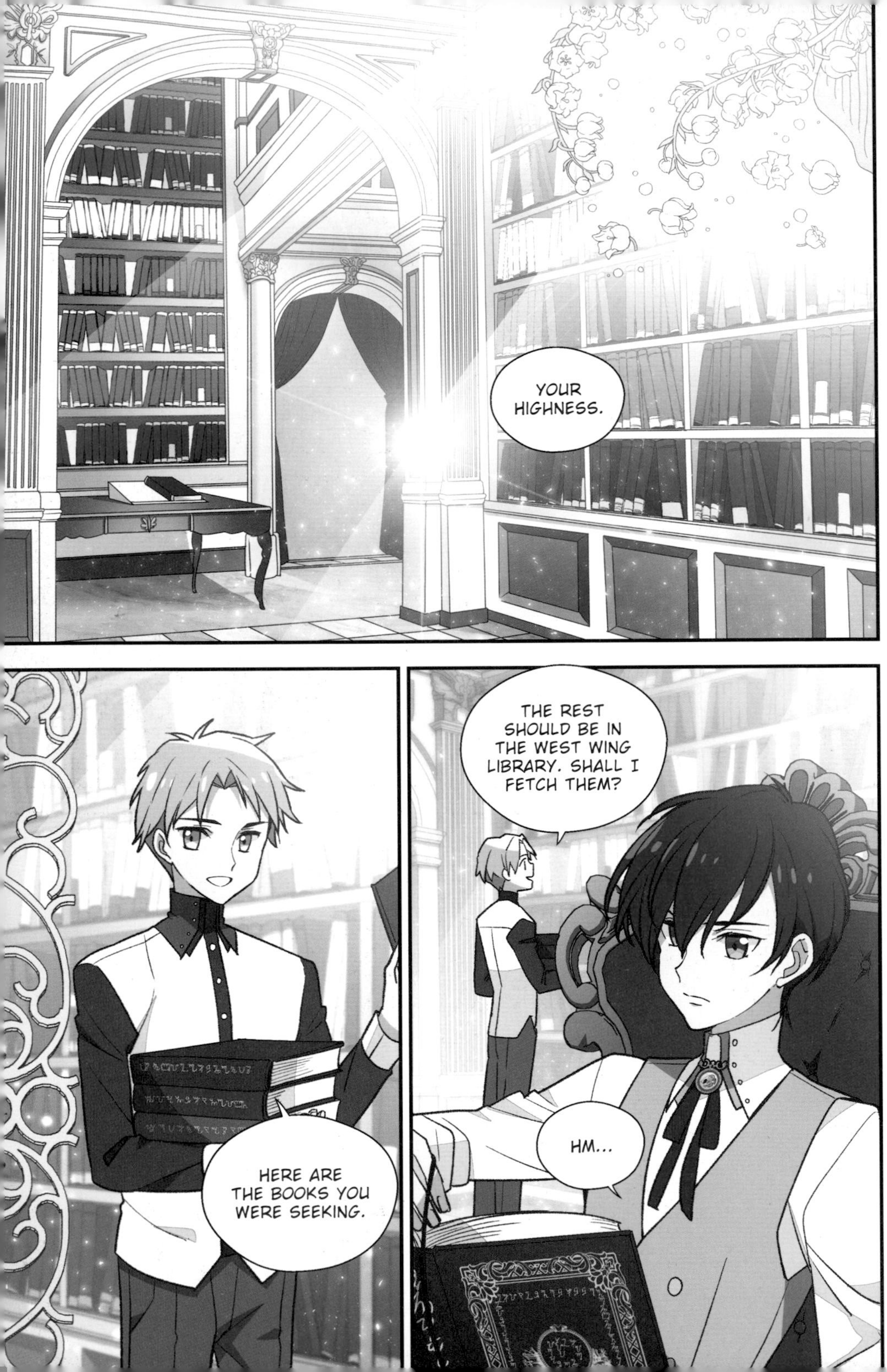
YOUR HIGHNESS.
HERE ARE THE BOOKS YOU WERE SEEKING.
THE REST SHOULD BE IN THE WEST WING LIBRARY. SHALL I FETCH THEM?
HM...

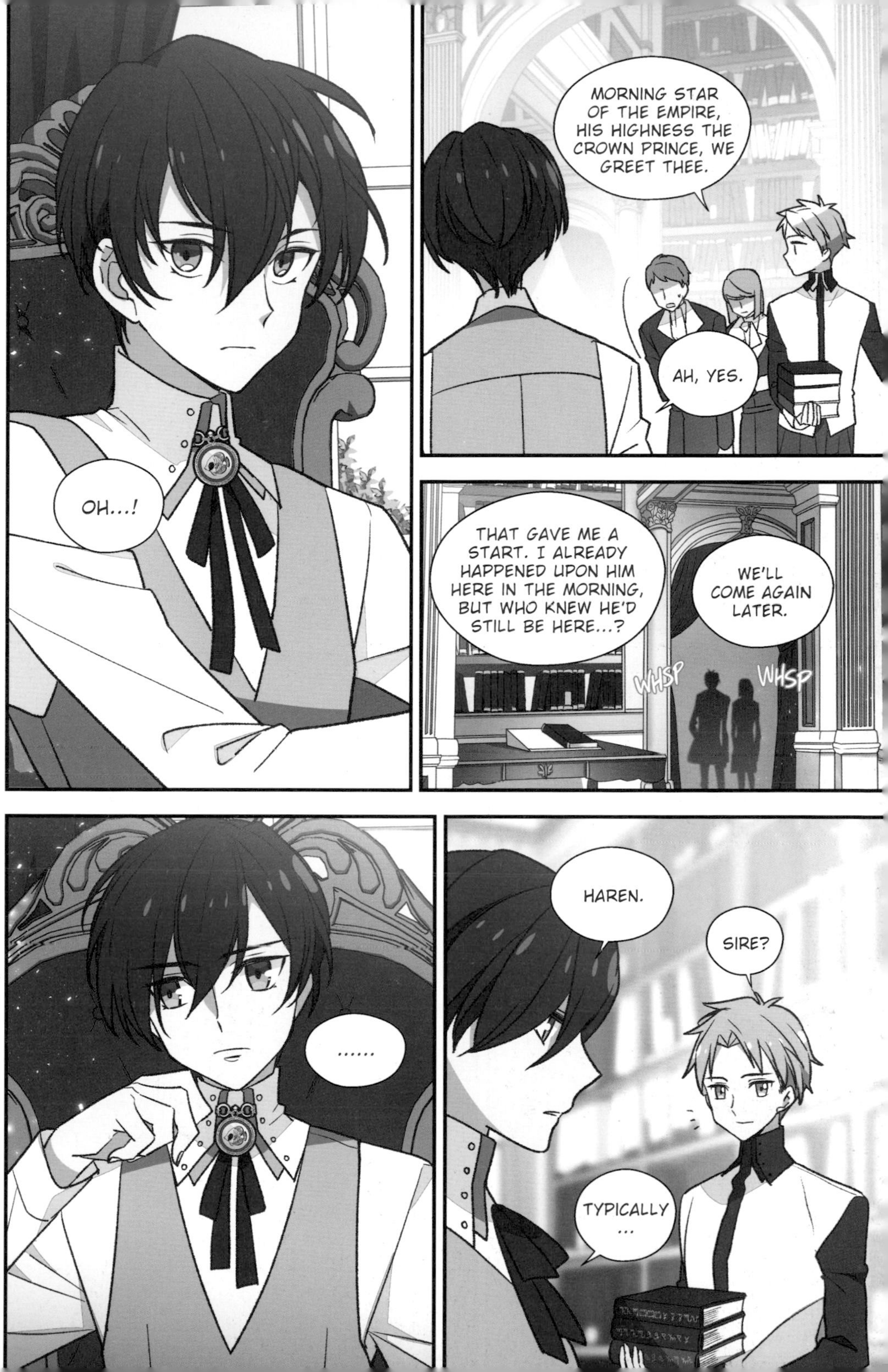
OH...!
MORNING STAR OF THE EMPIRE, HIS HIGHNESS THE CROWN PRINCE, WE GREET THEE.
AH, YES.
THAT GAVE ME A START. I ALREADY HAPPENED UPON HIM HERE IN THE MORNING, BUT WHO KNEW HE'D STILL BE HERE...?
WE'LL COME AGAIN LATER.
WHSP
WHSP
......
HAREN.
SIRE?
TYPICALLY...

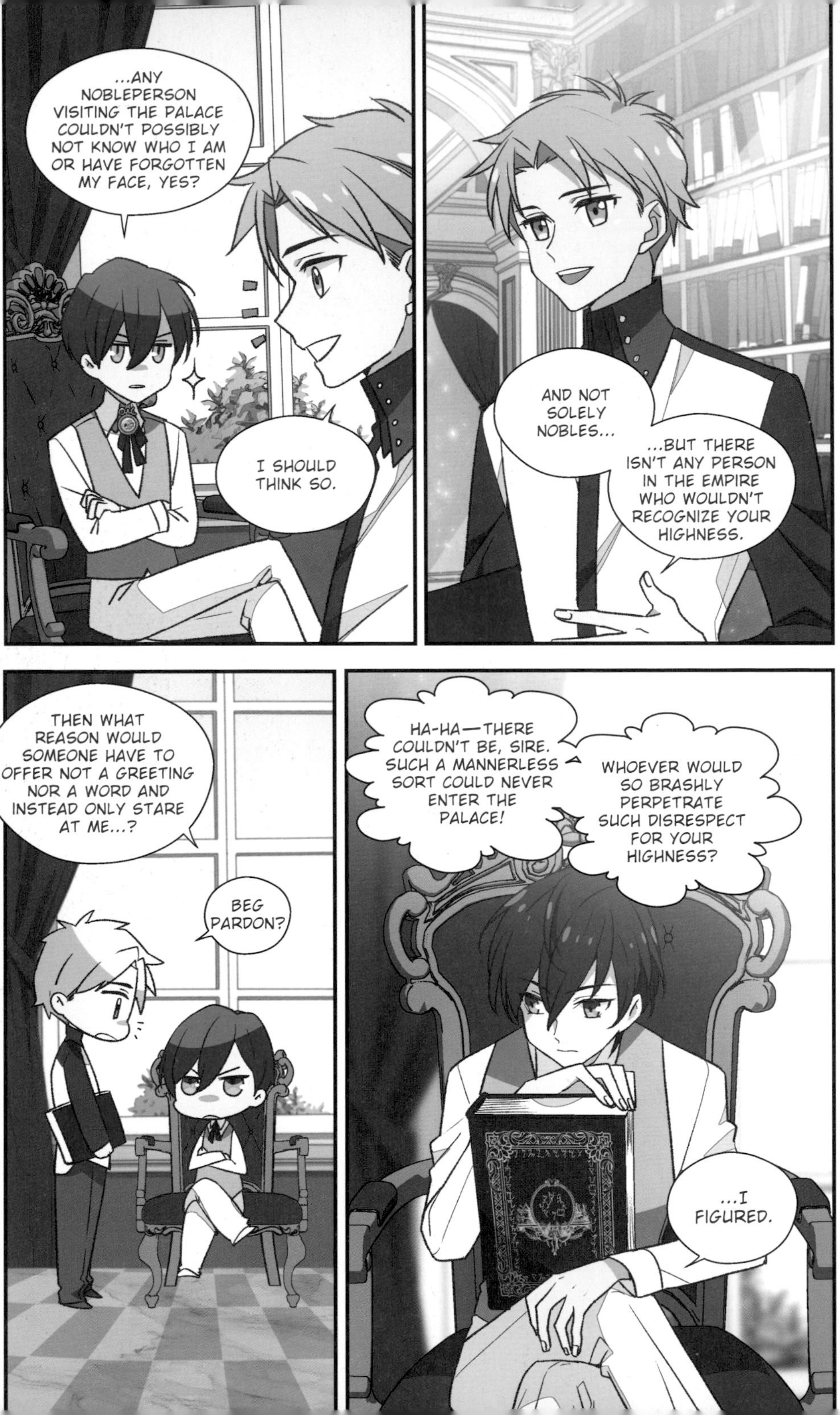
...ANY NOBLEPERSON VISITING THE PALACE COULDN'T POSSIBLY NOT KNOW WHO I AM OR HAVE FORGOTTEN MY FACE, YES?
I SHOULD THINK SO.
AND NOT SOLELY NOBLES...
...BUT THERE ISN'T ANY PERSON IN THE EMPIRE WHO WOULDN'T RECOGNIZE YOUR HIGHNESS.
THEN WHAT REASON WOULD SOMEONE HAVE TO OFFER NOT A GREETING NOR A WORD AND INSTEAD ONLY STARE AT ME...?
BEG PARDON?
HA-HA—THERE COULDN'T BE, SIRE. SUCH A MANNERLESS SORT COULD NEVER ENTER THE PALACE!
WHOEVER WOULD SO BRASHLY PERPETRATE SUCH DISRESPECT FOR YOUR HIGHNESS?
...I FIGURED.

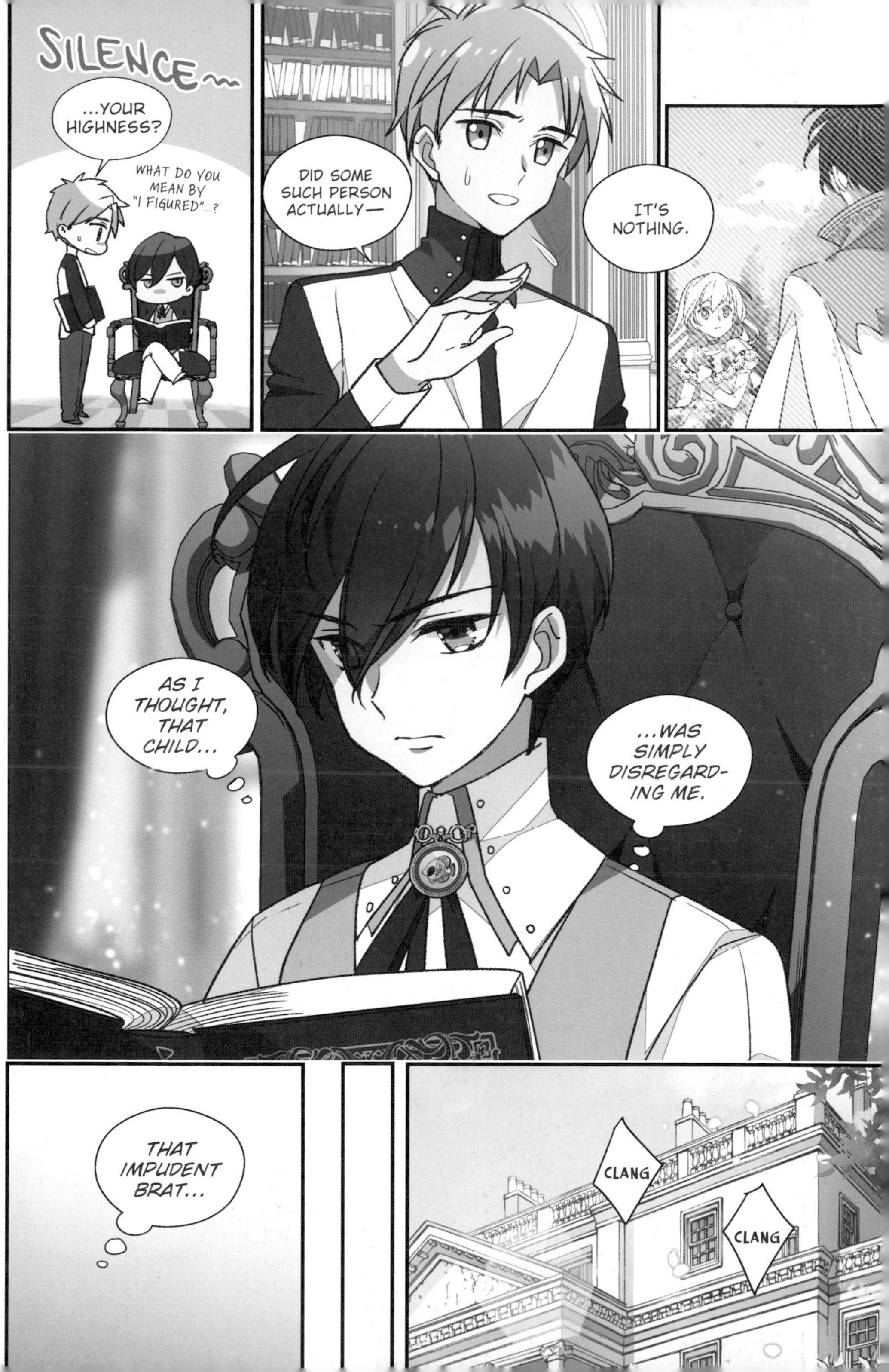
SILENCE~
...YOUR HIGHNESS?
WHAT DO YOU MEAN BY "I FIGURED"...?
DID SOME SUCH PERSON ACTUALLY—
IT'S NOTHING.
AS I THOUGHT, THAT CHILD...
...WAS SIMPLY DISREGARDING ME.
THAT IMPUDENT BRAT...
CLANG
CLANG

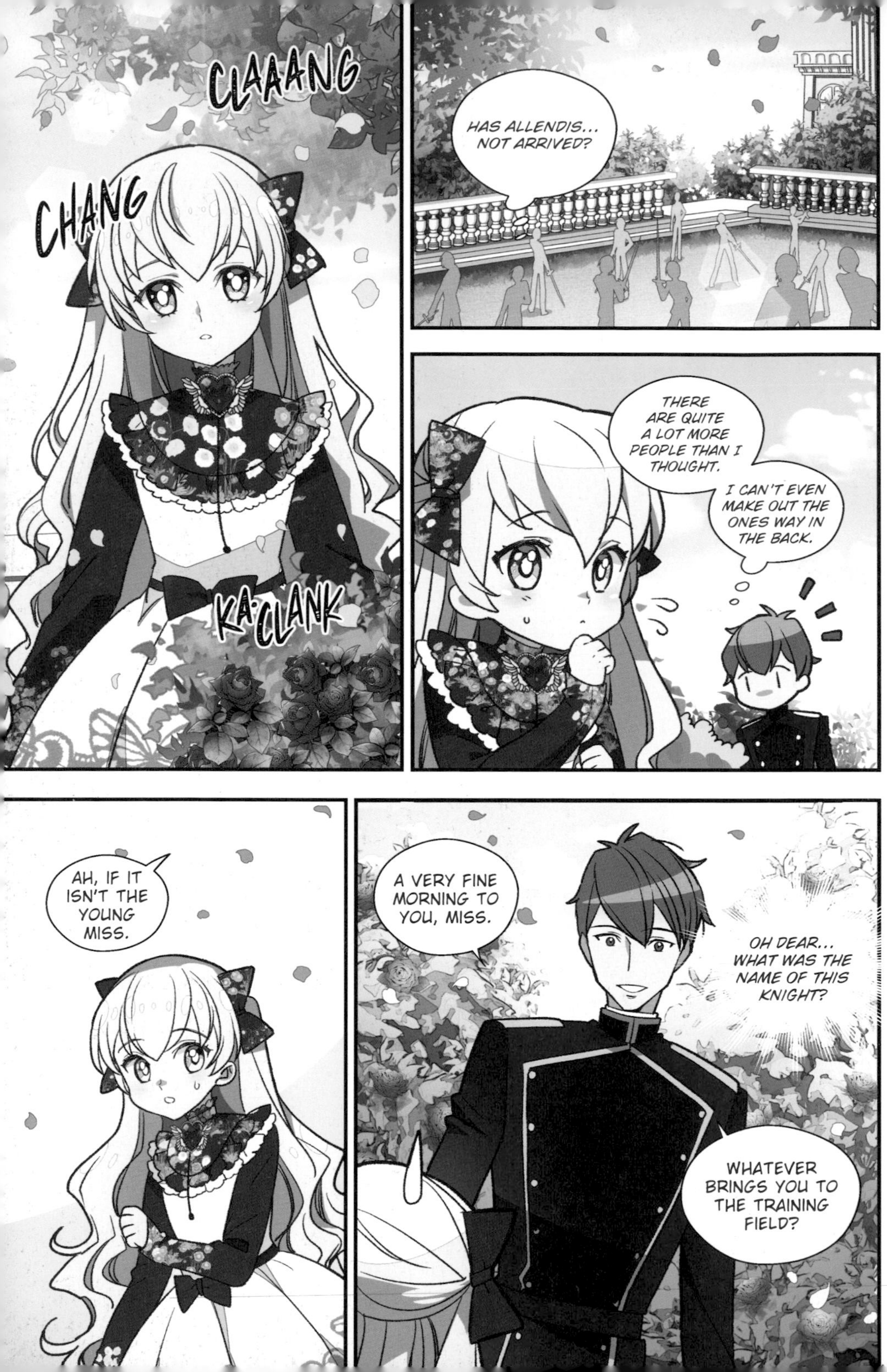
CLAAANG
CHANG
KA-CLANK
HAS ALLENDIS... NOT ARRIVED?
THERE ARE QUITE A LOT MORE PEOPLE THAN I THOUGHT.
I CAN'T EVEN MAKE OUT THE ONES WAY IN THE BACK.
AH, IF IT ISN'T THE YOUNG MISS.
A VERY FINE MORNING TO YOU, MISS.
OH DEAR... WHAT WAS THE NAME OF THIS KNIGHT?
WHATEVER BRINGS YOU TO THE TRAINING FIELD?

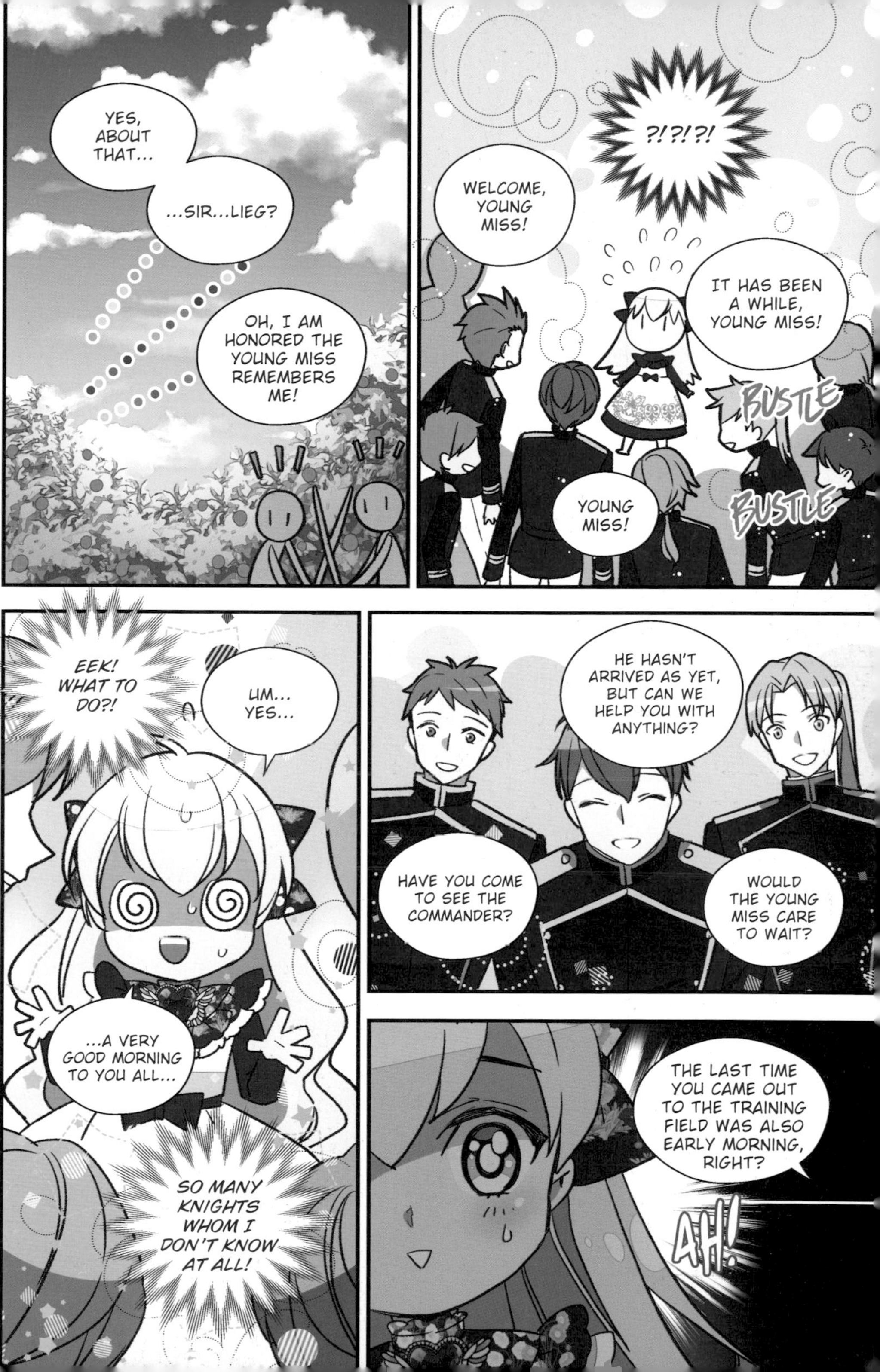
YES, ABOUT THAT...
...SIR...LIEG?
OH, I AM HONORED THE YOUNG MISS REMEMBERS ME!
?!?!?!
WELCOME, YOUNG MISS!
IT HAS BEEN A WHILE, YOUNG MISS!
BUSTLE
YOUNG MISS!
BUSTLE
EEK! WHAT TO DO?!
UM... YES...
...A VERY GOOD MORNING TO YOU ALL...
SO MANY KNIGHTS WHOM I DON'T KNOW AT ALL!
HE HASN'T ARRIVED AS YET, BUT CAN WE HELP YOU WITH ANYTHING?
HAVE YOU COME TO SEE THE COMMANDER?
WOULD THE YOUNG MISS CARE TO WAIT?
THE LAST TIME YOU CAME OUT TO THE TRAINING FIELD WAS ALSO EARLY MORNING, RIGHT?
AH!

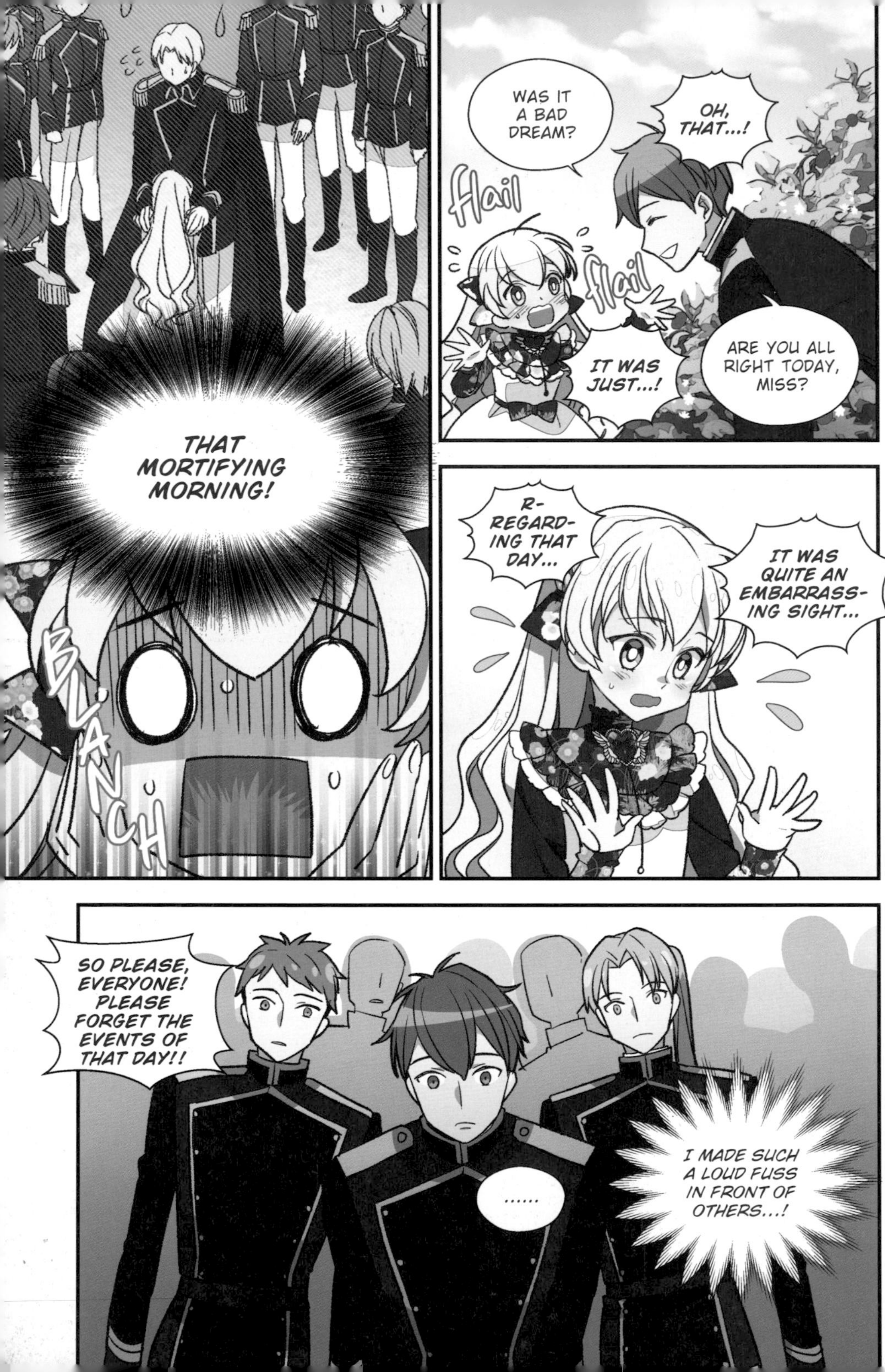

ARE YOU ALL RIGHT TODAY, MISS?
WAS IT A BAD DREAM?
OH, THAT...!
IT WAS JUST...!
flail
flail
IT WAS QUITE AN EMBARRASS-ING SIGHT...
R-REGARD-ING THAT DAY...
THAT MORTIFYING MORNING!
BLANCH
I MADE SUCH A LOUD FUSS IN FRONT OF OTHERS...!
......
SO PLEASE, EVERYONE! PLEASE FORGET THE EVENTS OF THAT DAY!!

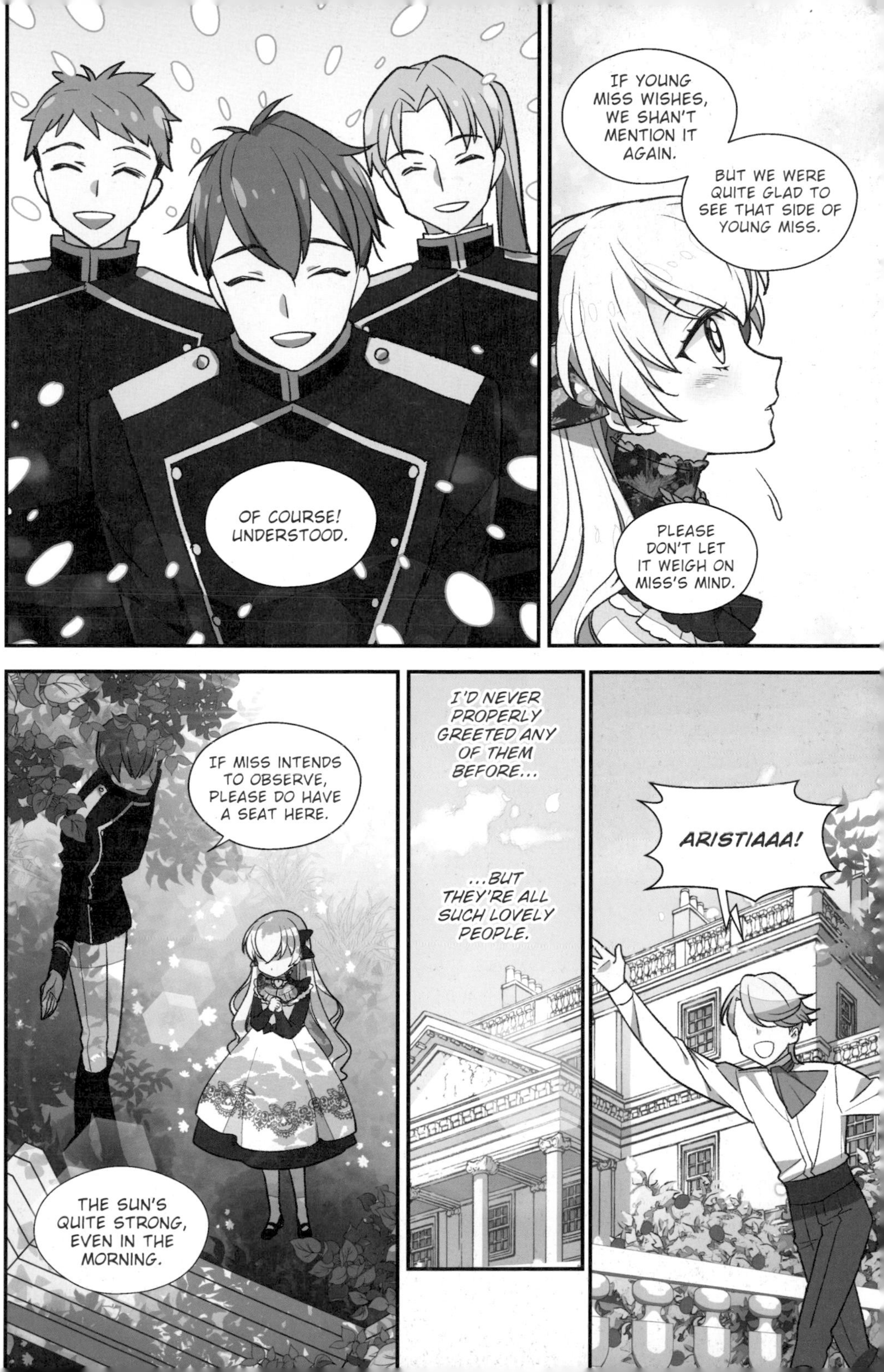
OF COURSE! UNDERSTOOD.
IF YOUNG MISS WISHES, WE SHAN'T MENTION IT AGAIN.
BUT WE WERE QUITE GLAD TO SEE THAT SIDE OF YOUNG MISS.
PLEASE DON'T LET IT WEIGH ON MISS'S MIND.
IF MISS INTENDS TO OBSERVE, PLEASE DO HAVE A SEAT HERE.
THE SUN'S QUITE STRONG, EVEN IN THE MORNING.
I'D NEVER PROPERLY GREETED ANY OF THEM BEFORE...
...BUT THEY'RE ALL SUCH LOVELY PEOPLE.
ARISTIAAA!

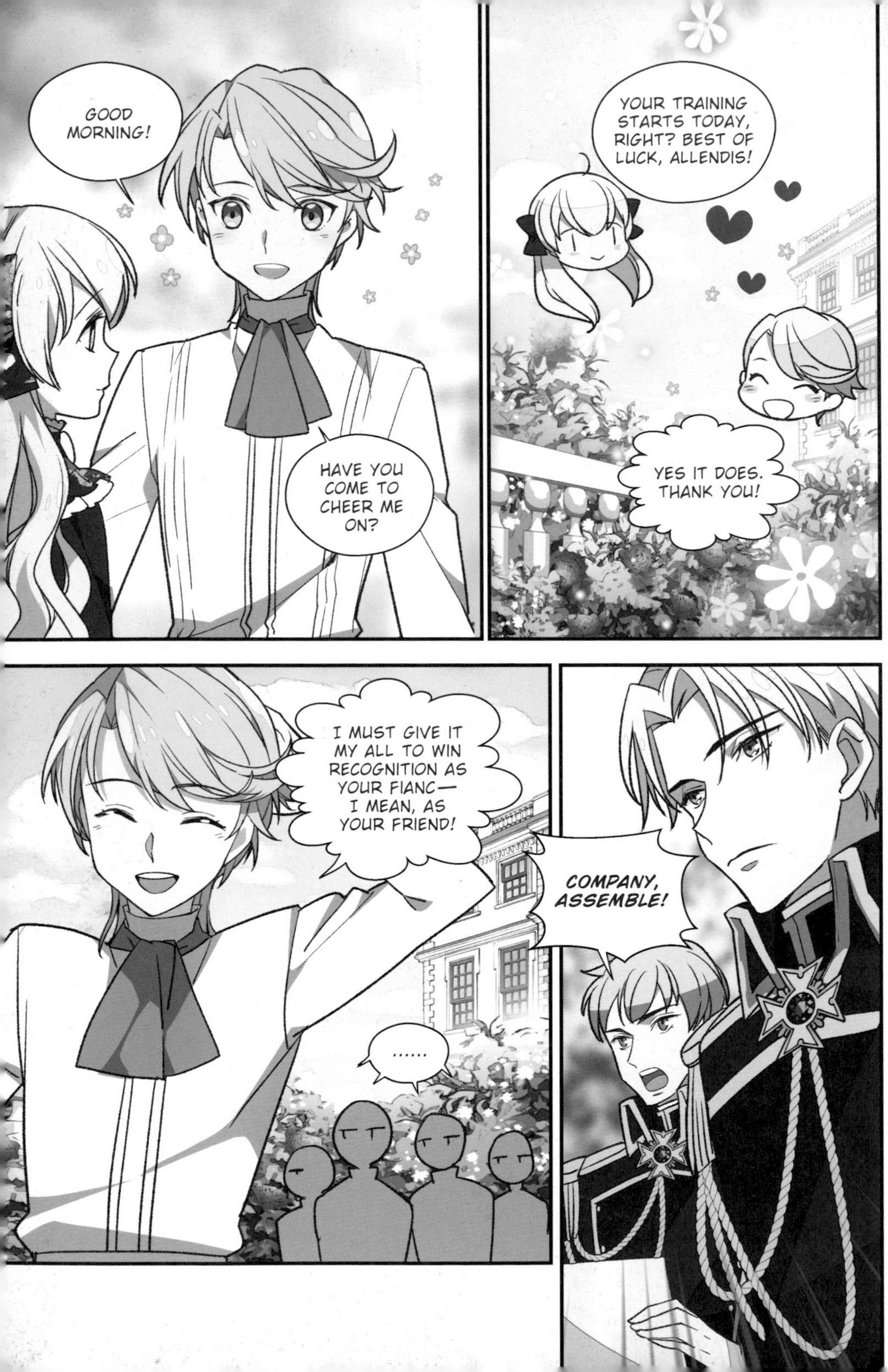
GOOD MORNING!
HAVE YOU COME TO CHEER ME ON?
YOUR TRAINING STARTS TODAY, RIGHT? BEST OF LUCK, ALLENDIS!
YES IT DOES. THANK YOU!
I MUST GIVE IT MY ALL TO WIN RECOGNITION AS YOUR FIANC— I MEAN, AS YOUR FRIEND!
......
COMPANY, ASSEMBLE!

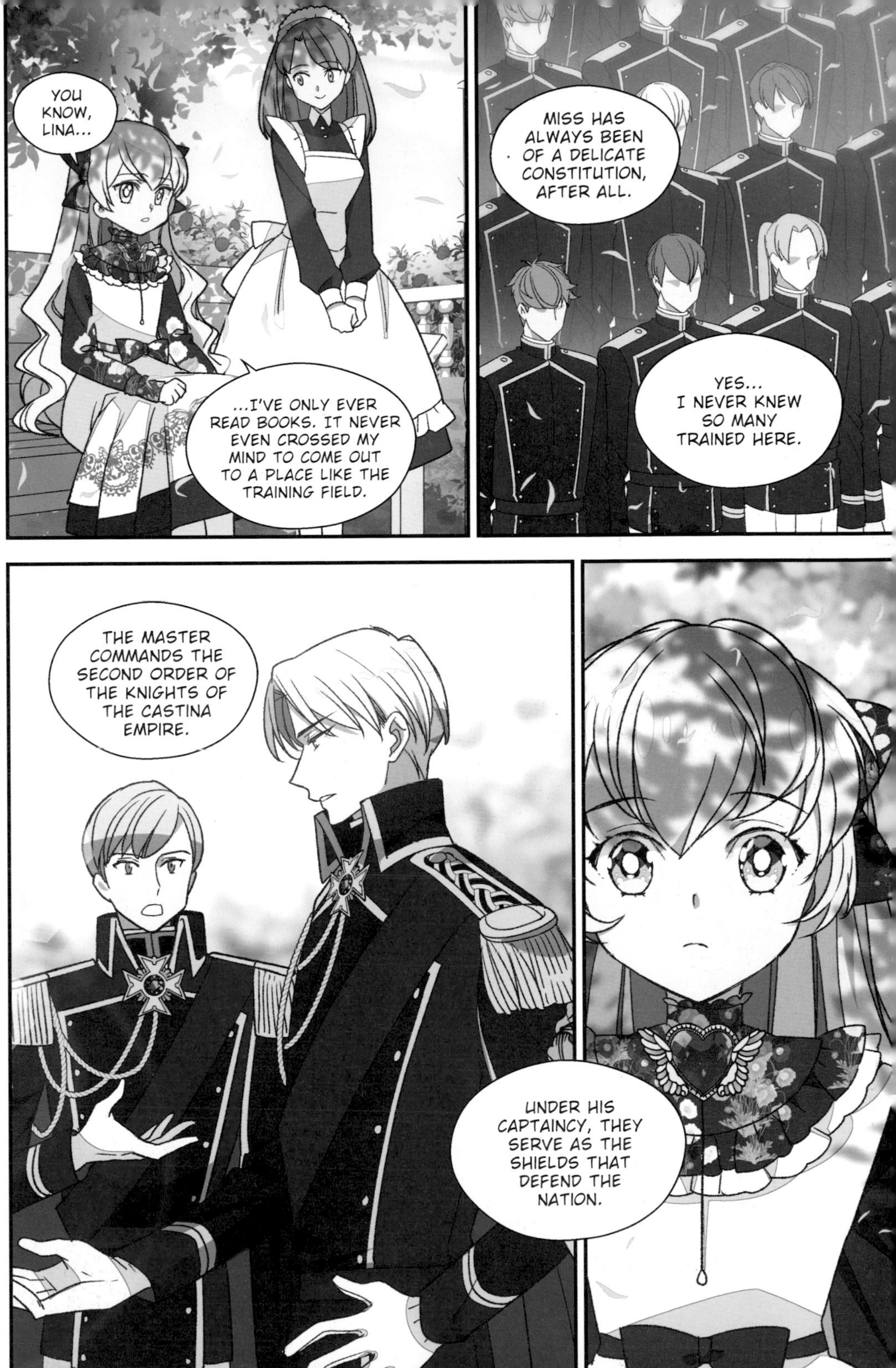
YOU KNOW, LINA...
...I'VE ONLY EVER READ BOOKS. IT NEVER EVEN CROSSED MY MIND TO COME OUT TO A PLACE LIKE THE TRAINING FIELD.
MISS HAS ALWAYS BEEN OF A DELICATE CONSTITUTION, AFTER ALL.
YES... I NEVER KNEW SO MANY TRAINED HERE.
THE MASTER COMMANDS THE SECOND ORDER OF THE KNIGHTS OF THE CASTINA EMPIRE.
UNDER HIS CAPTAINCY, THEY SERVE AS THE SHIELDS THAT DEFEND THE NATION.

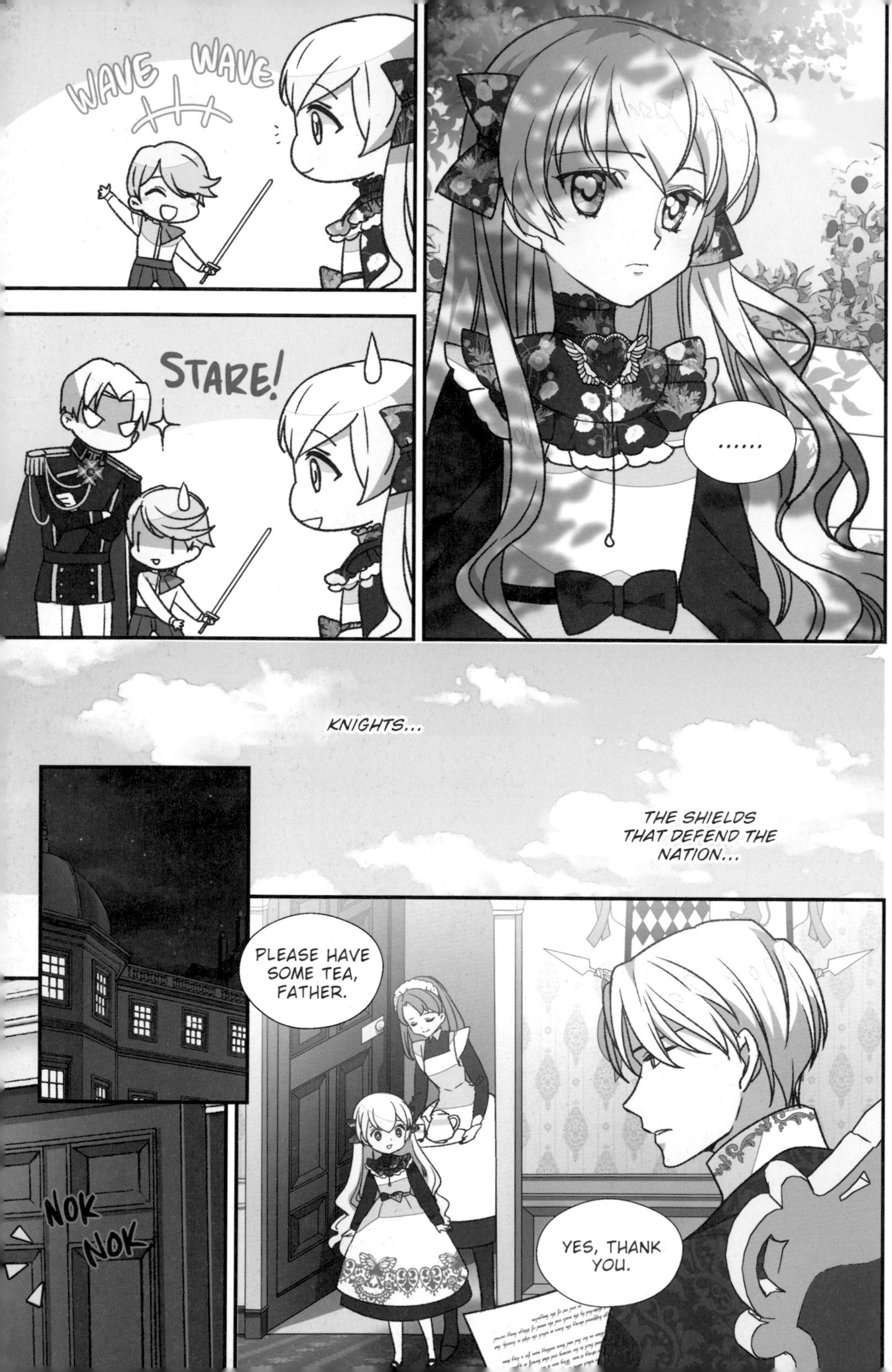
WAVE WAVE
STARE!
......
KNIGHTS...
THE SHIELDS THAT DEFEND THE NATION...
NOK NOK
PLEASE HAVE SOME TEA, FATHER.
YES, THANK YOU.

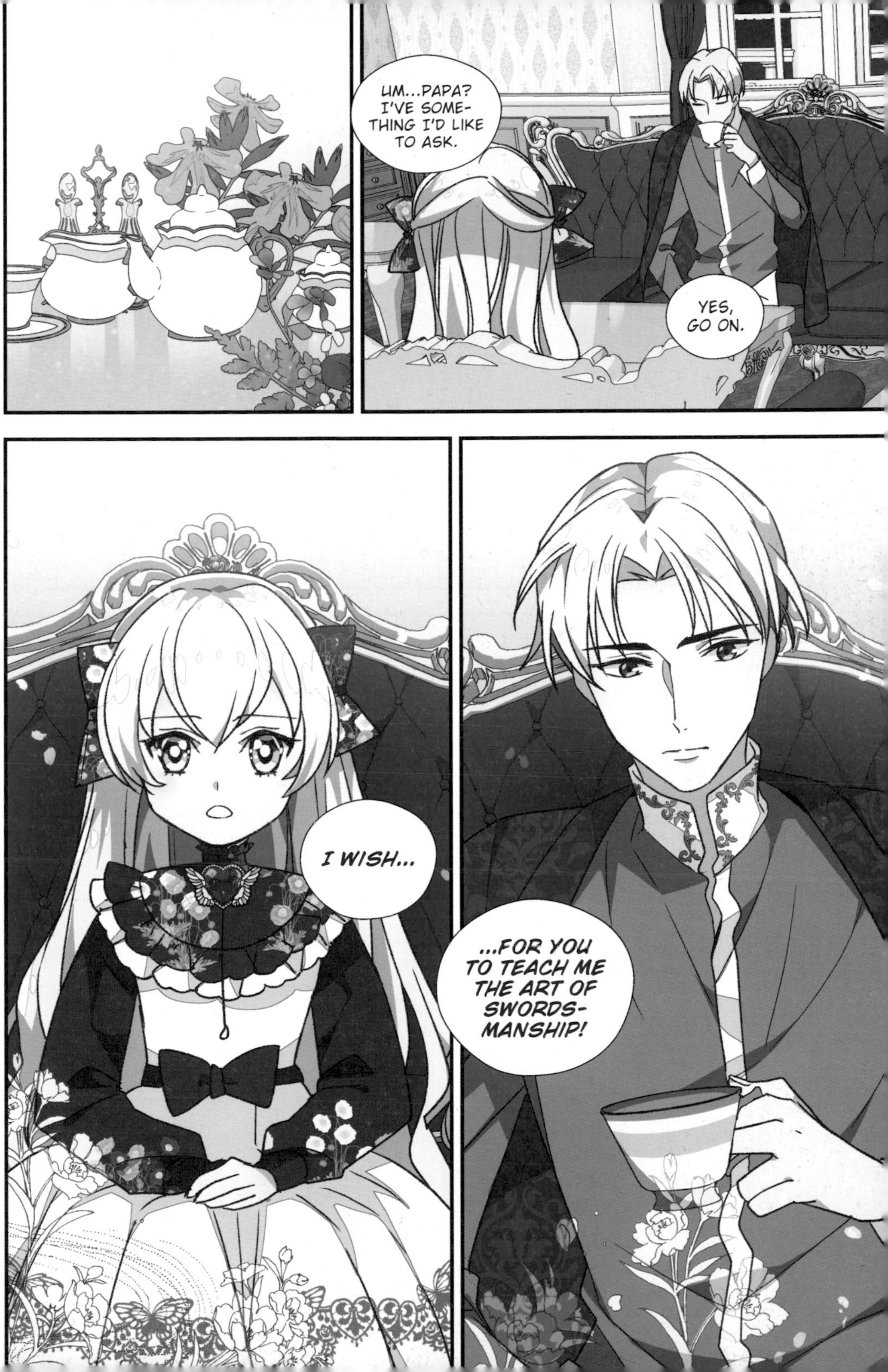
UM...PAPA? I'VE SOME-THING I'D LIKE TO ASK.
YES, GO ON.
I WISH...
...FOR YOU TO TEACH ME THE ART OF SWORDS-MANSHIP!

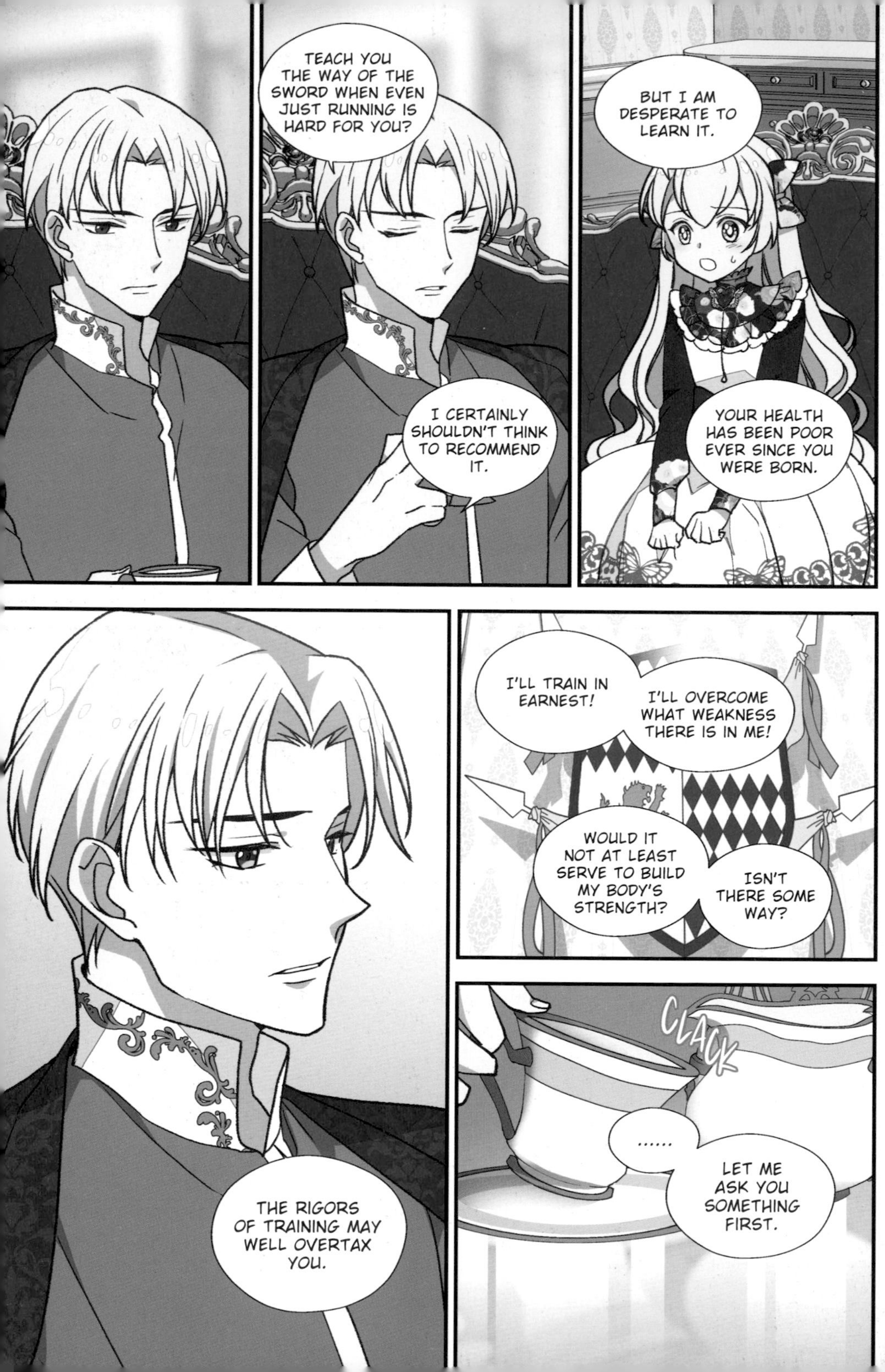

TEACH YOU THE WAY OF THE SWORD WHEN EVEN JUST RUNNING IS HARD FOR YOU?
I CERTAINLY SHOULDN'T THINK TO RECOMMEND IT.
BUT I AM DESPERATE TO LEARN IT.
YOUR HEALTH HAS BEEN POOR EVER SINCE YOU WERE BORN.
THE RIGORS OF TRAINING MAY WELL OVERTAX YOU.
I'LL TRAIN IN EARNEST!
I'LL OVERCOME WHAT WEAKNESS THERE IS IN ME!
WOULD IT NOT AT LEAST SERVE TO BUILD MY BODY'S STRENGTH?
ISN'T THERE SOME WAY?
CLACK
......
LET ME ASK YOU SOMETHING FIRST.

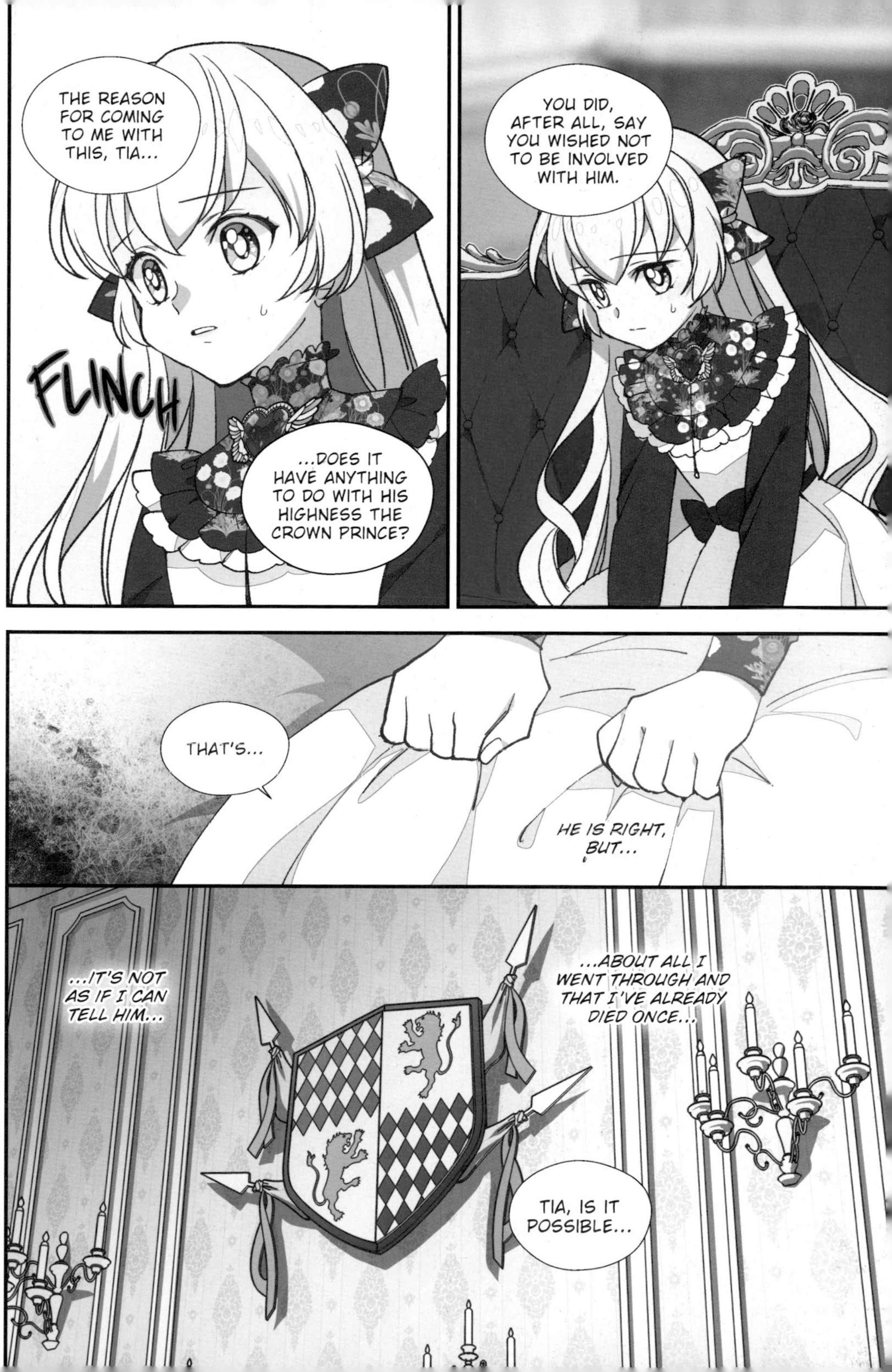
THE REASON FOR COMING TO ME WITH THIS, TIA...
FLINCH
...DOES IT HAVE ANYTHING TO DO WITH HIS HIGHNESS THE CROWN PRINCE?
YOU DID, AFTER ALL, SAY YOU WISHED NOT TO BE INVOLVED WITH HIM.
THAT'S...
HE IS RIGHT, BUT...
...IT'S NOT AS IF I CAN TELL HIM...
...ABOUT ALL I WENT THROUGH AND THAT I'VE ALREADY DIED ONCE...
TIA, IS IT POSSIBLE...

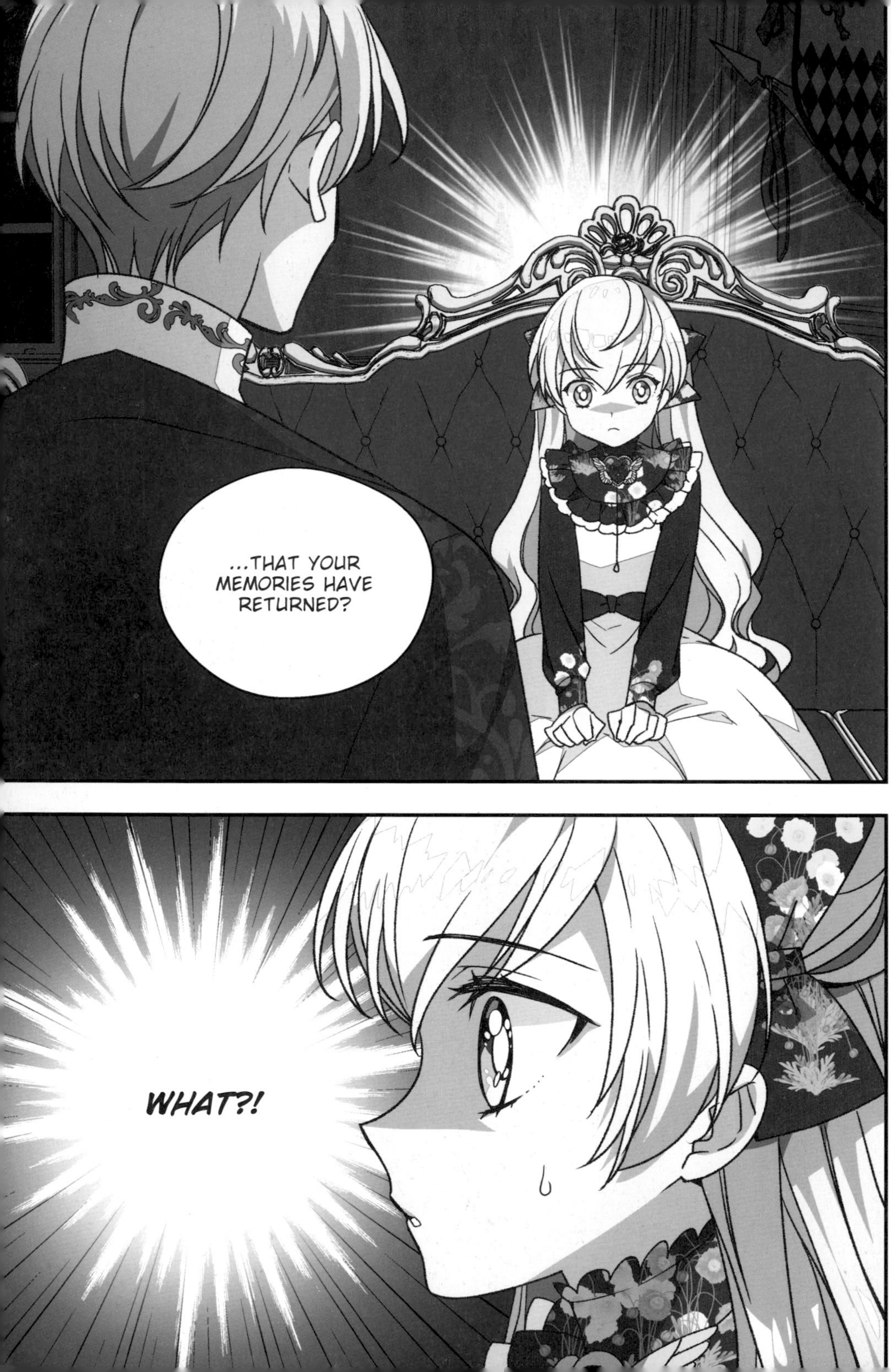
...THAT YOUR MEMORIES HAVE RETURNED?
WHAT?!

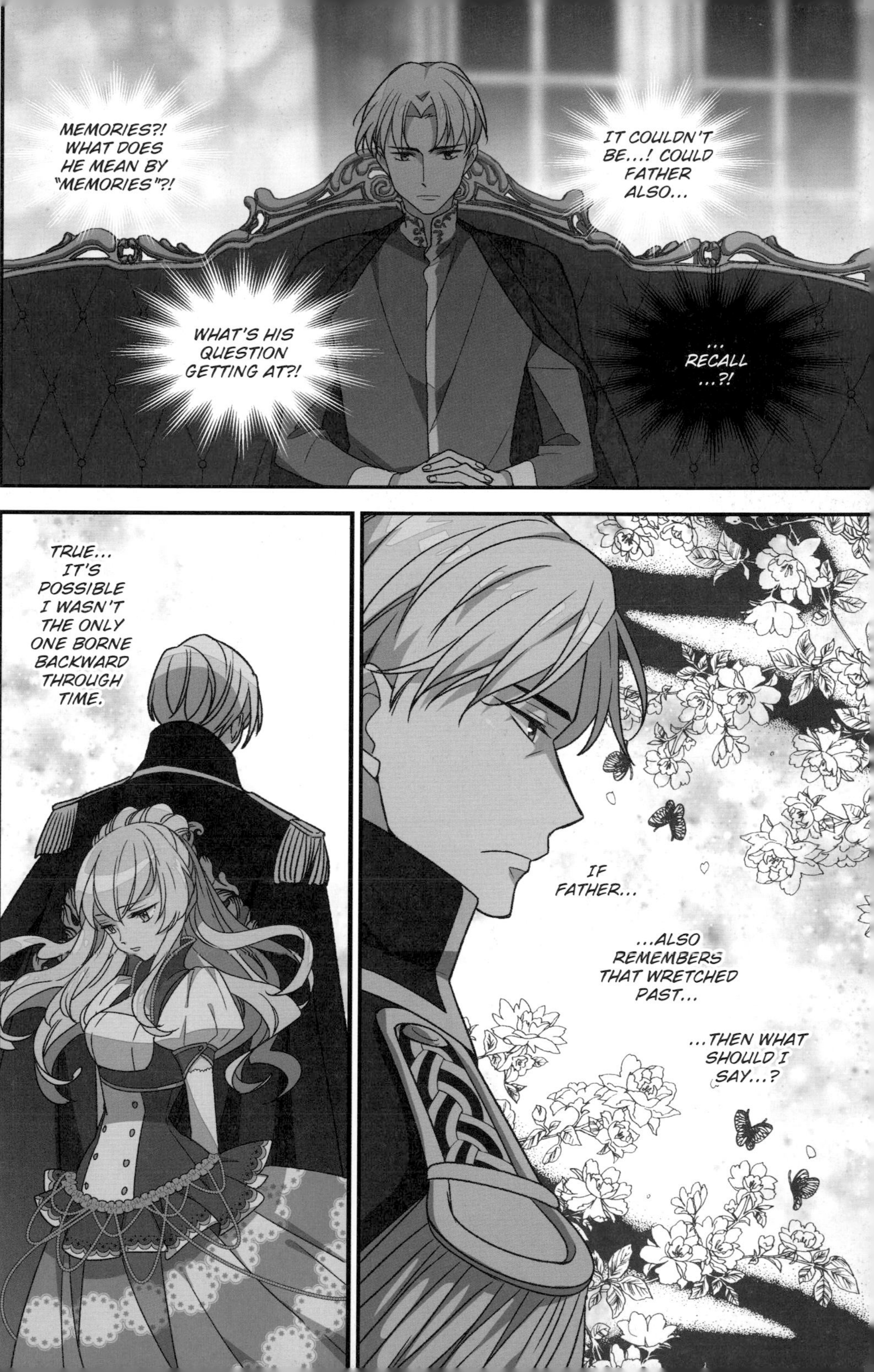
MEMORIES?! WHAT DOES HE MEAN BY "MEMORIES"?!
WHAT'S HIS QUESTION GETTING AT?!
IT COULDN'T BE...! COULD FATHER ALSO...
...RECALL...?!
TRUE... IT'S POSSIBLE I WASN'T THE ONLY ONE BORNE BACKWARD THROUGH TIME.
IF FATHER...
...ALSO REMEMBERS THAT WRETCHED PAST...
...THEN WHAT SHOULD I SAY...?

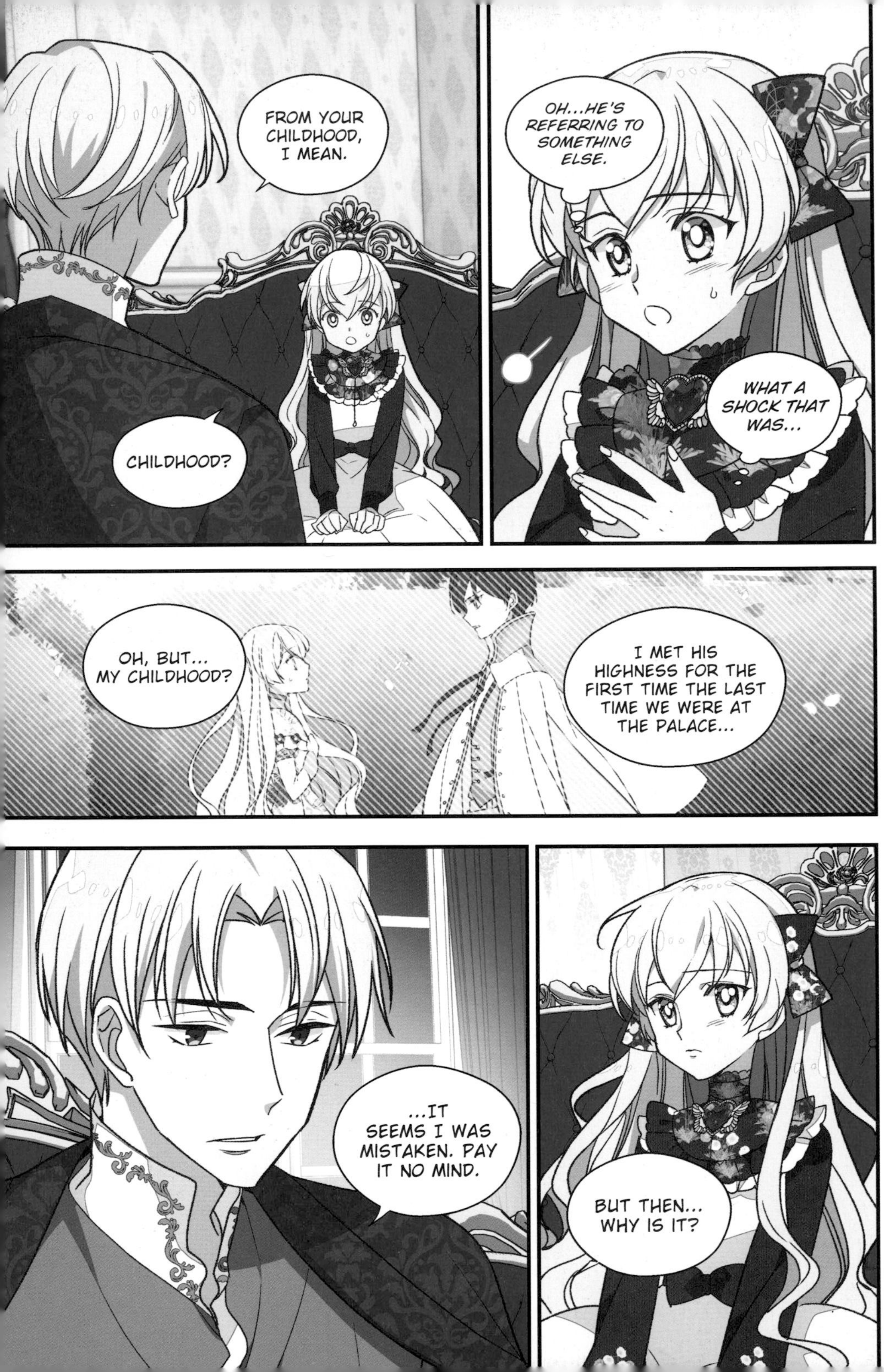
FROM YOUR CHILDHOOD, I MEAN.
CHILDHOOD?
OH...HE'S REFERRING TO SOMETHING ELSE.
WHAT A SHOCK THAT WAS...
OH, BUT... MY CHILDHOOD?
I MET HIS HIGHNESS FOR THE FIRST TIME THE LAST TIME WE WERE AT THE PALACE...
...IT SEEMS I WAS MISTAKEN. PAY IT NO MIND.
BUT THEN... WHY IS IT?

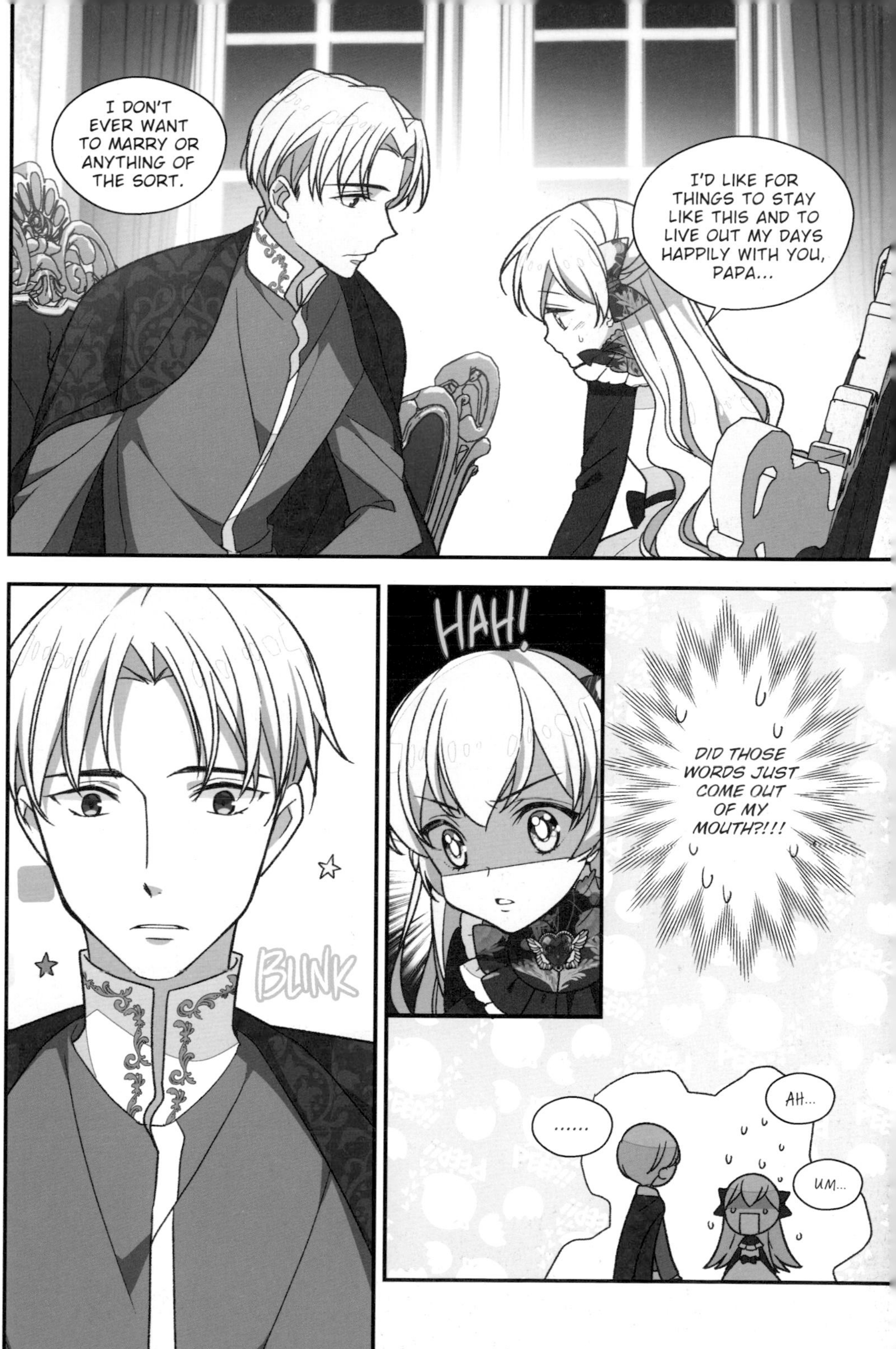
I DON'T EVER WANT TO MARRY OR ANYTHING OF THE SORT.
I'D LIKE FOR THINGS TO STAY LIKE THIS AND TO LIVE OUT MY DAYS HAPPILY WITH YOU, PAPA...
HAH!
DID THOSE WORDS JUST COME OUT OF MY MOUTH?!!!
BLINK
AH...
......
UM...

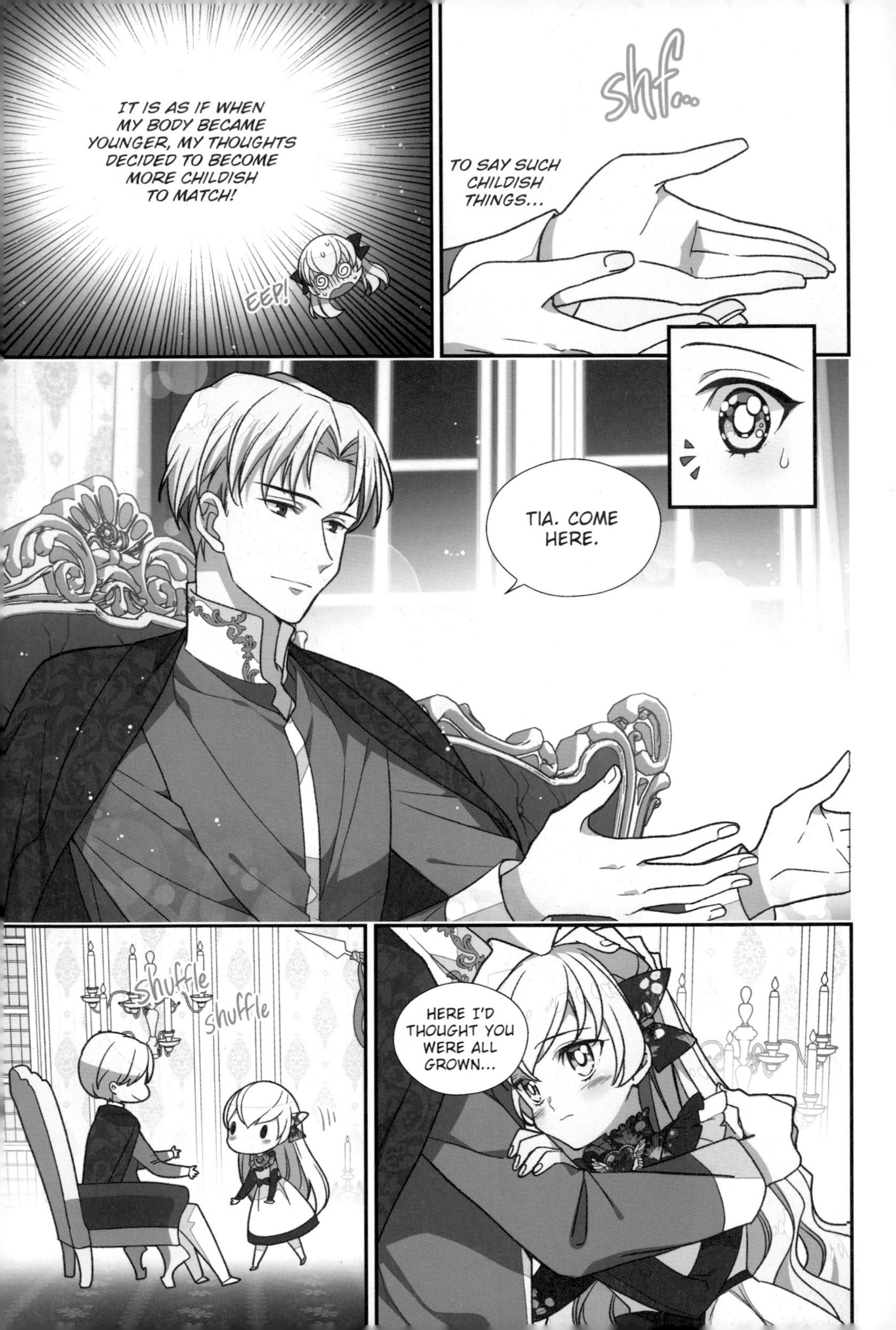
IT IS AS IF WHEN MY BODY BECAME YOUNGER, MY THOUGHTS DECIDED TO BECOME MORE CHILDISH TO MATCH!
EEP!
shf...
TO SAY SUCH CHILDISH THINGS...
TIA. COME HERE.
shuffle
shuffle
HERE I'D THOUGHT YOU WERE ALL GROWN...

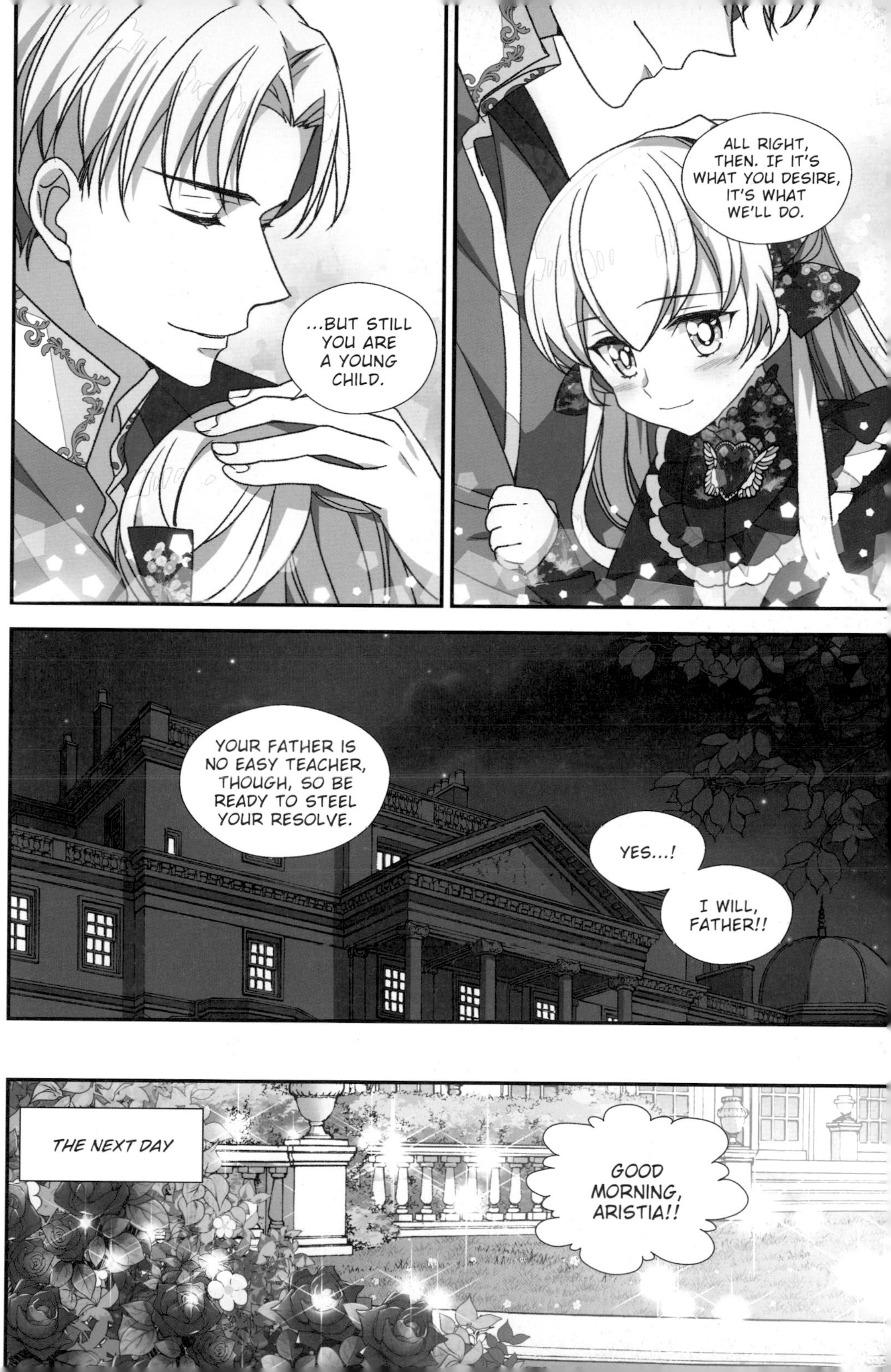
...BUT STILL YOU ARE A YOUNG CHILD.
ALL RIGHT, THEN. IF IT'S WHAT YOU DESIRE, IT'S WHAT WE'LL DO.
YOUR FATHER IS NO EASY TEACHER, THOUGH, SO BE READY TO STEEL YOUR RESOLVE.
YES...!
I WILL, FATHER!!
THE NEXT DAY
GOOD MORNING, ARISTIA!!

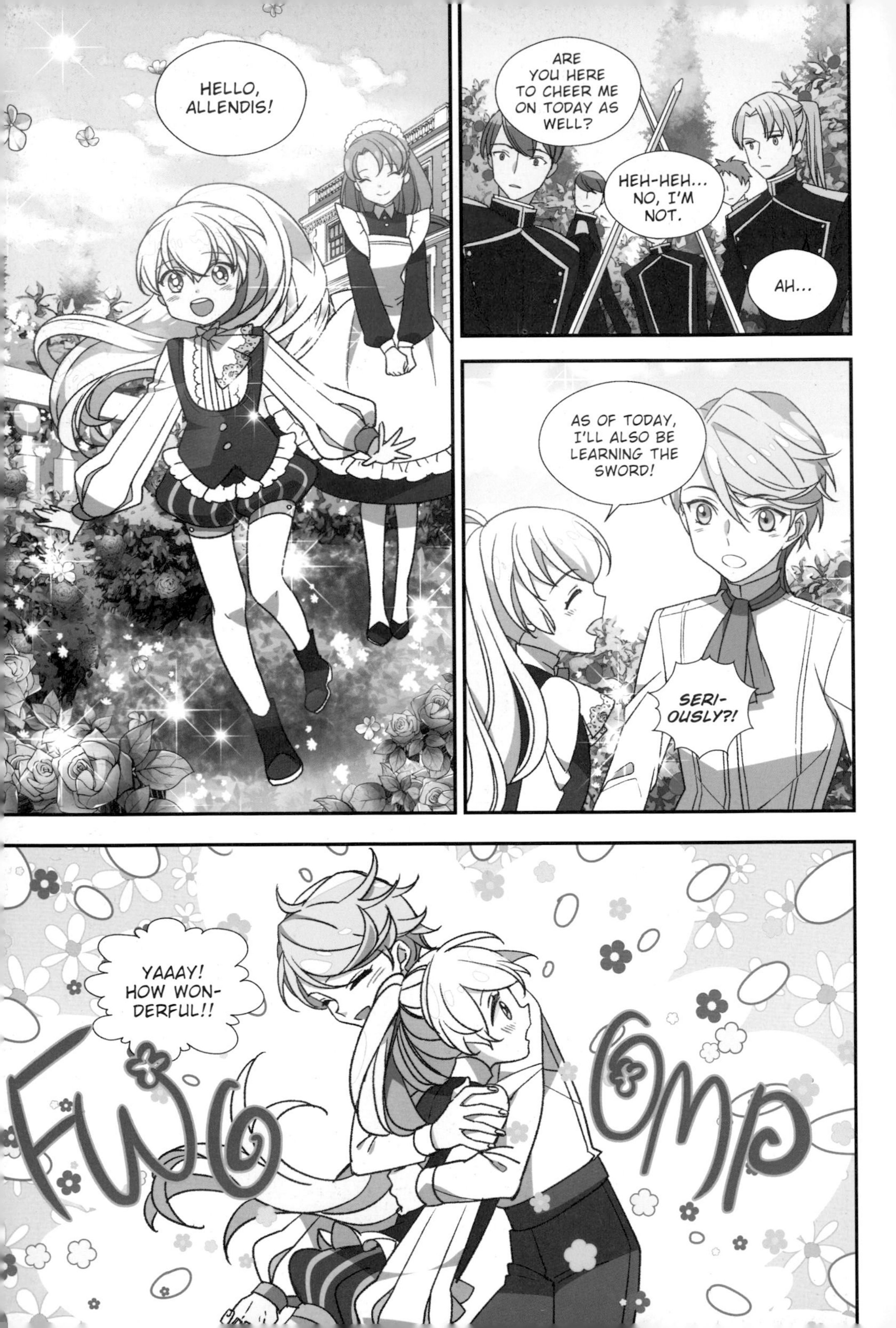
HELLO, ALLENDIS!
ARE YOU HERE TO CHEER ME ON TODAY AS WELL?
HEH-HEH... NO, I'M NOT.
AH...
AS OF TODAY, I'LL ALSO BE LEARNING THE SWORD!
SERI-OUSLY?!
YAAAY! HOW WON-DERFUL!!
FWOOMP

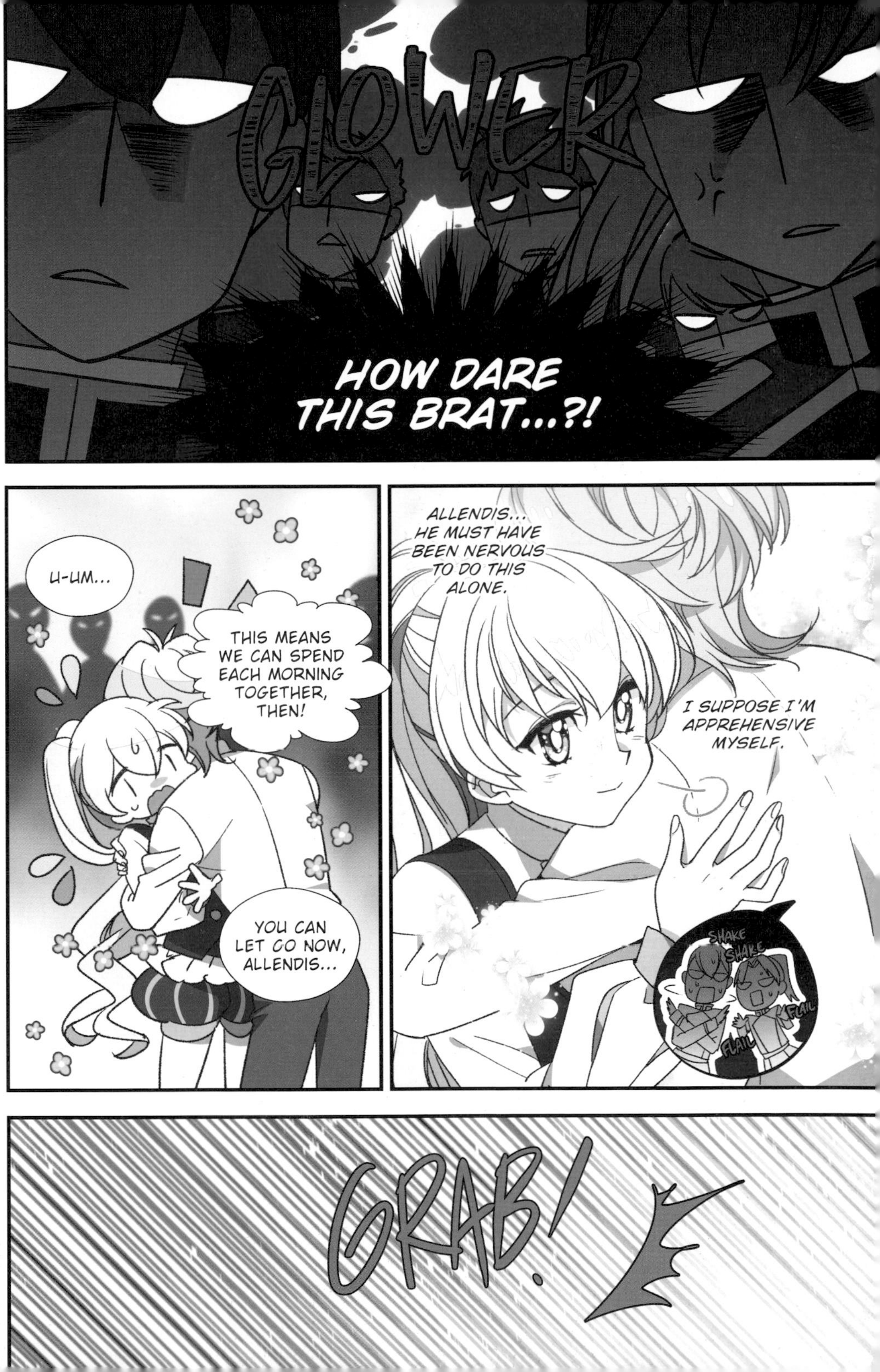
GLOWER
HOW DARE THIS BRAT...?!
U-UM...
THIS MEANS WE CAN SPEND EACH MORNING TOGETHER, THEN!
YOU CAN LET GO NOW, ALLENDIS...
ALLENDIS... HE MUST HAVE BEEN NERVOUS TO DO THIS ALONE.
I SUPPOSE I'M APPREHENSIVE MYSELF.
SHAKE
SHAKE
FLAIL
FLAIL
GRAB!

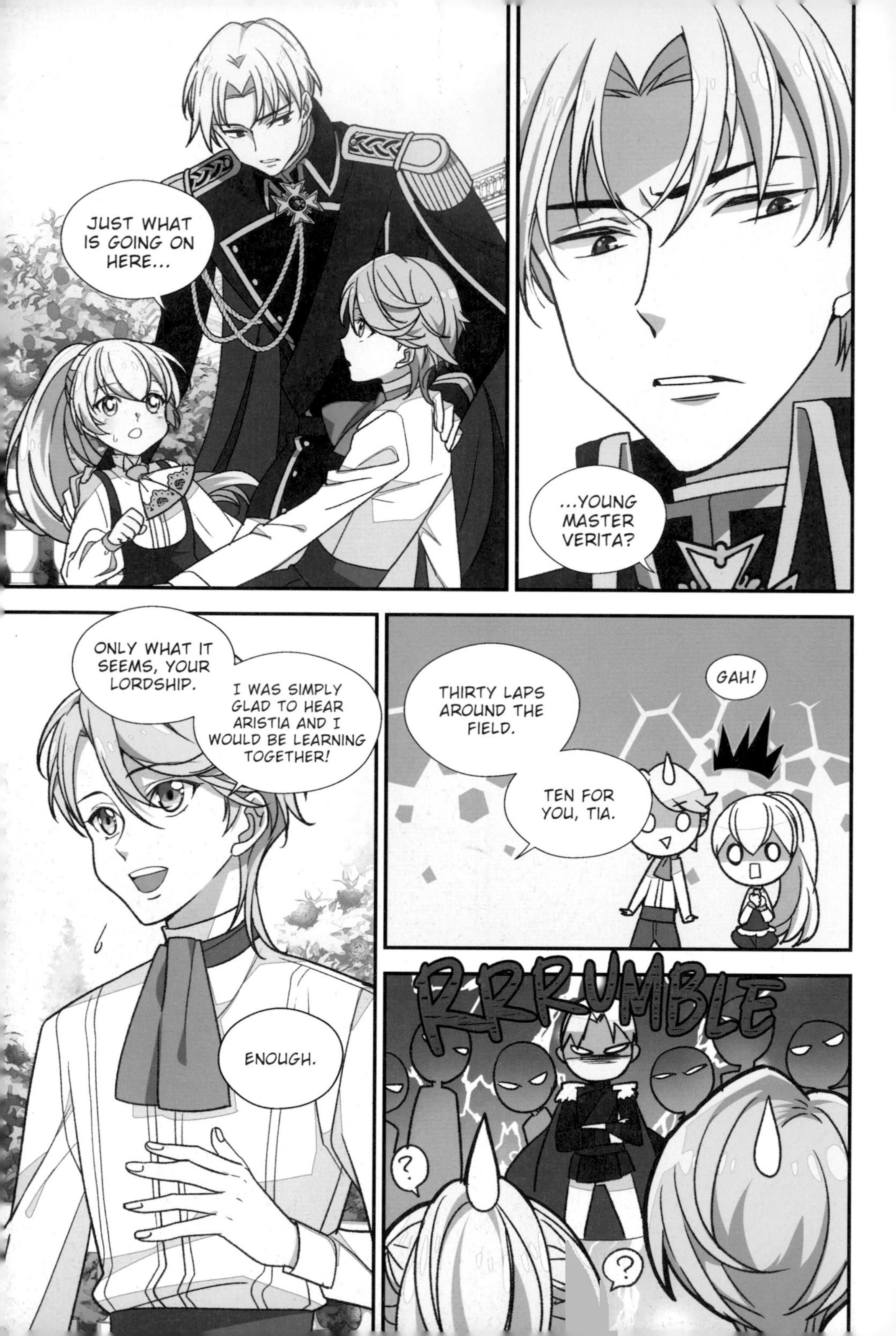
JUST WHAT IS GOING ON HERE...
...YOUNG MASTER VERITA?
ONLY WHAT IT SEEMS, YOUR LORDSHIP.
I WAS SIMPLY GLAD TO HEAR ARISTIA AND I WOULD BE LEARNING TOGETHER!
ENOUGH.
THIRTY LAPS AROUND THE FIELD.
GAH!
TEN FOR YOU, TIA.
RRRUMBLE
?
?

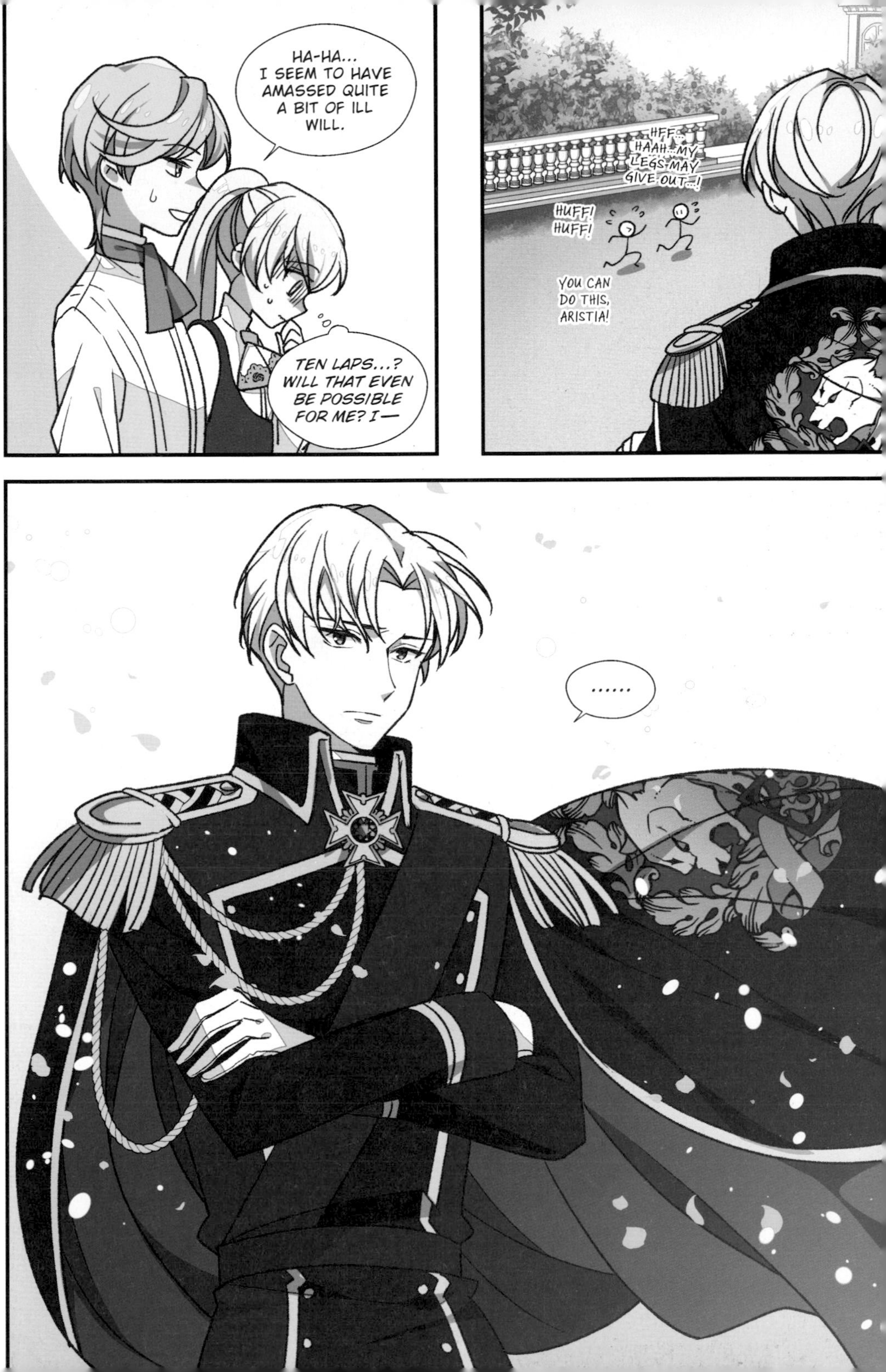
HA-HA... I SEEM TO HAVE AMASSED QUITE A BIT OF ILL WILL.
TEN LAPS...? WILL THAT EVEN BE POSSIBLE FOR ME? I—
HFF... HAAH... MY LEGS MAY GIVE OUT...!
HUFF! HUFF!
YOU CAN DO THIS, ARISTIA!
......

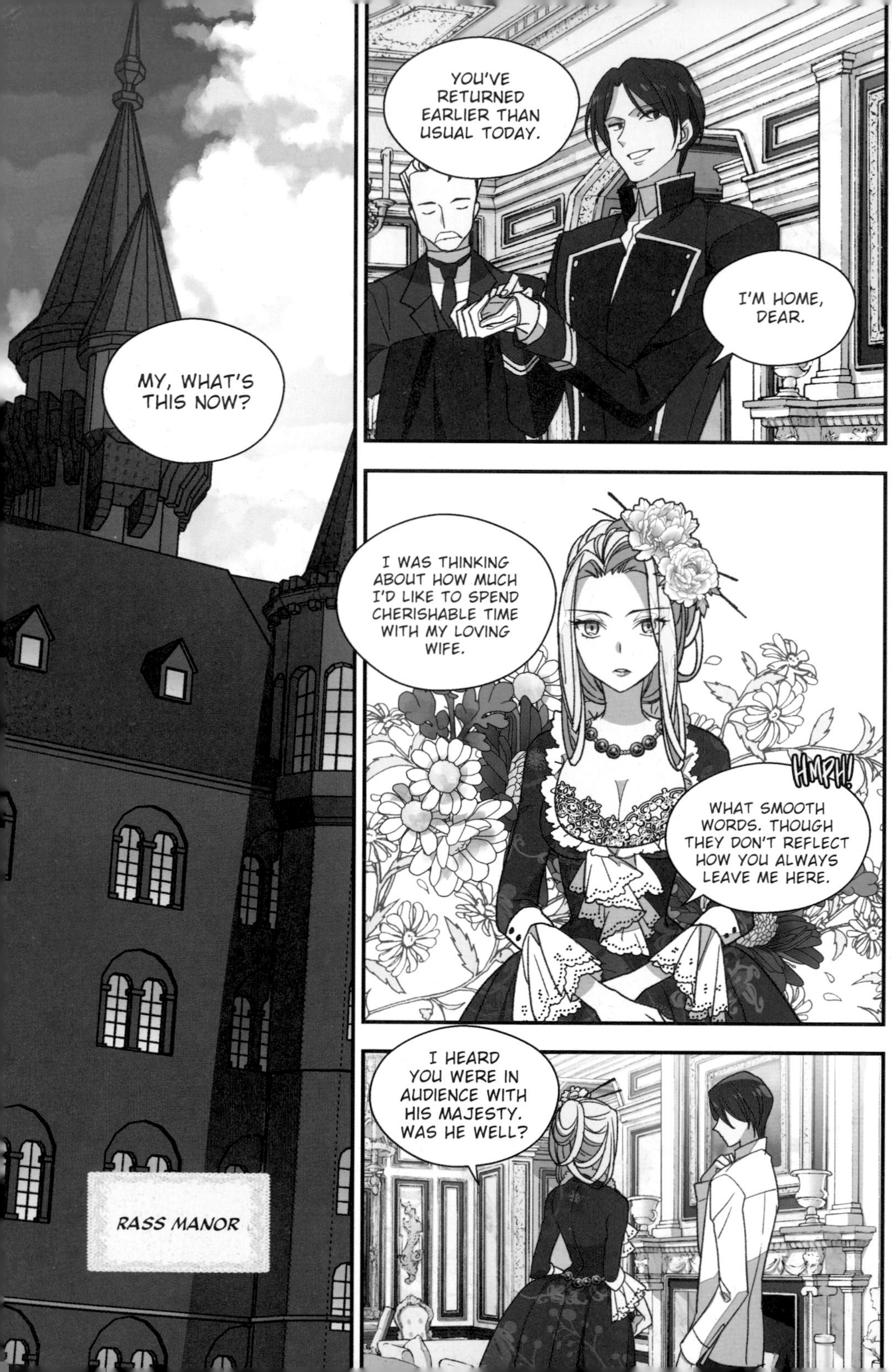

RASS MANOR
YOU'VE RETURNED EARLIER THAN USUAL TODAY.
I'M HOME, DEAR.
MY, WHAT'S THIS NOW?
I WAS THINKING ABOUT HOW MUCH I'D LIKE TO SPEND CHERISHABLE TIME WITH MY LOVING WIFE.
HMPH!
WHAT SMOOTH WORDS. THOUGH THEY DON'T REFLECT HOW YOU ALWAYS LEAVE ME HERE.
I HEARD YOU WERE IN AUDIENCE WITH HIS MAJESTY. WAS HE WELL?

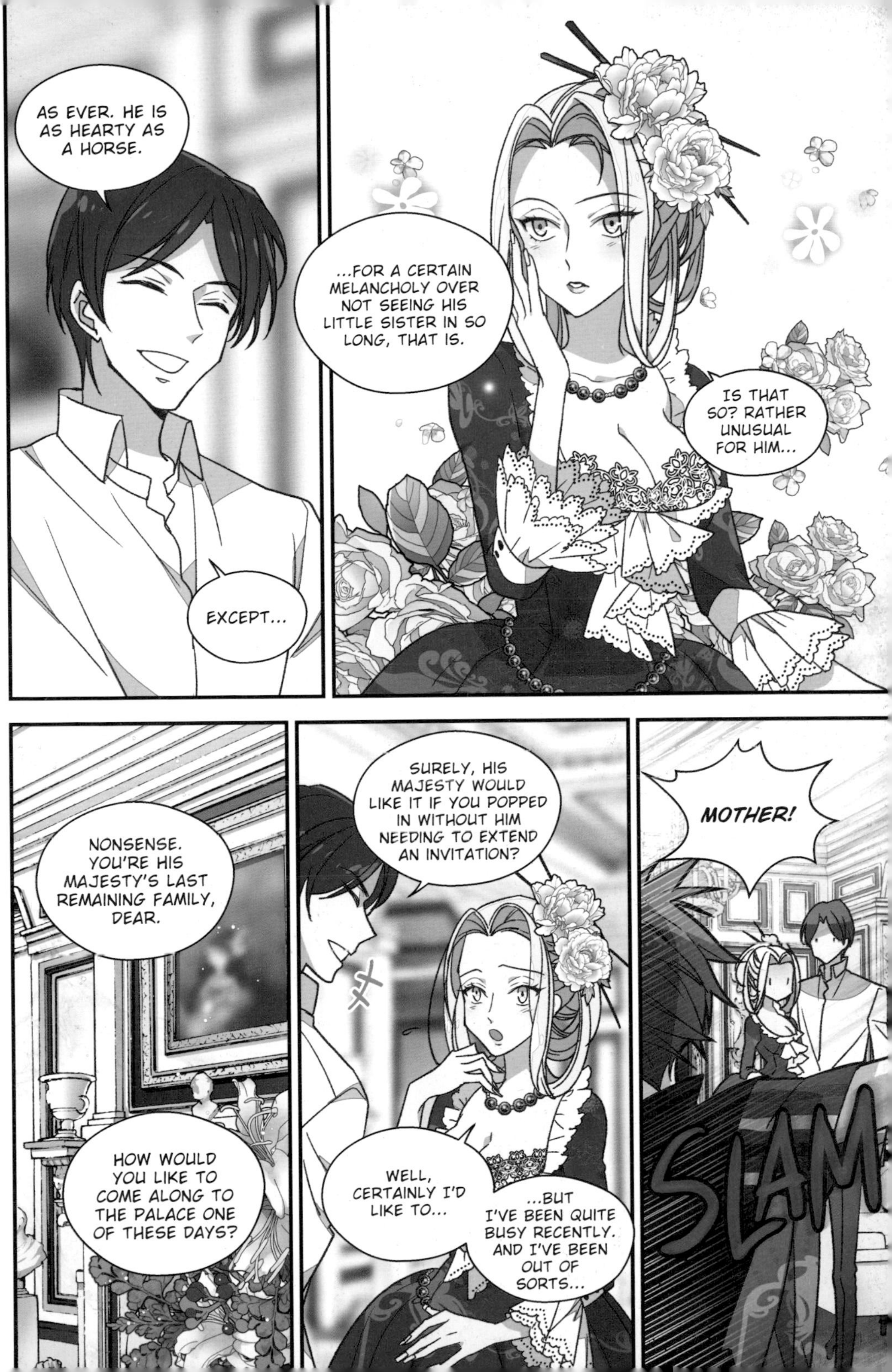
AS EVER. HE IS AS HEARTY AS A HORSE.
EXCEPT...
...FOR A CERTAIN MELANCHOLY OVER NOT SEEING HIS LITTLE SISTER IN SO LONG, THAT IS.
IS THAT SO? RATHER UNUSUAL FOR HIM...
NONSENSE. YOU'RE HIS MAJESTY'S LAST REMAINING FAMILY, DEAR.
HOW WOULD YOU LIKE TO COME ALONG TO THE PALACE ONE OF THESE DAYS?
SURELY, HIS MAJESTY WOULD LIKE IT IF YOU POPPED IN WITHOUT HIM NEEDING TO EXTEND AN INVITATION?
WELL, CERTAINLY I'D LIKE TO...
...BUT I'VE BEEN QUITE BUSY RECENTLY. AND I'VE BEEN OUT OF SORTS...
MOTHER!
SLAM

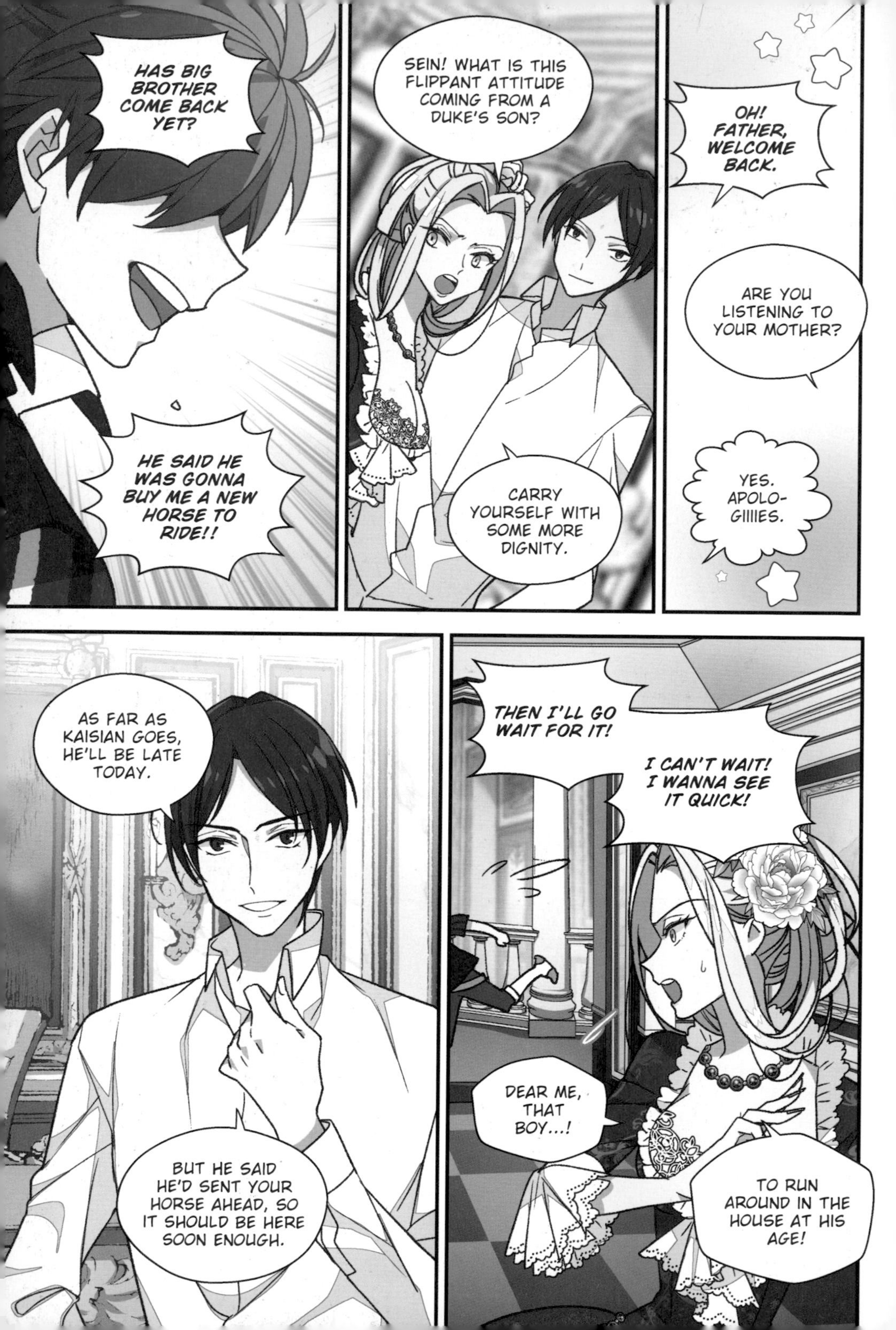
HAS BIG BROTHER COME BACK YET?
HE SAID HE WAS GONNA BUY ME A NEW HORSE TO RIDE!!
SEIN! WHAT IS THIS FLIPPANT ATTITUDE COMING FROM A DUKE'S SON?
CARRY YOURSELF WITH SOME MORE DIGNITY.
OH! FATHER, WELCOME BACK.
ARE YOU LISTENING TO YOUR MOTHER?
YES. APOLO-GIIIIES.
AS FAR AS KAISIAN GOES, HE'LL BE LATE TODAY.
BUT HE SAID HE'D SENT YOUR HORSE AHEAD, SO IT SHOULD BE HERE SOON ENOUGH.
THEN I'LL GO WAIT FOR IT!
I CAN'T WAIT! I WANNA SEE IT QUICK!
DEAR ME, THAT BOY...!
TO RUN AROUND IN THE HOUSE AT HIS AGE!

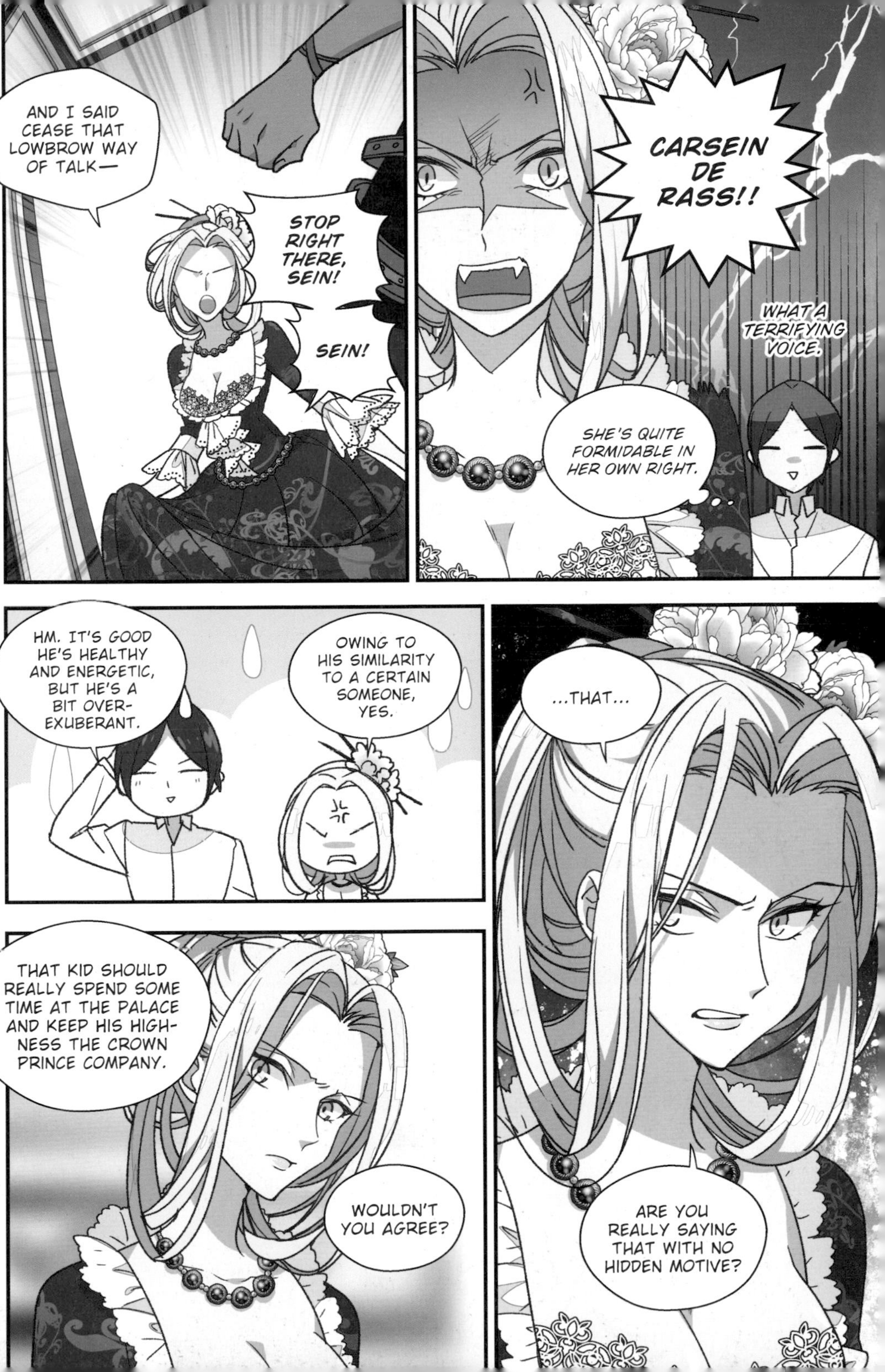
AND I SAID CEASE THAT LOWBROW WAY OF TALK—
STOP RIGHT THERE, SEIN!
SEIN!
CARSEIN DE RASS!!
WHAT A TERRIFYING VOICE.
SHE'S QUITE FORMIDABLE IN HER OWN RIGHT.
HM. IT'S GOOD HE'S HEALTHY AND ENERGETIC, BUT HE'S A BIT OVER-EXUBERANT.
OWING TO HIS SIMILARITY TO A CERTAIN SOMEONE, YES.
THAT KID SHOULD REALLY SPEND SOME TIME AT THE PALACE AND KEEP HIS HIGH-NESS THE CROWN PRINCE COMPANY.
WOULDN'T YOU AGREE?
...THAT...
ARE YOU REALLY SAYING THAT WITH NO HIDDEN MOTIVE?

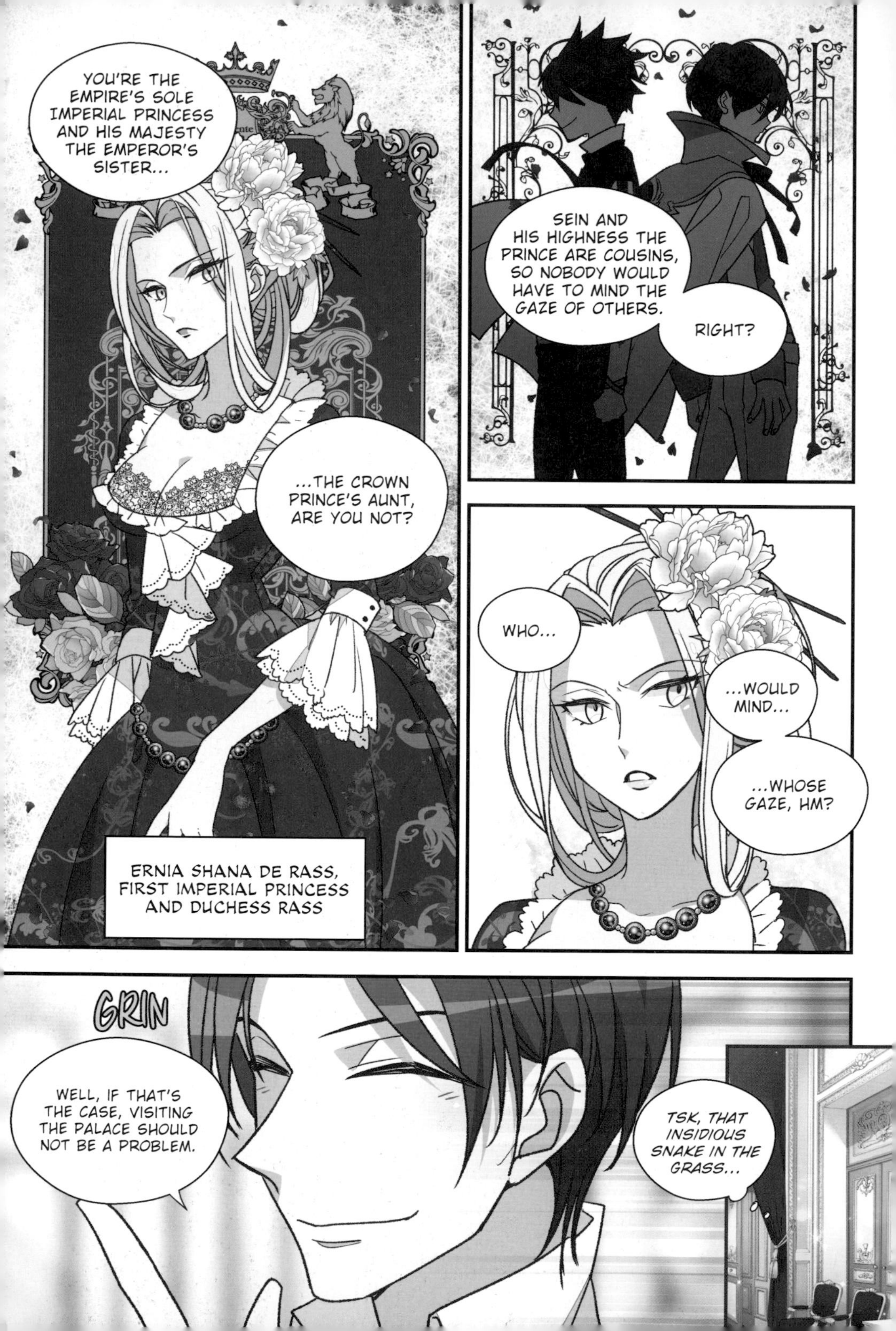
YOU'RE THE EMPIRE'S SOLE IMPERIAL PRINCESS AND HIS MAJESTY THE EMPEROR'S SISTER...
...THE CROWN PRINCE'S AUNT, ARE YOU NOT?
ERNIA SHANA DE RASS, FIRST IMPERIAL PRINCESS AND DUCHESS RASS
SEIN AND HIS HIGHNESS THE PRINCE ARE COUSINS, SO NOBODY WOULD HAVE TO MIND THE GAZE OF OTHERS.
RIGHT?
WHO...
...WOULD MIND...
...WHOSE GAZE, HM?
GRIN
WELL, IF THAT'S THE CASE, VISITING THE PALACE SHOULD NOT BE A PROBLEM.
TSK, THAT INSIDIOUS SNAKE IN THE GRASS...

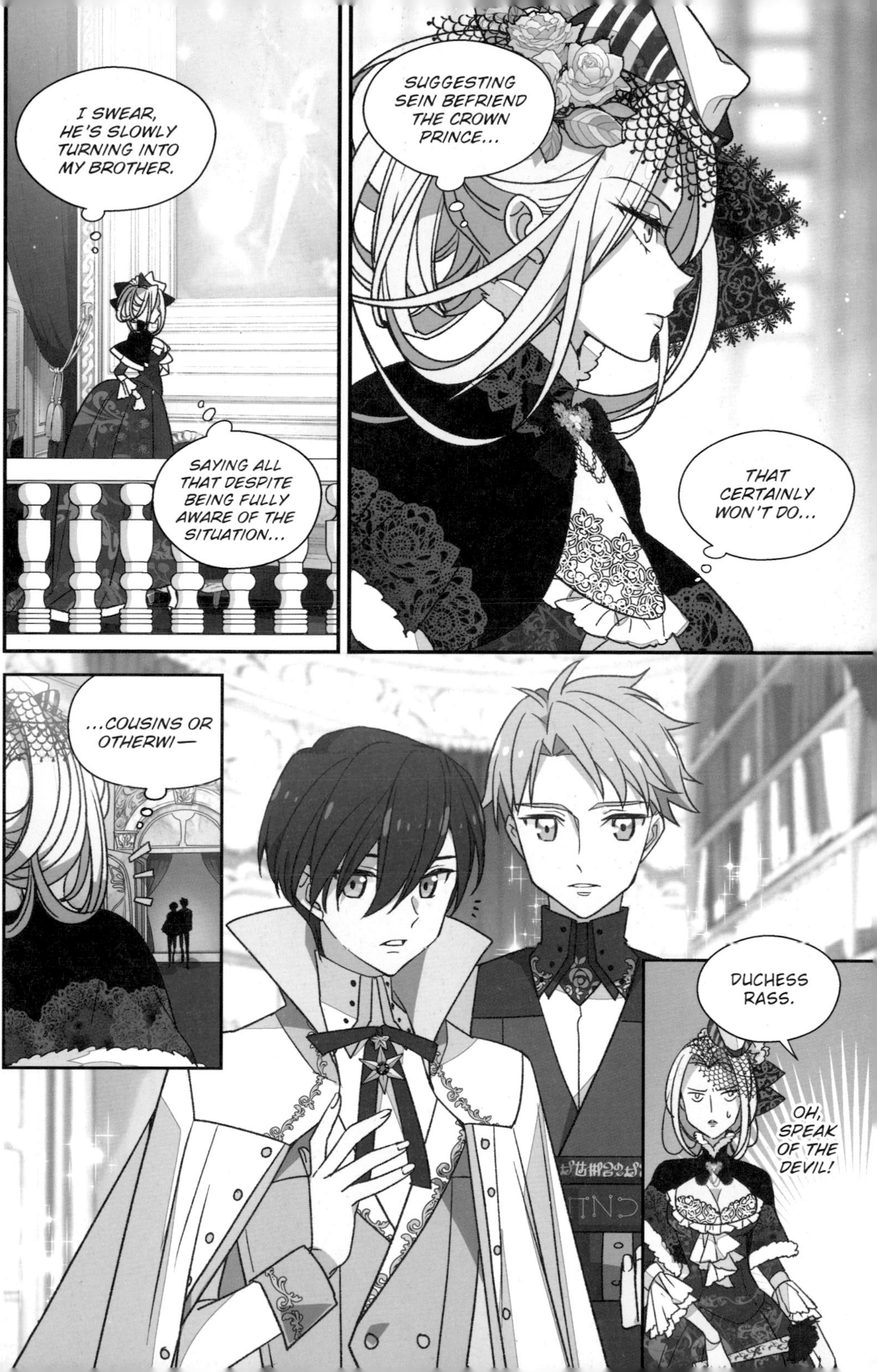
I SWEAR, HE'S SLOWLY TURNING INTO MY BROTHER.
SAYING ALL THAT DESPITE BEING FULLY AWARE OF THE SITUATION...
SUGGESTING SEIN BEFRIEND THE CROWN PRINCE...
THAT CERTAINLY WON'T DO...
...COUSINS OR OTHERWI—
DUCHESS RASS.
OH, SPEAK OF THE DEVIL!

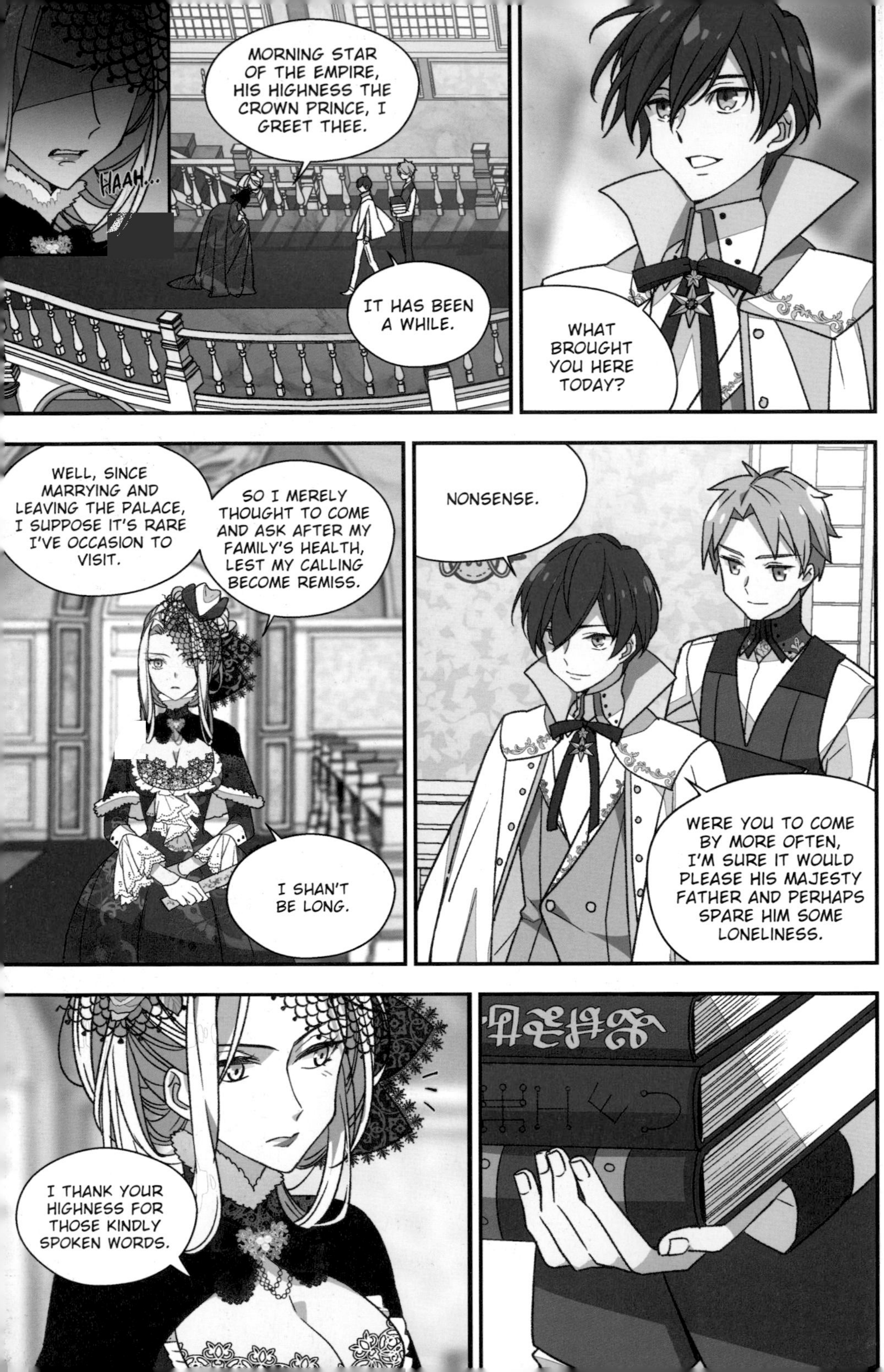
HAAH...
MORNING STAR OF THE EMPIRE, HIS HIGHNESS THE CROWN PRINCE, I GREET THEE.
IT HAS BEEN A WHILE.
WHAT BROUGHT YOU HERE TODAY?
WELL, SINCE MARRYING AND LEAVING THE PALACE, I SUPPOSE IT'S RARE I'VE OCCASION TO VISIT.
SO I MERELY THOUGHT TO COME AND ASK AFTER MY FAMILY'S HEALTH, LEST MY CALLING BECOME REMISS.
I SHAN'T BE LONG.
NONSENSE.
WERE YOU TO COME BY MORE OFTEN, I'M SURE IT WOULD PLEASE HIS MAJESTY FATHER AND PERHAPS SPARE HIM SOME LONELINESS.
I THANK YOUR HIGHNESS FOR THOSE KINDLY SPOKEN WORDS.

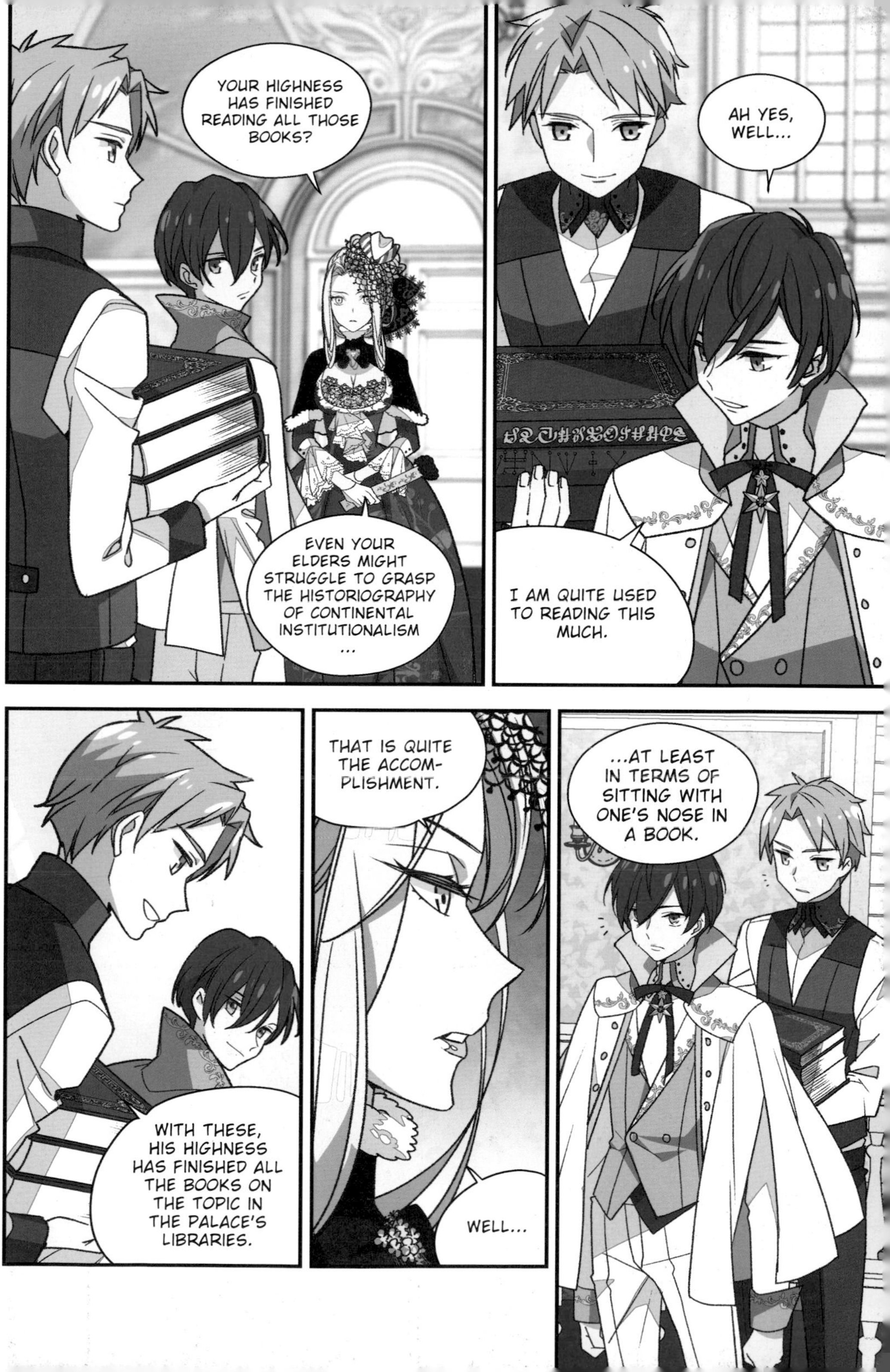
YOUR HIGHNESS HAS FINISHED READING ALL THOSE BOOKS?
EVEN YOUR ELDERS MIGHT STRUGGLE TO GRASP THE HISTORIOGRAPHY OF CONTINENTAL INSTITUTIONALISM ...
AH YES, WELL...
I AM QUITE USED TO READING THIS MUCH.
WITH THESE, HIS HIGHNESS HAS FINISHED ALL THE BOOKS ON THE TOPIC IN THE PALACE'S LIBRARIES.
THAT IS QUITE THE ACCOM-PLISHMENT.
WELL...
...AT LEAST IN TERMS OF SITTING WITH ONE'S NOSE IN A BOOK.

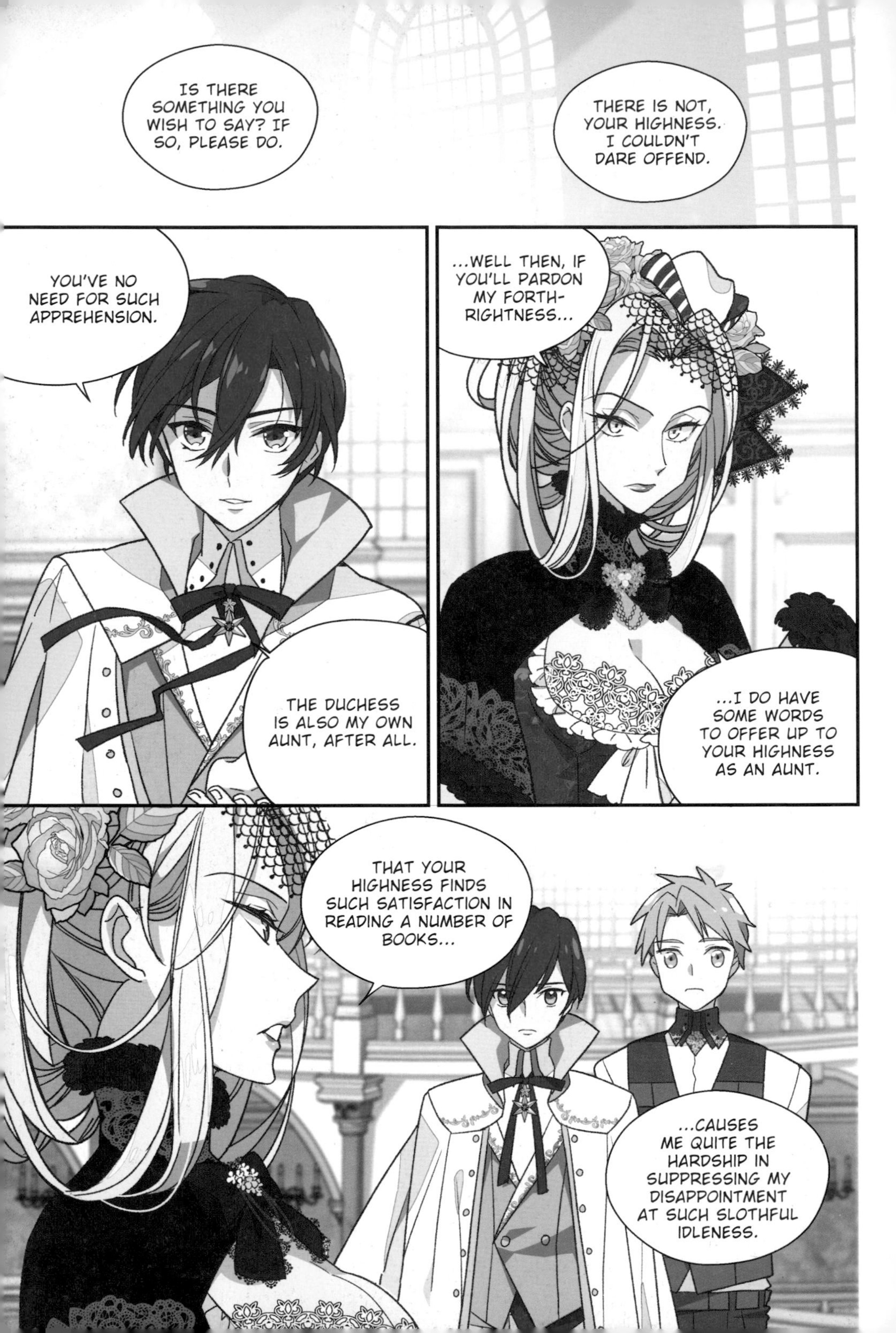
IS THERE SOMETHING YOU WISH TO SAY? IF SO, PLEASE DO.
THERE IS NOT, YOUR HIGHNESS. I COULDN'T DARE OFFEND.
YOU'VE NO NEED FOR SUCH APPREHENSION.
THE DUCHESS IS ALSO MY OWN AUNT, AFTER ALL.
...WELL THEN, IF YOU'LL PARDON MY FORTH-RIGHTNESS...
...I DO HAVE SOME WORDS TO OFFER UP TO YOUR HIGHNESS AS AN AUNT.
THAT YOUR HIGHNESS FINDS SUCH SATISFACTION IN READING A NUMBER OF BOOKS...
...CAUSES ME QUITE THE HARDSHIP IN SUPPRESSING MY DISAPPOINTMENT AT SUCH SLOTHFUL IDLENESS.

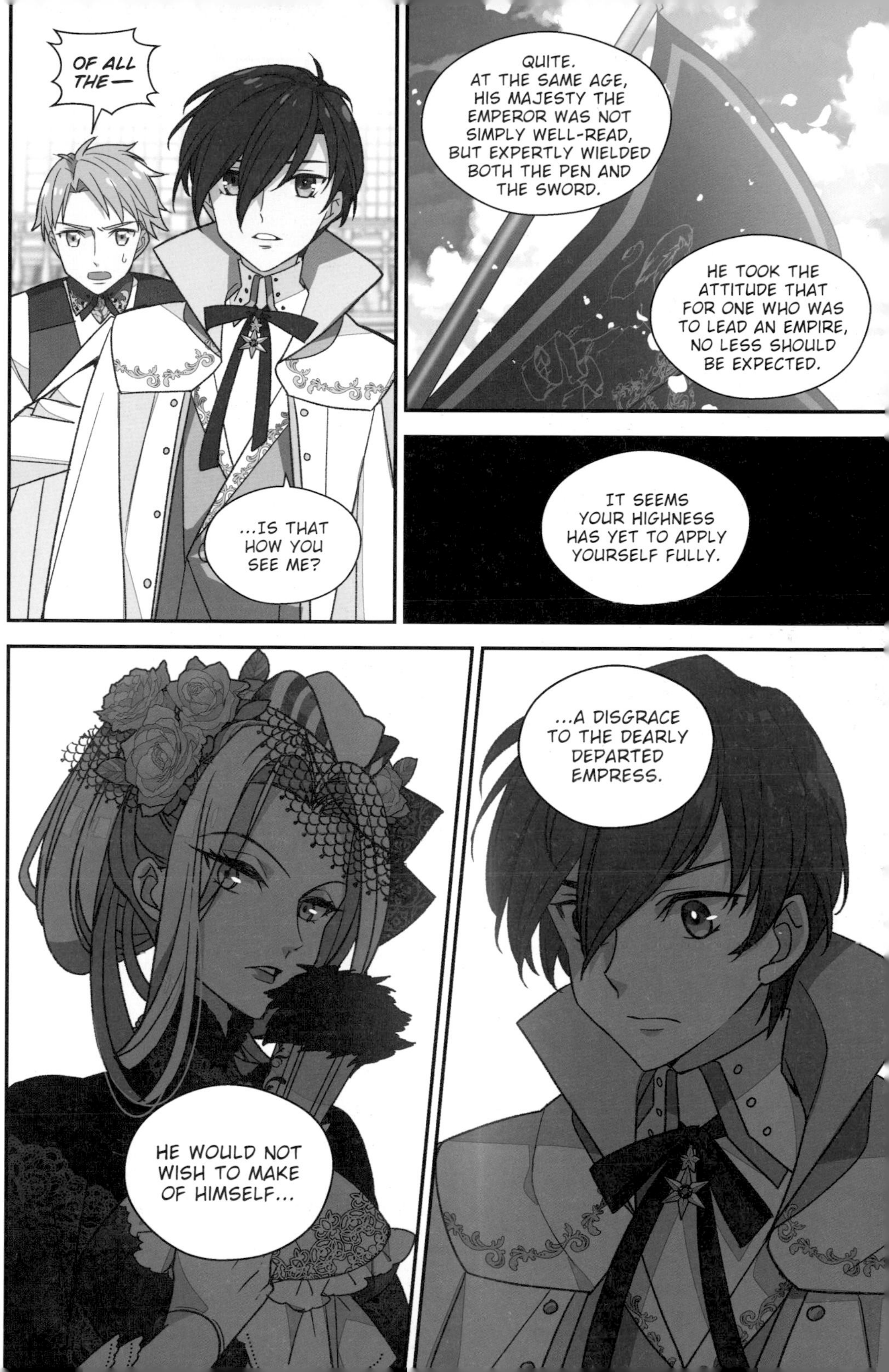
OF ALL THE—
...IS THAT HOW YOU SEE ME?
QUITE. AT THE SAME AGE, HIS MAJESTY THE EMPEROR WAS NOT SIMPLY WELL-READ, BUT EXPERTLY WIELDED BOTH THE PEN AND THE SWORD.
HE TOOK THE ATTITUDE THAT FOR ONE WHO WAS TO LEAD AN EMPIRE, NO LESS SHOULD BE EXPECTED.
IT SEEMS YOUR HIGHNESS HAS YET TO APPLY YOURSELF FULLY.
HE WOULD NOT WISH TO MAKE OF HIMSELF...
...A DISGRACE TO THE DEARLY DEPARTED EMPRESS.

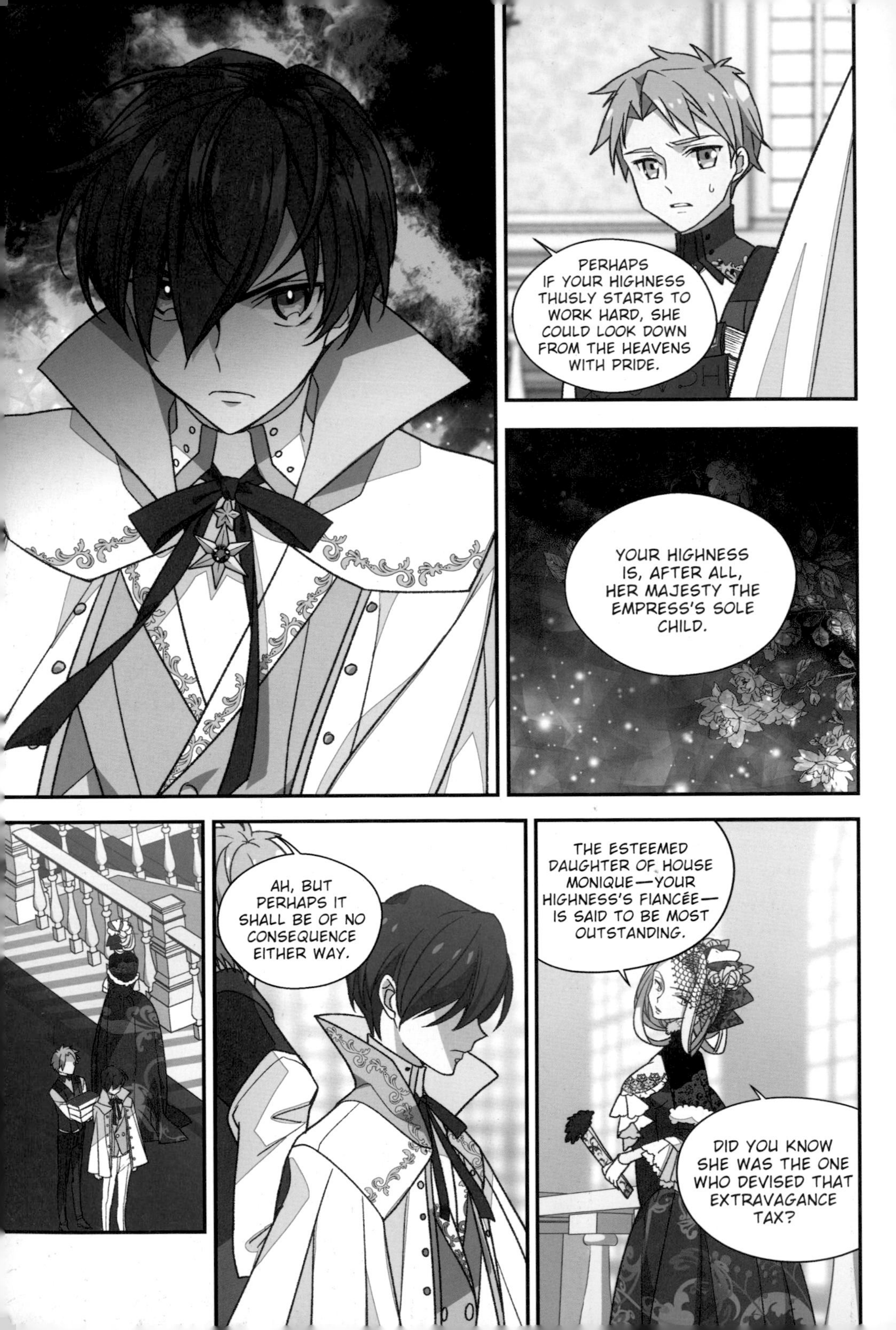
PERHAPS IF YOUR HIGHNESS THUSLY STARTS TO WORK HARD, SHE COULD LOOK DOWN FROM THE HEAVENS WITH PRIDE.
YOUR HIGHNESS IS, AFTER ALL, HER MAJESTY THE EMPRESS'S SOLE CHILD.
THE ESTEEMED DAUGHTER OF HOUSE MONIQUE—YOUR HIGHNESS'S FIANCÉE—IS SAID TO BE MOST OUTSTANDING.
DID YOU KNOW SHE WAS THE ONE WHO DEVISED THAT EXTRAVAGANCE TAX?
AH, BUT PERHAPS IT SHALL BE OF NO CONSEQUENCE EITHER WAY.

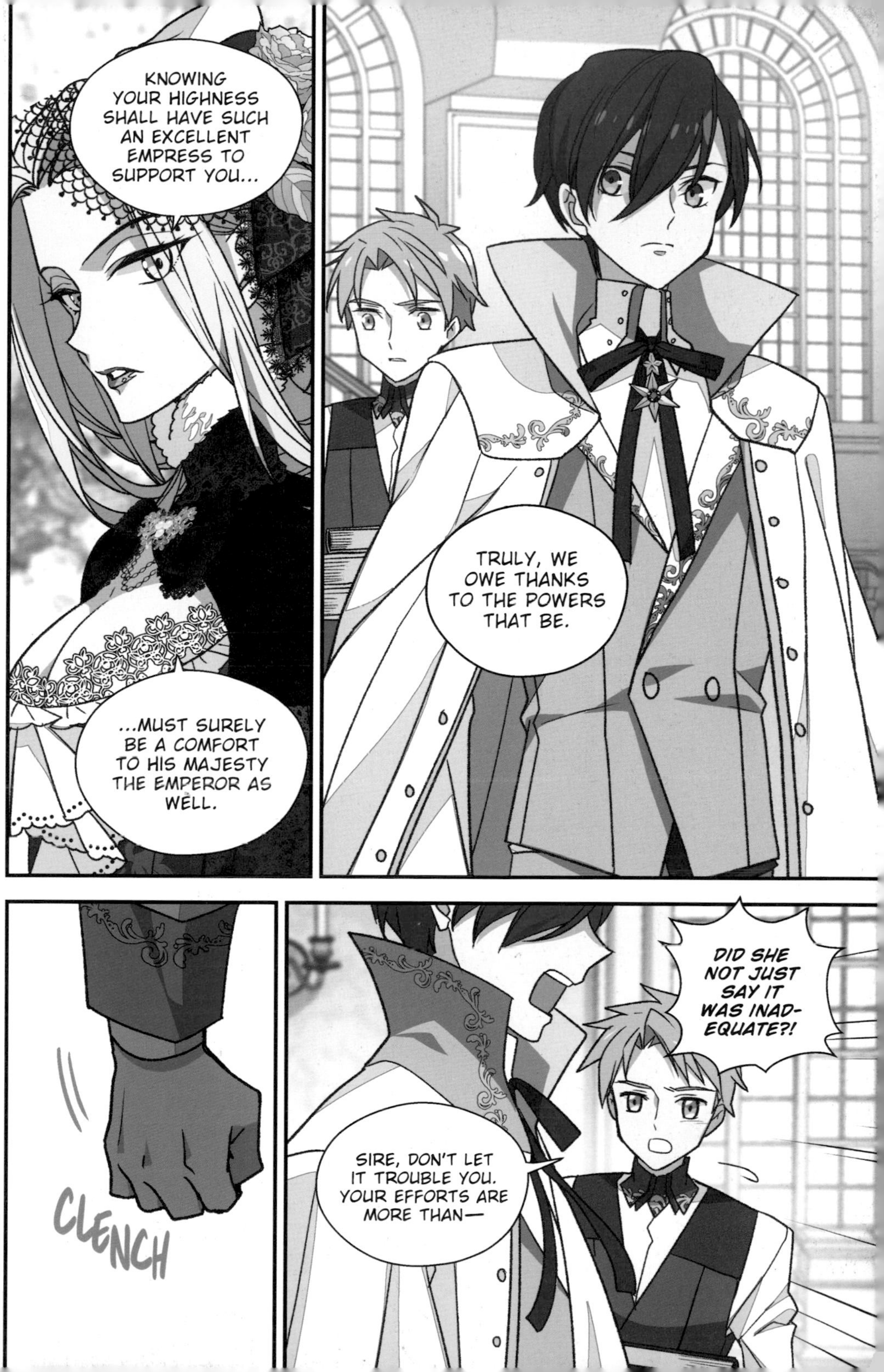
KNOWING YOUR HIGHNESS SHALL HAVE SUCH AN EXCELLENT EMPRESS TO SUPPORT YOU...
...MUST SURELY BE A COMFORT TO HIS MAJESTY THE EMPEROR AS WELL.
TRULY, WE OWE THANKS TO THE POWERS THAT BE.
CLENCH
DID SHE NOT JUST SAY IT WAS INAD-EQUATE?!
SIRE, DON'T LET IT TROUBLE YOU. YOUR EFFORTS ARE MORE THAN—

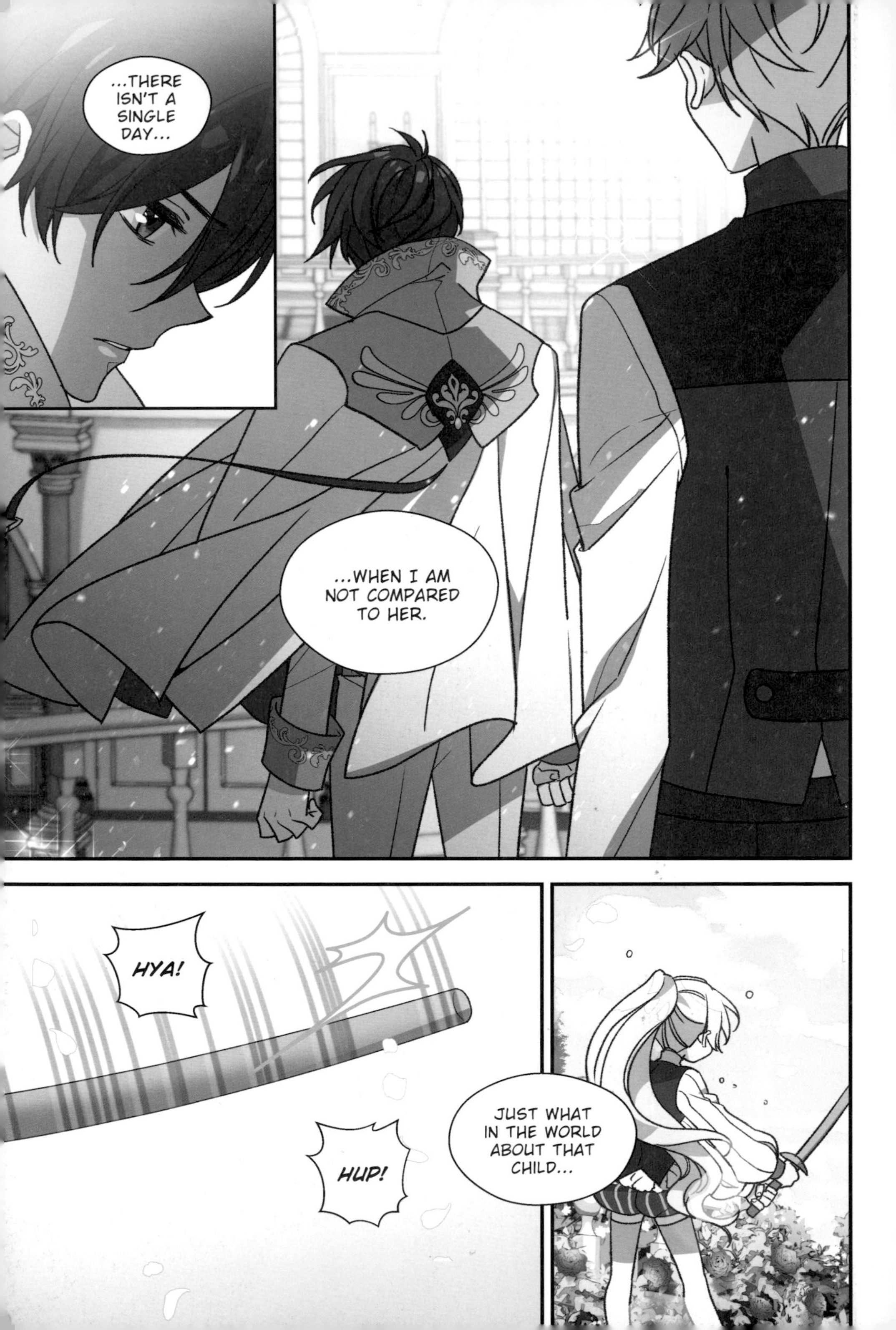
...THERE ISN'T A SINGLE DAY...
...WHEN I AM NOT COMPARED TO HER.
HYA!
HUP!
JUST WHAT IN THE WORLD ABOUT THAT CHILD...

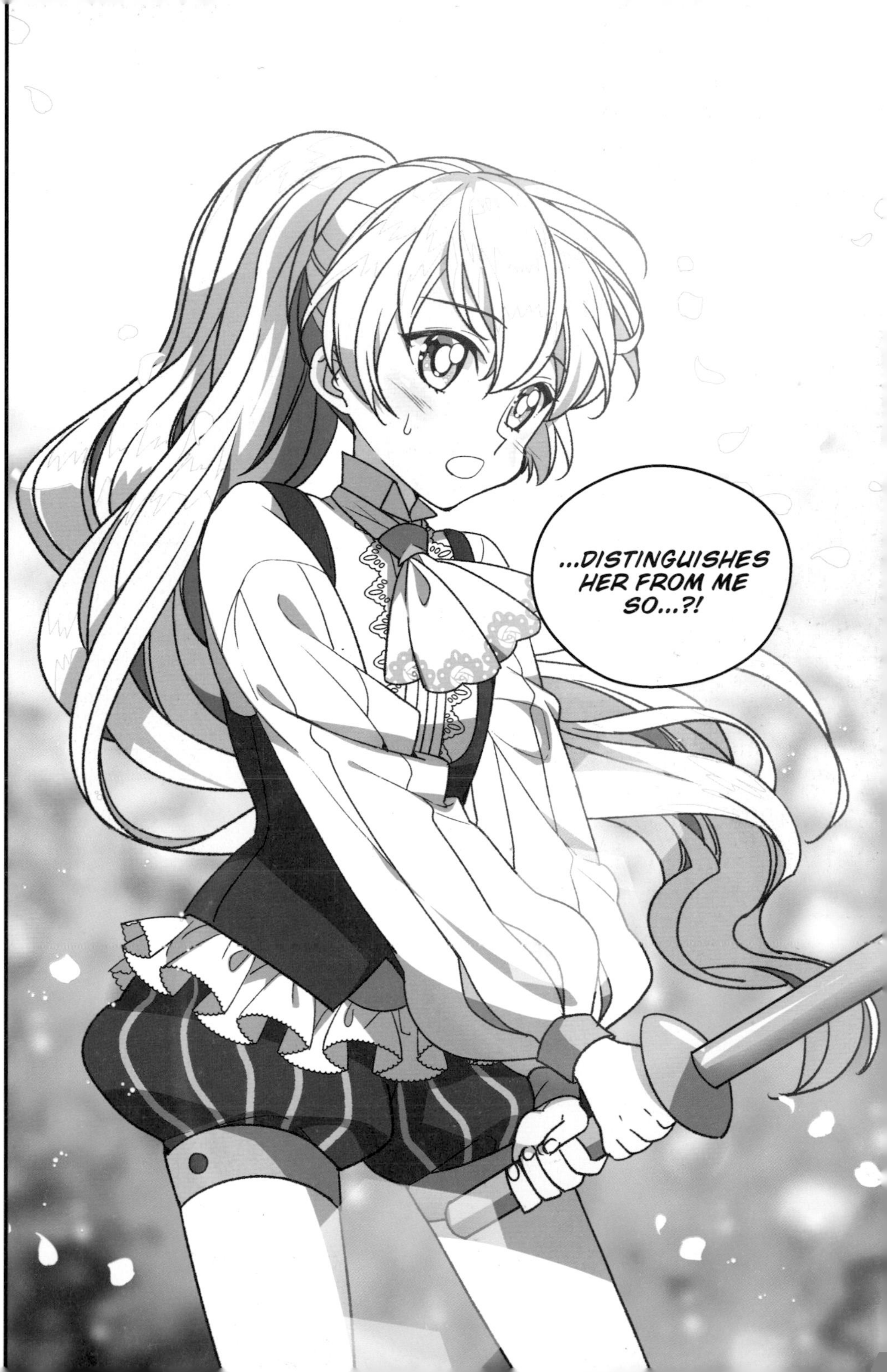
...DISTINGUISHES HER FROM ME SO...?!

# The Abandoned Empress

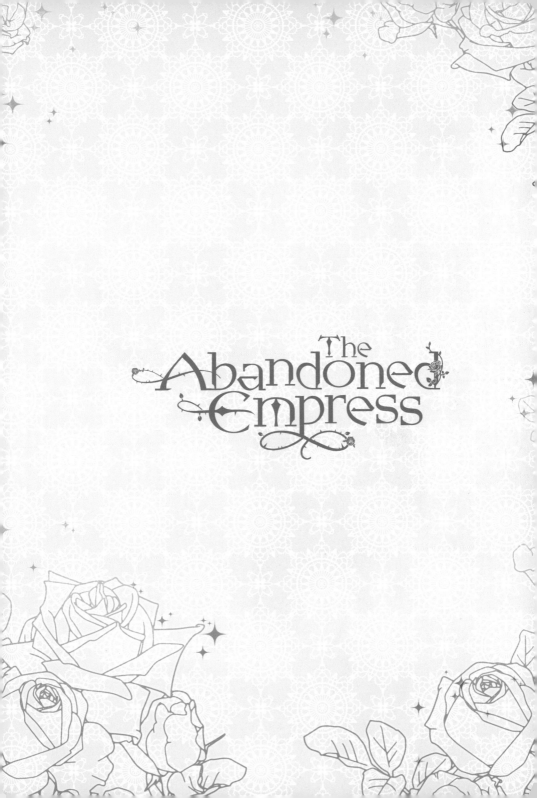

## VOLUME 2 PREVIEW

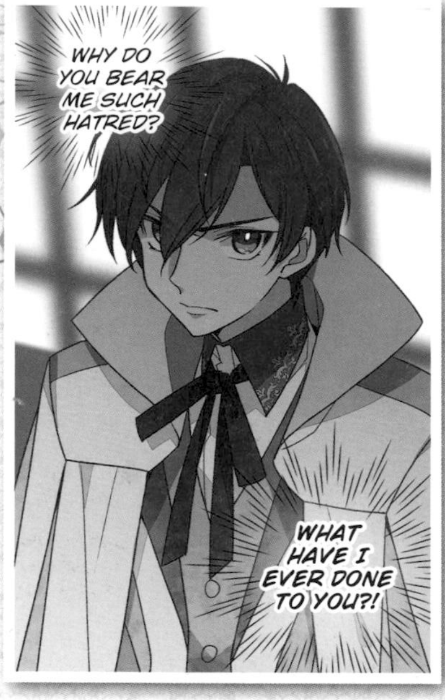
WHY DO YOU BEAR ME SUCH HATRED?
WHAT HAVE I EVER DONE TO YOU?!

RUVE'S GLARE IS AS COLD AS IN THE PAST LIFE!

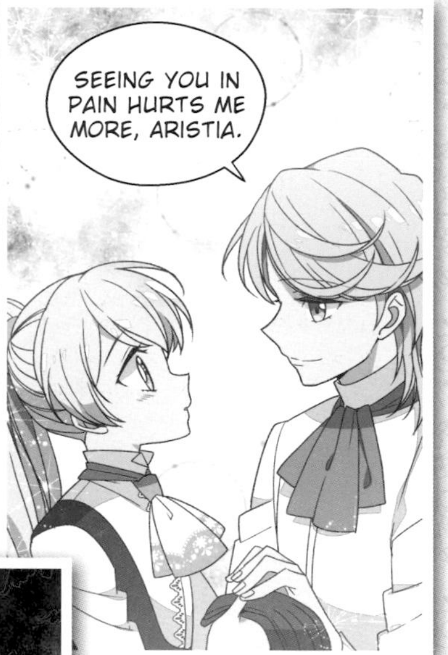
SEEING YOU IN PAIN HURTS ME MORE, ARISTIA.

ALLENDIS GROWS CLOSER AND CLOSER TO TIA!

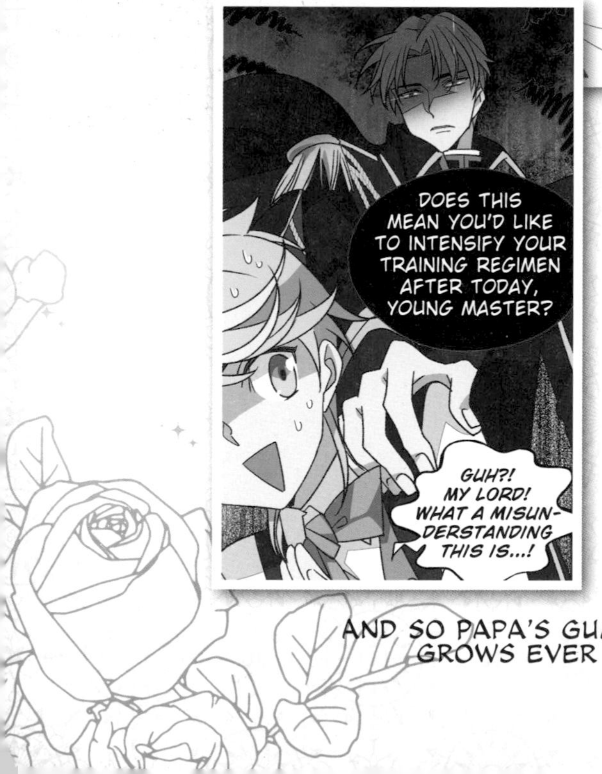
DOES THIS MEAN YOU'D LIKE TO INTENSIFY YOUR TRAINING REGIMEN AFTER TODAY, YOUNG MASTER?
GUH?! MY LORD! WHAT A MISUN-DERSTANDING THIS IS...!

AND SO PAPA'S GUARD GROWS EVER STRONGER...

I WISH WE COULD GROW UP QUICKLY...
...MY LADY.

THE PROMISED DAY
DRAWS NEAR...

FASTER ...
I MUST GROW MY SKILLS FASTER...!

TIA THROWS HERSELF INTO
TRAINING WITH NEW URGENCY
PRESENT IN HER HEART, BUT—

# The Abandoned Empress

VOLUME 2 OUT
EARLY 2022!

# The Abandoned Empress

## INA
### Original Story by **Yuna**

Translation: DAVID ODELL        Lettering: LYS BLAKESLEE

THE ABANDONED EMPRESS Volume 1
© INA, Yuna 2017 / D&C WEBTOON Biz
All rights reserved.
First published in Korea in 2017 by D&C WEBTOON Biz Co., Ltd.

English translation © 2021 by Yen Press, LLC

Yen Press
150 West 30th Street, 19th Floor
New York, NY 10001

Visit us at yenpress.com
facebook.com/yenpress
twitter.com/yenpress
yenpress.tumblr.com
instagram.com/yenpress

First Yen Press Edition: October 2021

Yen Press is an imprint of Yen Press, LLC.
The Yen Press name and logo are trademarks of Yen Press, LLC.

The publisher is not responsible for websites (or their content) that are
not owned by the publisher.

Library of Congress Control Number: 2021943164

ISBNs: 978-1-9753-3726-1 (paperback)
978-1-9753-3727-8 (ebook)

10  9  8  7  6  5  4  3  2  1

TPA

Printed in South Korea